Royal Geographical Society

Classified catalogue of the library of the Royal Geographical Society, to december, 1870

Royal Geographical Society

Classified catalogue of the library of the Royal Geographical Society, to december, 1870

ISBN/EAN: 9783741183768

Manufactured in Europe, USA, Canada, Australia, Japa

Cover: Foto ©Andreas Hilbeck / pixelio.de

Manufactured and distributed by brebook publishing software (www.brebook.com)

Royal Geographical Society

Classified catalogue of the library of the Royal Geographical Society, to december, 1870

CLASSIFIED CATALOGUE

OF

THE LIBRARY

OF THE

ROYAL GEOGRAPHICAL SOCIETY,

TO DECEMBER, 1870.

LONDON:
JOHN MURRAY, ALBEMARLE STREET.
1871.

PREFACE.

The present Catalogue has been made upon a plan which, it is hoped, will greatly increase the usefulness of the Library of the Royal Geographical Society. In it will be found, alphabetically arranged, entries under every division of the globe, country, or place treated of in the works which form the collection; such entries being chronologically sub-arranged, to aid the Geographer in comparing accounts of, or in tracing the history of, the particular locality which is the subject of his enquiry.

The Orthography generally has been determined by a collation of the best existing modern Gazetteers. For the spelling of African names, the works of Barth, Beke, Burton, Cooley, Livingstone, Rohlfs, and others, have been consulted; while for Indian names, the Gazetteers of Thornton must be held responsible.

Though no effort has been spared to detect and to rectify errors in the original Alphabetical Catalogue, upon which the present one is based, it is evidently possible that some of the less apparent of those inaccuracies may be reproduced here, as the certain avoidance of them would have involved nothing less than the bodily inspection of every book in the Library, a labour which the compiler was not called upon to undertake. For the correctness of the Supplement to that Catalogue, however, which is his own handiwork, and for the corresponding entries which this book contains, he alone is answerable.

GODFREY M. EVANS.

May 22, 1871.

ROYAL GEOGRAPHICAL SOCIETY.

CLASSIFIED CATALOGUE.

A.

Aachen.—*See* AIX-LA-CHAPELLE.
Abai.—*See* NILE.
Abeokuta.—BURTON, R. F. A. ... an Exploration. 1863.
    Var: Abbekuta, Abbeokoota, Abeokkeutah.
Abessinia.—*See* ABYSSINIA.
Abissina, Countries of the.—*See* ABYSSINIA.
Abyssinia.—BARATTI, G. The late Travels of S. G. Baratti ... into the remote Countries of the Abissins, *etc.*   *Lond.*, 1670.
——— LUDOLPHUS, J. Jobi Ludolfi ... Historia Æthiopica, sive Brevis ... descriptio Regni Habessinorum, *etc.*   *Franc. ad M.*, 1681.
——— LUDOLPHUS, J. A New History of Ethiopia. Being a full description of ... Abessinia, *etc.*   *Lond.*, 1684.
——— LOBO, FATHER J. Voyage to A., *etc.*   *Lond.*, 1735.
——— BRUCE, J. Travels into A., to discover the source of the Nile. 1790.
——— VALENTIA, VISCOUNT. Voyages and travels to ... A. ... 1802-6. 1811.
——— SALT, H. Voyage to A. ... in 1809-10, *etc.*   1814.
——— SALT, H. Voyage en Abyssinie ... 1809-10, *etc.*   *Par.*, 1816.
——— PEARCE, N. The Life and Adventures of N. Pearce ... during a residence in A. from ... 1810 to 1819, *etc.*   *Lond.*, 1831.
——— RUSSELL, BP. M. Nubia and A., *etc.*   *Edin.*, 1832.
——— GOBAT, S. Journal of a Three Years' Residence in A., *etc.*   1834.
——— BLUMHARDT, C. H. [Extracts from the Journal of C. H. B. during his Voyage to A.]   1838.
——— COMBES, E. and TAMISIER, M. Voyage en Abyssinie, *etc.*   *Par.*, 1838.
——— KATTE, A. VON. Reisein Abyssinien im Jahre 1836. *Stuttg.*, 1838.
——— RÜPPEL, E. Reise in Abyssinien. *Frankf. a. M.*, 1838-40.
——— ABBADIE, A. d'. Voyage en Abyssinie. *Par.*, 1839.
——— ISENBERG, C. W., and KRAPF, J. L. Journals ... with a Geographical Memoir of A., *etc.*   1843.

B

Abyssinia.

Abyssinia. ABYSSINIA. Voyage en Abyssinie, exécuté ... 1839-1843, par une Commission Scientifique, etc. *Par.* [1845.]
— BIRD, J. A. ... reviewed. *Bombay*, 1845.
— SANTAREM, VISCOUNT DE. Rapport sur un Mémoire de M. de Silveira, relativement à la découverte des Terres du Prêtre Jean et de la Guinée, par les Portugais. *Par.*, 1846.
— BEKE, C. T. Description of the ... Church of Mártula Máriam in A. 1847.
— BEKE, C. T. On the Korarima, or Cardamom of A. 1847.
— BEKE, C. T. On the Languages and Dialects of A., etc. 1847.
— FERRET, A., and GALINIER. Voyage en Abyssinie, etc. *Par.*, 1847.
— BEKE, C. T. On the Geographical Distribution of the languages of A., etc. *Edin.*, 1849.
— BEKE, C. T. Über die geographische Verbreitung der Sprachen von Abessinien, etc. 1849.
— ABBADIE, A. D'. Réponses de Falasha dits Juifs d'Abyssinie aux questions faites par M. LUZZATO. *Par.*, 1850.
— HOTH, J. R. Schilderung der Naturverhältnisse in Süd-A. *Münch.*, 1851.
— PARKYNS, M. Life in A., etc. 1853.
— VAYSSIÈRES, A. Souvenirs d'un Voyage en Abyssinie. *Brux.*, 1857.
— STERN, H. A. Wanderings among the Falashas in A., etc. *Lond.*, 1862.
— LEJEAN, G. Théodore II., le Nouvel Empire d'Abyssinie, etc. *Par.* [1865.]
— APEL, F. H. Drei Monate in Abyssinien, etc. *Zürich*, 1866.
— ABYSSINIA. Routes in A., etc. *Lond.*, 1867.
— BAKER, SIR S. W. The Nile Tributaries of A., etc. *Lond.*, 1867.
— BEKE, C. T. The British Captives in A., etc. *Lond.*, 1867.
— COZZIKA, J. Question d'Abyssinie, etc. *Constantin.*, 1867.
— DUFTON, H. Narrative of a Journey through A., in 1862-3, etc. *Lond.*, 1867.
— ABBADIE, A. D'. Douze Ans dans la Haute-Éthiopie (Abyssinie). *Par.*, 1868.
— ABYSSINIA. Report on the Survey Operations, A. *Lond.* [1868.]
— BLANC, B. A Narrative of Captivity in A., etc. *Lond.*, 1868.
— HEUGLIN, M. T. von. Reise nach Abessinien, etc. *Jena*, 1868.
— LEJEAN, G. L'Abyssinie en 1868. *Par.*, 1868.
— PLOWDEN, W. C. Travels in A., etc. *Lond.*, 1868.
— MARKHAM, C. R. A History of the A.n Expedition, etc. *Lond.*, 1869.
— RASSAM, H. Narrative of the British Mission to ... A.; with Notices of the Countries traversed, etc. *Lond.*, 1869.
— ROHLFS, G. Im Auftrage Sr. Majestät des Königs von Preussen mit dem Englischen Expeditionscorps in Abessinien. *Bremen*, 1869.

Abyssinia — Adel.

Abyssinia.—HOLLAND, T. J., and HOZIER, H. Record of the Expedition to A., etc. *Lond.*, **1870**.

—— HOZIER, J. C. Remarks on the A.n Expenditure, etc. *Lond.*, **1870**.

—— Abyssinie. Voyage au Darfour, 1793-99. EYRIÈS. Vol. XIV.

—— Lobo, Father J. Voyage to A. PINKERTON. Vol. XV.

—— Poncet's Journey to A. PINKERTON. Vol. XV.

—— An Armenian, his report of . . . the Emperor of the Abazins, etc. PURCHAS. Vol. II.

—— Relation du Père Jeronimo Lobo de l'Empire des Abyssins, etc. THEVENOT. Vol. IV.

—— Valentia, Viscount. Voyages and Travels to . . . A. . . . 1802-6. VOYAGES and TRAVELS. A Collection, etc. 1805. Vol. XI.

—— Valentia, Viscount. Voyages and Travels to . . . A. 1802-6. VOYAGES and TRAVELS. A Collection, etc. 1810. Vol. IV.

—— Portenger, H. N. Narrative of the sufferings and adventures of . . . who was wrecked on the Shores of A. . . . 1802. VOYAGES and TRAVELS, New. 1819. Vol. II.

See also SHOA.

——, **South.**—JOHNSTON, C. Travels in S.n A., etc. **1844.**

Acapulco.—Gualle, F. Voyage from . . . A. . . . to the Lucones . . . 1582-84. HAKLUYT. Vol. III.

Achanti.—*See* ASHANTEE.

Acheen.—Voyage of Capt. R. Bowles to A., etc. KERR. Vol. VIII.

—— Hores, W. Discourse of his Voyage from Surat to A. . . . 1618-19. PURCHAS. Vol. I.

—— Andere Reisen des P. van Caerden und J. van Neck nach Achin, 1600-1602. VOYAGES and TRAVELS. Allgemeine Historie, etc. Vol. VIII.

—— Beaulieu, A. Reise . . . 1619-21 . . . nach Achem, etc. VOYAGES and TRAVELS. Allgemeine Historie, etc. Vol. X.

Achem, Achen, Achin.—*See* ACHEEN.

Açorea.—*See* AZORES.

Acræ.—HOGG, J. On A. . . . and its principal Antiquities. **1852.**

Acuco.—*See* ACUCO.

Aculco.—Vasquez de Coronado, F. Voyage . . . . . to A. . . . . . 1540. HAKLUYT. Vol. III.

Adal.—*See* ADEL.

Adamawa.—JOMARD, E. F. Remarques an anjet du Voyage du Docteur Barth dans l'A. *Paris.*

Adea.—*See* CAMBAT.

Adel.—HERICOURT, C. R. D'. Considérations . . sur . . . le Pays d'A., etc. *Par.*, **1841.**

—— JOHNSTON, C. Travels . . . through . . . A. to . . . Shoa. **1844.**

—— HERICOURT, C. R. D'. Second Voyage . . . dans le Pays des Adels, etc. *Par.*, **1846.**

Adelaide.—EYRE, E. J. Journals of Expeditions . . . Overland from A. to King George's Sound, *etc.* **1845.**
—— ABBOTT, F. Results . . . To which is added a Meteorological Summary for A., *etc.* *Hob. Town*, **1866.**
Adelsberg.—AGAPITO, COUNT G. Le Grotte di Adlersberg, *etc.*
Vienna, **1823.**
—— SCHMIDL, A. A. Die Grotten und Höhlen von A., *etc.*
Wien, **1854.**
—— —— Guide du Voyageur dans la Grotte d'A., *etc.* *Vienne*, **1854.**
—— —— Wegweiser in die Adelsberger Grotte, *etc.* *Wien*, **1858.**
Aden.—MERRWETHER, W. L. [Report on places lately visited, between A. and Suez.]
—— INDIAN PAPERS. Correspondence relating to A. **1839.**
—— WILDE, R. T. Remarks . . . on his Topographic Model of . . . A.
1844.
—— Reise von Aden nach Mocka, *etc.* VOYAGES and TRAVELS. Allgemeine Historie, *etc.* Vol. XI.
——, **Gulf of.**—WARD, C. Y. Pilote du Golfe d'A., *etc.* *Par.*, **1866.**
Adirri, River. *See* VOLTA.
Adjunta.—ALEXANDER, Sir J. E. Visit to the Cavern Temples of A, *etc.* **1829.**
—— BURGESS, J. The Rock-cut Temples of Ajanta, *etc.* *Bombay*, **1868.**
Adlersberg.—*See* ADELSBERG.
Admiral's Bay.—AMERICA, CENTRAL. Description of . . . a Road . . . from A. B. . . . to . . . the Pacific, *etc.* *Phil.*, **1852.**
Adofoodiah.—DUNCAN, J. Travels . . . from Whydah . . . to A., *etc.*
1847.
Adriatic Sea.—PURDY, J. New Sailing Directory for the Gulf of Venice, *etc.* **1834.**
—— BEAUTEMPS-BEAUPRÉ, M. Rapports sur les Rades . . . de la Côte Orientale du Golfe de Venise. **1849.**
—— PATON, A. A. Highlands and Islands of the A., *etc.* **1849.**
—— GRAS, M. A. LE. Manuel de la Navigation dans la Mer Adriatique, *etc.* *Par.*, **1855.**
—— CAMPANA, VISCONTI, and SMYTH. A. Pilot, *etc.* **1861.**
—— STRANGFORD, VISCOUNTESS. The Eastern Shores of the A. in 1863, *etc.* *Lond.*, **1864.**
Adur, River.—THORNE, J. Rambles by Rivers; the A., *etc.* **1847.**
Aegyptus.—*See* EGYPT.
Æolian Islands.—*See* LIPARI ISLANDS.
Aethiopia.—*See* ETHIOPIA.
Affghanistan, Affghaunistaun. *See* AFGHANISTAN.
Afghanistan.—LONG, H. L. Campaign of Alexander in A.
—— WYLD, J. Notes on Map of A., *etc.*
—— FORSTER, G. Journey . . . through A., *etc.* **1798.**

Afghanistan — Africa.

Afghanistan.— FRASER, J. B. Historical ... account of Persia ... including ... A., etc. *Edin.*, 1834.
— CONOLLY, A. Journey ... through ... Affghaunistaun. 1838.
— DURNES, SIR A. Leech, Lord, and Woods; Reports ... on A., etc. *Calc.*, 1839.
— PERSIA. Correspondence relating to Persia and A., 1834-39. 1839.
— OUTRAM, J. Rough Notes of the Campaign in ... A. in 1838-9. 1840.
— VIGNE, G. T. A personal Narrative of a Visit to ... A., etc. *Lond.*, 1840.
— HOUGH, MAJOR W. Narrative of ... the Expedition to A. in 1838-39. 1841.
— WILSON, H. H. Ariana Antiqua. A descriptive account of the Antiquities ... of A., etc. 1841.
— ATKINSON, J. The Expedition into A., etc. *Lond.*, 1842.
— ZIMMERMANN, C. Der Kriegs-Schauplatz in Inner-Asien, oder Bemerkungen zu der Uebersichts-Karte von A., etc. *Berl.*, 1842.
— MASSON, C. Narrative of ... Journeys in ... A., etc. 1844.
— THORNTON, E. Gazetteer of ... A., etc. 1844.
— LAL, MOHAN. Travels in ... A., etc. 1846.
— GRIFFITH, W. Journals of Travels in ... A., etc. *Calc.*, 1847.
— FERRIER, J. P. Caravan Journeys ... in ... A., etc. 1856.
— ———— History of the Afghans, etc. 1858.
— RAVERTY, H. G. Dictionary of the ... Language of the Afghans, etc. 1860.
— ———— Grammar of the ... Language of the Afghans, etc. 1860.
— BELLEW, H. W. Journal of a Political Mission to A., etc. *Lond.*, 1862.
— EYRE, Sir V. A Retrospect of the Affghan War, etc. *Lond.*, 1869.
— Forster, G. Voyage ... dans l'A. EYRIES Vol. XIII.
— Elphinstone. Voyage dans l'A., 1808. EYRIES Vol. XIV.
— *See also* HERAUT.

Afghaunistan.— *See* AFGHANISTAN.

Africa.— AUMALE, LE DUC D'. Campagnes en Afrique, 1840-44. *Paris.*
— LEO AFRICANUS, JOHN. Geographical Historie of A., etc. 1600.
— ———— Africæ Descriptio, etc. *Lugd Bat.*, 1632.
— OGILBY, J. A., being an accurate description, etc. 1670.
— BURGO, G. B. DE. Viaggio di cinque anni in ... A., etc. *Milano* [1686.]
— DAPPER. Description de l'Afrique, etc. *Amst.*, 1686.
— TELLEZ, B. Travels ... Voyage to ... the ... Coast of Africk, by F. Cauche. 1710.

Africa.

Africa.—Lucas, P. Voyage de, dans ... l'Afrique. *Par.*, **1712.**
—— Motraye, A. de la. Travels through ... part of A., *etc.* **1723-32.**
—— Moore, F. Travels into the Inland Parts of A., *etc.* **1738.**
—— Astley, T. New ... Collection of ... Travels ... in ... A., *etc.* **1745-47.**
—— Osorio, J. History of the Portuguese ... containing all their discoveries, from the Coast of Africk to ... China, *etc.* **1752.**
—— Lindsay, J. Voyage to the Coast of A. in 1758, *etc.* **1759.**
—— Mann, M. l'Abbé. Mémoire ... sur les Découvertes et les Etablissemens faits le long des Côtes d'Afrique par Hannon, *etc.* **1779.**
—— Toriño de San Miguel, V. Derrotero de las Costas de España ... y su Correspondiente de A., *etc.* *Madr.*, **1787.**
—— Schlichthorst, H. Geographia Africæ Herodotea. *Gottingæ*, **1788.**
—— Lamiral, M. Affrique et le Peuple Affriquain, *etc.* *Par.*, **1789.**
—— Levaillant, F. Voyage dans l'Intérieur de l'Afrique ... 1780-85. *Par.*, **1790.**
—— Saugnier, M. Relations de plusieurs voyages à la Côte d'Afrique, *etc.* *Par.*, **1792.**
—— Thunberg, C. P. Reisen in ... A. ... 1770 bis 1779, *etc.* *Berl.*, **1792-94.**
—— Levaillant, F. Second Voyage dans l'Intérieur de l'Afrique, *etc.* *Par. An.* **3.**
—— —— Second Voyage dans l'Intérieur de l'Afrique ... 1783-85. *Par.* **[1796.]**
—— Africa. New Sailing Directions for ... A., *etc.* **1799.**
—— Bruns, P. J. Neue systematische Erdbeschreibung von A. *Nürnb.*, **1799.**
—— Park, M. Travels in ... A., in 1795-97. **1800.**
—— Damberger, C. F. Travels in the Interior of A., *etc.* **1801.**
—— Slave Trade. A Concise Statement of the Question regarding the Abolition of the S. T. **1804.**
—— St. Vincent, J. B. G. M. Bory de. Voyage dans les quatre principales Iles des Mers d'Afrique pendant 1801, *etc.* *Par.*, **1804.**
—— Browne, W. G. Travels in A., *etc.* **1806.**
—— Lamalle, M. Dureau de. Géographie physique ... de l'Intérieur de l'Afrique, *etc.* *Par.*, **1807.**
—— Mirza Abu Taleb Khan. Voyages en ... Afrique ... 1799-1803, *etc.* *Par.*, **1811.**
—— Keatinge, Col. Travels in ... A. **1816.**
—— Clarke, E. D. Travels in ... A. **1816-24.**
—— Leyden, J. Historical Account of ... Travels in A., *etc.* *Edinb.*, **1817.**
—— Murray, H. Historical Account of discoveries and travels in A., *etc.* *Edinb.*, **1818.**

Africa.

Africa.—Bowditch, T. E. Mission ... to Ashantee, with ... notices of other parts of ... A. 1819.
—— Smith, Capt. J. The True Travels ... of Capt. J. Smith, in ... A. ... beginning about ... 1593, etc. *Richmond, U. S.*, 1819.
—— Mollien, G. Travels in the Interior of A., etc. 1820.
—— Hutton, W. Voyage to A., etc. 1821.
—— M'Queen, J. Geographical ... View of Northern Central A., etc. *Edin.*, 1821.
—— Bowditch, T. E. Excursions in Madeira ... with occurrences ... in A., etc. 1825.
—— Owen, W. F. W. Tables of Latitudes and Longitudes ... of places ... principally on the W. and E. Coasts of A., etc. 1827.
—— Clapperton, Comm. Journal of a second expedition Into the Interior of A., etc. 1829.
—— Ibn Batuta. Travels of [in ... A., 1324, 5], etc. *Or. Trans. Fund*, 1829.
—— Africa. Narrative of Discovery and Adventure in A., from the earliest ages. ... By Professor Jameson, etc. *Edin. and Lond.*, 1830.
—— Denniée, Baron. Précis ... de la Campagne d'Afrique. *Par.*, 1830.
—— Lander, R. Records of Capt. Clapperton's last Expedition to A., etc. 1830.
—— Rennell, J. The Geographical System of Herodotus examined ... with dissertations on ... the Ancient Circumnavigation of A., etc. 1830.
—— Douville, J. B. Ma Défense ... avec Projet de Voyage en Afrique. *Par.*, 1832.
—— —— Voyage ... dans l'Intérieur de l'Afrique Equinoxiale, etc. *Par.*, 1832.
—— Estancelin, L. Recherches sur les voyages ... des Navigateurs Normands en Afrique, etc. *Par.*, 1832.
—— Owen, W. F. W. Narrative of Voyage to explore the shores of A., etc. 1833.
—— Leovard, J. Travels ... and his Exploratory Mission to A. 1834.
—— Ritter, C. Géographie générale Comparée ... Afrique, etc. *Par.*, 1836.
—— Aubel, M. L'Importance de la question d'Afrique, etc. *Par.*, 1837.
—— Avezac, d'. Esquisse générale de l'Afrique. *Par.*, 1837.
—— Laird, M. and Oldfield, R. A. K. Narrative of an Expedition into the Interior of A., etc. 1837.
—— Alexander, Sir J. E. Expedition ... into the Interior of A., etc. 1838.
—— Banister, J. W. Memoir respecting British Interests ... in S. E. A. 1838.
—— Davidson, G. Notes taken ... in A. 1839.

Africa.

Africa.—Gurley, R. R. Address on African Colonization *Philad.*, 1839.
—— Martin, R. M. Statistics of the Colonies ... in ... A., etc.
Lond., 1839.
—— Buxton, T. F. The A. n Slave Trade, etc. 1840.
—— M'Queen, J. Geographical Survey of A., etc. *Lond.*, 1840.
—— —— Supplement to the Geographical Survey of A., etc.
Lond., 1840.
—— Murray, H., and others. Narrative of discovery and adventure in A., etc.
Edin., 1840.
—— Rummegger, Herr. Beiträge zur Physiognomik ... und Geographie des Afrikanischen Tropenlandes. 1840.
—— Bleek, G. De Nominum generibus linguarum Africae, etc.
Bonnae, 1841.
—— Ebn-Khaldoun. Histoire de l'Afrique sous la dynastie des Aghlabites, etc.
Par., 1841.
—— Russegger, J. Reisen in ... A., etc. *Stuttg.*, 1841.
—— Ternaux-Compans, H. Bibliothèque Asiatique et Africaine, etc.
Par., 1841.
—— Völter, D. Die Grundlinien der mathematischen Geographie von A., etc.
Esslingen, 1841.
—— Dandinel, J. Some account of the trade in Slaves from A., etc.
1842.
—— Buret, E. Question d'Afrique, etc. *Par.*, 1842.
—— Beaumont, G. de. État de la Question d'Afrique, etc. *Par.*, 1843.
—— Isenberg, C. W. and Krapf, J. L. Journals ... with a geographical Memoir of ... S. E. n A., etc. 1843.
—— Lopes de Lima, J. J. Ensaios sobre a Statistica das Possessões Portuguezas na A. Occidental e Oriental, etc. *Lisboa*, 1844-62.
—— Avezac, d'. Description ... de l'Afrique ancienne, etc.
Par., 1845.
—— Duvivier, Gén. Abolition de l'Esclavage, Civilisation du Centre de l'Afrique. 1845.
—— Koelle, S. W. Polyglotta Africana, etc. 1845.
—— Africa. La France en Afrique. *Par.*, 1846.
—— Forbes, F. E. Six Months' Service in the African Blockade. 1849.
—— Slave Trade. Resolutions of the Select Committee of the House of Lords in 1849 to consider ... the A. n Slave Trade. 1849-50.
—— Bonaparte, P. N. Un Mois en Afrique. *Par.*, 1850.
—— Winniett, Sir W. Papers respecting the Danish Possessions on the Coast of A., etc. 1850.
—— Yule, H. The A. n Squadron vindicated. 1850.
—— Slave Trade. African Slave Trade. African Squadron. 1851.
—— —— Extracts from ... Evidence ... relative to the Slave Trade. 1851.
—— Storks, R. Regulated Slave Trade. Evidence, etc. 1851.
—— Wilson, J. L. The British Squadron on the Coast of A., etc. 1851.

Africa.—COOLEY, W. D.   Inner A. laid open, *etc.*   1852.
—— GUMPRECHT, T. E.   Barthund Overwegs Untersuchungs-Reise . . . in das Innere A.   *Berl.*, 1852.
—— WERNE, F.   A. n Wanderings, *etc.*   1852.
—— KUNSTMANN, F.   Afrika vor den Entdeckungen der Portugiesen.   *Münch.*, 1853.
—— PETERMANN, A.   A. n Discovery.   1854.
—— ALFRED THE GREAT.   A description . . . of A., *etc.*   1855.
—— ANDERSSON, C. J.   Lake 'Ngami, or explorations in . . . S. W. A.   1856.
—— SCHIRREN, C.   Der Niandsha und die Hydrographischen Merkmale A.'s.   *Riga*, 1856.
—— HEUGLIN, T. VON.   Reisen in Nord-Ost-A., *etc.*   *Gotha*, 1857.
—— SNIDER-PELLEGRINI, A.   Du Développement du Commerce de l'Algérie avec l'Intérieur de l'Afrique, *etc.*   *Par.*, 1857.
—— CAVE, L. T.   The French in A.   1859.
—— JAMIESON, R.   The inefficacy of Treaties for the suppression of the A. n Slave Trade, *etc.*   1859.
—— ZIEGLER, J. M.   Ueber die neuesten Reisen und Entdeckungen in Inner-A.   *Winterl.*, 1859.
—— DUNSTERVILLE, E.   The Admiralty List of the Lights on the W. and S. Coasts of A. Corrected to 1860, 61, 62.   1860-62.
—— AUCAPITAINE, BARON H.   Étude sur . . . le commerce de l'Intérieur de l'Afrique.   *Par.*, 1861.
—— CHAILLU, P. B. DU.   Explorations . . . in Equatorial A., *etc.*   1861.
—— SLAVE TRADE.   Papers relative to Free Labour and the Slave Trade.   1861.
—— BALDWIN, W. C.   African Hunting, *etc.*   1863.
—— BENJAMIN, J. B.   Eight years in . . . A., *etc.*   *Hanov.*, 1863.
—— CHAILLU, P. B. DU.   Voyages . . . dans l'Afrique Équatoriale, *etc.*   *Par.*, 1863.
—— GRAS, M. A. LE.   Routier de la Côte Sud et Sud-est d'Afrique, *etc.*   *Par.*, 1863.
—— BAINES, T.   Explorations in S.W. A., *etc.*   *Lond.*, 1864.
—— FAIDHERBE, L.   Chapitres de Géographie sur le Nord-Ouest de l'Afrique.   *Saint Louis*, 1864.
—— GRANT, J. A.   A Walk across A., *etc.*   *Edin., Lond.*, 1864.
—— HOGG, J.   On some Old Maps of A., *etc.*   1864.
—— HOSSET, A. F. R. DE.   Routier des Côtes Sud, Sud-est et Est d'Afrique, *etc.*   *Par.*, 1866.
—— MACQUEEN, J.   The A.n Slave Trade.   [1867.]
—— ROHLFS, G.   Neueste Nachrichten aus dem Innern A.'s.   [*Gotha*] 1867.

Africa.

Africa.—HAMILTON, A. On the Trade with the Coloured Races of A. *Lond.*, **1868**.

—— BERLIOUX, E. F. La Traite Orientale. Histoire des Chasses à l'Homme ... en Afrique, *etc.* *Par.*, **1870**.

—— CANTILHO, A. M. de. Études ... sur les Colonnes ou Monuments commémoratifs des découvertes Portugaises en Afrique. *Lisb.*, **1870**.

—— HAMILTON, C. Sketches of Life and Sport in S.E.n A., *etc.* *Lond.*, **1870**.

—— JOHNSTON, A. K. Atlas of the British Empire in ... A. ... with ... letterpress. *Edin. and Lond.*, [**1870**.]

—— ROHLFS, G. Land und Volk in A. Berichte, *etc.* *Bremen*, **1870**.

—— Cada Mosto, A. da. Two Voyages to ... A. ... 1455-56. ASTLEY. Vol. I.

—— V. de Gama's Voyage to India, round A., 1497. ASTLEY. Vol. I.

—— Voyages to several parts of A., *etc.* ASTLEY. Vol. I.

—— Voyages of the Portuguese along the Coast of A., as far as the Cape of Good Hope. ASTLEY. Vol. I.

—— Moore, F. Travels into the inland parts of A., *etc.* ASTLEY. Vol. II.

—— Of the Trees, fruits ... and ... animals in this part of A. ASTLEY. Vol. II.

—— Two Voyages to Cape de Verde and the neighbouring Coast of A., *etc.* ASTLEY. Vol. II.

—— Villault, Sieur. Abstract of a Voyage to the Coast of A. ... in 1666. ASTLEY. Vol. II.

—— Smith, Capt. J. True Travels ... in ... A. ... from 1592 to 1629. CHURCHILL. Vol. II.

—— Biddulph, W. Travels of four Englishmen ... into A. ... in 1600 and 1611. CHURCHILL. Vol. VII.

—— Froger, Sieur. Relation of a Voyage made in 1695-7 on the Coasts of A., *etc.* CHURCHILL. Vol. VIII.

—— Houghton. Voyage dans l'intérieur d'Afrique. EYRIÈS. Vol. X.

—— Voyages en A. EYRIÈS. Vol. X.

—— Park, M. Voyage dans l'intérieur de l'Afrique. EYRIÈS. Vol. XI.

—— Siouah, Fezzan, et Intérieur de l'Afrique. EYRIÈS. Vol. XIV.

—— Voyage dans l'est et dans le nord de l'Afrique. Mozambique. Thoman. Salt. EYRIÈS. Vol. XIV.

—— The Fardle of Facions, conteining the ... customes ... of ... Affricke and Asie, 1555. HAKLUYT. Vol. V.

—— Benjamin, Rabbi. Travels through ... A. ... 1160-1173. HARRIS, J. Vol. I.

—— Cada Mosto and P. de Cintra. Original Journals of the Voyages of, to the Coast of A., 1455-56. KERR. Vol. II.

—— Portuguese Discoveries along the Coast of A. ... 1463 ... 1466. KERR. Vol. II.

Africa.

Africa.—Découvertes et Conquêtes des Portugais. Gama. Cabral. Albuquerque. LAHARPE, J. F. Vol. I.

——— Voyages des Anglais sur les Côtes d'Afrique. LAHARPE, J. Vol. I.

——— Europe, A., India. LATHAM, R. G. Descriptive Ethnology. Vol. II.

——— Possessions in A., etc. MARTIN, R. M. History of the British Colonies. Vol. IV.

——— Park, M. Travels into the Interior . . . of A., in 1795-97. PELHAM. Vol. I.

——— Park's Travels in A. PINKERTON. Vol. XVI.

——— Of Tharsis . . . Of the Ancient Navigations about A., etc. PURCHAS. Vol. I.

——— A. n Possessions of the King of Spaine and the Turke. PURCHAS. Vol. II.

——— Gramaye, J. B. Relations of the Christianitie of A. . . . 1619. PURCHAS. Vol. II.

——— João dos Sanctos, Friar. Collections out of . . . his Æthiopia Orientalis . . . and . . . other Portugals, for the better knowledge of A., etc. PURCHAS. Vol. II.

——— Leo, J. Observations of A., etc. PURCHAS. Vol. II.

——— Sandys, G. Relations of A. . . . 1610. PURCHAS. Vol. II.

——— Smith, Capt. J. Travels . . . on the Sea Coasts of . . . A. . . . about 1596. PURCHAS. Vol. II.

——— Barkley, G. Travels . . . in . . . A. . . . 1605. PURCHAS. Vol. III.

——— Hannone. Navigatione nelle parti dell' A., etc. RAMUSIO. Vol. I.

——— Leone Africano, G. Della descrittione dell' A., 1520. RAMUSIO. Vol. I.

——— Cada Mosto, A. da. Reise . . . längst der Africanischen Küste bis Rio Grande, 1455-56. VOYAGES and TRAVELS. Allgemeine Historie, etc. Vol. II.

——— Brock, P. van den. Reise nach . . . der Küste von A., 1606. VOYAGES and TRAVELS. Allgemeine Historie, etc. Vol. III.

——— Moore, F. Reisen in die Inländischen Theile von A., etc. VOYAGES and TRAVELS. Allgemeine Historie, etc. Vol. III.

——— Villault, Ritter. Auszug aus einer Reise nach den Küsten von A. . . . 1666. VOYAGES and TRAVELS. Allgemeine Historie, etc. Vol. III.

——— Ovington, J. Reise . . . in A. . . . 1690-93. VOYAGES and TRAVELS. Allgemeine Historie, etc. Vol. X.

——— Vocabulaires appartenant à diverses Contrées . . . de l'Afrique, par M. Koenig, etc. VOYAGES and TRAVELS. Recueil, etc. Vol. IV.

——— Dumont, P. J. Narrative of Thirty-four Years' Slavery and Travels in A., etc. VOYAGES and TRAVELS. New. 1819. Vol. II.

——— Travideani, or Aveiro, Signor. Letters from A. . . . 1818-20. VOYAGES and TRAVELS, New. 1819. Vol. V.

——— Moore, F. Travels into the Inland Parts of A. 1730. VOYAGES and TRAVELS. The World displayed. Vol. XVII.

Africa, Central.

Africa, Central.—Hodgson, W. B. Remarks on the recent Travels of Dr. Barth in C. A., etc.

—— —— Denham, D. and Clapperton, H. Narrative of Travels ... in Northern and C. A. **1826.**

—— —— Jomard, E. F. Remarques sur les Decouvertes Géographiques faites dans l'Afrique Centrale. *Par.*, **1827.**

—— —— Caillié, R. Travels through C. A., etc. **1830.**

—— —— Smith, A. Report of the Expedition for exploring C. A. from the Cape ... 1834. *Cape Town*, **1836.**

—— —— Cooley, W. D. Negroland ... or an Inquiry into the Early History ... of C. A. **1841.**

—— —— Hodgson, W. B. The Foulahs of C. A., etc. *N. Y.*, **1843.**

—— —— Jamieson, R. Is C. A. to remain sealed, etc. *Liverp.*, **1844.**

—— —— Jomard, E. F. Renseignements Géographiques sur une partie de l'Afrique Centrale, etc. *Par.*, **1846.**

—— —— Ungar, A. C.-A., ein neuer ... Ansiedlungspunkt, etc. *Stuttg.*, **1850.**

—— —— Abbadie, A. d'. Observations relatives ... aux lacs de l'Afrique Centrale. *Par.*, **1851.**

—— —— Castelnau, F. de. Renseignements sur l'Afrique Centrale, etc. *Par.*, **1851.**

—— —— Hogg, J. Notice on Recent Discoveries in C. A., etc. **1851.**

—— —— Richardson, J. Narrative of a Mission to C. A., in 1850-51. **1853.**

—— —— Bruk-Rollet, M. Le Nil Blanc et le Soudan, études sur l'Afrique centrale, etc. *Par.*, **1855.**

—— —— Malte-Brun, V. A. Résumé historique de la Grande Exploration de l'Afrique Centrale faite de 1850 à 1855, par J. Richardson, etc. *Par.*, **1856.**

—— —— Barth, H. Travels ... in ... C. A., etc. *Lond.*, **1857.**

—— —— Roscher, A. Ptolemæus und die Handelsstrassen in C.-A. *Gotha*, **1857.**

—— —— Laird, M. Statement made to the C. A.n Company. *Lond.*, **1858.**

—— —— Malte-Brun, V. A. Résumé historique de l'Exploration faite dans l'Afrique Centrale de 1853 à 1856 par. ... E. Vogel. *Par.*, **1858.**

—— —— Schauenburg, E. Reisen in Central-Afrika von Mungo Park bis auf Dr. H. Barth, etc. *Lahr.*, **1859.**

—— —— Burton, R. F. The Lake Regions of C. A., etc. *Lond.*, **1860.**

—— —— Burton, R. F. The Lake Regions of C. A., etc. *N. Y.*, **1860.**

—— —— Campbell, R. Pilgrimage to my Motherland ... a Sojourn among the Egbas and Yorubas of C. A., etc. **1861.**

—— —— Petherick J. Egypt ... and C. A., etc. *Edin. and Lond.*, **1861.**

Africa, Central — Africa, East Coast.

Africa, Central.—BAIKIE, W. B. Despatches ... relative to ... C. A. as a future Cotton-field. 1862.

―――― BARTH, H. Sammlung ... Central-Afrikanischer Vokabularien, etc. *Gotha*, 1862.

―――― BARTH, H. Collection of Vocabularies of C.-A. Languages, etc. *Gotha*, 1863.

―――― TINNE, J. A. Geographical Notes of Expeditions in C. A., etc. *Liverp.*, 1864.

―――― ROWLEY, H. The Story of the Universities' Mission to C. A., etc. *Lond.*, 1866.

―――― ROSCHER, A. Ptolemæus und die Handelsstrassen in Central-Afrika. GERMANY. Anzeige, etc.

―――― See also BABL.

——, **East.**—AFRICA. English and French Rivalry in E.n A.

―――― GUILLAIN, M. Documents sur ... l'Afrique Orientale, etc. *Paris.*

―――― BOTELHO, S. X. Memoria ... sobre os dominios Portuguezes na A. Oriental. *Lisb.*, 1835.

―――― BIRD, J. Abyssinia, E. A. ... reviewed. *Bombay*, 1845.

―――― FROBERVILLE, M. DE. Rapport sur les Races Nègres de l'Afrique Orientale au Sud de l'Équateur. *Par.*, 1850.

―――― COOLEY, W. D. Claudius Ptolemy. ... his knowledge of E.n A., etc. *Lond.*, 1854.

―――― BURTON, R. F. First Footsteps in E. A., etc. 1856.

―――― MACLEOD, J. L. On the Resources of E.n A. 1858.

―――― MALTE-BRUN, V. A. Résumé historique de l'Exploration à la recherche des Grands Lacs de l'Afrique Orientale, faite 1857-58 par R. F. Burton et J. H. Speke. *Par.*, 1859.

―――― KRAPF, J. L. Travels ... during an Eighteen Years' Residence in E. A., etc. 1860.

―――― MACLEOD, J. L. Travels in E.n A., etc. 1860.

―――― COOLEY, W. D. Memoir of the Lake Regions of E. A. reviewed, etc. 1864.

―――― HORSBURGH, J. Instructions Nautiques ... Côte Est d'Afrique, etc. *Par.*, 1864.

―――― MUNZINGER, W. Ostafrikanische Studien. *Schaffh.*, 1864.

―――― WAKEFIELD, T. Footprints in E.n A., etc. *Lond.*, 1866.

―――― KERSTEN, O. Ueber Colonisation in Ost-Afrika, etc. *Wien*, 1867.

―――― DECKEN, BARON C. C. VON DER. Reisen in Ost-Afrika ... 1859 bis 1865. *Leip. u. Heid.*, 1869, 70.

―――― See also AJAN.-MOMBAS.

——, **East Coast.**—SALT, H. Voyage to Abyssinia ... an Account of the Portuguese Settlements on the E. C. of A., etc. 1814.

―――― A Description of the ... E. Coast of A., etc. ASTLEY. Vol. III.

Africa, East Coast—Africa, North Coast.

Africa, East Coast.—Lancaster, J. Memorable Voyage ... along the E. Coast of A. ... 1591. HAKLUYT. Vol. II.

———— Almeyda, F. de. Voyage ... with an account of ... the E.n C. of A., *etc.* KERR. Vol. VI.

———— Course of the Indian Trade ... with some account of the Settlement of the Arabs on the E. C. of A. KERR. Vol. VI.

———— Beschreibung der Länder längst der östlichen Küste von A., *etc.* VOYAGES and TRAVELS. Allgemeine Historie, *etc.* Vol. V.

———— Prior, J. Voyage along the E.n Coast of A. ... 1813. VOYAGES and TRAVELS, Now. 1819. Vol. II.

————, **North.**—Hogg, J. On some Roman Antiquities recently discovered by Dr. Barth in N. A.

———— AFRICA. Historical ... sketch of the ... Europeans in N. and W. A. at the close of the Eighteenth Century. *Edin.*, **1799.**

———— HORNEMANN, F. Voyage ... dans l'Afrique Septentrionale, *etc.* *Par.*, **1803.**

———— LYON, G. F. Narrative of Travels in N. A., in 1818-20, *etc.* **1821.**

———— WALCKENAER, BARON C. A. Recherches géographiques sur l'Intérieur de l'A. Septentrionale, *etc.* *Par.*, **1821.**

———— DENHAM, D. and CLAPPERTON H. Narrative of Travels in N. and Central A., *etc.* **1826.**

———— EBN-ED-DIN EL-EGHWAATI, HAWL Notes of a Journey into the Interior of N. A., *etc.* *Wash.*, **1830.**

———— GRÄBERG, COUNT J. Carta geografica del.'Africa settentrionale di G. Segato. *Gennaio*, **1830.**

———— AFRICA. Excursions dans l'Afrique Septentrionale, par la Société pour l'exploration de Carthage, *etc.* *Par.*, **1838.**

———— HODGSON, W. B. Notes on N. A., *etc.* *N. Y.*, **1844.**

———— BARTH, H. Wanderungen ... Bd. 1. Das Nordafrikanische Gestadeland. *Berl.*, **1849.**

———— TRÉMEAUX, M. Voyage ... dans l'Afrique Septentrionale ... 1847-48. *Par.*, **1853.**

———— HAMILTON, J. Wanderings in N. A. **1856.**

———— BARTH, H. Travels ... in N. ... A., *etc.* *Lond.*, **1857.**

———— GERARD, J. Life and Adventures ... among the Lions of N. A., *etc.* **1857.**

———— SAINT-MARTIN, V. DE. Le Nord de l'Afrique dans l'Antiquité Grecque et Romaine, *etc.* *Par.*, **1863.**

———— ORMSBY, J. Autumn Rambles in N. A. *Lond.*, **1864.**

———— Rennell, J. Observations on Mr. Scott's Routes in N. A. VOYAGES and TRAVELS, Now. 1819, *etc.* Vol. IX.

———— Réponse aux Questions proposées par la Société de Géographie sur l'A. Septentrionale, par M. Delaporte. VOYAGES and TRAVELS, Recueil, *etc.* Vol. II.

———— **North Coast.**—BEECHY, F. W. and H. W. Proceedings of ... Expedition to ... the N. C. of A., *etc.* **1828.**

Africa, North-west.—BOWDITCH, T. E. Essay on the Geography of N. W. A. *Par.*, 1821.
——, South.—BARROW, SIR J. Account of Travels into the Interior of S. A., *etc.* 1801-4.
—— —— BARROW, SIR J. Voyage to . . . S. A., *etc.* 1806.
—— —— LICHTENSTEIN, H. Travels in S.n A. in 1803-6, *etc.* 1812-15.
—— —— CAMPBELL, J. Travels in S. A., *etc.* 1815.
—— —— LATROBE, C. J. Journal of a Visit to S. A. in 1815 and 1816, *etc.* 1818.
—— —— BURCHELL, W. J. Travels in the Interior of S. A. 1822.
—— —— CAMPBELL, J. Second Journey into S. A., *etc.* 1822.
—— —— THOMPSON, G. Travels . . . in S.n A., *etc.* 1827.
—— —— AFRICA. Report . . . relating to the condition of the . . . Native Tribes of S. A., *etc.* 1830.
—— —— AFRICA. S. African Directory Advertiser for 1831. *Cape Town*, 1831.
—— —— HERSCHEL, SIR J. F. W. Instructions for making . . . Meteorological Observations in S. A., *etc.* 1835.
—— —— MOODIE, J. W. D. Ten Years in S. A., *etc.* 1835.
—— —— STEEDMAN, A. Wanderings . . . in the Interior of S. A. 1835.
—— —— HARRIS, SIR W. C. Narrative of an Expedition into S. A., in 1836-7, *etc.* *Bombay*, 1838.
—— —— MOODIE, D. The Record; or, a Series of Official Papers relative to . . . the Native Tribes of S. A., *etc.* *Cape Town*, 1838.
—— —— SHAW, B. Memorials of S. A. *Lond.*, 1840.
—— —— MOFFAT, R. Missionary Labours and Scenes in S.n A. 1842.
—— —— METHUEN, H. H. Life in the Wilderness; or Wanderings in S. A. *Lond.*, 1846.
—— —— DELEGORGUE, A. Voyage dans l'Afrique Australe, *etc.* *Par.*, 1847.
—— —— AFRICA. The Lights of S. A. . . . corrected to 1849, 51, 52, 56, 57, 58, 59. 1849-59.
—— —— CUMMING, R. G. Five Years in the Far Interior of S. A. 1850.
—— —— NAPIER, E. E. Excursions in S.n A., *etc.* 1850.
—— —— FREEMAN, J. J. Tour in S. A., *etc.* 1851.
—— —— GALTON, F. Narrative of an Explorer in Tropical S. A. 1853.
—— —— GAMITTO, A. C. P. O Muata Cazembe e os povos Maraves . . . da A. Austral, *etc.* *Lisb.*, 1854.
—— —— MOFFAT, R. Letter to . . . A. Tidman, on his Journey to . . . S. A. 1855.
—— —— FLEMING, F. Southern A. A Geography, *etc.* 1856.

Africa, South — Africa, West.

Africa, South. LIVINGSTONE, D. Missionary Travels and Researches in S. A., etc. Lond., 1857.

—— —— LIVINGSTONE, D. Outlines of Missionary Journeys and Discoveries in Central S. A. Lond., 1857.

—— —— MAGYAR, L. M. L. Délafrikai levelei és naplokivonatai. Kiadta Hunfalvy János. Pest, 1857.

—— —— MALTE-BRUN, V. A. Résumé historique des Explorations faites dans l'Afrique Australe de 1849 à 1850 par ... Livingstone. Par., 1857.

—— —— CORTAMBERT, E. Esquisse de la Géographie ... d'une partie d'Afrique Australe Intérieure, etc. Par., 1858.

—— —— DRAYSON, A. W. Sporting Scenes amongst the Kaffirs of S. A. 1858.

—— —— HALL, H. Manual of S. A.n Geography. Cape T., 1859.

—— —— DUNSTERVILLE, E. The Admiralty List of the Lights of S. A. ... corrected to 1860, 61, 62. 1860-62.

—— —— CASALIS, E. The Basutos; or, Twenty-three years in S. A. 1861.

—— —— LAYARD, E. L. The Birds of S. A., etc. Cape T. and Lond., 1867.

—— —— AFRICA. [Newspaper Cuttings relating to Karl Mauch's discovery of Gold in S. A.] [1867, 68.]

—— —— AFRICA. [Newspaper Cuttings relating to the S. A.n Gold-Fields] 1868.

—— —— BAMANG-WATO. To Ophir direct: or, the S. A.n Gold-Fields, etc. Lond., 1868.

—— —— CHAPMAN, J. Travels in the Interior of S. A., etc. Lond., 1868.

—— —— CORNELISSEN, J. F. On the Temperature of the Sea at the Surface near the S. point of A. Utrecht [1868.]

—— —— AFRICA. South A. and its Resources, etc. Lond., 1870.

—— —— Voyage to ... Countries in ... S. ... A. in 1682, by J. Merolla da Sorrento. ASTLEY. Vol. III.

—— —— Merolla da Sorrento, J. Voyage to ... several ... countries in the Southern Africk. CHURCHILL. Vol. I.

—— —— Merolla, H. Eine Reise ... in den südlichen Theilen von A., 1682-88. VOYAGES and TRAVELS. Allgemeine Historia, etc. Vol. IV.

—— **South Coast.** AFRICA. The Lights on the W. and S. Coasts of A. Corrected to 1848, 51, 55, 57, 59. 1848-59.

—— —— ERDEN, J. The Coast of S. A., etc. Grahamst., 1862.

—— **West.** AFRICA. Historical ... sketch of the ... Europeans 'n N. and W. A. at the close of the Eighteenth Century. Edin., 1793.

—— —— GOLDBERRY, S. M. X. Fragmens d'un Voyage en Afrique fait pendant ... 1785-1787, dans les contrées Occidentales, etc. Par., 1802.

—— —— DUFUR, J. Journal ... comprising Notes ... relative to the ... Interior of W. A., etc. 1824.

Africa, West.—LAING, G. A.   Travels in the Timannee, Kooranko, and
  Soolima Countries in W. n A.   **1825.**
——— ———   GRAY, W. and DOCHARD.   Travels in W. A. in 1818-21. etc.
  1826.
——— ———   ALEXANDER, SIR J. E.   Narrative of a voyage . . . among
  the Colonies of W. A., etc.   **1837.**
——— ———   MACBRAIR, R. M.   Sketches of a Missionary's Travels in . . .
  W. n A., etc.   **1839.**
——— ———   FREEMAN, T. B.   Extracts from the Journal of . . . a visit
  . . . to Ashantee, in the Interior of W. A.   **1840.**
——— ———   EAST, D. J.   Western A.; its condition, etc.   **1844.**
——— ———   WALKER, S. A.   Missions in W. n A., etc.   Dubl., **1845.**
——— ———   BOUET-VILLAUMEZ, COUNT E.   Description Nautique des
  Côtes . . . comprises entre le Sénégal et l'Equateur.   Par., **1846.**
——— ———   DUNCAN, J.   Travels in W. A., etc.   **1847.**
——— ———   HUTCHINSON, T. J.   Narrative of the Niger . . . Explora-
  tion . . . with remarks on the Malaria . . . of W. n. A.   **1855.**
——— ———   WILSON, J. L.   W. n A., its History, etc.   **1856.**
——— ———   DANIELL, W. F.   Observations on the Copals of W. A.
  1857.
——— ———   HUTCHINSON, T. J.   Impressions of W. n. A., etc.   **1858.**
——— ———   VALDEZ, F. T.   Six Years of a Traveller's Life in W. n A.
  Lond., **1861.**
——— ———   GRAS, M. A. LE.   Phares des Côtes Occidentales d'Afrique
  . . . Corrigés, 1862-63.   Par., **1862, 63.**
——— ———   BURTON, R. F.   Wanderings in W. A., etc.   **1863.**
——— ———   VALDEZ, F., T.   A. Occidental   Noticias, etc.   Lisbon, **1864.**
——— ———   HORTON, J. A. B.   W. A. n Countries and Peoples, etc.
  Lond., **1868.**

——— ———   See also BENIN.

———, **West Coast.**—ADAMS, R.   The Narrative of; who was wrecked
  on the W. C. of A. in 1810, etc.   **1816.**
——— ———   COCHELET, C.   Narrative of the Shipwreck of the *Sophia* in
  1819, on the W. C. of A., etc.   **1822.**
——— ———   ADAMS, CAPT. J.   Remarks . . . with an Account of the
  European Trade with the W. C. of A.   **1823.**
——— ———   ROUSSIN, CONTRE-AMIRAL LE BARON.   Memoir on the
  Navigation of the W. C. of A. . . . 1817, 18, etc.   **1827.**
——— ———   GAMA, A. DE S. DA.   Memoria sobre as Colonias de Portugal
  . . . na Costa Occidental d'A., em 1814, etc.   Par., **1839.**
——— ———   SLAVE TRADE.   Practical Remarks on the Slave Trade of
  the W. C. of A., etc.   **1839.**
——— ———   SANTAREM, VISCOUNT DE.   Memoria sobre a Prioridade dos
  Descobrimentos Portuguezes na Costa d'A. Occidental.   Par., **1841.**
——— ———   SANTAREM, VISCOUNT DE.   Atlas . . . devant servir de
  preuves à l'ouvrage sur la Priorité de la Découverte . . . sur la Côte
  Occidentale d'Afrique . . . par les Portugais, etc.   Par., **1842.**

C

Africa, West Coast.—Santarem, Viscount de. Recherches sur ... la découverte des Pays situés sur la Côte Occidentale d'Afrique, au-delà du Cap Bojador, etc. *Par.*, **1842.**

———— Africa.—The Lights on the W. and S. Coasts of A. Corrected to 1848, 51, 52, 57, 59. **1848-59.**

———— ———— Africa.—Sailing Directions for the W. C. of A. **1849.**

———— ———— Kerhallet, C. P. de. Description Nautique de la Côte Occidentale d'Afrique, etc. *Par.*, **1849.**

———— ———— Africa.—Renseignements sur la partie de la Côte entre le Cap Négro et le Cap Lopez. *Par.*, **1850.**

———— ———— Fox, W. Brief History of the Wesleyan Missions on the W. C. of A., etc. **1851.**

———— ———— Kerhallet, C. P. de. Manuel de la Navigation à la Côte Occidentale d'Afrique. *Par.*, **1851-2.**

———— ———— Anderson, C. J. A Journey to Lake 'Ngami ... from the W. Coast, etc. **1854.**

———— ———— African Pilot; or Sailing Directions for the W. C. of A., etc. **1856.**

———— ———— Santarem, Viscount de. Statement ... proving the Right of the Crown of Portugal to ... Territories ... on the W.n C. of A., etc. **1856.**

———— ———— Vallon, A. Influence des Courants sur la Navigation à la Côte Occidentale d'Afrique. *Par.*, **1860.**

———— ———— Horton, J. A. B. Physical and Medical Climate and Meteorology of the W. Coast of A., etc. *Lond.*, **1867.**

———— ———— Account of the French Settlements between Cape Blanco and Sierra Leona. Astley. Vol. II.

———— ———— Brue, A. Voyages ... along the W. C. of A., etc. Astley. Vol. II.

———— ———— Voyages ... along the W. C. of A., etc. Astley. Vol. II.

———— ———— Voyages ... by the Portuguese along the W-n. C. of A. ... under the direction of Don Henry. Kerr. Vol. II.

———— ———— Brüe, A. Reisen ... längst den westlichen Küsten von A., 1697. Voyages and Travels. Allgemeine Historie. Vol. II.

———— ———— Spilsbury, F. B. Account of a Voyage to the W. C. of A. ... 1805. Voyages and Travels. A Collection, etc. 1805. Vol. VI.

———— ———— Cochelet, C. Narrative of the Shipwreck of the *Sophia*, 1819, on the W.n C. of A., etc. Voyages and Travels, New. 1819, etc. Vol. IX.

———— ———— Misrab, M. Narrative of a Journey ... to the W.n C. of A., 1821. Voyages and Travels, New. 1819, etc. Vol. IX.

————, **Windward Coast of.**—Corry, J. Observations upon the W. C. of A., etc. *Lond.*, **1807.**

Africa Francese.—See Algeria.

Aggetelek.—See Aotelek.

Agimere.—See Ajmere.

Agogna.—Lizzoli, L. Osservazioni sul Dipartimento dell' A. *Mil.*, **1802.**

Agra.—LLOYD, SIR W. Narrative of a Journey... viâ... A., etc.
   Lond., 1840.
—— Bernier F. Voyage to Surat... and a description of... A., etc.
   CHURCHILL. Vol. VIII.
—— Finch, W. Observations... in 1607... Journey to A., etc.
   PURCHAS. Vol. I.
—— Mandelslo, J. A. Reise... nach A., etc. VOYAGES and TRAVELS.
   Allgemeine Historie, etc. Vol. X.
Agria.—*See* EGER.
Agro Pontino.—See PONTINE MARSHES.
Agro Trojano.—*See* TROAD.
Agtelek.—SCHMIDL, A. A. Die Baradla-Höhle bei A., etc.   *Wien*, 1857.
Aguignan.—Byron, Comm. Voyage... to... A.... 1764-66.
   HAWKESWORTH, J. Vol. I.
Ägypten.—*See* EGYPT.
Ahmedabad.—Mandelslo, J. A. Reise bis nach A., etc. VOYAGES and
   TRAVELS. Allgemeine Historie, etc. Vol. XI.
Ai.—NEWBOLD, T. J. On the Site of Hai, or A., etc.
Aigle.—RAZOUMOWSKY, COUNT G. DE.   Œuvres. Contenant, Voyage miné-
   ralogique... à... A., etc.   *Lausanne*, 1784.
—— RAZOUMOWSKY, COUNT G. DE.   Voyages Minéralogiques dans le
   Gouvernement d'A., etc.   *Lausanne*, 1784.
Ain-es-Salah.—*See* INSALAH.
Ain Salah.—*See* INSALAH.
Ait Fraoucen.—AUGAPITAINE, BARON H. Notice sur la Tribu des A. F.
   Alger.
Aix-la-Chapelle.—BILDEBBECK, L. VON. Wegweiser für... Aachen,
   etc.   *Aachen*, 1825.
Aix-les-Bains.—MORTILLET, G. Guide du Baigneur et de l'Etranger à
   A.-les-B., etc.   *Chambéry*, 1855.
Ajan.—BUSSEN, G. De Azania... commentatio, etc.   *Bonnæ*, 1852.
Ajanta.—*See* ADJUNTA.
Ajmeer.—*See* AJMERE.
Ajmere.—Steel, R. and Crowther J. Journey from A. to Ispahan, 1615-16.
   KERR. Vol. IX.
—— —— Journal of a Journey from Azmere... to Spahan...
   1615-16. PURCHAS. Vol. I.
Ajmir.—*See* AJMERE.
Alaba.—TELLEZ, B. Travels... and an Account of... A., etc.   1710.
Alabama.—KING, Hon. T. B. A.... and Georgia Railroad.   *Wash.*, 1848.
Aland Islands.—BUNBURY, S. A. A Summer in... the A. I., etc.
   1856.

Alaahka.—*See* ALASKA.
Alaska.—DALL, W. H. A. and its resources,   *Amst.*, 1816.
—— PERREY, A. Documents sur les Tremblements de Terre... de la
   péninsule d'Aljaska, etc.   *Dijon*, 1866.

   c 2

Alaska — Aleppo.

Alaska.—WHYMPER, F. Travel and Adventure in the Territory of A., *etc.*
Lond., 1868.

Alata.—BEKE, C. T. Mémoire justificatif en réhabilitation des Pères P. Paez et J. Lobo en ce qui concerne leurs visites . . . à la Cataracte d'Alata.
Par., 1849.

Albania.—HOBHOUSE, J. C. Journey through A., *etc.* 1813.
—— HOLLAND, H. Travels in . . . A., *etc.* 1819.
—— HUGHES, T. S. Travels in . . . A. 1820.
—— ———— Travels in Greece and A. 1830.
—— SPENCER, E. Travels . . . through . . . A., *etc.* 1851.
—— LEAR, E. Journal of a Landscape Painter in A., *etc.* 1852.
—— WINGFIELD, W. F. Tour in . . . A., *etc.* 1859.
—— ISTRIA, D. D'. Fyletia e Arbenoré proj Kanekate Laoshima. Enkethyeme ne Shkjipe perel D. C. *Livourne*, 1867.
—— Pouqueville, F. C. H. L. Travels through . . . A. . . . 1798-1801, *etc.* VOYAGES and TRAVELS. A Collection, *etc.* 1805. Vol. III.
—— ———— Travels in . . . A. . . . 1805. VOYAGES and TRAVELS, New, 1819. Vol. IV.
——, **South.**—BERESFORD, G. DE LA P. Sketches of Scenes in S. A. 1855.

Albany.—PHILIPPS, T. Advantages of Emigration to . . . A., S. Africa.
Lond., 1834.

Alben.—*See* PLANINA.

Albert N'yanza.—BAKER, SIR S. W. The A. N., *etc.* *Lond.*, 1866.

Albreda.—BRUE, A. Journey from A. to Kachao . . . in 1700. ASTLEY. Vol. II.

—— ———— Reise von A. . . . nach Karhao zu Lande, 1700. VOYAGES and TRAVELS. Allgemeine Historie, *etc.* Vol. II.

Alcaçar Kebir.—COMELIN, F. P. DE LA MOTTE, and BERNARD, J. Voyage to Barbary . . . with . . . exact draughts of . . . Alcasar, *etc.* 1725.

Alcalá de Henares.—LOPEZ Y RAMAJO, A. M. Breve descripcion de . . . la insigne Ciudad de A. de H. *Madrid*, 1861.

Alcasar.—*See* ALCAÇAR KEBIR.

Alder, River.—*See* Adur.

Alderney.—ALDERNEY. The Alderney Island Pilot, *etc.* *Lond.*, 1864.
—— ALDERNEY. Routier de l'Ile Aurigny, *etc.* *Par.*, 1865.

Aleppo.—ALEPPO. Journey from A. to Damascus, *etc.* 1737.
—— PLAISTED, B. Journal from Calcutta . . . to A., *etc.* 1758.
—— RUSSELL, A. The Natural History of A., *etc.* *Lond.*, 1794.
—— TAYLOR, J. Travels . . . to India, in 1789, by . . . A., *etc.* 1799.
—— MAUNDRELL, H. Journey from A. to Jerusalem . . . A.D. 1697, *etc.* 1810.
—— BUCKINGHAM, J. S. Travels . . . Journey from A. to Bagdad, *etc.* 1827.
—— Maundrell, H. Journey from A. to Jerusalem, 1696. HARRIS, J. Vol. II.

Aleppo — Algeria.

Aleppo.—Maundrell's Journey from A. to Jerusalem. PINKERTON. Vol. X.
—— Biddulph, W. Part of a letter from A. PURCHAS. Vol. II.
—— Cartwright, J. Observations in his Voyage from A. to Hispaan . . . about 1603. PURCHAS. Vol. II.
—— Coryates, T. Travels to . . . A. . . . 1612-14. PURCHAS. Vol. II.
—— Newbery, J. Letters relating to his . . . last Voyage into . . . A. . . . 1583. PURCHAS. Vol. II.
—— Notice sur la Carte Générale des Paschaliks de Hhaleb, etc. VOYAGES and TRAVELS. Recueil, etc. Vol. II.
—— Maundrell, Henry. Travels from A. to Jerusalem, 1096. VOYAGES and TRAVELS. The World displayed. Vol. XI.
—— Russell, Alexander. A Description of A., etc. VOYAGES and TRAVELS. The World displayed. Vol. XIII.

Alessandria.—See ALEXANDRIA.

Aleutian Islands.—PERREY, A. Documens sur les Tremblements de Terre . . . des Iles Aleutiennes, etc. *Dijon*, 1866.
—— Langsdorff, G. H. de. Voyage aux Iles Aléoutiennes . . . 1805-6. EYRIÈS. Vol. VI.

Alexandretta.—Dandini, J. Voyage to . . . also a description of . . . A., etc. CHURCHILL. Vol. VII.

Alexandria.—BUSCO, G. B. de. Viaggio . . . Con la descrittione di . . . . Alexandria, etc. *Milano* [1636].
—— DENHAM, H. M. Hydrographic Notices . . . A. Harbour, etc. 1856-59.
—— Alderney, L. Voyage to . . . A. . . . 1586. HAKLUYT. Vol. II.
—— Foxe, J. Voyage . . . and his . . . enterprize in delivering 266 Christians from captivitie . . . at A., 1577. HAKLUYT. Vol. II.
—— Scholz, J. M. A. Travels in the Countries between A. and Paraetonium . . . 1821. VOYAGES and TRAVELS, New. 1819, etc. Vol. VIII.
—— Walpole, R. The Catacombs of A. WALPOLE, R. Memoirs, etc.

Algarve.—CARDOSO, L. Diccionario geografico . . . de . . . A., etc. *Lisb.*, 1747-51.
—— BALBI, A. Essai . . . sur . . . l'A. *Par.*, 1822.

Alger.—See ALGERIA.

Algeria.—AVEZAC, D'. Esquisse d'Alger. *Par.*
—— ALGIERS. Aperçu . . . topographique, sur l'état d'Alger, etc. *Par.*, 1830.
—— ALGIERS. Itinéraire du royaume d'Alger. *Toulon*, 1830.
—— SAINT-DENYS, BARON J. DE. Considerations . . . sur la Régence d'Alger. *Par.*, 1831.
—— HAIN, V. A. La Nation sur Alger. *Par.*, 1832.
—— CLAUZEL, MARÉCHAL. Nouvelles observations sur la Colonisation d'Alger. *Par.*, 1833.
—— BÉRARD, A. Description Nautique des Côtes de l'Algérie, etc. *Par.*, 1837.

Algeria.

Algeria.—Desjobert, A. La Question d'Alger, etc.   *Par.*, 1837.
—— Grand, E. Défense et Occupation . . . d'Alger.   *Toulon*, 1837.
—— Dombasle, C. J. A. M. de. De l'Avenir de l'Algérie.   *Par.*, 1838.
—— Pélion, M. D. Considerations . . . sur l'Algérie.   *Par.*, 1838.
—— Algiers. Tableau de la situation des établissements Français dans l'Algérie, 1837-49, 1852-54.   *Par.*, 1839-55.
—— Bussy, G. de. De l'établissement des Français dans la Régence d'Alger, etc.   *Par.*, 1839.
—— Algiers. Notes sur . . . le centre de l'Algérie.   *Par.*, 1840.
—— Blanqui, M. Algérie. Rapport, etc.   *Par.*, 1840.
—— Baroux, E. Alger, etc.   *Par.*, 1841.
—— Baude, Baron. L'Algérie.   *Par.*, 1841.
—— Duvivier, Gén. Solution de la Question de l'Algérie.   *Par.*, 1841.
—— Buret, E. Question d'Afrique, de la double conquête de l'Algérie, etc.   *Par.*, 1842.
—— Gomot, F. Annuaire de l'Algérie, etc.   *Par.*, 1842.
—— Scott, Colonel. A Journal . . . of Travels in . . . A.   *Lond.*, 1842.
—— Enfantin. Colonisation de l'Algérie.   *Par.*, 1843.
—— Desjobert, A. L'Algérie en 1844-en 1846.   *Par.*, 1844, 46.
—— Algiers. Exploration scientifique de l'Algérie . . . 1840-42, etc.   *Par.*, 1844-48.
—— Landmann, Abbé. Mémoires au Roi sur la Colonisation de l'A.   *Par.*, 1845.
—— Moll, L. Colonisation et Agriculture de l'Algérie.   *Par.*, 1845.
—— Bourjolly, Gén. Projets sur l'Algérie.   *Par.*, 1847.
—— Galerao, Count J. Cenni sull' Agricoltura . . . dell' Africa Francese, etc.   *Firenze*, 1847.
—— Quétin. Guide du Voyageur en Algérie, etc.   *Par.*, 1847.
—— Larfeuil, M. de. Guide du Colon en Algérie, etc.   *Par.*, 1848.
—— Panet, M. Instructions . . . pour le Voyage de M. Panet du Sénégal en Algérie.   *Par.*, 1849.
—— Hedde, I. De l'Industrie Sérigène en Algérie.   *Lyon*, 1851.
—— Prus, Mdme. Residence in A.   1852.
—— Fitch, A. Insects of Algiers, etc.   *N. Y.*, 1853.
—— Reinaud, M. Rapport sur le Tableau des Dialectes de l'A. . . . de M. Geslin.   *Par.*, 1856.
—— Gerard, J. Life . . . with a . . . description of A.   1857.
—— —— Lion Hunting . . . in A.   1857.
—— Snider-Pellegrini, A. Du Développement du Commerce de l'Algérie avec l'Intérieur de l'Afrique, etc.   *Par.*, 1857.
—— Algiers. Annuaire de l'Algérie, etc.   *Par.*, 1859.
—— Blakesley, J. W. Four Months in A., etc.   *Camb.*, 1859.

Algeria — Alps.

Algeria.—AUCAPITAINE, BARON H. Les Kabyles et la colonisation de l'Algérie. *Par.*, 1864.
——— MARES, P. Nivellement barométrique dans les provinces d'Alger, *etc.* *Versailles*, 1864.
——— *See also* ORAN.

Algiers.—BERTHÉZÈNE, BARON. Dix-huit Mois à Alger, *etc.* *Montp.*, 1834.
——— TEMPLE, SIR G. T. Excursions in . . . A., *etc.* 1835.
——— CAMPBELL, T. Letters . . . during a Journey to A. *Phil.*, 1836.
——— RANG, SANDER, et F. DENIS. Fondation de la Régence d'Alger . . . Chronique Arabe du xvie siècle, *etc.* *Par.*, 1837.
——— PEYSONNEL et DESFONTAINES. Voyages dans les Régences de Tunis et d'Alger. *Par.*, 1838.
——— WILDE, W. R. Narrative . . . including a Visit to A., *etc.* *Dubl.*, 1852.
——— DAVIES, E. W. L. A. in 1857, *etc.* 1858.
——— Davis, W. A True . . . description of . . . A., *etc.* CHURCHILL. Vol. VII.
——— Knight, F. Relation of . . . Slavery . . . with a description of A. CHURCHILL. Vol. VIII.
——— Chaloner, Sir T. Voyage to A., 1541. HAKLUYT. Vol. II.
——— Gramaye, J. B. Relations of the Christianitie of . . . A., 1619. PURCHAS. Vol. II.
——— Nicholay, N. Description of the City of Algor, *etc.* PURCHAS. Vol. II.
——— *See also* ALGERIA.

Algoa Bay.—PHILIPPS, T. Advantages of Emigration to A. B., *etc.* *Lond.*, 1834.

Aljaska.—*See* ALASKA.

Allée-Blanche.—DESOR, E. Nouvelles Excursions . . . Accompagnées d'une Notice sur les glaciers de l'A.-B., *etc.* *Neuch., Par.*, 1846.

Alleghany Mountains.—MICHAUX, F. A. Travels to the Westward of the A. M. . . . 1802. VOYAGES and TRAVELS. A Collection, *etc.* 1805. Vol. I.

Alleghany, River.—Ashe, T. Travels . . . 1806, for . . . exploring the . . . A., *etc.* VOYAGES and TRAVELS. A Collection, *etc.* 1805. Vol. X.

Alps.—MURCHISON, SIR R. I. On the distribution of the superficial Detritus of the A., *etc.*
——— SCHLAGINTWEIT, A. Ueber die Temperatur des Bodens und der Quellen in den Alpen.
——— SIMLER, J. L Simleri . . . Alpium descriptio. *Lugd. Bat.*, 1633.
——— SCHEUCHZER, J. J. Helveticus, sive Itinera per Helvetiæ Alpinas Regiones facta annis 1702-11. *Lugd. Bat.*, 1723.
——— SAUSSURE, H. B. de. Voyages dans les A., *etc.* *Neuchâtel*, 1779-96.
——— BOURRIT, M. Description des . . . Alpes Pennines et Rhétiennes. *Genève*, 1783.

Alps.—BEAUMONT, J. F. A. Description des A. Grecques, etc.
Par., 1802-8.
—— BOURRIT, M. Description des Cols, ou Passages des Alpes.
Genève, 1803.
—— ALPI. Dei Passaggi Alpini, etc. *Mil.*, 1804.
—— DOUCETTE, M. DE LA. Histoire ... des Hautes-Alpes. *Par.*, 1820.
—— HANNIBAL. A Dissertation on the passage of, over the A.
Oxf., 1820.
—— HANNIBAL. Dissertation sur le passage du Rhone et des Alpes par Annibal, etc. *Par.*, 1821.
—— DE LUC, J. A. Histoire du Passage des Alpes par Annibal, etc.
Genève, 1825.
—— BROCKEDON, W. Illustrations of the Passes of the A., etc. 1828.
—— GUÉRIN, J. Mesures Barométriques ... faites dans les Alpes Françaises, etc. *Avignon*, 1829.
—— MURCHISON, SIR R. I. On the relations of the Tertiary and Secondary Rocks forming the S.n Flank of the Tyrolese A. near Bassano. 1829.
—— SEDGWICK, A., and Murchison Sir R. I. A Sketch of the Structure of the E.n A., etc. 1831.
—— FORBES, J. D. Travels through parts of the Pennine Chain, etc.
Edin., 1843.
— — ALPI. Le Alpi che cingono l'Italia. *Torino*, 1845.
—— DESOR, E. Nouvelles Excursions ... dans les ... Alpes de M. Agassiz, etc. *Neuch., Par.*, 1845.
—— LAW, W. J. Some Remarks on the Alpine Passes of Strabo.
Lond., 1846.
—— MURCHISON, Sir R. I. On the Geological Structure of the A., etc.
1849.
—— SCHLAGINTWEIT, H. Untersuchungen über die Vertheilung der mittleren Jahrestemperatur in den Alpen. *Münch.*, 1850.
—— SCHLAGINTWEIT, H. and A. Hypsometrische Bestimmungen in den Östlichen Alpen. *Leipz.*, 1850.
—— ULRICH, M. Die Seitenthäler des Wallis und der Monterosa.
Zürich, 1850.
—— —— Das Lötschenthal, der Monte Leone, der Portiengrat und die Diablereta. *Zürich*, 1851.
—— ZIGNO, A. da. Sui Terreni Jurassici delle Alpi Venete, etc.
Padova, 1852.
—— LITTROW, K. v. Die Culminations-punkte der Östlichen Central-Alpen. *Wien*, 1853.
—— ULRICH, M. Der Geltengrat, das Heremence- und Bagnethal, das Einfischthal und der Weissthorpass. *Zürich*, 1853.
—— SCHLAGINTWEIT, A. and H. Hypsometrische Bestimmungen in den Westlichen Alpen. *Leipz.*, 1854.
— — WILLS, A. Wanderings among the High A. *Lond.*, 1856.
—— HINCHLIFF, T. W. Summer Months among the A., etc. 1857.
—— KING, S. W. Italian Valleys of the Pennine A. 1858.

Alps — Amarapoora.

Alps.—Peaks, Passes, and Glaciers ... Excursions ... Edited by J. Ball. 1859.
——— Pugaard, C. Mémoire sur les calcaires plutonisés des Alpes Apuennes, etc. *Par.*, 1860.
——— Tyndall, J. Glaciers of the A., etc. 1860.
——— Sonklar, K. von. Von den Gletschern der Diluvialzeit. *Wien*, 1862.
——— Glaciers. Expeditions on the Glaciers, etc. 1864.
——— Sonklar, C. A. von. Von den Alpen. [1864.]
——— ——— K. von. Von den Alpen. *Wien*, 1864.
——— Law, W. J. The A. of Hannibal. *Lond.*, 1866.
——— Ellis, R. An Enquiry ... with an Examination of the theory of Hannibal's Passage of the A., etc. *Camb. and Lond.*, 1867.
——— Payer, J. Die Ortler-Alpen, etc. *Gotha*, 1867.
——— Ziegler, J. M. Notice sur ... l'Orographie des Alpes. *Genève*, 1867.
——— Gastaldi, B. Alcuni dati sulle Punte Alpini situate fra la Levanna ed il Rocciamelone. *Torino*, 1868.
——— Caraboeuf, M. Notice sur ... la hauteur ... de quelques Sommités des Alpes. Voyages and Travels. Recueil, etc. Vol. II.
——— Montèmont, A. Tour over the A. ... 1820. Voyages and Travels, New. 1819, etc. Vol. IX.
——— *See also* Mont Blanc.

Alsace.—Michaelis, E. H. Barometrische Höhenbestimmungen in Elsass, etc. *Berlin*.

Altai.—Ledebour, C. F. von. Reise durch das A. Gebirge, etc. *Berl.*, 1830.
——— Tchihatcheff, P. de. Mémoire relatif à la Constitution Géologique de l'A. *Par.*, 1845.
——— Csengery, A. Az Altaji Népek Ösvallása tekintettel a Magyar Ösvallásra. *Pest.*, 1858.

Alten.—Roquette, M. de la. Notice sur les Mines de Cuivre d'A. (Norvège) *Par.*, 1839.

Alto-Douro.—Forrester, J. J. Papers relating ... to the Maps ... of the A.-D. *Op.*, 1844.
——— ——— Documents relating to Mr. F.'s Topographical Works of the ... A.-D. and River Douro, etc. *Op.*, 1848.
——— ——— The Oliveira Prize-Essay on Portugal; with ... Surveys of the Wine Districts of the A.-D. 1853.

Alvarado.—Iberri, J. I.—Prospectus of a Navigable Canal between Vera Cruz and A. *N. Y.*, 1827.

Alyaska.—*See* Alaska.

Amadabad.—*See* Ahmedabad.

Amalfi.—Niccolini, A. Tavola Metrica-Chronologica delle varie Alterze ... fra la Costa di A. ed il Promontorio di Gaeta. *Nap.*, 1839.

Amarapoora, Amarapurah.—*See* Umerapoora.

Amasonas.—See AMAZON.

Amat.—See TAHITI.

Amazon.—MAW, H. L. A Letter to the Editor of the 'Edinburgh Review,' in answer to his criticism on a 'Journal of a Passage down the ... Marañon,' etc. *Lond.*

—— CONDAMINE, M. DE LA. Relation ... d'un Voyage ... en descendant la Rivière des Amazones. *Par., 1745.*

—— —— A succinct Abridgment of a Voyage ... down the River of Amazons. *1747.*

—— MAW, H. L. Journal of a Passage ... descending the ... A. *1829.*

—— POEPPIG, E. Reise ... auf dem Amazonenstrome ... 1827–32. *Leipz., 1836.*

—— PENTLAND, J. B. and PARISH, SIR W. Notices of the ... 8,n Affluents of the ... A. etc. *Lond., 1836.*

—— SMYTH, W. and LOWE, F. Narrative of a Journey ... down the A., etc. *1836.*

—— MONTRAVEL, M. L. DE TARDY DE. Instructions pour naviguer ... le fleuve des Amazones. *Par., 1847.*

—— ADALBERT, PRINCE. Travels ... with a voyage up the A., etc. *1849.*

—— WALLACE, A. R. Narrative of Travels on the A., etc. *1853.*

—— —— Palm Trees of the A., and their uses. *1853.*

—— HERNDON, W. L. and GIBBON, L. Exploration of the Valley of the A. *Wash., 1853-4.*

—— HERNDON, W. L. Exploration of the Valley of the A. *Wash., 1854.*

—— OSCULATI, G. Esplorazione delle Regioni Equatoriali lungo ... il fiume delle Amazoni, etc. *Milano, 1860.*

—— BATES, H. W. The Naturalist on the ... A., etc. *1863.*

—— HASLEWOOD, E. New Colonies on the Uplands of the A. *Lond., 1863.*

—— MARKHAM, C. R. A List of the Tribes in the Valley of the A., etc. *Lond., 1864.*

—— TAVARES BASTOS. A livre Navegação do Amazonas. *Para, 1864.*

—— MICHELENA Y RÓJAS, F. Exploracion Oficial ... del ... Amazonas, etc. *Bruselas, 1867.*

—— APPUN, C. F. Unter den Tropen. Wanderungen ... am Amazonenstrome, etc. *Jena, 1871.*

—— Barbot, J. Description of the ... A., etc. CHURCHILL. Vol V.

—— Davis, W. A True ... description of ... the River of Amazons, etc. CHURCHILL. Vol. VII.

—— Roteiro da Viagem da ... Pará até a's ultimas Colonias dos Dominios Portuguezes em os Rios Amazonas, etc. PORTUGAL. Collecção de Noticias, etc. Vol. VL

Amazon — America.

Amazon.—Davies, W. Description ... of the ... A. Purchas. Vol. IV.
—— Rivers from Brabisse to the A. Purchas. Vol. IV.
—— Oviedo, G. F. Relatione della Navigatione per il grandissimo Fiume Maragnon ... 1543. Ramusio. Vol. III.
—— — Reisen auf dem ... Amazonenflusse. Orsua, 1560.—Carvallo, 1633.—Teixeira, 1637.—Acunja and Artieda, 1639-40.—Condamine, 1743-45. Voyages and Travels. Allgemeine Historie, etc. Vol. XVI.

Amazons, Valley of the.—Expeditions into the Valley of the A., 1539, 1540, 1639 ... Edited ... by C. R. Markham. 1859. Hakluyt Soc. Pub. Vol. XXIV.

Amboina, Amboine.—*See* Amboyna.

Amboyna.—Stavorinus, J. S. Voyage ... à Amboine ... 1774-78. Par., 1800.
——— Account of the Massacre of A., 1623. Kerr. Vol. IX.
—— — Stavorinus. Account of ... A., etc., from the Voyages of. Pinkerton. Vol. XI.
——— The Dutch late proceedings at A. ... 1613-22. Purchas. Vol. II.
——— Zusatz zu der Beschreibung des Eylandes A. Voyages and Travels. Allgemeine Historie, etc. Vol. XVIII.

America.—Rafn, C. C. The Discovery of A. by the Northmen, etc.
——— Hornius, G. De Originibus Americanis libri quatuor.
Hag. Comitis, 1652.
——— Ogilby, J. A.; being the ... most accurate description, etc.
1671.
——— Dampier, W. A New Voyage ... describing particularly ... A.
1697.
— · — Gage, T. Survey of the Spanish West Indies; being a Journal of 3300 miles on the Continent of A., etc.
1702.
·—— Jesuits, Travels of several ... into ... A., etc.
1714.
——— Dampier, W. A New Voyage ... describing particularly ... A., etc.
1729.
——— Astley, T. New ... Collection of ... Travels ... in ... A., etc.
1745-47.
—— — Green, J. Remarks in support of the new Chart of N. and S. A.
1753.
——— Lettres édifiantes et curieuses, etc. Vol. 6-9. Amérique.
Par., 1780-83.
—— Coxe, W. Account of the Russian discoveries between Asia and A., etc.
1804.
——— Janson, C. W. Stranger in A., etc.
1807.
—— — Humboldt, A. von and Bonpland, A. Recueil d'Observations de Zoologie ... faites ... dans l'Intérieur du Nouveau Continent ... en 1799-1803
1811.
——— Alcedo, A. de. Geographical ... dictionary of A., etc. 1812.
——— Humboldt, A. von. Researches concerning the Ancient Inhabitants of A., etc.
1814.

America.—HUMBOLDT, A. VON and BONPLAND, A. Voyage aux Régions Équinoxiales du Nouveau Continent, fait en 1799-1804, etc. *Par.*, 1814.

—— LEWIS, and CLARKE, Capts. Travels . . . across the An Continent . . . in 1804-6. 1814.

—— LEWIS, and CLARKE, Capts. Travels . . . across the An Continent . . . in 1804-6. 1815.

—— BRADBURY, J. Travels in the Interior of A., etc. *Liver.*, 1817.

—— SMITH, Capt. J. The True Travels . . of Capt. J. Smith, in . . . A. . . . beginning about . . . 1593, etc. *Richmond, U.S.*, 1819.

—— HUMBOLDT, A. VON and BONPLAND, A. Personal Narrative of Travels to the Equinoctial Regions of the New Continent, during 1799-1804, etc. 1822-29.

—— NAVARETTE, M. F. de. Relations des quatre voyages . . . pour la découverte du Nouveau-Monde de 1492 à 1504, etc. *Par.*, 1828.

—— TREVELYAN, SIR W. C. Notions of the Americans, etc. 1828.

—— GRÄBERG, COUNT J. Pellegrinaggio in . . . A. di G. C. Beltrami. *Firenze*, 1829.

—— ESTANCELIN, L. Recherches sur les voyages . . . des Navigateurs Normands . . . en Amérique, etc. *Par.*, 1832.

—— RICH, O. A Catalogue of Books relating principally to A., etc. 1832.

—— ENGLAND AND A., a Comparison, etc. 1833.

—— LANG, J. D. View of the Origin . . . of the Polynesian Nation; demonstrating their . . . discovery . . . of . . . A. 1834.

—— RICH, C. J. Bibliotheca Americana Nova; or a Catalogue of Books relating to A., etc. 1835.

—— HUMBOLDT, A. VON. Examen critique de l'Histoire de la Géographie du Nouveau Continent . . . aux quinzième et seizième Siècles. 1836-39.

—— TERNAUX-COMPANS, H. Voyages, Relations et Mémoires Originaux, pour servir à l'histoire de la découverte de l'Amérique. *Par.*, 1837-41.

—— RAFINESQUE, C. S. The Ancient Monuments of N. and S. A. *Phil.*, 1838.

—— RAFN, C. C. Mémoire sur la Découverte de l'Amerique au dixième siècle, etc. *Par.*, 1838.

—— RAFN, C. C. Wiadomość o odkryciu Ameryki wdzieciątym wieku, etc. *W Krakowie*, 1838.

—— THOMASON, A. Men and Things in A. 1838.

—— BIONDELLI, B. Scoperta dell' A. fatta nel Secola x. da alcuni Scandinavi. *Mil.*, 1839.

—— DELAFIELD, J. J. An Inquiry into the Origin of the Antiquities of A., etc. *N.Y.*, 1839.

—— HAYWARD, J. New England Gazetteer, etc. *Concord*, 1839.

—— MARTIUS, C. F. P. de. Die Vergangenheit und Zukunft der Amerikanischen Menschheit. *München*, 1839.

—— RAFN, C. C. Memoria sulla scoperta dell' A. nel secolo decimo, etc. *Pisa*, 1839.

America.

America.—BUCKINGHAM, J. S. A., etc.   1841.
—— RAFN, C. C. A.'s Opdagelse i det tiende Aarhundrede Kjöb., 1841.
—— —— Supplement to the Antiquitates Americanæ. Copenh., 1841.
—— BANDINEL, J. Some Account of . . . Slaves . . . as connected with A., etc.   1842.
—— BUCKINGHAM, J. S. The Slave States of A.   1842.
—— BRADFORD, A. W. American Antiquities, etc.   N.Y., 1843.
—— EICHTHAL, G. D'. Mémoire sur l'histoire primitive des Races . . . Américaines. Par., 1843.
—— MORTON, S. G. Crania Americana, etc.   Phil., 1844.
—— PARAVEY, CHEVALIER DE. L'Amérique sous le nom de Pays de Fou Sang, etc. Par., 1844-7.
—— EICHTHAL, G. D'. Études sur l'histoire primitive des Races . . . Américaines. Par., 1845.
—— LONG, PROF., and OTHERS. A. . . . geographically described. 1845.
—— RAFN, C. C. Antiquités Américaines d'après les Monuments Historiques des Islandais, etc. Copenh., 1845.
—— —— A.'s Arcktiske Landes gamle Geographie, etc.   Kjöb., 1845.
—— JOMARD, E. F. Les Antiquités Américaines au point de vue des progrès de la Géographie. Par., 1847.
—— —— Fragments . . . les sur Antiquités Américaines, etc.   Par., 1847.
—— PARAVEY, CHEVALIER DE. Nouvelles preuves que le pays de Fou-Sang mentionné dans les livres Chinois est l'Amérique. 1847.
—— RAFN, C. C. Aperçu de l'Ancienne Géographie des Régions Arctiques de l'Amérique. Copenh., 1847.
—— PARAVEY, CHEV. DE. Réfutation de l'opinion émise par M. Jomard que les Peuples d'Amérique n'ont jamais eu aucun rapport avec ceux de l'Asie. Par., 1849.
—— BARTLETT, W. H. American Scenery, etc.   1852.
—— HUMBOLDT, A. VON, and BONPLAND, A. Personal Narrative of Travels to the Equinoctial Regions of A., during 1790-1604, etc. 1852, 3.
—— CHAMBERS, W. Things as they are in A.   Lond., Edin., 1854.
—— BECHER, A. B. The Landfall of Columbus on his first voyage to A., etc. 1856.
—— FERGUSON, W. A. by River and Rail, etc.   1856.
—— RADLINSKI L'A. prima di C. Colombo.   Mantova, 1857.
—— HITCHCOCK, E. Ichnology of New England, etc.   Bost., 1858.
—— HISTORICAL MAGAZINE, and Notes and Queries concerning . . . A. N. Y., 1859.
—— JAY, J. Statistical View of A.n Agriculture, etc.   N. Y., 1859.
—— CORTAMBERT, E. Tableau général de l'Amérique, etc. Par., 1860.
—— ?SQUIER, E. G. Collection of Rare . . . Documents concerning . . . A., etc.   N. Y., 1860.

America.

America.—D'EICHTHAL, G. Étude sur les Origines Bouddhiques de la Civilisation Américaine. *Par.*, 1865.
—— DIXON, W. H. New A. *Lond.*, 1867.
—— LECLERC, C. Bibliotheca Americana. Catalogue d'une ... Collection de Livres ... sur l'Amérique, etc. *Par.*, 1867.
—— MARTIUS, C. F. P. VON. Beiträge zur Ethnographie und Sprachenkunde A.'s, etc. *Leipz.*, 1867.
—— PEYTON, J. L. The A.n Crisis, etc. *Lond.*, 1867.
—— BLUNDELL, B. The Contributions of J. L. Peyton to the History ... of the Civil War in A. ... reviewed. *Lond.*, 1868.
—— COMMERCE de Coton du Globe. Production de l'Amérique, etc. *Memphis*, 1869.
—— COSTA, D. F. DE. Notes on a Review of "The Pre-Columbian Discovery of America by the Northmen," etc. *Charlest.*, 1869.
—— ADAMS, J. W. American Interoceanic Ship Canals. *N. Y.*, 1870.
—— BURRITT, E. Washington's Words to Intending English Emigrants to A., etc. *Lond.*, 1870.
—— JOHNSTON, A. K. Atlas of the British Empire in ... A., with ... letterpress. *Edin. and Lond.*, [1870.]
—— Smith, Capt. J. True Travels ... in ... A., from 1502 to 1629. CHURCHILL. Vol. II.
—— Barbot, J. Description ... and ... account of the first discoveries of A. in the XIV. century. CHURCHILL. Vol. V.
—— Castle, W. A short discovery of ... A., etc. CHURCHILL. Vol. VIII.
—— Considerations on ... affairs between England and A., 1778. DALRYMPLE, A. Tracts, from 1764 to 1808. Vol. I.
—— Columbus, C. Select Letters ... relating to his four Voyages to the New World: translated and edited by R. H. Major. 1847. HAKLUYT Soc. PUB. Vol. II.
—— Hakluyt, R. Divers Voyages touching the discovery of A. ... edited ... by J. Winter Jones. 1850. HAKLUYT Soc. PUB. Vol. VII.
—— Benzoni, G. History of the New World, showing his travels in A., from 1541 to 1556 ... edited by Rear-Adml. W. H. Smyth. 1857. HAKLUYT Soc. PUB. Vol. XXI.
—— Columbus, C. Fourth Voyage; his discoveries on the Continent, and of the Islands in A., 1502-5. HARRIS, J. Vol II.
—— The Discoveries ... and present state of the Dutch Colonies in A. ... 1642-1714. HARRIS, J. Vol. II.
—— The Discoveries and Settlements made by the English in ... A. ... 1495-1603. HARRIS, J. Vol. II.
—— An historical account of the British Settlements in A. ... 1060-1688. HARRIS, J. Vol. II.
—— The History of the British Colonies in A. ... 1688-1714. HARRIS, J. Vol. II.
—— The History of the Discoveries ... of the English Nation in A. ... 1603-1660. HARRIS, J. Vol. II.

America. 31

America.—History of the discoveries . . . of the French in A., 1523-1713. HARRIS, J. Vol. II.

—— Of the importance of the new-discovered Continent of A., etc. HARRIS, J. Vol. II.

—— Early discovery of Winland, or A., by the Icelanders, 1001. KERR. Vol. I.

—— Columbus, C. Account of the discovery of A., by A. de Herrera. KERR. Vol. III.

—— —— History of the discovery of A., etc. KERR. Vol. III.

—— Diaz del Castillo, B. History of the discovery . . . of A. in 1568, etc. KERR. Vol. III.

—— Vespucius Americus. Voyage to the New World. KERR. Vol. III

—— Butrigarius, G. Discourse respecting the discoveries in A. by S. Cabot. KERR. Vol. VI.

—— Amérique. Prémières Découvertes . . . Espagnols . . . C. Colomb, LAHARPE, J. Vol. IX.

—— A., Discoveries made by the English in; from . . . Henry VII. to . . . Elizabeth. PINKERTON. Vol. XII.

—— Smith's History of . . . New England, etc. PINKERTON. Vol. XIII.

—— Columbus, C. Conjectures touching a New World. PURCHAS. Vol. I.

—— —— First Voyage. . . . 1492. PURCHAS. Vol. I.

—— Of A., whether it were then peopled. PURCHAS. Vol. I.

—— Barkley, O. Travels . . . in . . . A . . . 1605. PURCHAS. Vol. III.

—— Benzon, J. Briefe extracts . . . out of his three books of the New World, touching the Spaniards' cruell handling of the Indians . . . 1041. PURCHAS. Vol. IV.

—— A briefe Relation of the discoverie and Plantation of New England, etc. PURCHAS. Vol. IV.

—— The first Voyages to divers parts of A. by Englishmen . . . 1517-05. PURCHAS. Vol. IV.

—— Smith, Capt. J. Extracts of a Booke called "New England's Trialls," printed 1622. PURCHAS. Vol. IV.

—— Vaz, L. Historie of . . . 1586 . . . touching A.n places, etc. PURCHAS. Vol. IV.

—— Winslow, E. Good Newes from New England . . . 1621-23. PURCHAS. Vol. IV.

—— Staden de Homberg, H. Véritable Histoire et Description d'un Pays . . . situé dans le Nouveau Monde . . . 1547-55. TERNAUX-COMPANS. Voyages. Vol. III.

—— Hulsius, L. Histoire véritable d'un Voyage curieux fait par U. Schmidel . . . dans l'Amérique . . . 1534-54. TERNAUX-COMPANS. Voyages. Vol. V.

—— Entdeckungen . . . der Europäer in A.—Columbus, Reisen, 1492-1506.—Reise des A. Ojeda, J. de la Cosa, A. Vesputius.—A. Niño und der beyden Guerren.—Y. Pinzon.—D. de Lopez.—A. von Cabral.—G. von Corte Real.—J. Cabot und seiner . . . Söhne.—D. de Solis, and Y. Pinzon, 1507.—VOYAGES and TRAVELS—Allgemeine Historie, etc. Vol. XIII.

America.—Engel. Nachrichten . . . über die Lage der mitternächtlichen Länder von . . . A., *etc.* Voyages and Travels. Allgemeine Historie, *etc.* Vol. XIX.

—— Lewis and Clark, Capts. and others. Travels in the Interior Parts of A. . . . 1805. Voyages and Travels. A Collection, *etc.* 1805. Vol. VI.

—— Ashe, T. Travels in A., 1806, *etc.* Voyages and Travels. A Collection, *etc.* 1805. Vol. X.

—— —— Travels in A., 1806. Voyages and Travels. A Collection, *etc.* 1810. Vol. V.

—— The Discoveries of the English in A. Voyages and Travels. The World displayed. Vol. IV.

—— The Discoveries and Settlements of the French . . . and . . . of the Dutch in A. A Danish Settlement in A. Voyages and Travels, The World displayed. Vol. V.

—— *See also* United States of America.

——, **British.** Mac Gregor, J. British A. *Edin.*, 1832.

—— —— Murray, H. Historical . . . Account of B. A., *etc.* *Edin.*, 1839.

—— —— Purdy, J. and Findlay, A. G., British A.'n Navigator, *etc.* 1847.

—— —— Alexander, Sir J. E. L'Acadie; or, Seven years' explorations in British A. 1849.

—— —— Doull, A. Report and Outline of a . . . Railway . . in the British N.A.'n Colonies, *etc.* 1850.

—— —— Isbister, A. K. A Proposal for a new Penal Settlement in . . . British N. A. *Lond.*, 1850.

—— —— Synge, M. H. Great Britain one Empire . . . by intercommunication . . . *viâ* British N. A. 1852.

—— —— Andrews, I. D. Report on . . . the British N. A.n Colonies, *etc.* *Wash.*, 1853.

—— —— America. The Lighthouses of . . . British N. A. Corrected to 1853, 56, 58, 59. 1853-59.

—— —— Dunsterville, E. The Lights of the Coasts and Lakes of British N. A. Corrected to 1856. 1856.

—— —— Morris, A. Nova Britannia: or British N. A., *etc.* *Montr.*, 1858.

—— —— Hind, H. Y. British N. A. Reports, *etc.* *Lond.*, 1860.

—— —— Dunsterville, E. The Admiralty List of the Lights on the Coasts and Lakes of British N. A. Corrected to 1860, 61, 62. 1860-62.

—— —— Hector, J. On the Physical Features of the Central part of British N. A., *etc.* *Edin.*, 1861.

—— —— Gras, M. A. Le. Phares des Côtes Orientales de l'Amérique Anglaise, *etc.* *Par.*, 1863-64.

—— —— Palliser, J. Journals . . . and Observations relative to the exploration of . . . British N. A., *etc.* 1863.

America, British — America, North. 33

America, British.—PALLISER, J. Papers ... relative to the exploration of ... British N. A., etc. **1863.**

——— RAWLINSON, J. The Confederation of the B. N. A.n Provinces, etc. *Lond.*, **1865.**

——— WADDINGTON, A. Overland Communication ... through B. N. A. *Victoria, V. I.*, **1867.**

——— ——— Sketch of the proposed Line of Overland Railroad through B. N. A. *Lond.*, **1869.**

——— **Central.**—CHAIX, P. Isthme de l'Amérique Centrale.

——— ——— AMERICA, CENTRAL. Brief statement ... of Grants ... to ... E. Coast of C. A. Commercial and Agricultural Company, etc. **1831.**

——— ——— HAEFKENS, J. Centraal Amerika, etc. *Dordr.*, **1832.**

——— ——— GALINDO, J. On C. A. **1836.**

——— ——— STEPHENS, J. L. Incidents of Travel in C. A., etc. **1842.**

——— ——— BAILY, J. Central A., etc. **1850.**

——— ——— BYAM, G. Wanderings in ... A.; with remarks upon ... the Great Ship Canal through C. A. **1850.**

——— ——— CHALONER and FLEMING. The Mahogany-Tree ... in ... C. A., etc. *Liverp.*, **1850.**

——— ——— AMERICA, CENTRAL. Description of the facilities ... which a Road across C. A. ... would afford, etc. *Phil.*, **1852.**

——— ——— HARDMAN, F. Scenes and Adventures in C. A. *Edin.*, **1852.**

——— ——— ÖRSTED, A. S. Centralamerikas Rublaceer. **1852.**

——— ——— SQUIER, E. G. Travels in C. A., etc. *N. Y.*, **1853.**

——— ——— LAPELIN, T. DE. Reconnaissance Hydrographique des Côtes Occidentales du Centre-Amérique. *Par.*, **1854.**

——— ——— SQUIER, E. G. Notes on C. A., etc. *N. Y.*, **1855.**

——— ——— SCHERZER, K. VON. Travels in the Free States of C. A., etc. **1857.**

——— ——— WELLS, W. V. Explorations and Adventures ... comprising ... a review of the history and general resources of C. A. *N. Y.*, **1857.**

——— ——— BRASSEUR DE BOURBOURG, E. C. Histoire des Nations civilisées ... de l'Amérique-Centrale, devant les siècles antérieurs à C. Colomb., etc. *Par.*, **1857-59.**

——— ——— FRÖBEL, J. Seven Years' Travel in C. A., etc. **1859.**

——— ——— VIELET D'AOUST, M. Coup-d'œil général sur la topographie ... de l'Amérique Centrale. *Par.*, [**1865**].

——— ——— BELLY, F. À travers l'Amérique Centrale, etc. *Par.*, **1867.**

——— ——— BOYLE, F. The Free Indian Tribes of C. A. *Lond.*, [**1867**].

——— ——— PAEZ, R. Travels and Adventures in S. and C. A., etc. *Lond.*, **1868.**

———, **Isthmus of.**—See PANAMA, ISTHMUS OF.

———, **North.**—REDFIELD, W. C. Remarks on the prevailing Storms of the Atlantic Coast of the N. A. States.

America, North.—Say, T. Descriptions of new species of Heteropterous Hemiptera of N. A., etc.

——— ——— Marquette, le P. Voyage et découverte de quelques Pays ... de l'Amérique Septentrionale, etc.   *Par.*, 1681.

——— ——— Lahontan, Baron. New Voyages to N. A., etc.   1703-35.

——— ——— Charlevoix, Père de. Histoire ... d'un voyage ... dans l'Amérique Septentrionale.   *Par.*, 1744.

——— ——— Benaduci, L. B. Idea de una nueva Historia General de la A. Septentrionale.   *Madrid*, 1746.

——— ——— Charlevoix, Father. Journal of a Voyage to N.-A., etc.   *Lond.*, 1761.

——— ——— Kalm, P. Travels into N. A., etc.   *Lund.*, 1772.

——— ——— Burnaby, A. Travels through the Middle Settlements of N. A., etc.   1775.

——— ——— Long, J. Voyages and Travels ... describing ... the N. A.n Indians, etc.   *Lond.*, 1791.

——— ——— Mackenzie, A. Voyages ... through ... N. A. ... in 1789 and 1793, etc.   1801.

——— ——— Pike, Z. M. Exploratory Travels through the Western Territories of N. A., etc.   1811.

——— ——— Hodgson, A. Letters from N. A., etc.   1824.

——— ——— Hall, B. Travels in N. A. in 1827-28.   *Edin.*, 1829.

——— ——— Head, G. Forest Scenes ... in the Wilds of N. A., etc.   1829.

——— ——— Murray, H. Historical Account of discoveries and travels in N. A., etc.   1829.

——— ——— Richardson, Sir J., and others. Fauna Boreali-Americana, etc.   1829-36.

——— ——— Bouchette, J. The British dominions in N. A., etc.   1832.

——— ——— Alexander, Sir J. E. Transatlantic Sketches, comprising ... scenes in N. and S. A., etc.   1833.

——— ——— Colton, C. Tour of the A.n Lakes ... in 1830, etc.   1833.

——— ——— Hoffman, C. F. A Winter in the Far West.   1835.

——— ——— Pickering, J. Remarks on the Indian languages of N. A.   1836.

——— ——— Richardson, Sir J. Report on N. A.n Zoology.   1837.

——— ——— Martin, R. M. Statistics of the Colonies ... in ... N. A., etc.   *Lond.*, 1839.

——— ——— Davison, G. M. Traveller's Guide through the Middle and Northern States, etc.   *Saratoga Springs*, 1840.

——— ——— Vail, E. A. Notice sur les Indiens de l'Amérique du Nord.   *Par.*, 1840.

——— ——— Wied-Neuwied, Prince M. de. Voyage dans l'Intérieur de l'Amérique du Nord pendant 1832-34.   *Par.*, 1840.

——— ——— Abert, Col. J. J. Report on the Commerce of the Lakes and Western Rivers.   *Wash.*, 1841.

America, North. 35

America, North.—CATLIN, G. Letters ... on ... the N. A. Indians.
1841.

———— ———— RICHARDSON, Sir J. On the Frozen Soil of N. A.
Edin., 1841.

———— ———— CASTELNAU, F. DE. Vues et souvenirs de l'Amérique du
Nord. *Par.*, 1842.

———— ———— KING, R. On the Unexplored Coast of N. A. 1842.

———— ———— WOODBRIDGE, W. C. Report on the Navigation of the Great
Lakes, etc. *Wash.*, 1843.

———— ———— LYALL, Sir C. Travels in N. A., etc. 1845.

———— ———— BYAM, G. Wanderings in some of the W. Republics of A.,
etc. 1850.

———— ———— BRASSEUR DE BOURBOURG, E. C. Lettres pour servir d'introduction à l'Histoire Primitive ... de l'Amérique Septentrionale.
Mex., 1851.

———— ———— DAROUDEAU, M. B. Tableau Général des Phares et Fanaux
des Côtes Orientales de l'Amérique du Nord. *Par.*, 1851.

———— ———— STANLEY, J. M. Catalogue of the Portraits of N. A.n Indians,
with sketches of Scenery, &c., painted by J. M. S. *Wash.*, 1852.

———— ———— AMERICA, SOUTH. The Lighthouses on the ... W. Coast
of N. A. Corrected to 1853, 55, 57, 58, 59. 1853-59.

———— ———— LAXMAN, C. Adventures in the Wilds of N. A., etc. 1854.

———— ———— WHIPPLE, T. E., and TURNER. Report upon the Indian
Tribes, with Vocabularies of N. A.n Languages. *Wash.*, 1855.

———— ———— BAILY, F. Journal of a Tour in ... N. A. In 1796, 97.
1856.

———— ———— OLMSTED, F. L. Journey in the Seaboard Slave States, etc.
1856.

———— ———— MARCOU, J. Geology of N. A., etc. *Zurich*, 1858.

———— ———— DOMENECH, E. Seven Years ... in the Great Deserts of
N. A. 1860.

———— ———— DUNSTERVILLE, F. The Admiralty List of the Lights on
the ... W. Coast of N. A. Corrected to 1860. 1861-62.

———— ———— DUNSTERVILLE, F. The Admiralty List of the Lights ...
on the W. Coast of N. A. Corrected to 1861, 62. 1861-62.

———— ———— EWBANK, T. N. A.n Rock-writing, etc.
Morrisania, N. Y., 1866.

———— ———— PALMER, W. J. Report of Surveys across the Continent
... for a Route extending the Kansas Pacific Railway to the Pacific
Ocean, etc. *Phil.*, 1868.

———— ———— BELL, W. A. New Tracks in N. A., etc. *Lond.*, 1870.

———— ———— NORTH PACIFIC PILOT. Pt. I. Sailing Directions for the
W. Coast of N. A., etc. *Lond.*, 1870.

———— ———— Langsdorff, G. H. de. Voyage à la côte de l'Amérique
septentrionale, 1805-8. EVRIÈS. Vol. VI.

———— ———— Hearne. Voyage dans la partie boréale de l'Amérique,
1769-72. EVRIÈS. Vol. VII.

D 2

36 America, North — America, North-west Coast.

America, North.—Mackenzie. Voyage dans l'Amérique septentrionale ... 1789-93. ÉTRILÈS. Vol. VII.

―――― Cabot, S. Voyage to the N. part of A. 1497. HAKLUYT. Vol. III.

―――― Voyages ... for the finding of a N.W. Passage to the N. parts of A., etc. HAKLUYT. Vol. III.

―――― Amérique Septentrionale. Floride. Colonies Anglaises, etc. LAHARPE, J. Vol. XII.

―――― Colonies Françaises ... Caractère des Habitans, et Histoire naturelle, etc. LAHARPE, J. Vol. XIII.

―――― Possessions in N. A., 1834-35. MARTIN, R. M. History of the British Colonies. Vol. III.

―――― A., Memoirs of N. PINKERTON. Vol. XIII.

―――― Burnaby's Travels through the Middle Settlements in N. A., in 1759-60. PINKERTON. Vol. XIII.

―――― Kalm's Travels in N. A. PINKERTON. Vol. XIII.

―――― Voyage & découverte du P. Marquette & sieur Jolliet dans l'Amérique Septentrionale. THEVENOT. Vol. IV.

―――― Verazzani, J. Reise und Entdeckungen von Nord-A., 1523-24. VOYAGES and TRAVELS. Allgemeine Historie, etc. Vol. XV.

―――― Fortsetzung der Reisen, Entdeckungen und Niederlassungen der Franzosen in Nord-A. VOYAGES and TRAVELS. Allgemeine Historie, etc. Vol. XVI.

―――― Reisen, Entdeckungen und Niederlassungen der Engländer in dem Nordlichen A., etc. VOYAGES and TRAVELS. Allgemeine Historie, etc. Vol. XVI.

―――― Reisen und Niederlassungen in dem Nordlichen A. VOYAGES and TRAVELS. Allgemeine Historie, etc. Vol. XVI.

―――― Naturgeschichte von Nord-A. VOYAGES and TRAVELS. Allgemeine Historie, etc. Vol. XVII.

―――― Reisen und Niederlassungen auf den Inseln des Nordlichen A. in dem Nordmeere. VOYAGES and TRAVELS. Allgemeine Historie, etc. Vol. XVII.

―――― Von den Gebräuchen ... der Indianer in dem Nordlichen A. VOYAGES and TRAVELS. Allgemeine Historie, etc. Vol. XVII.

―――― Muntule, E. Voyage to N. A. and the West Indies, 1817. VOYAGES and TRAVELS, New. 1819, etc. Vol. IX.

See also AMERICA, British.
AMERICA, Russian.
CANADA.
META INCOGNITA.
WEST.

――――, **North Coast.**—SIMPSON, T. Narrative of the Discoveries on the N. Coast of A. ... during 1836-39.   1843.

―――― PERREY, A. Documents sur les Tremblements de Terre .. ' de la Côte No. d'Amérique.   *Dijon*, 1868.

――――. **North-west Coast.**—DIXON, G. Voyage ... more particularly to the N.W. Coast of A., etc.   1789.

America, North-west Coast.—America, South. 37

America, North-west Coast.—Portlock, N. Voyage . . . more particularly to the N.W. Coast of A., 1785-88.   **1789.**

—— —— Meares, J. Voyages . . . from China to the N.W. Coast of A., etc.   *Lond.,* **1790.**

—— —— Wrangell, F. von. Statistische . . . Nachrichten über die Russischen Besitzungen an der Nordwestküste von A. *St. Pet.,* **1839.**

—— —— Greenhow, R. Memoir . . . on the N.W. Coast of A., etc.   *Wash.,* **1840.**

—— —— Greenhow, R. The History of Oregon . . . and the other Territories of the N.W. Coast of A., etc.   *Bost., U. S.,* **1844.**

—— —— Grewinck, C. Beitrag zur Kenntniss der orographischen . . . Beschaffenheit der Nord-West-Küste Amerika's, etc.   *St. Pet.,* **1850.**

—— —— Dickie, G. Notes of Algæ collected on the Coast of N.W. A., by Mr. R. Brown.   **[1868.]**

—— —— Dickie, G. Notes of Mosses and Hepaticæ, collected by R. Brown, Esq., on the N.W. Coast of A.   **[1868.]**

—— —— Meares. Voyage de la Chine à la Côte Nord-Ouest de l'Amérique, 1788, 89. Extraits. Vol. I.

—— —— Portlock et Dixon. Voyage à la Côte Nord-Ouest de l'Amérique, 1785-88. Extraits. Vol. I.

—— —— Douglas, Capt. Voyage à la Côte Nord-Ouest de l'Amérique, 1798, 99. Extraits. Vol. II.

—— —— Marchand, F. Voyage . . . à la Côte Nord-Ouest de l'Amérique, 1790-2. Extraits. Vol. II.

—— —— Harmon de Montreal, D. W. Voyage aux Côtes nord-ouest de l'Amérique. Extraits. Vol. VIII.

—— —— Gualle, F. Voyage . . . by the N.W. part of A. . . . to Acapulco, 1582-84. Hakluyt. Vol. III.

—— —— **Russian.**—Holmberg, H. J. Ethnographische Skizzen über die Völker des Russischen A.   *Helsingfors,* **1855.**

—— —— Kittlitz, F. H. v. Denkwürdigkeiten einer Reise nach dem Russischen Amerika, etc.   *Gotha,* **1858.**

—— —— Sumner, Hon. C. Speech . . . on the cession of R. A. to the United States.   *Wash.,* **1867.**

—, **South.**—Dauxou, P. C. F. De la A. Meridional, etc.
   Buen. Ayres.

—— —— King, P. P. Selections from a Meteorological Journal kept . . . during the Survey of the S.n Coasts of S. A., 1827-30.

—— —— Trevet, A. Historia dell' India America, detta altramente Francia Antarctica, etc.   *Vinegia,* **1561.**

—— —— Feuillée, L. Journal des Observations . . . faites sur les Côtes Orientales de l'Amérique Méridionale, etc.   *Par.,* **1725.**

—— —— Condamine, M. de la. Relation . . . d'un Voyage fait dans l'Intérieur de l'Amérique Méridionale, etc.   *Par.,* **1745.**

—— —— Condamine, M. de la. A succinct Abridgment of a Voyage . . . within the Inland parts of S. A., etc.   **1747.**

America, South.—JUAN, G., and ULLOA, A. Voyage historique de l'Amérique Méridionale, etc. *Amst. et Par.*, 1752.

—— ULLOA, A. DE. Voyage historique de l'Amérique Méridionale, etc. *Par.*, 1752.

—— BANCROFT, E. Essay on ... Guiana, in S. A., etc. 1769.

—— FALKNER, T. Description of Patagonia, and the adjoining parts of S. A., etc. *Hereford*, 1774.

—— ULLOA, A. DE. Mémoires ... concernant la découverte de l'Amérique, etc. *Par.*, 1787.

—— ULLOA, A. DE. Voyage to S. A., etc. 1806.

—— DEPONS, F. Travels in S. A., etc. 1807.

—— AZARA, F. de. Voyages dans l'Amérique méridionale, etc. *Par.*, 1809.

—— BAUZA, P. Ueber ... Süd Amerika, etc. ' *Madr.*, 1814.

—— HIPPISLEY, G. Narrative of the Expedition to the Rivers Orinoco and Apuré, in S. A. 1819.

—— BRACKENRIDGE, H. M. Voyage to S. A., etc. 1820.

—— DANIELL, J. F. Sketches ... of S. A. 1820.

—— CALDCLEUGH, A. Travels in S. A., etc. 1825.

—— STEVENSON, W. B. Historical ... Narrative of Twenty Years' Residence in S. A. 1825.

—— ULLOA, A. DE. Noticias Secretas de A., etc. *Lond.*, 1826.

—— WATERTON, C. Wanderings in S. A., etc. 1826.

—— ALEXANDER, SIR J. E. Transatlantic Sketches, comprising ... scenes in N. and S. A., etc. 1833.

—— EMPSON, C. Narratives of S. A., etc. *Lond.*, 1836.

—— HAWKSHAW, J. Reminiscences of S. A., etc. *Lond.*, 1838.

—— SCARLETT, HON. P. C. S. A. and the Pacific, etc. 1838.

—— KING, P. P., and FITZ-ROY, R. Narrative ... describing their examination of the S.n Shores of S. A., etc. 1839.

—— MARTIN, R. M. Statistics of the Colonies ... in ... S. A., etc. *Lond.*, 1839.

—— ROBERTSON, J. P. and W. P. Letters on S. A., etc. 1843.

—— WAPPÄUS, J. E. Die Republiken von Südamerika, etc. *Göttingen*, 1843.

—— DARWIN, C. Geological Observations on S. A., etc. *Lond.*, 1846.

—— FITZ-ROY, REAR-ADML. R. Sailing Directions for S. A., etc. 1848.

—— KING, P. P. and FITZROY, R. Sailing Directions for S. A., etc. 1850.

—— CASTELNAU, F. DE. Expédition dans les parties centrales de l'Amérique du Sud, etc. *Par.*, 1850-57.

—— ANGELIS P. DE. Memoria ... sobre los derechos de Soberanía ... de la Confederacion Argentina, á la parte Austral del Continente Americano, etc. *Buen. Aires*, 1852.

America, South.

America, South.—Chalx, P. Histoire de l'Amérique méridionale au seizième siècle, etc. *Par.*, **1853**.

—— —— Amunategui, M. L. Titulos de . . . Chile á la soberanía de la extremidad austral del Continente Americano, etc. *Sant.*, **1853-55**.

—— —— America, South. The Lighthouses on the E. and W. Coasts of S. A. . . . Corrected to 1853, 55, 57, 58, 59. **1853-59**.

—— —— Foetterle, F. Die Geologische Uebersichtskarte des mittleren Theiles von Süd-Amerika, etc. *Wien*, **1854**.

—— —— King, P. P. and Fitzroy, R. S. A. Pilot, etc. **1860**.

—— —— Dunsterville, E. The Admiralty List of the Lights on the E. and W. Coasts of S. A. . . . Corrected to 1860. **1861-62**.

—— —— The Admiralty List of the Lights in S. A. . . . Corrected to 1861, 62. **1861-62**.

—— —— Gras, M. A. Le. Phares des Côtes Orientales de l'Amérique du Sud. 1861-64. *Par.*, **1861-64**.

—— —— Hinchliff, T. W. S. A.-n Sketches, etc. **1863**.

—— —— America. Intereses, peligros y garantías de los Estados del Pacífico . . . de la A. del Sud. *Par.*, **1866**.

—— —— Tschudi, J. J. von. Reisen durch Südamerika. *Leip.*, **1866-1869**.

—— —— Michelena y Rójas, F. Exploracion Oficial por la primera vez desde el Norte de la A. del Sur siempre por Rios, etc. *Bruselas*, **1867**.

—— —— Hutchinson, T. J. The Paraná . . . and S. A.-n recollections, etc. *Lond.*, **1868**.

—— —— Paez, R. Travels and Adventures in S. and Central A., etc. *Lond.*, **1868**.

—— —— Marcoy, P. Voyage à travers l'Amérique du Sud. etc. *Par.*, **1869**.

—— —— Amérique Méridionale . . . Histoire Naturelle, depuis l'Isthme de Panama jusqu'au Brésil. Lacharpe, J. Vol. XI.

—— —— Condamine's Travels in S. A. Pinkerton. Vol. XIV.

—— —— Ulloa's Voyage to S. A. Pinkerton. Vol. XIV.

—— —— Folque, F. Reflexões acerca . . . dos dominios de Portugal e Hespanha na A. Meridional. Portugal. Collecção de Noticias, etc. Vol. VII.

—— —— Beschreibungen der erstern entdeckten Länder in dem mittäglichen A., etc. Voyages and Travels. Allgemeine Historie, etc. Vol. XV.

—— —— Reisen . . . an den Küsten von Süd A. Voyages and Travels. Allgemeine Historie, etc. Vol. XVI.

—— —— Depons, F. Travels in . . . S. A., 1801-4. Voyages and Travels. A Collection, etc. 1806. Vol. IV.

—— —— Keith, Sir G. M. Voyage to S. A. . . . 1805-6. Voyages and Travels. A Collection, etc. 1805. Vol. XI.

—— —— Depons, F. Travels in parts of S. A., 1801-4. Voyages and Travels. A Collection, etc. 1810. Vol. I.

America, Spanish.—LOREZ, J. J. Ueber die ... Beziehungen ... Europas mit den ... Hispano-Amerikanischen Republiken. *Berlin,*
——— ——— AMERICA, SPANISH. Outline of ... Revolution in S. A., etc. 1817.
——— ——— DONNYCASTLE, SIR R. H. S. A., etc. 1818.
——— ——— SHILLIBEER, J. Narrative ... including a Sketch of the present state of ... Spanish S. A. 1818.
——— ——— HASSAUREK, F. Four Years among Spanish Americans. *N. Y.,* 1868.
——— ——— Naturgeschichte der Spanischen Landschaften in dem Südlichen A., etc. VOYAGES and TRAVELS. Allgemeine Historie, etc. Vol. XVI.
American Isthmus.—*See* PANAMA, ISTHMUS OF.
Ameryka.—*See* AMERICA.
Amhara.—FERRET, A. and GALINIER. Voyage ... dans les provinces ... de l'A. *Par.,* 1847.
Amman.—JERICHO. An Excursion from Jericho to the Ruins of ... A., etc. 1852.
Ammon.—HOSKINS, G. A. Visit to ... the Oasis of Amun, etc. 1837.
Amoor, River.—*See* AMUR.
Amravati, Amrawutti.—*See* UMARAWUTTY.
Amsterdam, Island.—MORTIMER, G. Observations ... during a Voyage to ... A., etc. *Lond.,* 1791.
——— ——— Prior, J. Voyage ... to ... A., 1810-11. VOYAGES and TRAVELS, New. 1819. Vol. I.
Amu, River.—*See* OXUS.
Amun.—*See* AMMON.
Amur, River.—HABERSHAM, A. W. My last Cruise ... Visits to ... the mouth of the A. R. *Phil.,* 1857.
——— ——— SCHRENCK, L. v. Reisen und Forschungen im A.-Lande, etc. *St. Pet.,* 1858.
——— ——— MAACK, R. Journey on the A. in 1855. *Russ. St. Pet.,* 1859.
——— ——— ATKINSON, T. W. Travels in the Regions of the Amoor, etc. 1860.
——— ——— COLLINS, P. McD. A Voyage down the Amoor, etc. *N. Y. and Lond.,* 1860.
——— ——— RAVENSTEIN, A. The Russians of the A., etc. 1861.
——— ——— CIRCOURT, COUNT A. DE. The Russians on the A., etc. *Par.,* 1862.
Ana.—KULCZYCKI, A. Determination des Longitudes ... Observations pour ... A., etc. *Par.,* 1851.
Anadir, Gulf of.—STAEHLIN, J. VON. An Account of the New Northern Archipelago lately discovered ... in the Seas of Kamtschatka and A., etc. *Lond.,* 1774.
Anahuc.—*See* MEXICO.

Anatolia.—MACARIUS. Travels of . . . Pt. I. A., *etc.* **1849.**
——— Jackson, J. Journey . . . in 1797, through . . . Natolia, *etc.*
PELHAM. Vol. II.
Ancholme.—RENNIE, SIR J. An Account of the drainage of the Level of A., Lincolnshire. **1845.**
Andalousie, Andalucia.—*See* ANDALUSIA.
Andalusia.—LAMALLE, M. DUREAU DE. Climatologie comparée de l'Italie et de l'Andalousie, *etc.* *Par.*, **1849.**
——— MURRAY, HON. R. D. Cities and Wilds of A. **1853.**
Andalusia, New.—*See* NEW ANDALUSIA.
Andaman Islands.—KURZ, S. Report on the Vegetation of the A. I. **[1867.]**
Andes.—HUMBOLDT, A. VON. Researches concerning . . . America, with descriptions . . . of . . . the Cordilleras, *etc.* **1814.**
——— SCHMIDTMEYER, P. Travels . . . over the A., *etc.* *Lond.*, **1824.**
——— HEAD, F. B. Rough Notes . . . along the A. **1828.**
——— MAW, H. L. Journal of a Passage . . . crossing the A., *etc.* **1829.**
——— PENTLAND, J. B., and PARISH, SIR W. Notices of the Bolivian A., *etc.* *Lond.*, **1836.**
——— SMYTH, W., and LOWE, F. Narrative of a Journey . . . across the A., *etc.* **1836.**
——— SCARLETT, HON. P. C. South America . . . comprising a Journey across . . . the A., *etc.* **1838.**
——— BOUSSINGAULT, M. Viajes cientificos á los A. Ecuatoriales, *etc.* *Par.*, **1849.**
——— DOMEYKO, D. I. Viaje á las Cordilleras de Talca i de Chillan. **1849.**
——— HOPKINS, E. On the structure of the Crystalline Rocks of the A., *etc.* **1850.**
——— RICHARD, F. I. A Mining Journey across the Great A. **1863.**
——— SILVA COUTINHO, J. M. DE. Considerações geraes sobre os rios que descem da cordilheira dos A., *etc.* **1863.**
——— ROSETTI, E. Ferrovia Trasandina. Relazione sulla praticabilità, *etc.* *Buen. A.*, **1870.**
——— Schmidtmeyer, P. Voyage au Chili, à travers la chaine des A., 1820–21. EYRIES. Vol. IX.
Andorre.—SPAIN. Border Lands of Spain . . . with an account of a Visit to the Republic of A. **1856.**
Anglea.—Description of the divers Nations . . . in Brasill . . . also . . . A., *etc.* PURCHAS. Vol. IV.
Anglesea.—Edwin, the Saxon King of Northumberland. Conquest of . . . Anglesey, *etc.* HAKLUYT. Vol. I.
Angol Nemzet.—*See* ENGLAND.
Angola.—BOWDITCH, T. E. Account of the Discoveries of the Portuguese in the Interior of A., *etc.* **1824.**

Angola.—Cardozo de Castellobranco e Torres, J. C. F. Memorias contendo ... Descripção geographica ... de A., *etc.* *Par.*, 1825.
—— Fleming, F. Southern Africa ... from the Cape of Good Hope to A. 1856.
—— A Description of ... A., *etc.* Astley. Vol. III.
—— Voyages and Travels to ... A. Astley. Vol. III.
—— Barbot, J. Description of ... Ethiopia Inferior, vulgarly A., *etc.* Churchill. Vol. V.
—— Battel, A. Strange Adventure of, sent by the Portuguese prisoner to A. Pinkerton. Vol. XVI.
—— Catalogo dos Governadores do Reino de A. *etc.* Portugal. Collecção de Noticias, *etc.* Vol. III.
—— Description of the divers Nations ... in Brasill ... also A., *etc.* Purchas. Vol. IV.
—— Battels, A. Die Reisen und Begebenheiten in A., 1589. Voyages and Travels. Allgemeine Historie, *etc.* Vol. IV.
—— Eine Beschreibung der Königreiche ... A., *etc.* Voyages and Travels. Allgemeine Historie, *etc.* Vol IV.

Anguilla Islands.—Murchison, Sir R. I. On the ... value of certain Phosphate Rocks of the A. I., *etc.* 1859.
—— Engländische Inseln. Reisen ... in ... A. Voyages and Travels. Allgemeine Historie, *etc.* Vol. XVII.

Anhulwara.—*See* Nehrwalla.

Anian, Strait of.—*See* Behring's Strait.

Animalaya Mountains.—Hamilton, D. Report on the High Ranges of the Annamullay Mountains. *Madras*, 1866.

Animally Mountains.—*See* Animalaya Mountains.

Ankova.—Oliver, S. P. Madagascar ... with Sketches in the Provinces of Tamatave ... and A. *Lond.* [1865.]

Annamullay Mountains.—*See* Animalaya Mountains.

Assyria.—Walpole, Hon. F. The A. and the Assassins, *etc.* 1851.

Antartic France.—*See* America, South.
—— **Ocean.**—Morrell, B. Narrative of four Voyages to the ... A. O., *etc.* *N. Y.*, 1832.
—— —— Hooker, Sir W. J. Notes on the Botany of the A. Voyage, conducted by Capt. J. C. Ross, *etc.* *Lond.*, 1843.
—— **Regions.**—Report ... relative to ... Observations to be made in the A. Expedition, *etc.* 1840.
—— —— Ross, Sir J. C. Voyage ... in ... the A. R., 1839-43. 1847.
—— —— Sabine, Major-Gen. E. Observations made ... by the A. Naval Expedition, 1841-48, *etc.* 1848-53.

Anticosti.—Bocur, A. R. Notes on ... A. 1855.
—— Billings, E. Catalogues of the Silurian Fossils of ... A., *etc.* *Montreal*, 1866.
—— Anticosti. The Island of A., *etc.* *Lond.*, 1867.

Anticosti.—Voyage of the *Grace* . . . as far as the Isle of Assumption or Natiscotec, 1594. HAKLUYT. Vol. III.

Antigo.—*See* ANTIGUA.

Antigua.—EDWARDS, B. Historical Survey of . . . Saint Domingo . . . Also a Tour through . . . A., *etc.* 1801.

——— Engländische Inseln. Reisen . . . in . . . A., *etc.* VOYAGES and TRAVELS. Allgemeine Historie, *etc.* Vol. XVII.

Antilles.—WATERTON, C. Wanderings in . . . the A., *etc.* 1828.

——— POEY, A. Catalogue . . . suivi d'une Bibliographie sismique concernant les travaux relatifs aux Tremblements de Terre des A. *Versailles*, 1858.

——— DEVILLE, C. SAINTE-CLAIRE. Recherches sur les principaux Phénomènes . . . aux A., *etc.* *Par.*, 1860.

——— GRAS, M. A. LE. Phares de la Mer des A. . . . Corrigés, 1862, 63. *Par.*, 1862, 63.

——— Antilles. EYRIÈS. Vol. X.

——— Antilles. Mœurs . . . Commerce . . . Histoire Naturelle, *etc.* LAHARPE, J. Vol. XIV.

——— Reisen und Niederlassungen auf den Antillen. VOYAGES and TRAVELS. Allgemeine Historie, *etc.* Vol. XVII.

——— Von den Reisen nach den Antillen . . . 1635-63. VOYAGES and TRAVELS. Allgemeine Historie, *etc.* Vol. XVII.

——— Zusatz zu den Reisen und Niederlassungen auf den Antillen. VOYAGES and TRAVELS. Allgemeine Historie, *etc.* Vol. XVII.

———, **Sea of the.**—*See* CARIBBEAN SEA.

Antioch.—ARUNDELL, F. V. J. Discoveries . . . including a description of . . . A., *etc.* 1834.

——— HUG, A. Antiochia und der Aufstand des Jahres 387 n. Chr. *Winterth.*, 1863.

Antrim.—HAMILTON, W. Letters concerning the N. Coast of . . . A., *etc.* *Dubl.*, 1790.

——— DUBOURDIEU, J. Statistical Survey of . . . A., *etc.* *Dubl.*, 1812.

Antwerp.—VANDER MAELEN, P. Dictionnaire Géographique de la Province d'Anvers. *Brux.*, 1834.

Anuradhapura.—*See* ANURAJAPURA.

Anurajapura.—CHAPMAN, J. J. Some . . . Remarks upon the ancient city of A. . . . In . . . Ceylon.

Anvers.—*See* ANTWERP.

Anzio.—*See* ANZO, PORTO D'.

Anzo, Porto d'.—CIALDI, A. Osservazioni Idraulico-Nautiche sui Porti Neroniano ed Innocenziano in Anzio. *Roma*, 1848.

Anzuan.—*See* JOHANNA.

Apalache.—Soto, F. von. Reise nach . . . der Provinz A., *etc.* 1537-43. VOYAGES and TRAVELS. Allgemeine Historie, *etc.* Vol. XVI.

Apennines.—SPALLANZANI, L. Travels in . . . some parts of the A., *etc.* 1798.

Apennines.—Murchison, Sir R. I. On the Geological Structure of the ... A. 1849.
Appenzell.—Gemälde der Schweiz ... A., *etc.* *Bern*, 1834-38.
Apulia.—Cagnazzi, L. de S. Saggio sulla Popolazione ... di Puglia. *Nap.*, 1820.
Apure.—Hippisley, G. Narrative of the Expedition to the ... A., *etc.* 1819.
Aquitaine.—Avezac, d'. Notice sur l'A. *Par.*
—— Lartet, E. and Christy, H. Reliquiæ Aquitanicæ, *etc.* *Lond.*, [1865.]
Arabia.—Ritter, C. Der Arabische Weihrauch, *etc.*
—— Bellonius, P. Plurimarum ... rerum in ... A. ... conspectarum observationes, *etc.* *Antw.*, 1589.
—— Dapper. Naukeurige Beschryving van ... A., *etc.* *Amst.*, 1680.
—— La Roque, M. de. Voyage dans la Palestine ... Avec la description générale d'Arabie faite par le Sultan Ismael Abulfeda. *Amst.*, 1718.
—— Niebuhr, C. Beschreibung von Arabien, *etc.* *Kopenh.*, 1772.
—— Niebuhr, C. Voyage en Arabie, *etc.* *Amst.*, 1774-80.
—— Irwin, E. A Series of Adventures ... on the Coasts of A., *etc.* *Lond.*, 1780.
—— Griffiths, J. Travels in ... A. 1805.
—— Pocock, E. Specimen Historiæ Arabum, *etc.* *Oxonii*, 1806.
—— Ali Bey. Travels in ... A., *etc.* 1816.
—— Price, D. Essay towards the History of A. prior to the birth of Mahommed. 1824.
—— Burckhardt, J. L. Travels in A., in 1814-15, *etc.* 1829.
—— —— Arabic Proverbs, *etc.* 1830.
—— Stocqueler, J. H. Fifteen Months' Pilgrimage through ... parts of Turkish A., *etc.* 1832.
—— Berghaus, H. Asia ... nebst Bemerkungen über ... A., *etc.* *Gotha*, 1832-35.
—— Owen, W. F. W. Narrative of Voyage to explore the shores of ... A., *etc.* 1833.
—— Arabic Grammar, *etc.* *Bombay*, 1834.
—— Niebuhr, C. Reisebeschreibung nach Arabien, *etc.* *Hamb.*, 1837.
—— Wellsted, J. R. Travels in A. 1838.
—— Jomard, E. F. Etudes ... sur l'Arabie, *etc.* *Par.*, 1839.
—— Hammer-Purgstall, Baron. Geographie von Arabien. *Wien*, 1840.
—— Wellsted, J. R. Travels ... including a Voyage to the Coast of A., *etc.* 1840.
—— Forster, C. Historical Geography of A., *etc.* 1844.
—— Plate, W. Ptolemy's Knowledge of A., *etc.* 1845.

Arabia. 45

Arabia.—JOMARD, E. F.   Note sur la Carte d'Arabie publiée en 1847.
Par., **1847.**

—— ATTAD, El T. M.   Traité de la langue Arabe vulgaire.   *Leips.,* **1848.**

—— HAMMER-PURGSTALL, BARON.   Uebersicht der Literaturgeschichte der Araber.   *Wien,* **1850.**

—— CARTER, H. J.   A geographical description of . . . the S.E. Coast of A., *etc.*   *Bombay,* **1851.**

—— FORSTER, C.   The One Primeval Language traced . . . from the Monuments of . . . South A., *etc.*   **1851.**

—— KENNEDY, J.   Idumæa, with a survey of A., *etc.*   **1851.**

—— CARTER, H. J.   Memoir on the Geology of the S.E. Coast of A.
Bombay, **1852.**

—— HAMMER-PURGSTALL, BARON.   Über die Namen der Araber.
Wien, **1852.**

—— LOWTH, G. T.   Wanderer in A., *etc.*   **1855.**

—— WRIGHT, T.   Early Christianity in A., *etc.*   **1855.**

—— INDIA.   Geological Papers on W.n India, including . . . the N.E. Coast of A., *etc.*   *Bomb.,* **1857.**

—— PHILLIPS, J. S.   Interpretations . . . the Re-settlement of the Seed of Abraham in . . . A., *etc.*   **1860.**

—— HOMMAIRON, J.   Instructions Nautiques . . . Côte Sud d'Arabie, *etc.*
Par., **1864.**

—— PALGRAVE, G., Notes d'un Voyage au travers de l'intérieur de l'Arabie, *etc.*   [A Review.]   **[1864.]**

—— PALGRAVE, W. G., Narrative of a year's Journey through Central and Eastern A., 1862-63.   *Lond. und Cam.,* **1865.**

—— WARD, C. Y.   Pilote du Golfe d'Aden . . . Côtes . . . d'Arabie, *etc.*   *Par.,* **1866.**

—— AVRIL, A. D'.   L'Arabie contemporaine, *etc.*   *Par.,* **1868.**

—— Cartwright, J.   The Preacher's Travels . . . through . . . A., *etc.*   CHURCHILL.   Vol. VII.

—— BISSELL, A.   Voyage . . . along the E. Coast of A. to Bombay, 1798-99.   DALRYMPLE, A.   Collection of Nautical Memoirs, *etc.*

—— Arabie.   EYRIÈS.   Vol. XIV.

—— Athelard of Baths.   Voyage to . . . A., 1130.   HAKLUYT.   Vol. II.

—— Vertomannus, L.   Navigation and Voyages to . . . A. . . . 1503. HAKLUYT.   Vol. IV.

—— Baumgarten, M.   Travels through . . . A., *etc.*   CHURCHILL.   Vol. I.

—— Varthema, L. di.   Travels in . . . A. Deserta and A. Felix . . . 1503 to 1508 . . . Edited . . . by G. P. Badger.   1863.   HAKLUYT Soc. Pub.   Vol. XXXII.

—— —— Voyages and Travels in . . . A. . . . in 1503-8.   KERR.
Vol. VII.

—— Niebuhr's Travels in A.   PINKERTON.   Vol. X.

—— Iambulus, his Navigation to A., *etc.*   PURCHAS.   Vol. I.

Arabia.—Saltbanke, J. Voyage through . . . A., 1609. Purchas. Vol. I.
——— Barthema or Vertoman, L. Travels into . . . A. . . . 1503. Purchas. Vol. II.
——— Collections . . . especially of A., gathered out of an Arabike booke . . . written by a Nubian, 470 yeeres ago, *etc.* Purchas. Vol. II.
——— Mount Sinai . . . and the adjoining parts of A. described out of Breidenbach, *etc.* Purchas. Vol. II.
——— Of the Arabians . . . and of their Religions. Purchas. Vol. V.
——— Barthema, L. Itinerario dell' Egitto . . . A. Deserta et Felice, *etc.* Ramusio. Vol. I.
——— Jordan, ou Jourdain Catalani, P. Mirabilia descripta, sequitur de . . . A., *etc.* Voyages and Travels. Recueil, *etc.* Vol. IV.
——— **Deserta.**—Valle, P. della. Travels in . . . A. D., *etc.* 1665.
——— **Felix.**—Tellez, B. Travels . . . in A. F., *etc.* 1710.
——— ——— La Roque. A Voyage to A. the Happy . . . in 1708-10. 1730.
——— ——— Salt, H. Voyage to Abyssinia . . . a narrative of late events in A. F., *etc.* 1814.
——— ——— Combes, E. and Tamisier, M. Voyage en Abyssinie . . . précédé d'une excursion dans l'Arabie-Heureuse, 1835-37.
Pur., 1838.
——— ——— Middleton, Sir H. Observations in A. F. Hay, J.
——— ——— Erste Reisen der Franzosen nach dem glücklichen Arabien durch das Morgenländische Meer, 1708. Voyages and Travels. Allgemeine Historie, *etc.* Vol. XI.
——— See also Yemen.
——— **Petræa.**—Rüppel, E. Reisen in . . . dem Peträischen Arabien, *etc.*
1829.
——— ——— Laborde, N. L. de. Journey through A. P., *etc.* 1836.
——— ——— Stephens, G. Incidents of Travel in . . . A. P., *etc.* 1838.
——— ——— Robinson, E. Biblical Researches in . . . A. P., *etc.*
1841.
——— ——— Seetzen, U. J. Reisen durch . . . A. P., *etc. Berl.,* 1854.
——— ——— Figari, A. Studii scientifici sull' Egitto e . . . la Penisola dell' A. P., *etc. Lucca,* 1864-65.
Arabian Gulf.—*See* Red Sea.
Arabistan.—De Bode, Baron C. A. Travels in . . . A. 1845.
Aracan.—*See* Arracan.
Arafura Sea.—Stokes, J. L. Discoveries . . . Also a Narrative of Capt. O. Stanley's Visits to the Islands in the A. S. *Lond.,* 1846.
Araguaya.—Silva Coutinho, J. M. de. Annexo P. Exploração do Rio . . . A., *etc.* [1865.]
Aral, Sea of.—Khanikoff, T. V. Notes explanatory of a Map of the Lake of A., *etc. Russ. St. Pet.,* 1851.
——— Butakoff, A. Survey of the Sea of A. *Lond.,* 1852.

Aral, Sea of — Archipelago, Indian. 47

Aral, Sea of.—Lamansky, E. Esquisse Géographique du Bassin de la Mer d'A., etc. *Par.*, 1858.
Ararat.—Abich, H. Geognostiche Reise zum A., etc. *Berlin.*
Aran.—Jordan, ou Jourdain Catalani, P. Mirabilia descripta, sequitur ... de terra A., etc. Voyages and Travels. Recueil, etc. Vol. IV.
—— **Islands of.** See Arran.
Ararat.—Parrot, F. Reise zum A. *Berl.*, 1834.
—— Parrot, F. Journey to A., etc. 1845.
—— Freshfield, D. W. Travels ... including Visits to A., etc. *Lond.*, 1869.
Arauca.—Robinson, J. H. Journal of an Expedition ... up the A. 1822.

Araxe, River.—See Araxes.
Araxes, River. Caspian Sea. Description ... Mémoire sur le Cours de l'Araxe ... Par St. Croix. *Par.*, 1793.
—— Baer, K. E. von. Der alte Lauf des Armenischen A. 1857.
Arcadia.—Sibthorp, Dr. Journal relating to ... A., etc. Walpole, R. Travels, etc.
Archangel.—Vesselowsky, C. Époques des Débacles et de la prise par les Glaces de la Dwina à A. *St. Pet.*, 1856.
—— M'Dougall, G. F. Directions for ... the White Sea, including ... A., etc. 1858.
—— Allison's Voyage from A. Pinkerton. Vol. I.
Archipelago.—Borghini, M. L'Arcipelago, etc. *Ven.*, 1656.
—— Dapper. Beschryving van Eilanden der Archipel, etc. 1688.
—— Jesuits, Travels of several ... into ..., the A., etc. 1714.
—— Pococke, R. Description of ... the A., etc. 1743-45.
—— Mac Gill, T. Travels ... with an Account of some of the Greek Islands. 1808.
—— Aulnjo, J. Visit to ... some of the Greek Islands, etc. 1835.
—— Spratt, T. A. B. Report of Deep Soundings between Malta and the A., etc. 1857.
—— Thevenot, J. Account of ... various Islands in the A., etc. Harris, J. Vol. II.
—— Vernon, F. Travels ... through .... the A., etc. Ray, J.
—— Hawkins, Mr. On a Law of Custom which is peculiar to the Islands of the A. Walpole, R. Travels, etc.
—— Sibthorp, Dr. Voyage in the Grecian Seas, etc. (Second Voyage, etc.) Walpole, R. Travels, etc.
——, **Eastern.**—See Archipelago, Indian.
——, **Indian.**—Walckenaer, C. A. Le Monde Maritime, ou Tableau ... de l'Archipel d'Orient, etc. *Par.*, 1818.
—— —— Crawfurd, J. History of the I. A., etc. *Edin.*, 1820.
—— —— Earl, G. W. The Eastern Seas; or Voyages ... in the I. A. in 1832-34, etc. 1837.

Archipelago, Indian.—Moor, J. H. Notices of the I. A. and adjacent countries, etc. *Singapore*, 1837.
—— —— Bennett, F. D. Narrative . . . comprising Sketches of . . . the I. A., etc. 1840.
—— —— Hinderstein, G. F. von Derfelden de. Mémoire . . . des Possessions Neerlandaises dans le Grand Archipel Indien. *La Haye*, 1841.
—— —— Derfelden de Hinderstein, Baron G. F. von. Mémoire . . . pour servir d'explication à la Carte Générale des Possessions Néerlandaises dans le Grand Archipel Indien. *La Haye*, 1844.
—— —— Indian A., Journal of the, etc. *Singapore*, 1847-58.
—— —— Belcher, Sir E. Narrative of . . . Voyage . . . employed surveying the . . . E. A., etc. 1848.
—— —— Marryat F. S. Borneo and the I. A. *Lond.*, 1848.
—— —— Philopatris.—Commerce and Free Trade promoted in the I. A., etc. *Lond.*, 1848.
—— —— Keppel, Hon. G. Visit to the I. A., etc. 1853.
—— —— St. John, H. The I. A., its history, etc. 1853.
—— —— Gibson, W. M. The Prison of Weltevreden; and a glance at the E. I. A. *N. Y.*, 1855.
—— —— Logan, J. R. Ethnology of the Indo-Pacific Islands, etc. *Pinang*, 1855-56.
—— —— Crawfurd, J. A descriptive Dictionary of the Indian Islands, etc. 1856.
—— —— Denham, H. M. Hydrographic Notices . . . E. A., etc. 1856-59.
—— —— Boucher, F. The I. A., etc. 1857.
—— —— Müller, S. Reizen . . . in den Indischen Archipel . . . in 1828 en 1836. *Amst.*, 1857.
—— —— Reinwardt, C. G. C. Reis naar het oostelijk Gedeelte van den Indischen Archipel, in 1821, etc. *Amst.*, 1858.
—— —— Hügel, Baron C. von. Der Stille Ocean und die Spanischen Besitzungen im Ostindischen Archipel. *Wien*, 1860.
—— —— Sallot des Noyers, M. Instructions sur les Iles et les Passages du grand Archipel d'Asie, etc. *Par.*, 1867, 68.
—— —— Bickmore, A. S. Travels in the E. I. A. *Lond.*, 1868.
—— —— Îles de la Mer des Indes. Voyage . . . de F. Pyrard, etc. Laharpe, J. Vol. III.
——, **Louisiade.**—*See* Louisiade Archipelago.
——, **Low.**—*See* Low Archipelago.
——, **Malay.**—Wallace, A. R. The M. A.: the land of the Orang-Utan, etc. *Lond.*, 1869.
——, **Pomotou.**—*See* Low Archipelago.
Arcipelago.—*See* Archipelago.
Arcot, South.—India. Reports of the . . . effects of the . . . Coleroon Anicuts, in . . . S. A. *Madras*, 1858.

Arctic Ocean. 49

Arctic Ocean.—HEARNE, S. A Journey from . . . Hudson's Bay to the Northern Ocean . . . 1769-72. **1795.**

—— MACKENZIE, A. Voyages . . . to the Frozen and Pacific Oceans, in 1789 and 1793, etc. **1801.**

—— SARYCHEF, CAPT. Voyages along the . . . A. and Pacific Oceans . . . 1785 to 1793. *Russ.* *St. Pet.*, **1802.**

—— FRANKLIN, SIR J. Narrative of a Journey to the shores of the Polar Sea, in 1819-22, etc. **1823.**

—— COCHRANE, J. D. Narrative of a pedestrian Journey . . . to the Frozen Sea, etc. **1824.**

—— KING, R. Facts and Arguments in favour of a New Expedition to . . . the A. O. **1836.**

—————— Narrative of a Journey to . . . the A. O. in 1833-35, etc. **1836.**

—— FABVRE, CAPT. Retour en France de . . . *la Recherche*; Rapport sur la seconde campagne dans les Mers du Nord, etc. *Par.*, **1839.**

—— WRANGELL, F. VON. Reise . . . auf dem Eismeere in 1820-24, etc. *Berlin*, **1839.**

—————— Narrative of an Expedition to the Polar Sea in 1820-23, etc. **1840.**

—————— Narrative of an Expedition to the Polar Sea in 1820-23, etc. **1844.**

—— RAE, J. Narrative of an Expedition to the Shores of the A. Sea in 1846 and 1817. *Lond.*, **1850.**

—— KANE, E. K. Access to an open Polar Sea, etc. *N. Y.*, **1853.**

—— BELLOT, J. R. Journal d'un voyage aux Mers Polaires, etc. *Par.*, **1854.**

—— KANE, E. K. Astronomical Observations in the A. Seas, etc. *Phil.*, **1860.**

—————— Tidal Observations in the A. Seas, etc. *Wash.*, **1860.**

—— HAYES, I. I. The Open Polar Sea, etc. *Lond.*, **1867.**

—— BROWN, R. Notes on the . . . Pinnipedia frequenting the Spitzbergen and Greenland Seas. [*Lond.*, **1868.**]

—————— On the Nature of the Discoloration of the A. Seas. *Edin.*, **1868.**

—— M'CLINTOCK, SIR F. L. Fate of Sir John Franklin. The Voyage of the "Fox" in the A. Seas, etc. *Lond.*, **1869.**

—— Franklin, J. Voyage aux côtes de la Mer Polaire . . . 1819-21. EYRIÈS. Vol. VIII.

—— Parry, W. E. Voyage à la Mer Glaciale au nord de l'Amérique, 1819-20. EYRIÈS. Vol. VIII.

—— Beobachtungen wegen des Eises in denen Meeren, welche an die Pole gränzen. VOYAGES and TRAVELS. Allgemeine Historie, etc. Vol. XVIII.

—— Reisen . . . durch die Lena in das Eismeer. . . . zu gehen. VOYAGES and TRAVELS. Allgemeine Historie, etc. Vol. XIX.

—— Müller. Auszug aus . . . Reisen und Entdeckungen längst den Küsten des Eismeers, etc. VOYAGES and TRAVELS. Allgemeine Historie, etc. Vol. XX.

E

Arctic Ocean — Arctic Regions.

Arctic Ocean.—Kerguelen Tremarec, Von. Nachricht von seiner Reise in die Nordsee, 1707-68. Voyages and Travels. Allgemeine Historie, etc. Vol. XXI.

—— Sarytschew, G. Account of a Voyage ... to ... the Frozen Ocean ...1785. Voyages and Travels. A Collection, etc. 1806. Vol. V.

—— Parry, Capt. Letters written during the late Voyage ... in the W.n A. Sea, 1819-20, etc. Voyages and Travels, New. 1819. Vol. V.

Arctic Regions.—Belcher, Sir E. The last of the A. Voyages, etc.

—— Fitz James, J. The last Journals of, of the lost Polar Expedition, etc. *Brighton.*

—— Petermann, A. Historical Summary of the Five Years' Search after Sir J. Franklin, etc.

—— Phipps, C. J. Arctic Voyage ... 1773. **1774.**

—— Barrow, Sir J. Chronological history of Voyages into the A. R., etc. **1818.**

—— Scoresby, W. Account of the A. R., etc. *Edin.*, **1820.**

—— Fisher, A. A Journal of a Voyage ... to the A. R. ... in 1819-20. **1821.**

—— Scoresby, W. Journal of a Voyage to the N.n Whale Fishery, etc. *Edin.*, **1823.**

—— Sabine, Major-Gen. E. Account of Experiments to determine the figure of the Earth. ... (Also ... a brief account of Capt. Clavering's Voyage to the A. R.) **1825.**

—— Arctic Expeditions. A. Expeditions from England, from 1497 to 1838. **1834.**

—— Huish, R. The last Voyage of Capt. Sir J. Ross, to the A. R., etc. **1835.**

—— Ross, Capt. Sir J. Narrative ... of a Residence in the A. R. during 1829-33, etc. **1835.**

—— Back, Sir G. Narrative of the A. Land Expedition to ... Great Fish River, etc. **1836.**

—— Back, Sir G. Narrative of an expedition ... to ... the A. Shores, etc. **1838.**

—— Baer, K. E. von. Sur la fréquence des orages dans les régions Arctiques. *St. Pet.*, **1839.**

—— Rafn, C. C. Americas Arctiske Landes gamle Geographie, etc. *Kjöb.*, **1845.**

—— Barrow, Sir J. Voyages ... within the A. R., from ... 1818, etc. **1846.**

—— Rafn, C. C. Aperçu de l'ancienne Géographie des Régions Arctiques de l'Amérique. *Copenh.*, **1847.**

—— Arctic Expeditions. A Collection of papers relative to the recent A. expeditions, etc. **1848-56.**

—— Goodsir, R. A. Arctic Voyage to Baffin's Bay, etc. **1850.**

—— Kellet, H., and others. The A. Expedition of 1849, etc. **1850.**

Arctic Regions.—Scoresby, W. The Franklin Expedition; or Considerations ... for the discovery ... of our ... Countrymen in the A. R. **1850.**

—— Shillinglaw, J. J. Narrative of A Discovery from the earliest period, etc. **1850.**

—— Arctic Expeditions. A. Searching Expeditions of 1850-51, etc. **1851.**

—— Richardson, Sir J. Arctic Searching Expedition, etc. **1851.**

—— Snow, W. P. Voyage of the *Prince Albert*, in search of Sir J. Franklin, etc. **1851.**

—— Force, P. Remarks on the English Maps of A. Discoveries in 1850 and 1851. *Wash.*, **1852.**

—— Franklin, Sir J. Additional Papers relative to the A. Expedition, under Captain Austin, etc. **1852.**

—— Franklin, Sir J. Further Correspondence ... connected with the A. Expedition, etc. **1852.**

—— Franklin, Sir J. Report of the Committee appointed ... to inquire into the Report on the recent A. Expeditions in search of Sir J. F., etc. **1852.**

—— Petermann, A. The Search for Franklin. A Suggestion, etc. *Lond.*, **1852.**

—— Sutherland, P. C. Journal of a Voyage ... in 1850-51 ... in search of the Missing Crews, etc. **1852.**

—— Hooper, W. H. Ten Months among ... the Tuski, with ... an A. Boat Expedition, etc. **1853.**

—— Inglefield, E. A. A Summer Search for Sir J. Franklin, etc. **1853.**

—— Kane, E. K. The U. S. Grinnell Expedition in search of Sir J. Franklin, etc. *N. Y.*, **1853.**

—— Seemann, B. Narrative of ... Three Cruizers to the A. R., etc. **1853.**

—— Franklin, Sir J. Papers relative to the recent A. Expeditions in search of Sir J. F., etc. **1854.**

—— Irminger, C. Den Arctiske Strömning. **1854.**

—— Maltebrun, V. A. Coup-d'œil d'ensemble sur les différentes Expéditions Arctiques, etc. *Par.*, **1855.**

—— Mayne, F. Voyages ... in the A. R. **1855.**

—— Kane, E. K. Arctic Explorations. The second Grinnell Expedition, etc. *Phil.*, **1856.**

—— Kennedy, W. A Short Narrative of the second voyage of the *Prince Albert*, in search of Sir J. Franklin. *Lond.*, **1856.**

—— Rae, J. Voyages and Travels of, in the A. R. Copy of a Letter, etc. **1856.**

—— White, R. On the Open Water at the Great Polar Basin. **1856.**

—— Armstrong, A. Personal Narrative of ... travel ... in the A. R. etc. **1857.**

—— M'Dougall, G. F. The Voyage of H.M. ... *Resolute* to the A. R., 1852-54. **1857.**

Arctic Regions — Argentine Republic.

Arctic Regions.—Petersen, C.   Erindringer fra Polarlandene . . . 1850-55, etc. *Kjöb.,* **1857.**
——— Pim, B.   An Earnest Appeal to the British Public on behalf of the missing A. Expedition. **1857.**
——— Smucker, S. M.   A. Explorations and Discoveries during the Nineteenth century. *N. Y. and Auburn,* **1857.**
——— M'Clintock, F. L.   Reminiscences of A. Ice-Travel, *etc.*
Dubl., **1859.**
——— ——— The Voyage of the *Fox* in the A. Seas, *etc.* *Lond.,* **1859.**
——— Richardson, Sir J.   Polar Regions. [Art. from the Encyc. Brit.]
Edin., **1859.**
——— Chaix, P.   Explorations Arctiques, *etc.* **1860.**
——— Hayes, I. J.   Arctic Boat Journey in 1854, *etc.* **1860.**
——— Malte-Brun. V. A.   La Destinée de Sir J. Franklin dévoilée. Rapport du Capit. Mac Clintock, *etc.* **1860.**
——— Osborn, S.   The Career, last Voyage and fate of Sir J. Franklin. **1860.**
——— Petersen, C.   Den sidste Franklin-Expedition med *Fox,* etc. *Kjöb.,* **1860.**
——— Shaw, N.   Introductory Notice to Dr. I. L. Hayes's "Boat Journey," with Lists of A. Expeditions and Works. **1860.**
——— Snow, W. P.   On the Lost Polar Expedition, *etc.* **1860.**
——— Richardson, Sir J.   The Polar Regions. *Edin.,* **1861.**
——— Heer, O.   Ueber die Polarländer. *Zürich,* **1867.**
——— Maupertius's Journey to the Polar Circle.   Pinkerton.   Vol. I.
——— Fisher, A.   Journal of a Voyage . . . to the A. R., 1818, *etc.* Voyages and Travels, New. 1819. Vol. I.
——— ——— *See also* Arctic Ocean — Esquimaux — Greenland — North Pole — Spitzbergen — Wellington Channel.
——— Seas.—*See* Arctic Ocean.

Ardennes.—Joanne, A.   Collection des Guides-Joanne . . . A., *etc.*
Par., **1868.**
Ardra.—D'Elbée, Sieur.   Voyage to A. . . . in 1669-70.   Astley.   Vol. III.
Ardrah.—*See* Ardra.
Arecan.—*See* Arracan.
Arequipa.—Raimondi, A.   Analisis de las . . . Aguas potables de A.
Areq., **1864.**
———, Volcano of.—Rouaud y Paz Soldan, M.   Estudio sobre la Altura de las Montañas aplicado especialmente al Misti o Volcan de A.
Lima, **1868.**
Argentiera.—Sibthorp, Dr.   Voyage . . . A., *etc.*   Walpole, R.   Travels, *etc.*

Argentine Confederation.—*See* Argentine Republic.
——— **Republic.**—Angelis, P. de.   Memoria . . . sobre los derechos de Soberania . . . de la Confederacion Argentina, á la parte Austral del Continente Americano, *etc.* *Buen. Aires,* **1852.**

Argentine Republic. 53

Argentine Republic.—Oraty, A. M. du. Mémoire sur les productions minérales de la Confédération Argentine. *Par.*, 1855.

―――― Hopkins, E. A. Memoria . . . proveyendo los medios de disponer de las tierras publicas de la Confederacion Argentina, *etc.*
Buen. Ay., 1857.

―――― Alberdi, J. B. Organizacion de la Confederacion Argentina.
Besançon, 1858.

―――― Page, T. J. La Plata, the A. Confederation, *etc.* *N. Y.*, 1859.

―――― Mousey, V. M. de. Description Géographique . . . de la Confédération A. *Par.*, 1860-64.

―――― Argentine Railway. Central A. Railway, *etc.* 1863.

―――― Argentine Republic. Reglamentos de Policia Maritima . . . de la Nacion Arjentina. *Buen. A.*, 1863.

―――― Perkins, O. Las Colonias de Santa Fé . . . Con observaciones generales sobre la Emigracion a la Repúblíca Argentina, *etc.*
Rosario de S. F., 1864.

―――― Hutchinson, T. J. Buenos Ayres and A. Gleanings, *etc.*
Lond., 1865.

―――― Argentine Republic. Rejistro estadístico de la República Arjentina. 1864, 65. *Buen. A.*, 1865-67.

―――― Argentine Railway. Terrenos cedidos . . . con destino a la venta o permuta de los que han de expropiarse para ceder a la Empresa del Ferro-Carril Central Argentino, *etc.* 1866.

―――― Argentine Republic. La Republica Argentina, sus Colonias Agrícolas, *etc.* *Buen. A.*, 1866.

―――― Ford, F. C. A. R. Reports, *etc.* *Buen. Ay.*, 1866.

―――― Lacroze, J. Los Ferro-Carriles económicos y el Porvenir de la Republica Argentina. *Buen. Air.*, 1866.

―――― Argentine Railway. Central A. Railroad. Report, *etc.*
Lond., 1867.

―――― Argentine Republic. Anuario de Correos de la República Arjentina. *Buen. A.*, 1867.

―――― Argentine Republic. Datos Officiales. La Republica Arjentina. Poblacion, *etc.* *Par.*, 1867.

―――― Granel, J. Discursos pronunciados en el Senado Argentino en la discusion del Proyecto para fijar la Capital de la Nacion.
Buen. Aires, 1867.

―――― Labrador Argentino, El. Revista de Agricultura, *etc.*
Buen. Air., 1867.

―――― Johnson, H. C. R. A Long Vacation in the A. Alps, *etc.*
Lond., 1868.

―――― Poucel, B. Rapport sur le Rejistro Estadístico de la République Argentine. *Marseille*, 1868.

―――― Argentine Republic. Letters concerning the country of the A. R., *etc.* *Lond.*, 1869.

―――― Rickard, F. J. The Mineral and other Resources of the A. R. . . . in 1869. *Lond.*, 1870.

Argentine Republic.—*See also* BUENOS AYRES—LA PLATA.

Argolis.—Sibthorp, Dr. Journal relating to ... A., *etc.* WALPOLE, R. Travels, *etc.*

Arguin.—HOXEY, W. Narrative of ... Captivity ... on the Island of A., *etc.* *Lond.*, 1845.

——— Relation concerning the Estate of the Island and Castle of A. ... 1401. HAKLUYT. Vol. III.

Arguri.—ABICH, H. Geognostische Reise zum Ararat und Verschüttung des Thales von A. *Berlin.*

Arizona.—MOWRY, S. The Geography and Resources of A., *etc.* *San F. and N. Y.*, 1863.

Arkansa, River.—*See* ARKANSAS.

Arkansas.—PECK, J. M. Guide for Emigrants to ... A., *etc.* *Bost.*, 1836.

——— MARCOU, J. Geology of North America; with Reports on the Prairies of A., *etc.* *Zurich*, 1858.

——— OWEN, D. D. Reports of a Geological Reconnoissance of ... A., made during 1857-60. *Little Rock and Phil.*, 1858-60.

——— Schoolcraft, H. R. Journal of a Tour into the Interior of ... A. ..., 1818, 19. VOYAGES and TRAVELS, New. 1819. Vol. IV.

——— *See also* FORT SMITH.

——— **River.**—ABERT, LIEUT. J. W. Report of an expedition on the Upper A., *etc.* *Wash.*, 1846.

——— ——— EMORY, W. H. Notes of a Military Reconnoissance ... including parts of the A., *etc.* *N. Y.*, 1848.

——— ——— Pike. Voyage ... aux sources de l'A. ... 1805-7. EYRIÈS. Vol. IX.

Arkansaw.—*See* ARKANSAS.

Arkhangel.—*See* ARCHANGEL.

Armagh.—COOTE, SIR C. Statistical Survey of the County of A., *etc.* *Dubl.*, 1804.

Armenia.—KOCH, C. Erläuterungen zur Karte des ... Armeniens. *Berlin.*

——— MORIER, J. Journey through ... A. ... in 1808-9. 1812.

——— KINNEIR, J. M. Journey through ... A. ... in 1813-14, *etc.* 1818.

——— MORIER, J. A Second Journey through ... A., *etc.* *Lond.*, 1818.

——— JAUBERT, P. A. Voyage en Arménie ... 1805 et 1806, *etc.* *Par.*, 1821.

——— PORTER, Sir R. K. Travels in ... A., *etc.* *Lond.*, 1821, 22.

——— CHAMICH, M. History of A., *etc.* *Calc.*, 1827.

——— STOCQUELER, J. H. Fifteen Months' Pilgrimage through ... A., *etc.* 1832.

——— PRICE, W. Journal of Travels of the British Embassy to ... A., *etc.* 1833.

Armenia — Arracan. 55

Armenia.—SMITH, E. and DWIGHT, H. G. O. Missionary Researches in A., etc. 1834.
—— MONTPÉREUX, F. D. DE. Voyage . . . en . . . Arménie, etc. Par., 1839.
—— AINSWORTH, W. F. Travels . . . in . . A. 1842.
—— HAMILTON, W. J. Researches in . . . A., etc. 1842.
—— LAYARD, A. H. Discoveries . . . with Travels in A., etc. 1853.
—— CURZON, HON. R. A., etc. 1854.
—— VINCKE, and OTHERS. Memoir über die Construction der Karte von . . . Türkisch Armenien, etc. Berl., 1854.
—— PETACHIA, RABBI. Travels of; who, in the . . . Twelfth Century visited . . . A., etc. 1856.
—— SANDWITH, H. Narrative of . . . Travels in A., etc. 1856.
—— ABICH, H. Ueber das Steinsalz . . . im Russischen Armenien. St. Pet., 1857.
—— TCHIHATCHEFF, P. DE. Études sur la Végétation des Hautes-Montagnes . . . de l'Arménie. Par., 1857.
—— ALISHAN, R. L. M. Physiographie de l'Arménie. Ven., 1861.
—— STRECKER, W. Topographische Mittheilungen über Hoch-A. Berl., 1861.

—— Cartwright, J. The Preacher's Travels . . . through . . . A., etc. CHURCHILL. Vol. VII.
—— Odoricus, Friar B. Voyage to . . . A. . . . about 1325. HARLUYT. Vol. II.
—— Chardin, Sir J. Travels . . . through . . . A. 1672. HARRIS, J. Vol. II.
—— Jackson, J. Journey . . . in 1797, through . . . A., etc. PELHAM. Vol. II.
—— Of the Armenians . . . and of their Religions. PURCHAS. Vol. V.
—— Rauwolf, L. Journey into . . . A., etc. RAY, J.
—— Jordan ou Jourdain Catalani, l'. Mirabilia descripta, sequitur de A., etc. VOYAGES and TRAVELS. Recueil, etc. Vol. IV.

Arno, River.—BELLONI, A. Memoria idrometrica sopra il Fiume A. Ven., 1778.
—— —— CIALDI, A. Sul nuovo emissario del Lago di Bientina e sulla Rotta sotto l'A. Roma, 1857.

Arpino.—KELSALL, C. Classical Excursion from Rome to A. Geneva, 1820.
—— —— Classical Excursion from Rome to A., 1820. VOYAGES and TRAVELS, New. 1819. Vol. IV.

Arracan.—Relation des Royaumes de . . . Arecan, par wilhem Methold, etc. THEVENOT. Vol. I.
—— Ovington, J. Beschreibung des Königreichs A. VOYAGES and TRAVELS. Allgemeine Historie, etc. Vol. X.
—— Schouten, G. Reisen nach . . . A. . . . 1658-65. VOYAGES and TRAVELS. Allgemeine Historie, etc. Vol. XII.

Arrakan — Asia.

Arrakan.—See ABRACAN.

Arran, Island of [Scotland].—HEADRICK, J. View of the Mineralogy ... of the Island of A., etc. *Edin.*, **1807.**

——, **Islands of** [Ireland.]—HAVERTY, M. The A. Isles, etc. *Dubl.*, **1859.**

Arsina.—Willoughby, Sir H. Voyage, wherein he ... perished at A. Recs in Lapland, 1553. HAKLUYT. Vol. I.

Aruba.—REINWARDT, C. G. C. Waarnemingen aangaande de gesteldheid van den Grond van het Eiland A., etc.

Arun.—THORNE, J. Rambles by Rivers; the ... A., etc. **1847.**

Arzina.—See ARSINA.

Asam.—See ASSAM.

Aschaffenburg.—HESSLEIN, A. VON. A. und seine Umgegend, etc. *Aschaff.*, **1857.**

Asele-Lappmark.—Ehrenmalm, A. Reise ... nach der L. A. ... 1741. VOYAGES and TRAVELS. Allgemeine Historic, etc. Vol. XIX.

Asem.—See ASSAM.

Aserada, River.—See VOLTA.

Asfi.—See SAFFI.

Ashango Land.—DU CHAILLU, P. B. A Journey to A.-L., etc. *Lond.*, **1867.**

Ashantee.—BOWDITCH, T. E. Mission from Cape Coast Castle to A., etc. **1819.**

—— HUTTON, W. Voyage ... to A. in 1820, etc. **1821.**

—— DUPUIS, J. Journal of a Residence in A., etc. **1824.**

—— FREEMAN, T. B. Extracts from the Journal of ... a visit from Cape Coast to A., etc. **1840.**

—— BEECHAM, J. A., etc. **1841.**

—— WINNIETT, SIR W. Journal of a Visit to the King of A., etc. **1849.**

—— Bowdich, M. Voyage dans le pays d'Achanti, 1817. EXTRS. Vol. XI.

—— Hutton, M. Voyage en Achanti, 1820. EXTRS. Vol. XI.

—— Bowdich, T. E. Mission from Cape Coast Castle to A., 1817. VOYAGES and TRAVELS. New. 1819. Vol. I.

Asia.—RITTER, C. Löwen-und-Tiger-Land in Asien, etc. *Berlin.*

—— SEIDENZUCHT. Ueber Ausbreitung der, in Asien.

—— BELLONIUS, F. Plurimarum ... rerum in ... A. ... conspectarum observationes, etc. *Antw.*, **1589.**

—— DAPPER. A., of Naukeurige Beschryving van het rijk des Grooten Moguls, etc. *Amst.*, **1672.**

—— DAPPER. Naukeurige Beschryving van Asie, etc. *Amst.*, **1680.**

—— BEGNO, G. B. de. Viaggio di cinque anni in A., etc. *Milano* [**1686.**]

KAEMPFER, E. Amoenitatum exoticarum ... fasciculi V. quibus continentur variae relationes ... rerum ... Ulterioris Asiae, etc. *Lemgoviae*, **1712.**

Asia.

Asia.—LUCAS, P. Voyage fait en 1714 dans . . . l'Asie, etc.   *Amst.*, **1720.**

——— MOTRAYE, A. de la. Travels through . . . A., *etc.*   **1723-32.**

——— VOYAGES and TRAVELS. Voyages faits principalement en Asie dans les XII., XIII., XIV., et XV. siècles, par Benjamin de Tudèle, *etc.*
La Haye, **1735.**

——— ASTLEY, T. New . . . Collection of . . . Travels . . . in . . . A. *etc.*   **1745-47.**

——— DRUMMOND, A. Travels through . . . several parts of A., *etc.*
1754.

——— BARROS, J. DE. Da A. de J. de Barros, *etc.*   *Lisb.*, **1778-1781.**

——— ASIATIC RESEARCHES, *etc.*   *Calc.*, **1788-1836.**

——— THUNBERG, C. P. Reisen in . . . Asien . . . 1770 bis 1779, *etc.*
Berl., **1792-94.**

——— COXE, W. Account of the Russian discoveries between A. and America, *etc.*   **1804.**

——— MIRZA ABU TALEB KHAN. Voyages en Asie . . . 1799-1803, *etc.*
Par., **1811.**

——— BARBER, G. D. Ancient . . . Records of the Cimri . . . in A., *etc.* **1815.**

——— CLARKE, E. D. Travels in . . . A., *etc.*   **1816-24.**

——— SMITH, CAPT. J. The True Travels . . . of Capt. J. Smith, in . . . A . . . beginning about . . . 1593, *etc.*   *Richmond, U. S.,* **1819.**

——— MURRAY, H. Historical Account of discoveries and travels in A., *etc.*   *Edinb.,* **1820.**

——— EAST INDIA. Papers respecting the cultivation of Sugar in . . . parts of A., *etc.*   **1822.**

——— KLAPROTH, J. A. Polyglotta, Sprachatlas.   *Par.*, **1823.**

——— ——— Mémoires relatifs à l'Asie, *etc.*   *Par.*, **1824.**

——— ——— Magasin A.tique, ou Revue Géographique, *etc.*   *Par.*, **1825.**

——— ARUNDELL, F. V. J. A visit to the Seven Churches of A., *etc.* **1828.**

——— KLAPROTH, J. Mémoires relatifs à l'Asie, *etc.*   *Par.*, **1828.**

——— IBN BATUTA, Travels of [in A., 1324-5], *etc.*
Or. Trans. Fund, **1829.**

——— WILLIAMS, J. Two Essays on the Geography of Ancient A., *etc.*
1829.

——— HUMBOLDT, A. VON. Fragmens de Géologie et de Climatologie Asiatiques.   *Par.*, **1831.**

——— BEROHAUS, H. A., *etc.*   *Gotha,* **1832-35.**

——— MARTIN, R. M. Statistics of the Colonies . . . in . . . A., *etc.*
Lond., **1839.**

——— BAER, K. E. VON, and HELMERSEN, COUNT VON. Beiträge zur Kenntniss des Russischen Reiches und der angränzenden Länder Asiens.
St. Pet., **1839-58.**

——— RUSSEGGER, J. Reisen in . . . Asien, *etc.*   *Stuttg.,* **1841.**

——— TERNAUX-COMPANS, H. Bibliothèque Asiatique et Africaine, *etc.*
Par., **1841.**

Asia.

Asia.—VÖLTER, D. Die Grundlinien der mathematischen Geographie . . . von . . . Asien. *Esslingen*, 1841.

—— ZIMMERMANN, C. Geographische Analyse der Karte von Inner-Asien, *etc.* *Berl.*, 1841.

—— —— Der Kriegs-Schauplatz in Inner-Asien, *etc.* *Berl.*, 1842.

—— RITTER, C. Ueber die Asiatische Heimat, *etc.* *Berl.*, 1844.

—— PARAVEY, CHEV. DE. Réfutation de l'opinion émise par M. Jomard que les peuples d'Amérique n'ont jamais eu aucun rapport avec ceux de l'Asie. *Par.*, 1849.

—— CHRISTMAS, H. Shores and Islands of the Mediterranean, including a visit to the Seven Churches of A. 1851.

—— DUNCAN, C. Campaign with the Turks in A. 1855.

—— BALFOUR, E. Cyclopædia of . . . E. n and S. n A., *etc.* *Madras*, 1857.

—— KIEPERT, H. Über die Persische Königsstrasse durch Vorderasien nach Herodotus. *Berl.*, 1857.

—— BROWN, SIR R. European and Asiatic Intercourse, *etc.* 1858.

—— SCHLAGINTWEIT, H., A. and R. DE. Results of a Scientific Mission to . . . High A. . . . between . . . 1854 and 1858, *etc.* *Leips. and Lond.*, 1861-63.

—— BENJAMIN, J. B. Eight Years in A., *etc.* *Hanov.*, 1863.

—— NEUMANN, C. F. Geschichte des Englischen Reiches in Asien. *Leipzig*, 1867.

—— RITTER, C. [Geography of Asia, *etc.*] *Russ.* [*St. Pet.*] 1867.

—— HUNTER, W. W. A Comparative Dictionary of the (Non-Aryan) Languages of India and High A., *etc.* *Lond.*, 1868.

—— CATALOGUES. A Catalogue of Maps of the British Possessions in India and other parts of A. *Lond.*, 1870.

—— JOHNSTON, A. K. Atlas of the British Empire in . . . A. . . . with . . . letterpress. *Edin. and Lond.* [1870.]

—— Smith, Capt. J. True Travels . . . in . . . A. . . . from 1593 to 1629. CHURCHILL. Vol. II.

—— Biddulph, W. Travels of four Englishmen . . . into . . . A. . . . in 1600 and 1611. CHURCHILL. Vol. VII.

—— Usher, Abp. J. Geographical and historical disquisition touching . . . A., *etc.* CHURCHILL. Vol. VII.

—— Voyages en Asie. Japon. EYRIÈS. Vol. XII.

—— Constantine, the Great. Voyage to . . . A. . . . 339. HAKLUYT. Vol. II.

—— Richard I. Famous Voyage into A. for the recovering of Jerusalem . . . 1190. HAKLUYT. Vol. II.

—— Robert, Ketensis. Voyage to . . . A., 1143. HAKLUYT. Vol. II.

—— The Fardle of Facions, conteining the . . . customes . . . of . . . Affricke and Asie, 1555. HAKLUYT. Vol. V.

—— Benjamin, Rabbi. Travels through . . . A. . . . 1160-1173. HARRIS, J. Vol. I.

Asia — Asia, Central. 59

Asia.—Marco Polo. The curious . . . Travels of, in the middle of the XIIIth century through a great part of A., etc. HARRIS, J. Vol. I.

—— Thevenot, J. Account of several . . . Cities in A. . . . 1666. HARRIS, J. Vol. II.

—— Asia. LAHARPE, J. Vol. III.

—— E. n and N. n A. Europa. LATHAM, R. G. Descriptive Ethnology. Vol. I.

—— Possessions in A. MARTIN, R. M. History of the British Colonies. Vol. I.

—— Bell's Travels in A. PINKERTON. Vol. VII.

—— Noticia summaria do Gentilismo da A. PORTUGAL. Collecção de Noticias, etc. Vol. I.

—— Benjamin, the Son of Jonas. Peregrination of . . . and relations of . . . A., etc. PURCHAS. Vol. II.

—— Collections of A. . . . gathered out of an Arabike booke . . . written by a Nubian, 470 yeers ago, etc. PURCHAS. Vol. II.

—— Smith, Capt. J. Travels . . . on the Sea Coasts of . . . A. . . . about 1608. PURCHAS. Vol. II.

—— Barkley, G. Travels . . . in . . . A. . . . 1605. PURCHAS. Vol. III.

—— Historie of Ayton, or Anthonie the Armenian, of A., etc. PURCHAS. Vol. III.

—— Ovington, J. Reise . . . in . . . A. . . . 1690-93. VOYAGES and TRAVELS. Allgemeine Historie, etc. Vol. X.

—— Engel. Nachrichten . . . über die Lage der mitternächtlichen Länder von A., etc. VOYAGES and TRAVELS. Allgemeine Historie, etc. Vol. XIX.

—— Jordan, ou Jourdain Catalani, P. Description des Merveilles d'une partie de l'Asie, etc. VOYAGES and TRAVELS. Recueil, etc. Vol. IV.

—— See also EAST.

—— **Central.**—HUMBOLDT, A. VON. Asie Centrale. Recherches, etc.
Par., 1843.

—— —— MAHLMANN, W. Ergänzungen zu A. von Humboldt's Central-Asien. Berl., 1844.

—— —— KRASNIKOFF, J. and TOLSTOI, P. List of Positions in the S. W. n Parts of C. A. determined astronomically. Russ.
St. Pet., 1850.

—— —— ATKINSON, T. W. Oriental . . . Siberia . . . Adventures in . . . C. A. 1858.

—— —— SAINT-MARTIN, V. DE. Mémoire analytique sur la Carte de l'Asie Centrale . . . construite . . . pour les Voyages de Hiouen-Thsang, 629-645. Par., 1858.

—— —— KRASNIKOFF, N. DE. Mémoire sur la Partie Méridionale de l'Asie Centrale. Par., 1861.

—— —— DAVIES, R. H. Central A. Report, etc. 1864.

Asia, Central — Asia Minor.

Asia, Central.—Vambéry, A.   Travels in C. A., etc.   *Lond.*, **1864.**

————   **East.**—Indian Archipelago, Journal of the and E. n A.
Singapore, **1847-58.**

————   ————   Balfour, E.   The Timber Trees . . . of E. . . . A.
Madras, **1862.**

————   ————   Reinaud, M.   Relations politiques et commerciales de l'Empire Romain avec l'Asie Orientale . . . pendant les cinq premiers siècles, etc.   *Par.*, **1863.**

————   ————   Asia, East.   Die Preussische Expedition nach Ost-Asien, etc.   *Berl.*, **1866, 67.**

————   ————   Bastian, A.   Die Voelker des Oestlichen Asien, etc.
Leipz., **1866-67.**

————   ————   Camper, M. de N. du.   Remarques sur . . . plusieurs établissemens des Européens dans l'Asie Orientale, 1821-25.   Eysirs. Vol. XII.

————   ————   Joctans posteritie seated in the E. parts of A., etc.   Purchas. Vol. I.

————   **, North.**—Pallas, P. S.   Voyages . . . dans l'Asie Septentrionale, etc.   *Par.*, **1769-93.**

————   **, Russian.**—Venyukov, M.   [Travels on the Confines of R. A., etc.]   *Russ.*   *St. Pet.*, **1868.**

————   **, South.**—Balfour, E.   The Timber Trees . . . of . . . S. A.
Madras, **1862.**

————   ————   Dalrymple, A.   Memoir of a Chart of the Passages at the S. Extremity of A.   Dalrymple, A.   Collection of Nautical Memoirs, etc.

————   **, West.**—Rennell, J.   Treatise on the Comparative Geography of W. n A.   **1831.**

————   ————   Hagemeister, J. de.   Essai sur les ressources . . . de l'Asie Occidentale, etc.   *St. Pet.*, **1839.**

————   ————   Lopes de Lima, J. J.   Ensaios sobre a Statistica das Possessões Portuguezas . . . na A. Occidental, etc.   *Lisbon*, **1844-62.**

————   ————   Gerstfeldt, Herr.   Der Verkehr Russlands mit West-asien.   [**1862.**]

————   ————   Engel, C.   The Music of the most ancient Nations . . . with special reference to recent discoveries in W. n A., etc.
Lond., **1864.**

Asia Minor.—Dapper.   Naukeurige Beschryving van . . . Klein Asie, etc.
Amst., **1680.**

————   Lucas, P.   Voyage de, dans l'Asie Mineure, etc.   *Par.*, **1712.**

————   Pococke, R.   Description of . . . A. M., etc.   **1743-45.**

————   Griffiths, J.   Travels in . . . A. M., etc.   **1805.**

————   Morier, J.   Journey through . . . A. M. . . . in 1808-9. **1812.**

————   Chandler, R.   Travels in A. M., etc.   **1817.**

————   Beaufort, F.   Karamania; or a . . . description of the S. Coast of A. M., etc.   **1818.**

Asia Minor.

Asia Minor.—KINNEIR, J. M.   Journey through A. M. . . . in 1813-14, etc.   1818.

——— MORIER, J.   A Second Journey through . . . A. M., etc.
   Lond., 1818.

——— IRBY, HON. C. L., and MANGLES, J.   Travels in . . . A. M. . . . 1817 and 1818.   1823.

——— LEAKE, W. M.   Journal of a Tour in A. M., etc.   1824.

——— ALEXANDER, SIR J. E.   Travels . . . through . . . A. M., etc. 1827.

——— PROKESCH, A. von.   Erinnerungen aus . . . Kleinasien.
   Wien, 1829-30.

——— KEPPEL, HON. G.   Narrative of . . . a visit to . . . newly-discovered Ruins in A. M., etc.   Lond., 1831.

——— CRAMER, J. A.   Geographical . . . description of A. M.
   Oxford, 1832.

——— PRICE, W.   Journal of Travels of the British Embassy . . . through . . . A. M., etc.   1833.

——— ARUNDELL, F. V. J.   Discoveries in A. M., etc.   1834.

——— SMITH, E., and DWIGHT, H. G. O.   Missionary Researches . . . including a Journey through A. M., etc.   1834.

——— BARTLETT, W. H.   Syria . . . A. M., etc.   1836-38.

——— NIEBUHR, C.   Reisebeschreibung . . . durch Kleinasien, etc.
   Hamb., 1837.

——— FELLOWS, SIR C.   Journal . . . during an excursion in A. M.   1839.

——— FRANZ, J.   Fünf Inschriften und fünf Städte in Kleinasien.
   Berl., 1840.

——— MURRAY.   Hand-Book for Travellers in . . . A. M., etc.
   Lond., 1840.

——— AINSWORTH, W. F.   Travels . . . in A. M., etc.   1842.

——— HAMILTON, W. J.   Researches in A. M., etc.   1842.

——— STRUVE, F. G. W.   Astronomische Ortsbestimmungen in . . . Klein-Asien.   St. Pet., 1845.

——— SAINT-MARTIN, V. de.   Histoire des découvertes géographiques des Nations Européennes . . . Vols. II. III. Asie Mineure.   Par., 1845-6.

——— BIANCONI, J. J.   De Mari olim occupante planities et colles . . . Asiæ Minoris, etc.   Bonon., 1846-52.

——— TCHIHATCHEFF, P. DE.   Notice of Researches in A. M.   1849.

——— TCHIHATCHEFF, P. de.   L'Asie Mineure et l'Empire Ottoman, état actuel, etc.   Par., 1850.

——— FELLOWS, SIR C.   Travels and Researches in A. M., etc.   1852.

——— NEALE, F. A.   Eight Years in . . . A. M., etc.   1852.

——— TCHIHATCHEFF, P. DE.   Asie Mineure: description physique, etc.
   Par., 1853-60.

——— ——— Lettre sur les Antiquités de l'Asie Mineure, etc.
   Par., 1854.

——— VINCKE and others.   Memoir über die Construction der Karte von Klein-Asien, etc.   Berl., 1854.

Asia Minor.—TCHIHATCHEFF, P. DE. Études sur la Végétation des Hautes Moutagnes de l'Asie-Mineure, *etc.* *Par.,* 1867.

—— TEXIER, C., and PULLAN, R. P. The Principal Ruins of A. M. illustrated and described. *Lond.,* 1865.

—— WEAKLEY, R. H. Narrative of a Journey into the Interior of A. M. 1867.

—— Odoricus, Frier B. Voyage to A. M. . . . about 1325. HAKLUYT. Vol II.

—— Of the . . . Ancient Inhabitants of A. M. and of their Religions. PURCHAS. Vol. V.

—— Wheeler, Sir G. Plants observed in his Voyage to . . . A. M. RAY, J.

—— Collins, F. Voyages to . . . A. M., *etc.,* 1706-1801. VOYAGES and TRAVELS. A Collection, *etc.,* 1805. Vol. X.

—— —— Voyages to . . . A. M., *etc.,* 1706-1801. VOYAGES and TRAVELS. A Collection, *etc.* 1810. Vol. VI.

—— Browne, W. G. Journey . . . through A. M. . . . 1802. WALPOLE, R. Travels, *etc.*

—— Cockerell, Mr. Letter respecting the . . . Sepulchral Monuments and Inscriptions discovered by him on the S.n Coast of A. M. WALPOLE, R. Travels, *etc.*

—— Leake, Col. Journey through . . . A. M. in 1800. WALPOLE, R. Travels, *etc.*

—— —— Remarks on the . . . Geography of parts of A. M. WALPOLE, R. Travels, *etc.*

—— *See also* ANATOLIA.

Asiatic Mediterranean.—*See* CARPENTARIA, GULF OF.

Asie Turque.—*See* TURKEY, ASIATIC.

Asof, Asoph.—*See* AZOV.

Asowsches Meer.—*See* AZOV, SEA OF.

Assada.—EVERARD, R. Relation of three years' sufferings upon the Coast of A., *etc.* CHURCHILL. Vol. VI.

Assam.—BERGHAUS, H. Asia . . . Memoir zur Erklärung . . . der redukirten Karte von . . . A., *etc.* *Gotha,* 1832-35.

—— ASSAM. A.; Sketch of its History, *etc.* *Lond.,* 1839.

—— ROBINSON, W. Descriptive Account of A., *etc.* *Calc.,* 1841.

—— ASSAM. A sketch of A., *etc.* 1847.

—— GRIFFITH, W. Journals of Travels in A., *etc.* *Calc.,* 1847.

—— BUTLER, J. Travels and Adventures in . . . A. 1855.

—— MEDLICOTT, H. B. The Coal of A., *etc.* 1865.

—— JENKINS, H. L. Notes on the Burmese Route from A. to the Hookoong Valley. 1869.

—— Tavernier. Reisen nach . . . Asem, 1652. VOYAGES and TRAVELS. Allgemeine Historie, *etc.* Vol. X.

Assassins.—WALPOLE, Hon. F. The Ansayrii and the A., *etc.* 1851.

Asserbo.—FREDERICK VII., KING OF DENMARK. Vestiges d'A. et de Sohorg, découverts par . . . Frédéric VII., etc. *Copenh.*, **1855**.
Assinee.—LOYER, G. Abstract of a Voyage to Issini . . . in 1701, etc. ASTLEY. Vol. II.
――― ――― Kurze Nachricht von einer Seefahrt nach Issini, 1701. VOYAGES and TRAVELS. Allgemeine Historie, etc. Vol. III.
Assiniboine.—HIND, H. Y. Narrative of the A. . . . Exploring Expedition of 1858. **1859**.
――― DAWSON, S. J. Report on . . . the Country between . . . the Red River Settlement, and . . . the A., etc. *Toronto*, **1859**.
Assos.—Hunt, Dr. Journey . . . Ruins of A., 1799. WALPOLE, R. Memoirs, etc.
Assumpcao.—Schnirdel, H. Travels, from 1534-54 . . . March from Assumption into Peru. PURCHAS. Vol. IV.
Assumption.—*See* ASSUMPCAO.
―――, **Isle of.**—*See* ANTICOSTI.
Assyria.—DAPPER. Naukeurige Beschryving van . . . A., etc. *Amst.*, **1680**.
――― BUCKINGHAM, J. S. Travels in A., etc. **1830**.
――― AINSWORTH, W. F. Researches in A., etc. **1838**.
――― LÖWENSTERN, I. On the A.n Inscriptions. *Par.*, **1847**.
――― FLETCHER, J. P. Notes . . . and Travels in . . . A., etc. **1850**.
――― RAWLINSON, SIR H. C. Outlines of A.n History, etc. **1852**.
――― PETACHIA, RABBI. Travels of; who, in the. . . Twelfth Century visited . . . A., etc. **1856**.
――― Cartwright, J. The Preacher's Travels . . . through . . . A., etc. CHURCHILL. Vol. VII.
――― Of the . . . Regions and Religions of . . . A., etc. PURCHAS. Vol. V.
――― Rauwolf L. Journey into A., etc. RAY, J.
Astrakhan.—KEPPEL, Hon. G. Personal Narrative of a Journey from India . . . by . . . A., etc. **1827**.
――― POTOCKI, COUNT J. Voyage dans les Steps d'A., etc. *Par.*, **1829**.
Asuncion.—*See* ASSUMPCAO.
Atagama.—MEMORIA . . . de la provincia de A. . . . dando cuenta de todos los llamos de la Administracion. *Copiapó*, **1854**.
Atbara.—BELLEFONDS, L. DE. L'Etbaye, pays habité par les Arabes Bicharieh, etc. *Paris.*
――― LINANT, M. Journal . . . Description of a Journey across the Province of A., etc. **1828**.
Athens.—WILKINS, W. Atheniensia, or Remarks on . . . A. **1816**.
――― LEAKE, W. M. The Topography of A., etc. *Lond.*, **1821**.
――― STUART, J. and REVETT, R. The Antiquities of A., etc. **1825-33**.
――― PITTAKYS, K. S. L'Ancienne Athènes, etc. *Athènes*, **1835**.
――― GIFFARD, E. A Short Visit to . . . A., etc. *Lond.*, **1837**.
――― FORCHHAMMER, P. W. Topographie von Athen. *Kiel*, **1841**.

Athens.—Sommer, J. A. Répertoire analytique . . . pour la Carte d'Athènes et ses environs publiée en 1841. *Munich,* **1841.**

——— Borber, D. A Journey from Naples to Jerusalem, by way of A., etc. **1845.**

——— Penrose, F. C. On certain Anomalies in the construction of the Parthenon, A. **1847.**

——— Ulrichs, H. N. Topography of the Harbours . . . of A., etc. **1847.**

——— Erigen, J. Voyage to A., in 885. Hakluyt. Vol. II.

——— Erigena, J. Travels to A., in the ninth century. Kerr. Vol. I.

——— Hawkins, Mr. On the Topography of A., etc. Walpole, R. Memoirs, etc.

——— Haygarth, W. Panoramic View of A. illustrated. Walpole, R. Memoirs, etc.

Äthiopien.—*See* Ethiopia.

Athos, Mount.—Tozer, H. F. Researches . . . including Visits to Mounts . . . A., etc. *Lond.,* **1869.**

——— Belon, Mr. Remarks in . . . Crete . . . Description of Mount Athos, commonly called Monte Santo, etc. Ray, J.

——— Hunt, Dr. Mount A. An account, etc. Walpole, R. Memoirs, etc.

——— Sibthorp, Dr. Voyage . . . Mount A. etc. Walpole, R. Travels, etc.

Atlantic Ocean.—Navarette, M. F. de. Examination . . . and Notices of the principal Expeditions . . . in search . . . of a communication between the A. O. and the S. Seas. *MS. Port.*

——— Redfield, W. C. On the Gales and Hurricanes of the Western A.

——— Humboldt, A. von, and Bonpland, A. Recueil d'Observations de Zoologie . . . faites dans l'Océan Atlantique . . . en 1799-1803. **1811.**

——— Tofiño de San Miguel, V. España Marítima, or Spanish Coasting Pilot . . . for . . . the A., etc. **1814.**

——— Purdy, J. Memoir . . . to accompany the New Chart of the A. O., etc. **1817.**

——— Pitman, R. B. On the Practicability of joining the A. and Pacific Oceans by a Ship Canal, etc. **1825.**

——— Owen, W. F. W. Tables of Latitudes and Longitudes . . . of places in the A., etc. **1827.**

——— Maw, H. L. Journal of a Passage from the Pacific to the A., etc. **1829.**

——— Flint, T. History . . . with a Physical Geography of the A., etc. *Cincin.,* **1832.**

——— Rennell, J. Investigation of the Currents of the A. O., etc. **1832.**

——— Mercer, Hon. C. F. Report on the . . . connection of the A. and Pacific Oceans by . . . Lake Nicaragua, etc. *Wash.,* **1839.**

——— Avezac, d'. Notice des découvertes faites au Moyen-age dans l'Océan Atlantique, etc. *Par.,* **1845.**

——— Moro, G. Communication between the . . . Oceans through . . . Tehuantepec. Additional Observations, etc. **1845.**

Atlantic Ocean.—Moro, G. Report of the Communication between the A. and Pacific Oceans through the Isthmus of Tehuantepec. 1845.

——— Garay, J. de. An Account of . . . Tehuantepec . . . with proposals for . . . a communication between the A. and Pacific, etc. 1846.

——— Redfield, W. C. On three several Hurricanes of the A., etc. New Haven, 1846.

——— Carmichael-Smyth, R. On . . . the construction of a . . . Railway between the A. and the Pacific, etc. 1849.

——— Liot, W. B. Panama . . . Considerations upon the Communication between the A. and Pacific Oceans, etc. 1849.

——— Rockwell, J. A. Report on Canal and Railway Routes between the A. and Pacific, etc. Wash., 1849.

——— A. and Pacific Oceans. Official Report . . . on the communications between the A. and Pacific, etc. Wash., 1850.

——— Doull, A. Employment . . . for the Million, based upon . . . Railway Communication from the A. to the Pacific, etc. Lond., 1851.

——— America, Central. Description of . . . a Road . . . from the A. to the Pacific, etc. Phil., 1852.

——— Doull, A. Project for . . . a . . . passage between the A. and Pacific Oceans by means of a Railway, etc. 1852.

——— Erman, A. Ortsbestimmungen bei einer Fahrt durch den . . . Atlantischen Ocean, etc. 1852.

——— Kerhallet, C. P. de. Considérations générales sur l'Océan Atlantique, etc. Par., 1854.

——— Redfield, W. C. Cape Verde . . . Hurricane . . . 1853, with . . . notices of various Storms in the A., etc. New Haven, U.S., 1854.

——— A. and Pacific Oceans. The Practicability . . . of a . . . canal to connect the A. and Pacific, etc. N. Y., 1855.

——— Maury, M. F. Letter concerning Lanes for the Steamers crossing the A. N. Y., 1855.

——— Totten, G. M. Communication . . . containing . . . Observations upon the Levels of the A. and Pacific Oceans. N. Y., 1855.

——— Kelley, F. M. On the Junction of the A. and Pacific Oceans, etc. 1856.

——— Kerhallet, C. P. de. The A. O. considered with reference to the Wants of Seamen, etc. 1856.

——— Maury, M. F. Observations sur la Navigation des Paquebots qui traversent l'Atlantique, etc. Par., 1856.

——— Kelley, F. M. Projet d'un Canal Maritime . . . entre l'Océan Atlantique et l'Océan Pacifique, etc. Par., 1857.

——— Brown, Sir R. European and Asiatic Intercourse . . . by . . . Railway from the A. to the Pacific. 1858.

——— Nolloth, M. S. On the Submergence of the A. Telegraph Cable. Lond., 1858.

——— Thomassy, M. R. Note sur l'Hydrologie Maritime . . . de l'Océan Atlantique. Par., 1860.

Atlantic Ocean.—Gras, M. A. le. Phares des ... Iles étrangères de l'Océan Atlantique. Corrigés 1862, 63. *Par.*, **1862, 63.**

—— Wallich, G. C. The A. Deep-Sea Bed and its denizens. **1864.**

—— Toynbee, H. On the Normal Circulation and Weight of the Atmosphere in the N. and S. A. Oceans, *etc.* **1865.**

—— Davis, Rear-Admiral C. H. Report on Interoceanic Canals and Railroads between the A. and Pacific, *etc.* *Wash.*, **1867.**

—— Verney, Sir H. A Route from the A. to the Pacific through British Territory. *Lond.*, **1868.**

——, **North.**—Purdy, J., and Findlay, A. G. Memoir ... to accompany the Charts of the N. A. O., *etc.* **1845.**

—— —— Shade, J. M. Great Circle Tables for the N. A., *etc.* **1852.**

—— —— Blunt, G. W. Memoirs of the Dangers and Ice in the N. A. O. *N. Y.*, **1856.**

—— Dayman, J. Deep-Sea Soundings in the N. A. O., *etc.* **1858.**

—— —— Purdy, J., and Findlay, A. G. Memoir ... to accompany the Charts of the N. A. O., *etc.* **1861.**

—— —— Poey, A. Table chronologique de quatre cents Cyclones qui ont sévi ... dans l'Océan Atlantique Nord. *Par.*, **1862.**

—— —— Wallich, G. C. The N.—A. Sea-Bed, *etc.* **1862.**

—— —— Toynbee, H. Report ... on the Meteorology of the N. A., *etc.* *Lond.*, **1869.**

——, **South.**—Colnett, J. Voyage to the S. A., *etc.* **1798.**

—— —— Purdy, J. New Sailing Directory for the Ethiopic, or S.ern A. O., *etc.* **1822.**

—— —— Morrell, B. Narrative of four Voyages to the ... S. A. O., *etc.* *N. Y.*, **1832.**

—— —— Webster, W. H. B. Narrative of a Voyage to the S.n A. O. in ... 1828-30, *etc.* *Lond.*, **1834.**

—— —— Purdy, J. New Sailing Directory for the ... S.ern A. O., *etc.* **1837.**

—— —— —— New Sailing Directory for the ... S.ern A. O., *etc.* **1845.**

—— —— Rosser, H. W. Notes on the Physical Geography ... of the S. A., *etc.* **1862.**

Atlas Mountains.—Shabeeny, El Hage Abd Salam. Account of Timbuctoo ... Letters descriptive of Travels ... across the Mountains of A., by J. Grey Jackson. **1820.**

—— Tristram, H. B. The Great Sahara: Wanderings South of the A. M. *Lond.*, **1860.**

—— Rohlfs, G. Reise ... Uebersteigung des grossen A., *etc.* *Bremen*, **1868.**

Atrato, River.—Trautwine, J. C. Rough Notes of an Exploration ... of the ... A., *etc.* *Phil.*, **1854.**

Atrato, River.—LANE, J. C. Report of the Surveys of the .... A., *etc.*
N. Y., 1858.

———— ———— KELLEY, F. M. The Union of the Oceans ... viâ the A. Valley. *N. Y.*, 1859.

———— ———— WARD, HON. E. A Ship-Canal: its importance, *etc.*
Wash., 1859.

Attica.—CELL, SIR W. Itinerary of Greece; containing ... Routes in A., *etc.* 1819.

———— STUART, J., and REVETT, N. The Antiquities of Athens ... together with the ... Antiquities of A., *etc.* 1825-33.

———— Sibthorp, Dr. Remarks respecting A. WALPOLE, R. Memoirs, *etc.*

Auckland.—HOCHSTETTER, F. Lecture on the Geology of A., *etc.*
Auck., 1859.

———— LINDSAY, W. L. On the Geology of the Gold-Fields of A., New Zealand. 1862.

———— AUCKLAND. Sketch of ... A., *etc.* 1863.

———— ABBOTT, F. Results ... To which is added a Meteorological Summary for ... A., *etc.* *Hob. Town*, 1866.

———— HOCHSTETTER, F. VON. New Zealand ... with special reference to ... A., *etc.* *Stutlg.*, 1867.

Auckland Islands.—ENDERBY, C. The A. I., *etc.* 1849.

———— NORMAN, W. H., and MUSGRAVE, T. Journals of the Voyage ... of H. M. C. S. *Victoria* in search of Shipwrecked People at the A. and other Islands. *Melb.*, [1865.]

Aude.—BARANTE, C. J. Essai sur ... l'A. *Genève*, 1802.

Augusta, Port.—STUART, J. M'D. Journal of an Expedition into the Unexplored Country to the N.-W. and S.-W. of Port A., South Australia. 1858.

Aurigny.—*See* ALDERNEY.

Aurungabad.—BURGESS, J. The Rock-cut Temples of Ajanta, with an Account of a Trip to A., *etc.* *Bombay*, 1868.

Aussig.—DRESDEN und die umliegende Gegend bis ... A., *etc.*
Dresd., 1804.

Australasia.—MARTIN, R. M. Statistics of the Colonies ... in A., *etc.* *Lond.*, 1839.

———— MUNDY, G. C. Our Antipodes; or a Residence ... in the A.n Colonies, *etc.* 1852.

———— MOSSMAN, S. A. and Australia, *etc.* *Edin.*, 1853.

———— Possessions in ... A. MARTIN, R. M. History of the British Colonies. Vol. IV.

———— Brosses, President de. A., Introductory Observations from the Work of. PINKERTON. Vol. XI.

Australia.—AUSTRALIA. A.: a Popular Account, *etc.* [By G. F. Angas.]
Lond.

———— AUSTRALIA, Report of ... Aborigines Protection Society on.

———— CORTAMBERT, E. Dernières Explorations en Australie, *etc.* *Paris.*

Australia.—History of the Expedition of three Ships . . . to Terra Australis in 1721, *etc.*

—— Maconochie, A. On the Management of Prisoners in the A. n Colonies.

—— Westmacott, R. M. Sketches in A. *Exeter.*

—— Wyld, J. Notes on the distribution of Gold throughout . . . A., *etc.*

—— Péron, F. and Freycinet, L. Voyage de découvertes aux Terres Australes . . . 1800-1804. *Par.*, **1807-16.**

—— Flinders, M. Voyage to Terra Australis . . . in 1801-3, *etc.* **1814.**

—— Walckenaer, C. A. Le Monde Maritime, ou Tableau . . . de l'Australie, *etc.* *Par.*, **1819.**

—— King, P. P. Narrative of a Survey of the Intertropical and W. n Coasts of A., *etc.* *Lond.*, **1827.**

—— Australia. The Friend of A., *etc.* **1830.**

—— Threlkeld, E. L. Australian Grammar, *etc.* *Sydney*, **1834.**

—— Lhotsky, J. A Journey from Sydney to the A.n Alps, *etc.* *Syd.*, **1835.**

—— Australia. Aborigines of A., *etc.* *Hobart T.*, **1836.**

—— Horsburgh, J. India Directory, or Directions for . . . A., *etc.* **1836.**

—— Meinicke, C. E. Das Festland Australien, *etc.* *Prenzlau*, **1837.**

—— Gould, J. The Birds of A., *etc.* **1837, 38.**

—— Maconochie, A. Australiana, *etc.* **1839.**

—— Grey, Sir G. Vocabulary of the Dialects of S. W. A. **1840.**

—— Bleek, G. De Nominum generibus linguarum . . . Australia, *etc.* *Bonnae*, **1841.**

—— Grey, Sir G. Journals of two Expeditions . . . in N. W. and W. A. . . . 1837-39, *etc.* **1841.**

—— Backhouse, J. Narrative of a visit to the A. Colonies. **1843.**

—— Sutton, G. The Culture of the Grape-Vine and the Orange in A., *etc.* **1843.**

—— Darwin, C. Geological Observations . . . together with . . . notices on the Geology of A., *etc.* *Lond.*, **1844.**

—— Hodgkinson, C. A., from Port Macquarie to Moreton Bay, *etc.* **1845.**

—— Davidson, G. F. Trade and Travel . . . Recollections of . . . A., *etc.* *Lond.*, **1846.**

—— Stokes, J. L. Discoveries in A., *etc.* *Lond.*, **1846.**

—— Leichhardt, L. Journal of an Overland Expedition in A. 1844-45. **1847.**

—— Australia. Competence . . . by . . . An. colonization, *etc.* **1848.**

—— Boour, A. Steam to A., *etc.* *Sydney*, **1848.**

—— Gould, J. An Introduction to the Birds of A. **1848.**

Australia.

Australia.—MITCHELL, Sir T. L. Journal of an Expedition into the Interior of Tropical A., etc. *Lond.*, 1848.

—— WELLS, W. H. Geographical Dictionary . . . of the A.n Colonies, etc. *Sydney*, 1848.

—— CARRON, W. Narrative of an expedition . . . for . . . exploration of . . . country . . . between Rockingham Bay and Cape York. *Syd.*, 1849.

—— AFRICA. The Lights of . . . A. . . . Corrected to 1849, 51, 52, 56, 57, 58, 59. 1849-59.

—— AUSTRALIA. Report of Proceedings . . . for . . . establishment of Steam Communication with the A. Colonies, etc. 1850.

—— BOYD, B. Steam to A., etc. 1850.

—— JUKES, J. B. A Sketch of the Physical Structure of A., etc. 1850.

—— INDIA. First Report . . . on Steam Communications with . . . A. *Lond.*, 1851.

—— MELVILLE, H. The present state of A., etc. 1851.

—— HUGHES, W. The A.n Colonies, etc. 1852.

—— EARL, G. W. A Correspondence relating to the discovery of Gold in A. 1853.

—— MOSSMAN, S. Australasia and A., etc. *Edin.*, 1853.

—— MOSSMAN, S. and BANISTER, T. A. visited and revisited. 1853.

—— POWER, W. T. Recollections . . . including Peregrinations in . . . A., etc. *Lond.*, 1853.

—— SIDNEY, S. The Three Colonies of A. . . . their Pastures, etc. 1853.

—— BURWOOD, J. and YULE, C. B. A. Directory. 1853-63.

—— FOREMAN, H. The Routes to A., etc. 1854.

—— HADFIELD, W. Brazil . . . with the Cape Horn Route to A., etc. 1854.

—— GRAS, M. A. l.E. Routier de l'Australie. Instructions pour . . . la Côte Sud et Est, etc. *Par.*, 1855-61.

—— TOWSON, J. C. On Ice Impediments in A.n Voyages. 1855.

—— WATHEN, G. H. The Golden Colony . . . with Remarks on the Geology of the A.n Gold-Fields. 1855.

—— LAMING, J. Steam Communication with A., etc. 1856.

—— ZUCHOLD, E. A. Dr. L. Leichhardt . . . Nebst einem Berichte über dessen zweite Reise im Innern des Austral-Continents, etc. *Leip.*, 1856.

—— DENHAM, H. M. Hydrographic Notices. A., etc. 1856-59.

—— MUELLER, F. An Historical Review of the Explorations of A. 1857.

—— —— Fragmenta Phytographiæ Australiæ. *Melb.*, 1858.

—— PUSELEY, D. The Rise and Progress of A., etc. 1858.

—— DALRYMPLE, G. E. Report of the proceedings of the . . . *Spitfire* . . . on the N. E. Coast of A., etc. *Brisb.*, 1860.

Australia.

Australia.—SMITH, J. W. and DALRYMPLE, G. F. Report of the Proceedings of the . . . *Spitfire* . . . on the N. E.n Coast of A., etc.
Brisbane, 1860.

―― DUNSTERVILLE, E. The Admiralty List of the Lights of . . . A. . . . Corrected to 1860, 61, 62. 1860-62.

―― BRODRIBB, W. A. A plain Statement of Facts . . . on the . . . advantages of the A.n Colonies . . . for Emigration. *Lond.*, 1862.

―― GREGORY, F. T. Journal of the N.-W. Australian Exploring Expedition; Ap. to Nov. 1861. 1862.

―― M'KINLAY, J. Journal of Exploration in the Interior of A.
Melb., 1862.

―― GAAS, M. A. LE. Phares . . . de l'Australie . . . Corrigés 1862, 63. *Par.*, 1862, 63.

―― BOURNE, G. A. Expedition . . . in search of Burke and Wills.
Melb., 1863.

―― LEFROY, H. M. Memoir and Journal of an Expedition . . . for exploring the interior of the Colony Eastward. *W. Aust.*, 1863.

―― MACDONNELL, Sir R. G. A.; what it is, etc. *Dubl.*, 1863.

―― MUELLER, F. A Record of the Plants collected . . . during Mr. F. Gregory's Exploring Expedition into N.-W. A. [1863.]

―― STUART, J. M'D. Explorations across the Continent of A.
Melb., 1863.

―― WILLS, W. J. Successful Explorations through the Interior of A., etc. 1863.

―― GRAD, A. C. L'Australie Intérieure, etc. *Par.*, 1864.

―― HORSBURGH, J. Instructions Nautiques . . . Côtes Sud, Ouest, et N. O. de l'Australie, etc. *Par.*, 1864.

―― STUART, J. M'D. Journals of Explorations in A., in 1858-62, etc.
1864.

―― WILSON, J. A. Remarks on A.n and New Zealand Climatology, etc.
1864.

―― CRINOLE, T., pseud. A. n Sand-bar Harbours and Rivers, etc.
Melb., 1866.

―― HOOLEY, T. Journal of an overland journey from Perth to Port Walcott on the N.-W. Coast of A., etc. [1866.]

―― MUELLER, F. Notes sur la Végétation indigène et introduite de l'Australie, etc. *Melb.*, 1866.

―― YULE, C. B. Routier de l'Australie (Cotes Nord, N. O. et Ouest), etc.
Par., 1866.

―― MUELLER, F. Fragmenta Phytographiæ Australiæ. *Melb.*, 1867, 68.

―― MARCET, E. Australie. Un Voyage à travers le Bush.
Genève, 1868.

―― INDIA. The projected Sub-Marine Telegraph Cable to . . . A. considered, etc. *Lond.*, 1869.

―― THEORY. The True Theory of the Earth . . . considered as elucidating the origin and distribution of Auriferous Deposits in A., etc.
Edin., 1869.

Australia.—Flinders. Voyage à la Terre Australe . . . 1801-3. ETBIAS. Vol. IV.

—— Early Voyages to Terra Australis . . . Edited . . . by R. H. Major. 1859. HAKLUYT SOC. PUB. Vol. XXV.

—— Giros or De Quir, P. F. Petition . . . touching the discoveries of . . . Terra Australis Incognita . . . 1610. PURCHAS. Vol. IV.

—— Découverte de la Terre Australe, *etc.* THEVENOT. Vol. I.

—— *See also* GIFFS' LAND—GLENELG RIVER—NEW HOLLAND—VICTORIA.

——, **Central.**—EYRE, E. J. Journals of Expeditions . . . into C. A., *etc.* 1845.

—— —— STURT, C. Narrative of an Expedition into C. A. . . . 1844-46, *etc.* 1849.

—— —— LOCKE, J. Remarkable discoveries in C. A. *Dubl.*, 1863.

—— —— NEUMAYER, G. On a Scientific Exploration of C. A. 1869.

——, **East.**—MITCHELL, SIR T. L. Three Expeditions into the Interior of E. n A., *etc.* 1839.

——, **North.**—WOODS, J. E. T. N. A.; its physical Geography, *etc.* Adel., 1864.

—— —— SNOLL, T. C. The N. W. Settlements, *etc.* 1866.

——, **South.**—KINGSLEY, H. Eyre, the S.-A. n Explorer.

—— —— AUSTRALIA. Plan of . . . a Colony in S. A. 1832.

—— —— STURT, C. Two Expeditions into the Interior of S. n. A. . . . 1829-31, *etc.* 1834.

—— —— JAMES, T. H. Six Months in S. A., *etc.* 1838.

—— —— LEES, F. R. Sailing Directions for S. A. *Syd.*, 1839.

—— —— LEIGH, W. H. Reconnoitering Voyages . . . with adventures in the new Colonies of S. A., *etc.* *Lond.*, 1839.

—— —— WILLIAMS, W. Vocabulary of the Language of the Aborigines of . . . S. A. Adel., 1839.

—— —— LEIGH, W. H. Reconnoitering Voyages . . . in . . . S. A., *etc.* 1840.

—— —— TEICHELMANN, C. G. and SCHÜRMANN, C. W. Outlines of . . . the Aboriginal language of S. A., *etc.* Adel., 1840.

—— —— BENNETT, J. F. The S. A. . . . General Directory. Adel., 1841.

—— —— MEYER, H. A. E. Vocabulary of the Language spoken by the Aborigines of the S. n and E. n Portions . . . of S. A., *etc.* Adel., 1843.

—— —— COTTER, T. Y. The S. A. Almanack and . . . Directory. Adel., 1844.

—— —— DUTTON, F. S. A. and its Mines, *etc.* 1846.

—— —— WILKINSON, G. B. S. A.: its advantages . . . resources, *etc.* *Lond.*, 1848.

—— —— AGRICOLA. Description of the Barossa Range and its neighbourhood in S. A., *etc.* *Lond.*, 1849.

Australia, South.—STURT, C. Narrative ... together with a Notice of the Province of S. A. in 1847. **1849.**

—— —— SIDNEY, S. The Three Colonies of Australia ... S. A. etc. **1853.**

—— —— AUSTRALIA, SOUTH. Summary of ... discoveries during 1857, to the W. and N. of Eyria, S. A., etc. *Derby,* **1858.**

—— —— SOUTH, AUSTRALIA. Statistical Register of S. A. for 1863, etc. *Adel.,* **1864.**

—— —— McKINLAY, J. Journal of Exploring Expedition ... to examine the country of the N. n Territory recently annexed to S. A., etc. [*Adelaide*] **1866.**

—— —— CADELL, F. Exploration N. n Territory [S. A.]. **1868.**

—— —— *See also* AUGUSTA, PORT.

——, **West.**—DUBLACHER, A. Report on ... the Colony of W. A. ... Dec. 81, 1859. *Freemantle.*

—— —— NEW SOUTH WALES. Copies of the Royal Instructions to the Governors of ... W. n A., as to the ... disposing of Crown Lands. **1831.**

—— —— BRETON, LIEUT. Excursions in ... W. A., etc. **1834.**

—— —— IRWIN, F. C. State and position of W. A., etc. **1835.**

—— —— AUSTRALIA, WESTERN. Second Report of the W. A. Association. **1837.**

—— —— AUSTRALIA, WESTERN. Report of ... Committee ... to take into consideration the ... state ... of W. A., etc. *Perth,* **1838.**

—— —— OGLE, N. The Colony of W. n. A., etc. *Lond.,* **1839.**

—— —— MARTIN, D. and PANTER, F. K. Report for the ... Promoters of the N.-W. n Expedition of 1864, etc. *Perth,* **1864.**

—— —— HUNT, C. C. Journal of an Expedition to the E. n Interior of W. n A. **1866.**

—— —— *See also* SWAN RIVER.

——, **West Coast.**—GOWEN, J. R. Hints on Emigration to ... the W. C. of A. **1829.**

Australia Felix.—MITCHELL, Sir T. L. Three Expeditions ... with descriptions of ... A. F., etc. **1839.**

Australian Colonies.—*See* AUSTRALIA.

Austria.—HERMANN, D. F. Abriss der physikalischen Beschaffenheit der Oesterreichischen Staaten. *St. Pet. u. Leip.,* **1782.**

—— —— EMBEL, J. X. Schilderung der Gebirgs-Gegenden um den Schneeberg in Oesterreich. *Wien,* **1803.**

—— —— SARTORI, F. Naturwunder des Oesterreichischen Kaiserthumes. *Wien,* **1810.**

—— —— KLEYLE, F. F. Rückerinnerungen an eine Reise in Oesterreich, 1810. *Wien,* **1814.**

—— —— LIECHTENSTERN, J. M. F. VON. Handbuch der neuesten Geographie des Oesterreichischen Kaiserstaates. *Wien,* **1817-18.**

Austria.—TROMMSDORFF, J. B. Pharmacoporia Austriaca. *Wien*, 1818.
—— AUSTRIAN MONARCHY. Umriss von der Oesterreichischen Monarchie, etc. *Leip.*, 1834.
—— GROSS, A. J. Handbuch für Reisende durch die Österreichische Monarchie, etc. *München*, 1834.
—— SCHMIDL, A. A. R. von Jenny's Handbuch für Reisende in dem Österreichischen Kaiserstaate. *Wien*, 1834-36.
—— —— Das Kaiserthum Oesterreich. Die gefürstete Grafschaft Tirol mit Vorarlberg. *Stuttg.*, 1837.
—— ELLIOTT, C. B. Travels in A., etc. 1838.
—— SCHMIDL, A. A. Das Kaiserthum Oesterreich. Das Erzherzogthum Oesterreich mit Salzburg, etc. *Stuttg.*, 1838, 39.
—— SOMMER, J. G. Das Kaiserthum Oesterreich, geographisch-statistisch dargestellt. *Prag.*, 1839.
—— KOHL, J. G. A. Vienna, etc. *Lond.*, 1844.
—— CODEMO, G. Descrizione ... della Monarchia Austriaca, etc. *Ven.*, 1845.
—— BALBI, E. L'A. e le primarie Potenze. *Mil.*, 1846.
—— HAIDINGER, W. Bericht über die geognostische Uebersichts- Karte der Oesterreichischen Monarchie. *Wien*, 1847.
—— PATON, A. A. Highlands ... of the Adriatic, including the S. Provinces of the A. n Empire. 1849.
—— SCHMIDL, A. A. Handbuch der Geographie des Österreichischen Kaiserstaates. *Wien*, 1850.
—— SPENCER, E. Travels in European Turkey ... with ... a homeward Tour through ... the Slavonian Provinces of A. on the Lower Danube. 1851.
—— BARROW, J. Tour ... through ... A., etc. 1853.
—— REPERTOIRE de Cartés (A.) publié par l'Institut Royal des Ingenieurs Néerlandais. *La Haye*, 1854.
—— SCHMIDL, A. A. Die Oesterreichischen Höhlen, etc. *Pest*, 1858.
—— SONKLAR, K. von. Grundzüge einer Hyetographie des Österreichischen Kaiserstaates. *Wien*, 1860.
—— CZOERING, BARON C. VON. Die Vertheilung der Voelkerstaemme und deren Gruppen, in der Oesterreichischen Monarchie, etc. *Wien*, 1861.
—— Browne, E. Voyage ... to Holland, with a Journey ... through A. ... 1668. HARRIS, J. Vol. II.
—— Küttner, C. G. Travels through ... A. ... 1798-99. VOYAGES and TRAVELS. A Collection, etc. 1805. Vol. I.
——, **Lower.**—WEISKERN, F. W. Topographie von Niederösterreich. *Wien*, 1770.

Austrian Netherlands.—*See* NETHERLANDS, AUSTRIAN.

Auura.—KOLCZYCKI, A. Determination des Longitudes ... Observations pour ... A., etc. *Par.*, 1851.

Auvergne.—COSTELLO, L. S. A Pilgrimage to A., etc. 1842.

Ava.—Symes, M. Account of an Embassy to ... A. in 1795. **1800.**
—— Ava. Two Years in A., etc. *Lond.*, **1827.**
—— Crawfurd, J. Journal of an Embassy to A. ... in 1827, etc. **1829.**
—— Pemberton, R. B. Report ... with ... a supplement by Dr. Bayfield, on the British Political Relations with A. *Calc.*, **1835.**
—— Yule, H. Narrative of Major Phayre's Mission to ... A., etc. *Calc.*, **1856.**
—— —— Narrative of the Mission ... to ... A., in 1855, etc. **1858.**
—— Symes, M. Account of an Embassy to ... A., in 1795. Pelham. Vol II.
—— Syme's Embassy to A. Pinkerton. Vol. IX.

Avignon.—Gutain, J. Mesures Barométriques ... et ... Précis de la Météorologie d'A. *Avign.*, **1829.**

Aylesbury.—Smyth, Admiral W. H. Notice of certain Relics found near A., etc. **1859.**

Asach.—*See* Azov.
Asaffi.—*See* Saffi.
Asani.—Keppel, Hon. G. Narrative of ... a visit to A., etc. *Lond.*, **1831.**

Asania.—*See* Ajan.
Asmaveth.—Newbold, T. J. On the Site of ... A., etc.
Asmeer, Asmere.—*See* Ajmere.
Asoff, Sea of.—*See* Azov.
Azores.—Bartholomew, D. E. Voyage to the ... Western Islands. **1819.**
—— Bullar, J. and H. Winter in the A., etc. **1841.**
—— Kerhallet, C. P. de. Description de l'Archipel des Açores. *Par.*, **1858.**
—— Burrough, Sir J. Cruising Voyage to the A. in 1592, etc. Astley. Vol. I.
—— Flicke, R. Cruising Voyage to the A. in 1591. Astley. Vol. I.
—— Wright, E. Cruising Voyage to the A. in 1589, by the Earl of Cumberland. Astley. Vol. I.
—— Cumberland, Earle of. Voyage to the A., 1589. Hakluyt. Vol. II.
—— Raleigh, Sir W. Voyage to the A. ... in 1586. Hakluyt. Vol. II.
—— Voyage ... to ... the A., 1591. Reported by R. Flick. Hakluyt. Vol. II.
—— Burrough, Sir J. Cruising Voyage to the A., 1592. Kerr. Vol. VII.
—— Cumberland, Earl of. Cruising Voyage to the A., 1589. Kerr. Vol. VII.
—— Evesham, J. Cruising Voyage to the A. ... 1586. Kerr. Vol. VII.
—— Flicke, R. Report of a Cruizing Voyage to the A. in 1591, etc. Kerr. Vol. VII.

Azores — Babylon.

Azores.—Cumberland, Earl of. Voyage to the A. PINKERTON. Vol. I.
—— Essex, Earle of. Relation of the Voyage to the Iles of A., 1597. PURCHAS. Vol. IV.
—— Gorges, Sir A. Larger relation of the said Iland Voyage [A.] 1507. PURCHAS. Vol. IV.
—— Linschoten. Description of the .. A. or the Flemish Ilands, etc. PURCHAS. Vol. IV.
—— See also FURNAS.

Azov.—Barbaro, J. Travels from Venice to Tanna, now called Asof, 1436. KERR. Vol. I.
—— Pegoletti. Itinerary between A. and China, 1355. KERR. Vol. I.
—— Barbaro, J. Viaggio della Tana ... 1436-87. RAMUSIO. Vol. II.
—— **Sea of.**—BLACK SEA. A Geographical ... account of the Russian Ports of ... the Sea of Asoph, etc. 1837.
—— —— DABONDEAU, M. B. Tableau Général des Phares et Fanaux des Côtes ... de la Mer d'Azoff. Par., 1852.
—— —— CLOUÉ, G. C. Renseignements hydrographiques sur la Mer d'Azof. Par., 1856.
—— —— MEDITERRANEAN. The Lighthouses of the ... Sea of A. Corrected to 1856. 1856.
—— —— MEDITERRANEAN. The Lights of the ... Sea of A. Corrected to 1857, 58, 59. 1857-59.
—— —— DUNSTERVILLE, E. The Admiralty List of the Lights of the ... Sea of A. Corrected to 1860, 61, 62. 1860-62.
—— —— BAER, K. E. VON. Über das behauptete Seichter-Werden des Asowschen Meeres. 1861.
—— —— GRAS, M. A. LE. Phares de ... la Mer d'Azof ... Corrigés 1862, 63. Par., 1862, 63.
—— —— HELMERSEN, G. VON. Zur Frage über das behauptete Seichterwerden des Asow'schen Meeres. 1867.

B.

Baalbec.—RICHARDSON, H. Travels ... as far as ... B., etc. Lond., 1822.
—— Hogg, J. On the supposed Scriptural names of B., etc. 1862.
—— An Account of the Ruins of B., the ancient Heliopolis, etc. VOYAGES and TRAVELS. The World displayed. Vol. XI.
Babel.—MIGNAN, R. Travels ... with Observations on the Sites of B., etc. 1829.
—— BEKE, C. T. On the Non-identity of Babylon and B. 1836.
Babylon.—MARTYR, P. De rebus Oceanicis ... decades tres. Item ... de B. ica Legatione, lib. III., etc. Colonia, 1574.
—— MAURICE, T. Observations ... on the Ruins of B., etc. 1816.
—— BUCKINGHAM, J. S. Travels ... with Researches on the Ruins of ... B., etc. 1827.

Babylon.—Keppel, Hon. G. Personal Narrative of a Journey from India
 . . . by . . . the Ruins of B., *etc.* 1827.
—— Mignan, R. Travels . . . including a Journey from Bussorah to . . .
 B., *etc.* 1829.
—— Rennell, J. The Geographical System of Herodotus examined . . .
 with dissertations on . . . Ancient B., *etc.* 1830.
—— Beke, C. T. On the . . . Non-identity of B. and Babel. 1836.
—— Layard, A. H. Discoveries in the Ruins of . . . B., *etc.* 1853.
—— Eldred, J. Voyage . . . to B. . . . 1583. Hakluyt. Vol. II.
Babylonia.—Dapper. Naukeurige Beschryving van . . . R, *etc.*
 Amst., 1680.
—— Rennell, J. Illustrations . . . of the Expedition of Cyrus . . . to
 B., *etc.* 1816.
—— Porter, Sir R. K. Travels in . . . Ancient B., *etc.*
 Lond., 1821, 22.
—— Ainsworth, W. F. Researches in . . . B., *etc.* 1838.
—— Beke, C. T. On the Alluvia of B., *etc.* 1839.
—— Of . . . the Regions and Religions of B., *etc.* Purchas, Vol. V.
Bacola.—*See* Bakul.
Bactria.—Ritter, C. Die Stupa's oder die Architektonischen Denkmale
 an der grossen Königsstrasse zwischen Indien . . . und Baktrien.
 Berlin.
—— Lassen, C. Zur Geschichte der Griechischen und Indo-skythischen
 Könige in Baktrien, *etc.* *Bonn*, 1838.
—— Ritter, C. Stupa's (Topen) oder die Architectonischen Denkmale an
 der Indo-baktrischen Königstrasse, *etc.* *Berl.*, 1838.
—— Reinaud, M. Relations Politiques et Commerciales de l'Empire
 Romain avec . . . (la Bactriane) pendant les cinq premiers siècles, *etc.*
 Par., 1863.
—— Jenkinson, A. Voyage from . . . Mosco . . . to Boghar in B.
 Hakluyt. Vol. I.
Badakhshan.—Wood, J. Personal Narrative of a Journey to the Source
 of the . . . Oxus, by . . . B. 1841.
Badamee.—Marshall, T. Statistical Reports on . . . Badamy, *etc.*
 Bomb., 1822.
Badamy.—*See* Badamee.
Baden.—Michaelis, E. H. Barometrische Höhenbestimmungen in . . .
 B., *etc.* *Berlin*
—— Hennisch, A. J. v. Handbuch für . . . B. *Stutt.*, 1837.
—— Undine. Our Cruise in the *Undine* . . . through . . . B., *etc.*
 Lond., 1854.
—— Baden. Beitrage zur Statistik der inneren Verwaltung des Gross-
 herzogthums B. *Carls.*, 1855-62.
—— Baden. Festschrift . . . Beiträge zur Kenntniss der Land- und
 Forstwirthschaft im Grossherzogthum B. *Heidelb.*, 1860.
—— Dietz, R. Die Gewerbe im Grossherzogthum B., *etc.*
 Karlsr., 1863.

Baffin's Bay.—Ross, Capt. Sir J. Voyage . . . for . . . exploring B. B., etc. 1819.
—— ——. Goodsir, R. A. Arctic Voyage to B. B., etc. 1850.
—— Sutherland, P. C. Journal of a Voyage in B. B. . . . 1850-51, etc. 1852.
—— Allen, R. C., Snow, W. P., and Inglefield, E. A. Remarks on B. B. 1853.
—— Ross. Voyage dans la Mer de B. 1818. Eyriès. Vol. VII.
Bagdad.—Buckingham, J. S. Travels . . . Journey from Aleppo to B., etc. 1827.
—— Keppel, Hon. G. Personal Narrative of a Journey from India . . . by . . . B., etc. 1827.
—— Mignan, R. Travels . . . including a Journey from Bussorah to B., etc. 1829.
—— Buckingham, J. S. Travels . . . from B. . . . to Hamadan, etc. 1830.
—— Rich, C. J. Narrative of . . . a Voyage down the Tigris to B., etc. 1836.
—— Eldred, J. Voyage . . . to B. . . . 1583. Kerr. Vol. VIII.
—— Eldred J. and Shales, W. Letters from B. . . . 1583. Purchas. Vol. II.
—— Notice sur la Carte générale des Paschaliks de . . . B., etc. Voyages and Travels. Recueil, etc. Vol. II.
Bagdat, Bagdet, Baghdad.—See Bagdad.
Bagshot.—Rennie, G. Report on the supply of Water to be obtained from the District of B. 1850.
Bagulkot.—See Bagulkota.
Bagulkota.—Marshall, T. Statistical Reports on . . . B., etc. Bomb., 1822.
Bahama Channel.—Hawkins, Sir J. Voyages . . . thorow the chanel of B., 1562-68. Hakluyt. Vol. III.
Bahama Islands.—Purdy, J. and Findlay, A. G. Sailing Directory for the . . . B. Islands and Channels, etc. 1849.
—— Barnett, E. West India Pilot . . . with the B., etc. 1859-61.
—— Îles Lucayes. Eyriès. Vol. X.
—— Columbus, C. First Voyage, in which he discovered the Lucayan Islands, etc. Harris, J. Vol. II.
—— Reisen und Niederlassungen auf den Lucayischen Eylanden. Voyages and Travels. Allgemeine Historie, etc. Vol. XVII.
Bahawulpore.—Boileau, A. W. E. Tour through . . . Rajwara . . . and visit to . . . Buhawulpoor. Calc., 1837.
Bahia.—Navarro e Campos, Sa. Itinerary of a Journey . . . in 1808, from B. to Rio de Janeiro. MS. Portug.
—— Prior, J. Voyage . . . to . . . B. . . . 1813. Voyages and Travels, New. 1819. Vol. II.
Bahia de Todos os Santos.—Wilkins, J. A true Description of the Bay T. los S. in Brazil, etc. Purchas. Vol. II.

Bahiouda.—MARNO, E. Von Dabbeh nach Omderman durch die westliche Bajuda-Steppe. *Wien* [1870.]

Bahr-el-Abiad.—*See* NILE, WHITE.

Bahr-el-Ghazal.—KOTSCHY, T. and PEYRITSCH, J. Plantae Tinneanae ... Description de ... Plantes recueillies ... sur les bords du B., *etc.*
Vienne, **1867.**

Bajuda.—*See* BAHIOUDA.

Bak-Thian.—*See* CACHAO.

Baktrien.—*See* BACTRIA.

Bakul.—Fitch, R. The long ... voyage of ... to ... Bacola, *etc.* 1583-1591. HAKLUYT. Vol. II.

Balambangan.—FORREST, T. Voyage to New Guinea ... from B., *etc.*
1780.

—— An Account of ... a plan for ... an Establishment at B. 1760. DALRYMPLE, A. Tracts, from 1764 to 1808. Vol. I.

—— A full and clear proof that the Spaniards can have no claim to B., 1774. DALRYMPLE, A. Tracts, from 1764 to 1808. Vol. I.

Balbec.—*See* BAALBEC.

Balcan.—*See* BALKAN.

Balearen.—*See* BALEARIC ISLANDS.

Balearic Islands.—BALEARIC ISLANDS. Die Balearen, *etc. Leip.,* **1859.**

—— St. Sauveur, A. G. de. Travels through the B. ... I., 1801-6. VOYAGES and TRAVELS. A Collection, *etc.* 1805. Vol. VIII.

—— —— Travels through the B. ... I., 1801-6. VOYAGES and TRAVELS. A Collection, *etc.* 1810. Vol. III.

Bali.—Moor, J. H. Notices of ... B., *etc.* *Singapore,* **1837.**

Balk.—*See* BALKH.

Balkan.—DANUBE. Observations sur les Routes ... du Danube ... à travers le B., *etc.* *Par.,* **1828.**

—— KEPPEL, HON. G. Narrative of a Journey across the B., *etc.*
Lond., **1831.**

Balkan Bay.—*See* BALKHAN BAY.

Balkh.—LAL, MOHUN. Travels ... to B., *etc.*

—— SÉDILLOT, M. Notice sur une Carte Routière ... de Bokhara à B., *etc.* *Par.,* **1852.**

Balkhan Bay.—ZIMMERMANN, C. Denkschrift ... über die Stromlahn des Ochus ... zur B. B. *Berl.,* **1845.**

Ballston.—MEADE, W. An ... Inquiry into the chemical properties, &c., of the Mineral Waters of B., *etc.* *Phil.,* **1817.**

Ballybunian.—AINSWORTH, W. Account of the Caves of B., *etc.*
Dubl., **1834.**

Balochistan.—*See* BELOOCHISTAN.

Balsara.—*See* BASSORAH.

Baltic Sea.—MANN, M. L'ABBÉ. Mémoire dans lequel on examine l'opinion ... que les Mers ... Baltique & Blanche, ont anciennement communiqué ensemble. **1779.**

Baltic Sea.—Braumüller, J. G. Der wichtigste Kanal in Europa, durch eine Vereinigung des Schwarzen Meeres mit der Ost-und Nord-See, etc.
Berl., 1815.

——— Schubert, Lieut.-Gen. Chronometric Expedition round the B.
St. Pet., 1836.

——— Hill, S. S. Travels on the Shores of the B., etc.   1854.
——— Klint, G. Sailing Directions for the B. S., etc.   1854.
——— Baltic Pilot. Supplementary Sailing Directions.   1855.
——— Hooues, R. E. Two Summer Cruises with the B. Fleet, etc.
Lond., 1855.

——— Klint, G. Pilote de la Mer Baltique, etc.   *Par.*, 1856.
——— ——— Supplément au Pilote de la Mer Baltique, etc. *Par.*, 1857.
——— Gras, M. A. le. Phares de ... la Mer Baltique ... Corrigés 1850,
61, 62, 64.   *Par.*, 1859-64.
——— Dunsterville, E. The Admiralty List of Lights in the ... B.
... Corrected to 1861 and 1862.   1861-2.
——— Norie, J. W. Guide du Marin ... sur les Côtes de la Mer
Baltique, etc.   *Par.*, 1863.
——— Gras, A. Le. Instructions nautiques sur la Mer Baltique, etc.
Par., 1864.

——— ——— Phares de ... la Mer Baltique, etc. *Par.*, 1869.
——— Ohthere, Voyages of, to ... the B., in the ninth century. Kerr.
Vol. I.
——— Wulfstein. Voyage in the B., etc. Kerr. Vol. I.
——— Carr, J. A Northern Summer; or, Travels round the B. ...
1804. Voyages and Travels. A Collection, etc., 1805. Vol. III.

Bamba.—Carlius Widerwärtigkeiten zu B., 1668. Voyages and Travels.
Allgemeine Historie, etc. Vol. IV.

Bambook, Bambouk.—See Bambuk.

Bambuk.—Compagnon, Sieur. Account of the discovery of ... B. ...
in 1716, etc. Antley. Vol. II.

——— Compagnon. Eine Nachricht von der Entdeckung des Königreichs
B. ... 1716, etc. Voyages and Travels. Allgemeine Historie, etc.
Vol. II.

Bamian.—Ritter, C. Stupa's (Topes) ... und die Colosse von B.
Berl., 1838.

Bamiyan.—See Bamian.

Banca.—Palembang. De Heldhaftige Bevreding van Palembang ...
en ... korte beschrijving van ... B., etc.   *Rotter.*, 1822.

——— Anderson, J. Observations on ... restoration of B. ... to ...
Dutch, etc.   *P. of W. I.*, 1824.
——— Lange, H. M. Het Eiland Banka, etc.   *s'Hertog.*, 1850.
——— Croockewit, J. H. B. ... in 1849-50.   *Te Syrav.*, 1852.
——— **Strait.**—Melvill of Carnbee, and Smits, H. D. A. Seaman's
Guide ... through the Straits of B., etc.   1853.

Banca Strait — Bantam.

Banca Strait.—DENHAM, H. M. Hydrographic Notices . . . B. S., etc. 1858-59.
Banda.—Keeling, W. Voyage to . . . B. in 1607. ASTLEY. Vol. I.
——— Voyage of Captain D. Middleton to . . . B. in 1609. ASTLEY. Vol. I.
——— Fifth Voyage, in 1609 . . . Occurrences at . . . B., etc. KERR. Vol. VIII.
——— Voyage of Captain Colthurst to B. KERR. Vol. VIII.
——— Account of the Wrongs done to the English at B. . . . 1617-18. KERR. Vol. IX.
——— Courthop, N. Journal of his Voyage from Bantam to . . . B. . . . 1616-20, etc. PURCHAS. Vol I.
——— Fitz-Herbert, H. Pithy description of the chiefe Ilands of D. and Moluccas, 1621. PURCHAS. Vol. I.
——— Middleton, D. Voyage to Java and B., 1609. PURCHAS. Vol. I.
——— Spurway, T. Letter touching the wrongs done at B. to the English by the Hollanders, 1617. PURCHAS. Vol. I.
——— The Dutch late proceedings at Amboyna . . . with other like Acts . . . in B., 1613-22. PURCHAS. Vol. II.
——— Eylande, die unter der Regierung zu B. stehen. VOYAGES and TRAVELS. Allgemeine Historie, etc. Vol. XVIII.
——— Zusatz zu der Beschreibung der Insel D. VOYAGES and TRAVELS. Allgemeine Historie, etc. Vol. XVIII.
Ban de la Roche.—OBERLIN, H. G. Propositions Géologiques du B. de la R. Strasb., 1806.
Bandi, River.—BARBOT, J., and GRAZILHIER, J. Abstract of a Voyage to . . . B. and Doni Rivers in 1609. ASTLEY. Vol. III.
——— ——— Beschreibung von einer Seefahrt nach der Flüssen . . . B., etc. 1609. VOYAGES and TRAVELS. Allgemeine Historie, etc. Vol. IV.
Bangkok.—BANGKOK CALENDAR, 1859, 61, 64, etc. Bangkok, 1859-64.
Baniak Islands.—Low's Discovery of the Baniana. PINKERTON. Vol. VIII.
Baniana.—See BANIAK ISLANDS.
Banka.—See BANCA.
Bantam.—Keeling, W. Voyage to B . . . in 1607. ASTLEY. Vol. I.
——— Marten, N. Voyage of Capt. A. Hippon to . . . B. . . . in 1611. ASTLEY. Vol. I.
——— Saris, J. Occurrences at B. . . . 1605-9, etc. ASTLEY. Vol. I.
——— Scot, E. Account of . . . first Settlement of the English at B. . . . 1602-5. ASTLEY. Vol. I.
——— Voyage of . . . D. Middleton to B. . . . in 1607. ASTLEY. Vol. I.
——— Voyage of Sir E. Michelburne to B. in 1604. ASTLEY. Vol. I.
——— Middleton, Sir H. Voyage to B. . . . edited by B. Corney. 1855. HAKLUYT SOC. PUB. Vol. XIX.

Bantam — Barbary.

Bantam.—Middleton, D. Voyage to B. ... 1607. KERR. Vol. VIII.
—— Fifth Voyage, in 1609 ... Occurrences at B., etc. KERR. Vol. VIII.
—— Second Voyage in 1604 ... to B., etc. KERR. Vol. VIII.
—— Voyage to ... B., etc. KERR. Vol. VIII.
—— Pring, Capt. Voyage from B. to Patania, etc. KERR. Vol. IX.
—— Tenth Voyage, in 1612 ... to B. KERR. Vol. IX.
—— Courthop, N. Journal of his Voyage from B. to ... Banda ... 1616-20, etc. PURCHAS. Vol. I.
—— Floris, P. W. Extracts of his Journal ... 1610-15. Voyage to ... B., etc. PURCHAS. Vol. I.
—— Hores, W. Discourse of his Voyage from Surat to ... B., 1618-19. PURCHAS. Vol. I.
—— Saris, J. Observations of occurrents ... at B., 1605-9. PURCHAS. Vol. I.
—— Brown, A. Extracts of a Journal ... sayling divers times ... to B. ... 1617-22. PURCHAS. Vol. II.
—— Drey Reisen ... nach B., 1599-1602. VOYAGES and TRAVELS. Allgemeine Historie, etc. Vol. VIII.
—— Rhodes, A. Reise nach ... B., etc. VOYAGES and TRAVELS. Allgemeine Historie, etc. Vol. X.

Barbadoes.—SLOANE, H. Voyage to ... B., etc. - 1707.
—— EDWARDS, B. Historical Survey of ... Saint Domingo ... Also a Tour through ... B., etc. 1801.
—— SCHOMBURGK, R. The History of B., etc. 1848.
—— Roberts, G. Account of a Voyage to ... B. in 1721. ASTLEY. Vol. I.
—— Phillips, T. Abstract of a Voyage ... to B. in 1693. ASTLEY. Vol. II.
—— Phillips, Capt. Journal of ... Voyage ... to ... B. CHURCHILL. Vol. VI.
—— Roberts, G. Bericht von einer Reise nach ... B., 1721. VOYAGES and TRAVELS. Allgemeine Historie, etc. Vol. II.
—— Phillips, T. Beschreibung einer Reise ... nach B., 1693. VOYAGES and TRAVELS. Allgemeine Historie, etc. Vol. III.
—— Engländische Inseln. Reisen ... in ... B., etc. VOYAGES and TRAVELS. Allgemeine Historie, etc. Vol. XVII.

Barbados.—See BARBADOES.

Barbary.—COMELIN, F. P. DE LA MOTTE, and BERNARD, J. Voyage to B. ... in 1720, etc. 1725.
—— SHAW, T. Travels, or Observations relating to several parts of B., etc. 1757.
—— POIRET, Abbé. Voyage en Barbarie ... 1785-86, etc. Par., 1789.
—— SHABEENY, EL HAGE ABD SALAM. Account of Timbuctoo ... Letters descriptive of ... West and South B. ... by J. Grey Jackson. 1820.
—— GREENHOW, R. History ... of Tripoli, with some accounts of the other B. States. Richmond, U.S., 1835.

Barbary — Basque Provinces.

Barbary.—Russell, Dr. M. History of the present condition of the B. States, *etc.* *Edin.*, 1835.
—— Pananti, F. Avventure e Osservazioni sopra le Coste di Barberia. *Mendrisio*, 1841.
—— Barbary, Leaves from a Lady's diary of . . . Travels in. 1850.
—— Thomas, J. Second Voyage to B. in 1552, *etc.* Astley. Vol. I.
—— First two Voyages to B., 1551-2. Hakluyt. Vol. II.
—— Gurney, M. Voyage against the Moores of Alger to B., *etc.* Hakluyt. Vol. II.
—— Stukeley, T. Voyage into B., 1578. Hakluyt. Vol. II.
—— Windham, T. Second Voyage to B., 1552. Kerr. Vol. VII.
—— Shaw's Travels in B. Pinkerton. Vol. XV.
—— Collections of things most remarkable in the historie of B., by Ro. C. Purchas. Vol. II.
—— Gramaye, J. B. Relations of the Christianitie . . . of B. . . . 1610. Purchas. Vol. II.
—— Of Ægypt, B. . . . and of their Religions. Purchas. Vol. V.
—— Shaw, T. Travels through B. Voyages and Travels. The World displayed. Vol. XVII., XVIII.
—— *See also* Tripoli.—Tunis.
——, **West**. Addison, L. West B., *etc.* *Oxf.*, 1671.
—— —— Addison's Account of W. B. Pinkerton. Vol. XV.

Barberia.—*See* Barbary.

Barbuda.—Engländische Inseln. Reisen . . . in . . . B., *etc.* Voyages and Travels. Allgemeine Historie, *etc.* Vol. XVII.

Bären Insel.—*See* Bear Islands.

Bari.—Mittrrbutzner, J. C. Die Sprache der B. in Central-Afrika. Grammatik, *etc.* *Brixen*, 1867.

Barmudas.—*See* Bermuda Islands.

Barnstaple.—Sedgwick, A. and Murchison, Sir R. I. Description of a Raised Beach in B. or Bideford Bay, *etc.* 1836.

Barossa Mountains.—Agricola. Description of the B. Range, *etc.* *Lond.*, 1849.

Barrier Island.—New Zealand Geological Survey. Abstract Report . . . Together with reports on B. I., *etc.* *Well.*, 1869.

Barrow, Point.—Simpson, J. Results of Thermometrical Observations made at . . . P. B. 1857.

—— **Straits.**—Sutherland, P. C. Journal of a Voyage in . . . R. S. in 1850-51, *etc.* 1852.

Basa.—Werne, F. African Wanderings: or an Expedition from Sennaar to . . . B., *etc.* 1852.

Bashan.—Buckingham, J. S. Travels . . . through . . . B., *etc.* 1822.
—— Freshfield, D. W. Travels in . . . B., *etc.* *Lond.*, 1869.

Basora.—*See* Bassorah.

Basque Provinces.—Zamacola, D. J. A. Historia de las Naciones Bascas, *etc.* *Auch*, 1818.

Basque Provinces.—ABBADIE, A. D'. and CHAHO, J. A. Études grammaticales sur la langue Euskarienne. *Par.*, 1836.

Bassorah.—PLAISTED, R. Journal from Calcutta . . . to Busserah, *etc.* 1758.

—— TAYLOR, J. Travels . . . to India, in 1789, by . . . B., *etc.* 1799.

—— KEPPEL, HON. G. Personal Narrative of a Journey from India . . . by B., *etc.* 1827.

—— MIGNAN, R. Travels . . . including a Journey from B. to Bagdad, *etc.* 1829.

—— Eldred, J. Voyage to . . . Balsara, 1583. HAKLUYT. Vol. II.

—— —— Voyage . . . to . . . B., 1583. KERR. Vol. VIII.

—— Eldred, J. and Shales, W. Letters from . . . B., 1583. PURCHAS. Vol. II.

—— Newbery, J. Letters relating to his . . . last Voyage into . . . B. . . . 1583. PURCHAS. Vol. II.

—— Newberie, J. Two Voyages. One . . . to B. . . . 1580-82. PURCHAS. Vol. II.

—— Commencement d'un Livre des Chaldéens de B. . . . avec . . . une Carte Arabe du païs. THEVENOT. Vol. I.

Bass' Strait.—Tuckey, J. H. Voyage pour établir une colonie au Port Phillip dans le détroit de B., 1803-4. EYRIÈS. Vol. IV.

Batavia.—STAVORINUS, J. S. Voyage par . . . B., à Samarang, *etc.*, 1774-78. *Par.*, 1800.

—— STREHLER, DR. Bijzonderheden wegens B., *etc.* *Haarlem*, 1833.

—— BENNETT, G. Wanderings in . . . B., *etc.* 1834.

—— CHIMMO, W. Voyage . . . from Sydney to . . . B. 1857.

—— Brampton et Alt. Voyage de l'île Norfolk à B. . . . 1793. EYRIÈS. Vol. IV.

—— Tavernier, J. B. Remarks . . . together with his . . . Voyage . . . from B. to Europe. HARRIS, J. Vol. I.

—— Byron, Comm. Voyage . . . to . . . B. . . . 1764-66. HAWKESWORTH, J. Vol. I.

—— Carteret, Capt. Voyage . . . to . . . B. . . . 1766-69. HAWKESWORTH, J. Vol. I.

—— Wallis, Capt. Voyage to . . . B. . . . 1766-68. HAWKESWORTH, J. Vol. I.

—— Stavorinus. Account of . . . B., from the Voyages of. PINKERTON. Vol. XI.

—— Rhodes, A. Reise nach . . . B., *etc.* VOYAGES and TRAVELS. Allgemeine Historie, *etc.* Vol. X.

—— Kampfern, E. Reise nach . . . B. 1690-91. VOYAGES and TRAVELS. Allgemeine Historie, *etc.* Vol. XI.

—— Schouten, G. Reisen nach B. . . . 1658-65. VOYAGES and TRAVELS. Allgemeine Historie, *etc.* Vol. XII.

—— Belagerung der Stadt B. von dem Kaiser in Java, 1628-29. VOYAGES and TRAVELS. Allgemeine Historie, *etc.* Vol. XVIII.

Batavia — Bechuanas.

Batavia.—Broeck, Van den. Stiftung der Stadt B., 1618-19. Voyages and Travels. Allgemeine Historie, etc. Vol. XVIII.

Baudo, River.—Lane, J. C. Report of the Surveys of the ... B., etc. *N. Y.*, 1856.

Baussen.—*See* Dautzen.

Bautzen.—Dresden und die umliegende Gegend bis ... Baussen, etc. *Dresd.*, 1804.

Bavaria.—Bavaria. Handbuch des Königreichs Bayern. *Münch.*, 1840.

——— Barrow, J. Tour in ; ... B., etc. 1841.

——— Hermann, F. B. W. von. Ueber die Bewegung der Bevölkerung im Königreiche Bayern. *Mün.*, 1853.

——— ——— Ueber die Gliederung der Bevölkerung des Königreichs Bayern. *Mün.*, 1855.

——— Gistel, J. Neueste Geographie ... des Königreichs Bayern. *Straubing*, 1856.

——— Hermann, F. B. W. von. Ueber den Anbau und Ertrag des Bodens im Königreiche Bayern. *Mün.*, 1857.

——— Bavaria. Die Forstverwaltung Bayerns, etc. *Münch.*, 1861.

——— Murchison, Sir R. I. On the Gneiss and other Azoic Rocks of B., etc. 1863.

———, Browne, E. Voyage ... to Holland, with a Journey ... through ... B. ; ... 1668. Harris, J. Vol. II.

———, **Rhenish.**—Michaelis, C. H. Barometrische Höhenbestimmungen in ... Rheinbayern, etc. *Berlin.*

——— Undine. Our Cruise in the *Undine* ... through ... R. B., etc. *Lond.*, 1854.

———, **South.**—Schafhäutl, K. Geognostische Untersuchungen des Südbayerischen Alpengebirges, etc. *Münch.*, 1851.

Bavatoubé.—Jehenne, Capit. Sur ... B., etc. *Par.*, 1847.

Baya.—*See* Bayao.

Bayao.—Pudsey. Voyage to B. in Brasil, 1542. Hakluyt. Vol. IV.

Bayonne.—Bayonne, Barre de. Instruction pour aborder ... la Barre de B. *Par.*, 1850.

Bayuda.—*See* Bahiouda.

Bear Island.—Buch, L. von. Die Bären-Insel ... geognostisch beschrieben. *Berl.*, 1847.

——— Poole, J. Voyages set forth by Sir T. Smith ... to Cherry Island ... 1610-12. Purchas: Vol. III.

——— ——— ——— Voyages to Cherie Iland, 1604-9. Purchas. Vol. III.

——— Supplement, Description of Cherry ... I., etc. 1711. Voyages. Account of several late, etc.

Bechuanas.—Barrow, Sir J. Voyage to ... the Booshuana Nation ... in S. Africa, etc. 1806.

——— Archbell, J. Grammar of the B. Language. *Graham's T.*, 1837.

——— Truter et Somerville. Voyage au pays des Betjuanas, 1801. Erails. Vol. XI.

Bedford.—SMYTH, ADMIRAL W. H. Account of a Private Observatory recently erected at B. 1851.

Bedford Level.—ELSTOBB, W. Historical Account of the Great Level of the Fens, called B. L., *etc.* 1793.

Beejapoor.—Methold, W. Reise nach den Diamantgruben in ... Visapur, *etc.* VOYAGES and TRAVELS. Allgemeine Historie, *etc.* Vol. X.

Beekaneer.—BOILEAU, A. W. E. Tour through ... Beekaner, *etc.* Calc., 1837.

Beekaner.—*See* BEEKANEER.

Beersheba.—BONAR, H. The Land of Promise ... a Journey from B. to Sidon. 1858.

Beheda.—*See* BAHIOUDA.

Behrings' Strait.—NAVARETTE, M. F. DE. Examination of the account given by L. Ferrer Maldonado, of the discovery of the Strait of Anian, *etc. MS. Port.*

—— — KOTZEBUE, O. VON. A Voyage of Discovery into ... D. S. ... 1815-1818, *etc.* *Lond.,* 1821.

—— - BEECHEY, F. W. Narrative of a Voyage to ... D. S., *etc.* 1831.

—— — SNEDDEN, R. Nautical Observations, &c., taken during the Voyage of the *Nancy Dawson* to D. S., *etc. MS.* 1848-49.

—— Kotzebue, O. von. Voyage ... to B. S. ... 1815-18. VOYAGES and TRAVELS, New. 1819. Vol. VI.

Bekhur.—LLOYD, SIR W. Narrative ... And Captain A. Gerard's account of an attempt to penetrate by B. to Garoo, *etc.* *Lond.,* 1840.

Beled-al-Sur.—*See* DERKA.

Beled Beny Yass.—WREDE, A. VON. Reise in Hadramaut, B. B. Y., *etc.* *Braunsch.,* 1870.

Beled el Hadschar.—WREDE, A. VON. Reise in Hadramaut ... B. el H., *etc.* *Braunschw.,* 1870.

Belem.—MICHELENA Y ROJAS, F. Exploracion Oficial ... Vinje a Rio de Janeiro desde Belen, *etc.* *Bruselas,* 1867.

Belen.—*See* BELEM.

Belgam.—*See* BELGAUM.

Belgaum.—MARSHALL, T. Statistical Reports on ... B., *etc.* *Bomb.,* 1822.

Belgium.—GÖLNITZIUS, A. Itinerarium Belgico-Gallicum. *Lugd.,* 1631.

—— DESSIOU, J. P. Le Petit Neptune Français; or French Coasting Pilot for the Coast of Flanders (B.) Channel, *etc.* 1805.

—— GALIGNANI. Guide through B. *Par.,* 1824.

—— VANDER MAELEN, P. Statistique du Royaume de Belgique, *etc.* *Brussels,* 1830.

—— BELGIUM. Recueil de Documens Statistiques de la Belgique. 1833.

—— MURRAY. Hand-Book for Travellers ... through ... B., *etc.* *Lond.,* 1836.

—— HEUSCHLING, X. Statistique Générale de la Belgique, *etc.* *Bruss.,* 1838.

Belgium — Bengal.

Belgium.—WAUTERS, A. Atlas Pittoresque des Chemins de Fer de la Belgique. *Brux.*, 1840.
—— PETSCHLING, X. Essai sur la Statistique Générale de la Belgique, *etc.* 1841-44.
—— SEDGWICK, A., and MURCHISON, SIR R. I. On the Distribution and Classification of the Older ... Deposits of ... B., *etc.* 1842.
—— QUIN, M. J. Steam Voyages ... with ... Visits to the principal Cities of D. 1843.
—— BELGIUM. Belgian ... Lighthouses, corrected to 1843, 51, 54, 57, 58, 59. 1843-59.
—— BELL, R. Wayside Pictures through ... B., *etc.* 1849.
—— DARONDEAU, M. B. Tableau Général des Phares et Fanaux des Côtes ... de Belgique. *Par.*, 1849.
—— UNDINE. Our Cruise in the *Undine* ... through ... B., *etc.* *Lond.*, 1854.
—— LAMONT, J. Untersuchungen über den Erdmagnetismus in ... Belgien ... 1858 *Münch.*, 1858.
—— D'HALLOY, J. J. D'OMALIUS. Comp d'œil sur la Géologie de la Belgique. *Par.*, 1860.
—— DUNSTERVILLE, E. The Admiralty List of the Belgian ... Lights. Corrected to 1860. 1860.
—— JAMES, SIR H. Extension of the Triangulation of the Ordnance Survey into ... B., *etc.* 1863.
—— QUETELET, A. Sur ... les Orages observés en Belgique, pendant l'été de 1867, *etc.* *Brux.*, [1867.]

Belgrade.—PATON, A. A. Servia ... or, a residence in B., *etc.* *Lond.*, 1845.

Beloochistan.—POTTINGER, H. Travels in B., *etc.* 1816.
—— FRASER, J. B. Historical ... account of Persia ... including ... It., *etc.* *Edin.*, 1834.
—— MASSON, C. Narrative of ... Journeys in B., *etc.* 1844.
—— THORNTON, E. Gazetteer of ... B., *etc.* 1844.
—— FERRIER, J. P. Caravan Journeys ... in ... B., *etc.* 1856.
—— Beloutchistan. Pottinger. Christie. ETRIES. Vol. XIV.

Beloutchistan.—*See* BELOOCHISTAN.

Belts.—LÖVENORN CHEV. DE. New Sailing Directory for ... the B., *etc.* 1844.

Benatek.—HABANT, K. Gesta ... do B., *etc.* *v. Praze*, 1854.

Bengal.—PLAISTED, B. Journal ... An Account of the Countries ... adjacent to B., *etc.* 1758.
—— SCRAFTON, L. Reflections ... with a short sketch of the History of B., from 1739 to 1758, *etc.* *Lond.*, 1770.
—— BENGAL. A Narrative of ... Transactions in B., *etc.* *Calc.*, 1788.
—— FRANCKLIN, W. Observations made on a Tour from B. to Persia ... 1786-7, *etc.* *Lond.*, 1790.
—— FORSTER, G. Journey from B. to England, *etc.* 1798.

Bengal.—STEWART, C. History of B., *etc.* **1813.**
―――― SHAKESPEAR, A. Memoir of the Statistics of the N.-W.n Provinces of the B. Presidency. *Calc.*, **1848.**
―――― INDIA. Selections from the Records of the B. Government. *Calc.*, **1853**, *etc.*
――― - HOOKER, J. D. Himalayan Journal, or Notes ... in B., *etc.* **1854.**
―――― THUILLIER, H. L. General Report on the Revenue Survey Operations of ... B. ... 1858-61. *Calc.*, **1863.**
― - ―――― General Report on the Topographical Surveys of the B. Presidency ... 1862-63. *Calc.*, **1864.**
―――― LEES, W. N. Another Word on Tea Cultivation in E.n B. *Calc.*, **1867.**
―――― Bruton, W. News from the East Indies; or a Voyage to Bengalla, *etc.* CHURCHILL. Vol. VIII.
― - ― Fitch, R. The long ... voyage of ... to ... Bengala, *etc.* 1588-1591. HAKLUYT. Vol. II.
―――― Bruton, W. News from the East Indies; or, a Voyage to Bengalla ... 1638. HAKLUYT. Vol. V.
―――― Franklin, W. Observations made on a Tour from B. to Persia, in 1786-7, *etc.* PELHAM. Vol. II.
―――― Fitch, R. Voyage to ... Bengala ... 1583-91. PURCHAS. Vol. II.
―――― Methold, W. Reise nach den Diamantgruben in ... B., 1622. VOYAGES and TRAVELS. Allgemeine Historie, *etc.* Vol. X.
― - ― *See also* SILHET.
―――― **Bay of.**—PIDDINGTON, H. Researches on the Gale and Hurricane in the B. of B., June 3-5, 1839. *Calc.*, **1839.**
―――― ――――― Relation de Floris Villiamson du Golfe de B. THEVENOT. Vol. I.
―――― ――――― Floris, W. Reise nach dem B. ischen Meerbusen, 1611-13. VOYAGES and TRAVELS. Allgemeine Historie, *etc.* Vol. X.
―――― ――――― Luillier. Reise nach dem B. ischen Seebusen, 1722-23. VOYAGES and TRAVELS. Allgemeine Historie, *etc.* Vol. X.
――――, **Upper.** HOOKER, J. D. Observations made ... across the Hills of Upper B., *etc.* *Calc.*, **1848.**
Bengala, Bengalla.—*See* BENGAL.
Bengalischer Seebusen.—*See* BENGAL, BAY OF.
Benguela.—CARDOZO DE CASTELLOBRANCO E TORRES, J. C. F. Memorias contendo ... Descripção geographica ... de ... B. *Par.*, **1825.**
―――― A Description of ... B., *etc.* ASTLEY. Vol. III.
―――― Eine Beschreibung der Königreiche ... B., *etc.* VOYAGES and TRAVELS. Allgemeine Historie, *etc.* Vol. IV.
Benguella.—*See* BENGUELA.
Beni.—PENTLAND, J. B. and PARRIS, SIR. W. Notices of the ... S.n. Affluents of the ... B. *Lond.*, **1836.**
Beni Amer.—WERNE, F. African Wanderings : or, an Expedition from Sennaar to ... B. A., *etc.* **1852.**

Benin.—FAWCKNER, J.   Travels on the Coast of B., West Africa.   **1837.**
——— JAMIESON, R.   The inefficacy of Treaties . . . with . . . a short notice of . . . B.   **1859.**
——— Voyage to . . . B. in 1553, *etc.*   ASTLEY.   Vol. I.
——— Welsh, J.   Two Voyages to B. . . . in 1588 and 1590.   ASTLEY. Vol. I.
——— Voyages . . . to . . . B., *etc.*   ASTLEY.   Vol. II.
——— Voyages and Travels to B., *etc.*   ASTLEY.   Vol. III.
——— Welsh, J.   Two Voyages to B. . . . 1588-90.   HAKLUYT.   Vol. II.
——— Windam, T.   Voyage to Guinea and B., 1553.   HAKLUYT.   Vol. II.
——— Ingram, A.   Supplement to Welsh's Voyage to B., 1588.   KERR. Vol. VII.
——— Welsh, J.   Voyages to B. . . . 1588-90.   KERR.   Vol. VII.
——— Windham, Capt. and Pinteado, A. A.   Voyage to . . . B. in 1553. KERR.   Vol. VII.
——— The Passage from the Golden Coast to . . . Benal, *etc.*   PURCHAS. Vol. II.
——— Schiffahrten und Reisen nach . . . B., *etc.*   VOYAGES and TRAVELS. Allgemeine Historie, *etc.*   Vol. IV.
BennL.—*See* BENIN.
Benuê, River.—*See* CHADDA.
Berar.—BURGESS, J.   Memorandum . . . with lists of the Rock-Excavations, Temples, &c. in . . . B., *etc.*   *Bombay*, **1870.**
Berbers.—AUCAPITAINE, BARON H.   Lettre à M. F. Denor sur les origines des B.
——— ———   Notions ethnographiques sur les B. Touaregs.
——— NEWMAN, F. W.   Essay towards a Grammar of the B. language. **1836.**
——— PARADIS, V. DE.   Grammaire et dictionnaire abrégés de la langue Berbère.   *Par.*, **1844.**
——— AUCAPITAINE, BARON H.   Ethnographie : Nouvelles Observations sur l'Origine des B.-Shamou, *etc.*   *Par.*, **1867.**
Berbice.—PETLEY, J.—Remarks on the Rivers of B. and Demerara.   **1645.**
——— Bolingbroke, H.   Voyage . . . containing a Statistical Account of the Settlements . . . on the . . . B. . . . 1799.   VOYAGES and TRAVELS.   A Collection, *etc.*   1805.   Vol. X.
Berenice.—BELZONI, G.   Narrative of . . . a Journey . . . in search of the ancient B., *etc.*   **1822.**
Beresow.—*See* BEREZOW.
Beresow.—Lisle, de.   Auszug aus der Beschreibung einer Reise nach B. . . . 1740.   VOYAGES and TRAVELS.   Allgemeine Historie, *etc.* Vol. XIX.
Bergamo.—PONTE, G. M. DA.   Dizionario . . . della Provincia Bergamasca.   *Berg.*, **1819.**
Bergen.—HIORTDAHL, T. and IRGENS, M.   Geologiske Undersögelser i B. Omegn, *etc.*   *Christ.*, **1862.**

Bergenhus.—*See* BERGENHOUS.
Bergenhuus, North.—IRGENS, M. and HIORTDAHL, T. Om de Geologiske Forhold paa Kyststrækningen af Nordre Bergenhus amt.
Christ., **1864.**
Berlin.—BRALIN. Guide de B., *etc.* *Berl.*, **1793.**
——— WIEBE, E. Ueber die Reinigung und Entwässerung der Stadt B.
Berl., **1861.**
Bermejo, River.—*See* VERMEJO.
Bermuda Islands.—SMITH, CAPT. J. The True Travels ... of Capt. J. Smith ... The General Historie of ... the Summer Isles, *etc.*
Richm. U.S., **1819.**
——— WELLESLEY, HON. W. Private Letter-Book of H.M.S. *Sapphire*, during her Voyage ... to B., *etc.* **1830-33.**
——— LLOYD, S. H. Sketches of B. **1835.**
——— PURDY, J. and FINDLAY, A. G. Colombian Navigator. Vol. I. Sailing Directory for the B. I., *etc.* **1847.**
——— BERMUDA ... or Eighteen Months in the Somers' Islands. **1857.**
——— BARNETT, E. West India Pilot ... with the ... B., *etc.*
1859-61.
——— GODET, T. L. B.; its history, *etc.* *Lond.*, **1860.**
— — Jourdan, S. Discovery of the Bermudas ... 1610. HAKLUYT. Vol. V.
— — — Smith's History of ... the Summer Isles. PINKERTON. Vol. XIII.
——— Argal, S. Voyage ... to seek the Ile of B. ... 1610. PURCHAS. Vol. IV.
——— May, H. Shipwracke on the Summer Ilands, 1593, *etc.* PURCHAS. Vol. IV.
——— Norwood, R. Relations of Summer Ilands ... 1622. PURCHAS. Vol. IV.
——— Smith, Capt. J. Historie of B.s, or Summer Ilands ... 1613-23. PURCHAS. Vol. IV.
— — Strachy, W. True reportorie of the Wracke ... of Sir T. Gates, upon ... the B.s ... 1610. PURCHAS. Vol. IV.
— — Reisen und Niederlassungen auf den Inseln B.s oder den Commerrylanden. VOYAGES and TRAVELS. Allgemeine Historie, *etc.* Vol. XVII.
Berne.—FORBES, J. D. Norway ... with Excursions in the High Alps of ... B., *etc.* *Edin.*, **1853.**
——— HILDEBRAND, B. Beiträge zur Statistik des Kantons B. **1860.**
Bernese Oberland.—BERNE. Hand Atlas für Reisende in das Berner O.
Bern, **1816.**
——— BERNE. Nouvelle description de l'Oberland Bernois, *etc.*
Bern, **1838.**
Berwick.—JOHNSON, E. J. Sailing Directions from Sunderland Point to B., *etc.* **1836.**

Bessarabia.—GRIMM. Anzeige, *etc.* Die Salzseen Bessarabiens ... von G. v. Helmersen.

—— —— Anzeige, *etc.* Rapport ... sur ... l'Expédition de Bessarabie entreprise en 1852 ... par M. Praxmovski.

—— PRAXMOVSKI, A. Rapport sur les Travaux de l'Expédition de B., en 1852, *etc.* **1853.**

—— HELMERSEN, G. VON. Die Salzseen Bessarabiens, *etc.* **1854.**

— —— Campenhausen, Baron. Travels through ... B. ... **1805.** VOYAGES and TRAVELS. A Collection, *etc.* 1805. Vol. VIII.

Betanimena.—OLIVER, S. P. Madagascar ... with Sketches in the Provinces of ... B., *etc.* *Lond.* [**1885.**]

Betjuanas.—*See* BECHUANAS.

Beverley.—TURNER, M. The B. Guide, *etc.* *Bev.*, **1830.**

Bhilsa.—CUNNINGHAM, A. The B. Topes, *etc.* *Lond. and Bomb.*, **1854.**

Bhooj.—BURNES, J. A Narrative ... and some Remarks on the Medical Topography of B. *Edin. and Lond.*, **1831.**

Bhotan.—TURNER, S. Account of ... a Journey through Bootan, *etc.* **1806.**

—— BERGHAUS, H. Asia ... Memoir zur Erklärung ... der reduzirten Karte von ... B., *etc.* *Gotha*, **1839-35.**

—— PEMBERTON, R. B. Report on B., *etc.* *Calc.*, **1839.**

—— —— —— Ambassade au B. Journal abrégé, *etc.* *Par.*, **1840.**

— — GRIFFITH, W. Journals of Travels in ... B., *etc.* *Calc.*, **1847.**

— — BOOTAN. Political Missions to B., *etc.* *Calc.*, **1865.**

— — — RENNIE, D. B. B. and the Story of the Dooar War, *etc.* *Lond.*, **1866.**

—— Tibet et Boutan. Royle. Turner. ETHIKS. Vol. XIV.

— — Tavernier. Reisen nach ... Butan ... 1652. VOYAGES and TRAVELS. Allgemeine Historie, *etc.* Vol. X.

Bhutan.—*See* Bhotan.

Biana.—Finch, W. Observations ... in 1607 ... Description of ... B., *etc.* PURCHAS. Vol. I.

Bideford.—SEDGWICK, A., and MURCHISON, SIR R. I. Description of a Raised Beach in Barnstaple or B. Bay, *etc.* **1836.**

Bientina, Lake of.—CIALDI, A. Sul nuovo emissario del Lago di B., *etc.* *Roma*, **1857.**

Bijayanagar.—Nachrichten von Carnate (B.), durch einige Jesuiten-Missionarien. VOYAGES and TRAVELS. Allgemeine Historie, *etc.* Vol. XI.

—— Beschreibung der Königreiche ... Carnate (B.). VOYAGES and TRAVELS. Allgemeine Historie, *etc.* Vol. XVIII.

—— Zusatz zu der Nachricht von Carnate (B.), 1703-36. VOYAGES and TRAVELS. Allgemeine Historie, *etc.* Vol. XVIII.

Billiton.—CROOCKEWIT, J. H. Banka ... en B. ... in 1849-50. *Te Sgrav.*, **1852.**

Binuë, River.—*See* CHADDA.

Birma.—See BURMAH.
Birmingham.—SMITH, W. H. B. and its Vicinity, *etc.* **1836.**
Biscay, Bay of.—DESSIOU, J. F. Le Petit Neptune Français . . . for . . . the B. of B., *etc.* **1805.**
Bisnagar.—See BIJAYANAGAR.
Bissagos.—KERHALLET, C. P. DE. Description Nautique . . . comprenant l'Archipel des B. *Par.*, **1849.**
—— Brue, A. Voyage to the Isles of Bissao and B. . . . in 1700. ASTLEY. Vol. II.
—— Brüe, A. Reise nach den Inseln . . . B., 1700. VOYAGES and TRAVELS. Allgemeine Historie, *etc.* Vol. II.
Bissao.—Brue, A. Voyage to the Isles of B. and Bissagos . . . in 1700. ASTLEY. Vol. II.
—— Reise nach . . . B. . . . 1700. VOYAGES and TRAVELS, Allgemeine Historie, *etc.* Vol. II.
Bithynia.—Smith, T. Historical . . . Account of the City of Prusa in B. HAY, J.
Black Sea.—GRIBERG, COUNT J. Notes statistiques sur le Littoral de la Mer Noire, 1833.
—— PEYSSONNEL, M. DE. Observations . . . sur les peuples barbares qui ont habité les bords . . . du Pont-Euxin. *Par.*, **1765.**
—— MANN, M. L'ABBÉ. Mémoire dans lequel on examine l'opinion . . . que les Mers Noire . . . et Blanche, ont anciennement communiqué ensemble. **1779.**
—— CASPIAN SEA. Description des Pays situés entre la Mer Noire et la Mer Caspienne. *Par.*, **1793.**
—— POTOCKI, COUNT J. Mémoire sur un Nouveau Péryple du Pont Euxin. *Vienne*, **1796.**
—— LECHEVALIER, J. B. Voyage . . . du Pont-Euxin. *Par.*, **1800.**
—— ARRIAN. Voyage round the Euxine Sea, *etc.* **1805.**
—— REUILLY, J. Voyage . . . sur les bords de la Mer Noire . . . 1803, *etc.* *Par.*, **1806.**
—— LAMALLE, M. DUREAU DE. Géographie Physique de la Mer Noire, *etc.* *Par.*, **1807.**
—— BRAUMÜLLER, J. G. Der wichtigste Kanal in Europa, durch eine Vereinigung des Schwarzen Meeres mit der Ost- und Nordsee, *etc.* *Berl.*, **1815.**
—— ANDREOSSY, COUNT. Voyage à l'embouchure de la Mer-Noire, *etc.* *Par.*, **1818.**
—— FLOTTE D'ARGENÇON, COUNT M. DE. Nouveau Portulan de la Méditerranée . . . depuis Cadix jusqu'à la Mer Noire. *Toulon*, **1820.**
—— GRIBERG, COUNT J. Memoria sulle Colonie del Mar Nero. *Pisa*, **1832.**
—— PURDY, J. New Sailing Directory for the . . . B. S., *etc.* **1834.**
—— BLACK SEA. A Geographical . . . account of the Russian Ports of the B. S., *etc.* **1837.**

Black Sea.—Marigny, Chev. Taitbout de. Three Voyages to the B. S., etc. *Lond.*, 1837.

—— Spencer, E. Travels . . . including a Steam Voyage . . . round the B. S., etc. 1837.

—— Birago, Gen. On the projected Canal between the Danube and the B. S. 1839.

—— Fuss, G., and others. Beschreibung der zur Ermittelung des Höhenunterschiedes zwischen dem Schwarzen und dem Caspischen Meere . . . ausgeführten Messungen, etc. *St. Pet.*, 1849.

—— Darondeau, M. B. Tableau Général des Phares et Fanaux des Côtes . . . de la Mer Noire, etc. *Par.*, 1852.

—— Macintosh, A. F. Military Tour . . . on the E.n Shores of the B. S. 1854.

—— Oliphant, L. The Russian Shores of the B. S. in 1852, etc. 1854.

—— Spencer, E. Turkey . . . the B. S., etc. 1854.

—— Wyld, J. Geographical Notes to accompany . . . Maps of . . . the B. S. 1854.

—— Danube. Advantages . . . to the Trade of the D. from . . . a Free Port on the B. S. 1855.

—— Marigny, Chev. Taitbout de. B. S. Pilot. 1855.

—— Tchihatchef, P. de. Considérations historiques sur les phénomènes de congélation constatés dans le Bassin de la Mer Noire. *Versailles*, [1855.]

—— Mediterranean. The Lighthouses of the . . . B. S. . . . Corrected to 1856. 1856.

—— O'Reilly, Comm. Twelve Views in the B. S., etc. 1856.

—— Liddell and Gordon, Messrs. Report on the proposed Railway between the Danube and the B. S., etc. 1857.

—— Mediterranean. The Lights of the . . . B. S. . . . Corrected to 1857, 58, 59. 1857-59.

—— Bergsträsser, Dr. Die Verbindung des Caspischen mit dem Schwarzen Meere. *Gotha*, 1859.

—— Dunsterville, E. The Admiralty List of the Lights of the . . . B. S. . . . Corrected to 1860, 61, 62. 1860-62.

—— Bergsträsser, Dr. De la Réunion de la Mer Caspienne à la Mer Noire. *Par.*, 1861.

—— Gras, M. A. le. Phares de . . . la Mer Noire . . . Corrigés 1862, 63. *Par.*, 1862, 63.

—— Arnold, R. A. From the . . . B. S., etc. *Lond.*, 1868.

—— Biddulph, W. Travels of four Englishmen . . . into . . . the B. S. . . . in 1600 and 1611. Churchill. Vol. VII.

—— Cartlin, Sir J. Travels by way of the B. S. . . . into Persia Proper, 1072. Harris, J. Vol. II.

—— Arriano. Lettera, della sua Navigatione d'intorno al Mar Maggiore. Ramusio. Vol. II.

—— Reuilly, J. Travels . . . along the Shores of the B. S., 1803. Voyages and Travels. A Collection, etc. 1805. Vol. V.

Blenheim.—OXFORD UNIVERSITY and City Guide: to which is added a description of B., etc. *Oxf.*, **1831.**
Blue Mountains.—BURTON, R. F. Goa and the B. M., etc. **1851.**
———— **N. S. W.**—OXLEY, J. Voyages à l'ouest des Montagnes Bleues dans . . . la Nouvelle Galles du Sud, 1817-18. EYRIÈS. Vol. V.
Boca Chica.—PARSONS, J. West India Directory. Sailing directions . . . for B. C., etc. **1854.**
Bodega Bay.—BLAKE, W. P. Observations on the . . . Coast of California, from B. B. to San Diego. *Wash.*, **1855.**
Bœotia.—GELL, SIR W. Itinerary of Greece; containing . . . Routes in . . . B., etc. **1819.**
———— Raikes, Mr. Journal through parts of B., etc. WALPOLE, R. Memoirs, etc.

Boeton.—*See* BOUTONG.
Boghar.—*See* BOKHARA.
Bogota.—GRÄBERG, COUNT J. Recueil de Voyages . . . and Historical Researches on the Conquest of . . . B. . . . in the thirteenth Century, by J. Ranking. **1828.**
———— PARAVEY, CHEV. DE. Mémoire sur l'origine . . . de la Civilisation des Peuples du Plateau de B., etc. *Par.*, **1835.**
———— HUMBOLDT, A. VON. Ueber die Hochebene von B. *Berl.*, **1838.**
Bohemia.—LINDAU, W. A. Vergissmeinnicht. Ein Taschenbuch für . . . Theile Böhmens. *Dresden*, **1823.**
———— KOHL, J. G. Austria . . . B., etc. *Lond.*, **1844.**
———— BATAILLARD, P. Nouvelles recherches sur l'apparition . . . des Bohémiens en Europe. *Par.*, **1849.**
———— HABANT, K. Gesta z Královstvi Ceského do Benátek, etc. *v. Praze*, **1854.**
———— MURCHISON, SIR R. I. On the Gneiss and other Azoic Rocks . . . of . . . B. **1863.**
———— ———— On the Permian Rocks of N.-E. B. **1863.**
———— Browne, E. Voyage . . . to Holland, with a Journey . . . through . . . B. . . . 1668. HARRIS, J. Vol. II.
———— De Bric, J. Appendix to Stolberg's Travels, extracted from a Journey in . . . B in 1804. PELHAM. Vol. II.
———— Salvo, Marquis de. Travels . . . through . . . B. . . . 1806. VOYAGES and TRAVELS. A Collection, etc. 1805. Vol. VI.

Bohus.—*See* GOTTENBURG.
Bojador, Cape.—AVEZAC, D'. Note sur la . . . situation du Mouillage marqué au Sud du Cap du Bugeder. *Par.*, **1846.**
Bokaro.—Hughes, T. W. H. On the B. Coal-Field. INDIA GEOLOGICAL SURVEY. Memoirs. Vol. VI.
Bokhara.—MEYENDORFF, BARON G. DE. Voyage d'Orenbourg à B. . . . 1820, etc. *Par.*, **1826.**
———— BURNES, SIR A. Travels into B., etc. **1834.**
———— GENS, GENERAL MAJOR. Nachrichten über . . . Buchara, etc. *St. Pet.*, **1839.**

Bokhara.—HELMERSEN, G. VON. Nachrichten über . . . Buchara, etc.
St. Pet., 1839.
——— MEYENDORFF, BARON G. DE. Journey of the Russian Mission from Orenbourg to B., etc. *Madras*, 1840.
——— MOORCROFT and TREBECK. Travels . . . in . . . B. . . . 1819 to 1825. 1841.
——— GROVER, J. An Appeal to the British Nation in behalf of Col. Stoddart and Capt. Conolly, now in captivity at B. 1843.
——— KHANIKOFF, N. DE. Description of the Khanate of B. *Russ. St. Pet.*, 1843.
——— GROVER, J. B. Victims. 1845.
——— ——— Lord Aberdeen and the Ameer of B., etc. 1845.
——— KHANIKOFF, N. DE. B.; its Amir, etc. 1845.
——— LAL, MOHAN. Travels . . . to . . . B., etc. 1846.
——— WOLFF, J. Narrative of a Mission to B. in 1843-45, etc. 1846.
——— SÉDILLOT, M. Notice sur une Carte Routière de Meschel à B., etc.
Par., 1852.
——— LAMANSKY, F. Esquisse Géographique . . . et quelques traits des Mœurs des Habitants de B., etc. *Par.* 1858.
——— VAMBÉRY, A. Travels . . . to . . . B., etc. *Lond.*, 1864.
——— Description of . . . Bukhária, etc. ASTLEY. Vol. IV.
——— Travels through . . . Bukhária to . . . China. ASTLEY. Vol. IV.
——— Voyages and Travels of A. Jenkinson from Russia to Boghár . . . in 1557, etc. ASTLEY. Vol. IV.
——— Boukharie. ETHIER. Vol. XIV.
——— Jenkinson, A. Voyage from . . . Mosco . . . to Boghar, etc.
HAKLUYT. Vol. I.
——— Jenkinson's Travels to Bucharia. PINKERTON. Vol. IX.
——— Jenkinson, A. Voyage from . . . Mosco . . . to . . . Boghar, etc. 1558. PURCHAS. Vol. III.
——— Beschreibung der grossen Bokharey. VOYAGES and TRAVELS. Allgemeine Historie, etc. Vol. VII.
——— Jenkinson, A. Reise aus Russland nach . . . B., 1557. VOYAGES and TRAVELS. Allgemeine Historie, etc. Vol. VII.

Bokhara, Little.—*See* KASHGAR.
Bokhara.—*See* BOKHARA.
Bolgárország.—*See* BULGARIA.
Bolivia.—PACIFIC OCEAN. Three Years in the Pacific; containing Notices of . . . B., etc. 1835.
——— PENTLAND, J. B. and PARISH, SIR W. Notices of the Bolivian Andes, etc. *Lond.*, 1836.
——— PERU. Pacto y Ley Fundamental de la Confederacion Péru-Boliviana, 1837.
——— BACH, M. Descripcion . . . de Otuquis en B. *Buen. Aires*, 1843.

Bolivia.—BOLIVIAN ASSOCIATION, a few words on the, etc. 1843.
——— FITZROY, REAR ADML. R. Sailing Directions for . . . B., etc.
1848.
——— DALENCE, J. M. Bosquejo Estadistico de B. *Chuquisaca*, 1851.
——— WEDDELL, H. A. Aperçu d'un Voyage dans le Nord de la Bolivie,
etc. *Paris*, 1853.
——— ——— Voyage dans le Nord de la Bolivie, etc. *Par.*, 1853.
——— BONELLI, L. H. DE. Travels in B., etc. 1854.
——— BOLIVIA. Notizen über den Minenbetrieb in Bolivien, etc.
Berl. [1867.]
Bologna.—BIANCONI, G. Guida . . . per la Città di B., etc. *Bol.*, 1820.
——— ——— Guida di B. 1828.
Bombay.—BOMBAY. An historical account of the Settlement . . . of B.
by the . . . East India Company, etc. 1781.
——— MORIER, J. A Second Journey . . . with a Journal of the voyage
by . . . B. to the Persian Gulf, etc. *Lond.*, 1818.
——— HEBER, BISHOP. Narrative of a Journey . . . from Calcutta to B.,
etc. 1829.
——— BOURCHIER, W. Narrative of a Passage from B. to England, etc.
1834.
——— BOMBAY. Report of the Chamber of Commerce for 1837-40.
Bom., 1838-39.
——— ROBERTS, G. De Delhi à B., etc. *Par.*, 1843.
——— BOMBAY.—Observations made at the . . . Observatory at B. . . .
1846-1862. *Bom.*, 1849-63.
——— BERNCASTLE, DR. A Voyage to China; Including a Visit to the
B. Presidency, etc. *Lond.*, 1850.
——— INDIA. Selections from the Records of the B. Government.
Bom., 1854, etc.
——— BARBER, W. C. On the lighting up . . . B. Harbour, etc.
Bomb., 1862.
——— FERGUSSON, E. F. T. Account of . . . a Cyclone . . . at B., Nov.,
1862. *Bomb.*, 1862.
——— BURGESS, J. Remarks on the B. Tidal Observations for 1861.
1863.
——— ——— Memorandum . . . with lists of the Rock-Excavations,
Temples, &c. in the B. Presidency, etc. *Bomb.*, 1870.
——— B., some reasons for the Unhealthiness of. CHURCHILL. Vol. VI.
——— DALRELL, A. Voyage . . . to B., 1798-99. DALRYMPLE, A. Collection of Nautical Memoirs, etc.
——— Wynne, A. B. On the Geology of the Island of B. INDIA GEOLOGICAL SURVEY. Memoirs. Vol. V.
——— *See also* COLABA.
——— **Island.**—WYNNE, A. B. On Frog-Beds in B. I. INDIA GEOLOGICAL
SURVEY. Memoirs, etc. Vol. VI.

Bon.—TRIPLETT, R. B. Harbour . . . its Advantages, *etc.*
St. Louis, 1849.
Bongo.—Of the Provinces of B., *etc.* PURCHAS. Vol. II.
Bonny, River.—Barbot, J. and Grazilhier, J. Abstract of a Voyage to . . . Bandi and Doni Rivers in 1699. ANTLEY. Vol. III.
——— ——— Beschreibung von einer Seefahrt nach den Flüssen . . . D., 1699. VOYAGES and TRAVELS. Allgemeine Historie, *etc.* Vol. IV.
Bonpland, Cape.—MÜLLER, J. Die Humboldts-Bai und Cap B. in Neu-Guinea ethnographisch und physikalisch untersucht, *etc. Berl.*, 1884.
Boondelas.—*See* BUNDELCUND.
Boorendo Pass.—*See* BURENDA PASS.
Booshuana Nation.—*See* BECHUANAS.
Bootan.—*See* BHOTAN.
Booton.—*See* BOUTONG.
Borandia.—A Voyage . . . containing an Account of . . . B., *etc.*
HARRIS, J. Vol. II.
Bordeaux.—BORDEAUX. Notice sur les Vins de B., *etc. Bord.*, 1834.
Borneo.—EARL, G. W. The Eastern Seas . . . comprising . . . visits to B., *etc.* 1837.
——— Moor, J. H. Notices of . . . B., *etc. Singapore*, 1837.
— — BLUME, C. L. Toelichtingen aangaande de Nasporingen op It. van O. Müller. *Leyden*, 1842.
——— BROOKE, J., RAJAH OF SARAWAK. Letter from B., with notices of the country, *etc.* 1842.
——— BRERETON, C. D. An Address, with a proposal for . . . a Church at Sarawak, on the N. W. Coast of B. 1846.
— — KEPPEL, HON. G. Expedition to B. of H.M.S. *Dido*, *etc.* 1846.
——— FORBES, F. E. Five Years in China . . . with an Account of the Occupation of . . . B., *etc.* 1848.
——— HOOKER, J. D. Notes of a Tour in . . . B., *etc. Lond.*, 1848.
——— MARRYAT, F. S. B. and the Indian Archipelago, *etc. Lond.*, 1848.
— · — MUNDY, R. Narrative of the events in B. . . . down to the occupation of Labuan, *etc.* 1848.
——— CHAMEROVZOW, L. A. B. facts versus B. fallacies, *etc.* 1851.
——— SCHWANER, C. A. L. M. B., beschrijving, *etc. Amst.*, 1853.
——— BELCHER, SIR E. and BATE, W. T. China Pilot . . . Observations on the Coasts of B., *etc.* 1859.
——— BOYLE, F. Adventures among the Dyaks of B. *Lond.*, 1865.
——— Sumatra . . . B., *etc.* EYRIES. Vol. XII.
——— Beeckman's Voyage to B. PINKERTON. Vol. XI.
— — Beschreibung der Insel B. VOYAGES and TRAVELS. Allgemeine Historie, *etc.* Vol. XVIII.
Bornu.—BORNU. Grammar of the B. . . . Language, *etc.* 1853.
——— NORRIS, E. Grammar of the B. or Kanuri language, *etc.*
Lond. 1853.

Borriquen.—*See* Puerto Rico.
Bosforo.—*See* Bosphorus.
Bosnia.—Spencer, E. Travels . . . through B., etc. 1851.
—— Érdy. J. A Boszna és Szerb Régi Érmek. *Pest*, 1858.
—— Thoemmel, G. Geschichtliche . . . Beschreibung des Vilajet Bosnien, etc. *Wien*, 1867.
—— Roumeau, G. Géographie générale de la Bosnie, etc. 1868.
Bosphorus.—Andréossy, Count. Voyage . . . ou Essai sur le Bosphore, etc. *Par.*, 1818.
—— Indizi, L. Villeggiature de' Bizantini sul Bosforo Tracio, etc. *l'eurzia*, 1831.
—— Tchihatcheff, P. de. Dépôts Tertiaires . . . Dépôts Paléozoïques . . . du Bosphore. *Par.*, 1854.
—— Graa, M. A. le. Sailing Directions for . . . the B. 1855.
—— O'Reilly, Comm. Twelve Views in . . . the B., etc. *Lond.*, 1856.
—— M'Pherson, D. Antiquities of Kertch, and Researches in the Cimmerian B., etc. 1857.
—— Tchihatcheff, P. de. Le Bosphore et Constantinople, etc. *Par.*, 1864.
—— Pertusier, C. Picturesque Promenades . . . on . . . the B., 1820. Voyages and Travels, New. 1810, etc. Vol. VIII.
Bosrna.—*See* Bosnia.
Botany Bay.—Phillip, A. Voyage to B. B., etc. 1789.
—— A serious Admonition to the Public on the intended Thief-Colony at B. B. 1786. Dalrymple, A. Tracts, from 1764 to 1808. Vol. II.
—— Philip, Governor. Voyage to B. B., etc. Pelham. Vol. I.
Bothnia, Gulf of.—Ledyard, J. Travels . . . round the G. of B., etc. 1834.
—— —— Djorth, J. Description . . . de l'Entrée du Golfe de B., etc. *Par.*, 1854.
—— —— Klint, G. B. Pilot. 1855.
Boukara, Boukhara, Boukharie.—*See* Bokhara.
Boulac Canal.—Galloway, J. A. Communication with India . . . with remarks on the B. C., etc. 1844.
Boulogne.—Bertrand, P. J. B. Précis de l'histoire . . . de B.-sur-Mer, etc. *Boul.*, 1828, 29.
—— Brunet, J. New Guide to B., etc. *Boul.*, 1858.
Boulonnais.—Topley, W. On the Lower Cretaceous Beds of the Bas-B., etc. 1898.
Bourbon, Island of.—Mauritius. A Voyage to . . . B., etc. *Lond.*, 1775.
—— —— —— Papers . . . relative to the Slave Trade at . . . B. . . . 1811-25. 1826.
—— —— Thomas, P. U. Essai de Statistique de l'Île de B., etc. *Par.*, 1828.

H

Bourbon, Island of — Brazil.

Bourbon, Island of.—Mouat, F. J. Rough Notes of a trip to Reunion, etc. *Calc.*, **1852.**

—————— Beschreibung der Eylande B. und Frankreich. VOYAGES and TRAVELS. Allgemeine Historic, *etc.* Vol. X.

—————— St. Vincent, J. B. G. M. Bory de. Voyage to . . . [B.] 1801-2, *etc.* VOYAGES and TRAVELS. A Collection, *etc.* 1805 Vol. II.

—————— Prior, J. Voyage . . . to . . . D. . . . 1810-11. VOYAGES and TRAVELS, New. 1819. Vol. I.

Boutan.—*See* BHOTAN.

Boutong.—Fifth Voyage, in 1609 . . . Occurrences at . . . Booton, etc. KERR. Vol. VIII.

Brabant.—HEURNITIUS, G. and OBTELIUS, A. Itinerarium . . . Gallo-Brabanticum. *Lugd. Bat.*, **1630.**

—————— VANDER MAELEN, P. Statistique . . . du B., *etc. Bruxels*, **1830.**

Brablisse.—Rivers from B. to the Amazones. PURCHAS. Vol. IV.

Brachmans.—*See* BRAHMINS.

Braemar.—MACGILLIVRAY, W. Natural History of the Dee Side and B. **1855.**

Brahmapootra.—RENNELL, J. Memoir . . . containing an account of the . . . Burrampooter, *etc.* **1785.**

—————— Memoir . . . with an Account of the . . . Burrampooter, etc. **1793.**

Brahmins.—The Learning, discipline . . . and privileges of the Brachmans, *etc.* HARRIS, J. Vol. I.

Bramport.—*See* BURHAMPORE.

Brasill.—*See* BRAZIL.

Brazil.—MARTIUS, C. F. P. DE. Das Naturell . . . der Urbewohner Brasiliens. *München.*

—————— OSORIO, J. History of the Portuguese . . . including also their discovery of the Bs, *etc.* **1752.**

—————— ULLOA, A. DE. Voyage to S. America . . . and an account of the Bs, by J. Adams. **1806.**

—————— MAWE, J. Travels in . . . B., *etc.* **1812.**

—————— CAZAL, P. M. A. DE. Corografia Brazilica, *etc. Rio de Jan.*, **1817.**

—————— KOSTER, H. Travels in B. **1817.**

—————— MORIER, J. A Second Journey . . . with a Journal of the voyage by the Bs . . . to the Persian Gulf. *Lond.*, **1818.**

—————— SHILLIBEER, J. Narrative . . . including a Sketch of the present state of the Bs, *etc.* **1818.**

—————— HENDERSON, J. History of B., *etc.* **1821.**

—————— SPIX, J. B. VON, and MARTIUS, C. F. P. VON. Reise in Brasilien . . . 1817-20. *München*, **1823.**

—————— GRAHAM, M. Journal of a . . . Voyage from Chile to B. in 1823. **1824.**

—————— SPIX, J. B. VON, and MARTIUS, C. F. P. VON. Travels in B. in 1817-20, *etc.* **1824.**

Brazil.

Brazil.—CALDCLEUGH, A. Travels in ... B., etc. 1825.
— MATHISON, G. F. Narrative of a Visit to B., etc. 1825.
— ROUSSIN, CONTRE-AMIRAL LE BARON. Pilote du Brésil, etc.
  Par., 1827.
— MARTIUS, C. F. P. DE. Von dem Rechtszustande unter den Ureinwohnern Brasiliens. Münch., 1832.
— POHL, J. E. Reise im Innern von Brasilien, etc. Wien, 1832.
— DOUVILLE, J. B. Trente Mois de ma Vie ... suivie de détails sur les ... habitans du Brésil, etc. Par., 1833.
— PACIFIC OCEAN. Three years in the Pacific; containing notices of B., etc. 1835.
— HORSBURGH, J. India Directory, or Directions for ... B., etc. 1836.
— SOUSA, L. DE. Diario da Navegação da Armada que foi á ... Brasil, em 1530, etc. Lisboa, 1839.
— VARNHAGEN, F. A. DE. Reflexões Criticas sobre o Escripto do Seculo XIV. Impresso com o titulo de Noticia do Brasil, no tomo 3º da Collecção de Not. Ultr. Lisbon, 1839.
— SANTAREM, VISCOUNT DE. Analyse du Journal de la Navigation de la Flotte qui est allée à la Terre du Brésil en 1530-32, etc. 1840.
— PURDY, J. Brasilian Navigator, etc. 1844.
— HORNER, G. R. B. Medical Topography of B., etc. Phil., 1845.
— ADALBERT, PRINCE. Travels ... in B., etc. 1849.
— MARTIUS, C. F. P. DE. Versuch eines Commentars über die Pflanzen, in den Werken von Marcgrav and Piso über Brasilien. Münch., 1853.
— HADFIELD, W. B., etc. 1854.
— MANSFIELD, C. B. Paraguay, B. ... in 1852-53, etc.
  Camb., 1856.
— AVEZAC, D'. Considérations ... sur ... Brésil, etc.
  Par., 1857.
— JENZSCH, G. Considérations relatives à ... l'Expédition Scientifique Brésilienne. Dresde, 1857.
— KIDDER, D. P. and FLETCHER, J. C. B. and the B.ians, etc.
  Phil., 1857.
— VARNHAGEN, F. A. DE. Examen de quelques points de l'histoire géographique du Brésil, etc. Par., 1858.
— MOURE, J. G. A. and MALTE-BRUN, V. A. Tratado de Geographia ... do B. Par., 1861.
— BRAZIL. Brasilianische Zustände und Aussichten im Jahre 1861, etc. Berl., 1862.
— MARTIUS, C. F. P. DE. Glossaria Linguarium Brasiliensium, etc.
  Erlangen, 1863.
— STUCK, J. J. Neue Beiträge über Brasilien, etc. Berlin, 1865.
— DUNLOP, C. B. as a Field for Emigration, etc. Lond. [1866.]
— SCULLY, W. B.; its Provinces and chief Cities, etc. Lond., 1866.

H 2

Brasil.—BRAZIL. La Politique du Brésil, ou la fermeture des Fleuves, etc. *Par.*, 1867.

—— MARTIUS, C. F. P. VON. Beiträge zur Ethnographie . . . , Brasiliens. *Leipz.*, 1867.

—— AGASSIZ, L. and MRS. A Journey in B. *Bost., Lond.*, 1868.

—— BURTON, R. F. Explorations of the Highlands of the B., etc. *Lond.*, 1869.

—— SCHRAMM, H. C. F. P. v. Martins . . . Insbesondere seine Reiseerlebnisse in Brasilien. *Leipz.*, 1869.

—— Atkins, J. Voyage to . . . B. . . . in 1721. ASTLEY. Vol. II.

—— Nieuhoff, J. Voyages and Travels into B., etc. CHURCHILL. Vol. II.

—— Brésil. EYRIES. Vol. IX.

—— Pert, Sir T. and Cabot, S. Voyage to B. . . . 1516. HAKLUYT. Vol. III.

—— Hare, S. Voyage to B., 1580. HAKLUYT. Vol. IV.

—— Hawkins, W. Voyages to B., 1530-32. HAKLUYT. Vol. IV.

—— Reniger, R. and Borey, T. Voyage to B., 1540. HAKLUYT. Vol. IV.

—— History of the discovery . . . of B. by the Portuguese . . . 1500-1709. HARRIS, J. Vol. II.

—— Pert, Sir T. and Cabot, S. Voyage to B. . . . about 1516. KERR. Vol. VI.

—— Brésil. Etablissements, Description, et Histoire Naturelle. LAHARPE, J. Vol. XII.

—— Nieuhoff's Voyages and Travels into B. PINKERTON. Vol. XIV.

—— Noticia do B., etc. PORTUGAL. Collecção de Noticias, etc. Vol. III.

—— The Second Fleet sent to the E. Indies; their discoveries of B. . . . 1500. PURCHAS. Vol. I.

—— Description of the divers Nations of Savages in B., etc. PURCHAS. Vol. IV.

—— Lerius, J. Extracts out of the Historie of B., 1558. PURCHAS. Vol. IV.

—— A Treatise of B., written by a Portugall, etc. PURCHAS. Vol. IV.

—— Turner, T. Relations of . . . B., etc., about 1601. PURCHAS. Vol. IV.

—— Of Cumana . . . B. . . . and of their Religions. PURCHAS. Vol. V.

—— Discorso d'un gran Capitano di Mare Francese . . . sopra la terra del B., etc. RAMUSIO. Vol. III.

—— Magalhanes de Gandavo, P. de. Histoire de la Province de . . . Brésil, 1576. TERNAUX-COMPANS. Voyages. Vol. II.

—— Atkins, J. Reise nach . . . Brasilien . . . 1721. VOYAGES and TRAVELS. Allgemeine Historie, etc. Vol. III.

—— Carlins Rückreise nach Brasilien und Europa, 1608. VOYAGES and TRAVELS. Allgemeine Historie, etc. Vol. IV.

—— Beschreibung von Brasilien, etc. VOYAGES and TRAVELS. Allgemeine Historie, etc. Vol. XVI.

Brazil.—Küste der Statthalterschaft Rio de la Plata bis nach Brasilien. VOYAGES and TRAVELS. Allgemeine Historie, *etc.* Vol. XVI.

—— Reisen nach Brasilien. Reisen ... der Portugiesen,—der Franzosen,—der Holländer, *etc.* VOYAGES and TRAVELS. Allgemeine Historie, *etc.* Vol. XVI.

—— The Settlement of B. by the Portuguese, *etc.* VOYAGES and TRAVELS. The World displayed. Vol. III.

—— *See* also BAYAO.—PERNAMBUCO.—SAŌ PAULO.

——, **Coast of.**—FREZIER, M. Relation du Voyage de la Mer du Sud aux Côtes ... du Brésil ... 1712-14. *Amst.*, 1717.

—— —— PURDY, J. New Sailing Directions for the ... S. Atlantic Ocean; including the Coasts of B., *etc.* 1837.

—— —— KERHALLET, C. P. de. Instruction pour remonter la Côte du Brésil, *etc.* *Par.*, 1841.

—— —— MONTRAVEL, M. L. de TARDY de. Instructions pour naviguer sur la Côte Septentrionale du Brésil, *etc.* *Par.*, 1847.

—— —— MOUCHEZ, M. Longitudes chronométriques des principaux points de la Côte du B. *Par.*, 1869.

—— —— —— Les Côtes du Brésil, *etc.* *Par.*, 1869.

—— —— Fenton, E. and Ward, L. Voyage to the Coast of B. ... 1582. HAKLUYT. Vol. IV.

—— —— A Ruttier which declareth the situation of the Coast of B., from the Isle of Santa Catalina unto the mouth of the River of Plate, *etc.* HAKLUYT. Vol. IV.

Brazos, River.—MARCY, R. B. Report of his Explorations of the Big Witchita and Head Waters of the B. River. *Wash.*, 1856.

Brecon.—MURCHISON, SIR R. I. The Silurian System, founded on Geological Researches in ... B., *etc.* 1839.

Breslau.—RENCKE, K. C. B. Ein Wegweiser, *etc.* *Bresl.*, 1808.

—— Reinbeck, G. Travels ... through ... B. ... 1805. VOYAGES and TRAVELS. A Collection, *etc.* 1806. Vol. VI.

Brest.—ROUJOUX, H. DE. Essai sur l'atterrage et l'entrée de la Rade de B. par temps brumeux, *etc.* *Par.*, 1866.

Breton, Cape.—SHIRLEY, W. Letter ... with a Journal of ... Operations ... during the Expedition against ... C. B. 1746.

—— **Island.**—PURDY, J. and FINDLAY, A. G. British American Navigator. Sailing Directory for ... B. I., *etc.* 1847.

Bridlington.—PRICKETT, M. History of the Priory Church of B., *etc.* *Camb.*, 1836.

Brimham Crags.—RIPON. The Tourist's Companion; being a ... description ... of ... B. C., *etc.* *Ripon*, 1828.

Brisbane.—LOGAN, P. Journal of a Journey from B. Town to St. George's Pass, *etc.* *Sydney*, 1828-30.

Bristol—OWEN, E. Observations on the Earths ... and Minerals about B. 1754.

—— **Channel.** TELFORD, T. and NICHOLLS, G. Ship Canal for the Junction of the English and B. Channels: Reports, *etc.* 1824.

Bristol Channel.—HUDDART, J. Piloting Directory for B. C., *etc.* **1837.**
——— DENHAM, H. M. Sailing Directions for the B. C. **1839.**
——— WHITE, M. and PURDAY, J. Portulan . . . du Canal de B., *etc.*
Par., **1855.**
Britain, Britannia.—*See* GREAT BRITAIN.
British Colonies.—NAPIER, C. J. The C. . . . generally, *etc.* **1833.**
——— MARTIN, R. M. History of the B. C. **1834-35.**
——— ——— Colonial Policy of the B. Empire. **1837.**
——— ——— Statistics of the Colonies, *etc.* Lond., **1839.**
——— PRIDHAM, C. England's Colonial Empire, *etc.* **1846.**
——— BYRNE, J. C. Twelve Years' Wanderings in the B. C., *etc.* **1848.**
——— SABINE, MAJOR-GEN. E. Observations on Days of Unusual Magnetic Disturbance, made at the B. Colonial Magnetic Observatories . . . 1840-44. **1851.**
——— ——— Some of the Results obtained at the B. Colonial Magnetic Observatories. **1854.**
——— BRITISH COLONIES, The B. C. A Synopsis of their . . . condition, *etc.*
Edinb., **1857.**
——— STATISTICAL TABLES relating to the Colonial . . . Possessions of the United Kingdom. **1862.**
——— **Columbia.**—BROWN, SIR R. European and Asiatic Intercourse *viâ* B. C., *etc.* **1858.**
——— RICHARDS, G. H. Vancouver Island Pilot. Sailing Directions for . . . B. C., *etc.* **1861.**
——— BARRETT-LENNARD, C. E. Travels in B. C., *etc.* **1862.**
——— MACDONALD, D. G. F. B. C. and Vancouver's Island, *etc.* **1862.**
——— MAYNE, R. C. Four Years in B. C., *etc.* Lond., **1862.**
——— RATTRAY, A. Vancouver Island and B. C., *etc.* **1862.**
——— MACFIE, M. Vancouver Island and B. C., *etc.* Lond., **1865.**
——— MILTON, VISCOUNT, and CHEADLE, W. B. The North-West Passage by Land. Being . . . a Route . . . to B. C., *etc.* Lond., [**1865.**]
——— RAWLINGS, T. The Confederation of the British N. American Provinces . . . Including also B. C., *etc.* Lond., **1865.**
——— TRUTCH, J. W. B. C. Overland Coach Road, *etc.*
New Westm., **1866.**
——— **Empire.** *See* GREAT BRITAIN.
——— **Islands.** *See* GREAT BRITAIN.
Brittany.—TROLLOPE, T. A. A Summer in B., *etc.* Lond., [**1840.**]
——— WELD, C. R. A Vacation in B. **1856.**
——— JEPHSON, J. M. Narrative of a Walking Tour in B., *etc.*
Lond., **1859.**
Broang Pass.—*See* DURENDA PASS.
Brosah, Broussa.—*See* BRUSAH.
Brusah.—Smith, T. Historical Account of the City of Prusa, *etc.* RAY, J.

Brussels.—QUETELET, E. Sur l'État de l'Atmosphère à Bruxelles, pendant
. . . 1865. *Brux.*
——— RAZOUMOWSKY, COUNT G. DE. Œuvres. Contenant, Voyage Minéralogique . . . de Bruxelles à Lausanne, *etc.* *Lausanne*, 1784.
——— LOUIS XVIII., KING OF FRANCE. Relation d'un Voyage à Bruxelles et à Coblentz, 1791. *Par.*, 1823.
——— VANDER MAELEN, P. L'Établissement Géographique de Bruxelles. *Brux.*, 1831.
——— ——— Lettre sur l'Etablissement Géographique de D., *etc. Brux.*, 1836.
——— DRAPIEZ, M. Notice sur l'Établissement Géographique de Bruxelles. *Brux.*, 1842.

Buchara, Bucharia.—*See* BOKHARA.

Budukhshan.—*See* BADAKHSHAN.

Buenos Ayres.—DAVIE, J. C. Letters . . . describing . . . B. A., *etc.* 1805.
——— HELMS, A. Z. Travels from B. A. . . . to Lima. 1806.
——— WILCOCK, S. H. History of . . . B. A., *etc.* 1807.
——— VIDAL, E. E. Picturesque Illustrations of B. A., *etc.* 1820.
——— BUENOS AIRES. Registro Estadístico de . . . B. A.
Buen. A., 1822-24.
——— CALDCLEUGH, A. Travels in . . . B. A., *etc.* 1825.
——— ANDREWS, CAPT. Journey from B. A. . . . to Potosi, *etc.* 1827.
——— DOUVILLE, J. B. Trente Mois de ma Vie . . . suivis de détails sur les . . . habitans . . . de B. A., *etc.* *Par.*, 1833.
——— SCARLETT, HON. P. C. South America . . . comprising a Journey . . . from B. A. to Valparaiso, *etc.* 1838.
——— PARISH, SIR W. B. A. and the Provinces of the Rio de la Plata, *etc.* 1839.
——— ——— B. A. and the Provinces of the Rio de la Plata, *etc.* 1852.
——— ——— Buenos Aires y las Provincias del Rio de la P., *etc. Buen. A.*, 1853.
——— BONELLI, L. H. DE. Travels . . . across the Pampas to B. A. 1854.
——— DALGARCE, M. B.-A.; sa situation présente, *etc. Par.*, 1857.
——— HEUSSER, J. C. and CLARAZ, G. Beiträge zur . . . Kenntniss der Provinz B. A. *Zurich*, 1864.
——— MOUSSY, M. DE. Voyage à la Frontière Indienne de B.-A. en 1863. [*Par.*, 1864.]
——— HUTCHINSON, T. J. B. A. and Argentine Gleanings, *etc. Lond.*, 1865.
——— BUENOS AIRES. Registro Estadístico de Buenos Aires. 1864. *Buen. A.*, 1866.
——— HANNAH, J. Review of "Sheep Farming in B. A.," *etc. Buen. A.*, 1867.

Buenos Ayres.—Beschreibung . . . der Stadt B. A. Voyages and Travels. Allgemeine Historie, etc. Vol. XVI.

―――― Helms, A. Z. Travels from B. A. . . . to Lima, etc. Voyages and Travels. A Collection, etc. 1805. Vol. V.

―――― Brackenridge, H. M. Voyage to B. A., 1817-18. Voyages and Travels, New. 1819. Vol. III.

―――― See also Argentine Confederation.—La Plata.

Bugeder, Cap du.—See Bojador.
Buhawulpoor.—See Bahawulpore.
Bukhara, Bukharey, Bukhâria.—See Bokhara.
Bukovina.—See Bukowina.
Bukowina.—Kohl, J. G. Austria . . . B., etc.   Lond., 1844.
Bulgaria.—Spencer, E. Travels . . . through . . . B., etc.   1851.

―――― Moltke, Baron von. The Russians in B. . . . in 1828-29. 1854.

―――― Kiss, K. Hunyadi János Utolsó Hadjárata Bolgár és Szerborszagban 1454-ben, etc.   Pest, 1857.

―――― Jackson, J. Journey . . . in 1797, through . . . B., etc. Pelham. Vol. II.

Bulka.—Döllen, W. Resultate einer astronomisch-geodätischen Verbindung zwischen Pulkowa und den Ufern des Ladogasees.   1858.

Bullom.—Nylander, G. R. Grammar . . . of the B. Language. 1814.

Bundelcund.—Pogson, Captain W. R. A History of the Boondelas. Calc., 1828.

―――― Mallet, F. R. Copper in B. India Geological Survey. Records, etc. Vol. I.

Bundelkhand, Bundlecund.—See Bundelcund.
Buona Esperanza, Cape.—See Cape of Good Hope.
Burdekin, River.—Dalrymple, G. E. Report of the proceedings of the . . . Spitfire, in search of the Mouth of the . . . B., etc.
Brisb., 1860.

―――― ―――― Mueller, F. Victoria. Essay on the Plants collected . . . during Lieut. Smith's Expedition to the Estuary of the B.
Melb., 1860.

―――― ―――― Smith, J. W. and Dalrymple, G. E. Report of the Proceedings of the . . . Spitfire, in search of the Mouth of the River B., etc. Brisbane, 1860.

Burenda Pass.—Lloyd, Sir W. Narrative of a Journey from Caunpoor to the Boorendo Pass, etc.   Lond., 1840.

Burhampooter.—See Brahmapootra.
Burhampore.—Report of W. Nicols, which travelled by land from Bramport to Masulipatan . . . 1612. Purchas. Vol. I.

Burhou.—Alderney. The Alderney Island Pilot; comprising . . . B., etc.
Lond., 1864.

―――― Aldernet. Routier de l'Ile Aurigny, comprenant . . . B., etc.
Par., 1865.

Burmah.—Cox, H.—Journal of a Residence in the Burman Empire, *etc.*
 1821.
——— Alexander, Sir J. E. Travels ... to the Burman Empire, *etc.*
 1827.
——— Snodgrass, Major. Narrative of the Burmese War, *etc.* 1827.
——— Berghaus, H. Asia ... nebst Bemerkungen über die nördlichen Provinzen des Birma-Reichs, *etc.* *Gotha*, 1832-35.
——— Sangermano, Rev. Father. Description of the Burmese Empire, *etc.* *Rome*, 1833.
——— Griffith, W. Journals of Travels in ... B., *etc.* *Calc.*, 1847.
——— Spete, R. H. F. and C. H. F. The British and China Railway ... through ... B., *etc.* 1858.
——— Winter, C. T. Six Months in British B., *etc.* [*Lond.*] 1858.
——— Blandford, W. T. Account of a Visit to Puppá-doung ; an extinct Volcano in Upper B. *Calc.*, 1862.
——— Williams, C. Memorandum on the Question of British Trade with W.n China *viâ* B. 1864.
——— ——— Through B. to W.n China, *etc.* *Edin. and Lond.*, 1868.
——— Jenkins, H. L. Notes on the Burmese Route from Assam to the Hookoong Valley. 1869.
——— McLeod, W. C. Copy of Papers relating to ... the Route of Dr. Richardson on his Fourth Mission to the Shan Provinces of B., *etc.*
 Lond., 1869.
——— Empire Burman. Symes. Cox. Eyries. Vol. XIII.

Burrampooter.—*See* Brahmapootra.
Bursah.—*See* Brusah.
Burtscheid.—Dildessec, L. von. Wegweiser für ... B., *etc.*
 Aachen, 1825.
Bury Saint Edmund's.—Battely, J. Opera posthuma. Antiquitates S. Edmundi Burgi, *etc.* *Oxon.*, 1745.
Bushehr.—*See* Bushire.
Bushire.—Pelly, L. Remarks on ... the Country between B. and Shiraus, *etc.* *Bomb.*, 1863.
Busserah, Bussora.—*See* Bassorah.
Butan.—*See* Bhotan.
Byana.—*See* Biana.
Bythinia.—Biddulph, W. Travels of four Englishmen ... into ... B. ... in 1600 and 1611. Churchill. Vol. VII.

C.

Cabenda.—Abstract of a Voyage to ... Kabinda in 1700, by J. Barbot and J. Cassenueve. Astley. Vol. III.
——— Barbot, J., and Casseneure, J. Auszug aus einer Reise ... nach Kabinda, 1700. Voyages and Travels. Allgemeine Historie, *etc.* Vol. IV.

Cabool.—See KABOOL.
Cabo-Verde.—See Cape Verde.
Cabul.—See KABOOL.
Cachao.—BRUE, A. Journey from Albreda to Kachao ... in 1700. ASTLEY. Vol. II.

—— Brüe, A. Reise von Albreda ... nach Kachao zu Lande, 1700. VOYAGES and TRAVELS. Allgemeine Historie, etc. Vol. II.

Cachemir.—See CASHMERE.
Cachao.—See CACHAO.
Caconga.—See CACONGO.
Cacongo.—Proyart's History of ... Kakongo, etc. PINKERTON. Vol. XVI.

Cadiz.—FLOTTE D'ARGENÇON, COUNT M. DE. Nouveau Portulan de la Méditerranée ... depuis Cadix jusqu'à la Mer Noire.
Toulon, 1820.

—— Drake, Sir F. Voyage to C. ... 1587. HAKLUYT. Vol. II.

—— The honourable Voyage to C., 1590. HAKLUYT. Vol. II.

—— A briefe and true report of the honourable Voyage unto C., 1590, etc. PURCHAS. Vol. IV.

Caen.—TOUSSAINT, M. Indicateur complet de la Ville de C., etc.
Caen, 1835.

Caermarthen.—MURCHISON, Sir R. I. The Silurian System, founded on Geological Researches in ... C., etc. 1839.

Caesarea.—FALCONER, W. Dissertation on St. Paul's Voyage from C. to Puteoli, etc. *Oxf.*, 1817.

—— Dissertation on St. Paul's Voyage from C. to Puteoli, etc.
Lond., 1870.

Caffraria.—PATERSON, W. A Narrative of Four Journeys into ... C. In ... 1777, 78, 79. *Lond.*, 1789.

—— BOYCE, W. B. Grammar of the Kafir language.
Graham's T., 1834.

—— KAFFIR WAR, Summary of the, of 1834-5, etc. *Cape T.*, 1836.

—— ALEXANDER, Sir J. E. Narrative ... of a Campaign in Kaffir Land, etc. 1837.

—— COOLEY, W. D. Negroland of the Arabs examined, etc. 1841.

—— KING, R. W. Campaigning in Kaffirland, etc. 1855.

Cairo.—BUSCO, G. B. DE. Viaggio ... Con la descrittione di ... Gran C., etc. *Milano* [1686.]

—— CLOGHER, ROBERT, BISHOP OF. A Journal from Grand C. to Mount Sinai, etc. *Lond.*, 1753.

—— HORNEMAN, F. Travels from C. to Mourzouk ... in 1797, 8. 1802.

—— MAUNDRELL, H. Journey ... from Grand C. to Mount Sinai, etc. 1810.

—— JOMARD, E. F. Jours de pluie observés au Caire. *Par.*, 1839.

Cairo.—KINNEAR, J. C. . . . in 1839, etc.   *Lond.*, **1841.**
——— BARTLETT, W. H. Forty days in the Desert . . . a Journey from C., etc.   **1851.**
——— CLAYTON, BP. R. Journal from Grand C. to Mount Sinai, etc.
                 Lond., **1853.**
——— Aldersey, L. Voyage to . . . C. . . . 1580. HAKLUYT. Vol. II.
——— Cairo, Journey from, to Mount Sinai. PINKERTON. Vol. X.
——— Sanderson, J. Voyages to . . . C. . . . 1584-1602. PURCHAS. Vol. II.
——— Timberley, H. Report of the Voyage from C. . . . to Jerusalem, 1601. PURCHAS. Vol. II.
——— Viaggio scritto per un Comito Venetiano . . . fino al Diu . . . col suo ritorno poi al C., 1537-8. RAMUSIO. Vol. I.
——— Journey from Grand C. to Mecca. RAY, J.

Calabar, River, New.—Barbot, J., and Grazilhier, J. Abstract of a Voyage to New Kalabar . . . in 1699. ASTLEY. Vol. III.
——— ———— Beschreibung von einer Seefahrt nach den Flüssen Neu-Kalabar, etc. 1699. VOYAGES and TRAVELS. Allgemeine Historie, etc. Vol. IV.
——— ———, Old.—The Coast, from O. Kalabar R. to Cape Lope Gonsalvo. ASTLEY. Vol III.
——— Gonsalvo, L. Die Küste vom Alt-Kalabarflusse nach dem Vorgebirge. VOYAGES and TRAVELS. Allgemeine Historie, etc. Vol. IV.

Calabria.—FIORE, R. P. G. Della C. illustrata, opera varia, etc.
                 Napoli, **1691.**
——— CALABRIA. Istoria . . . del Tremoto avvenuto nelle Calabrie . . . 1783, etc.   *Napoli*, **1784.**
——— CALABRIA, during a Military Residence of Three Years, etc.
                 Lond., **1832.**
——— LEAR, E. Journals of a Landscape Painter in S.n C., etc. **1852.**
——— Dolomieu's Account of the Earthquakes in C. in 1783. PINKERTON. Vol. V.

Calamina.—*See* ST. THOME.

Calcutta.—PLAISTED, B. Journal from C. . . . to Busserah, etc. **1758.**
——— HEBER, BISHOP. Narrative of a Journey . . . from C. to Bombay, etc.   **1829.**
——— LUSHINGTON, MRS. C. Narrative of a Journey from C. to Europe, etc.   **1829.**
——— LEIGH, W. H. Reconnoitering Voyages . . . including visits to . . . C., etc.   *Lond.*, **1839.**
——— MARTIN, J. R. Official Report on the Medical Topography and Climate of C., etc.   *Calc.*, **1839.**
——— LEIGH, W. H. Reconnoitering Voyages . . . including visits to . . . C., etc.   **1840.**
——— EDEN, HON. A. Evidence of, taken before the Indigo Commission sitting in C.   *Calc.*, **1860.**

108   Calcutta — California.

Calcutta.—CALCUTTA. Cyclone Report.   *Calc.*, **1865.**
——— GASTRELL, J. E., and BLANFORD, H. F. Report on the C. Cyclone
   of the 5th October, 1864.   *Calc.*, **1866.**
——— CALCUTTA. Abstract of the Results of the Hourly Meteorological
   Observations taken at . . . C., etc.   [**1869.**]
Caldea.—*See* CHALDEA.
Calemplny.—Pinto, F. M. Reisen nach . . . der Insel C., etc. VOYAGES
   and TRAVELS. Allgemeine Historie, etc. Vol. X.
Callout.—Payton, W. Voyage . . . in 1615. Occurrences at C., etc.
   KERR. Vol. IX.
——— Gama's Acts at C., etc. PURCHAS. Vol. I.
——— Alvarez, P. Navigatione da Lisbona in C. RAMUSIO. Vol. I.
——— Gama, V. di. Navigatione . . . fino in C., 1497. RAMUSIO.
   Vol. I.

California.—BLAKE, W. P. On the . . . Geology of C., etc.   *Wash.*
——— WYLD, J. Notes on the Distribution of Gold throughout . . . C.,
   etc.
——— CHAPPE D'AUTEROCHE, J. Voyage en Californie, etc. *Par.*, **1772.**
——— AUTEROCHE, ABBÉ CHAPPE D'. A Voyage to C., etc.   *Lond.*, **1778.**
——— CLAVIGERO, F. S. Storia della C.   *Venezia*, **1789.**
——— BENNETT, F. D. Narrative . . . comprising Sketches of . . . C.,
   etc.   **1840.**
——— GREENHOW, R. The History of . . . C., etc.   *Bost. U. S.*, **1844.**
——— MOFRAS, DUFLOT DE. Exploration du Territoire . . . des Cali-
   fornies, etc.   *Par.*, **1844.**
——— KING, T. B. C. : the Wonder of the Age, etc.   *N. Y.*, **1850.**
——————— Report on C.   *Wash.*, **1850.**
——— SMITH, GEN. P. F., and RILEY, GEN. B. Report on the Geology
   and Topography of C.   *Wash.*, **1850.**
——— TYSON, P. T. Report in relation to the Geology and Topography of
   C.   *Wash.*, **1850.**
——— BRODIE, W. Pitcairn's Island . . . and a few hints upon C., etc.
                                                                     1851.
——— HOFFMAN, D. The Fremont Estate; an Address to the British
   Public, etc.   **1851.**
——— RYAN, W. R. Personal Adventures in Upper and Lower C., in
   1848-9.   **1851.**
——— COKE, HON. H. J. A Ride . . . to . . . C., etc.   **1852.**
——— HOFFMAN, D. C. Fremont's Estates, etc.   **1852.**
——— MAYER, B. Mexico . . . Notices of . . . C.
                                                         Hartf. U. S., **1852.**
——— HOLINSKI, A. La Californie et les Routes Interocéaniques.
                                                             Brux., **1853.**
——— BARTLETT, J. R. Personal . . . explorations . . . in . . . C.,
   etc.   *N. Y.*, **1854.**

California.—CAPRON, E. S. History of C., etc. *Bost.*, 1854.
——— WILLIAMSON, R. S. Report of a Reconnaissance and Survey in C., etc. *Wash.*, 1854.
——— WILSON, J. S. On the Gold Regions of C. 1854.
——— BLAKE, W. P. Description of . . . Fossils and Shells collected in C. *Wash.*, 1855.
——— ——— Observations on . . . the Coast of C. from Bodega Bay to San Diego. *Wash.*, 1855.
——— ——— On the Rate of Evaporation on the Tulare Lakes of C. *Wash.*, 1856.
——— FREMONT, J. C. Life . . . and Adventures in . . . C., etc. *N. Y.*, 1856.
——— TRASK, J. B. Report on the Geology of Northern and Southern C., etc. *Wash.*, 1856.
——— BORTHWICK, J. D. Three Years in C. *Edinb.*, 1857.
——— SEYD, E. C. and its Resources, etc. 1858.
——— BURTON, R. F. City of the Saints and across the Rocky Mountains to C. 1861.
——— HUTCHINGS, J. M. Scenes of Wonder . . . in C. *Lond.*, 1865.
——— UNION PACIFIC RAILROAD: the great National Highway between the Missouri River and C., etc. *Chicago*, 1868.
——— Drake, Sir F. Voyage . . . from . . . Guatulco . . . to the N.W. of C., etc. HAKLUYT. Vol. III.
See also MONTEREY.—SIERRA NEVADA.
———, **Gulf of.**—MOREAU, DUFLOT DE. Exploration . . . de la Mer Vermeille, etc. *Par.*, 1844.
——— ——— DERBY, G. H. Report of the Reconnaissance of the G. of C. . . . made in 1850-51. *Wash.*, 1852.
——— ——— Alarchon, F. Voyage . . . to the bottome of the Gulfe of C. . . . 1540. HAKLUYT. Vol. III.
——— ——— Ulloa, F. de. Voyage . . . into the G. of C. . . . 1539. HAKLUYT. Vol. III
——— ——— Ulloa, F. Navigatione per discoprire l'Isole delle Specierie fino al Mare detto Vermeio, 1532-39. RAMUSIO. Vol III.
———, **North.**—FREMONT, J. C. Report of the Exploring Expedition to . . . N. C. in 1843-4. *Wash.*, 1845.
———, **Upper.**— ——— Geographical Memoir upon Upper C., etc. *Wash.*, 1848.
——— ——— KUNZEL, H. Ober-Californien; eine geographische Schilderung, etc. *Darmst.*, 1848.
——— ——— *See also* SAN DIEGO.
Callao.—LIMA. A True . . . Relation of the . . . Earthquake . . . at . . . C., on the 28th October, 1740, etc. 1748.
——— Reisen von dem Hafen C. nach Europa, etc. VOYAGES and TRAVELS, Allgemeine Historie, etc. Vol. IX.

Callirhoe.—See OBYAH.

Calongo.—Of the Provinces of Bongo, C., etc. PURCHAS. Vol. II.

Calvados.—MOSCROVE, G. M. Ramble through Normandy; or Scenes ... in a Sketching Excursion through C. *Lond.*, 1855.

Camanche.—ABERT, LIEUT. J. W. Report of an expedition ... through the country of the C. Indians in 1845. *Wash.*, 1846.

Camaroons Mountains.—BURTON, R. F. Abeokuta and the C. M., etc. 1863.

Cambaia.—See CAMBAY.

Cambalu.—See PEKING.

Cambat.—TELLEZ, B. Travels ... and an Account of ... C., etc. 1710.

Cambate.—See CAMBAT.

Cambay.—Fitch, R. The long ... voyage of ... to ... Cambaia, etc., 1583-1591. HAKLUYT. Vol. II.

——— ——— Voyage ... to C. ... 1583-01. PURCHAS. Vol. II.

Cambodia.—HIMACHÈRE, M. DE LA. État actuel ... des royaumes de Camboge, etc. *Par.*, 1812.

——— SPRYE, R. H. F., and C. H. F. The British and China Railway; from ... Rangoon ... to ... C., etc. 1858.

——— MOUHOT, H. Travels in ... C., etc. *Lond.*, 1864.

——— THOMSON, G. The Antiquities of C., etc. *Edin.*, 1867.

——— ——— Notes on C. and its Races. 1867.

——— Beschreibung der Königreiche Laos und C., 1691. VOYAGES and TRAVELS. Allgemeine Historie, etc. Vol. XVIII.

———, **River.**—See MEKONG.

Camboge, Cambogia, Camboja.—See CAMBODIA.

Cambria.—See WALES.

Cambridge, Mass.—PEIRCE, B. The Latitude of the C. Observatory ... determined, etc.

Cameroons, River.—AFRICA. Africa Pilot ... from Cape Spartel to the River C. 1858.

Campeachy.—Parker, W. Voyage to Margarita ... with his surprise of Campeche ... 1596-07. HAKLUYT. Vol. IV.

Campeche.—See CAMPEACHY.

Canaan.—See PALESTINE.

Canada.—LAHONTAN, BARON. New Voyages ... a ... description of C., etc. 1703-35.

——— CHARLEVOIX, PÈRE DE. Histoire et description ... do la Nouvelle France, etc. *Par.*, 1744.

——— BARTRAM, J. Observations on ... C., etc. 1751.

——— VOLNEY, C. F. Tableau ... des États-Unis d'Amérique; suivi d'éclaircissemens ... sur quelques Colonies Canadiennes, etc. *Par.*, 1803.

——— ——— AMERICA. Excursion through ... C., etc. 1824.

Canada.

Canada.—HODGSON, A. Letters ... written during a Tour in ... C. 1824.

——— DE ROOS, HON. F. F. Personal Narrative of Travels in ... C., etc. 1827.

——— CANADA.—Estimates of the Expense of ... Water Communications in the C.s, etc. 1828.

——— HEAD, G. Forest Scenes ... from Halifax to the C.s, etc. 1829.

——— CANADA. Reports of the Committee of Roads and Public Improvements. Quebec, 1831.

——— BOUCHETTE, J. The British dominions in N. America ... a ... description ... of Lower and Upper C., etc. 1832.

——— RICHARDS, J. Report ... respecting the Waste Land in the C.s, etc. 1832.

——— FINCH, J. Travels in ... C., etc. 1833.

——— LEBRUN, I. Tableau statistique ... des Deux C.s. Par., 1833.

——— DAVISON, G. M. Traveller's Guide through ... C. Saratoga Springs, 1840.

——— PRESTON, T. R. Three Years' Residence in C., etc. 1840.

——— DE VEAUX, S. The Traveller's Own Book to ... C., etc. Buf., 1841.

——— BARTLETT, W. H. Canadian Scenery Illustrated, etc. 1842.

——— TANNER, H. S. The Traveller's Handbook for ... C. N. Y., 1844.

——— GARNEAU, F. X. Histoire du C., etc. Queb., 1845.

——— LYELL, SIR C. Travels ... with Geological Observations on ... C., etc. 1845.

——— BONNYCASTLE, SIR R. H. C. ... in 1846. 1846.

——— CANADA. British Colonies in America. C., etc. 1847.

——— BIGSBY, J. J. The Shoe and Canoe; or ... Travel in the C.s. 1850.

——— WARBURTON, E. Conquest of C. 1850.

——— SMITH, W. C.; Past, Present, and Future, etc. Toronto, 1851.

——— WILLIAMS, W. Traveller's ... Guide through ... C., etc. Phil., 1851.

——— LACHLAN, R. On the periodical Rise and Fall of the Great Canadian Lakes. Toronto, 1854.

——— HOGAN, J. S. Le C. Essai, etc. Montreal, 1855.

——— WELD, C. R. Vacation Tour in the United States and C. 1855.

——— MURRAY, HON. A. M. Letters from ... C. 1856.

——— SHAW, J. Ramble through ... C., etc. 1856.

——— CANADA. Appendix to Report of the Commissioner of Crown Lands. Toronto, 1857.

——— ——— C. Directory for 1857-58, etc. Montreal, 1857.

——— MURRAY, HON. H. A. Lands of the Slave and the Free; or Cuba ... and C. 1857.

Canada.

Canada.—CANADA. Geological Survey of C. Report of Progress . . . 1853-58. *Toronto*, 1857-58.

—— JESUITS. Relations des Jésuites, contenant ce qui s'est passé . . . dans les Missions . . . dans la Nouvelle France, 1611 à 1672.
Québec, 1858.

—— HOPE, H. The Canadian Settlers' Guide. 1860.
—— GIBB, G. D. On Canadian Caverns. 1861.
—— KOHL, J. G. Travels in C., etc. *Lond.*, 1861.
—— KING, W. R. The Sportsman and Naturalist in C., etc.
Lond., 1866.

—— CARTIER, J. Relation originale du Voyage de Jacques Cartier au C. en 1534, etc. *Par.*, 1867.

—— BROWN, R. A History . . . of the Discovery . . . of C., etc.
Lond., 1869.

—— CANADA. Second Report . . . on Immigration and Colonization.
Ottawa, 1869.

—— Nova Francia; or the description of . . . New France, etc. CHURCHILL. Vol. VIII.

—— C. ETBIÂR. Vol. VIII.

—— La Roche, J. F. de. Voyage . . . to . . . C. . . . 1542. HAKLUYT. Vol. III.

—— Cartier, J. Voyages . . . to . . . C. . . . 1534-37. KERR. Vol. VI.

—— Cartier's Discovery of New France. PINKERTON. Vol. XII.

—— Lahontan's Travels in C. PINKERTON. Vol. XIII.

—— Champlaine, S. Voyage made unto C., 1603. PURCHAS. Vol. IV.

—— Collections out of a French Booke, called Additions to Nova Francia; containing the accidents there, from 1607-11. PURCHAS. Vol. IV.

—— Lescarbot, M. Voyage into New France . . . 1603-9. PURCHAS. Vol. IV.

—— Notes of Voyages and Plantations of the French . . . in . . . C., 1524-82. PURCHAS. Vol. IV.

—— Of New France . . . with other Regions . . . and of their Religions. PURCHAS. Vol. V.

—— Carthier, J. Prima Relatione della . . . Nuova Francia, 1534. RAMUSIO. Vol. III.

—— Seconda Relatione, della navigatione per lui fatta all' Isole di C., etc. RAMUSIO. Vol. III.

—— Discorso d'un gran Capitano di Mare Francese, sopra le navigationi fatte alla Nuova Francia, etc. RAMUSIO. Vol. III.

—— Charlevoix, P. F. X. Beschreibung von Neu-Frankreich, etc. VOYAGES and TRAVELS. Allgemeine Historie, etc. Vol. XIV.

—— Beschreibung . . . von C., etc. VOYAGES and TRAVELS. Allgemeine Historie, etc. Vol. XVI.

—— Heriot, G. Travels through the C., etc. VOYAGES and TRAVELS. A Collection, etc., 1805. Vol. VII.

Canada — Canary Islands.   113

Canada.—*See also* OTTAWA.
———, **Lower.**—BOUCHETTE, J. Topographical Dictionary of ... L. C.
  1832.
——— ——— TEMPLETON, F. Statement ... on the Eastern Townships
  of L. C. 1838.
——— ——— Sanson, J. 'Travels in L. C., 1817. VOYAGES and TRAVELS,
  New. 1819. Vol. III.
———, **River of.**—*See* SAINT LAWRENCE.
———, **Upper.**—BANISTER, J. W. On Emigration to U. C., *etc.* 1831.
——— ——— CANADA, UPPER. Letters from Settlers in U. C., *etc.*
  1831.
——— ——— CANADA, UPPER. Report on the Indians of U. C., *etc.*
  1839.
——— ——— CANADA, UPPER. Remarks on U. C. Surveys, *etc.*
  Quebec, 1861.
Canara.—HAMILTON, F. Journey ... through ... C., *etc.* 1807.
——— Buchanan's Journey through C., *etc.* PINKERTON. Vol. VIII.
Canaries.—*See* CANARY ISLANDS.
Canary Island.—The Conquest of the Grand Canaries ... 1599.
  HAKLUYT. Vol. V.
——— Benzoni, G. History of the New World ... with some particulars of the Island of C. ... edited by Rear-Adm. W. H. Smyth.
  1857. HAKLUYT Soc. PUB. Vol. XXI.
——— **Islands.**—GLAS, G. History of the Discovery and Conquest of the
  C. I., *etc.* 1764.
——— MACGREGOR, F. C. Die Canarischen Inseln nach ihren gegenwärtigen Zustande. *Hannover*, 1831.
——— BUCH, L. VON. Description physique des Îles Canaries, *etc.*
  Par., 1836.
——— PURDY, J. Brazilian Navigator ... with ... Directions for
  the ... C. ... I., *etc.* 1844.
——— AVEZAC, D'. Note sur la première expédition de Béthencourt aux
  Canaries, *etc.* *Par.*, 1846.
——— KERHALLET, C. P. DE. Description ... des Canaries, *etc.*
  Par., 1851.
——— HADFIELD, W. Brazil ... including notices of ... the C., *etc.*
  1854.
——— KERHALLET, C. P. DE. Description Nautique ... des Canaries.
  Par., 1858.
——— MURRAY, Mrs. E. Sixteen Years ... in ... the C. I. 1859.
——— Nichols, T. Description of the C. I., *etc.* ASTLEY. Vol. I.
——— Roberts, G. Account of a Voyage to ... the C. ... in 1721.
  ASTLEY. Vol. I.
——— Le Maire, Sieur. Voyages of, to the C. I., *etc.* CHURCHILL.
  Vol. VIII.

I

Canary Islands.—Account of the discovery and conquest of the C. I. KERR. Vol. II.

―――― Voyages des Anglais . . . dans les Îles Canaries. LAHARPE, J. Vol. I.

―――― Glas's History of the C. I. PINKERTON. Vol. XVI.

― ― Nicols, T. Beschreibung der Canarischen Eylande . . . 1560. VOYAGES and TRAVELS. Allgemeine Historie, *etc.* Vol. II.

― ― Roberts, G. Bericht von einer Reise nach den Canarieninseln . . . 1721. VOYAGES and TRAVELS. Allgemeine Historie, *etc.* Vol. II.

― ― Le Maire. Reise nach den Canarieninseln . . . 1682. VOYAGES and TRAVELS. Allgemeine Historie, *etc.* Vol. III.

―――― St. Vincent, J. B. G. M. Bory de. Voyage to . . . the . . . [C.] 1801-2, *etc.* VOYAGES and TRAVELS. A Collection, *etc.* 1805. Vol. II.

Canavese.—*See* IVREA.

Candia.—*See* CRETE.

Canelos.—PERU. Documentos . . . que acreditan la posesion del Peru sobre los Territorios de . . . C., *etc.*   *Lima*, **1860**.

Canning River.—GOWEN, J. R. Hints on Emigration to the Swan and C. Rivers, *etc.*   **1829**.

Canterbury.—CANTERBURY GUIDE, *etc.*   *Cant.*, **1830**.

―――― **New Zealand.**—DOYNE, W. T. Report upon the Plains and Rivers of C., N. Z.   *Christch.*, **1864**.

―――― ―――― HAAST, J. Report on the formation of the C. Plains. *Christch.*, **1864**.

―――― ――― ――― ――― Report on the Geological Survey of . . . C. *Christch.*, **1864**.

Canton.—MORTIMER, G. Observations . . . during a Voyage to . . . C., *etc.*   *Lond.*, **1791**.

― ― BARROW, SIR J. Travels . . . from Pekin to C.   **1804**.

― ― ELLIOTT, R. Views in the East; comprising . . . C., *etc.*   **1833**.

―――― Journey of A. Gaubil . . . from Kanton to Peking in 1722. ASTLEY. Vol. III.

―――― Journey of J. Bouvet . . . from Peking to Kanton . . . in 1693. ASTLEY. Vol. III.

Cany.—NOEL, S. B. J. Premier Essai sur . . . C., *etc.*   *Rouen*, **1795**.

Cap de Bonne-Esperance.—*See* CAPE OF GOOD HOPE.

Cape Breton.—BOUCHETTE, J. The British dominions in N. America . . . a . . . description of C. B., *etc.*   **1832**.

―――― BROWN, R. A History of the Island of C. B., *etc.* *Lond.*, **1869**.

― ― Fisher, R. Voyage . . . unto C. B. . . . 1593. HAKLUYT. Vol. III.

― ― Hore, M. Voyage to . . . C. B., in 1536. HAKLUYT. Vol. III.

― ― Leigh, C. Voyage to Cape B . . . 1597. HAKLUYT. Vol. III.

―――― **Coast Castle.**—CAPE COAST CASTLE. Letters from C. C. C. . . . March, 1767, to March, 1769. *MS.*

Cape Coast Castle — Cape of Good Hope. 115

Cape Coast Castle.—Letters . . . to the Governors, Council, &c. of C. C. C. . . . Aug. 21st, 1751, to Nov. 10th, 1768. *MS.*

—— Bowditch, T. E. Mission from C. C. C. to Ashantee, *etc.* 1819.

—— Freeman, T. B. Extracts from the Journal of . . . a visit from C. C. to Ashantee, *etc.* 1840.

—— Bowdich, T. E. Mission from C. C. C. to Ashantee, 1817. Voyages and Travels, New. 1819. Vol. I.

— - **Colony.**—*See* Cape of Good Hope.

— - **de Verde Islands.**—*See* Cape Verde Islands.

    Horn.—Hadfield, W. Brazil . . . with the C. H. Route to Australia, *etc.* 1854.

— - **Monday.**—Byron, Comm. Voyage . . . to . . . C. M. . . . 1764-66. Hawkesworth, J. Vol. I.

   - **Negro.**—Africa. Renseignements sur la partie de la Côte entre le Cap N. et le Cap Lopez. *Par.*, 1850.

— - **of Good Hope.**—Darwin, C. Geological Observations . . . together with . . . notices on the Geology of . . . the C. of G. H.

— — Mauritius. A Voyage to . . . the C. of G. H., *etc. Lond.*, 1775.

— — Sparrmann, A. Voyage to the C. of G. H. . . . 1772-76., *etc.* 1785.

— — Van Reenan, J. A Journal of a Journey from the C. of G. H. . . . in search of the Wreck of the . . . *Grosvenor, etc.* 1792.

—— Levaillant, F. Second Voyage dans . . . l'Afrique par le Cap, *etc. Par., An* 3. [1795.]

— — Thunberg, C. P. Voyages au Japon, par le Cap de Bonne Espérance . . . 1770-1778, *etc. Par.*, 1796.

— — Africa. New Sailing Directions . . . from Cape Spartel . . . to the Cape of G. H., *etc.* 1799.

— — Stavorinus, J. S. Voyage par le Cap de Bonne Espérance . . . à Samarang . . . 1774-78. *Par.*, 1800.

— — Dambeboer, C. F. Travels . . . from the C. of G. H. to Morocco, *etc.* 1801.

— Barrow, Sir J. Account of . . . Tribes surrounding . . . the C. of G. H. 1801-4.

— - Cape of Good Hope.—Extracts of Correspondence relative to . . . the C. of G. H., *etc.* 1827.

—— - Cape of Good Hope. Report of Inquiry upon the . . . C. of G. H., *etc.* 1829.

—— — Bannister, J. W. On Emigration to . . . the C. of G. H., *etc.* 1831.

— - Horsburgh, J. India Directory, or Directions for . . . C. of G. H., *etc.* 1836.

  - Smith., A. Report of the Expedition for exploring Central Africa from the C. of G. H. *Cape Town*, 1836.

—— — Leigh, W. H. Reconnoitering Voyages . . . including visits to . . . the C. of G. H., *etc. Lond.*, 1839.

Cape of Good Hope.

Cape of Good Hope.—LEIGH, W. H. Reconnoitering Voyages . . . including visits to . . . the C. of G. H., etc. 1840.

—— ARBOUSSET, T. and DAUMAS, F. Relation d'un voyage . . . au Nord-est . . . du Cap de Bonne Espérance, etc. *Par.*, 1842.

—— BUNBURY, C. J. F. Journal of a Residence at the C. of G. H., etc. 1848.

—— BERNCASTLE, DR. A Voyage to China; including a Visit to . . . the C. of G. H. *Lond.*, 1850.

—— CAPE OF GOOD HOPE. Despatches relative to the Reception of Convicts at the C. of G. H. *Lond.*, 1850.

—— NAPIER, E. E. Excursions . . . including a history of the Cape Colony, etc. 1850.

—— CAPE OF GOOD HOPE. Correspondence . . . relative to the State of the Kaffr Tribes, etc. *Lond.*, 1851.

—— CAPE OF GOOD HOPE, COLONY OF THE. Universal Exhibition, 1855. Vade-Mecum. *Cape Town*, 1855.

—— SABINE, MAJOR-GEN. E. On the Magnetic Variation in the Vicinity of the C. of G. H. 1855.

—— FLEMING, F. Southern Africa . . . from the C. of G. H. to Angola. 1856.

—— MARTIN, W. Notes on the C. of G. H., etc. *Calc.*, 1856.

—— PAPPE, L. Floræ Capensis medicæ Prodromus, etc. *Cape Town*, 1857.

—— ROUZET, E. DU. Instructions . . . aux batiments venant en Nouvelle-Calédonie par le Cap de Bonne Espérance. *Par.*, 1858.

—— IRONS, W. The Settlers' Guide to the C. of G. H., etc. 1858.

—— Account of the Portuguese possessions from the C. of G. H. to China. ASTLEY. Vol. I.

—— Voyages of the Portuguese along the Coast of Africa, as far as the C. of G. H. ASTLEY. Vol. I.

—— A Description of the Countries . . . from the C. of G. H. to Cape Guarda Fuy, etc. ASTLEY. Vol. III.

—— Description of the Dutch Possessions at the C. ASTLEY. Vol. III.

—— Hamilton, A. Remarks on . . . Maritime Countries . . . between the Capes of G. H. and Guarda Fuy. ASTLEY. Vol. III.

—— Ten Rhyne's account of the C. of G. H., etc. CHURCHILL. Vol. IV.

—— Barrow, M. Voyages au Cap de Bonne Espérance, 1797. EYRIÈS. Vol. XI.

—— Campbell, M. Voyages au Cap de Bonne Espérance, 1812-21. EYRIÈS. Vol. XI.

—— Latrobe. Voyage au Cap de Bonne Espérance, 1805. EYRIÈS. Vol. XI.

—— Lichtenstein, M. Voyage au Cap de Bonne Espérance, 1803-6. EYRIÈS. Vol. XI.

—— Gordon, Lady Duff. Letters from the C. GALTON, F. Vacation Tourists . . . in 1862-3.

Cape of Good Hope — Cape Verde Islands.

Cape of Good Hope.—Lancaster, J. Memorable Voyage about the Cape of Buona Esperanza, along the E. Coast of Africa . . . 1591. Hakluyt. Vol. II

—— Stevens, T. Voyage about the Cape of Buona Esperanza onto Goa . . . 1579. Hakluyt. Vol. II.

—— Byron, Comm. Voyage . . . to . . . C. of G. H. . . . 1764-66. Hawkesworth, J. Vol. I.

—— Carteret, Capt. Voyage . . . round the C. of G. H. . . . 1766-69. Hawkesworth, J. Vol. I.

—— Wallis, Capt. Voyage to . . . the C. of G. H. . . . 1766-68. Hawkesworth, J. Vol. I.

—— A short account of the Portuguese Possessions between the C. of G. H. and China. Kerr. Vol. VII.

—— Peyton, W. Voyage . . . in 1615 . . . with the Ports . . . between the C. of G. H. and Japan, 1616. Kerr. Vol. IX.

—— Cap de Bonne Espérance, etc. Laharpe, J. Vol. III.

—— Thunberg's Account of the C. of G. H. Pinkerton. Vol. XVI.

—— Gama, V. di. Navigatione dal Capo Buona Speranza, fino in Calicut, 1497. Ramusio. Vol. I.

—— Gonsalvo, L. Beschreibung der Küsten von Rio da Volta bis an das Vorgebirge. Voyages and Travels. Allgemeine Historie, etc. Vol. IV.

—— Die Küste vom Alt-Kalabarflusse nach dem Vorgebirge. Voyages and Travels. Allgemeine Historie, etc. Vol. IV.

—— Hamilton, A. Einige Anmerkungen über die Küsten und Inseln zwischen dem Vorgebirge der guten Hoffnung und Capo Guarda Fuy. Voyages and Travels. Allgemeine Historie, etc. Vol. V.

—— Keith, Sir G. M. Voyage to . . . the C. of G. H., 1805-6. Voyages and Travels. A Collection, etc. 1805. Vol. XI.

—— Prior, J. Voyage . . . to the C. of G. H. . . . 1810-11. Voyages and Travels, New. 1819. Vol. I.

—— Kolben, Peter. Voyage to the C. of G. H. 1705. Voyages and Travels. The World displayed. Vol. X.

Capetown.—Matson, J. S. The Malays of C. *Manchester*, 1861.

Cape Verde.—Redfield, W. C. C. V. and Hatteras Hurricane, of Aug.-Sept., 1853, etc. *New Haven, U. S.*, 1854.

—— Le Maire, Sieur. Voyages of, to . . . C. V., etc. Churchill. Vol. VIII.

—— Roberts, G. Bericht von einer Reise nach . . . dem grünen Vorgebirge . . . 1721. Voyages and Travels. Allgemeine Historie, etc. Vol. II.

—— Broek, P. van den. Reise nach dem grünen Vorgebirge . . . 1606. Voyages and Travels. Allgemeine Historie, etc. Vol. III.

—— Le Maire. Reise nach . . . dem grünen Vorgebirge . . . 1682. Voyages and Travels. Allgemeine Historie, etc. Vol. III.

—— —— **Islands.**—Bartholomew, D. E. Voyage to the C. V. I., etc. 1819.

Cape Verde Islands.—Brunner, S. Reise nach . . . den Inseln des grünen Vorgebürges, *etc.* *Bern*, 1840.
——— Chelmicki, J. C. C. de. Corografia Cabo-Verdiana, *etc.* *Lisb.*, 1841.
——— Purdy, J. Brasilian Navigator . . . with . . . Directions for the . . . C. V. I. . . . *etc.* 1844.
— Kerhallet. C. P. de. Description . . . de l'Archipel des Îles du Cap Vert. *Par.*, 1851.
— — Hadfield, W. Brazil . . . including notices of . . . C. V. 1854.
— — Kerhallet, C. P. de. Description Nautique des Îles du Cap Vert. *Par.*, 1858.
— Cada Mosto, A. da. Two Voyages . . . In which the C. de V. Islands were discovered, 1455-56. Astley. Vol. I.
— Description of the C. de V. I. Astley. Vol. I.
— Roberts, G. Account of a Voyage to . . . C. de V. . . . In 1721. Astley. Vol. I.
— Wren, W. Voyage of . . . G. Fenner to the Islands of C. de V. in 1566. Astley. Vol. I.
— — Two Voyages to the C. de V., *etc.* Astley. Vol. II.
— Fenner, G. Voyage to . . . the Isles of Capo V., 1566. Hakluyt. Vol. II.
— Fenner, G. Voyage to . . . the C. de V. I., 1566. Kerr. Vol. VII.
— Silva, M. da. Voyage from C. V. I. to Guatulco, *etc.* Kerr. Vol. X.
— Beschreibung der Eylande des Grünen Vorgebirges. Voyages and Travels. Allgemeine Historie, *etc.* Vol. II.
— A Voyage to the C. de V. I., by Capt. George Roberts. 1721. Voyages and Travels. The World displayed. Vol. X.

Cape York.—Macgillivray, J. Narrative . . . To which is added the account of E. B. Kennedy's Expedition for the Exploration of the C. Y. Peninsula.
——— Bonus, A. Steam to Australia . . . the expediency of . . . a settlement at C. Y. . . . pointed out, *etc.* *Sydney*, 1848.

Capo Verde.—*See* Cape Verde.
Cappadocia.—Tchihatcheff, P. de. Dépôts Tertiaires . . . de la Cappadoce, *etc.* *Par.*, 1854.
Cap Vert.—*See* Cape Verde.
Caqueta, River.—*See* Jappa.
Caraccas.—Depons, F. Travels . . . containing a description of the C., *etc.* 1807.
Caramania.—Beaufort, F. Karamania, *etc.* 1818.
——— ——— Memoir of a Survey of the Coast of Karamania, *etc.* 1820.
Caranja.—Andrews, Capt. Journey . . . by the Deserts of C. to Arica, *etc.* 1827.

Cardiff.—SMYTH, ADMIRAL W. H. Nautical Observations on ... C. *Card.*, 1840.

Caria.—TCHIHATCHEFF, P. DE. Dépôts Tertiaires ... du Midi de la Carie, *etc.* *Par.*, 1854.

Caribbean Sea.—BARNETT, E. West India Pilot ... with ... the C. S., *etc.* 1859-61.

—— KERHALLET, C. P. DE. Manuel de la Navigation dans la Mer des Antilles, *etc.* 1862-3.

—— —— GRAS, A. LE. Phares de la Mer des Antilles, *etc.* *Par.*, 1869.

—— —— **Islands.**—Ursprung, Gemüthsart und Gebräuche der Caraïben VOYAGES and TRAVELS. Allgemeine Historie, *etc.* Vol. XVII.

—— *See also* SAINT LUCIA.

Carie.—*See* CARIA.

Carinthia.—Browne, E. Journey ... through ... C., *etc.* HARRIS, J. Vol. II.

Carlsbad.—HOFER, C. E. Beschreibung ... (von Karlsbad.) *Prag*, 1797.

—— MANNL, R. C. and its Mineral Springs, *etc.* *Leipz.*, 1847.

—— GRIEBEN, T. Grieben's Reise-Bibliothek. No. 38. ... C., *etc.* *Berl.*, 1861.

Carlskrona.—TOPOGRAFISKA och Statistiska Uppgifter om C. Län, *etc.* *Stockh.*, 1849.

Carnata.—*See* BIJAYANAGAR.

Carniola.—CADELL, W. A. Journey in C., *etc.* *Edin.*, 1820.

—— Browne, E. Journey ... through ... C. HARRIS, J. Vol. II.

——, **Upper.**—SEEN, Die, der Vorzeit in Oberkrain ... von F. B. M. *Laibach*, 1863.

——, **South.**—CARROL, B. R. Historical Collections of S. C., *etc.* *N. Y.*, 1836.

Carpathians.—MURCHISON, SIR R. I. On the Geological Structure of the ... C., *etc.* 1849.

Carpentaria.—LANDSBOROUGH, W. Journal of an Expedition from C., in search of Burke and Wills. *Melb.*, 1862.

—— —— [Newspaper Cuttings, containing the Journal of his Expedition to C. in 1866.] 1866.

——, **Gulf of.**—SAUNDERS, T. W. The Asiatic Mediterranean ... the G. of C., *etc.* 1853.

—— —— CHIMMO, W. Voyage ... from Sydney to the G. of C., *etc.* 1857.

—— —— MACDONALD, J. G. Journal ... on an Expedition from Port Denison to the G. of C., *etc.* *Brisbane*, 1865.

Cartagena.—*See* CARTHAGENA.

Carthage.—HEEREN, A. H. L. Historical Researches into the Politics ... of the Carthaginians, *etc.* *Oxf.*, 1836.

—— BLAKESLEY, J. W. Four Months in Algeria, with a visit to C. *Camb.*, 1859.

Carthage.—DAVIS, N. Ruined Cities within . . . Carthaginian Territories.
Lond., 1861.

Carthagena.—JACK, T. Survey of the Spanish West Indies . . . describing . . . C., *etc.*
1702.

——— Ursachen . . . Schiffahrt . . . nach . . . Cartagena . . . Beschreibung derselben, *etc.* VOYAGES and TRAVELS. Allgemeine Historie, *etc.* Vol. IX.

——— Von der Reise von C. nach Terra Firma, *etc.* VOYAGES and TRAVELS. Allgemeine Historie, *etc.* Vol. IX.

——— Beschreibungen . . . von . . . C., *etc.* VOYAGES and TRAVELS. Allgemeine Historie, *etc.* Vol. XV.

———, **Bay of.**—PARSONS, J. West India Directory. Sailing directions . . . for . . . B. of C.
1854.

Casbin.—Mindenhall, J. Second Letter . . . from C. in Persia, 1606. PURCHAS. Vol. I.

Cashmere.—FORSTER, G. Journey . . . through . . . Kashmire, *etc.*
1798.

——— HÜGEL, BARON C. VON. Kaschmir und das Reich der Siek.
Stutt., 1840, 41.

——— MOORCROFT and TREBECK. Travels in . . . Kashmir . . . 1819 to 1825.
1841.

——— VIGNE, G. T. Travels in Kashmir, *etc.*
1842.

——— HÜGEL, BARON C. VON. Travels in Kashmir and the Panjab, *etc.*
1845.

——— HONIGBERGER, J. M. Thirty-five Years in the East. Adventures relating to . . . C., *etc.*
1852.

——— SCHONBERG, BARON E. VON. Travels in India and Kashmir. 1853.

——— MARKHAM, F. Shooting in . . . C., *etc.*
Lond., 1854.

——— HIMALAYAN. A Summer Ramble . . . with Sporting Adventures in the Vale of C., *etc.*
Lond., 1860.

——— TORRENS, H. D. Travels in . . . Kashmir.
Lond., 1862.

——— KNIGHT, CAPTAIN. Diary of a Pedestrian in C., *etc.* *Lond.*, 1863.

——— LEITNER, G. W. Results of a Tour in . . . Kashmir, *etc.*
Lahore, Lond. [1868.]

——— THORP, R. C. Misgovernment.
Lond., 1870.

——— Bernier, F. Voyage to Surat . . . with the Emperor's Voyage to Kachemire in 1644, *etc.* CHURCHILL. Vol. VIII.

——— Forster, G. Voyage à Cachemir, *etc.* EYRIÈS. Vol. XIII.

——— Voyage de Bernier à C. LAHARPE, J. Vol. V.

——— Bernier. Reise in . . . Kachemir, 1664. VOYAGES and TRAVELS. Allgemeine Historie, *etc.* Vol. XI.

Casiquiare, River.—*See* CASSIQUIARE.

Caskets.—ALDERNEY. The Alderney Island Pilot; comprising the . . . Casquets, *etc.*
Lond., 1864.

——— ——— Routier de l'Ile Aurigny, comprenant . . . les Casquets, *etc.*
Par., 1865.

Caspian Sea.—HANWAY, J. Historical Account of the British Trade over the C. S., etc. **1753.**
—— MANN, M. L'ABBÉ. Mémoire dans lequel on examine l'opinion ... que les Mers ... Caspienne ... & Blanche, ont anciennement communiqué ensemble, etc. **1779.**
—— CASPIAN SEA. Description des Pays situés entre la Mer Noire et la Mer Caspienne. *Par.*, **1793.**
—— FORSTER, G. Journey ... into Russia, by the C. S. **1798.**
—— FRASER, J. B. Travels ... on the S. Bank of the C. S., etc. **1826.**
—— KEPPEL, HON. G. Personal Narrative of a Journey from India ... by ... the W.n Shore of the C. S., etc. **1827.**
—— EICHWALD, E. Reise auf dem Caspischen Meere ... in 1825-26. *Stutt. u. Tüb.*, **1834.**
—— BAER, K. E. VON. Kaspische Studien. *St. Pet.*, **1839.**
—— HELL, X. H. DE. Travels in the Steppes of the C. S., etc. **1847.**
—— FUSS, G. and others. Beschreibung der zur Ermittelung des Höhenunterschiedes zwischen dem Schwarzen und dem Caspischen Meere ... ausgeführten Messungen, etc. *St. Pet.*, **1849.**
—— HUMBOLDT, A. VON. Travels ... including his Journey to ... the C. S., etc. **1853.**
—— BAER, K. E. VON. Dattel-Palmen an den Ufern des Kaspischen Meeres, etc. **1859.**
—— BERGSTRAESSER, DR. Die Verbindung des Caspischen mit dem Schwarzen Meere. *Gotha*, **1859.**
—— BAER, K. E. VON. Kaspische Studien, etc. **1860.**
—— BERGSTRAESSER, DR. De la Réunion de la Mer Caspienne à la Mer Noire. *Par.*, **1861.**
—— IVASHINTZOV, N. A. [Hydrographical Researches upon the C. S. Astronomical part.] *Russ.* *St. Pet.*, **1866.**
—— Jenkinson, A. Voyage ... over the C. S. ... 1501. HAKLUYT. Vol. I.
—— Sherley, Sir A. Voyage over the C. S. ... 1601. PURCHAS. Vol. II.
—— The beginning of the English Discoveries towards the North ... also Voyages ... over the C. S., etc. PURCHAS. Vol. III.
—— Borough, C. Reports of sixt voyage ... more especially over the C. S. ... 1579-81. PURCHAS. Vol. III.
—— *See also* KARABOGHAZ BAY.

Caspii Montes.—*See* ELBRUZ.
Casquets.—*See* CASKETS.
Cassiquiare, River.—MICHELENA Y ROJAS, F. Exploracion Oficial ... del ... C., etc. *Bruselas*, **1867.**
Castilla del Oro.—The discoveries made by the Spaniards in ... Golden Castile ... 1513-26. HARRIS, J. Vol. II.
—— — The discovery of Golden Castile. 1572. VOYAGES and TRAVELS. The World displayed. Vol. III.

Castle Del Mina.—*See* Saint George Del Mina.
Casvin.—*See* Cabbin.
Catamarca.—Poccei, B. Mes Itinéraires . . . Province de C.
Par., 1864.
———— La Province de C. [*Par.*, 1864.]
Catania.—Catania. Sn' Lavori pel Molo di C., *etc.* *Cat.*, 1846.
———— Peyssa, C. E. F. Memoria sulla Latitudine Geografica di C., *etc.*
Cat., 1849.
Cataya.—*See* China.
Cathaia.—**Cathay.**—*See* China.
Cat Island.—Bache, A. D. Additional notes of . . . Tidal Observations . . . at C. I., *etc.* *New Hav.*, 1852.
Cattegat.—Löveworn, Chev. de. New Sailing Directory for the C., *etc.*
1844.
Caubul.—*See* Kabool.
Caucasus.—Koch, C. Erläuterungen zur Karte des Kaukasischen Isthmus und Armeniens. *Berlin.*
— — Reineggs, Dr., and Marshal Biebersten. General . . . description of Mount C., *etc.* 1807.
— — Klaproth, J. Travels in the C. . . . in 1807-8, *etc.*
Lond., 1814.
— — Engelhardt, M. von, and Parrot, F. Reise in . . . den Kaukasus. *Berl.*, 1815.
— — Freygan, M. and Mme. Letters from the C., *etc.* 1823.
— Potocki, Count J. Voyage dans les Steps . . . du Caucase, *etc.*
Par., 1829.
— Kupffer, M. Voyage . . . dans le Caucase, en 1829.
St. Pet., 1830.
— Eichwald, E. Reise . . . in den C. in 1825-20.
Stutt. u. Tüb., 1834.
— Spencer, E. Travels in the Western C., *etc.* 1838.
— Mignan, R. Winter Journey through . . . the Caucasian Alps, *etc.* 1839.
— Montpéreux, F. D. de. Voyage autour du Caucase, *etc.*
Par., 1839.
— Struve, F. G. W. Astronomische Ortsbestimmungen . . . in Kaukasien, *etc.* *St. Pet.*, 1845.
- Hxli, X. H. de. Travels in . . . the C., *etc.* 1847.
—— · Saint-Martin, V. de. Mémoire Historique sur la Géographie ancienne du Caucase, *etc.* *Par.*, 1847.
———— ———— Recherches sur les populations primitives . . . du Caucase.
Par., 1847.
— — — Golovin, I. The C. 1854.
- - Haxthausen, Baron von. Tribes of the C., *etc.* 1855.
—— — Moser, L. The C. and its People, *etc.* 1856.

Caucasus.—Wagner, M. Travels ... with Sketches of ... the C., *etc.*
1856.
——— Chodyko, General. Survey of the C. 1857-63.
——— Moritz, A. Lebenslinien der meteorologischen Stationen am Kaukasus, *etc.* *St. Pet.*, 1859.
——— Abich, H. Beiträge zur geologischen Kenntniss der Thermalquellen in den Kaukasischen Ländern. *Tiflis*, 1865.
——— Radde, G. Berichte über die biologisch-geographischen Untersuchungen in den Kaukasuslaendern, *etc.* *Tiflis*, 1866.
——— Pollington, Viscount. Half round the Old World ... a Tour in ... the C., *etc.* *Lond.*, 1867.
——— Freshfield, D. W. Travels in the Central C., *etc.* *Lond.*, 1869.

Caunpoor.—*See* Cawnpore.

Cauvery, River.—Jervis, A. Narrative of a Journey to the Falls of the C., *etc.* *Lond.*, 1834.

Cavery, River.—*See* Cauvery.

Cawnpoor.—*See* Cawnpore.

Cawnpore.—Lloyd, Sir W. Narrative of a Journey from Caunpoor to the Boorendo Pass, *etc.* *Lond.*, 1840.
——— Montgomery, R. Statistical Report of ... C., 1848. *Calcutta*, 1849.

Cayari, River.—*See* Madeira, River.

Cayor.—*See* Kayor.

Casembe.—Cooley, W. D. Inner Africa laid open ... with the routes to ... the C., *etc.* 1852.

Cecina.—Grázzro, Count J. Cenni storici ... sulla ... Cava di Caporciano ... nella Valle di C. *Firenze*, 1847.

Cefalonia.—*See* Cephalonia.

Ceillo.—*See* Ceylon.

Celebes.—Woodard, D. The Narrative of ... in ... C., *etc.* 1805.
——— Moor, J. H. Notices of ... C., *etc.* *Singapore*, 1837.
——— Mundy, R. Narrative of the events in ... C., down to the occupation of Labuan, *etc.* 1848.
——— Van der Hart, C. Reize rondom ... C., *etc.* *Te 'Sgrav.* 1853.
- Sumatra ... C., *etc.* Eureka. Vol. XII.
- Carteret, Capt. Voyage ... to ... C., ... 1766-69. Hawkesworth, J. Vol. I.
- Stavorinus. Account of C. ... from the Voyages of. Pinkerton. Vol. XI.
- Beschreibung der Insel C., *etc.* Voyages and Travels. Allgemeine Historie, *etc.* Vol. XI.
- Zweytes Unternehmen der Holländer wider ... C. ... 1666-69. Voyages and Travels. Allgemeine Historie, *etc.* Vol. XVIII.
- Woodward, D. Narrative of the sufferings of ... in ... C., 1804. Voyages and Travels. A Collection, *etc.* 1805. Vol. I.

Celebes — Ceylon.

Celebes.—*See also* MACASSAR.
Cephalonia.—DAPPER. Naukeurige Beschryving van ... C., *etc.*
                                  Amst., 1688.
—— GOODISSON, W. Historical ... Essay upon ... C., *etc.* 1822.
—— MOUSSON, A. Ein Besuch auf ... C., in 1858. *Zurich*, 1859.
Cerigo.—CASTELLAN, A. L. Lettres sur la Morée ... C., *etc.*
                                  Par., 1808.
Cervi.—LEAKE, W. M. On the claim to the Islands of C. and Sapienza.
                                  Lond., 1850.
Cetina, Mons.—*See* KAHLEN MOUNTAINS.
Ceuta.—MOROCCO. Observations on ... Morocco ... 1830 ... Description of ... C., *etc.* MS.
Cevola.—*See* ZUNI.
Ceylan.—*See* CEYLON.
Ceylon.—BALDÆUS, P. Naauwkeurige Beschryvinge van ... C., *etc.*
                                  Amst., 1672.
—— RIBEYRO, J. Histoire de l'Isle de Ceylan, *etc.* *Amst.*, 1701.
—— THUNBERG, C. P. Travels ... in ... C., *etc.* 1796.
—— PERCIVAL, R. Account of ... C., *etc.* 1803.
—— CORDINER, J. Description of C., *etc.* 1807.
—— VALENTIA, VISCOUNT. Voyages and Travels to ... C. 1802-6
                                  1811.
—— PHILALETHES. The History of C., *etc.* *Lond.*, 1817.
—— DAVY, J. An Account of ... C., *etc.* 1821.
—— RASK, R. K. Singalesisk Skriftlære. *Kolombo*, 1821.
—— UPHAM, E. The ... Sacred and Historical Books of C., *etc.*
                                  1823.
—— HEBER, BISHOP. Narrative ... with Notes upon C., *etc.* 1829.
—— HEEREN, A. H. L. De Ceylone insula, *etc.* *Getting.*, 1831.
—— COLEBROOKE, LIEUT.-COL. Report upon ... C., *etc.* 1832.
—— FORBES, MAJOR. Eleven Years in C., *etc.* 1840.
—— BENNETT, J. W. C. and its Capabilities, *etc.* 1843.
—— CAMPBELL, J. Excursions ... in C., *etc.* 1843.
—— KNIGHTON, W. History of C., *etc.* 1845.
—— HOFFMEISTER, W. Travels in C., *etc.* *Edin.*, 1848.
—— PRIDHAM, C. Historical ... and Statistical Account of C., *etc.*
                                  1849.
—— DICKENSON, W. B. Dudu-Massa, Coco-Reedi, or Hook Money of C.
                                  1850.
—— FREEMAN, J. J. Tour in S. Africa, with notices of ... C, *etc.*
                                  1851.
—— MOUAT, F. J. Rough Notes of a trip to ... C., *etc.*
                                  Calc., 1852.
—— SULLIVAN, E. The Bungalow and the Tent; or a Visit to C. 1854.

Ceylon.—BAKER, S. W. Eight Years' Wanderings in C. 1855.
── BARROW, SIR G. C., etc. 1857.
── BINNING, R. B. M. Journal of two years' Travel in ... C., etc. 1857.
── TENNENT, SIR J. E. C.; an Account, etc. 1860.
── ── Sketches of the Natural History of C., etc. *Lond.*, 1861.
── STEUART, J. Notes on C., etc. 1862.
── POWER, E. R. On the Agricultural ... Statistics of C. 1863.
── Baldaeus, P. A true ... description of ... C., etc. CHURCHILL. Vol. III.
── Ceylon. Percival. Boyd. Davy. EYRIES. Vol. XIII.
── Ribeiro, J. Fatalidade Historica da Ilha de Ceilão, 1685. PORTUGAL. Collecção de Noticias, etc. Vol. V.
── Halens, de la. Reise ... 1670-72. Fahrt nach C., etc. VOYAGES and TRAVELS. Allgemeine Historie, etc. Vol. VIII.
── Knoxen, R. Reise nach ... C., 1657-59. VOYAGES and TRAVELS. Allgemeine Historie, etc. Vol. VIII.
── Spilberg, G. Reise nach ... C., 1601-3. VOYAGES and TRAVELS. Allgemeine Historie, etc. Vol. VIII.
── Zusatz zur Beschreibung der Insel C., etc. VOYAGES and TRAVELS. Allgemeine Historie, etc. Vol. XVIII.
── Valentia, Viscount. Voyages and Travels to ... C. ... 1802-0. VOYAGES and TRAVELS. A Collection, etc. 1805. Vol. XI.
── ── Voyages and Travels to ... C. ... 1802-6. VOYAGES and TRAVELS. A Collection, etc. 1810. Vol. IV.
── Haafner, J. Travels on foot through ... C. VOYAGES and TRAVELS, New. 1819. Vol. V.
── *See also* ANURAJAPURA.—MAHAVILLAGANGA.

Chaco, Gran.—ARENALES, J. Noticias sobre el gran pais del C., etc. *Buen. Aires*, 1833.
── ── Dalrymple, A. Catalogue of Authors ... on ... C. DALRYMPLE, A. Collection of Nautical Memoirs, etc.
── ── Beschreibung von C., etc. VOYAGES and TRAVELS. Allgemeine Historie, etc. Vol. XVI.

Chad, Lake.—GUMPRECHT, T. E. Barth und Overwegs Untersuchungs-Reise nach dem Tschad-See, etc. *Berl.*, 1852.

Chadda, River.—BARTH, H. Dr. B. Baikie's Thätigkeit am ... Niger, mit besonderer Berücksichtigung der Flusschwellen ... des Tsad- und Nilbeckens. *Berlin.*
── ── HUTCHINSON, T. J. Narrative of the ... Tshadda Exploration, etc. 1855.
── ── BAIKIE, W. B. Narrative of ... Voyage up the ... Tsádda, etc. 1856.

Chagos Archipelago.—MORESBY, R. Nautical Directions for ... the C. A. 1840.

Chagres.—EMORY, W. H. Observations ... made at C., etc. *Camb. U. S.*, 1850.

Chaldea.—LANDSEER, J. Sabæan Researches ... Essays ... on the engraved Hieroglyphics of C., etc. 1823.
— MIGNAN, R. Travels in C., etc. 1829.
— — AINSWORTH, W. F. Researches in ... C. 1838.
— — BEKE, C. T. On the Alluvia of ... C. 1839.
— — AINSWORTH, W. F. Travels ... In ... C., etc. 1842.
— — LOFTUS, W. K. Travels ... in C., etc. 1857.
— - Cartwright, J. The Preacher's Travels ... through ... C., etc. CHURCHILL. Vol. VII.
— — Odoricus, Frier B. Voyage to ... C. ... about 1325. HAKLUYT. Vol. II.
— — Of Simon Sulaka, a Papal Easterne Patriarke, amongst the Chaldæans, etc. PURCHAS. Vol. I.
— — Strozza, P. Treatise of the opinions of the Chaldæans, touching the Patriarke of Babylon, etc. PURCHAS. Vol. I.
— - Rauwolf, L. Journey Into ... C., etc. RAY, J.
— — Jordan, ou Jourdain Catalani, P. Mirabilia descripta, sequitur de ... C., etc. VOYAGES and TRAVELS. Recueil, etc. Vol. IV.

Chambery.—CHAMBERY. Notice sur ... les environs de C., etc.
Chambery, 1824.

Chamouni.—MAKOET, J. L. C., le Mont Blanc, etc. *Geneva,* 1843.

Champagne.—RAZOUMOWSKY, COUNT G. DE. Œuvres. Contenant, Voyage Minéralogique ... à ... C., etc. *Lausanne,* 1784.

Champlain, Lake.—GRAHAM, J. D. Report on the Improvement of the Harbours of Lakes Michigan ... and C. *Wash.,* 1860.

Chandah.—BLANFORD, W. T. On the Coal Seams of the Neighbourhood of C., etc. INDIA GEOLOGICAL SURVEY. Records, etc. Vol. I.

Chandgurh.—MARSHALL, T. Statistical Reports on ... C., etc.
Bomb., 1822.

Channel Islands.—INGLIS, H. D. The C. I. 1835.
— - WHITE, M. Sailing Directions ... and a detailed Account of the C. I. 1850.
——- DENDY, W. C. Islets of the Channel. 1858.
——— ANSTED, D. T. and LATHAM, R. G. The C. I., etc. *Lond.,* 1862.

Characene.—REINAUD, M. Mémoire sur le Commencement et la Fin du Royaume ... de la Kharacène, etc. *Par.,* 1861.

Charlton Island.—James, Capt. T. Voyage ... his wintering in C. I. ... 1631-32. HARRIS, J. Vol. II.

Charmettes.—CHAMBERY. Notice sur les C., etc. *Chambery,* 1824.

Charran.—See HARRAN.

Chartum.—See KHARTUM.

Chasseral.—DENZLER, H. H. Die Meereshöhe des C., etc. 1864.

Chateegaon.—See CHITTAGONG.

Chatham Islands.—MUELLER, F. The Vegetation of the C. I.
Melb., 1864.

Chaturgrama.—*See* CHITTAGONG.
Cheltenham.—MURCHISON, SIR R. I. Outline of the Geology of the neighbourhood of C., *etc.* *Chelt.*, **1834.**
———— ———— Outline of the Geology of the neighbourhood of C., *etc.* *Lond., Chelt.*, **1845.**
Cher.—LUÇAY, CITOYEN. Statistique du Département du C. *Par.* [**1802.**]
Cherbourg.—PIM, B. Notes on C. **1859.**
———— KELLER, F. A. E. Notice sur la Carte des Environs de C., *etc.* *Par.*, **1861.**
Cherie Island.—*See* BEAR ISLAND.
Cherry Island.—*See* BEAR ISLAND.
Cherso.—FORTIS, A. Travels . . . to which are added . . . Observations on . . . C., *etc.* *Lond.*, **1778.**
Chersonesus Taurica.—*See* TARTARY.
Chester.—PENNANT, T. The Journey from C. to London, *etc.* *Lond.*, **1811.**
Chiapas.—STEPHENS, J. L. Incidents of Travel in . . . C., *etc.* **1842.**
Chica.—*See* CHICO.
Chi-Chen.—NORMAN, B. W. Rambles in Yucatan . . . including a Visit to . . . C.-C., *etc.* *N. Y.*, **1843.**
Chico.—Of Cumana . . . C. . . . and of their Religions. PURCHAS. Vol. V.
Chihuahua.—BARTLETT, J. R. Personal . . . explorations . . . in . . . C., *etc.* *N. Y.*, **1854.**
———— AUMAILE, R. L. D'. Report in detail . . . of Explorations and Surveys of the . . . Mines of . . . C., *etc.* *N. Y.*, **1861.**
Chile.—*See* CHILI.
Chilecito.—METEOROLOGY. Meteorological Tables. Famatina and C. Observations, 1827-8. *MS.*
Chili.—FRÉZIER, M. Relation du Voyage de la Mer du Sud aux Côtes du C. . . . . 1712-14. *Amst.*, **1717.**
———— ———— Relation du Voyage de la Mer du Sud aux Côtes du C. . . . 1712-14, *etc.* *Par.*, **1732.**
———— MOLINA, G. I. Saggio sulla Storia Civile del C. *Bologna*, **1787.**
———— MOLINA, J. The Geographical . . . History of C., *etc.* *Lond.*, **1809.**
———— GRAHAM, M. Journal of a Residence in C. during 1822, *etc.* **1824.**
———— SCHMIDTMEYER, P. Travels into Chile, *etc.* *Lond.*, **1824.**
———— CALDCLEUGH, A. Travels in . . . C. **1825.**
———— HALL, B. Extracts from a Journal written on the Coasts of C. . . . in 1820-22. *Edin.*, **1825.**
———— MATHISON, G. F. Narrative of a Visit to . . . C., *etc.* **1825.**
———— PACIFIC OCEAN. Three Years in the Pacific; containing Notices of . . . C., *etc.* **1835.**
———— POEPPIG, E. Reise in C. . . . 1827-32. *Leipz.*, **1835.**

Chili — Chimborazo.

Chili.—GARDINER, A. F. A Visit to the Indians on the Frontiers of C.
Lond., **1841**.

——— SUTCLIFFE, T. Sixteen Years in C. and Peru from 1822 to 1839, *etc.*
Lond. [**1841.**]

——— WHEELWRIGHT, W. Report . . . with an Account of the Coal Mines of C., *etc.* **1843.**

——— CHILE. Notice sur le Chile, par un Voyageur Français.
Par., **1844.**

——— GAY, C. Historia fisica e politica de Chile, *etc.* *Par.*, **1844-54.**

——— FITZROY, REAR-ADML. R. Sailing Directions for . . . C., *etc.*
1848.

——— DOMEYKO, I. Memoria sobre la Colonizacion en Chile. [**1850.**]

——— AMUNATEGUI, M. L. Titulos de . . . Chile á la soberanía . . . de la estremidad austral del Continente Americano, *etc.* *Sant.*, **1853-55.**

——— CHILE. Estadistica Comercial de . . . Chile . . . 1853.
Valp., **1854.**

——— PERREY, A. Documens relatifs aux Tremblements de Terre au C.
Lyon, **1854.**

——— CHILE. Estadistica Comercial . . . de C. del año 1854, 58.
Valparaiso, **1854-59.**

——— MACKENNA, B. V. Le C. considéré sous le rapport de son Agriculture, *etc.* *Par.*, **1855.**

——— PEREZ-ROSALES, V. Essai sur le C. *Hambourg*, **1857.**

——— CHILE. Censo jeneral . . . de Chile . . . 1854. *Santiago*, **1858.**

——— BOLLAERT, W. Antiquarian . . . Researches in . . . C., *etc.*
1860.

——— Brawern, D. and Herckemann, C. Voyage to . . . C., *etc.* CHURCHILL.
Vol. I.

——— Ovalle, A. de. Historical relation of . . . C. CHURCHILL. Vol. III.

——— Techo, F. N. del. History of . . . Chile, *etc.* CHURCHILL. Vol. IV.

——— Schmidtmeyer, P. Voyage au C. . . . 1820-21. EYRIES. Vol. IX.

——— Pizarro, F. The History of the discovery . . . of C. . . . 1535. HARRIS, J. Vol. II.

——— History of the discovery . . . of C. KERR. Vol. V.

——— Ovalle's Historical Relation of C. PINKERTON. Vol. XIV.

——— Ursino, A. Relation concerning . . . the secrets of . . . C., 1581. PURCHAS. Vol. IV.

——— Of Cumana . . . C. . . . and of their Religions. PURCHAS. Vol. V.

——— Beschreibungen . . . von . . . C., *etc.* VOYAGES and TRAVELS. Allgemeine Historie, *etc.* Vol. XIII.

——— Almagro, D. von. Entdeckung von C. VOYAGES and TRAVELS, Allgemeine Historie, *etc.* Vol. XV.

Chilicito.—*See* CHILECITO.

Chillan.—DOMEYKO, D. I. Viaje á las Cordilleras de . . . C. **1849.**

Chimborazo.—HUMBOLDT, A. VON. Notice de deux tentatives d'ascension du C. *Par.*, **1838.**

China.

China.—CHINA. Description of . . . C. *Chinese.*
——— CHINA. Memoires sur la Chine, *etc.* [*Paris.*]
——— JAPAN. Nuovi Avvisi del Giapone con alcuni altri della Cina, *etc.* *Venetia,* 1586.
——— MENDOCE, J. G. DE. Histoire du Grand Royaume de la Chine, *etc.* *Par.,* 1588.
——— VERA, G. DI. Tre Navigationi fatte dagli Olandesi . . . verso il . . . Regno de Sini, *etc.* *Venet.,* 1599.
——— GUZMAN, P. L. Historia de las Missiones . . . de la Compañia de Jesus . . . en . . . la C., *etc.* *Alcalá,* 1601.
——— MENDEZ PINTO, F. Historia Oriental de las peregrinaciones de F. Mendez Pinto . . . en . . . C., *etc.* *Madrid,* 1627.
——— NIEUHOFF, J. L'Ambassade de la Compagnie Orientale des Provinces Unies vers l'Empereur de la Chine, *etc.* *Leyde,* 1665.
——— NIEUHOF, J. Legatio Batavica ad . . . Sinæ Imperatorem, *etc.* *Amst.,* 1668.
——— PALLU F. Breve e compendiosa Relatione de' Viaggi di tre Vescovi Francesi . . . à i Regni della Cina, *etc.* *Roma,* 1669.
——— DAPPER. Beschryving . . . van . . . Sina, *etc.* *Amst.,* 1670.
——— ——— Gedenkwaerdig Bedryf der Nederlandsche Oost-Indische Maetschappye, op de Kuste en in het Keizerrijk van . . . Sina, *etc.* *Amst.,* 1670.
——— KIRCHER, A. La Chine, *etc.* *Amst.,* 1670.
——— WAGNER, J. C. Das mächtige Kayser-Reich Sina . . . vor Augen gestellet, *etc.* *Augsp.,* 1688.
——— NIEUHOF, J. Het Gezandtschap der Neerlandtsche Oost-Indische Compagnie, aan den . . . Keizer van C., *etc.* *Amst.,* 1693.
——— CARLIERI, J. Notizie varie . . . della C., *etc.* *Firenze,* 1697.
——— MOXON, J. A Brief Discourse of a Passage by the North Pole to . . . C., *etc.* *Lond.,* 1697.
——— IDES, E. Y. Three Years' Travels from Moscow . . . to C., *etc.* *Lond.,* 1706.
——— JESUITS, Travels of several . . . into . . . C., *etc.* 1714.
——— MANDELSLO, J. A. DE. Voyage . . . Contenants une description . . . de la Chine, *etc.* *Amst.,* 1727.
——— RENAUDOT, E. Ancient Accounts of India and C. . . . in the 9th century, *etc.* *Lond.,* 1733.
——— DU HALDE, J. B. Description . . . de la Chine, *etc.* *Hague,* 1736.
——— ——— A Description of . . . C., *etc.* *Lond.,* 1738.
——— LECOMTE, L. Memoirs and Remarks made in above Ten Years' Travels through . . . C. 1738.
——— OSORIO, J. History of the Portuguese . . . containing all their Discoveries, from . . . Africk to . . . C., *etc.* 1752.
——— OSBECK, P. A Voyage to C., *etc.* *Lond.,* 1771.
——— CHINA. Mémoires concernant l'histoire . . . des Chinois, par les Missionaires de Pekin. *Par.,* 1776.

China.—MOYRIAC DE MAILLA, J. A. M. DE. Histoire générale de la Chine, etc. *Par.*, 1777-85.

—— LETTRES edifiantes et curieuses, etc. Vol. 16-24, 20. Chine. *Par.*, 1780-83.

—— SONNERAT, M. Voyage . . . à la Chine, 1774-81. *Par.*, 1782.

—— MEARES, J. Voyages . . . from C. to the N. W. Coast of America, etc. *Lond.*, 1790.

—— ROCHON, ABBÉ. A Voyage to Madagascar . . . To which is added, a Memoir on the Chinese Trade. *Lond.*, 1792.

—— ANDERSON, Æ. A Narrative of the British Embassy to C., in 1792-94, etc. *Lond.*, 1796.

—— STAUNTON, SIR G. Authentic Account of an Embassy to . . . C., etc. 1797.

—— BARROW, SIR J. Travels in C., etc. 1804.

—— COXE, W. Account of the . . . Commerce between Russia and C. 1804.

—— JOHNSON, J. The Oriental Voyager . . . a Voyage to . . . C., etc. *Lond.*, 1807.

—— FROBISHER, SIR M. Instructions when going on a Voyage to . . . Cathay, etc. 1816.

—— RICCIUS, M. Histoire de l'Expédition Chrestienne au Royaume de la Chine, entreprise par . . . la Compagnie de Jésus, etc. *Lyon*, 1818.

—— ELLIS, H. Journal of the Proceedings of the late Embassy to C., etc. 1818.

—— MACLEOD, J. Voyage of H.M.S. *Alceste* to C., etc. 1819.

—— STAUNTON, SIR G. T. Miscellaneous Notices relating to C., etc. 1822-50.

—— COCHRANE, J. D. Narrative of a pedestrian Journey . . . from the Frontiers of C., etc. 1824.

—— TIMKOWSKI, G. Travels of the Russian Mission . . . to C. 1820-21, etc. 1827.

—— INDIA and CHINA, Papers relating to the Trade with, etc. 1829.

—— DOBELL, P. Travels . . . with a Narrative of a residence in C. 1830.

—— NEUMANN, C. F. Pilgerfahrten Buddhistischer Priester von C. nach Indien. *Leipz.*, 1833.

—— URMSTON, SIR J. B. Observations on the C. Trade, etc. 1833.

—— BENNETT, G. Wanderings in . . . C., etc. 1834.

—— GUTZLAFF, C. Journal of three Voyages along the Coast of C., 1831-33. 1834.

—— —— Sketch of Chinese History, etc. 1834.

—— ANDRADE, J. I. Memoria dos feitos Macaenses contra los piratas da C., etc. *Lisb.*, 1835.

—— DAVIS, SIR J. F. The Chinese, etc. 1836.

—— HORSBURGH, J. India Directory, or Directions for . . . C., etc. 1836.

China.—Murray, H., and others. Historical ... account of C., &c.
   Edin., 1836.
——— Pauthier, Chev. de. Réponse à l'Article de M. Riambourg sur l'Antiquité Chinoise.
   Epernay, 1836.
——— Gutzlaff, C. C. opened, *etc.*
   Lond., 1838.
——— Medhurst, W. H. C., its State and Prospects, *etc.*
   1838.
——— Gens, General Major. Nachrichten über ... den N. W. Theil des Chinesischen Staates, *etc.*
   St. Pet., 1839.
——— Helmersen, G. von. Nachrichten über ... den nord-westlichen Theil des Chinesischen Staates.
   St. Pet., 1839.
——— Slade, J. Narrative of the late Proceedings ... in C.
   Canton, 1839.
——— Wise, H. Analysis of One Hundred Voyages to and from ... C., *etc.*
   1839.
——— Biot, E. Études sur les Montagnes et les Cavernes de la Chine.
   Par., 1840.
——— ——— Recherches sur la Hauteur de quelques points remarquables du Territoire Chinois.
   Par., 1840.
——— ——— Recherches sur la temperature ancienne de la Chine.
   Par., 1840.
——— Ternaux-Compans, H. De ... l'expédition contre Chine.
   Par., 1840.
——— Lay, G. T. Chinese as they are, *etc.*
   1841.
——— Bingham, J. E. Narrative of ... Expedition to C., *etc.*
   1842.
——— Biot, E. Dictionnaire des Noms ... des Villes et Arrondissements compris dans l'Empire Chinois.
   Par., 1842.
——— Müller, G. F. and Pallas, P. S. Conquest of Siberia and the History of the Transactions ... between Russia and C. from the earliest period.
   1842.
——— Belcher, Sir E. Narrative ... including details of ... Naval Operations in C., *etc.*
   1843.
——— Biot, E. Sur la direction de l'Aiguille aimantée en Chine, *etc.*
   Par., 1844.
——— Chinese Topography, *&c.*
   Canton, 1844.
——— Galloway, J. A. Communication with ... C., *etc.*
   1844.
——— Lopes de Lima, J. J. Ensaios sobre a Statistica dos Possessõe Portuguezas ... na C., *etc.*
   Lisboa, 1844-62.
——— Reinaud, M. Relation des Voyages faits par les Arabes et les Persans dans ... la Chine dans le IX°. siècle.
   1845.
——— Davidson, G. F. Trade and Travel ... Recollections of ... C.
   Lond., 1846.
——— Martin, R. M. Reports, Minutes, and Despatches on the British Position and Prospects in C.
   Lond., 1846.
——— Smith, Br. G. Narrative of an explanatory Visit to each of the Consular Cities of C., *etc.*
   1847.
——— Erman, A. Travels in Siberia, including excursions ... to the Chinese frontier, *etc.*
   1848.

China.

China.—FORBES, F. E. Five Years in C., etc. 1848.
—— HALL, W. H., and BERNARD, W. D. The Nemesis in C., etc. 1848.
—— HEDDE, I. Description ... des Produits ... recueillis dans un Voyage en Chine. St. Étienne, 1848.
—— WILLIAMS, S. W. The Middle Kingdom; a survey of the ... Chinese Empire, etc. N. Y. and Lond., 1848.
—— SIRR, H. C. C. and the Chinese, etc. 1849.
—— BERNCASTLE, DR. A Voyage to C., etc. Lond., 1850.
—— PEET, Mr. Letter from, on a new Chinese Geography. Doc. U. S., 1850.
—— INDIA. First Report ... on Steam Communications with ... C., etc. Lond., 1851.
—— SOARES, J. P. C. Bosquejo das Possessões Portuguezas no ... India e ... C. Lisb., 1851.
—— FORTUNE, R. Journey to the Tea Countries of C., etc. 1852.
—— HUC, M. Souvenirs d'un Voyage dans ... la Chine ... 1844-46. 1852.
—— —— Recollections of a Journey through ... C. ... 1844-46, etc. 1852.
—— BUTTON, SIR T. Some particulars ... of a North-West Passage to C., etc., 1012. 1853.
—— POWER, W. T. Recollections of a Three Years' Residence in C., etc. Lond., 1853.
—— SUMMERS, J. Lecture on the Chinese Language and Literature, etc. Lond., 1853.
—— HUC, M. L'Empire Chinois, etc. Par., 1854.
—— STANLEY, H. Chinese Manual ... Recueil de Phrases Chinois, etc. 1854.
—— BATE, W. J. C. Pilot, etc. 1855.
—— HUC, M. The Chinese Empire, etc. Lond., 1855.
—— TAYLOR, B. Visit to ... C. ... in 1853. 1855.
—— MEADOWS, T. T. The Chinese and their Rebellions, etc. 1856.
—— RICHARDS, O. C. Pilot. Appendix 13, 14, 16-18, etc. 1856-7.
—— DAVIS, SIR J. F. C.: a general description, etc. 1857.
—— FORTUNE, R. Residence among the Chinese, etc. 1857.
—— HABERSHAM, A. W. My last Cruise ... Visits to ... C., etc. Phil., 1857.
—— MARTIN, R. M. Report ... and Minute on the British Position and Prospects in C., etc. 1857.
—— MILNE, W. C. Life in C. 1857.
—— HUC, M. Christianity in C., etc. 1857-8.
—— AFRICA. The Lights of ... C. ... Corrected to 1857, 58, 59. 1857-59.
—— COLLINSON, ADMIRAL. The Coasts of C. and Tartary, etc. 1858.

China. 133

China.—Cooke, G. W. C.; etc. 1858.
—— Richards, J. C. Pilot. Appendix N°. 1. Gulf of Siam, etc. 1858.
—— Rondot, M. N. Notice du Vert de Chine, etc. Par., 1858.
—— Belcher, Sir E., and Bate, W. T. C. Pilot, etc. 1859.
—— China. Journal of the first French Embassy to C., 1698-1700, etc. 1859.
—— Oliphant, L. Narrative of the Earl of Elgin's Mission to C. . . . in 1857-59. Edin., 1859.
—— Tronson, J. M. Narrative of a Voyage to . . . various parts of the Coast of C. 1859.
—— Atkinson, T. W. Travels . . . on the confines of . . . C. 1860.
—— Osborn, S. The Past and Future of British Relations in C. 1860.
—— Rondot, M. N. Commerce de la France avec la Chine, etc. Lyon, 1860.
—— Spate, R. Commerce with Western and Interior C., etc. 1860.
—— Dunsterville, E. The Admiralty List of the Lights of . . . C. . . . Corrected to 1860, 61, 62. 1860-62.
—— Duckworth, H. New Commercial Route to C. 1861.
—— King, J. W. C. Pilot, etc. 1861.
—— Lockhart, W. The Medical Missionary in C., etc. Lond., 1861.
—— Proudfoot, W. J. Barrow's Travels in C.; an Investigation, etc. 1861.
—— Rondot, M. N. Pé-King et la Chine; Mésures, Monnaies, etc. Par., 1861.
—— Sykes, W. H. Notes on . . . the Trade of England with C., etc. 1861.
—— Brine, L. The Taeping Rebellion in C., etc. 1862.
—— Lauture, Count d'Escayrac de. Notice sur les Déplacements des deux principaux Fleuves de la Chine. Par., 1862.
—— Sainsbury, W. N. Calendar of State Papers . . . C. . . . 1513-1616, etc. Lond., 1862.
—— Spate, D. and R. H. F. Aërial Telegraph to . . . the Open Ports of C., etc. Lond., 1862.
—— —— The Western-Inland-Provinces of C. Proper . . . considered, etc. 1862.
—— Reinaud, M. Relations Politiques et Commerciales de l'Empire Romain avec . . . (la Chine) pendant les cinq premiers siècles, etc. Par., 1863.
—— Sykes, W. H. The Taeping Rebellion in C., etc. 1863.
—— Lauture, Count d'Escayrac de. Mémoires sur la Chine, etc. Par., 1864.
—— Stephenson, Sir M. Railways in C. Report, etc. 1864.
—— Davis, Sir J. F. Chinese Miscellanies, etc. Lond., 1865.
—— Doolittle, J. Social Life of the Chinese, etc. N. Y., 1865.

China.

China.—Pumpelly, R. Notice of an Account of Geological Observations in C., etc. [1866.]

—— Courcy, Marquis de. L'Empire du Milieu [C.], description, etc. *Par.*, 1867.

—— Ferrari, J. La Chine et l'Europe, leur histoire, etc. *Par.*, 1867.

—— Lamprey, Dr. Further Remarks on the Ethnology of the Chinese. 1867.

—— Alabaster, C. and others. Reports of Journeys in C., etc. *Lond.*, 1869.

—— Jenner, T. Mnemonic Geography. Part I. The Provinces of C. *Lond.*, 1869.

—— McLeod, W. C. Copy of Papers relating to ... Route ... from Moulmein to ... C., etc. *Lond.*, 1869.

—— Account of the Portuguese possessions from the Cape of Good Hope to C. Astley. Vol. I.

—— Embassy of the Lord Van Hoorn to ... C., etc. Astley. Vol. III.

—— The first attempts of the Dutch to trade to C., etc. Astley. Vol. III.

—— Navarrette's Travels through C. in 1658. Astley. Vol. III.

—— Nieuhoff, J. Embassy of P. de Goyer and J. de Keyzer ... to ... C. in 1655. Astley. Vol. III.

—— Travels of Dr. J. F. Gemelli Careri in C. in 1695. Astley. Vol. III.

—— Travels of E. Isbrand Ides ... in C. in 1693. Astley. Vol. III.

—— Travels of L. Lange ... in C. in 1717. Astley. Vol. III.

—— Voyages and Travels in ... C. Astley. Vol. III.

—— Description of C., etc. Astley. Vol. IV.

—— Embassy of Shâh Rokh ... to ... C. in 1419, etc. Astley. Vol. IV.

—— Travels of B. Goëz ... from Lahor ... to China in 1602. Astley. Vol. IV.

—— Travels through Tartary ... to ... C. Astley. Vol. IV.

—— Travels through Tibet, to and from C., etc. Astley. Vol. IV.

—— Voyage and Travels ... from Russia to Boghâr ... in 1557 ... Information concerning the Road thence to Katay or C. Astley. Vol. IV.

—— Navarrette, D. F. Account of ... C., etc. Churchill. Vol. I.

—— Backhoff, F. I. Voyage into C. Churchill. Vol. II.

—— Wagener, Z. Voyage ... into C. Churchill. Vol. II.

—— Bandier, M. History of the Court ... of C. Churchill. Vol. VIII.

—— Bernardine. Account of ... C., etc. Churchill. Vol. VIII.

—— Meares. Voyage de la Chine à la Côte Nord-Ouest de l'Amérique, 1788, 89. Eyriès. Vol. I.

—— Chine. Ambassade des Anglais, 1792 et 1816. Eyriès. Vol. XII.

China.   135

China.—Mandevil, Sir J. Voyage ... to ... C. ... 1322-1355. HAKLUYT. Vol. II.
— Odoricus, Frier B. Voyage to ... C. ... about 1325. HAKLUYT. Vol. II.
— Frobisher, M. Voyages ... in search of a Passage to C., 1576-78. HAKLUYT. Vol. III.
— Gilbert, Sir H. Discourse to prove a passage by the N.W. to Cataya, etc. HAKLUYT. Vol. III.
— Rundall, T. Narratives of Voyages ... in search of a passage to Cathay and India, 1496 to 1631, etc. HAKLUYT Soc. Pub. Vol. V.
— Veer, G. de. True Description of three Voyages ... towards Cathay and C. ... in 1594-96. ... Edited by C. T. Beke. 1853. HAKLUYT Soc. Pub. Vol. XIII.
— Mendoza, Padre J. G. da. History of ... C. ... Edited by Sir G. T. Staunton, etc. 1853. HAKLUYT Soc. Pub. Vol. XIV. XV.
— An Account of the Travels of two Mahommedans through ... C. in the ninth Century, etc. HARRIS, J. Vol. I.
— Benjamin, Rabbi. Travels ... from Spain to C., 1160-1173. HARRIS, J. Vol. I.
— Rubruquis, W. de. The remarkable Travels of ... into Tartary and C., 1253. HARRIS, J. Vol. I.
— Kao, D. An Authentick Account ... of C., etc. HARRIS, J. Vol. II.
— —— A Geographical description of ... C., etc. HARRIS, J. Vol. II.
— Ysbrants Ides, E. Travels ... to the frontiers of C. ... 1692-95. HARRIS, J. Vol. II.
— Benjamin, Rabbi. Travels from Spain to C. in the twelfth Century. KERR. Vol. I.
— Marco Polo. Travels into C. from 1260 to 1295. KERR. Vol. I.
— Oderic, of Portenau. Travels into C. ... 1318. KERR. Vol. I.
— Pegoletti. Itinerary between Azof and C., 1355. KERR. Vol. I.
— Travels of Two Mahometans into ... C. in the ninth century. KERR. Vol. I.
— A short account of the Portuguese Possessions between the Cape of Good Hope and C. KERR. Vol. VII.
— Cunningham, J. Observations ... with some early notices respecting C. KERR. Vol. IX.
— Description des quinze Provinces de la Chine. LAHARPE, J. Vol. VI.
— Précis de differens Voyages à la Chine, depuis le treizième siècle, etc. LAHARPE, J. Vol. VI.
— Voyages ... des Hollandais à la Chine. LAHARPE, J. Vol. VI.
— Mœurs des Chinois, etc. LAHARPE, J. Vol. VII.
— Histoire Naturelle de la Chine. LAHARPE, J. Vol. VIII.
— Staunton, Sir G. Account of the Earl of Macartney's Embassy ... to ... C. PELHAM. Vol. I.

China.

China.—Goes. Travels from Lahor to C. PINKERTON. Vol. VII.
—— Nieuhoff's Travels in C. PINKERTON. Vol. VII.
—— Brown, A. Extracts of a Journal . . . sayling divers times . . . to . . . the Coast of C. . . . 1617-22. PURCHAS. Vol. II.
—— Trigautius, N. Letter touching . . . the state of Christianitie in C. . . . 1618. PURCHAS. Vol. II.
—— Cruz, G. da. Treatise of C. . . . about 1556. PURCHAS. Vol. III.
—— Description of the Empires of Catay, etc. PURCHAS. Vol. III.
—— A general collection . . . of the Jesuites entrance into Japon and C. . . . 1542-99. PURCHAS. Vol. III.
—— Goes, B. Travels from Lahore to C. . . . 1603. PURCHAS. Vol. III.
—— Herrada, Friar M. de, and other Spaniards entertainment in C. . . . about 1580. PURCHAS. Vol. III.
—— Mendez Pinto, F. Observations of C. . . . 1521-45. PURCHAS. Vol. III.
—— Monfart. Continuation of the Jesuites Acts . . . in C. . . . 1618. PURCHAS. Vol. III.
—— Perera, G. Relations of C. PURCHAS. Vol. III.
—— Pontoia, Father D. Letter written in . . . 1602. Description of C., etc. PURCHAS. Vol. III.
—— Relation of two Russe Cossacks Travailes out of Siberia to Catay . . . 1619. PURCHAS. Vol. III.
—— Riccios and Trigautius. Discourse of C., etc. PURCHAS. Vol. III.
—— Veer, G. de. Voyages of W. Barents . . . to . . . C., 1594-96. PURCHAS. Vol. III.
—— Of the . . . Chinois, and of their Religions. PURCHAS. Vol. V.
—— Navigationi fatte da gli Olandesi . . . verso il . . . Regno de' Sini, etc. 1594-97. RAMUSIO. Vol. III.
—— Extrait de la Relation de l'Ambassade que les Hollandois envoyèrent en 1656 & 1657, au . . . Maistre de la Chine. THEVENOT. Vol. I.
—— Voyage d'Antoine Jenkinson au Cathay. THEVENOT. Vol. I.
—— Flora Sinensis . . . avec . . . figures, etc. THEVENOT. Vol. II.
—— Ambassade des Hollandois à la Chine.—Route . . . des Ambassadeurs, etc. THEVENOT. Vol. III.
—— Ambassade des Moscovites à la Chine, etc. THEVENOT. Vol. IV.
—— Voyage à la Chine des Pères Grueber & d'Orville, etc. THEVENOT. Vol. IV.
—— Wood, J. Attempt to discover a N.-E. Passage to C., etc. 1711. VOYAGES. Account of several late, etc.
—— Ihnovet, J. Reise von Peking nach Kanton . . . 1693. VOYAGES and TRAVELS. Allgemeine Historie, etc. Vol. V.
—— Comte et Fontaney. Reise von Siam nach Ning po fu, etc. VOYAGES and TRAVELS. Allgemeine Historie, etc. Vol. V.
—— Fontaney, J. Reise von Peking nach Kyangchew . . . und . . . Nan King, 1688. VOYAGES and TRAVELS. Allgemeine Historie, etc. Vol. V.

China. 137

China.—Fünf Französischer Jesuiten Reisen von Ning po fu nach Peking, 1687. VOYAGES and TRAVELS. Allgemeine Historie, etc. Vol. V.

——— Gaubils, A. Reise von Kanton nach Peking, 1722. VOYAGES and TRAVELS. Allgemeine Historie, etc. Vol. V.

——— Gemelli Careri, J. F. Reise in C., 1695, etc. VOYAGES and TRAVELS. Allgemeine Historie, etc. Vol. V.

——— Ishrand Ides, E. Reise nach C., 1693. VOYAGES and TRAVELS. Allgemeine Historie, etc. Vol. V.

——— Langens, L. Reise nach C., 1717. VOYAGES and TRAVELS. Allgemeine Historie, etc. Vol. V.

——— Mezzabarba, C. A. Legation . . . an den Kaiser . . . im C., 1720. VOYAGES and TRAVELS. Allgemeine Historie, etc. Vol. V.

——— Montanus, A. Die Gesandtschaft des Herrn van Hoorn an . . . C. . . . 1666-7. VOYAGES and TRAVELS. Allgemeine Historie, etc. Vol. V.

——— Die Gesandtschaft J. von Campen und C. Nobles, an den Unterkönig von Fokyen Sing la mong, 1662. VOYAGES and TRAVELS. Allgemeine Historie, etc. Vol. V.

——— Navarette, F. Reisen des, durch C., 1058. VOYAGES and TRAVELS. Allgemeine Historie, etc. Vol. V.

— — Neuhof, J. P. von Goyer und J. von Keyzer Gesandtschaft . . . an den Kaiser in C., 1655. VOYAGES and TRAVELS. Allgemeine Historie, etc. Vol. V.

——— Reisen nach dem C. VOYAGES and TRAVELS. Allgemeine Historie, etc. Vol. V.

——— Van Rechteren. Erste Versuche der Holländer, nach C. zu handeln, etc. VOYAGES and TRAVELS. Allgemeine Historie, etc. Vol. V.

——— Beschreibung von C., etc. VOYAGES and TRAVELS. Allgemeine Historie, etc. Vol. VI.

——— Gesandtschaft des Sohnes Tamerlans . . . an den Kaiser in . . . C., 1419-22. VOYAGES and TRAVELS. Allgemeine Historie, etc. Vol VII.

——— Goes, B. Reisen . . . nach C., 1602. VOYAGES and TRAVELS. Allgemeine Historie, etc. Vol. VII.

——— Gruber, J. Reisen von C. nach Europa, 1661. VOYAGES and TRAVELS. Allgemeine Historie, etc. Vol. VII.

——— Matelief, C. Reise . . . 1605-8 . . . Reise nach C. VOYAGES and TRAVELS. Allgemeine Historie, etc. Vol. VIII.

— - Fonteuay, P. von. Reise von Siam nach C., 1686. VOYAGES and TRAVELS. Allgemeine Historie, etc. Vol. X.

——— Pinto, F. M. Reise nach . . . C., etc. VOYAGES and TRAVELS. Allgemeine Historie, etc. Vol. X.

——— Schouten, G. Reisen nach . . . C. . . . 1658-65. VOYAGES and TRAVELS. Allgemeine Historie, etc. Vol. XII.

——— India. An Account of a Voyage to India, C., etc. in H.M.S. Caroline, 1803-5, etc. VOYAGES and TRAVELS. A Collection, etc. 1805. Vol. V.

——— Diary of a Journey Overland through the Maritime Provinces of C. . . . 1819-20. VOYAGES and TRAVELS, New. 1819. Vol. VI.

China — Chinese Tartary.

China.—Le Comple, Louis, and Du Halde, P. A. Description of C., 1665.
Voyages and Travels. The World displayed. Vol. XVI.
———, **East Coast.**—Biot, E. Mémoire sur l'extension progressive des Côtes Orientales de la Chine, etc. *Par.*, 1844.
——— ——— Collinson, Admiral. C. Pilot, East Coast, etc. 1855.
———, **North.**—Fortune, R. Three Years' Wanderings in the N. Provinces of C., etc. 1847.
——— ——— Swinhoe, R. Narrative of the N. C. Campaign of 1860, etc. *Lond.*, 1861.
——— ——— Dennys, N. D. Notes for Tourists in the N. of C. *Hongkong*, 1866.
——— ——— Williamson, A. Notes on the N. of C., etc. 1867.
——— ——— ——— Journeys in N. C., etc. *Lond.*, 1870.
———, **West.**—Sprye, R. and R.-H.-F. The Western-Inland-Provinces of C. Proper ... considered in connection with British-E.n-Pegue, etc. *Lond.*, 1862.
——— ——— China. Memorial ... on ... Commerce with the W. of C. from ... Rangoon. 1864.
——— ——— Williams, C. Memorandum on the Question of British Trade with W.n C. viâ Burmah. 1864.
——— ——— Williams, J. M. Memorandum on Railway Communication with W.n C. ... from ... Rangoon, etc. *Lond.*, 1865.
——— ——— Williams, J. M. and Luard, C. H. Copies of ... Survey Report ... respecting Rangoon and W.n C., etc. *Lond.*, 1867.
——— ——— Williams, C. Through Burmah to W.n C., etc. *Edin. and Lond.*, 1868.
——— ——— Sprye, R. The Sprye Route to W.n C. [*Lond.*] 1869.
——— ——— Wakefield Chamber of Commerce. Direct Commerce with the ... W. of C. ... Memorial, etc. *Lond.*, 1869.

China Sea.—Redfield, W. C. Whirlwinds excited by Fire, with further Notices of the Tyfoons of the C. S.
——— Morrell, B. Narrative of four Voyages to the ... C. S., etc. *N. Y.*, 1832.
——— Redfield, W. C. On the Course of Hurricanes, with Notices of the Tyfoons of the C. S., etc. *N. Y.*, 1838.
——— Piddington, H. Ten Memoirs on the law of Storms as applying to the Tempests of the Indian and Chinese Seas. *Calc.*, 1839-43.
——— ——— The Horn-Book of Storms for the Indian and C. Seas. *Calc.*, 1845.
——— Lagravière, J. de. Rapport sur la Campagne de la Corvette *La Bayonnaise* dans les Mers de Chine. *Par.*, 1851.
——— Perry, M. C. Narrative of the Expedition of an American Squadron to the C. S. ... in 1852-54, etc. *Wash.*, 1856.
——— Denham, H. M. Hydrographic Notices ... C. S., etc. 1856-59.
——— Gras, M. A. le. Phares des Mers ... de Chine ... Corrigés 1862, 63. *Par.*, 1862, 63.

Chinese Tartary.—See Tartary, Chinese.

Chio.—*See* Scio.
Chipionyan, Fort.—*See* Chippewayan.
Chippewa.—Owen, D. D. Reports of a Geological Reconnoissance of the C. Land District of Wisconsin, *etc.* *Wash.*, 1848.
Chippewayan, Fort.—Mackenzie. Voyage . . . du Fort Chipionyan aux côtes du Grand Océan, 1789-93. Eyriès. Vol. VII.
Chiquimula.—Palacio, D. G. de. Description of the Ancient Province of . . . C. . . . 1576. Squier, Collection. No. I.
Chira.—Spruce, R. Notes on the Valleys of Piura and C., *etc.*
Lond., 1864.
Chiriqui Bay.—America, Central. Description of . . . a Road . . . from Admiral's Bay . . . to C. B., *etc.* *Phil.*, 1852.
——— **Lagoon.**—America, Central. Description of . . . a Road . . . from . . . C. L. . . . to . . . the Pacific, *etc.* *Phil.*, 1852.
Chittagong.—Poason, Capt. W. R. Narrative during a tour to Chateegaon, 1831. *Serump.*, 1831.
Chiwa.—*See* Khiva.
Choa.—*See* Shoa.
Chokand.—*See* Krokan.
Cho-Lagan.—Strachey, H. Narrative of a Journey to the Lakes C.-L., *etc.* *Calc.*, 1848.
Cholmondeley, River.—*See* Ramaia.
Cho-Mapan, Lake.—*See* Manasarowar.
Choromandel.—*See* Coromandel.
Christiania.—Hansteen, C., and Fearnley, C. Beschreibung und Lage der Universitats-Sternwarte in C., *etc.* *Christ.*, 1849.
——— Kjerulf, T. Das C.-Silurbecken, chemisch-geognostisch untersucht. *Christ.*, 1855.
——— Murchison, Sir R. I. Additional Observations on the Silurian and Devonian Rocks near C., *etc.* 1855.
——— Norman, J. M. Quelques Observations de Morphologie Végétale faites au Jardin Botanique de C. *Christ.*, 1857.
——— Meteorologische Beobachtungen aufgezeichnet auf C.s Observatorium. *Christ.*, 1862.
——— Mohn, H. Den Magnetiske Declination i C. . . . 1842-62. 1863.
——— Kjerulf, T. Veiviser ved Geologiske Excursioner i C. Omegn.
Christ., 1865.
Christmas Island.—Besson, G. Sketch of C. I. 1838.
——— Trevelyan, F. H. Remarks on C. I. 1838.
Churssachsische Lande.—*See* Saxony.
Chusan.—Smith, Bp. G. Narrative of an Explanatory Visit to . . . C. *etc.* 1847.
——— Martin, R. M. Report on . . . C., *etc.* 1857.
——— Cunningham, J. Observations . . . during his residence on the Island of C. . . . 1701. Harris, J. Vol. I.

Chusan.—Cunningham J. Observations during a Residence in . . . C., in 1701, etc. Kerr. Vol. IX.

Cibola.—See Zuni.

Cibyra.—Spratt, T. A. B., and Forbes, E. Travels in . . . the Cibyratis. 1847.

Cilicia.—Barker, W. B. Lares and Penates; or, C. and its Governors, etc. 1853.

――― Tchihatcheff, P. de. Dépôts Tertiaires d'une partie de la Cilicie Trachée, de la Cilicie Champêtre, etc. Par., 1854.

――― Biddulph, W. Travels of four Englishmen . . . into . . . C. . . . in 1600 and 1611. Churchill. Vol. VII.

Cina.—See China.

Cinaloa.—Perez, M. Extracts out of certain Letters of, from the New Mission of . . . C. . . . 1501, etc. Purchas. Vol. IV.

Cinoloa.—See Cinaloa.

Circars.—Observations on the Copper Coinage wanted for the C. 1794. Dalrymple, A. Tracts, from 1764 to 1808. Vol. II.

――― Memoir on Watering the C. Dalrymple, A. Tracts, from 1769 to 1798.

Circassia.—Marigny, Chev. Taitbout de. Three Voyages . . . to the Coast of C., etc. Lond., 1837.

――― Spencer, E. Travels in C., etc. 1837.

――― Bell, J. S. Journal of a Residence in C. during . . . 1837-39. Lond., 1840.

――― Neumann, C. F. Russland und die Tscherkessen. Stutt. und Tüb., 1840.

――― Spencer, E. Turkey . . . and C. 1854.

――― Chardin, Sir J. Travels . . . through . . . C. . . . 1672. Harris, J. Vol. II.

Circumnavigation.—See World.

City of the Saints.—See Utah.

Ciudad de los Angelos.—See Puebla de los Angelos.

Civita Vecchia.—Davis, W. A true . . . description of C. V., etc. Churchill. Vol. VII.

Coahuila.—See Cohahuila.

Coblenz.—Louis XVIII., King of France. Relation d'un Voyage à Bruxelles et à C., 1791. Par., 1823.

Cochin.—Lawson, C. A. British and Native C. 1861.

――― Corsali, A. Lettera scritta in C. . . . 1515, etc. Ramusio. Vol. I.

――― China.—Pallu, F. Breve, e compendiosa Relatione de' Viaggi di tre Vescovi Francesi . . . à i Regni della . . . Cocincina, etc. Roma, 1669.

――― Barrow, Sir J. Voyage to C.-C., etc. 1806.

――― Bissachère M. de la. État actuel . . . de la Cochinchine, etc. Par., 1812.

Cochin China.—CRAWFURD, J. Journal of an Embassy to . . . C. C. etc. 1830.
—— Moor, J. H. Notices of . . . C. C., etc. *Singapore*, 1837.
—— SPEYE, R. H. F. and C. H. F. The British and China Railway; from Rangoon . . . to . . . C.-C. 1858.
—— GRAMMONT, L. DE. Onze Mois de Sous-Préfecture en Basse-Cochinchine, etc. *Napoléon-Vendée*, 1863.
—— PRUNER-BEY, DR. Note sur les Usages des Populations Indigènes de la Cochinchine Française. 1863.
—— COINCY, L. DE. Quelques Mots sur la Cochinchine en 1866. *Par.*, 1866.
—— THOREL, C. Notes Médicales du Voyage d'Exploration . . . de Cochinchine. *Par.*, 1870.
—— Dorri, R. F. C. Account of C., etc. CHURCHILL. Vol. II.
—— Cochin-chine. ETATS. Vol. XIII.
—— Bovis's History of C. C. PINKERTON. Vol. IX.
—— Rhodes, A. Reise nach C., etc. VOYAGES and TRAVELS. Allgemeine Historie, etc. Vol. X.
—— Rey, Capt. Voyage from France to C. C., 1819-20. VOYAGES and TRAVELS, New. 1819. Vol. IV.

Cœle-Syria.—Squire, Col. Travels through part of the ancient C.-S., etc. WALPOLE, R. Travels, etc.

Cohahuila.—EDWARDS, C. Texas and C., etc. *N. Y.*, 1834.

Colaba.—BUIST, G. Provisional Report on the Meteorological Observations made at C. . . . for 1844. *Cupar*, 1845.

Colchis, Colchide.—*See* MINGRELIA.

Col du Geant.—BARROW, J. Expeditions on . . . C. du G., etc. 1864.
—— GLACIER. Expeditions . . . including an ascent of . . . C. du G., etc. 1864.

Coleroon.—INDIA. Reports of the . . . effects of the . . . C. Annicuts in Tanjore, etc. *Madras*, 1858.

Colmogro.—*See* KHOLMOGORY.

Cologne.—Browne, E. Voyage . . . to Holland; with a Journey through the Electorates of C. . . . 1666. HARRIS, J. Vol. II.

Colombia.—BOLDUC, J. B. Z. Mission de la Colombie . . . 1842-43.
—— COLOMBIA. Being a geographical . . . account of that Country. 1822.
—— MOLLIEN, G. Travels in . . . C., etc. 1824.
—— COCHRANE, C. S. Journal of a Residence and Travels in C. during 1823-24. 1825.
—— HALL, F. C. in its present state, etc. 1827.
—— COLOMBIA. The Present State of C., etc. 1827.
—— COLOMBIA. Noticia sobre la Geografía Política de C. *Caracas*, 1830.

——, **River.** *See* COLOMBIA, RIVER.

Colong.—ANDERSON, J. Observations . . . the result of a . . . Mission to . . . C., *etc.* *P. of W. I.*, **1824.**

Colonia Georgico-Anglicana.—*See* GEORGIA.

Colonies.—*See* BRITISH COLONIES.

Colonnæ.—CALVERT, F. Contributions to . . . Ancient Geography. . . . Investigations relative to . . . C., *etc.* **1861.**

Colorado.—WHITNEY, J. P. C., in the U. S. of America. Schedule of Ores contributed to the Paris Universal Exposition of 1867, *etc.* *Lond.*, **1867.**

—— HAYDEN, F. V. Preliminary Field Report of the U. S. Geological Survey of C., *etc.* *Wash.*, **1869.**

——, **River.**—IVES, LIEUT. J. C. Voyage d'Exploration du C. en 1857 et 1858.

—— —— WHIPPLE, A. W. Report of an Expedition from San-Diego to the C., *etc.* *Wash.*, **1851.**

—— —— DERBY, G. H. Report of the Reconnaissance of . . . the C. R., made in 1850-51. *Wash.*, **1852.**

—— —— SITGREAVES, L. Report of an Expedition down the . . . C., *etc.* *Wash.*, **1854.**

—— —— HUMPHREYS, A. A. Report . . . Exploration of the Rio C., *etc.* *Wash.*, **1859.**

—— —— IVES, J. C. Report upon the C., *etc.* *Wash.*, **1861.**

Columbia, District of.—WARDEN, D. B. A Chorographical . . . Account of the District of C., *etc.* *Paris*, **1816.**

——, **River.**—COX, R. Adventures on the C. R., *etc.* **1831.**

—— —— MONTGOMERIE, J. E. and HOBNEY, A. F. R. DE. A few words collected from . . . the Indians in the Neighbourhood of C. River, *etc.* **1848.**

—— —— Lewis et Clarke. Voyage . . . à l'embouchure de la C. dans le Grand Océan, 1804-6. EYRIES. Vol. IX.

Columbian Isthmus.—*See* PANAMA, ISTHMUS OF.

Commereylande.—*See* BERMUDA ISLANDS.

Como, Lake of.—BERTOLOTTI, D. Viaggio ai . . . Laghi di C., *etc.* *Como*, **1825.**

Comores.—*See* COMORO ISLANDS.

Comorin, Cape.—Lancaster, J. Memorable Voyage . . . beyond Cape C. . . . 1591. HAKLUYT. Vol. II.

—— Beaulieu, A. Reise . . . 1619-21 . . . nach dem Vorgebirge C., *etc.* VOYAGES and TRAVELS. Allgemeine Historie, *etc.* Vol X.

Comoro Islands.—GEVREY, A. Essai sur les Comores. *Pondichéry*, **1870.**

—— Inverarity, D. Memoir . . . and C. I., by the Hon. T. Howe, 1766. DALRYMPLE, A. Collection of Nautical Memoirs, *etc.*

—— Pyrard, F. Fahrt und Begebenheiten . . . bis an die Inseln Comorres, *etc.* VOYAGES and TRAVELS. Allgemeine Historie, *etc.* Vol. VIII.

Comoro Islands — Congo.

Comoro Islands.—Spilberg, G. Reise nach ... den Comorrischen Inseln. 1601-3. VOYAGES and TRAVELS. Allgemeine Historie, etc. Vol. VIII.

Comorres.—See COMORO ISLANDS.

Compostella, Saint James of.—See SANTIAGO DE COMPOSTELLA.

Comstock Lode.—RICHTHOFEN, BARON F. The C. L.; its character, etc. *San. F.*, **1866**.

——— SUTRO, A. The Sutro Tunnel to the C. I., etc. *N. Y.*, **1866**.

Concan.—JERVIS, T. B. Geographical ... Memoir of the Konkun. *Calc.*, **1840**.

Concord, River.—THOREAU, H. D. A Week on the C. and Merrimack Rivers. *Bost. and Camb.*, **1849**.

Confederacion Argentina.—See ARGENTINE REPUBLIC.

Congo.—PELLICER DE TOVAR, J. Mission Evangelica al Reyno de C., etc. *Madrid*, **1649**.

——— MANDELSLO, J. A. DE. Voyage ... Contenants une description du C., etc. *Amst.*, **1727**.

——— DOUVILLE, J. B. Atlas du Voyage au C., etc. *Paris* [**1832**.]

——— ——— Voyage au C., etc. *Par.*, **1832**.

——— ——— Voyage au C., etc. [A Review.] **1832**.

——— Portuguese sent to ... East Indies by Land, with ... account of ... Kongo. ASTLEY. Vol. I.

——— A Description of ... K., etc. ASTLEY. Vol. III.

——— Voyage to K. in 1666-67 by M. Angelo and D. de Carli, etc. ASTLEY. Vol. III.

——— Voyage to K. ... in 1682, by J. Merolla de Sorrento. ASTLEY. Vol. III.

——— Voyages and Travels to Benin ... and ... Kongo. ASTLEY. Vol. III.

——— Voyages and Travels to Kongo and Angola. ASTLEY. Vol. III.

——— Angelo, M. and Carli, D. Curious ... account of a Voyage to C. in 1666-67. CHURCHILL. Vol. I.

——— Merolla da Sorrento, J. Voyage to C., etc. CHURCHILL. Vol. I.

——— Pigafetta, P. Report of the Kingdom of C., etc. CHURCHILL. Vol. VIII.

——— Congo. LABARRE, J. Vol. III.

——— Angelo and Carli's Voyage to C. PINKERTON. Vol. XVI.

——— Merolla's Voyage to C. PINKERTON. Vol. XVI.

——— Pigafetta, P. Report of the Kingdom of C., etc. PURCHAS. Vol. II.

——— Description of the divers Nations ... in Brasill ... also ... C., etc. PURCHAS. Vol. IV.

——— Angelo, M. Die Reise nach K., 1666. VOYAGES and TRAVELS. Allgemeine Historie, etc. Vol. IV.

——— Carli, D. Reisen der Missionarien in K., 1667. Fortsetzung, 1668. VOYAGES and TRAVELS. Allgemeine Historie, etc. Vol. IV.

Congo.—Eine Beschreibung der Königreiche . . . K., etc. VOYAGES and TRAVELS. Allgemeine Historie, etc. Vol. IV.
—— Lopes, E. Die Reise nach K., 1578. VOYAGES and TRAVELS. Allgemeine Historie, etc. Vol. IV.
—— Merolla, H. Eine Reise nach K. . . . 1682-88. VOYAGES and TRAVELS. Allgemeine Historie, etc. Vol. IV.
—— Schiffahrten und Reisen nach . . . K., etc. VOYAGES and TRAVELS. Allgemeine Historie, etc. Vol. IV.
——, River.—TUCKEY, J. K. Narrative of an Expedition to explore . . . the C. . . . in 1816, etc. 1818.
—— —— ADAMS, Capt. J. Remarks on the Country . . . from Cape Palmas to the River C., etc. 1823.
—— —— Abstract of a Voyage to K. R. . . . in 1700, by J. Barbot and J. Casseneuve. ASTLEY. Vol. IIII.
—— —— Tuckey. Voyage au Zaire ou fleuve du C., 1818. EYRIÈS. Vol. XI.
—— —— Barbot, J., and Casseneuve, J. Auszug aus einer Reise an den Fluss von K. . . . 1700. VOYAGES and TRAVELS. Allgemeine Historie, etc. Vol. IV.
Connaught.—GRIFFITH, G. D. Geological . . . Survey of the C. Coal District, etc. *Dubl.*, 1818.
—— C. Description of the Province of, 1612. 1837.
Connecticut.—HITCHCOCK, E. Ichnology of New England. A Report on the Sandstone of the C. Valley, etc. *Bost.*, 1858.
Constantina, Algeria.—See CONSTANTINE.
Constantine.—TEMPLE, Sir G. T. Sketch of the Campaign of Kostantinah. 1839.
—— MORICIÈRE ET BEDEAU. Projets de Colonisation pour les Provinces d'Oran et de C. *Par.*, 1847.
—— MALTE-BRUN, V. A. Itinéraire . . . de Philippeville à C. *Par.*, 1858.
—— MARÈS, P. Nivellement barométrique dans les provinces d'Alger et de C. *Versailles*, 1864.
Constantinople.—GYLLIUS, P. P. Gyllii de Constantinopoleos Topographia lib. IV. *Lugd. Batav.*, 1632.
—— BUSSO, G. B. da. Viaggio . . . Con la descrittione di . . . Constantinopoli, etc. *Milano* [1686.]
—— DRIESCH, G. C. VON DEN. Historische Nachricht von der Gross-Botschaft nach C., etc. *Nürnb.*, 1723.
—— MORIER, J. Journey . . . to C., in 1808-9. 1812.
—— HOBHOUSE, J. C. Journey . . . to C., in 1809-10. 1813.
—— MORIER, J. A Second Journey . . . to C., etc. *Lond.*, 1818.
—— MACMICHAEL, W. Journey from Moscow to C., etc. *Lond.*, 1819.
—— DANUBE. Observations sur les Routes . . . du Danube à C. à travers le Balcan, etc. *Par.*, 1828.
—— MAC FARLANE, C. C. in 1828, etc. 1829.
—— WALSH, R. Journey from C. to England. 1831.

Constantinople.—PRICE, W. Journal of Travels of the British Embassy
to . . . C., etc. 1833.
—— AULDJO, J. Visit to C., etc. 1835.
—— FRASER, J. B. Winter Journey from C. to Tehran, etc. 1838.
—— MURRAY. Hand-Book for Travellers in . . . C., etc. Lond., 1840.
—— DAVY, J. Notes . . . on C., etc. 1842.
—— SMITH, A. Month at C. 1850.
—— RAWLINSON, SIR H. C. Notes on the direct Overland Telegraph from
C. to Kurrachi. 1861.
—— TCHIHATCHEFF, P. DE. Le Bosphore et C., etc. Par., 1864.
—— Rolamb, N. Relation of a Journey to C. CHURCHILL. Vol. V.
—— Kennedy, C. M. The Turks of C. GALTON, F. Vacation Tourists
. . . in 1862-3.
—— Austel, H. Voyage . . . to C. . . . 1856. HAKLUYT. Vol. II.
—— Hareborne, W. Voyage overland from C. to London, 1588.
HAKLUYT. Vol. II.
—— Voyage of certaine Englishmen . . . to C. . . . about 500. HAK-
LUYT. Vol. II.
—— Voyage of three Ambassadors . . . unto C. . . . 1056. HAKLUYT.
Vol. II.
—— Voyage of the Susan to C. . . . 1582. HAKLUYT. Vol. II.
—— Wrag, R. Description of a Voyage to C. . . . 1593-95. etc.
HAKLUYT. Vol. II.
—— Thevenot, J. Voyages . . . from Italy to C., 1655. HARRIS, J.
Vol. II.
—— Voyage of three Ambassadors from England to C., about 1056.
KERR. Vol. I.
—— Coryates, J. Travels to . . . C. . . . 1612-14. PURCHAS. Vol. II.
—— Glover, Sir T. Account of the Journey of E. Barton, Esq., Ambas-
sador . . . in C., 1596. PURCHAS. Vol. II.
—— Sanderson, J. Pilgrimage from C. to the Holy Land . . . 1601.
PURCHAS. Vol. II.
—— —— Voyages to C. . . . 1584-1602. PURCHAS. Vol. II.
—— Belon, Mr. Remarks in . . . Creta . . . Journey from Mount
Athos to C., etc. RAY, J.
—— Greaves, J. Account of the Latitude of C., etc. RAY, J.
—— Smith, T. Historical Observations relating to C., etc. RAY, J.
—— Itinéraire de C. à la Mecque, etc. VOYAGES and TRAVELS. Recueil,
etc. Vol. II.
—— An Itinerary from London to C . . . 1794. VOYAGES and TRAVELS.
A Collection, etc. 1805. Vol. I.
—— Pouqueville, F. C. H. L. Travels . . . to C., 1708-1801, etc.
VOYAGES and TRAVELS. A Collection, etc. 1805. Vol. III.
—— Macmichel, W. Journey from Moscow to C., 1817-18. VOYAGES
and TRAVELS, New. 1819. Vol. I.

L

Constantinople.—Pertusier, C. Picturesque Promenades in and near C. . . . 1820. VOYAGES and TRAVELS, New. 1819, *etc.* Vol. VIII.
—— Browne, W. G. Journey from C. through Asia Minor . . . 1802. WALPOLE, R. Travels, *etc.*
—— Hawkins, Mr. Some particulars respecting the Police of C. WALPOLE, R. Travels, *etc.*

Coordistan.—*See* KURDISTAN.

Coorg.—COLE, R.A. An Elementary Grammar of the C. Language.
Bangalore, 1867.

Copenhagen.—WRAXALL, N. A Tour through . . . C., *etc.* 1776.
—— MARRYAT, H. Residence in . . . C. 1860.

Coquimbo.—ANDREWS, Capt. Journey . . . to C., *etc.* 1827.

Cordilleras.—*See* ANDES.

Cordova.—ANDREWS, Capt. Journey . . . through . . . C., *etc.* 1827.
—— WHEELWRIGHT, W. Introductory Remarks . . . Parana and C. Railway, Report, *etc.* 1861.
—— ARGENTINE RAILWAY. Central Argentine Railway from Rosario to C., *etc.* 1863.
—— MONETA, P. Informe sobre la Practicabilidad de la Prolongacion del Ferrocarril Central Argentino desde C. hasta Jujuy. *Buen. A.,* 1867.

Corea.—DU HALDE, J. B. A Description of . . . Korea, *etc.*
La Haye, 1736.
—— HALL, B. Account of a Voyage . . . to the W. Coast of C., *etc.*
1818.
—— MACLEOD, J. Voyage of H.M.S. *Alceste* to . . . C., *etc.* 1819.
—— GRAS, M. A. LE. Renseignements hydrographiques sur . . . la Corée, *etc.* *Par.,* 1859.
—— COREA. Description hydrographique de la Côte Orientale de la Corée, *etc.* *Par.,* 1861.
—— YOUNG, A. Remarks on Korea. *Lond.,* 1865.
—— WILLIAMSON, A. Journeys in North China . . . with some account of C. *Lond.,* 1870.
—— Description of Korea, *etc.* ASTLEY. Vol. IV.
—— Hamel, H. Travels of some Dutchmen in Korea, *etc.* ASTLEY. Vol. IV.
—— Regis, J. B. Geographical Observations and History of Korea. ASTLEY. Vol. IV.
—— An Account . . . of the Kingdom of C. CHURCHILL. Vol. IV.
—— Description of . . . C. HARRIS, J. Vol. II.
—— KAO, D. An Authentick . . . description of . . . C., *etc.* HARRIS, J. Vol. II.
—— De la Corée. LAHARPE, J. Vol. VIII.
—— Hamel's Travels in Korea. PINKERTON. Vol. VII.
—— Beschreibung von Korea, *etc.* VOYAGES and TRAVELS. Allgemeine Historie, *etc.* Vol. VI.

Corea — Corsica. 147

Corea.—Hamel, H. Reisen einiger Holländer nach Korea. . . . 1058–68.
 Voyages and Travels. Allgemeine Historie, *etc.* Vol. VI.
—— Regis, J. B. Geographische Beobachtungen . . . von Korea, 1720.
 Voyages and Travels. Allgemeine Historie, *etc.* Vol. VI.
Corfu.—Marmora, A. da. Historia di C. *Venice*, 1672.
—— Dapper. Naukeurige Beschryving van . . . Korfu, etc.
 Amst., 1688.
—— Goodisson, W. Historical . . . Essay upon . . . C., *etc.* 1822.
—— Mousson, A. Ein Besuch auf K. und Cefalonien, im 1858.
 Zurich, 1859.
Corinth.—Squire, Col. The Plain of Marathon, the Isthmus of C., *etc.*
 Walpole, R. Memoirs, *etc.*
—— Sibthorp, Dr. Voyage . . . Isthmus of C. Walpole, R. Travels,
 etc.
Cork.—Townsend, H. Statistical Survey of the County of C., *etc.*
 Dubl., 1810.
Cornwall.—Murchison, Sir R. I. Brief Review of the Classification of the
 Sedimentary Rocks of C.
—— Sedgwick, A. and Murchison, Sir R. I. Classification of the older
 Sedimentary Rocks of C. 1839.
—— —— Classification of the Older Stratified Rocks of . . . C. 1839.
Coro.—Pizarro, F. Reisen . . . an der Küste von . . . C., 1524–41.
 Voyages and Travels. Allgemeine Historie, *etc.* Vol. XV.
Coromandel.—Baldæus, P. Nauwkeurige Beschryvings van . . . Cho-
 romandel, *etc.* *Amst.*, 1672.
—— Marten, N. Voyage of Capt. A. Hippon to the Coast of Koromandel
 . . . in 1611. Astley. Vol. I.
—— Baldæus, P. A true . . . description of . . . C., *etc.* Churchill.
 Vol. III.
—— A short account of the Gentoo mode of collecting the Revenues on
 the Coast of C. 1753. Dalrymple, A. Tracts, from 1704 to 1803.
 Vol. I.
—— Explanation of the Map of the East India Company's Lands on the
 Coast of Choromandel. 1776. Dalrymple, A. Tracts, from 1769 to
 1793.
—— Pimenta, N. Indian Observations . . . principally relating to . . .
 the Coast of C. . . . 1597–99. Purchas. Vol. II.
—— Beschreibung der Küste C. Voyages and Travels. Allgemeine
 Historie, *etc.* Vol. XVIII.
Coronel.—Barrio, P. del. Noticia sobre el Terreno Carbonifero de C. i
 Lota. *Santiago*, 1857.
Corsica.—Corsica. A new description . . . of C., *etc.* 1738.
—— Chauchard, Capt. Geographical . . . description of . . . C., *etc.*
 Lond., 1800.
—— Dessiou, J. F. Le Petit Neptune Français . . . with . . . C.
 1805.
—— Benson, R. Sketches of C., *etc.* *Lond.*, 1825.

L 2

Corsica.—GREGOROVIUS, F. C., etc. 1855.
—— FORESTER, T. Rambles in ... C., etc. 1858.
—— CORSICA. Guide du Voyageur en Corse. *Ajaccio*, 1868.
Costa Rica.—GAGE, T. Survey of the Spanish West Indies ... describing ... C. R., etc. 1702.
—— BAILY, J. Central America ... C. R., etc. 1850.
—— MOLINA, F. Bosquejo de la República de C.-R. *Madr.*, 1850.
—— —— Memoria sobre las Cuestiones de Límites ... entre ... C.-R. y ... Nicaragua. *Madr.*, 1850.
—— Mosquito, Nicaragua, and C.-R. 1850.
—— MOLINA, F. C.-R. y Nueva Granada; Exámen de la cuestión de Límites, etc. *Wash.*, 1852.
—— NEW GRANADA and C. R. The Boundary Question ... examined, etc. *Lond.*, 1852.
—— MOLINA, F. C. R. and New Granada. An Inquiry into the question of Boundaries, etc. *Wash.*, 1853.
—— COSTA RICA RAILWAY, Account of the. *Liverpool*, 1855.
—— BOYLE, F. A Ride ... through ... C. R. *Lond.*, 1868.
Coteau des Prairies.—FEATHERSTONHAUGH, G. W. Report of a Geological Reconnaissance ... by Green Bay ... to the C. de P. *Wash.*, 1836.
Council Bluffs.—PENDLETON, N. G. On Military Posts from C. B. to the Pacific Ocean. *Wash.*, 1842.
Courlande.—*See* CURLAND.
Cranganore.—HAWES, R. Proceedings of the Factory at C. Kees. Vol. IX.
—— —— Memorialls ... touching the Proceedings of the Factorie of C. ... 1615. PURCHAS. Vol. I.
Creta.—*See* CRETE.
Crete.—POCOCKE, R. Description of ... Candia, etc. 1743-45.
—— PASHLEY, R. Travels in C. *Camb.*, 1837.
—— GRASSO, COUNT J. Relazioni Commerciali ... dell' Isola di Candia ... coi l'orti dell'Italia, etc. *Firenze*, 1841.
—— FLETCHER, F. T. The Twenty Years' Siege of Candia. 1855.
—— SPRATT, T. A. B. Instructions sur l'Ile de C. ou Candie, etc. *Par.*, 1861.
—— —— Sailing Directions for ... C., etc. 1861.
—— —— Travels and Researches in C. *Lond.*, 1865.
—— RAULIN, V. Description physique ... de l'Ile de C. *Par.*, 1867-69.
—— SKINNER, J. E. H. Roughing it in C. in 1867. *Lond.*, 1868.
—— Dandini, J. Voyage to ... also a description of Candia, etc. CHURCHILL. Vol. VII.
—— Another Voyage unto Candia ... 1535. HAKLUYT. Vol. II.
—— Bodenham, R. Voyage to Candia ... 1550. HAKLUYT. Vol. II.

Creta.—Voyage . . . to Candia . . . about 1534. HAKLUYT. Vol. II.
——— Soot, W. L. Travels in Candia . . . 1612. PURCHAS. Vol. II.
——— Belon, Mr. Remarks in the Island of C., etc. RAY, J.
——— Cockerell, Mr. On the Labyrinth of C. WALPOLE, R. Travels, etc.

Crimea.—GUTHRIE, M. Tour . . . in . . . 1795-6 through the Taurida or C. 1802.
——— REUILLY, J. Voyage en Crimée . . . 1803, etc. Par., 1806.
——— ENGELHARDT, M. VON, and PARROT, F. Reise in die Krym, etc. Berl., 1815.
——— MONTPÉREUX, F. D. DE. Voyage . . . en . . . Crimée. Par., 1839.
——— HELL, X. H. DE. Travels in . . . the C., etc. 1847.
——— MACINTOSH, A. F. Military Tour in . . . the C., etc. 1854.
——— DEMIDOFF, A. DE. Travels in . . . the C. . . . during 1837. 1855.
——— KOCH, C. C. and Odessa, etc. 1855.
——— SEYMOUR, H. D. Russia on the Black Sea . . . Travels in the C., etc. 1855.
——— PETACHIA, RABBI. Travels of; who, in the . . . Twelfth Century visited . . . the C., etc. 1856.
——— TAYLOR, G. C. Adventures with the British Army, from the commencement of the War, etc. 1856.
——— M'PHERSON, D. Antiquities . . . with Remarks on the Ethnological . . . History of the C. 1857.
——— Reuilly, J. Travels in the C. . . . 1803. VOYAGES and TRAVELS. A Collection, etc. 1805. Vol. V.
——— Campenhausen, Baron. Travels through . . . the C., about 1805. VOYAGES and TRAVELS. A Collection, etc. 1805. Vol. VIII.

Crimean Tartary.—See TARTARY, CRIMEAN.

Croatia.—BOUÉ, A. Les Serbes et les Croates.
——— PATON, A. A. Highlands . . . of the Adriatic, including . . . C., etc. 1849.
——— THOEMMEL, G. Geschichtliche . . . Beschreibung des . . . Bosnien nebst türckisch Croatien, etc. Wien, 1867.
——— Dutens, J. V. Travels in . . . C. . . . in 1806. PELHAM. Vol. II.

Ctesiphon.—MIGNAN, R. Travels . . . with Observations on the Site of . . . C. 1829.

Cuba.—PICHARDO, E. Memoria justificativa de la Carta . . . del departamento Occidental de . . . C., etc. Habana.
——— CUBA. Original Papers relating to . . . C. 1744.
——— CUBA. Cuadro estadistico . . . de C., etc. Habana, 1829.
——— SAGRA, R. DE LA. Historia . . . de la Isla de C., etc. Hab., 1831.
——— POEY, F. Compendio de la Geografia de la Isla de C. Hab., 1838.
——— TURNBULL, D. Travels in the West. C., etc. 1840.

Cuba.—HERNANDEZ, A. R. DEL V. Balanza general del Comercio . . . de C. . . . 1840. *Habana*, 1841.
—— CUBA. Guia de Forasteros, en . . . C., *etc. Habana*, 1842.
—— POEY, A. Compendio de la Geografía de la Isla de C. *Hab.*, 1842.
—— BONANY, S. Balanza General del Comercio de . . . en 1841-42. *Hab.*, 1842-43.
—— PURDY, J., and FINDLAY, A. G. Sailing Directory for . . . C., *etc.* 1848.
—— WILSON, T. W. The Island of C. in 1850, *etc. New Orleans*, 1850.
—— PICHARDO, E. Geografía de la Isla de C. *Habana*, 1854
—— TORRE, J. M. DE LA. Compendio de Geografía . . . de C. *Habana*, 1854.
—— HURLBUT, W. H. Pictures of C. 1855.
—— POEY, A. Sur les Tempêtes Électriques . . . à l'Île de C. *Versailles*, 1855.
—— —— Tableau chronologique des Tremblements de Terre ressentis à l'Île de C. de 1551 à 1855, *etc. Par.*, 1855.
—— BECHER, A. B. The Landfall of Columbus . . . and . . . his Track to C. 1856.
—— MURRAY, Hon. A. M. Letters from . . . C., *etc.* 1856.
—— TORRE, J. M. DE LA. Nuevos Elementos de Geografía . . . de C. *Habana*, 1856.
—— MURRAY, Hon. H. A. Lands of the Slave and the Free; or C., *etc.* 1857.
—— PHILIPPO, J. M. The United States and C. 1857.
—— PICHARDO, E. Nueva Carta Geotopografica de . . . C. *Habana*, 1870.
—— Hawkins, Sir J. Voyages to . . . the Cape of S. Anton, upon the W. end of C. . . . 1562-68. HAKLUYT. Vol. III.
—— Columbus, C. First Voyage, in which he discovered C., *etc.* HARRIS, J. Vol. II.
—— Ocampo. Reise um die Insel C., 1508. VOYAGES and TRAVELS. Allgemeine Historie, *etc.* Vol. XIII.
—— Weitere Eroberungen der Castilianer in . . . C., 1511. VOYAGES and TRAVELS. Allgemeine Historie, *etc.* Vol. XIII.

Cuddapah.—King, W. On the Kuddapah and Kurnool Formations. INDIA GEOLOGICAL SURVEY. Records, *etc.* Vol. II.

Culiacan.—Marco de Niça, Friar. Voyage from the town of S. Michael, in C., to . . . Cevola, *etc.*, 1539. HAKLUYT. Vol. III.
—— Ulloa, F. de. Voyage by the Coasts of . . . C., Into the Gulfe of California . . . 1539. HAKLUYT. Vol. III.

Cumana.—Of C., Guiana . . . and of their Religions. PURCHAS. Vol. V.
—— Las Casas, B. de. Reise . . . an der Küste von C., 1520-21. VOYAGES and TRAVELS. Allgemeine Historia, *etc.* Vol. XV.

Cumberland.—ROBINSON, T. Natural History of . . . C.   1709.
——— HUTCHINSON, W. Excursion to the Lakes in . . . C., *etc.*   1776.
——— CLARKE, J. Survey of the Lakes of C., *etc.*   1789.
——— MURRAY, HON. MRS. S. Guide to . . ., the Lakes of . . . C., *etc.*   1799.
——— HOUSMAN, J. Descriptive . . . Guide to . . . C., *etc.*
  Carlisle, 1818.

Cumbum Valley.—MARKHAM, C. R. Chinchona cultivation . . . Expedition . . . from Peermeade to the C. Valley, *etc.*   1865.

Cundinamarca.—TERNAUX-COMPANS, H. Essai sur l'Ancien C. *Paris.*

Curdistan.—*See* KURDISTAN.

Curland.—FERBER, J. J., and FISCHER, J. B. Physische Erdbeschreibung von Kurland, *etc.*   *Riga,* 1784.
——— POSSART, P. A. F. K. Statistik und Geographie des Kurland.
  Stutt., 1843.
——— HJORTH, J. Description des Côtes . . . de la Courlande, *etc.*
  Par., 1855.

Cuscatlan.—Palacio, D. G. de. Description of the Ancient Provinces of C. . . . 1576. SQUIER. Collection. No. 1.

Cuscho. Cusco.—*See* CUZCO.

Cutch.—BURNES, J. A Narrative . . . Sketch of the History of C., *etc.*
  Edin. and Lond., 1831.
——— INDIA. Geological Papers on W.n India, including C., *etc.*
  Bomb., 1857.
——— Blanford, W. T. On the Geology of a portion of C. INDIA GEOLOGICAL SURVEY. Memoirs. Vol. VI.

Cutchee Hills.—NAPIER, SIR W. History of General Sir C. Napier's . . . Campaign in the C. H.   *Lond.,* 1851.

Cuttack.—STERLING, A. An Account . . . of Orissa Proper, or C.

Cuxhaven.—ABENDROTH, SENATOR. Ritzebüttel und das Seebad zu C., *etc.*   *Hamb.,* 1818.

Cuzco.—MARKHAM, C. R. C.—a Journey to the ancient Capital of Peru, *etc.*   *Lond.,* 1856.
——— Xeres, F. de. Conquest of Peru and C. . . . 1524-33. PURCHAS. Vol. IV.
——— Relatione d'un Secretario di F. Pizarro . . . della gran Città del Cuscho, 1534. RAMUSIO. Vol. III.
——— Xeres, F. Relatione della Conquista . . . del C. . . . 1532-3. RAMUSIO. Vol. III.
——— Xérès, F. Relation véridique de la Conquête . . . de C. . . . 1524-33. TERNAUX-COMPANS. Voyages. Vol. IV.
——— Beschreibungen . . . von . . . C., *etc.* VOYAGES and TRAVELS. Allgemeine Historie, *etc.* Vol. XV.

Cypern.—*See* CYPRUS.

Cyprus.—DAPPER. Beschryving van . C., *etc.*   1668.
——— POCOCKE, R. Description of . . . C., *etc.*   1743-45.

Cyprus.—ALI BEY. Travels in . . . C., *etc.* 1816.
——— LIGHT, H. Travels in . . . C. . . . 1814. *Lond.*, 1818.
——— NIEBUHR, C. Reisebeschreibung . . . nach Cypern, *etc.*
Hamb., 1837.
——— WILDE, W. R. Narrative of . . . a Visit to . . . C., *etc.*
Dubl., 1852.
——— HOGG, J. On some Inscriptions from C., *etc.* 1862.
——— UNGER, F. Die Insel Cypern einst und jetzt, *etc.* *Wien*, 1866.
——— Davis, W. A True . . . description of . . . C. CHURCHILL.
Vol. VII.
——— Hume, Dr. Plants collected in C. WALPOLE, R. Memoirs, *etc.*
——— Sibthorp, Dr. Birds, Quadrupeds, and Fishes of . . . C. WAL-
POLE, R. Memoirs, *etc.*
——— ——— Observations on Natural History, relating to . . . C. WAL-
POLE, R. Memoirs, *etc.*
——— Hume, Dr. Extracts from . . . Journals relating to parts of C.,
etc. WALPOLE, R. Travels, *etc.*
——— Sibthorp, Dr. Voyage . . . C., *etc.* WALPOLE, R. Travels, *etc.*
Cyrenaica.—BEECHEY, F. W., and H. W. Proceedings . . . compre-
hending an account of . . . C., *etc.* 1828.
——— Cervelli, A. Relations inédites de la Cyrénaïque, *etc.* VOYAGES
and TRAVELS. Recueil, *etc.* Vol. II.
Cyrene.—SMITH, CAPT. R.M., and PORCHER, COMM. E. A. History of
the recent Discoveries at C., *etc.* *Lond.*, 1864.
Cyrus, River.—CASPIAN SEA. Description . . . Mémoire sur le Cours
. . . du C. . . . Par St. Croix. *Par.*, 1793.

D.

Dabbeh.—MARNO, E. Von D. nach Omderman, *etc.* *Wien* [1870].
Dabul.—Middleton, Sir H. Journey to Zenan . . . Voyage from Surat to
D. KERR. Vol. VIII.
Dacota. WARREN, G. K. Explorations in the D. Country, *etc.*
Wash., 1856.
Daghestan.—ABICH, H. Sur la Structure et Géologie du D.
St. Pét., 1862.
Dahoma.—*See* DAHOMEY.
Dahomey.—DALZELL, A. The History of D., *etc.* 1793.
——— DUNCAN, J. Travels . . . through D., *etc.* 1847.
——— WINNIETT, Sir W. Journal . . . and B. Cruickshank's Report of
his Mission to the King of D. 1849.
——— FORBES, F. E. Dahomey and the Dahomans, *etc.* 1851.
——— BURTON, R. F. A Mission to . . . Dahome, *etc.* 1864.
——— Conquêtes de D., Villault, Atkins, Smith, Snelgrave. LABARRE, J.
Vol. II.
Dakel.—*See* DAKHEL.

Dakhel — Danube.

Dakhel.—Drovetti. Itinerary of an Excursion to the Valley of D., 1818, etc. VOYAGES and TRAVELS, New. 1819. Vol. VII.

Dakhleh.—*See* DAKHEL.

Dalmatia.—FORTIS, A. Travels into D., etc. *Lond.*, **1778.**
——— WILKINSON, SIR J. G. D. and Montenegro, etc. **1848.**
——— PATON, A. A. Highlands . . . of the Adriatic, including D., etc. **1849.**
——— WINGFIELD, W. F. Tour in D., etc. **1859.**
——— Robert, Rotensis. Voyage to D. . . . 1143. HAKLUYT. Vol. II.
——— Vernon, F. Travels . . . through . . . D., etc. RAY, J.
——— CARVAS, L. F. Travels in D., 1702, etc. VOYAGES and TRAVELS. A Collection, etc. 1805. Vol. I.

Damascus.—HOGG, J. Further Account of . . . Turkey, with a notice of the Roman Remains at D.
——— ALEPPO. Journey from Aleppo to D., etc. **1737.**
——— RICHARDSON, R. Travels . . . as far as . . . D., etc. *Lond.*, **1822.**
——— ADDISON, C. G. D. and Palmyra, etc. **1838.**
——— KINNEAR, J. Cairo . . . and D. in 1839, etc. *Lond.*, **1841.**
——— PORTER, J. L. Five Years in D., etc. *Lond.*, **1855.**
——— MACGREGOR, J. The "Rob Roy" . . . A Canoe Cruise in . . . the Waters of D. *Lond.*, **1869.**
——— Biddulph, W. Travels of four Englishmen . . . into . . . D. . . . in 1600 and 1611. CHURCHILL. Vol. VII.
——— Benjamin, the Son of Jonas. Peregrination of . . . and relations of . . . D., etc. PURCHAS. Vol. II.
——— Coryates, T. Travels to . . . D. . . . 1612-14. PURCHAS. Vol. II.

Damiata.—*See* DAMIETTA.

Damietta.—Curson, Cardinal R. Voyage to Damiata . . . 1218. HAKLUYT. Vol. II.
——— Rainulph Glanville, Earle of Chester. Voyage . . . to Damiata, in Ægypt, 1218. HAKLUYT. Vol. II.

Dancali. TELLEZ, B. Travels . . . and an Account of . . . D., etc. **1710.**

Danemark, Danmark.—*See* DENMARK.

Danish Isles.—*See* DENMARK.

Dantzic.—DANTZIC. A particular description of the City of D., etc. *Lond.*, **1734.**

Danube.—PEYSSONNEL, M. DE. Observations historiques et géographiques sur les peuples barbares qui ont habité les bords du D., etc. *Par.*, **1765.**
——— DANUBE. Observations sur les Routes que conduisent du D. à Constantinople, etc. *Par.*, **1828.**
——— PLANCHE, J. R. Descent of the D. . . . during 1827, etc. **1828.**

Danube.—BLACK SEA. A Geographical . . . account of the Russian Ports of . . . the D. 1837.
—— SPENCER, E. Travels . . . including a Steam Voyage down the D., etc. 1837.
—— BIRAGO, GEN. On the projected Canal between the D. and the Black Sea. 1839.
—— KOHL, J. G. Austria . . . the D., etc. Lond., 1844.
—— DANUBE. Advantages likely to accrue to the Trade of the D. from the Canal, etc. 1855.
—— LEAHY, E. Report of the D. Canal. 1855.
—— RENNIE, G. B. Suggestions for the Improvement of the . . . D., etc. 1856.
—— LIDDELL and GORDON, Messrs. Report on the proposed Railway between the D. and the Black Sea, etc. 1857.
—— SPRATT, T. A. B. Report on the Delta of the D., etc. 1857.
—— HARTLEY, SIR C. A. Description of the Delta of the D., etc. 1862.
—— DANUBE. Mémoire sur le Régime Administratif établi aux embouchures du D., etc. Galatz, 1867.
—— DANUBE. Mémoire sur les travaux d'amélioration exécutés aux embouchures du D., etc. Galatz, 1867.
—— ARNOLD, R. A. From the . . . D. Lond., 1868.
—— DESJARDINS, F. Rhone et D., etc. Par., 1870.

Danubian Principalities.—O'BRIEN, P. Journal of a Residence in the D. P., in . . . 1853. Lond., 1854.

Dansig.—See DANTZIC.

Daour.—See DAOURIA.

Daouria.—IDES, E. Y. Three Years' Travels . . . thro' . . . Daour, etc. Lond., 1706.
—— Ysbrants Ides, E. Travels . . . through . . . D. . . . 1692-95, HARRIS, J. Vol. II.

Dardanelles.—KNIGHT, W. A Diary in the D., etc. Lond., 1849.
—— GRAS, M. A. LE. Sailing Directions for the D., etc. 1855.
—— Sibthorp, Dr. Voyage in the . . . D., etc. WALPOLE, R. Travels, etc.

Dardistan.—LEITNER, G. W. Results of a Tour in D., etc.
Lahore, Lond. [1868.]

Darfour.—See DARFUR.

Darfur.—EBN-OMAR EL-TOUNSY, CHEYKH MOHAMMED. Voyage au Darfour, etc. Par., 1845.
— ·— JOMARD, F. F. Observations sur le Voyage au D., etc. Par., 1845.
—— LAUTUR, COUNT D'ESCAYRAC DE. Notice sur le D., etc.
Par., 1859.
— — — Abysinie. Voyage au D., 1793-09. EYRIÈS. Vol. XIV.
⊥ — — Browne's Journey to D.-F. PINKERTON. Vol. XV.
—— Drovetti. Itinerary . . . from Syout to . . . Darfour. VOYAGES and TRAVELS, New. 1819. Vol. VII.

Darien, Gulf of.—OXNAM, J. Voyage . . . over the streight of D. into the South Sea, 1575. HAKLUYT. Vol. IV.

———, **Isthmus of.**—*See* PANAMA, ISTHMUS of.

———, **Province of.**—DARIEN. Memoirs of D., *etc.* *Glasgow*, 1715.

——— ——— POWER, J. Description of the Province of Sancto Domingo del D. in S. America . . . in . . . 1754, *etc.* **1868.**

——— ——— Drake, Sir F. Voyages to Nombre de Dios and D., about 1572. HAKLUYT. Vol. IV.

——— ——— Vespucio, A. Las cuatro Navegaciones, Establecimientos de los Españoles en el D. NAVARETTE. Coleccion. Vol. III.

——— ——— Ojeda, A. and Nicuesa. Reisen, 1510, Entdeckung des Landes D., *etc.* VOYAGES and TRAVELS. Allgemeine Historie, *etc.* Vol. XIII.

Darjeeling.—HOOKER, J. D. Notes . . . during an Excursion from Darjiling to Tonglo, *etc.* *Calc.*, **1849.**

Darjiling.—*See* DARJEELING.

Dauphiné.—FORBES, J. D. Norway . . . with Excursions in the High Alps of D., *etc.* *Edin.*, **1853.**

Davis' Straits.—ANDERSON, J. Nachrichten von . . . der Strasse D. *Hamb.*, **1746.**

Dead Sea.—SEETZEN, M. Brief Account of the Countries adjoining . . . the D. S. *Bath*, **1810.**

——— LYNCH, W. F. Report of an examination of the D. S. *Wash.*, **1849.**

——— RITTER, C. Der Jordan und die Beschiffung des Todten Meeres. *Berl.*, **1850.**

——— KENNEDY, J. The Jordan and the D. S. **1851.**

——— LYNCH, W. F. Official Report of the U. S. Expedition to explore the D. S., *etc.* *Balt., U. S.*, **1852.**

——— SAULCY, F. DE. Narrative of a Journey round the D. S., *etc.* **1854.**

——— ALLEN, W. The D. S., a new route for India. **1855.**

Debreczin.—PATON, A. A. The Goth and the Hun: or . . . D. . . . in 1850. **1851.**

Debretzin.—*See* DEBRECZIN.

Decoan.—SICÉ, E. Traité des Lois Mahométanes, ou Recueil des Lois, Usages et Coutumes des Musulmans du D. *Par.*, **1841.**

Dee Side.—MACGILLIVRAY, W. Natural History of D. S., *etc.* **1855.**

Delaware.—BOOTH, J. C. Memoirs of the Geological Survey of . . . D., *etc.* *Dover*, **1841.**

——— MARYLAND. Message . . . in relation to the Intersection of the Boundary Lines of . . . D. *Wash.*, **1850.**

——— GRAHAM, J. D. Reports in relation to the . . . Boundary Lines of . . . D., *etc.* *Chicago*, **1862.**

———, **River.**—BARBER, J. N. Sketches of . . . Primitive Settlements on the . . . D. *Phil.*, **1838.**

Delaware Bay.—READ, J. M. A historical enquiry concerning H. Hudson . . . in connection with the . . . discovery of D. B. *Albany*, **1866**.
Delhi.—LLOYD, SIR W. Narrative of a Journey . . . via . . . D., etc.
Lond., **1840**.
——— ROBERTS, G. De D. à Bombay, etc. *Par.*, **1843**.
——— BARR, W. Journal of a March from D. to Peshâwur, etc.
Lond., **1844**.
——— SCINDE RAILWAY. . . . The D. Railway: Reports of the Directors . . . Sept. 1863. **1863**.
——— DELHI RAILWAY. Opening of the Meerut and Umballa Section of the D. Railway, etc. *Lond.*, **1869**.
——— Bernier, F. Voyage to Surat . . . and a description of D., etc. CHURCHILL. Vol. VIII.
Del Norte, Rio.—*See* RIO BRAVO DEL NORTE.
Demerara.—PETLEY, J. Remarks on the Rivers of Berbice and D.
1845.
——— Bolingbroke, H. Voyage to the D. . . . 1799. VOYAGES and TRAVELS. A Collection, etc. 1805. Vol. X.
——— Voyage to the D., 1799. VOYAGES and TRAVELS. A Collection, etc. 1810. Vol. V.
Demerary.—*See* DEMERARA.
Denmark.—SAXO GRAMMATICUS. Danorum Regum heroumque Historiæ, etc. *Parrhis.*, **1514**.
——— LAHONTAN, BARON. New Voyages . . . an Account of . . . D., etc.
1703-35.
——— DENMARK. An Account of D.: as it was in . . . 1692, etc.
Lond., **1738**.
——— COXE, W. Travels into . . . D. **1784**.
——— WILSON, W. R. Travels in . . . D., etc. *Lond.*, **1826**.
——— PAULY, F. Topographie von Dänmark, etc. *Altona*, **1828**.
——— ELLIOTT, C. B. Letters from . . . D., etc. **1832**.
——— BARROW, J. Excursions in . . . D., etc. **1834**.
——— INGLIS, H. D. A Personal Narrative of a Journey through . . . D.
Lond., **1835**.
——— NIEBUHR, C. Reisebeschreibung . . . nach . . . Dännemark, etc.
Hamb., **1837**.
——— WELLINGTON, DUKE OF. Despatches, during his . . . Campaigns in . . . D., etc. **1837-39**.
——— CLARKE, E. D. Travels in . . . D., etc. **1838**.
——— BREMNER, R. Excursions in D., etc. **1840**.
——— SIMONSEN, VEDEL. Bidrag til Danske Slottes . . . Historie.
Odense, **1840**.
——— BELGIUM. Belgian . . . Danish . . . Lighthouses, corrected to 1843, 51, 54, 57-59. **1843-59**.
——— ROSS, W. A. Yacht Voyage to . . . D., etc. **1849**.
——— HÜBERTZ, J. R. De Sindssyge i Danmark. *Kjöb.*, **1851**.

Denmark — Derbyshire.

Denmark.—HAMILTON, A. Sixteen Months in the Danish Isles. 1852.
—— PUGAARD, C. Deux Vues géologiques ... du D. *Copenh.*, 1853.
—— ZAHRTMAN, C. C. Danish Pilot. 1853.
—— DENMARK. Pilote Danois, *etc.* *Par.*, 1855.
—— SCOTT, C. H. Danes and the Swedes ... a Visit to D., *etc.* 1856.
—— FORCHHAMMER, G. Bidrag til skildringen af Danmarks Geographiske Forhold, *etc.* *Kjöb.*, 1858.
—— TRAP, J. P. Statistisk-Topographisk Beskrivelse af ... D. *Kjöb.*, 1858-60.
—— LAMONT, J. Untersuchungen über den Erdmagnetismus in ... Dänemark ... 1858. *Münch.*, 1859.
—— DUNSTERVILLE, E. The Admiralty List of the ... Danish ... Lights. Corrected to 1860. 1860.
—— MARRYAT, H. Residence in ... the Danish Isles, *etc.* 1860.
—— STATISTICAL TABLES ... Part VII. ... D., *etc.* 1861.
—— IRMINGER, C. Notice sur les Pêches du D., *etc.* *Par.*, 1863.
—— ANDRÆ, C. G. Den Danske Gradmaaling. *Kjöb.*, 1867.
—— Lubbock, Mrs. The Ancient Shell Mounds of D. GALTON, F. Vacation Tourists ... in 1862-3.
—— Malgo, King. Voyage to ... D. ... 580. HAKLUYT. Vol. I.
—— Molesworth, and others. The present state of ... D., *etc.* HARRIS, J. Vol. II.
—— Nowel, T. Travels in D. ... in 1801. PELHAM. Vol. II.
—— Coxe's Travels in D. PINKERTON. Vol. VI.
—— Küttner, C. G. Travels through D. ... 1798-99. VOYAGES and TRAVELS. A Collection, *etc.* 1805. Vol. I.
—— Carr, J. A Northern Summer; or, Travels ... through D. ... 1804. VOYAGES and TRAVELS. A Collection, *etc.* 1805. Vol. III.
—— Seume, J. G. Tour through ... D., *etc.* 1805. VOYAGES and TRAVELS. A Collection, *etc.* 1805. Vol. VII.
—— Macdonald, J. Travels through D. ... 1809. VOYAGES and TRAVELS. A Collection, *etc.* 1805. Vol. XI.
—— —— Travels through D. ... 1809. VOYAGES and TRAVELS. A Collection, *etc.* 1810. Vol. VI.
—— Seume, J. G. Tour through ... D., *etc.* 1805. VOYAGES and TRAVELS. A Collection, *etc.* 1810. Vol. VI.
—— Hallberg, Baron von. Sentimental Sketches, written during a Journey through ... D. ... 1820. VOYAGES and TRAVELS, New. 1819. Vol. V.
—— Molesworth, Lord. An Account of D. VOYAGES and TRAVELS. The World displayed. Vol. XX.

Derbyshire.—PILKINGTON, J. View of the present state of D., *etc.* *Derby*, 1789.
—— MAWE, J. Mineralogy of D., *etc.* 1802.
—— Bray, W. Sketch of a Tour into D. PINKERTON. Vol. II.

Derbyshire.—Ferber's Oryctography of D. Pinkerton. Vol. II.
Derg, Lough.—Wolfe, J. Sailing Directions for ... L. D. 1843.
Derna.—Cervelli, A. Relations inédites ... Extrait du Journal d'une Expédition faite en 1811-12, de Tripoli à Derne, etc. Voyages and Travels. Recueil, etc. Vol. II.
Dernah.—See Derna.
Desert.—Chubb, J. H. See Nile, the D., etc. Lond., 1853.
——— Lautour, Count d'Escayrac de. Le Désert et le Soudan. Études, etc. Par., 1853.
——— Layard, A. H. Discoveries ... with Travels in ... the D., etc. 1853.
———, **Great.**—Plaisted, B. Journal ... across the G. D. to Aleppo, etc. 1758.
——— ——— Taylor, J. Travels ... to India, in 1789 ... over the G. D., etc. 1799.
——— ——— Adams, R. The Narrative of; who ... was detained three years in slavery by the Arabs of the G. D., etc. 1816.
——— ——— Caillié, R. Travels ... across the G. D. to Morocco, etc. 1830.
——— ——— Boileau, A. W. E. Tour through ... Rajwara ... with the passage of the G. D., etc. Calc., 1837.
——— ——— Hodgson, W. B. Notes on ... the Sahara, etc. N. Y., 1844.
——— ——— Daumas, Lieut-Col. Le Sahara Algérien, etc. Par., 1845.
——— ——— Prax, M. Instructions pour le Voyage de, dans le Sahara Septentrional. Par., 1847.
——— ——— Richardson, J. Travels in the Great Desert of Sahara, etc. 1848.
——— ——— Tristram, H. B. The Great Sahara, etc. Lond., 1860.
——— ——— Edwards, M. B. Through Spain to the Sahara. Lond., 1868.
——— ——— Rohlfs, G. Reise ... durch die grosse Wüste, etc. Bremen, 1868.
——— ——— Voyages en Africa. Sahara, etc. Eysies. Vol. X.
——— ——— Scott, A. Account of the Captivity of, among the wandering Arabs of the Great African D. ... 1810-16. Voyages and Travels, New. 1819, etc. Vol. IX.
———, **Little.**—Plaisted, B. Journal ... To which are added ... Directions for passing over the L. D. from Busserah, etc. 1758.
Devonshire.—Vancouver, C. General View of the Agriculture of ... Devon, etc. 1808.
——— Sedgwick, A. and Murchison, Sir R. I. On the Physical Structure of D., etc. 1837.
——— ——— Classification of the Older Stratified Rocks of D., etc. 1839.
Diacria.—Finlay, G. Remarks on the Topography of Oropia and D. Athens, 1838.

Diarbekir.—Jackson, J. Journey ... in 1797, through D., *etc.* PELHAM. Vol. II.

Diarbekr.—*See* DIARBEKIR.

Dieppe.—NOEL, S. B. J. Premier Essai sur ... D., *etc.* *Rouen*, 1785.

Disappointment Islands.—Byron, Comm. Voyage ... to ... [. of D. ... 1764-68. HAWKESWORTH, J. Vol. I.

Diu.—The second Siege of D. ... in 1546. ASTLEY. Vol. I.

—— Viaggio scritto per un Comito Venetiano, dal Mar Rosso fino al D. ... 1537-8. RAMUSIO. Vol. I.

Divels, Isle of.—*See* BERMUDA ISLANDS.

Djohor.—*See* JOHORE.

Djokjokarta.—*See* JOCJACARTA.

Djyntia.—*See* JYNTEEA.

Dniester, River.—BRAUMÜLLER, J. G. Der wichtigste Kanal in Europa ... vermittelst der D.a, *etc.* *Berl.*, 1816.

Dodabetta.—TAYLOR, T. G. Meteorological Observations made ... on D. ... in 1847-48. *Madras*, 1848.

—— SYKES, W. H. Discussion of Meteorological Observations taken ... at D., *etc.* 1850.

Dodona.—Hawkins, Mr. On the Site of D. WALPOLE, R. Travels, *etc.*

Dominica.—Hawkins, Sir J. Voyages to ... the Isle of D. ... 1562-68. HAKLUYT. Vol. III.

—— Newport, C. Voyage to ... D. ... 1591. HAKLUYT. Vol. IV.

—— Sherley, Sir A. Voyage to ... D. ... 1596. HAKLUYT. Vol. IV.

—— Jayfield, E. Large Relation ... with a description of D. ... 1500-98. PURCHAS. Vol. IV.

Dominican Republic.—*See* HAYTI.

Don.—STRUVE, O. Positions Géographiques déterminées en 1847, par ... Lemm, dans le Pays des Cosaques du D. *St. Pet.*, 1855.

Dona Ana.—PARKE, J. G. Report of Explorations for ... a Railway ... between D. A. on the Rio Grande, and Pimas Villages on the Gila. *Wash.*, 1854.

Donegal.—M'PARLAN, J. Statistical Survey of the County of D. *Dubl.*, 1802.

Dongola.—PONCET, MONSIEUR. A Voyage to Æthiopia ... describing ... likewise ... D, *etc.* *Lond.*, 1709.

—— DONGOLA and SENNAAR. Narrative of the Expedition to D. and Sennaar, *etc.* 1822.

—— Drovetti. Itinerary ... from Syout to D., *etc.* VOYAGES and TRAVELS, New. 1819. Vol. VII.

Dongolah.—*See* DONGOLA.

Doni, River.—*See* BONNY.

Dornburg.—THOMA, E. Das unterirdische Eisfeld, bei der D., *etc.* *Würzb.*, 1841.

Dorpat.—OETTINGEN, A. VON. Meteorologische Beobachtungen angestellt in D. ... 1867. *Dorp.*, 1868.

Dorset — Dutch East Indies.

Dorset.—BOSWELL, E. Civil Division of the County of D., etc.
Sherborne, 1795.

Douro.—FORRESTER, J. J. Papers relating to the Improvement of the Navigation of the . . . D., etc. *Op.*, 1844.

—— BULCHER, SIR E. Directions for the . . . D., 1833. 1847.

—— FORRESTER, J. J. Documents relating to Mr. F.'s Topographical Works of the . . . River D., etc. *Op.*, 1848.

—— CRAWFURD, MR. CONSUL. Report on the Bar and Navigation of the D. *Lond.*, 1866.

Dove, River.—THORNE, J. Rambles by Rivers: the . . . D. 1847.

Dover.—LAURIE, R. H., and WHITTLE, J. New Piloting Directory for the . . . Thames; with the Navigation . . . to D., etc.
Lond., 1816.

—— MACKIE, S. J. Thoughts on the D. Cliffs. 1863.

Down.—DUBOURDIEU, J. Statistical Survey of . . . D., etc.
Dubl., 1802.

Dresden.—LEHNINGER, J. A. Description de . . . D., etc. *Dresde*, 1782.

—— DRESDEN. D. und die umliegende Gegend, etc. *Dresd.*, 1804.

—— LINDAU, W. A. Merkwürdigkeiten D.s, etc.
Dresd. u. Leip., 1832.

Dreyeinigkeits-Insel.—*See* JAN MAYEN.

Drogeo.—Zeno, N. and A. Voyage to the yles of . . . D. . . . 1380.
HAKLUYT. Vol. III.

Drome.—DRONE. Le Petit Guide de l'Etranger dans le département de la D., etc. *Valence*, 1863.

Drontheim.—DRONTHEIM. Det Tronhiemske Wäysen-Huns, etc.
Tronhiem, 1742.

—— BARROW, J. Visit to Iceland, by way of Tronyem. 1835.

Drosacka.—*See* TROSACHS.

Druses.—*See* LEBANON.

Dualla.—SAKER, A. Dualla Lesson Book, No. 2. Cameroons River.
Dunfermline Press, Bimbia, 1847.

Dublin.—ARCHER, J. Statistical Survey of the County of D., etc.
Dubl., 1801.

—— DUTTON, H. Observations on Mr. Archer's Statistical Survey of the County of D. *Dubl.*, 1802.

Duddon.—THORNE, J. Rambles by Rivers; the . . . D., etc. 1847.

Due Siollie.—*See* NAPLES and SICILY.

Dumfries.—JAMESON, R. Mineralogical Description of the County of D.
Edinb., 1805.

Duna.—*See* DWINA.

Dunfermline.—MERCER, A. History of D. *Dunf.*, 1828.

Dura Den.—ANDERSON, J. D. D. A Monograph of the Yellow Sandstone, etc. *Edin., Lond.*, 1859.

Dutch East Indies.—*See* EAST INDIES.

Dvina.—*See* DWINA.
Dwina.—VESSÉLOWSKY, C. Époques des Débacles et de la prise par les Glaces de la D., à Arkhangel. *St. Pet.*, 1856.

E.

East.—D'HERBELOT, M. Bibliothèque Orientale, etc. *Par.*, 1697.
——— POCOCKE, R. Description of the E., etc. 1743-45.
——— D'HERBELOT, M. Bibliothèque Orientale, etc. *La Haye*, 1777.
——— EASTERN NATIONS, Dictionary of the Religious Ceremonies of the, etc. *Calc.*, 1787.
——— EBN HAUKAL. Oriental Geography, etc. 1800.
——— CHARDIN, SIR J. Voyages en Perse et autres lieux de l'Orient, etc., *Par.*, 1811.
——— OUSELEY, SIR W. Travels in various countries of the E. . . . in 1810-12. 1819.
——— MARIGNOLA, J. VON. Reise in das Morgenland v. J. 1339-1353, etc. *Prag*, 1820.
——— WALPOLE, R. Travels in various Countries of the E., etc. *Lond.*, 1820.
——— ELLIOTT, R. Views in the E., etc. 1833.
——— ADDISON, C. G. Damascus . . . a journey to the E., etc. 1838.
——— SCHUBERT, G. H. VON. Reise in das Morgenlande, etc. *Erlangen*, 1838.
——— URQUHART, D. The Spirit of the E. 1839.
——— AUCHER-ÉLOY, P. M. R. Relations de Voyages en Orient de 1830 à 1838. *Par.*, 1843.
——— DAVIDSON, G. F. Trade and Travel in the Far E., etc. *Lond.*, 1846.
——— MARTINEAU, H. E.n Life, etc. 1848.
——— PALMER, A. H. Letter . . . enclosing a Paper . . . on the Independent Oriental Nations, etc. *Wash.*, 1849.
——— SPENCER, J. A. The E. Sketches of Travels, etc. 1850.
——— BELDAM, J. Recollections of Scenes in . . . the E. 1851.
——— SOARES, J. P. C. Bosquejo das Possessões Portuguezas no Oriente, etc. *Lisb.*, 1851.
——— HONIGBERGER, J. M. Thirty-five Years in the E., etc. 1852.
——— SOARES, J. P. C. Documentos Comprovativos do Bosquejo das Possessões Portuguezas no Oriente. 1853.
——— RAFN, C. C. Antiquités de l'Orient, Monuments Runographiques, *Copenh.*, 1856.
——— ROTH, J. R. Bemerkungen zu den Meteorologischen Beobachtungen, auf seiner dermaligen Reise im Oriente. *Münch.*, 1858.
——— ROSNY, L. DE. L'Orient. *Par.*, 1860.
——— ST. JOHN, S. Life in the Forests of the Far E. 1862.

East — East Indies.

East.—Schläfli, A. Mittheilungen Schweizerischer Reisender. Pt. II. Reisen in den Orient. *Winterthur*, 1864.
— Nardi, F. Ricordi di un Viaggio in Oriente, *etc.* *Roma*, 1866.
— Tchihatchef, P. de. Une Page sur l'Orient. *Par.*, 1868.
—— Jordanus, Friar. Mirabilia descripta. The Wonders of the E. Translated . . . with a Commentary, by Col. H. Yule. 1863. Hakluyt Soc. Pub. Vol. XXXI.
—— Mandeville, Sir J. Travels into the E., 1322. Kerr. Vol. I.
—— Marco Polo. Travels into . . . the E., from 1260 to 1295. Kerr. Vol I.
—— Oderic of Portenau. Travels into . . . the E., 1318. Kerr. Vol. I.
— — Continuation of the Discoveries . . . of the Portuguese in the E., *etc.* Kerr. Vol. VI.
—— Pococke, Dr. Travels in the E. Pinkerton. Vol. X.
—— Collections of divers Mahometan authors . . . touching the most remarkable things in the E., *etc.* Purchas. Vol. II.
—— Rubriquis, Friar W. de. Journall of his Travels unto the E. . . . 1253. Purchas. Vol. III.
—— Rauwolf, L. Journey into the Eastern Countries, *etc.* Ray, J.
—— Rubruquis, W. Reisen in die ostlichen Gegenden der Welt, 1253. Voyages and Travels. Allgemeine Historie, *etc.* Vol. VII.
—— Voyage en Orient du Frère G. de Rubruk, 1253. Notice, *etc.* Voyages and Travels. Recueil, *etc.* Vol. IV.

East Cape.—New Zealand Geological Survey. Abstract Report. . . . Together with reports on . . . E. C., *etc.* *Well.*, 1869.

East Indies.—India. Lettere dell' India Orientale, *etc.* *Vinegia*, 1580.
—— Balbi, G. Viaggio dell' Indie Orientali, *etc.* *Venetia*, 1590.
—— Linschoten, J. H. van. Discourse of Voyages into the E. and W. I. *Lond.*, 1598.
——— Guzman, P. L. Historia de las Missiones . . . de la Compañia de Jesus, en la India Oriental, *etc.* *Alcala*, 1601.
——— Iarric, P. du. Troisiesme partie de l'histoire des . . . Indes Orientales . . . 1600 jusques à 1610. *Bordeaux*, 1614.
—— Valle, P. della. Travels in E. India, *etc.* 1665.
— — Chardin, Sir J. Travels into . . . the E. I., *etc.* 1686.
—— Thevenot, M. de. Travels into . . . the E. I. 1687.
—— Valentyn, F. Oud en Nieuw Oost-Indiën, *etc.* *Dordr., Amst.*, 1724-26.
——— Mandelslo, J. A. de. Voyage . . . de Perse aux Indes Orientales, *etc.* *Amst.*, 1727.
—— Osbeck, P. A Voyage to China and the E. I., *etc.* *Lond.*, 1771.
— — Terry, E. Voyage to E. India, *etc.* 1777.
— — Sonnerat, M. Voyage aux Indes Orientales . . . 1774-81. *Par.*, 1782.
— — Raynal, G. T. A Philosophical . . . History of the . . . Europeans in the E. and W. I., *etc.* *Lond.*, 1788.

East Indies.—BLIGH, W. Narrative of ... Voyage ... from Tofoa
... to Timor ... in the E. I. 1790.
———— ROCHON, Abbé. A Voyage to Madagascar, and the E. I., *etc.*
Lond., 1792.
———— HOGENDORP, D. VAN. Berigt van den tegenwoordigen Toestand der Bataafsche Bezittingen in Oost Indiën, *etc.* [1799.]
———— EAST INDIES. A demonstration of the Necessity ... of a Free Trade to the E. I., *etc.* 1807.
———— ———— Papers respecting the Culture and Manufacture of Sugar in British India, *etc.* 1822.
———— EAST AND WEST INDIA TRADE. Five Accounts of the ... Value of Exports to the E. I., *etc.* 1827.
———— HAMILTON, W. The E. India Gazetteer. 1828.
———— ALEXANDER, SIR J. E. Visit to Adjunta in the E. I. 1829.
———— ESTANCELIN, L. Recherches sur les voyages ... des Navigateurs Normands ... dans les Indes Orientales, *etc.* Par., 1832.
———— STRAUSENS, J. J. Reise durch ... Ostindien ... 1647-1673. Gotha, 1832.
———— OLIVIER, J. Tafereelen en Merkwaardigheden uit Oost-Indië.
Amst., 1836.
———— FAIRBAIRN, H. A Letter ... on the ... advantages of a Steam Passage to the E. I., by the Gulf of Mexico, *etc.* 1837.
———— OSCULATI, G. Note d'un Viaggio ... nelle Indie Orientali, *etc.*
Monza, 1844.
———— SIEBOLD, P. F. DE, AND CARNBEE P. MELVILL DE. Le Moniteur des Indes-Orientales ... recueil de Mémoires, *etc.*
La Haye et Bat., 1847-49.
———— AFRICA. The Lights of ... E. I. ... Corrected to 1849, 51, 52, 56, 57, 58, 59. 1849-59.
———— AVEZAC, D'. L'Expédition ... des frères Vivaldi, à la découverte ... des Indes Orientales au xIIIᵉ. siècle, *etc.* Par., 1859.
———— DUNSTERVILLE, E. The Admiralty List of the Lights of ... E. I. ... Corrected to 1860, 61, 62. 1860-62.
———— SAINSBURY, W. N. Calendar of State Papers ... E. I. ... 1513-1616, *etc.* Lond., 1862.
———— Barker, E. Report of a Voyage to the E. I. in 1591, *etc.* ASTLEY. Vol. I.
———— Davis, J. Voyage to the E. I. in 1598. ASTLEY. Vol. I.
———— The first Voyages of the English to ... the E. I. ASTLEY. Vol. I.
———— Portuguese sent to ... E. I. by Land, *etc.* ASTLEY. Vol. I.
———— Saris, J. Occurrences at ... parts of the E. I., 1605-9, *etc.* ASTLEY. Vol. I.
———— Unfortunate Voyage of Capt. B. Wood toward the E. I. in 1596. ASTLEY. Vol. I.
———— V. de Gama's Second Voyage to the E. I. in 1502. ASTLEY. Vol. I.

M 2

East Indies.

East Indies.—Voyages of the English to the E. I., *etc.* ASTLEY. Vol. I.
——— Voyage of J. de Nueva to the E. I. ASTLEY. Vol. I.
——— Voyages to the S. E. and E. I., till the Europeans settled there. ASTLEY. Vol. I.
——— Roe, Sir T. Journal of his Voyage to the E. I., *etc.* CHURCHILL. Vol. I.
——— Nieuhoff, J. Voyages and Travels into . . . the E. I. CHURCHILL. Vol. II.
——— Lord, H. Discovery of two foreign Sects in the E. I., *etc.* CHURCHILL. Vol. VI.
——— Cartwright, J. The Preacher's Travels to . . . the E. I., *etc.* CHURCHILL. Vol. VII.
——— Bruton, W. News from the E. I., *etc.* CHURCHILL. Vol. VIII.
——— Description of a Voyage . . . into the E. I. . . . 1595-97, *etc.* CHURCHILL. Vol. VIII.
——— Considerations on . . . "Thoughts on our Acquisitions in the E. I.," *etc.* 1772. DALRYMPLE, A. Tracts, from 1764 to 1808. Vol. I.
——— Voyage of Master Cæsar Frederick into the East India . . . 1563. HAKLUYT. Vol. II.
——— Gilbert, Sir H. A Discourse to prove a passage by the N. W. to . . . the E. I. HAKLUYT. Vol. III.
——— May, H. Voyage to the E. I. . . . 1591-93. HAKLUYT. Vol. IV.
——— Vertomannus, L. Navigation and Voyages to . . . E. India . . . 1503. HAKLUYT. Vol. IV.
——— Bruton, W. Newes from the E. I. . . . 1638. HAKLUYT. Vol. V.
——— Voyage made by certaine Ships of Holland into the E. I., 1595-97. HAKLUYT. Vol. V.
——— An Account of the most remarkable Fish and Fowl in the E. I., *etc.* HARRIS, J. Vol. I.
——— Beaulieu, A. de. Expedition to the E. I. . . . 1619-22. HARRIS, J. Vol. I.
——— The Discovery, settlement, and commerce of the E. I. HARRIS, J. Vol. I.
——— An historical Account of the Intercourse between . . . Great Britain and . . . the E. I., *etc.* HARRIS, J. Vol. I.
——— History of the . . . Portuguese Empire in the E. I., *etc.* HARRIS, J. Vol. I.
——— Laval, F. Pirard de. Voyage to the E. I. . . . 1601-11. HARRIS, J. Vol. I.
——— Maglianos or Magellan, F. Voyage from the South Seas to the E. I., 1519-22. HARRIS, J. Vol. I.
——— Of the Land Animals in the E. I., *etc.* HARRIS, J. Vol. I.
——— Tavernier, J. B. Account of the Commodities . . . of the E. I. HARRIS, J. Vol. I.
——— Wood, R. Unfortunate Voyage towards the E. I., 1596. KERR. Vol. VII.

East Indies.—Davis, J. Voyage to E. I. 1598. KERR. Vol. VIII.
—— First Voyage of the English E. I. Company 1601, etc. KERR. Vol. VIII.
—— Fifth Voyage of . . . the English E. I. Company in 1617, etc. KERR. Vol. IX.
—— Rochon, Abbé. Voyage to . . . the E. I. PELHAM. Vol. II.
—— Bernier's Voyage to the E. I. PINKERTON. Vol. VIII.
—— Hamilton's Account of the E. I. PINKERTON. Vol. VIII.
—— Breve Relação das Escrituras dos Gentios da India Oriental, e dos seus Costumes. PORTUGAL. Collecção de Noticias, etc. Vol. I.
—— Empoli, J. de. Viagem as Indias Orientaes, 1503. PORTUGAL. Collecção de Noticias, etc. Vol. II.
—— Lopes, T. Navegação a's Indias Orientaes, 1502. PORTUGAL. Collecção de Noticias, etc. Vol. II.
—— An Answer to the Hollander's declaration concerning the occurrents of the E. India. PURCHAS. Vol. I.
—— Best, T. Journal of the tenth Voyage to the E. I., 1611-14, etc. PURCHAS. Vol. I.
—— A briefe narration of the fourth Voyage to the E. I. under A. Sharpey, etc. PURCHAS. Vol. I.
—— Clayborne, T. Discourse of a Second Voyage to the E. I. under Sir H. Middleton, 1604-6, etc. PURCHAS. Vol. I.
—— Davis, J. A Ruter, or briefe direction for readie sayling into the E. India, etc. PURCHAS. Vol. I.
—— —— Third Voyage . . . to the E. I., 1604-6. PURCHAS. Vol. I.
—— —— Voyage to the Easterne India, 1598-1600. PURCHAS. Vol. I.
—— Davy, J. Journal of the Ninth Voyage to the E. I. . . . 1611-15. PURCHAS. Vol. I.
—— Dodsworth, E. Briefe Memorialls observed by, during a Voyage to the E. I., 1613-15. PURCHAS. Vol. I.
—— Downton, N. Extracts of the Journal of a Voyage to the E. I. . . . 1613-15. PURCHAS. Vol. I.
—— Dutch Navigations to the E. I., etc. PURCHAS. Vol. I.
—— Elkington, T. Collections taken out of the Journal of a Voyage to the E. I., 1613-15. PURCHAS. Vol. I.
—— First Voyage made to E. India by Sir J. Lancaster, 1600, etc. PURCHAS. Vol. I.
—— The Hollanders Declaration of the affaires of the E. I. . . . 1622. PURCHAS. Vol. I.
—— Keeling, W. Journal of the third Voyage to the E. I., 1607-10, etc. PURCHAS. Vol. I.
—— Marten, N. Seventh Voyage into E. India . . . 1610-15. PURCHAS. Vol. I.
—— Middleton, Sir H. Sixth Voyage, set forth by the E. I. Companie . . . 1610-12, etc. PURCHAS. Vol. I.

East Indies.

East Indies.—Millward, J. Memorial of a Voyage to the E. I., 1614-15. PURCHAS. Vol. I.

—— Mun, T. Discourse of Trade from England unto the E. I., etc. PURCHAS. Vol. I.

—— Of the first English Voyages to the E. I., etc. PURCHAS. Vol. I.

—— Peyton, W. Journal of all the principal matters passed in the Voyage to the E. India, 1612-14. PURCHAS. Vol. I.

—— —— Second Voyage into the E. I. 1614-16, etc. PURCHAS. Vol. I.

—— The Portugals Discontent ... and the first Discoveries of the E. I., 1493-4. PURCHAS. Vol. I.

—— Pring, M. Brief Notes of two Voyages into the E. I., 1614-16. Second Voyage ... 1610-21. PURCHAS. Vol. I.

—— Saris, J. Eighth Voyage set forth by the E. I. in Societie ... 1611-14. PURCHAS. Vol. I.

—— —— Observations of occurrents which happened in the E. I. ... 1605-9. PURCHAS. Vol. I.

—— The Second Fleet sent to the E. I. ... 1500. PURCHAS. Vol. I.

—— Spilbergen, G. Brief description of the ... E. I. ... 1616. PURCHAS. Vol. I.

—— Tatton, J. Journal of a Voyage ... to the E. I., 1612-13. PURCHAS. Vol. I.

—— Wilson, R. Journal of the eleventh Voyage to the E. I., 1611-13. PURCHAS. Vol. I.

—— Wood, B. Voyage into the E. I., 1596-1601. PURCHAS. Vol. I.

—— Fitch, R. Voyage to ... all the Coast of the E. I., 1583-91. PURCHAS. Vol. II.

—— Hulghen van Linschoten, J. Voyage to Goa and observations of the E. I., 1483. PURCHAS. Vol. II.

—— Pyrard de Laval, F. Voyage to the E. I. ... 1601-11, etc. PURCHAS. Vol. II.

—— Terry, E. Relation of a Voyage to the Easterne India, 1616. PURCHAS. Vol. II.

—— Nicolo di Conti. Voyage to Indies, etc. PURCHAS. Vol. III.

—— Of the E. I. ... with their Religions. PURCHAS. Vol. V.

—— Arriano. Navigatione del Mar Rosso, fino all' Indie Orientali, etc. RAMUSIO. Vol. I.

—— Barbosa, O. Libro dell' Indie Orientali, 1516. RAMUSIO. Vol. I.

—— Conti, N. di. Viaggio nelle Indie Orientali, 1449. RAMUSIO. Vol. I.

—— Lopez, T. Navigatione verso l'Indie Orientali, 1502. RAMUSIO. Vol. I.

—— Ramusio. Discorso sopra alcune lettere e navigationi fatte per li Capitani dell' armate ... di Portogallo, verso l'Indie Orientali. RAMUSIO. Vol. I.

—— —— Discorso sopra la Navigatione dal Mar Rosso, fino all' Indie Orientali, scritta per Arriano. RAMUSIO. Vol. I.

—— Sommario di tutti li Regni, Cittá, e Popoli dell' Indie Orientali. RAMUSIO. Vol. I.

East Indies. 167

East Indies.—Marco Polo. Viaggi delle cose . . . dell' Indie Orientali, 1250, etc. RAMUSIO. Vol. II.
———— Federici, C. de'. Viaggio nell' India Orientale . . . 1568-69. RAMUSIO. Vol. III.
———— Description des Plantes & des Animaux des Indes Orientales, par COMMAR, etc. THEVENOT. Vol. I.
———— Roatier des Indes Orientales par Aleixo da Motta, etc. THEVENOT. Vol. I.
———— Voyage aux Indes Orientales de Bontekoe, etc. THEVENOT. Vol. I.
———— Carte Portugaise de la Carres, ou Navigation des Indes Orientales. THEVENOT. Vol. II.
———— Vues des principales costes des Indes Orientales. THEVENOT. Vol. II.
———— Le Voyage de Beaulieu (aux Indes Orientales). THEVENOT. Vol. II.
———— Rapport que les Directeurs de la Compagnie Hollandoise des Indes Orientales ont fait . . . en l'an 1664. THEVENOT. Vol. III.
———— Bontekoes, W. I. Reise nach Ostindien, 1618-25. VOYAGES and TRAVELS. Allgemeine Historie, etc. Vol. VIII.
———— Broeck, P. van den. Reise nach Ostindien, 1613-27, etc. VOYAGES and TRAVELS. Allgemeine Historie, etc. Vol. VIII.
———— Caerden, P. van. Zweyte Reise nach Ostindien, 1607-11. VOYAGES and TRAVELS. Allgemeine Historie, etc. Vol. VIII.
———— Erste Reise nach Ostindien von C. Houtmann, 1595. VOYAGES and TRAVELS. Allgemeine Historie, etc. Vol. VIII.
———— Haiens, de la. Reise nach Ostindien, 1670-72, etc. VOYAGES and TRAVELS. Allgemeine Historie, etc. Vol. VIII.
———— Matelief, C. Reise nach Ostindien, 1605-8, etc. VOYAGES and TRAVELS. Allgemeine Historie, etc. Vol. VIII.
———— Pyrard, F. Reise, welche die Erste der Franzosen nach Ostindien ist, 1601-10. VOYAGES and TRAVELS. Allgemeine Historie, etc. Vol. VIII.
———— Spilberg, G. Reise nach Ostindien, 1601-3. VOYAGES and TRAVELS. Allgemeine Historie, etc. Vol. VIII.
———— Van der Hagen, S. Zweyte Reise nach Ostindien, 1604-5. VOYAGES and TRAVELS. Allgemeine Historie, etc. Vol. VIII.
———— Verhoeven, P. W. Reise nach Ostindien, 1607-11. etc. VOYAGES and TRAVELS. Allgemeine Historie, etc. Vol. VIII.
———— Warwyck, W. van. Reise nach Ostindien, 1602-4. VOYAGES and TRAVELS. Allgemeine Historie, etc. Vol. VIII.
———— Beaulieu, A. Reise nach Ostindien, 1619-21, etc. VOYAGES and TRAVELS. Allgemeine Historie, etc. Vol. X.
———— Carre. Reise nach Ostindien, 1668-71. VOYAGES and TRAVELS. Allgemeine Historie, etc. Vol. X.
———— L'Estra. Reise nach Ostindien, 1671-75. VOYAGES and TRAVELS. Allgemeine Historie, etc. Vol. X.
———— Ibboles, A. Reise nach Ostindien, 1619-19. VOYAGES and TRAVELS. Allgemeine Historie, etc. Vol. X.

168   *East Indies — Ecclesiastical State.*

East Indies.—Tachard, G. Zweyte Reise nach Ostindien, 1687. VOYAGES and TRAVELS. Allgemeine Historie, etc. Vol. X.

—— Reisen nach Ostindien durch Südwest. Magalhanes, F. 1519. Noort, O. von. 1598-1601. VOYAGES and TRAVELS. Allgemeine Historie, etc. Vol. XI.

—— Naturgeschichte von Ostindien. VOYAGES and TRAVELS. Allgemeine Historie, etc. Vol. XII.

—— Reisen nach Ostindien durch Südwest. Drake, 1577-79. Sarmiento, 1580. VOYAGES and TRAVELS. Allgemeine Historie, etc. Vol. XII.

—— Rogers, W. Reise nach Ostindien durch Südwesten, 1708-10. VOYAGES and TRAVELS. Allgemeine Historie, etc. Vol. XII.

—— Verschiedene Reisen nach Ostindien durch die Magellanische Strasse. Candish, 1586.—Noort and Weert, 1598-09.—Spilberg, 1614.— L'Hermite and Schapenham, 1624.—Narborough, 1669-71. VOYAGES and TRAVELS. Allgemeine Historie, etc. Vol. XII.

—— Anmerkungen, welche zur Verbindung des Fortganges der Holländer in Ostindien dienen. VOYAGES and TRAVELS. Allgemeine Historie, etc. Vol. XVIII.

—— The Voyage of Pedro Alvarez de Cabral, to the E. I. 1500.—The Voyage of Captain James Lancaster to the E. I. 1600.—The Expedition of Commodore Beaulieu to the E. I. 1619. VOYAGES and TRAVELS. The World displayed. Vol. VIII.

—— The Voyage of Sir Henry Middleton to the E. I. 1610.—The Voyage of Mr. Grose to the E. I. 1750. VOYAGES and TRAVELS. The World displayed. Vol. IX.

—— A New History of the E. I. VOYAGES and TRAVELS. The World displayed. Vol. XVI.

—— *See also* GOA.

——, **Dutch.**—ALMANACH. Almanak van Nederlandsch—Indie, etc.
Batavia, 1843.

—— —— EAST INDIES. Land-en Zeemagt in Nederlandsch Indie, 1844.
Batavia, 1843.

—— —— HANDLEIDING tot de Aardrijks-Kunde van Nederlands Oostindische Bezittingen, etc. *Leyd. Dev. en Gron.*, 1843.

—— —— VAN HEES, M. G. Handleiding tot de Aardrijkskunde van Nederlands Oostindische Bezittingen. *Leyden*, 1843.

—— —— AA, A. J. VAN DER. Nederlands Oost-India, etc.
Amst., 1846.

— —— —— TEENSTRA, M. D. Beknopte Beschrijving van do Nederlandsche Overzeesche Bezittingen . . . in Oost-en West-Indien, etc.
Gron., 1846.

—— —— BUDGET, BARON K. VAN. Beschouwingen over Nederlandsch India. *Grav.*, 1847.

East Sea.—*See* SOUND.
Eastern Archipelago.—*See* ARCHIPELAGO, INDIAN.
Ebro.—WALTON, W. Sketch of the River E., etc.   1852.
Ecbatana.—*See* HAMADAN.
Ecclesiastical State.—*See* STATES OF THE CHURCH.

Ecuador — Egypt.

Ecuador.—ECUADOR. E. Land Company, limited. [A Prospectus.]
Lond.

──── WRIGHT, R. A brief sketch of the . . . Republic of the Equator, etc. 1836.

──── PRITCHETT, G. J. E. Waste Lands. 1858.

──── ──── Report of his Mission to . . . E. 1858.

──── VILLAVICENCIO, M. Geografía de la Republica del E.
N. Y., 1858.

──── BOLLAERT, W. Antiquarian . . . Researches in . . . Equador, etc.
1860.

──── SPRUCE, R. Report on the Expedition to procure seeds and plants of the Cinchona Succirubra [in E.], etc. *Lond.*, 1861.

──── ECUADOR. E. und die E.-Land Compagnie. *Mannheim*, 1862.

Edessa.—*See* ORFAH.

Edinburgh.—SMYTH, C. P. Report . . . on the Royal Observatory of E., 1846. *Edin.*, 1846.

──── ──── Report to the Board of Visitors of the Royal Observatory of E., Nov. 1852. *Edin.*, 1852.

──── ──── Report read to the Special Meeting . . . of Visitors of the Royal Observatory, E., etc. *Edin.*, 1864.

Edom.—LINDSAY, Lord. Letters on . . . E., etc. 1847.

──── ──── KENNEDY, J. Idumæa, etc. 1851.

Egean Sea.—*See* ARCHIPELAGO.

Egeesche Zee.—*See* ARCHIPELAGO.

Eger.—GRIESEN, T. Griehen's Reise-Bibliothek. N°. 38 . . . E., etc.
Berl., 1861.

── ──── Barton, E. Two letters . . . from Agria, 1506. PURCHAS. Vol. II.

Egmont Island.—Carteret, Capt. Voyage . . . to . . . E. I. 1766-69. HAWKESWORTH, J. Vol. I.

Egypt.—CORRAUX, F. On the Comparative Physical Geography of the Arabian Frontier of E., at the earliest epoch, etc. [*Edinburgh*.]

──── ──── EGYPT. Relation de l'Expédition scientifique des Français en Égypte en 1798.

──── ──── JOMARD, E. F. Relation de l'Expédition Scientifique des Français en E. au 1798. *Paris.*

── ──── PELAGIUS CAMBRENSIS. Voyage into Æ. . . . 890.

──── BELLONIUS, P. Plurimarum . . . rerum in . . . Ægypto . . . conspectarum observationes, etc. *Antw.*, 1589.

──── SANDYS, G. A Relation of a Journey begun . . . 1610. Containing a description of . . . Æ., etc. 1615.

──── PONCET, MONSIEUR. A Voyage to Æthiopia . . . describing . . . likewise . . . part of E., etc. *Lond.*, 1709.

──── HASIUS, J. M. Regni Davidici . . . descriptio . . . una cum delineatione . . . Ægypti, etc. *Nurimb.*, 1739.

──── ──── LE MASCRIER, M. L'Abbé. Description de l'Egypte, etc.
La Haye, 1740.

Egypt.—Pococke, R. Description of . . . E., *etc.* 1743-45.
——— Norden, F. L. Travels in E. and Nubia, *etc.* 1757.
——— Irwin, E. A Series of Adventures . . . on the Coasts of . . . E., *etc.* Lond., 1780.
——— Savary, M. Letters on E., *etc.* 1786.
——— Volney, C. F. Voyage . . . en É., pendant 1783-85. Par., 1787.
——— Sonnini, C. S. Travels in Upper and Lower E., *etc.* 1800.
——— Denon, V. Voyage dans la Basse et la Haute Égypte, *etc.* Lond., 1802.
——— Browne, W. G. Travels in . . . E., *etc.* 1806.
——— Valentia, Viscount. Voyages and Travels to . . . E., in 1802-6. 1811.
——— Ali Bey. Travels in . . . E., *etc.* 1816.
——— Legh, T. Narrative of a Journey in E., *etc.* 1816.
——— Light, H. Travels in E. . . . 1814. Lond., 1818.
——— Belzoni, G. Narrative of . . . Operations . . . in E., *etc.* 1822.
——— Cella, P. della. Narrative of an expedition from Tripoli . . . to . . . E., *etc.* 1822.
——— Irby, Hon. C. L., and Mangles, J. Travels in E. . . . 1817 and 1818. 1823.
——— Landseer, J. Sabaean Researches . . . Essays . . . on the engraved Hieroglyphics of . . . E., *etc.* 1823.
——— Mengin, F. Histoire de l'Égypte sous le gouvernement de Mohammed-Aly, *etc.* Par., 1823.
——— Young, T. An Account of some recent discoveries in . . . E. ian Antiquities, *etc.* 1823.
——— Henniker, Sir F. Notes during a Visit to E., *etc.* 1824.
——— Lushington, Mrs. C. Narrative of a Journey . . . to Europe, by way of E. 1829.
——— Madden, R. R. Travels in . . . E., *etc.* 1829.
——— Prokesch, A. von. Erinnerungen aus Ægypten, *etc.* Wien, 1829-30.
——— Burckhardt, J. L. Arabic Proverbs; or the Manners . . . of the Modern Egyptians, *etc.* 1830.
——— Elwood, Mrs. Col. Journey Overland . . . by . . . E. . . . to India. 1830.
——— Grásszo, Count J. Tableau de l'Égypte, *etc.* Gennaio, 1830.
——— Tattam, H. Compendious Grammar of the E. ian language, *etc.* Lond., 1830.
——— Young, T. Rudiments of an E. ian Dictionary in the Ancient Enchorial Character, *etc.* Lond., 1830.
——— Russell, Bp. M. View of Ancient and Modern E., *etc.* Edin., 1832.
——— Yeates, T. Dissertation on . . . the principal Pyramids of E., *etc.* 1833.

Egypt. 171

Egypt.—FITZMAURICE, HON. W. E. Cruise to E., etc. 1834.
—— MADOX, J. Excursions in ... E., etc. 1834.
—— YEATES, T. Remarks on the History of Ancient E., etc. 1835.
—— BEKE, C. T. On the Complexion of the Ancient Egyptians. 1836.
—— HOSKINS, G. A. Ethiopia versus E. 1836.
—— JOMARD, E. F. Coup-d'œil impartial sur l'état présent de l'Égypte, etc. *Par.,* 1836.
—— LANE, E. W. Account of ... the Modern Egyptians, etc. 1836.
—— HOLROYD, A. T. E. and Mahomed Ali Pasha, in 1837. 1837.
—— HEEREN, A. H. L. Historical Researches into the Politics ... of the ... Egyptians, etc. *Oxf.,* 1838.
—— STEPHENS, G. Incidents of Travel in E., etc. 1838.
—— MACBRAIR, R. M. Sketches of a Missionary's Travels in E., etc. 1839.
—— DAMER, HON. MRS. G. L. D. Diary of a Tour in ... E., etc. *Lond.,* 1841.
—— GLIDDON, G. R. An Appeal ... on the destruction of the Monuments of E. 1841.
—— —— A Memoir on the Cotton of E. 1841.
—— GRÅBERG, COUNT J. Relazioni Commerciali del Egitto ... coi Porti dell' Italia, etc. *Firenze,* 1841.
—— INDIA. Hand-Book for ... E. 1841.
—— PARBURY, G. Hand-Book for India and E., etc. *Lond.,* 1841.
—— EGYPT. Notes from a private Journal of a Visit to E., etc. *Lond.,* 1844.
—— FONTANIER, V. Voyage dans l'Inde ... par l'Égypte, etc. *Par.,* 1844.
—— GALLOWAY, J. A. Communication with India ... viâ E., etc. 1844.
—— MORTON, S. G. Crania Ægyptiaca, etc. *Phil.,* 1844.
—— BORRER, D. A Journey from Naples to Jerusalem, by way of ... E., etc. 1845.
—— CURRBI, O. Storia fisica ... dell' Egitto, etc. *Firenze,* 1845.
—— HAHN-HAHN, COUNTESS I. Travels in ... E., etc. 1845.
—— PRUNER, F. Die Ueberbleibsel der altägyptischen Menschenrace. *Münch.,* 1846.
—— ROMER, MRS. Pilgrimage to ... E., etc. 1846.
—— SHARPE, S. History of E. ... till ... A.D. 640. 1846.
—— WILSON, T. Nozráui in E. and Syria. 1846.
—— LINDSAY, LORD. Letters on E., etc. 1847.
—— CORBAUX, F. On the Comparative Physical Geography of the Arabian Frontier of E., etc. *Edin.,* 1848.
—— LEPSIUS, R. Denkmäler aus Ägypten und Äthiopien, etc. *Berl.,* 1849.
—— BARTLETT, W. H. The Nile Boat; or, Glimpses of ... E. 1850.

Egypt.

Egypt.—SPENCER, J. A. The East. Sketches of Travels in E., etc. 1850.
— WILD, J. J. Letter . . . containing proposals for a scientific Exploration of E., etc. 1850.
— EGYPT. The Present Crisis in E., in relation to our Overland communication with India. 1851.
— FORSTER, C. The One Primeval Language traced . . . from the Monuments of E., etc. 1851.
— FREEMAN, J. J. Tour in S. Africa, with notices of . . . E., etc. 1851.
— POOLE, S. The Englishwoman in E., etc. 1851.
— LEPSIUS, R. Discoveries in E. . . . In 1842-45, etc. 1852.
— RUSSELL, BP. M. History of Ancient and Modern E., etc. 1852.
— ST. JOHN, B. Village Life in E., etc. Lond., 1852.
— WILDE, W. R. Narrative . . . including a Visit to . . . E., etc. Dubl., 1852.
— PFEIFFER, J. Visit to . . . E., etc. 1853.
— POWER, W. T. Recollections . . . including Peregrinations in . . . E., etc. Lond., 1853.
— HABANT, K. Gesta . . . do Egypto, etc. v. Prase, 1854.
— HORNER, L. Account of some recent Researches . . . undertaken with the view of throwing light upon the Geological History of the Alluvial Land of E. 1855.
— LOTTIN DE LAVAL, M. Voyage dans . . . l'Égypt Moyenne, etc. Par., 1855-59.
— FALKLAND, VISCOUNTESS. Chow-Chow; being Selections from a Journal kept in . . . E., etc. 1857.
— SAINT-HILAIRE, J. B. E. and the Great Suez Canal, etc. 1857.
— WILKINSON, SIR J. G. The Egyptians in the Time of the Pharaohs, etc. 1857.
— —— Popular Account of the Ancient Egyptians. 1857.
— LEPSIUS, R. The XXII. Egyptian Royal Dynasty, etc. 1858.
— PETHERICK, J. E., the Soudan, etc. Edin. and Lond., 1861.
— LANGE, D. A. Reflections on the E. lan Desert. 1862.
— HOSKINS, G. A. Winter in Upper and Lower E. 1863.
— ENGEL, C. The Music of the most ancient Nations . . . with special reference to recent discoveries in . . . E. Lond., 1864.
— FIGARI, A. Studii scientifici sull' Egitto, etc. Lucca, 1864-65.
— DUFF GORDON, LADY. Letters from E., etc. Lond., 1865.
— ARROW, SIR F. A Fortnight in E., etc. Lond., 1869.
— MACGREGOR, J. The "Rob Roy" . . . A Canoe Cruise in . . . E., etc. Lond., 1869.
— Baumgarten, M. Travels through E., etc. CHURCHILL. Vol. I.
— Greaves, J. Pyramidographia, etc. CHURCHILL. Vol. II.
— Egypts. Nubie. EYRIES. Vol. XIV.
— Athelard, of Bathe. Voyage to Æ. . . . 1130. HAKLUYT. Vol. II.

Egypt. 173

Egypt.—Constantine, the Great. Voyage to . . . Æ. . . . 339. HAK-
LUYT. Vol. II.

——— Evesham, J. Voyage . . . into Æ., 1586. HAKLUYT. Vol. II.

——— Voyage of William Long-espee into Æ. . . . 1249. HAKLUYT.
Vol. II.

——— Vertomannus, L. Navigation and Voyages to . . . E. . . . 1503.
HAKLUYT. Vol. IV.

——— Varthema, L. di. Travels in E. . . . 1503 to 1508 . . . Edited
. . . by G. P. Badger. 1863. HAKLUYT Soc. PUB. Vol. XXXII.

——— Varthema, L. Voyages and Travels in E. . . . in 1503-8. KERR.
Vol. VII.

——— Sonnini, C. S. Travels in Upper and Lower E., abridged. PEL-
HAM. Vol. I.

——— Volney, C. F. Travels through . . . E., in 1783-85. PELHAM.
Vol. II.

——— Allatif, A. Relation respecting E. PINKERTON. Vol. XV.

——— Pococke's Travels in E. PINKERTON. Vol. XV.

——— Barthema or Vertoman, L. Travels into E. . . . 1503. PURCHAS.
Vol. II.

——— Benjamin, the Son of Jonas. Peregrination of . . . and relations
of . . . E., etc. PURCHAS. Vol. II.

——— Scot, W. L. Travels in . . . E. . . . 1612. PURCHAS. Vol. II.

——— Of Æ., Barbary . . . and of their Religions. PURCHAS. Vol. V.

——— Barthema, L. Itinerario dell' Egitto, etc. RAMUSIO. Vol. I.

——— Belon, M. Observations made in a Voyage to E. RAY, J.

——— Greaves, J. Description of the Pyramids in E., 1638-39. RAY, J.

——— Huntingdon, R. Letter concerning the Porphyry Pillars in E.
RAY, J.

——— Vansleb, Father. Of the Pyramids . . . of E. RAY, J.

——— Description des Pyramides d'Egypte, par Jean Greaves, etc. THEVE-
NOT. Vol. I.

——— Collins, F. Voyages to . . . E., etc. 1706-1801. VOYAGES and
TRAVELS. A Collection, etc. 1805. Vol. X.

——— Valentia, Viscount. Voyages and Travels to . . . E., 1802-6.
VOYAGES and TRAVELS. A Collection, etc. 1805. Vol. XI.

——— Valentia, Viscount. Voyages and Travels to . . . E., 1802-6.
VOYAGES and TRAVELS. A Collection, etc. 1810. Vol. IV.

——— Collins, F. Voyages to . . . E., etc. 1706-1801. VOYAGES and
TRAVELS. A Collection, etc. 1810. Vol. VI.

——— Fitzclarence, Lt.-Col. Journal of a Route . . . through E. to
England, 1817-18. VOYAGES and TRAVELS, New. 1819. Vol. I.

——— Burckhardt, M. Some Account of the Travels of, in E., etc.
VOYAGES and TRAVELS, New. 1819. Vol. II.

——— Forbin, Count de. Travels in E. . . . 1817-18. VOYAGES and
TRAVELS, New. 1819. Vol. II.

Egypt.—Montulé, E. de. Travels in E., 1818-19. VOYAGES and TRAVELS, New. 1810. Vol. V.

——— Lelorrain, M. Journey in E., 1821, etc. VOYAGES and TRAVELS, New. 1819, etc. Vol. VIII.

——— Scholz, J. M. A. Travels in . . . E. . . . 1821. VOYAGES and TRAVELS, New. 1810, etc. Vol. VIII.

——— Misrah, M. Narrative of a Journey from E. to the W.n Coast of Africa, 1821. VOYAGES and TRAVELS, New. 1819, etc. Vol. IX.

——— Voyage de Bernard et de ses compagnons en E., etc. VOYAGES and TRAVELS. Recueil, etc. Vol. IV.

——— Pococke, Richard. Travels through E. 1737. VOYAGES and TRAVELS. The World displayed. Vol. XII., XIII.

——— Davison, Mr. Observations relating to . . . the Antiquities of E. WALPOLE, R. Memoirs, etc.

——— Hume, Dr. Remarks on . . . Modern . . . E. WALPOLE, R. Memoirs, etc.

——— *See also* DAMIETTA. SIUT.

———, **Lower.**—SENTZEN, U. J. Reisen durch . . . Unter-Aegypten, etc. etc. *Berl.*, 1854.

———, **Upper.**—LUCAS, P. Voyage au Levant. . . . description de la Haute-Égypte, etc. *La Haye*, 1709.

——— ——— UHLE, J. P. Der Winter in Oberägypten als Klimatischen Heilmittel. *Leipz.*, 1858.

Elanceer.—*See* ARCTIC OCEAN.

El-Ahkaf.—PLATE, W. Ptolemy's Knowledge . . . especially of . . . the Wilderness E.-A. 1845.

Elba, Isle of.—THIÉDAUT DE BERNEAUD, A. A Voyage to the Isle of E., etc. *Lond.*, 1814.

Elbing.—SCHMID, VON. Der E.-Oberlandische Canal. *Berl.*, 1861.

Elbrous.—*See* ELBRUZ.

Elbrus.—KUPFFER, M. Voyage dans les Environs de Mont Elbrous . . . en 1829. *St. Pét.*, 1830.

——— DOUGLAS, F. W. Travels . . . including . . . Ascents of Kazbak and E. *Lond.*, 1869.

——— Jordan ou Jourdain Catalani, P. Mirabilia descripta, sequitur de . . . Montibus Caspiis, etc. VOYAGES and TRAVELS. Recueil, etc. Vol. IV.

Elburj.—*See* ELBRUZ.

Eleusis.—STUART, J. and REVETT, N. The Antiquities of Athens . . . E., etc. 1825-33.

Elfsborg.—TOPOGRAPHISKA och Statistiska Uppgifter om E.s Län. *Stockh.*, 1860.

Ellis.—Sibthorp, Dr. Journal relating to parts of the ancient E., etc. WALPOLE, R. Travels, etc.

Ellora.—BURGESS, J. The Rock-cut Temples of Ajanta, with an Account of a Trip to . . . E. *Bombay*, 1868.

El-Medinah.—See MEDINA.
Elmira.—PETERS, C. H. F. Report on the determination of the Longitude of E. [1862.]
El Obéid.—See Lobeid.
Elora.—See ELLORA.
Eloth.—Of Exion Geber, E., and the Red Sea, *etc.* PURCHAS. Vol. I.
Elsass.—See ALSACE.
Elster.—GRIEBEN, T. Grieben's Reise-Bibliothek. No. 38 . . . E., *etc.*
Berl., **1861.**
Elsterwerda.—Dresden und die umliegende Gegend bis E., *etc.*
Dresd., **1804.**
Empire Burman.—See BURMAH.
Empire Chinois.—See CHINA.
Empire du Milieu.—See CHINA.
Empire Ottoman.—See TURKEY.
Engadine, Upper.—REY, W. Les Grisons et la Haute Engadine.
Genève, **1860.**

England.—OGILBY, J. Britannia; or . . . E . . . surveyed, *etc.*,
1698.

——— POLLNITZ, C. L., BARON DE. Memoirs . . . in his . . . Travels through . . . E., *etc.* **1737.**

——— SEWARD, W. Journal of a voyage . . . from Philadelphia to E., 1740. Lond., **1740.**

——— MARTIN, B. The Natural History of E., *etc.* Lond., **1759-63.**

——— OWEN, J. Britannia Depicta . . . an actual Survey of . . . E., *etc.*
1764.

——— Considerations on . . . affairs between E. and America. 1778. DALRYMPLE, A. Tracts, from 1764 to 1808. Vol. I.

——— ANDREWS, J. Historical Atlas of E., *etc.* **1797.**

——— FAUJAS SAINT-FOND, B. Voyage en Angleterre, *etc.* Par., **1797.**

——— FORSTER, G. Journey from Bengal to E., *etc.* **1798.**

——— FAUJAS SAINT-FOND, B. Travels in E., *etc.* **1799.**

——— MUDGE, W., and DALBY, J. Trigonometrical Survey of E. . . . , 1784-99. **1799-1801.**

——— PLAYFAIR, W. The Commercial and Political Atlas, representing . . . the progress of . . . E., during . . . the Eighteenth Century, *etc.* Lond., **1801.**

——— CARY, J. Itinerary of the Great Roads throughout E., *etc.* **1812.**

——— FRANK, G. Viaggio . . . per una gran parte dell' Inghilterra, *etc.*
Milano, **1813.**

——— CONYBEARE, W. D., and PHILLIPS, W. Outlines of the Geology of E. and Wales, *etc.* Lond., **1822.**

——— ALEXANDER, SIR J. E. Travels from India to E., *etc.* **1827.**

——— CARLISLE, N. Historical Account of . . . Charities in E. and Wales, *etc.* **1828.**

England.—Paterson's Roads in E. and Wales . . . improved by E. Mogg.
1829.
—— Elwood, Mrs. Col. Journey Overland from E . . . to India.
1830.
—— Walsh, R. Journey from Constantinople to E. 1831.
—— England. An Act to settle and describe the Divisions of Counties . . . in E., etc. 1832.
—— England. Reports from Commissioners on Proposed Division of Counties, etc. 1832.
—— England and America, a Comparison, etc. 1833.
—— Arctic Expeditions. Arctic Expeditions from E., from 1497 to 1833. 1834.
—— Bourchier, W. Narrative of a Passage from Bombay to E., etc.
1834.
—— Bell, J. New . . . Gazetteer of E., etc. *Glasg.,* 1837, 38.
—— Dechen. Anzeige der Geognostichen Karte von . . . E., etc.
Berl., 1839.
—— Murchison, Sir R. L. Map of the Silurian Region and adjacent counties of E., etc. 1839.
—— Greenough, G. B. Memoir of a Geological Map of E., etc. 1840.
—— England. Report of the Commissioners appointed to survey the Harbours (S.E. Coast). 1840.
—— Clark, Sir J. The Sanative Influence of Climate, with an account of . . . places of resort . . . in E., etc. 1841.
—— Parliamentary Gazetteer of E. and Wales, etc.
Lond., Edin., Glasg., 1843.
—— Registrar General, Reports of the, of Births, Deaths, and Marriages in E., 1844-5. *Lond.,* 1845-47.
—— Rónay, J. Jellemisme, vagy az Angol . . . Nemzet Jellemgése, etc. *Györött,* 1847.
—— Maury, L. F. A. Histoire . . . des Forêts de l'Angleterre, etc.
Par., 1850.
—— Murchison, Sir R. L. On the distribution of the Flint Drift of the S.E. of E., etc. *Lond.,* 1851.
—— Garc, F. Education in E., etc. 1852.
—— Worsaae, J. J. A. Account of the Danes and Norwegians in E., etc.
1852.
—— Black's Picturesque Tourist of E. and Wales. *Edin.,* 1854.
—— Hamel, J. E. and Russia, etc. 1854.
—— Whitley, N. On some Peculiarities of the Climate of the S.-W. of E., etc. 1855.
—— Glaisher, J. On the Meteorology of E., etc. 1857-59.
—— James, Sir H. Ordnance Survey. Abstracts of the principal Lines of Spirit Levelling in E. and Wales. 1861.
—— Sykes, W. H. Notes on . . . the Trade of E. with China, etc.
1861.
—— Domesday Book, or the Great Survey of E. . . . In Fac-simile, etc. 1861-63.

England.—MCAUGHION, SIR R. I., and HARKNESS, R. On the Permian Rocks of the N.-W. of E., *etc.* **1864.**

——— BALFOUR, MAJOR-GEN. On the Budgets and Accounts of E., *etc. Lond.*, **1866.**

——— PEACOCK, R. A. Physical and historical evidences of vast Sinkings of Land on the S.W. Coasts of E., within the Historical Period. *Lond.*, **1868.**

——— KING, J. W. Pilote de la Manche, Côtes Sud et Sud-Ouest d'Angleterre, *etc. Par.*, **1869.**

——— RAVENSTEIN, E. G. Denominational Statistics of E. and Wales. *Lond.*, **1870.**

——— ——— Reisehandbuch für E., *etc. Hildburgh.*, **1870.**

——— BETTS, J. Exercises on . . . E. and Wales, *etc.*

——— GERMANY. Anzeige der geognostischen Karte von . . . E, *etc.*

——— Phillips, Capt. Journal of . . . Voyage from E. to Cape Mounseradoe, *etc.* CHURCHILL. Vol. VI.

——— Bissell, A. Voyage from E. to the Red Sea . . . 1798-99. DALRYMPLE, A. Collection of Nautical Memoirs, *etc.*

——— Horsey, Master J. Voyage over land from Mosco . . . to E., 1584. HAKLUYT. Vol. I.

——— Austel, H. Voyage . . . through Germany into E., 1586. HAKLUYT. Vol. II.

——— Mandevil, Sir J. Voyage from E. to Judea . . . from 1322 to 1355. HAKLUYT. Vol. II.

——— Browne, E. Voyage from E. to Holland . . . 1668. HARRIS, J. Vol. II.

——— Gonzales. Voyage to E. and Scotland. PINKERTON. Vol. II.

——— Moritz, C. P. Travels through several parts of E. PINKERTON. Vol. II.

——— Ancient Commerce between E. and Norway, *etc.* PURCHAS. Vol. III.

——— Gleanings of a Wanderer, in . . . E. . . . 1804. VOYAGES and TRAVELS. A Collection, *etc.* 1805. Vol. I.

——— Wales, a Tour in, and several Counties of E. . . . 1805. VOYAGES and TRAVELS. A Collection, *etc.* 1805. Vol. IV.

——— Wales, a Tour in and through several Counties of E. 1805. VOYAGES and TRAVELS. A Collection, *etc.* 1810. Vol. I.

——— E., Journal of a Tour in the W.n Counties of, 1807. VOYAGES and TRAVELS. A Collection, *etc.* 1810. Vol. V.

——— A Sketch of Old E., by a New England Man, 1822. VOYAGES and TRAVELS, New. 1819, *etc.* Vol. VIII.

——— **North.**—YOUNG, A. Six Months' Tour through the N. of E. **1770.**

——— ——— MAWE, J. Mineralogy . . . with a description of . . . Mines in the N. of E., *etc.* **1802.**

——— ——— GREEN, J. A . . . Guide to the Beauties of the N. of E. **1810.**

——— **South.**—YOUNG, A. Six Weeks' Tour through the S.n Counties of E., *etc.* **1768.**

——— ——— ROBERTS, G. Social History of the People of the S.n Counties of E. in past centuries. **1856.**

England, West — Espartel, Cape.

England, West.—Shaw's Tour to the W. of E. PINKERTON. Vol. II.
—— —— England, Journal of a Tour to the W.n Counties of, 1807. VOYAGES and TRAVELS. A Collection, *etc.* 1805. Vol. X.
English Channel.—TELFORD, T., and NICHOLLS, G. Ship Canal for the Junction of the E. and Bristol Channels: Reports, *etc.* 1824.
—— English and Irish Channels and Ports Tide-Tables, *etc.* 1835-53.
—— PURDY, J., and FINDLAY, A. G. Sailing Directory for the E. C., *etc.* 1849.
—— WHITE, M. Sailing Directions for the E. C., *etc.* 1850.
—— BEECHEY, F. W. Report on ... Tidal Streams of the E. C., *etc.* 1851.
—— KING, J. W. Channel Pilot, *etc.* 1859-63.
Engoy.—*See* EN-GOYO.
En-Goyo.—Of the Province of Engoy, *etc.* PURCHAS. Vol. II.
Engroenland.—*See* GREENLAND.
Engronland.—*See* GREENLAND.
Ensala.—*See* INSALAH.
Entre-Rios.—Coleccion de Leyes ... de la Provincia de E. R.
Buen. A., 1864.
Ephesus.—Voyage of three Ambassadors ... unto E., 1056. HAKLUYT. Vol. II.
Epirus.—SPENCER, E. Travels ... through ... E., *etc.* 1851.
—— Pouqueville, F. C. H. L. Travels in E. ... 1805. VOYAGES and TRAVELS, New. 1819. Vol. IV.
Equador.—*See* ECUADOR.
Equator, Republic of the.—*See* ECUADOR.
Erde.—*See* WORLD.
Erdély.—*See* TRANSYLVANIA.
Erie, Lake.—CANADA. Estimates of the Expense of ... Water Communications ... from Lake E. to Lake Ontario. 1828.
—— —— GRAHAM, J. D. Report on the Improvement of the Harbours of Lakes ... E., *etc.* *Wash.*, 1860.
Erne, Lough.—WOLFE, J. Sailing Directions, *etc.*, with some Hydrographic Notices of L. E., *etc.* 1850.
Erythrean Sea.—REINAUD, M. Mémoire ... sur l'époque de la rédaction du Périple de la Mer Érythrée, *etc.* *Par.*, 1861.
Erzeroom.—*See* ERZERUM.
Erzerum.—CURZON, HON. R. Armenia; a Year at E., *etc.* 1854.
—— MONTEITH, W. Kars and E., *etc.* 1856.
Eskimo.—*See* ESQUIMAUX.
Eslanda.—*See* ICELAND.
Espagne, España.—*See* SPAIN.
Espartel, Cape.—*See* SPARTEL.

Esquimaux.—ARCTIC EXPEDITIONS. Eskimaux and English Vocabulary, etc. *Lond.*, 1850.
—— WASHINGTON, J. E. and English Vocabulary, etc. 1850.
—— ARCTIC EXPEDITIONS. Greenland—Eskimo Vocabulary, etc. *Lond.*, 1853.
—— HALL, C. F. Life with the E., etc. *Lond.*, 1864.
Essequebo.—BOLINGBROKE, H. Voyage ... containing a Statistical Account of the Settlements ... on the E. ... 1799. VOYAGES and TRAVELS. A Collection, etc. 1805. Vol. X.
Esthonia.—HJOARTU, J. Description des Côtes de l'Esthonie, etc. *Par.*, 1855.
Estotiland.—ZENO, N. and A. Voyage to the yles of ... E. ... 1390. HAKLUYT. Vol. III.
Etbaya.—See ATBARA.
Ethiopia.—MARTYR, P. De rebus Oceanicis ... Item de rebus Æthiopicis ... opuscula. *Colonia*, 1574.
—— PONCET, MONSIEUR. A Voyage to Æthiopia, made in ... 1698, 1699, and 1700, etc. *Lond.*, 1709.
—— TELLEZ, B. Travels of the Jesuits in E., etc. 1710.
—— WADDINGTON, G. and HANBURY, B. Journal of a Visit to some parts of E. 1822.
—— HOSKINS, G. A. Travels in E., etc. 1835.
—— —— E. versus Egypt. 1836.
—— HEEREN, A. H. L. Historical Researches into the Politics ... of the ... Ethiopians, etc. *Oxf.*, 1838.
—— HARRIS, SIR W. C. The Highlands of Æ. 1844.
—— LEPSIUS, R. Denkmäler aus ... Äthiopien, etc. *Berl.*, 1849.
—— WILD, J. J. Letter ... containing Proposals for a scientific Exploration of ... E. 1850.
—— BERNATZ, J. M. Scenes in E., etc. *Munich and Lond.*, 1852.
—— LEPSIUS, R. Discoveries in ... E. ... in 1842-45, etc. 1852.
—— HAMILTON, J. Sinai ... Wanderings ... across the Æthiopian Desert, etc. 1857.
—— HUTCHINSON, T. J. Ten Years' Wanderings among the E.ns, etc. 1861.
—— ABBADIE, A. D'. Géodésie d'Éthiopie, etc. *Par.*, 1863.
—— HARRIS, SIR W. C. Illustrations of the Highlands of Æ.
—— Vertomannus, L. Navigation and Voyages to ... E. ... 1503. HAKLUYT. Vol. IV.
—— Varthema, L. dl. Travels in ... E. 1503-1508 ... Edited ... by G. P. Badger. 1863. HAKLUYT Soc. Pub. Vol. XXXII.
—— Santo's History of E.n E. PINKERTON. Vol. XVI.
—— Iambulus, his Navigation to ... E., etc. PURCHAS. Vol. I.
—— Nunnez, Bareins, J. and Oviedo, A. Relations of the State and Religion in E., 1555-77, etc. PURCHAS. Vol. I.

Ethiopia.—Alvarez, Sir F. Voyage unto the Court . . . of E., 1520-23, etc. PURCHAS. Vol. II.
—— Benjamin, the Son of Jonas. Peregrination of . . . and relations of . . . E., etc. PURCHAS. Vol. II.
—— Brief Relation of the Embassage . . . from . . . E. to . . . Portugal, etc. PURCHAS. Vol. II.
—— João dos Sanctos, Friar. Collections out of . . . his Æthiopia Orientalis, etc. PURCHAS. Vol. II.
—— Of Æ., and the African Ilands, and of their Religions. PURCHAS. Vol. V.
— · — Alvarez, F. Viaggio fatto nell' E., 1520. RAMUSIO. Vol. I.
— — Barthema, L. Itinerario dell' Egitto . . . E., etc. RAMUSIO. Vol. I.
—— Ramusio. Discorso sopra il viaggio dell' E. RAMUSIO. Vol. I.
— · — Lobo, Father. Observations of E. RAY, J.
—— Michael, of Tripoli. Of E. RAY, J.
—— Remarques sur les Relations de l'Ethiopie des Pères Ieronimo Lobo & de Balthazar Tellez, Jesuites. THEVENOT. Vol. IV.
— — — *See also* ABYSSINIA.
·· — **Inferior.**—*See* ANGOLA.
· — **Interior.**—*See* ABYSSINIA.
—— **Upper.**—Histoire de la Haute-Ethiopie écrite sur les lieux par le Père Manoël d'Almeida, etc. THEVENOT. Vol. IV.
Etna.—Gourbillon, M. Travels . . . to Mount E., 1819. VOYAGES and TRAVELS, New. 1819. Vol. IV.
Eton.—WINDSOR. The Royal Windsor Guide, with a brief account of E., etc.   *Windsor*.
Etruria.—STEUB, L. Ueber die Urbewohner Rätiens und Ihren Zusammenhang mit den Etruskern.   *München*, **1843**.
—— FORSTER, C. The One Primeval Language traced . . . from the Monuments of E., etc.   **1851**.
Etymander.—*See* HELMUND.
Euboea.—Sibthorp, Dr. Voyage . . . E., etc. WALPOLE, R. Travels, etc.
Euphrate.—*See* EUPHRATES.
Euphrates.—DRUMMOND, A. Travels . . . as far as the Banks of the E., etc.   **1754**.
— D'ANVILLE, J. B. L'Euphrate et le Tigre.   *Par.*, **1779**.
— Arrian's Voyage of Nearchus, from the Indus to the E., etc. VINCENT, W. The Commerce, etc. Vol. I.   **1807**.
— —— CHESNEY, F. R. Reports on the Navigation of the E.   **1833**.
—— —— Expeditions for the Survey of the . . . E. . . . in 1835-37, etc.   **1850**.
— THOMPSON, J. B. The E. Valley Route to India.   **1853**.
— · —— ANDREW, W. P. The Scinde Railway and Its relations to the E. Valley and other routes to India.   **1856**.
— — — EUPHRATES VALLEY Route to India, etc.   **1856**.

Euphrates.—ANDREW, W. P. Memoir on the E. Valley Route to India, *etc.* 1857.

—— GRIFFITH, C. D. Speech on . . . the E. Railway, *etc.* 1857.

Europa.—*See* EUROPE.

Europa del Turco.—*See* TURKEY, EUROPEAN.

Europe.—BROWN, E. Travels in divers parts of E. 1685.

—— NORTHLEIGH, J. Observations made in two Voyages through most parts of E. 1702.

—— MOTRAYE, A. DE LA. Travels through E., *etc.* 1723-32.

—— ASTLEY, T. New . . . Collection of . . . Travels . . . in E., *etc.* 1745-47.

—— D'ANVILLE, J. B. BOURGUIGNON. États formés en E. après la Chute de l'Empire Romain en Occident. *Par.*, 1771.

—— BERCHTOLD, COUNT L. An Essay . . . To which is added a Catalogue of . . . European Travels up to 1787. 1788.

—— THUNBERG, C. P. Reisen in Europa . . . 1770 bis 1779, *etc.* *Berl.*, 1792-94.

—— ANDERSON, A. Historical . . . view of . . . E., *etc.* 1801.

—— PROSPETTO GEOGRAFICO-STATISTICO degli Stati Europei. *Milano,* 1802.

—— GRIFFITHS, J. Travels in E., *etc.* 1805.

—— FAWKES, W. Chronology of the History of Modern E. . . . A.D. 476, to . . . 1793. *York,* 1810.

—— MIRZA ABU TALEB KHAN. Voyages en . . . E. . . . 1799-1803, *etc.* *Par.*, 1811.

—— KRUSE, C. Kurze Anzeigen und Erläuterungen über meinen Atlas zur Geschichte aller Europäischen Länder, *etc.* *Halle,* 1812.

—— BARBER, G. D. Ancient . . . Records of the Cimri . . . in E., *etc.* 1815.

—— BRAUMÜLLER, J. G. Der wichtigste Kanal in Europa, *etc.* *Berl.*, 1815.

—— CLARKE, E. D. Travels in . . . E., *etc.* 1816-24.

—— KEATINGE, COL. Travels in E., *etc.* 1816.

—— SMITH, CAPT. J. The True Travels . . . of Capt. J. Smith, in E. . . . beginning about . . . 1593, *etc.* *Richmond, U.S.,* 1819.

—— HAHNZOG, A. G. Lehrbuch der Militar-Geographie von Europa. *Magdeburg,* 1820.

—— BENICKEN, F. W. Die Elemente der Militar-Geographie von Europa. *Weimar,* 1821.

—— EVERETT, E. Europe, or a General Survey, *etc.* 1822.

—— GANDINI, F. Itinéraire . . . de l'E. *Milan,* 1826.

—— ADOLPH, J. G. B. Mathematische . . . Erdbeschreibung mit besonderer Rücksicht auf Europa. *Mainz,* 1829.

—— ASPIN, J. Geo-Chronology von Europa. *Kempten,* 1829.

—— GALERRI, COUNT J. Pellegrinaggio in Europa . . . di G. C. Beltrami. *Firenze,* 1829.

—— LUSHINGTON, MRS. C. Narrative of a Journey from Calcutta to E., *etc.* 1829.

Europe.

Europe.—BRUGUIÈRE, L. Orographie de l'E. *Par.*, 1830.
—— ELWOOD, MRS. COL. Journey Overland ... by ... E. to India. 1830.
—— SCHOUW, J. F. Europa, en letfattelig Naturskildring. *Copenh.*, 1832.
—— MALCHUS, C. A. F. VON. Handbuch der Militär-Geographie von E. *Heidel. u Leip.*, 1833.
—— ZEUNE, A. Der Seeboden um Europa. *Berl.*, 1834.
—— Possessions in E. MARTIN, R. M. History of the British Colonies. Vol. V. 1834-35.
—— EICHHOFF, F. G. Parallèle des Langues de l'Europe et de l'Inde, etc. *Par.*, 1836.
—— MENDELSSOHN, G. B. Das Germanische Europa. *Berl.*, 1836.
—— GRÅBERG, COUNT J. L'Europa, Quadro fisiografico da Schouw. *Milan*, 1839.
—— MARTIN, R. M. Statistics of the Colonies ... in ... E., etc. *Lond.*, 1839.
—— SCHOW, J. C. L'Europa. Quadro fisiografico, etc. *Milano*, 1839.
—— MENZEL, W. E. In 1840, etc. *Edinb.*, 1841.
—— RUSSEGGER, J. Reisen in Europa, etc. *Stuttg.*, 1841.
—— BANDINEL, J. Some account of ... Slaves ... as connected with E., etc. 1842.
—— BALBI, A. Saggio ... delle strade ferrate Europee, etc. *Mil.*, 1848.
—— CATLIN, G. Notes of Eight Years' Travels ... in E. 1848.
—— BATAILLARD, P. Nouvelles recherches sur l'apparition ... des Bohémiens en E. *Par.*, 1849.
—— HUGHES, W. Manual of European Geography, etc. *Edin.*, 1851.
—— JUNGHUHN, F. Rückreise von Java nach Europa ... 1848, etc. *Leip.*, 1852.
—— LATHAM, R. G. The Ethnology of E. 1852.
—— ALISHAN, R. L. M. Introduction to ... the Geography of E. Arm. *Ven.*, 1853.
—— ROWELL, G. A. On the Change of Temperature in E., etc. 1853.
—— ALFRED, THE GREAT. A description of E., etc. 1855.
—— HEUFLER, L. VON. Asplenii Species Europææ. *Wien*, 1856.
—— HOUZEAU, J. C. Histoire du Sol de l'E. *Brux.*, 1857.
—— BROWN, SIR R. European and Asiatic Intercourse, etc. 1858.
—— LAMONT, J. Untersuchungen über die Richtung und Stärke des Erdmagnetismus an verschiedenen Puncten des südwestlichen Europa. *Münch.*, 1858.
—— Europa. Africa, India. LATHAM, R. G. Descriptive Ethnology. Vol. II. 1859.
—— ENQUIRY. An Enquiry into the Primeval State of E. *Lond.*, 1864.
—— HORSBURGH, J. Instructions Nautiques. Traversées d'E. aux différentes parties de l'Inde, etc. *Par.*, 1864.

Europe, Central — Europe, North. 183

Europe.—FERRARI, J. La Chine et l'E., leur histoire, etc. *Par.*, 1867.
——— EUROPÄISCHE GRADMESSUNG. Bericht, etc. *Berl.*, 1868.
——— JOHNSTON, A. K. Atlas of the British Empire in E. . . . with . . . letterpress. *Edin. and Lond.* [1870.]
——— BETTS, J. Exercises on . . . E., etc.
——— LOPEZ, J. J. Ueber die . . . Beziehungen . . . Europas mit den Hispano-Amerikanischen Republiken. *Berlin.*
——— SANSON, N. Géographie de l'E. *Paris.*
——— Smith, Capt. J. True Travels . . . in E. . . . from 1592 to 1629. CHURCHILL. Vol. II.
——— Careri, J. G. Travels through E. CHURCHILL. Vol. VI.
——— Osborne, T. Introductory discourse . . . and . . . . description of E. CHURCHILL. Vol. VII.
——— Arthur, King. Voyage to . . . the most N.E. parts of E., 517. HAKLUYT. Vol. I.
——— Benjamin, Rabbi. Travels through E. . . . 1160-1173. HARRIS, J. Vol. I.
——— A briefe and general Consideration of E. compared with the other parts of the World, etc. PURCHAS. Vol. I.
——— Smith, Capt. J. Travels . . . on the Sea Coasts of E. . . . about 1606. PURCHAS. Vol. II.
——— Barkley, G. Travels . . . in E. . . . 1605. PURCHAS. Vol. III.
——— Carlins Rückreise nach . . . Europa, 1668. VOYAGES and TRAVELS. Allgemeine Historie, etc. Vol. IV.
——— Gruber, J. Reisen von China nach Europa, 1661. VOYAGES and TRAVELS. Allgemeine Historie, etc. Vol. VII.
——— Mandelslo, J. A. Reise . . . nach Europa über Goa. VOYAGES and TRAVELS. Allgemeine Historie, etc. Vol. XI.
——— Tavernier. Reisen . . . 1665-68 . . . nach Europa. VOYAGES and TRAVELS. Allgemeine Historie, etc. Vol. XI.
——— Bruguière, L. Orographie de l'E. VOYAGES and TRAVELS. Recueil, etc. Vol. III.
———, **Central**.—POTENTI, G. Légende des Matières contenues dans la Carte Itinéraire . . . de l'E. Centrale. *Braz.*, 1848.
———, **North**.—WRAXALL, N. A Tour through . . . N.n . . . E., etc. 1776.
——— ——— ELLIOTT, C. B. Letters from the N. of E., etc. 1832.
——— ——— BARROW, J. Excursions in the N. of E., etc. 1834.
——— ——— LANDOR, E. W. Adventures in the N. of E., etc. *Lond.*, 1836.
——— ——— MURRAY. Hand-Book for N. E. *Lond.*, 1849.
——— ——— BUNBURY, S. A. A Summer in N. E., etc. 1856.
——— ——— MURCHISON, SIR R. I. On the distribution of the superficial Detritus of the Alps, as compared with that of N.ern E.
——— ——— North of Europe, Three Voyages of the Dutch to the. PINKERTON. Vol. I.

Europe, North.—Travels through the most N.n parts of E. ... Extracted from the Journal of a Gentleman employed . . . to make discoveries. 1654. Voyages and Travels. The World displayed. Vol. XX.

———, **South.**—Clark, Sir J. The Sanative Influence of Climate; with an account of . . . places of resort . . . in . . . the S. of E., *etc.* 1841.

——— ——— Adalbert, Prince. Travels in the S. of E., *etc.* 1849.

———, **West.** Long, H. L. Survey of the Early Geography of W.n E., *etc.* 1859.

Euskaria.—*See* Basque Provinces.

Eustatius, Saint.—Greveлинк, A. H. D. Beschrijving van het Eiland Sint E. 1846.

Euxine.—*See* Black Sea.

Eyria—Australia, South. Summary of . . . discoveries during 1857, to the W. and N. of E., *etc.* *Derby*, 1858.

Ezlongeber.—Of E. G., Eloth, and the Red Sea, *etc.* Purchas. Vol. I.

——— Salomons, King. Navis sent from E. to Ophir, *etc.* Purchas. Vol. I.

F.

Faaraya.—Kulczyckі, A. Determination des Longitudes . . . Observations pour . . . F., *etc.* *Par.*, 1851.

Falashas—Abbadie, A. d' Réponses de F. . . . aux questions faites par M. Luzzato. *Par.*, 1850.

——— Stern, H. A. Wanderings among the F.s in Abyssinia, *etc.* *Lond.*, 1862.

Falkland Islands.—Johnson, S. Thoughts on the late Transactions respecting F.s I. 1771.

——— Falkner, T. Description of Patagonia . . . and . . . the F. I. *Hereford*, 1774.

——— FitzRoy, Rear-Adml. R. Sailing Directions for . . . F. . . . I., *etc.* 1848.

——— Hadfield, W. Brazil . . . the F. I., *etc.* 1854.

——— Snow, W. P. Two Years' Cruise off . . . the F. I., *etc.* 1857.

——— Byron, Comm. Voyage . . . to F. I. . . . 1764-66. Hawkesworth, J. Vol. I.

——— *See also* Pepys' Island.

Falmouth.—James, Sir H. Note on the Block of Tin dredged up in F. Harbour. 1863.

Famatina.—Meteorology. Meteorological Tables. F. and Chilicito Observations, 1827-8. *MS.*

Fanagoria.—*See* Taman.

Farama.—Spratt, T. A. B. A Dissertation on the true position of . . . F. *Lond.*, 1859.

Faro Islands.—Kerguelen Trémarec, M. de. Relation d'une Voyage . . . aux Côtes . . . de Ferro, *etc.* *Par.*, 1771.

Faro Islands.—LANDT, G. Description of the Feroe Islands, etc. 1810.
—— PAULY, F. Topographie von Dännemarck einschliesslich Islands und der Färöer. *Altona*, 1828.
—— RAFN, C. C. Færeyinga Saga . . . I den Islandske Grundtext, etc. *Kjöb.*, 1832.
—— —— Færeyinga Saga . . . Im Isländischen Grundtext, etc. *Kopen.*, 1833.
—— — TREVELYAN, SIR W. C. Vegetation and Temperature of the F. I. *Edin.*, 1835.
—— —— Vegetation and Temperature of the F. I. *Florence*, 1837.
—— MAUCROIX, D'ESTR. DE. Note sur le Banc de Feroë. *Par.*, 1846.
—— CHAMBERS, R. Tracings of . . . the F. I. *Lond., Edin.*, 1856.
—— SYMINGTON, A. J. Pen and Pencil Sketches of F., etc. 1862.
—— IRMINGER, C. Notice sur les Pêches . . . des Isles Férod, etc. *Par.*, 1863.

Fars.—PELLY, L. Remarks . . . with . . . a brief account of . . . F. *Bomb.*, 1863.

Farsistan.—*See* FARS.
Fazogl.—CAILLIAUD, F. Voyage . . . de F. . . . a Syouah, etc. *Par.*, 1826.

Feejees.—*See* FIJI ISLANDS.
Feiran, Wadi.—BARTLETT, W. H. Forty days in the Desert . . . a Journey . . . by W. F., to . . . Sinai, etc. 1851.
Fellatahs.—EICHTHAL, G. D'. Histoire et Origine des Foulahs ou Fellahs. *Par.*, 1840.
—— —— Recherches sur l'histoire et l'origine des Foulahs, etc. *Par.*, 1840.

Ferdinandea.—MARZOLLA, B. Descrizione dell' Isola F., etc. *Nap.*, 1826.

Fermanagh.—PORTLOCK, J. E. Report on the Geology . . . of parts of . . . F. *Dubl.*, 1843.
Fernambuck.—*See* PERNAMBUCO.
Fernando Po.—SIERRA LEONE.—Report from the Select Committee on the Settlements of Sierra Leone and F. P. 1830.
—— BURTON, R. F. Wanderings . . . from Liverpool to F. P. 1863.
Feroe Islands.—*See* FARO ISLANDS.
Ferro.—*See* FARO ISLANDS.
Fetipore.—*See* FUTTEHPOOR.
Fes.—ADDISON, L. West Barbary; or a short Narrative of the Revolutions of . . . F., etc. *Oxf.*, 1671.
—— TELLEZ, B. Travels . . . Travels of the Sieur Mouette in . . . F., etc. 1710.
Fezzan.—SIOUAH, F., et Intérieur de l'Afrique. ETHNK. Vol. XIV.
—— *See* also MOURZUK.

Fiji Islands.—CARGILL, D. A brief Essay on the Feejean language. 1840.

Fiji Islands.—Erskine, J. E. Journal of a Cruise . . . including the Feejees, etc. 1853.
—— Arthur, W. What is F.? etc. 1859.
—— Seeman, B. Viti: an account of a Government Mission to the . . . Fijian Islands . . . 1860–61. *Camb. and Lond.*, 1862.

Finland.—Acerbi, J. Travels through . . . F. . . . to the North Cape, etc. 1802.
—— Elliott, C. B. Letters from . . . F., etc. 1832.
—— Barrow, J. Excursions in . . . F., etc. 1834.
—— Schnitzler, J. H. Russie . . . et la F. Tableau statistique, etc. *Par.*, 1835.
—— Clarke, E. D. Travels in . . . F. 1838.
—— F. and Russia. Murray. Hand-Book for Northern Europe. Part II. *Lond.*, 1849.
—— Galitzin, Prince E. La Finlande; Notes, etc. *Par.*, 1852.
—— Finland. Narrative of the Conquest of . . . in 1808-9, etc. 1854.
—— Dunsbury, S. A. A Summer in . . . F., etc. 1856.
—— Nordenskiöld, N. Beitrag zur Kenntniss der Schrammen in F. *Helsingf.*, 1863.
—— Helmersen, G. von. Das Vorkommen und die Entstehung der Riesenkessel in F. *St. Pet.*, 1867.

Finland, Gulf of.—Lljorth, J. Description du Golfe de F., etc. *Par.*, 1854.
—— Klint, G. Sailing Directions for . . . the G. of F., etc. 1854.
—— Gras, A. Le. Instructions Nautiques sur . . . le Golfe de F., etc. *Par.*, 1864.

Finmark.—Bravais, M. A. Sur les lignes d'ancien Niveau de la Mer dans le F. *Paris.*
—— Brooke, Sir A. de C., Bart. Travels through . . . F., etc. 1823.
—— Struve, W. Exposé historique des Travaux . . . 1851 . . . Suivi de deux Rapports de M. G. Lindhagen sur l'Expédition de Finnmarken, 1850, etc. *St. Pet.*, 1852.

Finnland.—*See* Finland.
Finnmarken.—*See* Finmark.
Fish River, Great.—Back, Sir G. Narrative of . . . Expedition to the . . . G. F. R., etc. 1836.
Fiume Bianco.—*See* Nile, White.
Fiumicino.—Cialdi, A. Navigazione del Tevere e della sua foce in F. *Roma*, 1845.

Flanders.—Pollnitz, C. L., Baron de. Memoirs . . . in his Travels . . . through . . . F., etc. 1737.
—— Bagnolds, L. du G. Mémoires sur l'Intendance de la Flandre. *Bruss.*, 1739.
—— Flanders. Plans et Journaux des Sièges de la dernière guerre de Flandres, etc. *Strasb.*, 1750.

Flanders.—BAILLIE, M. First Impressions of ... French F. **1819.**
——— RADCLIFF, T. On the Agriculture of E.n and W.n F. **1819.**
——— GRANVILLE, A. B. St. Petersburg, Travels to and from through F., *etc.* **1828.**
———, **East.**—VANDER MAELEN, P. Statistique ... de la Flandre Orientale, *etc.* *Brussels*, **1830.**
——— ——— ——— Dictionnaire Géographique de la Flandre Orientale. *Brux.*, **1834.**
———, **West.**—VANDER MAELEN, P. Dictionnaire Géographique de la Flandre Occidentale. *Brux.*, **1836.**

Flemish Islands.—*See* AZORES.
Fleuve Blanc.—*See* NILE, WHITE.
Florence.—STENDHALL, COURT DE. Rome ... and F., in 1817. **1818.**
——— GARGIOLLI, L. F. M. G. Description de ... F., *etc.* *Flor.*, **1819.**
——— FIRENZE, Guida di. *Fir.*, **1820.**
——— MARENIGH, J. Guide de F., *etc.* *Flor.*, **1822.**
——— FIRENZE. Guida della Città di Firenze. *Fir.*, **1833.**
——— DIX, J. A. A Winter in Madeira: and a Summer in ... F., *etc.* *N. Y.*, **1851.**

Florida.—BENZONI, H. Novæ Novi Orbis Historiæ ... adjuncta est, De Gallorum in Floridam expeditione ... historia. *Geneva*, **1600.**
——— CARDENAS, G. DE. Ensayo cronologico, para la Historia general de la F., *etc.* *Madrid*, **1723.**
——— VEGA, G. DE LA. La F. del Inca, *etc.* *Madrid*, **1723.**
——— VOLNEY, C. F. Tableau ... des États-Unis ... suivi d'éclaircissemens sur la Floride, *etc.* *Par.*, **1803.**
——— KING, HON. T. B. Alabama, F. and Georgia Railroad. *Wash.*, **1848.**
——— PURDY, J. and FINDLAY, A. G. Sailing Directory for ... the Coast of F., *etc.* **1848.**
——— BRINTON, D. G. A Guide-Book of F., *etc.* *Phil.*, **1869.**
——— Description ... more particularly of F. HAKLUYT. Vol. III.
——— Gourgues, D. Voyage to F., 1567. HAKLUYT. Vol. III.
——— Landonnière, R. Voyage to F., 1564. HAKLUYT. Vol. III.
——— Ribault, J. Voyages to F., 1562 and 65. HAKLUYT. Vol. III.
——— Verazzano, J. da. Voyage to the Coast of F. ... 1524. HAKLUYT. Vol. III.
——— Virginia richly valued, by the description of the Maine Land of F. ... 1609. HAKLUYT. Vol. V.
——— Soto, Don. F. de. The Discovery and Conquest of F. ... Edited ... by W. B. Rye. 1851. HAKLUYT Soc. Pub. Vol. IX.
——— Discovery of F., *etc.* KERR. Vol. V.
——— Las Casas, B. de. Briefe Narration of ... F., *etc.* PURCHAS. Vol. IV.
——— Notes of Voyages and Plantations of the French ... in F. ... 1524-82. PURCHAS. Vol. IV.

Florida.—Soto, F. de. Voyage to F. . . . 1539-43. Purchas. Vol. IV.
——— Of New France . . . F. . . . and of their Religions. Purchas. Vol. V.
——— Retcta, O. de. Relation de la Floride, 1549. Ternaux-Compans. Voyages. Vol. XX.
——— D'Escalante Fontanedo, H. Mémoire sur la Floride, etc. Ternaux-Compans. Voyages. Vol. XX.
——— Gourgue, Capit. La Reprinse de la Floride. Ternaux-Compans. Voyages. Vol. XX.
——— Lopez de Mendoza, F. Voyage . . . dans . . . la Floride, 1565. Ternaux-Compans. Voyages. Vol. XX.
——— Ribaut, J. Histoire Mémorable du dernier Voyage aux Indes, lieu appelé la Floride, en 1565. Ternaux-Compans. Voyages. Vol. XX.
——— Ponce de Leon. Reise und Entdeckung von F., 1512. Voyages and Travels. Allgemeine Historie, etc. Vol. XIII.
——— Soto, F. von. Reise nach F. . . . 1537-43. Voyages and Travels. Allgemeine Historie, etc. Vol. XVI.
———, **Gulf of.**—Description of the Windward Passage and G. of F., etc. 1739.
——— ——— Purdy, J. and Findlay, A. G. Sailing Directory for the Windward and Gulf Passages, etc. 1848.
——— ——— Andrews, L. D. Report on the . . . Straits of F., etc. Wash., 1853.
——— ——— Barnett, E. West India Pilot . . . with . . . F. Strait. 1859-61.
——— **Keys.**—Purdy, J. and Findlay, A. G. Sailing Directory for . . . the Martyrs, etc. 1848.
Formosa.—Richards, J. China. Harbours . . . at the S.-W. end of . . . F. 1855.
——— Habersham, A. W. My last Cruise . . . Visits to . . . F., etc. Phil., 1857.
——— Gras, M. A. le. Renseignements hydrographiques sur . . . Formose, etc. Par., 1859.
——— Jomard, E. F. Coup-d'œil sur l'Ile Formose. Par., 1859.
——— Swinhoe, R. Notes on . . . F. 1863.
——— Guérin, M. Vocabulaire du dialecte Tayal ou aborigène de l'Ile Formose. 1868.
——— Expedition of the Dutch for recovering F., etc. Astley. Vol. III.
——— Candidius, G. Account of . . . F., etc. Churchill. Vol. I.
——— Kao, D. An Authentick . . . description of . . . F., etc. Harris, J. Vol. I.
——— Relation de la prise de l'Isle F. par les Chinois . . . 1661. Thevenot. Vol. I.
——— Montanus, A. Die Seezug der Holländer, das Eyland F. . . . wieder zu erobern, 1663-4. Voyages and Travels. Allgemeine Historie, etc. Vol. V.

Formosa.—Van Rechteren. Erste Versuche der Holländer, nach China zu handeln, und ihr Handelssitz zu Taywan. VOYAGES and TRAVELS. Allgemeine Historie, etc. Vol. V.

Formosa.—See FORMOSA.

Fort Leavenworth.—EMORY, W. H. Notes of a Military Reconnoissance from F. L. in Missouri, to San Diego, etc. *N. Y.*, 1848.

—— **Smith.**—SIMPSON, J. H. Report of the Route from F. S., to Santa Fé, etc. *Wash.*, 1850.

Foulahs.—See FELLATAHS.

Fountains Abbey.—RIPON. The Tourist's Companion ... being a ... description ... of ... F. A., etc. *Ripon*, 1828.

Fou-Sang.—See AMERICA.

Fox Islands.—MORTIMER, G. Observations ... during a Voyage to ... the F. I., etc. *Lond.*, 1791.

Foyle, Lough.—YOLLAND, W. Ordnance Survey. An Account of the Measurement of the Lough F. Base in Ireland, etc. 1847.

France.—GERMANY. Anzeige der geognostischen Karte von ... Frankreich, etc.

—— GÖLNITZIUR, A. Itinerarium Belgico-Gallicum. *Lugd.*, 1631.

—— POLLNITZ, C. L., BARON DE. Memoirs ... in his ... Travels ... through ... F., etc. 1737.

—— PLAISTED, B. Journal from Calcutta ... through F., etc. 1758.

—— GUETTARD ET MONNET. Tableau representatif des diverses Cartes de l'Atlas Minéralogique de la France. *Par.*, 1766-70.

—— NUGENT, Mr. The Grand Tour ... through F., etc. 1778.

—— MONNET, M. Atlas et Description minéralogiques de la F. *Par.*, 1780.

—— TOWNSEND, J. A Journey through Spain in 1786-87; and remarks in passing through a part of F. *Lond.*, 1792.

—— FRANCE. Statistique de la F. *Par.*, 1801.

—— FRANCE. Geographie de la F. *Par.*, 1802.

—— LACOUSTURIER, A. F. and CHAUDOUET, F. Dictionnaire Géographique des Postes aux Lettres ... de la République Française. *Par.*, 1802.

—— FRANCE. Statistique générale et particulière de la F. et de ses Colonies, etc. *Par.*, 1803.

—— PEUCHET, J. Statistique Élementaire de la F. *Par.*, 1805.

—— —— and others. Description topographique ... de la F. *Par.*, 1811-17.

—— DEPPING, G. B. Merveilles et Beautés de la Nature en F. *Par.*, 1812.

—— BIRKBECK, M. Tour in F. in 1814. 1815.

—— DICTIONNAIRE Général des Communes de F., etc. *Par.*, 1819.

—— DAILLIE, M. First Impressions of ... F., etc. 1819.

—— LACOUSTURIER, A. F. Dictionnaire des Postes aux Lettres du Royaume de F., etc. *Par.*, 1819.

France.

France.—CADELL, W. A. Journey in . . . F., etc.   Edin., 1820.
—— JACOB, W. View of the Agriculture . . . of . . . F. in 1819.   1820.
—— FRANCE. Itinéraire de la F.   Par., 1823.
—— FRANCE. Itinéraire de la F.   Par., 1824.
—— RAVINET, T. Dictionnaire hydrographique de la F., etc.   Par., 1824.
—— BROCKEDON, W. Illustrations of the Passes . . . by which Italy communicates with F., etc.   1828.
—— BARBICHON, P. M. Dictionnaire complet . . . de la F., etc.   Par., 1831.
—— FRANCKLIN, L. Recherches . . . suivies d'observations sur la Marine . . . et les établissemens coloniaux des Français.   Par., 1832.
—— GOLDSMITH, L. Statistics of F.   1832.
—— GUERRY, A. M. Essai sur la Statistique Morale de la F.   Par., 1833.
—— LORIOL, M. La F.; Description géographique, etc.   Par., 1834.
—— FRENCH LIGHT-HOUSES. Translated from the Description Sommaire, &c., corrected to 1836.   1836.
—— JAMIESON, MRS. Topographical . . . History of F.   1836.
—— FRANCE. Statistique de la F. Territoire, Population.   Par., 1837.
—— WELLINGTON, DUKE OF. Despatches during his . . . Campaigns in . . . F., etc.   1837-39.
—— FRANCE. Statistique de la F. Commerce extérieur.   Par., 1838.
—— DECHEN. Anzeige der Geognostischen Karte von . . . Frankreich, etc.   Berl., 1839.
—— DENAIX, M. Geographie prototype de la F.   Par., 1841.
—— GIVRY, M. Pilote Français, etc.   Par., 1842-45.
—— MURRAY. Hand-Book for Travellers in F., etc.   Lond., 1843.
—— AFRICA. La F. en Afrique.   Par., 1846.
—— RÓNAY, J. Jellemisme, vagy az . . . Franczia . . . Nemzet . . . Jellemzése, etc.   Györött, 1847.
—— DELL, R. Wayside Pictures through F., etc.   1849.
—— MAURY, L. F. A. Histoire des Grandes Forêts de la Gaule et de l'ancienne F., etc.   Par., 1850.
—— GARC, F. Education in England. Revolutions in F., etc.   1852.
—— SPENCER, E. Tour of Inquiry through F., etc.   1853.
—— LAING, S. Notes . . . on . . . F., etc.   1854.
—— UNDINE. Our Cruise in the Undine . . . through F., etc.   Lond., 1854.
—— CHAMIER, CAPT. My Travels . . . through F., etc.   1855.
—— SMITH, C. R. Notes on some of the Antiquities of F., etc.   Lond., 1855.
—— SPAIN. Border Lands of Spain and F., etc.   1856.
—— MALTE-BRUN, V. A. La F. Illustrée, etc.   Par., 1858.

France — France, Coasts of. 191

France.—RONDOT, M. N. Commerce de la F. avec la Chine. *Lyon*, 1860.
——— BLOCK, M. Bevölkerung des Französischen Kaiserreichs, *etc.*
  Gotha, 1861.
——— JAMES, SIR H. Extension of the Triangulation of the Ordnance Survey, into F. and Belgium, *etc.* 1863.
——— STUCKLÉ, H. Le Commerce de la F. avec le Soudan. *Par.*, 1864.
——— BALFOUR, Major-Gen. On the Budgets and Accounts of ... F.
  Lond., 1866.
——— ELLIS, R. An Enquiry into the Ancient Routes between Italy and Gaul, *etc.* *Camb.* and *Lond.*, 1867.
——— Skippon, Sir P. Journey through ... F. CHURCHILL. Vol. VI.
——— F. and Italy, a Tour in, made by an English Gentleman, 1675. CHURCHILL. Vol. VII.
——— Puissant. Nouvelle description géométrique de la F. FRANCE. Memorial du Dépôt Général de la Guerre. Vol. VI. VII.
——— Bertram, J. G. Fish Culture in F. GALTON, F. Vacation Tourists ... 1862-3.
——— Bertrandon de la Brocquière. Voyage ... de Jérusalem en F. par la Voie de Terre ... 1432-33. HAKLUYT. Vol. IV.
——— Northleigh, J. Travels through F., 1702. HARRIS, J. Vol. II.
——— Skippon, Sir P. and Ray, J. Travels through ... F., 1664. HARRIS, J. Vol. II.
——— Young's Travels in F. PINKERTON. Vol. IV.
——— Benjamin, the Son of Jonas. Peregrination of ... and relations of ... F. PURCHAS. Vol. II.
——— Smith, Capt. J. Travels ... thorow F. ... about 1596. PURCHAS. Vol. II.
——— Ray, J. Travels through ... F., *etc.* RAY, J. Collection, *etc.*
——— Williams, T. Travels through F. during 1802-6. VOYAGES and TRAVELS. A Collection, *etc.* 1805. Vol. VIII.
——— Travels through F., 1802-6. VOYAGES and TRAVELS. A Collection, *etc.* 1810. Vol. III.
——— Rey, Capt. Voyage from F. to Cochin China, 1819-20. VOYAGES and TRAVELS, New. 1819. Vol. IV.
——— Switzerland and F. Letters from, *etc.* VOYAGES and TRAVELS, New. 1819. Vol. VI.
——— Stevens, Sacheverell. Travels through F. 1738. VOYAGES and TRAVELS. The World displayed. Vol. XIX.

——— Coasts of.—FRANCE. Reconnaissance hydrographique des Côtes de F., *etc.* *Par.*, 1832.
——— ———— DAUSSY, P. Second Mémoire sur les Marées des Côtes de F.
  Par., 1838.
——— ———— FRANCE. Description sommaire des Phares et Fanaux ... sur les Côtes de F. au 1839 et 1851. *Par.*, 1839.
——— ———— FRANCE. The Lighthouses on the N. and W. Coasts of F. ... Corrected to 1848, 52-54, 56, 57. 1848-57.

France, Coasts of.—FRANCE. The Admiralty Lists of the Lights of the N. and W. Coasts of F. . . . Corrected to 1850. 1859.
——— ——— DUNSTERVILLE, E. The Admiralty List of the Lights on the N. and W. Coasts of F. . . . Corrected to 1860, 61, 62.
1860-62.
——— ——— GRAS, M. A. LE. Phares des Côtes Nord et Ouest de la F. . . . Corrigés 1862-64. Par., 1862-64.
——— ——— PEACOCK, R. A. Physical and historical evidences of vast Sinkings of Land on the N. and W. Coasts of F. . . . within the Historical Period. Lond., 1868.
——— ——— GRAS, A. LE. Phares des Côtes Nord et Ouest de F., etc.
Par., 1869.
———, Isle of.—See MAURITIUS.
———, North Coast.—DÉCAT, P. Exposé des opérations géodésiques . . . sur les Côtes Septentrionales de F. Par., 1839.
———, South.—LARTET, E. and CHRISTY, H. Reliquæ Aquitanicæ; being Contributions to the Archæology and Palæontology of . . . S.n F.
Lond. [1865.]
——— ——— Millin, A. L. Travels through the Southern Departments of F., 1804-5. VOYAGES and TRAVELS. A Collection, etc. 1805. Vol. VII.
———, West Coast.—BEAUTEMPS-BEAUPRÉ, M. Exposé des travaux relatifs à la reconnaissance hydrographique des Côtes Occidentales de F., etc. 1829.
——— ——— VAUHELLO, M. LE SAULNIER DE. Mémoire sur les Atterages des Côtes Occidentales de F., etc. Par., 1833.
——— ——— BOUQUET DE LA GRYE, A. Pilote des Côtes Ouest de F.
Par., 1869.
Franche-Comté.—RAZOUMOWSKY, COUNT G. DE. Œuvres. Contenant, Voyage Minéralogique . . . à . . . F. C., etc. Lausanne, 1784.
Francia Antarctica.—See AMERICA, South.
Franconia.—TYLOR, C. A. Historical Tour in F., etc. Brighton, 1852.
Franconia Namzet.—See FRANCE.
Frankfort-on-the-Main.—ENGELMANN, J. B. Résumé de l'histoire . . . de Francfort, etc. Heidelb.
——— KRIEGK, G. L. Kurze . . . Beschreibung der Umgegend von Frankfurt am Main.
——— FRANKFORT. Tableau historique et topographique de Francfort, etc.
Francf., 1828.
——— FRANKFURT AM MAIN. Mittheilungen über Physisch-geographische . . . Verhältnisse von Frankfurt am Main, etc. 1839-41.
——— MEIDINGER, H. Statistische Uebersicht . . . nebst einigen Worten über Frankfurts Handel der Vorzeit. Frankf-a-M., 1841.
——— ——— Zur Statistik Frankfurts, etc. Frankf-a-M., 1848.
——— BIERSACK, H. L. Einige Worte . . . über die Statistik von Frankfort, etc. Frankf., 1855.
Franklin, County.—HOUGH, F. B. History of St. Laurence and F. Counties, etc. Albany, 1853.

Frankreich, Eyland.—*See* MAURITIUS.
Fransensbad.—GRIEBEN, T. Grieben's Reise-Bibliothek. No. 38.
F., *etc.* *Berlin,* **1861.**
Franzensbrunn.—HOFER, C. F. Beschreibung von F., *etc.* *Prag,* **1799.**
Französisches Kaiserreich.—*See* FRANCE.
Frederikagave.—*See* HAGENSKOV.
Freezland.—*See* FRIESLAND.
Freiburg.—GEMÄLDE DER SCHWEIZ ... F., *etc.* *Bern,* **1834-36.**
Frenberg.—DRESDEN und die umliegende Gegend bis ... F., *etc.*
Dresd., **1804.**
French Colonies.—TABLEAU DE L'OPULATION ... formant pour 1830-
62, la suite des Tableaux insérés dans les Notices Statistiques sur les
Colonies Françaises. *Par.,* **1842-64.**
Friendly Islands.—MARINER, W. Account of the ... Tonga I., *etc.*
Lond., **1818.**
—— FARMER, S. S. Tonga and the F. I., *etc.* **1855.**
—— Mariner, G. Voyage aux Iles Tonga, 1805-10. EYRIÈS. Vol. V.
—— *See also* TONGA.
Friesland.—HEGESITIUS, G. Itinerarium Frisio-Hollandicum.
Lugd. Bat., **1630.**
—— LAET, J. DE. Belgii Confœderati Respublica: seu ... Fris. ...
descriptio. *Lugd. Bat.,* **1630.**
—— Zeno, N. and A. Voyage to the yles of F., *etc.* 1380. HAKLUYT.
Vol. III.
—— Nicolo, M. M. and Zeni, A. Discoveries in ... F. ... 1380.
PURCHAS. Vol. III.
—— Zeno, N. and A. Dello scoprimento dell' Isola Frislanda, *etc.*
RAMUSIO. Vol. II.
—— Supplement. Description of ... Freezland, *etc.* VOYAGES. Ac-
count of several late, *etc.*
Friseland, Frisia, Frislanda. *See* FRIESLAND.
Friull.—Browne, E. Journey ... to Venice ... with an account of
the Quicksilver Mines in F., *etc.* HARRIS, J. Vol. II.
—— Odorico da Udine, Beato. Due Viaggi, di Porto Maggiore del F.,
1318. RAMUSIO. Vol. II.
Frozen Sea.—*See* ARCTIC OCEAN.
Fulfulde.—BAIKIE, W. B. Observations on the Hausa and F. languages,
etc.
Funday, Bay of.—*See* FUNDY.
Fundy, Bay of. PURDY, J. and FINDLAY, A. G. British American Navi-
gator. Sailing Directory for ... the B. of F., *etc.* **1847.**
————— SHORTLAND, P. F. Bay of F. ... Sailing Directions, *etc.*
1856.
————— Bay of F. Pilot, *etc.* **1857.**
————— GRAS, M. A. LE. Routier de la Baie de F., *etc.*
Par., **1861.**

O

Fundy, Bay of.—McDougall, G. F. Instructions nautiques pour ... la Baie de F. *Par.*, **1869.**
Furnas.—Bullar, J. and H. Winter in the Azores, and a Summer at the Baths of the F. **1841.**
Fûta.—*See* Futajallon.
Futajallon.—The remarkable captivity ... of J. ben Solomon ... with ... remarks relating to ... Fûta. Astley. Vol. II.
Futtehpoor.—Finch, W. Observations ... in 1607 ... Description of Fetipore, *etc.* Purchas. Vol. I.

G.

Gaboon.—Hutchinson, T. J. Ten Years' Wanderings ... from Senegal to G. **1861.**
Gadames.—*See* Ghadamis.
Gaeta.—Niccolini, A. Tavola Metrica-Chronologica delle varie Altezze ... fra la Costa di Amalfi ed il Promontorio di G. *Nap.*, **1839.**
Gago.—Two briefe Relations concerning ... Tombuto and G. ... written in 1594. Hakluyt. Vol. III.
——— The Trading of the Moores into Guinea and G. for gold ore, *etc.* Purchas. Vol. II.
Galam.—Saugnier, M. Relations de plusieurs voyages ... à G., *etc. Par.*, **1792.**
——— G. Eyries. Vol. X.
——— Brüe, A. Andere Reise den Sanagastrom hinauf in ... G., **1698.** Voyages and Travels. Allgemeine Historie, *etc.* Vol. II.
——— Durand, J. P. L. Voyage ... from Isle St. Louis to G., 1785-86. Voyages and Travels. A Collection, *etc.* 1806. Vol. IV.
Gallois.—Spencer, E. Travels ... including a Tour through ... G., *etc.* **1838.**
——— Kohl, J. G. Austria ... G., *etc. Lond.*, **1844.**
——— Salvo, Marquis de. Travels ... through ... G. ... 1806. Voyages and Travels. A Collection, *etc.* 1805. Vol. VI.
Galilee.—Biddulph, W. Travels of four Englishmen ... into ... G. ... in 1600 and 1611. Churchill. Vol. VII.
Galla.—Krapf, J. L. Imperfect Outline ... of the G. Language, *etc.* **1840.**
——— Tutschek, C. Dictionary of the G. Language, *etc. Munich*, **1844.**
——— ——— Grammar of the G. Language, *etc. Munich*, **1845.**
——— Beke, C. T. Christianity among the G.s **1847.**
——— ——— On the Origin of the G.s **1848.**
——— Heuglin, M. T. von. Reise nach ... den Gala-Ländern, *etc. Jena*, **1868.**
——— Plowden, W. C. Travels in ... the G. Country, *etc. Lond.*, **1868.**
Gambia.—Le Maire, Sieur, Voyages of, to ... G. Churchill. Vol. VIII.

Gambia, River.—BELCHER, SIR E. Directions for the ... G.

―― ―― ―― MOLLIEN, G. Travels ... to the Sources of the Senegal and G., etc. 1820.

―― ―― ―― BOWDITCH, T. E. Excursions in Madeira ... a description of the English Settlements on the ... G., etc. 1825.

―― ―― ―― POOLE, T. E. Life ... in Sierra Leone and the G. 1850.

―― ―― ―― BOREL, L. Voyage à la Gambie, etc. [1865.]

―― ―― ―― Voyages of R. Rainolds and T. Dassel to the ... G. ... 1591. ASTLEY. Vol. I.

―― ―― ―― Account of the Jalofs ... inhabiting towards the Gambra. ASTLEY. Vol. II.

―― ―― ―― Differences between the English and French about the Trade of the ... Gambra. ASTLEY. Vol. II.

―― ―― ―― A general description of the ... G., etc. ASTLEY. Vol. II.

―― ―― ―― Jobson, R. Voyage for the discovery of the ... Gambra ... in 1620-21. ASTLEY. Vol. II.

―― ―― ―― Letter concerning the discovery of the Gold Mines in a Voyage up the Gambra. ASTLEY. Vol. II.

―― ―― ―― Moore, F. Travels ... for 600 miles up the ... Gambra, etc. ASTLEY. Vol. II.

―― ―― ―― Of the Fūli inhabiting along the Gambra. ASTLEY. Vol. II.

―― ―― ―― Of the Trade ... in the ... Gambra, etc. ASTLEY. Vol. II.

―― ―― ―― Stibbs, B. Voyage up the Gambra in 1724, etc. ASTLEY. Vol. II.

―― ―― ―― Voyages ... containing ... an account of the ... G., etc. ASTLEY. Vol. II.

―― ―― ―― Mollien, M. Voyage aux sources ... de la Gambie, 1818. Extraits. Vol. XI.

―― ―― ―― Rainolds, R., and Dassell, T. Voyage to the ... Gambra ... 1591. HAKLUYT. Vol. III.

―― ―― ―― Voyage to the ... G., 1501. KERR. Vol. VII.

―― ―― ―― Adamson's Voyage to ... the River G. PINKERTON. Vol. XVI.

―― ―― ―― Jobson, R. Observations touching the River G., etc. PURCHAS. Vol. II.

―― ―― ―― Jobson, R. True Relation of a Voyage for the discovery of Gambra, etc. PURCHAS. Vol. II.

―― ―― ―― Eine Allgemeine Beschreibung von dem Flusse Gambra oder G. VOYAGES and TRAVELS. Allgemeine Historie, etc. Vol. III.

―― ―― ―― Jobson, R. Reise zur Entdeckung des Flusses Gambra ... 1620-21. VOYAGES and TRAVELS. Allgemeine Historie, etc. Vol. III.

―― ―― ―― Le Maire. Reise nach ... der Gambra, 1682. VOYAGES and TRAVELS. Allgemeine Historie, etc. Vol. III.

Gambia, River.—Solomons, Job hn. Die merkwürdige Gefangenschaft und Befreyung, eines muhammedanischen Priesters von Bunda, nahe bey der Gambra, 1732. VOYAGES and TRAVELS. Allgemeine Historie, etc. Vol. III.

—— Stibbs, B. Reise auf der Gambra, 1724. VOYAGES and TRAVELS. Allgemeine Historie, etc. Vol. III.

Gambra.—See GAMBIA.
Ganat.—See KANO.
Ganges.—SAINT MARTIN, V. DE. Étude sur . . . le Bassin du Gange.
Paris.

—— RENNELL, J. Memoir . . . containing an account of the G., etc. 1785.

—— —— Memoir . . . with an Account of the G., etc. 1793.

—— FRASER, J. B. Tour . . . to the sources of the Jumna and G. 1820.

—— SKINNER, T. Excursions in India, including a Walk . . . to the Sources of the . . . G. 1832.

—— —— GANGES CANAL, Short Account of the. 1853.

—— —— CAUTLEY, SIR P. T. G. Canal : a disquisition, etc. 1864.

—— —— G. Canal : a valedictory note, etc. *Lond.*, 1864.

—— Fitch, R. The long . . . voyage of . . . to . . . the River G., etc., 1583-1591. HAKLUYT. Vol. II.

—— Voyage to . . . G. . . . 1583-91. PURCHAS. Vol. II.

—— Graaf, N. Reise auf dem G., 1668-73. VOYAGES and TRAVELS. Allgemeine Historie, etc. Vol. X.

Gardokh.—See GARU.
Garonne.—LARTET, E. Note sur deux nouveaux Siréniens fossiles des terrains tertiaires du bassin de la G. *Par.*, 1866.
Garoo.—See GARU.
Garrow Hills.—Medlicott, H. B. On the prospects of useful Coal being found in the G. H., etc. INDIA GEOLOGICAL SURVEY. Records, etc. Vol. L

Gartokh.—See GARU.
Gartopa.—See GARU.
Garu.—LLOYD, SIR W. Narrative . . . And Captain A. G.'s account of an attempt to penetrate by Bekhar to Garoo, etc. *Lond.*, 1840.
Gasall.—See BAHR-EL-GHAZAL.
Gaspar, Strait.—MELVILL, of Cambee, and SMITH, H. D. A. Seaman's Guide . . . through the Straits of . . . G. 1853.
Gaspé.—GOULD and DOWIE. Instructions for making G. . . . in the River St. Lawrence. 1832.
Gaul.—See FRANCE.
Gea.—ZEUNE, A. G. : Versuch die Erdrinde . . . zu schildern.
Berl., 1830.
Gebel Nakus.—See NAKUS.
Geelong.—STONEY, H. B. Victoria ; with a description of . . . G., etc. 1856.

Gelderland.—LANT, J. DE. Belgii Confœderati Respublica: seu Gelriæ
 . . . descriptio. *Lugd. Bat.*, **1630**.

Gelria.—*See* GELDERLAND.

Gênes.—GÊNES. Description . . . de G., *etc.* *Gênes*, **1819**.

—— —— Nouvelle description de G. *Gênes*, **1826**.

—— CEVASCO, N. Statistique de . . . G. *Gênes*, **1838**.

Geneva.—SAUSSURE, H. B. DE. Voyages . . . précédés d'un Essai sur
 l'Histoire Naturelle des Environs de Genève. *Neuchâtel*, **1779-96**.

—— CANDOLLE, A. P. DE. Hypsométrie des environs de Genève.
 Par., **1839**.

——, **Lake of.**—JACKSON, J. R. Mémoire sur les Selches du Lac de
 Genève, *etc.* *Gen.*, **1804**.

Gennesareth.—MACGREGOR, J. The "Rob Roy" on . . . G., *etc.*
 Lond., **1869**.

Genoa.—RATTI, C. G. Istruzione di quanto può vedersi di più bello in
 Genova. **1780**.

—— ST. JOHN, B. Subalpine Kingdom; or, Experiences . . . in . . .
 G. **1856**.

George, Lake.—HOVELL, W. H. Reply to "A brief statement of facts,
 in connection with an Overland Expedition from Lake G. to Port
 Philip, in 1824, *etc.* *Sydney*, **1855**.

—— HUME, H. A brief statement of Facts in connection with an Overland Expedition from L. G. to Port Phillip in 1624, *etc.*
 Sydney, **1855**.

Georgetown.—SANDEMAN, P. Monthly Tables . . . deduced from Observations taken at the Observatory, G., Demerara . . . during eleven
 years, commencing Jan. 1846, *etc.* *Greenock*, **1857**.

Georgia.—MONTEITH, W. Notes on G., *etc.*

—— GEORGIA. A State of the Province of G., *etc.* **1742**.

—— GEORGIA. De præstantia Coloniæ Georgico-Anglicanæ, *etc.*
 Aug. Vindel., **1747**.

—— Persia. An Historical Account of the present Troubles of Persia
 and G., *etc.* **1756**.

—— KLAPROTH, J. Travels in . . . G. in 1807-8, *etc.* *Lond.*, **1814**.

—— PORTER, SIR R. K. Travels in G., *etc.* *Lond.*, **1821-22**.

—— FREYGAN, M. and Mme. Letters from . . . G., *etc.* **1823**.

—— SMITH, E., and DWIGHT, H. G. O. Missionary Researches . . .
 including a Journey . . . Into G., *etc.* **1834**.

—— MIGNAN, R. Winter Journey through . . . G., *etc.* **1839**.

—— MONTPÉREUX, F. D. DE. Voyage . . . en . . . Géorgie, *etc.*
 Par., **1839**.

—— KING, HON. T. D. Alabama . . . and G. Railroad. *Wash.*, **1848**.

—— WAGNER, M. Travels in . . . G., *etc* **1856**.

—— Chardin, Sir J. Travels . . . through . . . G. . . . **1672**.
 HARRIS, J. Vol. II.

—— The History of . . . G., 1732-12. HARRIS, J. Vol. II.

Georgia.—Informatione della G. di Pietro della Valle, *etc.* Trevenot. Vol. I.

—— Jordan ou Jourdain Catalani, P. .Mirabilia descripta, sequnitur de . . . Guorgiana, *etc.* Voyages and Travels. Recueil, *etc.* Vol. IV.

—— Chardin, Sir John. Travels through . . . G. into Persia. 1671. Voyages and Travels. The World displayed. Vol. XV. XVI.

Geram.—Jericho. An Excursion from Jericho to the Ruins of . . . G., *etc.* 1852.

Geraea.—*See* Gerara.

German Confederation.—Hassel, G. Staats-und Address- Handbuch der Teutschen Bundes- Staaten, 1816. *Weimar*, 1816.

—— **Ocean.**—*See* North Sea.

Germany.—Germany. Anzeige der geognostischen Karte von Deutschland, *etc.*

—— Lopez, J. J. Ueber die . . . Beziehungen Deutschlands mit den La-Plata Staaten, *etc.* *Berlin.*

—— Zeiller, M. Itinerarium Germaniæ, *etc.* *Ulmæ*, 1653.

—— Spener, J. C. Notitia Germaniæ Antiquæ, *etc.* *Halæ Magd.*, 1717.

—— Pollnitz, C. L., Baron de. Memoirs . . . In his . . . Travels . . . through G., *etc.* 1737.

—— Hanway, J. Historical Account . . . with . . . Travels . . . through . . . G., *etc.* 1753.

—— Drummond, A. Travels through . . . G., *etc.* 1754.

—— Nugent, Mr. The Grand Tour . . . through . . . G., *etc.* 1778.

—— Stolberg, Count F. L. zu. Reise in Deutschland, *etc.* *Königsb. u. Leip.*, 1794.

—— Chauchard, Capt. Geographical . . . description of . . . G., *etc.* *Lond.*, 1800.

—— Germany, Holland, the Netherlands . . . Geographical . . . description of, *etc.* 1800.

—— Repertorium aller Oerter . . . in der topographisch-militarischen Charte von Teutschland, *etc.* *Weimar*, 1812-13.

—— Baillie, M. First Impressions of . . . G. 1819.

—— Jacob, W., View of the Agriculture . . . *etc.* of G., *etc.* 1820.

—— Mannert, K. Germania . . . nach den Begriffen der Griechen und Römer, *etc.* *Leipzig*, 1820.

—— Wilson, W. R. Travels in . . . G., *etc.* *Lond.*, 1826.

—— Brockedon, W. Illustrations of the Passes . . . by which Italy communicates with . . . G. 1828.

—— Stocqueler, J. H. Fifteen Months' Pilgrimage through . . . G. 1832.

——. Mendelssohn, G. B. Das Germanische Europa. *Berl.*, 1836.

—— Niebuhr, C. Reisebeschreibung . . . nach Deutschland, *etc.* *Hamb.*, 1837.

Germany.—Zeuss, K. von. Die Deutschen und die Nachbarstämme.
Münch., **1837**.
———— Hawkins, B. G.: the Spirit of her History, *etc.* **1838**.
———— Dechen. Anzeige der geognostischen Karte von Deutschland, *etc.*
Berl., **1839**.
———— Hoffman, K. F. v. Das Vaterland der Deutschen. *Nürnb.*, **1839**.
———— Lal, Mohan. Travels ... and a Visit to ... G. **1846**.
———— Rónay, J. Jellemisme, vagyaz ... Német ... Nemzet ... Jellemzése, *etc.* *Györött*, **1847**.
———— Maury, L. F. A. Histoire ... des Forêts ... de l'Allemagne, *etc.* *Par.*, **1850**.
———— Meidinger, H. Die Deutschen Ströme in ihren Verkehrs- und Handels-Verhältnissen. *Leipz.*, **1853**.
———— Graham, W. The Jordan and the Rhine ... Five years ... in G. **1854**.
———— Skippon, Sir P. Journey through ... G., *etc.* Churchill. Vol. VI.
———— Austel, H. Voyage ... through ... G. ... 1586. Hakluyt. Vol. II.
———— Burnet, Bishop G. Travels through ... some Provinces of G. ... 1685-86. Harris, J. Vol. II.
———— Misson, M. Travels through ... G. ... 1687-88. Harris, J. Vol. II.
———— Ray, J. Travels through ... G. ... 1663. Harris, J. Vol. II.
———— Stolberg, Count F. L. Travels through G., *etc.* Pelham. Vol. II.
———— Riesbeck's Travels through G. Pinkerton. Vol. VI.
———— Benjamin, the Son of Jonas. Peregrinations of ... and relations of ... G., *etc.* Purchas. Vol. II.
———— Ray, J. Travels through ... G., *etc.* Ray, J. Collection, *etc.*
———— Carr, J. A Northern Summer; or, Travels ... through ... part of G., 1804. Voyages and Travels. A Collection, *etc.* 1805. Vol. III.
———— Reinbeck, G. Travels from St. Petersburgh ... to G., 1805. Voyages and Travels. A Collection, *etc.* 1806. Vol. VI.
———— Seume, J. G. Tour through part of G. ... 1805. Voyages and Travels. A Collection, *etc.* 1805. Vol. VII.
———— ———— Tour through part of G. ... 1805. Voyages and Travels. A Collection, *etc.* 1810. Vol. VI.
———— The Travels of Mr. Jonas Hanway ... through ... G. ... 1743. Voyages and Travels. The World displayed. Vol. XIV. XV.
———— Misson, M. Travels through G. and Italy. Voyages and Travels. The World displayed. Vol. XVIII, XIX.
———— Keysler, John George. Travels through ... G., *etc.* 1729. Voyages and Travels. The World displayed. Vol. XIX.

Germany, North.—MURRAY. Hand-Book for Travellers . . . through . . . N. G., etc. *Lond.*, 1836.
——— ——— KOCH, F. C. L., and DUNKER, W. Beiträge zur Kenntniss des Norddeutschen Oolithgebilden, etc. *Braunschw.*, 1837.
——— ——— SEDGWICK, A., and MURCHISON, SIR R. I. On the Distribution and Classification of the Older . . . Deposits of the N. of G., etc. 1842.
——— ——— BARROW, J. Tour . . . through N. G., etc. 1853.
——— ——— LAMONT, J. Untersuchungen über den Erdmagnetismus in Norddeutschland . . . 1858. *Münch.*, 1859.
——— ——— MITTHEILUNGEN aus der Norddeutschen Seewarte. 1870.
——— ——— Hallberg, Baron von. Sentimental Sketches, written during a Journey through the N. of G. . . . 1820. VOYAGES and TRAVELS, New. 1819. Vol. V.
———, **South.**—CARR, Sir J. Tour through Holland . . . to the S. of G., 1806. VOYAGES and TRAVELS. A Collection, etc. 1806. Vol. VIII.

Ghadames.—*See* GHADAMIS.

Ghadamis.—RICHARDSON, J. Touarick Alphabet . . . Vocabularies of the Ghadamsee and Touarghee Languages, etc. *Lond.*, 1847.
——— ——— Travels in the Great Desert . . . including a description of . . . G., etc. 1848.
——— CUERBONNEAU M. A. Relation du Voyage de M. . . . de Bonnemain à R'Dâmes 1856-57. *Par.*, 1857.
——— MIRCHER, H. Mission de G. . . . Rapports officiels, etc. *Alger*, 1863.
——— ROHLFS, G. Reise . . . über Rhadames nach Tripoli. *Bremen*, 1868.

Ghanat.—*See* KANO.

Ghasal, Bahr-el.—*See* BAHR-EL-GHASAL.

Ghat.—RICHARDSON, J. Travels in the Great Desert . . . including a description of . . . G., etc. 1848.

Ghauts.—CHAPLIN, W. Report . . . of . . . Administration introduced into . . . Territory above the G., etc. *Bomb.*, 1838.

Ghizni.—*See* GHUZNEE.

Ghuznee.—VIGNE, G. T. A personal Narrative of a Visit to Ghuzni, etc. *Lond.*, 1840.

Ghuzni.—*See* GHUZNEE.

Giant's Causeway.—WRIGHT, G. N. Guide to the G.'s C. 1823.

Giappan, Giappone.—*See* JAPAN.

Gibraltar.—LEMPRIERE, W. Tour from G. to Tangier, etc. 1791.
——— — SAYER, CAPT. History of G., etc. 1862.
——— — GIBRALTAR. [Cuttings from the 'Times' relative to the proposed cession to Spain of G., etc.] [1868-69.]

Gibraltar, Straits of.—HEINER, J. Sailing Directions for . . . the S. of G. 1826.
——— — PURDY, J. . New Sailing Directory for the S. of G., etc. 1832.
——— — PURDY, J. Sailing Directions for the S. of G. etc. 1846.

Gibraltar, Straits of.—Vincendon-Dumoulin, C. A. Manuel de la Navigation dans le Détroit de G. *Par.*, 1857.
—— Boland's Observations on the Streights of G., *etc.* Churchill. Vol. IV.
—— Foxe, J. Voyage to the Streight of G., 1563, *etc.* Hakluyt. Vol II.
—— Voyages made without the Straight of G. to the South, *etc.* Hakluyt. Vol. II.

Gierusalem.—*See* Jerusalem.

Gila, River.—Emory, W. H. Notes of a Military Reconnoissance... including parts of the ... G., *etc.* *N. Y.*, 1848.
—— Parke, J. G. Report of Explorations for ... a Railway ... between Dona Ana ... and Pimas Villages, on the G. *Wash.*, 1854.

Gilead.—Buckingham, J. S. Travels ... through ... G., *etc.* 1822.

Gingea.—Beschreibnng der Königreiche ... G., *etc.* Voyages and Travels. Allgemeine Historie, *etc.* Vol. XVIII.

Gingi.—*See* Gisgee.

Gingiro.—Tellez, B. Travels ... and an Account of ... G., *etc.* 1710.

Gipps' Land.—Gipps' Land. Plain statement of facts relating to G. L. 1840.
—— —— Progress of discovery in G. L., *etc.* 1840.

Girnar.—Burgess, J. Notes of a visit to ... G., *etc.* *Bombay*, 1869.

Gironde.—Linder, M. Étude sur les Terrains de Transport du Département de la G., *etc.* *Bord.*, 1868.

Glatz.—Martiny, F. W. Handbuch für Reisende nach ... G. *Breslau*, 1812.

Glenelg, River.—Martin, J. Journal of a Voyage to the G. R., *etc.* *Perth*, 1864.

Glen Roy.—Darwin, C. Observations on the Parallel Roads of G. R., *etc.* 1839.

Globe.—*See* World.

Gloucestershire.—Rudge, T. General View of the Agriculture of the County of G. 1807.
—— Murchison, Sir R. I. and Strickland, H. E. On the Upper Formations of the New Red Sandstone System in G., *etc.* 1837.
—— Murchison, Sir R. I. The Silurian System, founded on Geological Researches in ... G., *etc.* 1839.

Goa.—Burton, R. F. G. and the Blue Mountains, *etc.* 1851.
—— Stephens, T. Voyage ... to G. in 1579. Astley. Vol. I.
—— Voyage of Don S. de Gama, from G. to Suez in 1540, *etc.* Astley. Vol. I.
—— Fitch R. The long ... voyage of ... to ... G. in the East Indies, *etc.* 1583-1591. Hakluyt. Vol. II.
—— Stevens, T. Voyage ... unto G. ... 1579. Hakluyt. Vol. II.
—— Castro, J. de. Voyage of Don S. de Gama from G. to Suez, in 1540, *etc.* Kerr. Vol. VI.

Goa — Gondar.

Goa.—Stevens, T. Voyage to G., 1579. Kerr. Vol. VII.
——— Duart de Menezes, Don. Tractate of the Portugall Indies [G.], etc. Purchas. Vol. II.
——— Fitch, R. Voyage to . . . G. . . . 1583-91. Purchas. Vol. II.
——— Huighen van Linschoten, J. Voyage to G. . . . 1483. Purchas. Vol. II.
——— Mandelslo, J. A. Reise . . . nach Europa über G. Voyages and Travels. Allgemeine Historie, etc. Vol. XI.
——— Tavernier. Reisen . . . 1605-66 . . . nach G., etc. Voyages and Travels. Allgemeine Historie, etc. Vol. XI.

Gobernador, Straits of.—*See* Governador.

Godavery.—India. Reports of the . . . effects of the G. and Krishna Annicuts, etc. *Madras*, 1858.
——— Upper.—Oldham T. On the Agate Flake found . . . in the Pleiocene (?) Deposits of the Upper G. India, Geological Survey. Records, etc. Vol. I.

Goeree.—Van Rhijn, A. Beschrijving van de Hydrograp. Kaart der Zergaten van de G., etc. 1839.

Golconda.—Relation des Royaumes de G. . . . par Wilhem Methold, etc. Thevenot. Vol. I.
——— Beschreibung der Königreiche G. und Pegu. Voyages and Travels. Allgemeine Historie, etc. Vol. X.
——— Methold, W Reise nach den Diamantgruben in G. . . . 1622. Voyages and Travels. Allgemeine Historie, etc. Vol. X.
——— Zusatz zu der letzten Regierungsänderung in G. Voyages and Travels. Allgemeine Historie, etc. Vol. XVIII.

Gold Coast.—Dupuis, J. Journal . . . comprising Notes . . . relative to the G. C., etc.   1824.
——— Murphy, B. F. Memoir on the G. C., etc. *MS.*   1831.
——— Beecham, J. Ashantee and G. C., etc.   1841.
——— Cruickshank, B. Eighteen Years on the G. C., etc.   1853.
——— Clarke, R. Remarks on . . . the G. C.   1860.
——— G. C., Its discovery, etc. Astley. Vol. II.
——— Inland Countries behind the G. C. Astley. Vol. II.
——— Natural History of the G. C. Astley. Vol. II.
——— Of the G. C. Negroes, etc. Astley. Vol. II.
——— Meredith, H. Description de la Côte d'Or. Eyriès. Vol. XI.
——— The Passage from the G. C. to . . . Benni, etc. Purchas. Vol. II.

Golden Castile.—*See* Castilla del Oro.

Golfe Arabique.—*See* Red Sea.

Golkonda.—*See* Golconda.

Gomorrah.—Saulcy, F. de. Narrative . . . including an account of the discovery of the Sites of Sodom and G.   1854.

Gondar.—Pearce, N. The Life and Adventures of N. Pearce . . . Together with Mr. Coffin's account of his Visit to G., etc. *Lond.* 1831.

Gondogoro.—See GONDOKORO.
Gondokoro.—NARDI, F. Del Clima di G., Memoria. *Roma*, 1861.
Goodwin Sands.—CHOWNE, O. A Voice from the "G.," etc. 1857.
Gooserat.—See GUZERAT.
Goree.—PARK, M. Papers in MS. ... Observations for Longitude made during the passage to G.
———— LINDSAY, J. Voyage ... containing an account of the ... taking ... of G., etc. 1759.
———— SAUGNIER, M. Relations de plusieurs voyages ... à G., etc. *Par.*, 1792.
———— Brue, A. Attempt for a discovery of the Lake of Kayor in 1714; with an account of ... G. ASTLEY. Vol. II.
———— Sénégambie, Iles Saint Louis et G. EYRIES. Vol. X.
———— Adamson's Voyage to ... G., etc. PINKERTON. Vol. XVI.
Gorgona.—EMORY, W. H. Observations ... made at ... G., etc. *Camb. U. S.*, 1850.
Göteborg.—See GOTTENBURG.
Gothenburg.—See GOTTENBURG.
Gothland.—SWEDEN. Rambles in Sweden and G." ... by Sylvanus. 1847.
———— DUNBURY, S. A. A Summer in ... G. 1856.
———— MARRYAT, H. One Year in Sweden; including a visit to ... Gütland. *Lond.*, 1862.
———— Malgo, King. Voyage to ... Gotland ... 580. HAKLUYT. Vol. I.
Götland.—See GOTHLAND.
Gottenburg.—TOPOGRAFISKA OCH STATISTISKA Uppgifter von Göteborgs och Bohus Län. *Stockh.*, 1859.
Gottland.—See GOTHLAND.
Gournay.—NOEL, S. B. J. Premier Essai sur ... G., etc. *Rouen*, 1795.
Governador, Straits of.—Weg, welchen Man nehmen muss, um durch die Strassen von ... Golernador zu kommen. VOYAGES and TRAVELS. Allgemeine Historie, etc. Vol. XVIII.
Goyaz.—Bolivia. Notizen über den Minenbetrieb in ... G., etc. *Berl.*, [1867.]
Gozo.—ROINGELIN, L. DR. Ancient and Modern Malta; containing ... Account of ... G., etc. *Lond.*, 1805.
———— GIACINTO, P. C. Saggio di Agricoltura per le Isole di Malta e G. *Messina*, 1811.
———— BADGER, G. P. Description of ... G. *Malta*, 1838.
Graham Island.—SMYTH, W. H. Some remarks on an error respecting the Site and Origin of G. I. 1832.
Grain Coast.—The Malaghetta, G. or Pepper Coast. ASTLEY. Vol. II.
Granada. LAS CASAS, B. de. Briefe Narration of ... G. PURCHAS. Vol. IV.
————, **Island.**—See GRENADA.

Grand Bay.—Cartier, J. Voyages to . . . the G. B. . . . 1534, 40.
Hakluyt. Vol. III.

——— Notes and Observations . . . for the G. B., etc. Hakluyt.
Vol. III.

Grand Cairo.—See Cairo.

Grand Canaries.—See Canary Island.

Grande-Chartreuse.—Dupré Duloire, E. F. M. Voyage à la G.-C., etc.
Valence, 1830.

——— Pardoe, Miss. The River and the Desart; or, Recollections of the
Rhône and the C. Lond., 1838.

Grand Manan.—See Menan, Grand.

Grand Ocean.—See Pacific Ocean.

Graubünden.—Gemälde der Schweiz . . . G., etc. Bern, 1834-38.

——— Bergmann, J. Untersuchungen über die freien Walliser . . . in
G., etc. Wien, 1844.

Great Britain.—England. The Land we Live in, a Tour of the British
Islands, etc.

——— Land We Live In. A pictorial . . . Sketchbook of the British
Islands. Lond.

——— Stanford, C. Catalogue of the . . . Maps . . . of the Geological
Survey of G. B., etc.

——— Camden, W. Britannia, etc. Lond., 1695.

——— Steinoer, M. Opera Mineralia Explicata; or the Mineral Kingdom
. . . of G. B. display'd, etc. 1713.

——— Strachey, J. Observations on the different Strata . . . of G. B.
1727.

——— Horsley, J. Britannia Romana; or the Roman Antiquities of B.,
etc. 1732.

——— Baxter, W. Glossarium Antiquitatum Britanicarum, etc. 1733.

——— Campbell, J. Political Survey of G. B., etc. 1774.

——— Skrine, H. A General Account of all the Rivers of Note in G. B.,
etc. Lond., 1801.

——— England. Abstract of . . . Returns . . . to . . . "An Act for
taking an Account of the Population of G. B." . . . Enumeration
1801-2. 1801-2.

——— Navigable Rivers and Canals in . . . G. B., etc. Lond., 1808.

——— Capper, B. P. Topographical Dictionary of the United Kingdom,
etc. 1808.

——— Colquhoun, P. On . . . the British Empire. 1815.

——— Geography, Remarks touching, especially that of the British Isles, etc.
Lond., 1825.

——— Britain, Great. Historical account of . . . Rivers, Canals, and
Railways of G. B., etc. 1831.

——— Pebrer, P. Taxation, Revenue . . . Statistics and Debt of the
whole British Empire, etc. Lond., 1833.

——— England. Tables of the Revenue, Population, &c. of the United
Kingdom . . . 1820-1838, etc. 1834-40.

Great Britain.—British Islands, Lighthouses of the. Corrected to . . . 1836, 44, 49, 51, 54, 58, 59. 1836-59.
—— —— Jonnès, A. M. Statistique de la Grande Bretagne, etc. *Par.*, 1837.
—— —— Sabine, Major-Gen. E. Report on the Magnetic Inclinal and Isodynamic Lines in the British Islands. 1839.
—— —— Clark, J. A. Glimpses of the Old World, or Excursions . . . in G. B. 1840.
—— —— Nowrojee, Jehangeer, and Hirjeebhoy Merwanjee. Journal of a Residence of two years and a half in G. B. 1841.
—— —— Lal, Mohan. Travels . . . and a Visit to G. B., etc. 1846.
—— —— M'Culloch, J. R. Descriptive . . . Account of the British Empire, etc. 1847.
—— —— Banister, S. Classical sources of the history of the British Isles, etc. 1849.
—— —— Petermann, A. Statistical Notes to the Cholera Map of the British Isles. 1831-33. 1849.
—— —— Whitley, N. On the Climate of the British Islands, etc. *Lond.*, 1850.
—— —— Hughes, W. Manual of British Geography, etc. *Edin.*, 1851.
—— —— Life-Boats. Report . . . to which is added a list of the . . . Life-boat . . . Stations . . . of the British Isles, etc. 1851.
—— —— Imperial Cyclopædia. Sub-Division, Cyclopedia of the British Empire. 1852.
—— —— Latham, R. G. The Ethnology of the British Islands. 1852.
—— —— Sedgwick, A. A Synopsis of the Classification of the British Palæozoic Rocks, etc. *Lond. and Camb.*, 1852.
—— —— Stange, M. H. G. B. one Empire . . . by inter-communication, etc. 1852.
—— —— Calvert, J. Gold Rocks of G. B., etc. 1853.
—— —— Cheshire, E. The Results of the Census of G. B. in 1851, etc. 1853.
—— —— Burwood, J., and Yule, C. B. Tide Tables for the British . . . Ports, etc. 1855-63.
—— —— Twining, T. Memorandum on . . . enabling the Working Classes of G. B. . . . to improve their . . . comforts. 1855.
—— —— Dunsterville, E. The Lights of the British Islands. Corrected to 1856. 1856.
—— —— Denby, W. C. The Beautiful Islets of Britaine. 1857.
—— —— Imray, J. F. Pilotage Rates and Regulations of the Principal Ports in the United Kingdom, etc. 1858.
—— —— Poey, A. Sur le nombre de personnes tuées par la foudre dans . . . la Grande-Bretagne de 1852 à 1856, etc. *Par.*, 1858.
—— —— Tennant, J. Catalogue of Fossils found in the British Isles. 1858.
—— —— Lewin, T. The Invasion of Britain by Julius Cæsar. *Lond.*, 1859.
—— —— Murchison, Sir R. I. Table showing the Vertical Range of the Silurian Fossils of B. 1859.

Great Britain.—Tucker, L. H. American Glimpses of Agriculture in G. B. *Albany*, **1860.**

—— — Dunsterville, F. The Admiralty List of the Lights of the British Islands. Corrected to 1860, 61, 62. **1860-62.**

—— — Wright, T. The Celt, the Roman, and the Saxon; a history of the early Inhabitants of B., etc. *Lond.*, **1861.**

—— — Gras, M. A. Le. Phares des Côtes des Îles Britanniques. Corrigés 1861-63. *Par.*, **1861-63.**

—— — Trade and Navigation of the United Kingdom . . . in 1861 and 1862. **1862-63.**

—— — Hughes, W. The Geography of British History, etc. **1863.**

—— — Ravenstein, A. Geographie und Statistik des Britischen Reichs. *Leip.*, **1863.**

—— — Hull, E. The Coal Resources of G. B. **1864.**

—— — Tide Tables for the British and Irish Ports, for 1865, etc. **1864.**

—— — Johnston, A. K. Atlas of the British Empire . . . with . . . letterpress. *Edin. and Lond.*, **[1870.]**

—— — Gonzales, M. Voyage to G. B., etc. Churchill. Vol. VII.

—— — An historical Account of the Intercourse between . . . G. B. and . . . the East Indies, etc. Harris, J. Vol. I.

—— — Dupin, C. Tour through the Naval and Military Establishments of G. B., 1816-20. Voyages and Travels, New. 1819. Vol. VII.

Great Desert.—*See* Desert, Great.

Great Salt Lake.—Chandless, W. Visit to the S. L., etc. **1857.**

—— —— City.—*See* Utah.

Grecia.—*See* Greece.

Grecian Seas.—*See* Archipelago.

Greece.—Pausanias. Pausaniae de tota Græcia libri decem, etc. *Basil*, **1550.**

—— — Bellonius, P. Plurimarum . . . rerum in Græcia . . . conspectarum observationes, etc. *Antw.*, **1589.**

—— - Lucas, P. Voyage de, dans la Grèce, etc. *Par.*, **1712.**

—— — Pococke, R. Description of . . . G., etc. **1743-45.**

—— —— Potter, J., Abp. of Canterbury. Archæologia Græca, etc. **1751.**

—— —— Drummond, A. Travels through . . . G., etc. **1754.**

—— - Bas, L. Antiquities of G., etc. **1772.**

—— -- Barthélemy, Abbé. Voyage du jeune Anacharsis en Grèce, etc. *Par.*, **1790.**

—— — Pausanias. Viaggio Istorico della Grecia. *Roma*, **1792.**

—— — Robertson, W. History of Ancient G., etc. *Edin.*, **1793.**

—— — Pausanias. Græciæ descriptio, etc. *Lips.*, **1794-96.**

—— — Sonnini, C. R. Travels in G., etc. **1801.**

—— ·· Gell, Sir W. Itinerary of G., etc. **1810.**

—— — Chandler, R. Travels in . . . G. **1817.**

Greece.

Greece.—PAUSANIAS. Descrizione della Grecia, etc.   *Roma*, 1817.
—— -- DODWELL, E. A Classical . . . Tour through G. . . . 1801, 1805
  and 1800.   *Lond.*, 1819.
—— -- GELL, SIR W. Itinerary of G., etc.   1819.
—— —— HUGHES, T. S. Travels in . . . G., etc.   1820.
—— —— LAURENT, P. Classical Tour through . . . G. . . . in 1818-19.
   1821.
—— —— STUART, J., and REVETT, N. The Antiquities of Athens and other
  places in G., etc.   1825-33.
—— —— LEAKE, W. M. Historical Outline of the Greek Revolution, etc.
   Lond., 1826.
—— - — DANKOVSZKY, G. Die Griechen als Stamm- und Sprachverwandte
  der Slawen, etc.   *Presb.*, 1828.
—— —— GRIBERO, COUNT J. L'Empire Russe comparé aux principaux états
  du Monde . . . Quadro . . . della . . . Grecia, nel 1829.   1829.
—— —— HUGHES, T. S. Travels in G. and Albania.   1830.
—— —— ALCOCK, T. Travels in . . . G., etc.   1831.
—— —— STRACHSEN, J. J. Reise durch . . . Griechenland . . . 1647-
  1673.   *Gotha*, 1832.
—— -- FITZMAURICE, HON. W. E. Cruise to . . . G.   1834.
—— —— LEAKE, W. M. Travels in N. n G.   *Lond.*, 1835.
—— —— TEMPLE, SIR G. T. Travels in G., etc.   1836.
—— —— MURRAY. Hand-Book for Travellers in . . . G., etc.
   Lond., 1840.
—— —— DAMER, HON. MRS. G. L. D. Diary of a Tour in G., etc.
   Lond., 1841.
—— —— ST. JOHN, J. A. History of the Manners and Customs of Ancient G.
   1842.
—— —— STRONG, F. G. as a Kingdom, etc.   1842.
—— —— DROYSEN, J. G. Die Hellenistischen Colonien.   1843.
—— —— BIANCONI, J. J. De Mari olim occupante planities et colles . . .
  Graeciae, etc.   *Bonon*, 1846-52.
—— -- SPENCER, E. Travels in European Turkey . . . with a Visit to G.,
  etc.   1851.
—— - — WILDE, W. R. Narrative of . . . a Visit to . . . G.
   Dubl., 1852.
—— —— WORDSWORTH, C. G.; pictorial, descriptive, etc.   *Lond.*, 1853.
—— — CARLISLE, EARL OF. Diary in . . . Greek Waters.   1854.
—— — PETACHIA, RABBI. Travels of; who, in the . . . Twelfth Century
  visited . . . G., etc.   1856.
—— - — SMITH, W. Dictionary of Greek and Roman Geography.   1856.
—— — -- PARAVEY, CHEV. DE. Recherches sur le Népenthès des Grecs, etc.
   Versailles, 1860.
—— —— SCHMIDT, J. F. J. Beiträge zur physikalischen Geographie von
  Griechenland.   *Athen*, 1861.
—— —— LEWIS, T. State Rights: a Photograph from the Ruins of Ancient
  G., etc.   *Albany*, 1865.

Greece.—FINLAY, G. Παρατηρησεις επι της εν ... Ελλαδι προιστορικης αρχαιολογιας. Εν Αθηναις, 1869.
— —— CONSTANTINE THE GREAT. Voyage to G. ... 330. HARLUYT. Vol. II.
—— — RUBEST, KETENSIS. Voyage to ... G. ... 1143. HARLUYT. Vol. II.
—— — Angelos, C. Of the condition of life in which the Greeks now live, etc. PURCHAS. Vol. I.
—— — Scot, W. L. Travels in ... G. ... 1612. PURCHAS. Vol. II.
—— — Vernon, F. Travels ... through ... G., etc. Ray, J.
—— — Wheeler, Sir G. Plants observed in his Voyage to G., etc. RAY, J.
—— — Forbin, Count de. Travels in G. ... 1817-18. VOYAGES and TRAVELS, New. 1819 Vol. I.
— ·— Müller, C. Journey through G. ... 1821. VOYAGES and TRAVELS, New. 1819, etc. Vol. VIII.
—— — Sibthorp, Dr. Birds, Quadrupeds, and Fishes of G. WALPOLE, R. Memoirs, etc.
—— ·· —— Observations on Natural History, relating to parts of G., etc. WALPOLE, R. Memoirs, etc.
—— — Leake, Colonel. Inscriptions copied in various parts of G. WALPOLE, R. Travels, etc.
—— See also ATTICA.

Greek Islands.—See ARCHIPELAGO.

Green Bay—FEATHERSTONHAUGH, G. W. Report of a Geological Reconnaissance ... by ... G. H. and the Wisconsin Territory to the Coteau de Prairie. *Wash.*, 1836.

Greenland.—RINK, H. Om den formeentlige Opdagelse af Grönlands Nordkystog et saabent Polarhav, etc.
—— VERA, G. DL Tre Navigationi fatte dagli Olandesi ... doue scoprirsero ... un Paese ... creduto la Groenlandia. *Venet.*, 1599.
— — GREENLAND. Relation de Groenland. *Pur.*, 1663.
— -- EGEDE, H. Description of G., etc. 1745.
— - ANDERSON, J. Nachrichten von ... Grünland, etc. *Hamb.*, 1748.
—— — KERGUELEN TREMAREC, M. DE. Relation d'une Voyage ... aux Côtes ... du G., etc. *Par.*, 1771.
—— — SAABYE, H. E. Brackstükke eines Tagebuches gehalten in Grönland in 1770 bis 1778, etc. *Hamb.*, 1817.
—— — EGEDE, H. Description of G., etc. 1818.
— -— CRANTZ, D. History of G., etc. 1820.
— - SCORESBY, W. Journal ... including Researches ... on the E.n Coast of W. G., etc. *Edin.*, 1823.
—— — GRAAH, W. A. Undersögelses-Reise til Ostkysten af Grönland, etc. *Cop.h.*, 1832.
—— ROQUETTE, M. DE LA. Sur les Découvertes faites en Groenland. *Par.*, 1835.
—— GRAAH, W. A. Narrative of an Expedition to the E. Coast of G., etc. *Lond.*, 1837.

Greenland.

Greenland.—GAIMARD, P. Voyage en . . . Grœnland, pendant 1835 et 1836, etc. *Par.*, **1838-40**.

—— RINK, H. Om den geographiske Beskaffenhed af de danske Handels-distrikter i Nordgrønland, etc. *Kjøb.*, **1852**.

—— —— Grønland geographisk og statistisk beskrevet. *Kjøb.*, **1852-57**.

—— Arctic Expeditions. G.-Eskimo Vocabulary, etc. *Lond.*, **1853**.

—— MARKHAM, C. R. Franklin's Footsteps; a sketch of G., etc. *Lond.*, **1853**.

—— OSTERGAARD, C. C., and others. Observationes meteorologicæ per annos 1832-54 in Grönland factæ. *Haunie*, **1856**.

—— KANE, E. K. Astronomical Observations . . . made . . . on the N.W. Coast of G., etc. *Phil.*, **1860**.

—— IRMINGER, C. Notice sur les Pêches . . . du Grœnland. *Par.*, **1863**.

—— RAFN, C. C. Renseignements sur les premiers habitants de la Côte Occidentale du Grœnland, etc. **1864**.

—— HELMS, H. Grönland und die Grönlander, etc. *Leips.*, **1867**.

—— BROWN, R. Floræ Discoana: Contributions to the Phyto-Geography of G., etc. *Edin.*, **1868**.

—— —— On the Mammalian Fauna of G. [*Lond.*, **1868**.]

—— Monck, Capt. J. Account of a . . . Voyage . . . with a description of Old and New G. CHURCHILL. Vol. I.

—— La Peyrere. Account of G. CHURCHILL. Vol. II.

—— Two Journals. The first kept . . . in . . . G. in 1633-4, etc. CHURCHILL. Vol. II.

—— Pelham's preservation of eight Men in G., etc. CHURCHILL. Vol. IV.

—— Gudbrandus Thorlacina, Bishop of Holen. Letter concerning the ancient state of . . . Grœnland. HAKLUYT. Vol. I.

—— Voyage . . . of . . . the Ships Sunshine and Northstarre . . . to discover a passage betweene Grœnland and Iseland, 1587. HAKLUYT. Vol. III.

—— Zeno, N. and A. Voyage to . . . Engronland . . . 1380. HAKLUYT. Vol. III.

—— Collection of Documents on Spitzbergen and G. Edited . . . by A. White. 1855. HAKLUYT Soc. Pub. Vol. XVIII.

—— History of . . . G. . . . 1585-1746. HARRIS, J. Vol. II.

—— Original discovery of G. by the Icelanders in the ninth century. KERR. Vol. I.

—— Annales, ou Histoire civile du G., etc. LAHARPE. Vol. XVII.

—— G. Glaces, Climat, Minéraux, etc. LAHARPE, J. Vol. XVII.

—— Baffin, W. Fourth Voyage of J. Hall to Grœneland, 1612, etc. PURCHAS. Vol. III.

—— Baffin, W. Journall of the Voyage made to G., 1613. PURCHAS. Vol. III.

—— Blefkens, D. Voyages and history of . . . G., 1563. PURCHAS. Vol. III.

P

Greenland.—Edge, T. Northerne Discoveries . . . with a description of G., 1653-1622. PURCHAS. Vol. III.
—— Fotherbye, R. Voyage of Discovery to G., 1614. PURCHAS. Vol. III.
—— Hall, J. Voyages forth of Denmark for the Discovery of G., 1605-6. PURCHAS. Vol. III.
—— Heley, W. Divers Voyages to G. . . . 1617-23. PURCHAS. Vol. III.
—— Iver Boty. Treatise of the Course from Island to Groneland, 1608. PURCHAS. Vol. III.
—— Navigationi fatte da gli Olandesi . . . dove scopersero . . . un paese . . . creduto la Groenlandia, 1594-97. RAMUSIO. Vol. III.
—— Marten, F. Observations made in . . . G., etc. 1711. Voyages. Account of several late, etc.
—— Supplement. Description of G., etc. 1711. Voyages. Account of several late, etc.
—— Cranz. Historie und Beschreibung von Grönland, etc. VOYAGES and TRAVELS. Allgemeine Historie, etc. Vol. XIX.
—— **Sea.**—See ARCTIC OCEAN.
Greenwich.—AIRY, G. B. Plan of the . . . Royal Observatory, etc.
—— METEOROLOGICAL REGISTER for 1833; kept at G. Lond., 1834.
—— GREENWICH OBSERVATORY, Description of the Altitude and Azimuth Instrument erected at. 1847.
Grenada, Island.—EDWARDS, B. Historical Survey of . . . Saint Domingo. . . . Also a Tour through . . . G., etc. 1801.
—— Reisen nach . . . Insel G., etc. VOYAGES and TRAVELS. Allgemeine Historie, etc. Vol. XVII.
Grenoble.—GRENOBLE. Le Petit Guide de l'Étranger à G., etc. Grenoble, 1863.
Grisons.—REY, W. Les G. et la Haute-Engadine. Genève, 1850.
—— Ray, J. Travels through . . . the Country of the G., etc. HARRIS, J. Vol. II.
Groaneland.—See GREENLAND.
Grodno.—Reinbeck, G. Travels . . . through . . . G. . . . 1805. VOYAGES and TRAVELS. A Collection, etc. 1806. Vol. VI.
Groenland.—See GREENLAND.
Groninga.—See GRONINGEN.
Groningen.—LAET, J. DE. Belgii Confoederati Respublica; seu Groning. . . . descriptio. Lugd. Bat., 1630.
Grosser Ocean.—See PACIFIC OCEAN.
Guadeloupe.—Reisen nach G., etc. VOYAGES and TRAVELS. Allgemeine Historie, etc. Vol. XVII.
Guaicuhi.—See VELHAS, RIO DAS.
Guainia, River.—See RIO-NEGRO.
Guaira.—See LA GUAYRA.

Guanahani.—VARNHAGEN, F. A. DE. La verdadera G. de Colon. Memoria, etc. Santiago, 1864.

——— Das wahre G. des Columbus, etc. Wien, 1869.

Guardafui, Cape.—A Description of the Countries ... from the Cape of Good Hope to C. G., etc. ASTLEY. Vol. III.

——— ——— Hamilton, A. Remarks on ... Maritime Countries ... between the Capes of Good Hope and G. ASTLEY. Vol. III.

——— ——— Einige Anmerkungen über den Küsten und Inseln zwischen dem Vorgebirge der guten Hoffnung und Capo Guarda Fuy. VOYAGES and TRAVELS. Allgemeine Historie, etc. Vol. V.

Guarda Fuy, Cape.—See GUARDAFUL.

Guatemala.—GAGE, T. Survey of the Spanish West Indies ... Also ... Journey through ... G., etc. 1702.

——— PORTA, A. Relacion del Reconocimiento de la Costa do G., etc. 1792.

——— JUARROS, D. A Statistical ... History of ... G., etc. 1823.

——— HAEFKENS, J. Reize naar G. Gravenh., 1827.

——— THOMPSON, G. A. Narrative of an Official Visit to G., etc. 1829.

——— AMERICA, CENTRAL. Brief statement ... of Grants ... to E. Coast of Central America Commercial and Agricultural Company, by ... G. 1831.

——— BAILY, J. Central America ... G., etc. 1850.

——— BRASSEUR DE BOURBOURG, E. C. Aperçus d'un Voyage dans ... G. Par., 1857.

——— XIMENEZ, R. P. F. F. Las Historias del Orígen de los Indios de G., etc. Lond., 1857.

——— TEMPSKY, G. F. VON MITLA. A Narrative of ... a Journey in ... G., etc. 1858.

——— VALOIS, A. DE. Mexique ... et G. Notes de Voyage. Par., [1862.]

——— Palacio, D. G. de. Description of the Ancient Provinces of G., 1576. SQUIER. Collection. No. I.

——— See also SAN DOMINGO DE PALENQUE.

Guatulco.—Drake, Sir F. Voyage ... from ... G. ... to the N.W. of California, etc. HAKLUYT. Vol. III.

——— Voyage of N. de Silva ... as far as ... G. upon the Coast of New Spaine, etc. HAKLUYT. Vol. IV.

——— Silva, M. da. Voyage from Cape Verd Islands to G., etc. KERR. Vol. X.

Guaxaca.—See OAXACA.

Guayaquil.—Reise aus dem Hafen Perico nach G., etc. VOYAGES and TRAVELS. Allgemeine Historie, etc. Vol. IX.

——— Naturgeschichte ... des Landes G., etc. VOYAGES and TRAVELS. Allgemeine Historie, etc. Vol. XVI.

Guaynia, River.—See RIO-NEGRO.

P 2

Guayra — Guiana, British.

Guayra.—Beschreibung von . . . der Provinz G., etc. Voyages and Travels. Allgemeine Historie, etc. Vol. XVI.

Guazacapan.—Palacio, D. G. de. Description of the Ancient Provinces of G. . . . , 1576. Squier. Collection. No. I.

Guernsey.—Guernsey. The G. Island Pilot, etc. Lond., 1863.

——— Guernsey. Pilote de l'Ile de Guernesey, etc. Par., 1864.

Guiana.—Dellin, S. Description . . . de la Guyane, etc. Par., 1763.

——— Bancroft, E. An Essay on the Natural History of G., etc.
Lond., 1769.

——— Stedman, J. G. Narrative . . . with an account of the Indians of G., etc. 1796.

——— Montravel, M. L. de Tardy de. Instructions Nautiques pour . . . les Côtes des Guyanes. Par., 1851.

——— Brett, W. H. The Indian Tribes of G., etc. Lond., 1868.

——— Barbot, J. Description of . . . the Province of G., etc. Churchill. Vol. V.

——— Guyana. Eyries. Vol. IX.

——— Ralegh, Sir W. Voyages made for the discovery . . . of G., 1595-6. Hakluyt. Vol. IV.

——— The Discovery of the . . . Empire of G. . . . in 1595 . . . edited . . . by Sir R. H. Schomburgk. 1848. Hakluyt Soc. Pub. Vol. III.

——— Harcourt, R. Relation of a Voyage to G., 1608-11., etc. Purchas. Vol. IV.

——— Leigh, C. Voyage to G. . . . 1604. Purchas. Vol. IV.

——— Sparrey, F. Description of . . . G. . . . 1602. Purchas. Vol. IV.

——— Turner, W. Treatise touching the . . . voyage to G., 1605. Purchas. Vol. IV.

——— Wilson, J. Relation of his returne into England, from Wiapoco, in G., 1606. Purchas. Vol. IV.

——— Of Cumana, G. . . . and of their Religions. Purchas. Vol. V.

——— Keymis, L. Reise nach G., 1596. Voyages and Travels. Allgemeine Historie, etc. Vol. XVI.

——— Raleigh, Sir W. Reise in G., 1595. Voyages and Travels. Allgemeine Historie, etc. Vol. XVI.

——— Bolingbroke, H. Voyage . . . containing a Statistical Account of the Settlements . . . on the . . . Rivers of G., 1799. Voyages and Travels. A Collection, etc. 1805. Vol. X.

———, **British.**—Latrobe, C. J. Negro Education, B. G., etc. 1839.

——— ——— Guiana, British. Papers relative to the Affairs of B. G.
1840.

——— ——— Hancock, J. Observations on . . . B. G., etc.
Lond., 1840.

——— ——— Schomburgk, Sir R. H. Description of B. G., etc. 1840.

——— ——— Millioux, F. Émigration à la Guyane Anglaise.
Par., 1842.

Guiana, British — Guinea.

Guiana, British.—Schomburgk, R. Reisen in B.-G. in 1840-44, etc.
  Leips., **1847, 48.**

——— ——— Dalton, H. G. The History of British G., etc.
  Lond., **1855.**

——— ——— Veness, W. T. El Dorado; or, B. G. as a field for Colonisation.
  Lond., **1867.**

——— ——— Appun, C. F. Unter den Tropen. Wanderungen ... durch Britisch Guyana, etc.
  Jena, **1871.**

——— ——— *See also* Georgetown.

———, **French.** Millroux, F. Guyane Française. Examen et critique, etc.
  Par., **1846.**

——— ——— Französisches G. Voyages and Travels. Allgemeine Historie, etc. Vol. XVI.

———, **Venezuelan.** Class, J. L. Emigration to V. G., etc. **1868.**

——— ——— Guiana, Venezuelan. The Emigrant's Vade-Mecum, or Guide to the "Price Grant" in V. G.
  Lond., **1868.**

Guinea.—Smith, W. A New Voyage to G., etc. *Lond.*, **1745.**

——— Stedman, J. G. Narrative ... with an account of the Negroes of G. **1796.**

——— Rask, R. K. Vejledning til Akra-Sproget paa Kysten Ginea, etc.
  Kobenh., **1828.**

——— Azurara, G. E. de. Chronica do descobrimento ... de Guiné, etc.
  Par., **1841.**

——— Chelmicki, J. C. C. de. Corografia Cabo-Verdiana, ou descripção ... da Provincia das Ilhas de Cabo-Verde e Guiné. *Lisb.*, **1841.**

——— Trentepohl, J. J., and others. Observationes Meteorologicae per annos 1820-34 et 1838-42 in G. factae, etc. *Haunia*, **1845.**

——— Santarem, Viscount de. Rapport sur un Mémoire de M. de Silveira, relativement à la découverte ... de la Guinée, par les Portugais.
  Par., **1846.**

——— The first Voyages of the English to G., etc. Astley. Vol. I.

——— Lok, J. Second Voyage to G. Astley. Vol. I.

——— Portuguese sent to ... East Indies by Land, with ... account of ... G., etc. Astley. Vol. I.

——— Towrson, W. Three voyages to G. ... in 1555-57. Astley. Vol. I.

——— Voyages of R. Rainolds and T. Dassel to ... G. 1591. Astley. Vol. I.

——— Voyage to G. ... in 1553, etc. Astley. Vol. I.

——— Voyages to G. in 1561-66. Astley. Vol. I.

——— Atkins, J. Voyage to G. ... in 1721. Astley. Vol. II.

——— A description of G., etc. Astley. Vol. II.

——— Des Marchais, Chev. Voyage to G. ... in 1725. Astley. Vol. II.

——— Phillips, T. Abstract of a Voyage along the Coast of G. to Whidah ... in 1693. Astley. Vol. II.

Guinea.

Guinea.—Smith, W. Voyage to G. in 1726. ASTLEY. Vol. II.
—— Snelgrave, W. A new account of ... G. ... in 1730. ASTLEY. Vol. II.
—— Villault, Sieur. Abstract of a Voyage to ... G. in 1666. ASTLEY. Vol. II.
—— Voyages ... to G., etc. ASTLEY. Vol. II.
—— Voyages and Travels to G., etc. ASTLEY. Vol. III.
—— Barbot, J. Description of the Coasts of N. and S. G., etc. CHURCHILL. Vol. V.
—— Phillips, Capt. Journal of ... Voyage ... along the Coast of Guiney, etc. CHURCHILL. Vol. VI.
—— Baker, R. Two Voyages to G., 1562-3. HAKLUYT. Vol. II.
—— Fenner, G. Voyage to G. ... 1566. HAKLUYT. Vol. II.
—— Lok, J. Voyage to G., 1554. HAKLUYT. Vol. II.
—— The success of another Voyage to G., at the direction of Sir W. Gerard and others, 1564. HAKLUYT. Vol. II.
—— Towrson, W. Three Voyages to G. ... 1555-57. HAKLUYT. Vol. II.
—— Voyage made to G., at the charges of Sir W. Gerard ... 1562. HAKLUYT. Vol. II.
—— Windam, T. Voyage to G. and Benin, 1553. HAKLUYT. Vol. II.
—— Hawkins, Sir J. Voyages to ... the Coast of G. ... 1562-63. HAKLUYT. Vol. III.
—— Baker, R. Voyage to G., 1563. KERR. Vol. VII.
—— Carlet, D. Voyage to G., 1564. KERR. Vol. VII.
—— Fenner, G. Voyage to G. ... 1566. KERR. Vol. VII.
—— Lok, J. Voyage to G., 1554. KERR. Vol. VII.
—— Notices of an intended Voyage to G., 1561. KERR. Vol. VII.
—— Rutter, W. Voyage to G., 1562. KERR. Vol. VII.
—— Towerson, W. Voyages to G. ... 1555-58. KERR. Vol. VII.
—— Windham, Capt., and Pinteado, A. A. Voyage to G. ... in 1553. KERR. Vol. VII.
—— Voyages sur la Côte de Guinée. LAHARPE, J. Vol. II.
—— Bonnan's Description of the Coast of G. PINKERTON. Vol. XVI.
—— G., a description and historical declaration of the Kingdom of, etc. PURCHAS. Vol. II.
—— The Trading of the Moores into G. and Gago for gold ore, etc. PURCHAS. Vol. II.
—— Discorso d'un gran Capitano di Mare Francese ... supra ... G., etc. RAMUSIO. Vol. III.
—— Atkins, J. Reise nach G. ... 1721. VOYAGES and TRAVELS. Allgemeine Historie, etc. Vol III.
—— Beschreibung von G., etc. VOYAGES and TRAVELS. Allgemeine Historie, etc. Vol. III.
—— Des Marchais, Ritter. Eine Fahrt nach G. ... 1725. VOYAGES and TRAVELS. Allgemeine Historie, etc. Vol. III.

Guinea — Gwalior. 215

Guinea.—PHILLIPS, T. Beschreibung einer Reise längst der Küste von G. . . . 1693. VOYAGES and TRAVELS. Allgemeine Historie, *etc.* Vol. III.

———— Smith, W. Eine Reise nach G., 1726. VOYAGES and TRAVELS. Allgemeine Historie, *etc.* Vol. III.

———— Snelgrave, W. Neue Nachricht . . . von G. . . . 1730. VOYAGES and TRAVELS. Allgemeine Historie, *etc.* Vol. III.

———— Villault, Ritter. Auszug aus einer Reise nach . . . G., 1666. VOYAGES and TRAVELS. Allgemeine Historie, *etc.* Vol. III.

———— Beschreibung von G., fortlaufend. VOYAGES and TRAVELS. Allgemeine Historie, *etc.* Vol. IV.

———— Schiffahrten und Reisen nach G., *etc.* VOYAGES and TRAVELS. Allgemeine Historie, *etc.* Vol. IV.

———— A Description of G. VOYAGES and TRAVELS. The World displayed. Vol. XVII.

————, **Gulf of.** DANIELL, W. F. Sketches of the Medical Topography . . . of the G. of G., *etc.* 1849.

———— ———— CAPELLO, B. Guide pour l'usage des Cartes des Vents et des Courants, du Golfe de G. *Par.*, 1862.

————, **New.**—*See* NEW GUINEA.

Guiney, Guinie.—*See* GUINEA.

Gujarashtra.—*See* GUZERAT.

Gujarát.—*See* GUZERAT.

Gulf Passage.—*See* FLORIDA, GULF OF.

———— **Stream.**—PURDY, J., and FINDLAY, A. G. Colombian Navigator. Vol. II. . . . including the description of the . . . G. S. 1849.

———— ———— Sailing Directory for the . . . G. S., *etc.* 1848.

———— ———— BACHE, A. D. The Tides of the . . . U. S., the G. S., *etc.* *New Hav.*, 1856.

———— ———— Lecture on the G. S., *etc.* 1860.

———— ———— KOHL, J. G. Geschichte des Golfstroms, *etc.* *Bremen*, 1868.

Guntoor.—INDIA. Reports of the . . . effects of the Godavery and Krishna Annicuts, in . . . G., *etc.* *Madras*, 1856.

Gurhwal.—INDIA. Official Reports . . . with a Medical Report on the Mahamurree in G. in 1849-50, *etc.* *Agra*, 1851.

Guyana, Guyana.—*See* GUIANA.

Guzerat.—ALI MOHAMMED KHAN. The Political and Statistical History of Gujarát, *etc.* *Lond.*, 1836.

———— BRIGGS, H. G. The Cities of Gujarashtra, *etc.* *Bombay*, [1850.]

———— BURT, G. Notes on a Journey through . . . Goozerat, *etc.* 1855.

Gwalior.—LLOYD, SIR W. Narrative of a Journey . . . viâ G., *etc.* *Lond.*, 1840.

H.

Habana.—See HAVANA.

Hacha, Rio de la.—See RIO DE LA HACHA.

Hackfall.—RIPON. The Tourist's Companion; being a ... description ... of ... H., etc. *Ripon*, 1828.

Hadhramaut.—See HADRAMAUT.

——— FORSTER, C. Historical Geography of Arabia ... with ... Translations ... of the Hamyaritic Inscriptions recently discovered in H. 1844.

——— PLATZ, W. Ptolemy's Knowledge ... especially of H., etc. 1845.

——— WREDE, A. VON. Reise in H., etc. *Braunschw.*, 1870.

Hæthum.—Forster, J. R. Remarks on the situation of Sciringes-heal and H. KERR. Vol. I.

Hagenskov.—SIMONSEN, VEDEL. Samlinger til H. Slots ... Historie. *Odense*, 1840.

Hal.—See AL.

Haidarabad.—See HYDERABAD.

Hal-ling.—Macaulay, IL. Directions for entering the Harbour of Olinchy, on the W. Side of H., etc. DALRYMPLE, A. Collection of Nautical Memoirs, etc.

Hai-nan.—ROQUETTE, M. DE LA. Note sur l'Ile d' H., etc. *Paris.*

Hainault.—VANDER MAELEN, P. Statistique ... de H., etc. *Brussels*, 1830.

——— ——— Dictionnaire Géographique de la Province de H. *Brux.*, 1833.

Hainaut.—See HAINAULT.

Haïti.—See HAYTI.

Haleb.—See ALEPPO.

Halicarnassus.—ROSS, L. On the Topography of H., etc. *Cumb.*, 1854.

Halifax.—HEAD, G. Forest Scenes ... from H. to the Canadas, etc. 1829.

Halifax.—BAYFIELD, ADMIRAL H. W. Nova Scotia Pilot ... including H. Harbour. 1856.

Halland.—See HALMSTAD.

Halmstad.—TOPOGRAFISKA och Statistiska Uppgifter om H.s Län. *Stockh.*, 1847.

Hamadan.—BUCKINGHAM, J. S. Travels ... from Bagdad ... to H., etc. 1830.

Hamburg.—Browne, E. Voyage ... to Holland, with a Journey ... to H., 1668. HARRIS, J. Vol. II.

Hammerfest.—M'DOUGALL, G. F. Directions ... Including a description of H., etc. 1858.

Hanoeu.—See QUISSAY.

Hannek.—GOTTBERG, E. DE. Des Cataractes ... de H., etc. *Par.*, 1867.

Hanover.—SPITTLER, L. T. Geschichte des Fürstenthums H. ... bis zu Ende des siebzehnten Jahrhunderts, etc. *Hann.*, 1798.
—— WILSON, W. R. Travels in ... H., etc. *Lond.*, 1836.
—— REDEN, BARON F. VON. Das Königreich H. statistisch beschrieben, etc. *Hann.*, 1839.
—— BELOUM. Belgian ... Hanoverian ... Lighthouses, corrected to 1843, 51, 64, 57-59. 1843-59.
—— DUNSTERVILLE, E. The Admiralty List of the ... Hanoverian ... Lights. Corrected to 1860. 1860.
—— Mangourit, M. O. B. Travels in H., 1803-4. VOYAGES and TRAVELS. A Collection, etc. 1805. Vol. III.
—— —— Travels in H., 1803-4. VOYAGES and TRAVELS. A Collection, etc. 1810. Vol. VI.

Han-sur-Lesse.—WAUTERS, A. Guide pittoresque ...'. à la Grotte de H.-s-L. *Brux.*, 1841.

Haouran.—*See* HAURAN.

Haran.—*See* HARRAN.

Harar.—BURTON, R. F. First Footsteps in East Africa; or an Exploration of H. 1856.

Hardanger-Fiord.—SEXE, S. A. Mærker efter en Iistid i Omegnen af H.fjorden. *Christ.*, 1866.

Harran.—BEER, F. Jacob's Flight; or a Pilgrimage to H., etc. *Lond.*, 1865.

Harris, Sound.—OTTER, H. C. and STANTON, W. Western Hebrides ... Sailing directions for the Sound of H. 1859.
—— INSKIP, G. H. Instructions Nautiques sur le Sound de H., etc. *Par.*, 1862.

Harrogate.—RIPON. The Tourist's Companion; being a ... description ... of ... H., etc. *Ripon*, 1828.

Hartwell.—SMYTH, ADMIRAL W. H. Ædes Hartwellianæ: or Notices of the Manor and Mansion of H. 1851.

Hartz Mountains.—GATTERER, C. W. J. Beschreibung des Harzes. *Nuremb.*, 1792.
—— MURCHISON, SIR R. I. and MORRIS, J. On the Palæozoic ... Rocks of the ... H. 1855.

Hastings.—FITTON, W. H. A Geological sketch of the Vicinity of H. 1833.

Hatteras, Cape.—REDFIELD, W. C. Cape Verde and H. Hurricane, of Aug.-Sept., 1853, etc. *New Haven*, U. S., 1854.

Hauran.—MADOX, J. Excursions ... including a visit to ... the H. 1834.
—— PORTER, J. L. Five years in Damascus ... with Travels ... in ... the H. *Lond.*, 1855.
—— —— Greek Inscriptions from ... the H., etc. *Lond.*, 1855.
—— — GRAHAM, C. C. Additional Inscriptions from the Hauran, etc. 1859.
—— — HOGG, J. On Gebel H., etc. *Edinb.*, 1860.

Hausa.—See HOUSSA.
Haute-Éthiopie.—See ABYSSINIA.
Haut Fleuve Blanc.—See NILE, WHITE, UPPER.
Havana.—GAGE, T. Nouvelle Relation des Voyages dans la Nouvelle Espagne . . . et retour . . . jusques à la Havane, etc.
Amst., **1695.**
—— —— Survey of the Spanish West Indies . . . describing H., etc.
1702.
—— HABANA. Balanza Mercantil de la Habana . . . 1837 e 1840.
Hab., **1838-41.**
—— LÖWENSTERN, I. Les États-Unis et la H., etc.   *Par.,* **1842.**
—— VALOIS, A. DE. Mexique, Havane . . . Notes de Voyage.
Par., **[1862.]**
Havannah.—See HAVANA.
Havre.—PARIS. Itinéraire des bateaux à vapeur de Paris au H., etc.   *Par.*
Hawaii.—MORTIMER, G. Observations . . . during a Voyage to . . . Owhyhee, etc.
Lond., **1791.**
—— ELLIS, W. Narrative of a Tour through H., etc.   **1826.**
Hayti.—SAINT-MÉRY, L. E. MOREAU DE. Description topographique de la partie Espagnole de . . . Saint-Domingue, etc.   *Phil.,* **1796.**
—— EDWARDS, B. Historical Survey of the Island of Saint Domingo, etc.
1801.
—— FRANKLIN, J. The present state of H., etc.   **1828.**
—— BOUADIEU, L. DU. Notes sur quelques Ports . . . de H.
Par., **1844.**
—— PURDY, J. and FINDLAY, A. G. Sailing Directory . . . H., etc.
1846.
—— DOMINICAN REPUBLIC, the, and the Emperor Soulouque, etc.
Phil., **1852.**
—— ARDOUIN, B. Études sur l'histoire d'Haïti, etc.   *Par.,* **1853.**
—— Pert, Sir T. and Cabot, S. Voyage to . . . Santo Domingo . . . 1510. HAKLUYT. Vol. III.
—— Newport, C. Voyage to . . . Hispaniola . . . 1591. HAKLUYT. Vol. IV.
—— Columbus, C. First Voyage, in which he discovered . . . Hispaniola, etc. HARRIS, J. Vol. II.
—— Pert, Sir T. and Cabot, S. Voyage to . . . St. Domingo . . . about 1510. KERR. Vol. VI.
—— Beschreibung der Insel Hispaniola, etc. VOYAGES and TRAVELS. Allgemeine Historie, etc. Vol. XIII.
—— Weitere Eroberungen der Castiliane in . . . Hispaniola . . . 1511. VOYAGES and TRAVELS. Allgemeine Historie, etc. Vol. XIII.
—— Niederlassung der Franzosen in . . . Hispaniola . . . 1630-92. VOYAGES and TRAVELS. Allgemeine Historie, etc. Vol. XVII.
Hazareebagh.—MEDLICOTT, H. B. Memorandum on the Wells now being sunk at . . . H. INDIA GEOLOGICAL SURVEY. Records, etc. Vol. II.
—— See also RAMGURH.

Hebrides.—MARTIN, M. A Description of the Western Islands of Scotland, etc. *Lond.*, 1716.
——— FAUJAS SAINT-FOND, B. Voyage . . . aux Îles Hébrides. *Par.*, 1797.
——— ——— Travels in . . . the H. 1799.
——— MACCULLOCH, J. Description of the Western Islands of Scotland, etc. *Edin.*, 1819.
——— GALBRAITH, W. On Trigonometrical Surveying and its application to correct the maps and charts of the H. 1820.
——— MURCHISON, SIR R. I. Supplementary Remarks on the Strata of the Oolitic Series . . . in the H. 1827.
——— SCOTLAND. Scottish Tourist and Itinerary; or a Guide to . . . the Western Islands. *Edin.*, 1834.
——— OTTER, H. C. and STANTON, W. Western or Outer H., etc. 1859.
——— FRICKMANN, M. Instructions . . . 1ᵐ Partie. H., etc. *Par.*, 1869.
——— Martin's Description of the Western Islands. PINKERTON. Vol. III.
——— Saussure, L. A. Necker de. Voyage to the H. . . . 1822. VOYAGES and TRAVELS, New. 1819, etc. Vol. VIII.
——— See also RONA.—SAINT KILDA.

Hedjaz.—BURCKHARDT, J. L. Travels in Arabia . . . comprehending . . . H., etc. 1829.
——— HAMILTON, J. Sinai, the H., and Soudan, etc. 1857.

Heidelberg.—SCHREIBER, A. H. und seine Umgebungen, etc. *Heid.*, 1811.

Hejaz.—*See* HEDJAZ.
Helgoland.—*See* HELIGOLAND.
Heligoland.—WIEDEL, K. W. M. Die Insel Helgoland, etc. *Hamb.*, 1848.
Heliopolis.—*See* BAALBEC.
Helmund.—SEGISTAN ovvero Il Corso del Fiume Hindmend secondo Abu Ishak-el- Farssi-el- Istachri, etc. *Milano*, 1842.
Helvetia.—*See* SWITZERLAND.
Hemisphère Austral.—*See* SOUTH POLE.
He-ong-Kong.—*See* HONG-KONG.
Herat.—*See* HERAUT.
Heraut.—ABBOTT, CAPT. J. Journey from H. to Khiva, etc. 1843.
——— LAL, MOHAN. Travels . . . to . . . H., etc. 1846.
——— Travels of the Ambassadors . . . of Persia from H. to Khanbalek in Kathay, 1419. KERR. Vol. I.

Hereford.—MURCHISON, SIR R. I. The Silurian System, founded on Geological Researches in . . . H., etc. 1839.

Herm.—GUERNSEY. The Guernsey Island Pilot . . . H., etc. *Lond.*, 1863.

Hernosand.—Ehrenmalm, M. A. Travels into W. n. Nordland, etc. PINKERTON. Vol. I.

Herrnhut.—Dresden und die umliegende Gegend bis ... II., etc.
Dresd., **1804.**

Herzegovina.—Abbuthnot, G. II., etc. **1862.**

—— Thoemmel, G. Geschichtliche ... Beschreibung ... der Herzegovina, etc. *Wien*, **1867.**

—— Boursau, A. Géographie générale ... de l'Herzégovina. **1868.**

Hespanha.—See Spain.

Hesse Cassel.—Ludwig, R. Versuch einer geographischen Darstellung von Hessen in der Tertiärzeit. *Darmst.*, **1855.**

—— Geology. Geologische Specialkarte des Grossherzogthums Hessen, etc. *Darmst.*, **1856-60.**

Hhaleb.—See Aleppo.

Hillah.—Mignan, R. Travels ... including a Journey from Bussorah to ... H., etc. **1829.**

Himálá Mountains.—See Himalayas.

Himalayas.—Fraser, J. B. Tour through part of the Snowy Range of the Himálá Mountains, etc. **1820.**

—— Skinner, T. Excursions ... including a Walk over the H. Mountains, etc. **1832.**

—— Archer, Major. Tours in ... the H., etc. **1833.**

—— Vigne, G. T. Travels in ... the H., N. of the Panjab. **1842.**

—— Hoffmeister, W. Travels in Ceylon ... the H., etc.
Edin., **1848.**

—— Hooker, J. D. Notes of a Tour in ... the H., etc.
Lond., **1848.**

—— —— On the Climate and Vegetation of ... the Sikkim H. Mountains. *Lond.*, **1849.**

—— Hodgson, B. H. On the Physical Geography of the H. *Calc.*, **1850.**

—— Fortune, R. Journey to ... China ... with a short notice of the ... Tea Plantations in the H. Mountains. **1852.**

—— Thomson, A. S. Western H. and Tibet, a ... Journey, etc. **1852.**

—— Hooker, J. D. H. n Journal, etc. **1854.**

—— Markham, F. Shooting in the H., etc. *Lond.*, **1854.**

—— Dunlop, R. H. Hunting in the H., etc. *Lond.*, **1860.**

—— Himalayas. A Summer Ramble in the H., etc. *Lond.*, **1860.**

—— Rennie, D. R. Bhotan ... including Sketches of three months' residence in the H., etc. *Lond.*, **1866.**

—— Montgomerie, T. G. Report on the Trans-Himalayan Explorations ... 1865-67. *Dehra Doon*, **1867.**

—— Voyages au travers de l'H. ... Hardwicke, Webb, etc. Eraiga. Vol. XIV.

See also Burenda Pass.—Koonawur.

Himjar.—See Himyar.

Himyar.—Rödiger, E. Versuch über die Himjaritischen Schrift-Monumente, etc.
Halle, **1841.**

Hindmend.—See HELMUND.
Hindoo Koosh.—See HINDU KOOSCH.
Hindostan, Hindoustan.—See INDIA.
Hindu Kooach.—HUGEL, BARON C. VON. Das Kabul- Pecken und die Gebirge zwischen dem H. K. and dem Sutlej].　　　*Wien*, **1850.**
Hinlopen Strait.—NORDENSKIÖLD, A. E. Geografisk och geognostisk Beskrifning öfver . . . H. S.　　　*Stockh.*, **1863.**
Hinsuan.—See JOHANNA.
Hirta.—See SAINT KILDA.
Hispaan.—See ISPAHAN.
Hispaniola.—See HAYTI.
Hobarton.—See HOBART TOWN.
Hobart Town.—SABINE, MAJOR-GEN. E. Observations made at the Observatory at Hobarton . . . 1841-48, etc.　　　**1848-53.**
―――― ABBOTT, F. Results of Meteorological Observations . . . for H. T. . . . Jan. 1841 to Dec. 1860.　　　*Tasm.*, **1861.**
―――― ―――― Results of Twenty-five Years' Meteorological Observations for H. T., etc.　　　*Hob. T.*, **1866.**
Hochelaga.—WARBURTON, E. H. : or England in the New World, **1851.**
―――― Cartier, J. Voyages . . . to H. . . . 1534, 40. HAKLUYT. Vol. III.
―――― La Roche, J. F. de. Voyage . . . to . . . H. . . . 1542. HAKLUYT. Vol. III.
―――― Cartier, J. Voyages . . . to . . . H. . . . 1534-37. KERR. Vol. VI.
―――― Carthier, J. Seconda Relatione della navigatione per lui fatta all Isole di . . . H., etc. RAMUSIO. Vol. III.
Hoemus, Mont.—See BALKAN.
Holland.—GROTIUS, H. H. Grotii de Antiquitate Reipublicæ Batavicæ liber singularis.　　　[*The Hague*, **1610.**]
―――― LAET, J. DE. Belgii Confœderati Respublica: seu . . . H. . . . descriptio.　　　*Lugd. Bat.*, **1630.**
―――― POLLNITZ, C. L., BARON DE. Memoirs . . . in his . . . Travels through . . . H., etc.　　　**1737.**
―――― HANWAY, J. Historical Account . . . with . . . Travels through . . . H.　　　**1753.**
―――― CHACCHARD, CAPT. Geographical . . . description of . . . H., etc.　　　*Lond.*, **1800.**
―――― GERMANY. H. . . . Geographical . . . description of, etc.　　**1800.**
―――― JACOB, W. View of the Agriculture . . . of . . . H., etc. **1820.**
―――― GALIGNANI. Guide through H., etc.　　　*Par.*, **1824.**
―――― ELLIOTT, C. B. Letters from . . . H., etc.　　　**1832.**
―――― MURRAY. Hand-Book for Travellers . . . through H., etc. *Lond.*, **1836.**

Holland.—BELL, R. Wayside Pictures through H. **1849.**
——— DARONDEAU, M. B. Tableau Général des Phares et Fanaux des Côtes de Hollande, etc. *Par.,* **1849.**
——— BELGIUM. The Belgian, Dutch ... Lights. Corrected to 1854, 57-59. **1854-59.**
——— LAMONT, J. Untersuchungen über den Erdmagnetismus in ... H. ... 1858. *Münch.,* **1859.**
——— DUNSTERVILLE, E. The Admiralty List of the ... Dutch ... Lights ... Corrected to 1860. **1860.**
——— Browne, E. Voyage from England to H. ... 1668. HARRIS, J. Vol. II.
——— MISSON, M. Travels through part of H. ... 1687-88. HARRIS, J. Vol. II.
——— Holcroft, T. Travels ... through ... H., etc. VOYAGES and TRAVELS. A Collection, etc. 1805. Vol. II.
——— Carr, Sir J. Tour through H. ... 1806. VOYAGES and TRAVELS. A Collection, etc. 1805. Vol. VIII.
——— ——— Tour through H., 1806. VOYAGES and TRAVELS. A Collection, etc. 1810. Vol. III.
——— The Travels of Mr. Jonas Hanway ... through ... H. 1743. VOYAGES and TRAVELS. The World displayed. Vol. XIV. XV.

Hollandia.—*See* HOLLAND.

Holstein.—STURZ, J. J. Der Nord-und Ostsee-Kanal durch H., Deutschlands Doppelpforte zu seinen Meeren, etc. *Berl.,* **1864.**

Holyhead.—MALLET, R. Account of Experiments made at H. to ascertain the Transit-Velocity of Waves, etc. **1861.**

Holy Land.—*See* PALESTINE.

Ho-nan.—RICHTHOFEN, BARON F. F. VON. Reports on the Provinces of ... H., etc. *Shangh.,* **1870.**

Honduras.—HONDURAS INDIANS, Report ... on the Case of the, etc. **1828.**
——— BAILY, J. Central America ... H., etc. **1850.**
——— SQUIER, E. G. H. Interoceanic Railway. Preliminary Report. *N. Y.,* **1854.**
——— ——— Notes on ... H., etc. *N. Y.,* **1855.**
——— SCHERZER, K. VON. Travels in ... H., etc. **1857.**
——— WELLS, W. V. Explorations and Adventures in H., etc. *N. Y.,* **1857.**
——— SQUIER, E. G. H.; descriptive, historical, etc. *Lond.,* **1870.**

Honduras, Gulf of.—MAUSSION CANDÉ, DE. Notice sur le Golfe du H., etc. *Par.,* **1842.**
——— Parker, A. Voyage to ... the Bay of the H. ... 1576. HAKLUYT. Vol. IV.
——— Newport, C. Voyage to ... the Bay of the H., 1591. HAKLUYT. Vol. IV.
- ——— Shorley, Sir A. Voyage to the Bay of the H. ... 1596. HAKLUYT. Vol. IV.

Hong-Kong.—HONG-KONG. A Letter from H.-K. descriptive of that Colony, etc. 1845.
——— SMITH, BP. G. Narrative of an explanatory Visit to . . . H.-K., etc. 1847.
——— HALL, W. H. and BERNARD, W. D. The Nemesis in China . . . with an account of . . . H.-K. 1846.
——— HONG-KONG. Directions for making the Passage . . . to H.-K. through Sunda Strait, etc. 1857.
——— MARTIN, R. M. Report on H.-K., etc. 1857.
——— SPRYE, R. and R.-H.-F. Aërial Telegraph to H.-K., etc. Lond., 1862.
——— Howel, Mr. Memoir of the Harbour He-ong-K. DALRYMPLE, A. Collection of Nautical Memoirs, etc.
Hooghly.—HOOGHLY. Reports . . . of the Committee appointed to inquire into the State of the . . . H. Calc., 1854.
——— LONGBRIDGE, J. A. The H. and the Mutiny, etc. 1864.
Hookoong Valley.—JENKINS, H. L. Notes on the Burmese Route from Assam to the H. Valley. 1869.
Hoondgoond.—See HOONUGOONDA.
Hoonugoonda.—MARSHALL, T. Statistical Reports on . . . Hoondgoond, etc. Bomb., 1822.
Hor, Mount.—BERTOU, COMTE DE. Le Mont H., etc. Par., 1860.
Horeb.—HABANT, K. Gesta . . . na Horu Oreb, etc. v. Praze, 1854.
——— Mount Sinai, Oreb . . . described out of Breidenbach, etc. PURCHAS. Vol. II.
Hormus.—See ORMUZ.
Hottentot Country.—Kolben. Account of the Country of the H., etc. ASTLEY. Vol. III.
Housa.—See HOUSSA.
Houssa.—SHABEENY, EL HAGE ABD SALAM. Account of Timbuctoo and Hausa Territories, etc. 1820.
——— BAIKIE, W. B. Observations on the Hausa and Fulfúlde languages, etc. 1861.
——— SCHÖN, J. F. Grammar of the Hausa Language. 1862.
Hubertsburg.—DRESDEN und die umliegende Gegend bis . . . H., etc. Drcsd., 1840.
Hudson's Bay.—DOBBS, A. An Account of the Countries adjoining to H. B., etc. Lond., 1744.
——— ——— Remarks upon Capt. Middleton's . . . Voyage for discovering a passage from H. B. to the South Seas, etc. 1744.
——— ELLIS, H. Voyage to H. B. . . . in 1746-47, etc. 1748.
——— HEARNE, S. A Journey from Prince of Wales's Fort in H. B. to the Northern Ocean . . . 1769-72. 1795.
——— M'LEAN, J. Notes of a Twenty-five Years' Service in the H. B. Territory. Lond., 1849.
——— MARTIN, R. M. The H. B. Territories, etc. Lond., 1849.

Hudson's Bay.—RAWLINGS, T. The Confederation of the British North American Provinces . . . including also . . . H. B. Territory, etc.
Lond., 1865.

—— Cents, Capt. W. Geography of H. B. . . . Edited by J. Barrow. 1852. HAKLUYT SOC. PUB. Vol. XII.

—— Middleton, C. Attempts . . . for . . . a passage to the South Seas from H. B. . . . 1725-42. HARRIS, J. Vol. II.

—— Beschreibung der H. und dasiger Wilden, etc. VOYAGES and TRAVELS. Allgemeine Historie, etc. Vol. XVI.

—— McKeevor, T. Voyage to H. B., 1812, etc. VOYAGES and TRAVELS, New. 1819. Vol. II.

—— **Straits.**—Monck, Capt. J. Account of a . . . voyage to H. S., etc. CHURCHILL. Vol. I.

Hud.—FINLAYSON, G. The Mission to . . . H. . . . in 1821-2, etc.
Lond., 1826.

Humboldt Bay.—MÜLLER, J. Die Ha-Bai . . . in Neu-Guinea ethnographisch und physikalisch untersucht, etc. *Berl.*, 1864.

Hu-nan.—RICHTHOFEN, BARON F. VON. Reports on the Provinces of H., etc. *Shangh.*, 1870.

Hungary.—WINDISCH, K. G. v. Geographie des Königreichs Ungarn, etc.
Presburg, 1780-90.

—— KARABINSKY, J. M. Geographisch-Historisches . . . Lexikon von Ungarn. *Presburg*, 1786.

—— TOWNSON, R. Travels in H., etc. 1797.

—— SCHWARTNER, M. VON. Statistik des Königreichs Ungarn.
Ofen, 1809-11.

—— DECKER, W. G. E. Journal einer Reise durch Ungarn, etc.
Freyb., 1815.

—— NÉMETH, L. v. Reisen durch Ungern, etc. *Pesth*, 1825.

—— ELEK, P. G. A'Moldvai Magyar Telepekröl. *Buddn*, 1838.

—— KOHL, J. G. Austria . . . H., etc. *Lond.*, 1844.

—— RÓNAY, J. Jellemisme, vagy az . . . Magyar . . . Nemzet . . . Jellemzése, etc. *Györött*, 1847.

—— SPENCER, E. Travels in European Turkey . . . with . . . a homeward Tour through H., etc. 1851.

—— ARNOLD, I. A Középkori Emlékszerü Epitészet Magyarországon.
Pesten, 1852.

—— SZABAD, E. H., Past and Present, etc. *Edin.*, 1854.

—— DEMIDOFF, A. DE. Travels in . . . H. . . . during 1837. 1855.

—— PAGET, J. H. and Transylvania, etc. 1855.

—— CZENUKRY, A. Az Altaji Népek Osvallása tekintettel a Magyar Osvallásra. *Pest*, 1858.

—— KNAUZ, N. Az Orszagos Tanács és Országgyülések Történele, 1445-52. *Pest*, 1859.

—— MIKO IMRE, COUNT. Erdély Különválása Magyarországtol.
Budan, 1860.

—— SZLEMENICS, P. Törvényeink Története a Dicső Ausztriai Ház Országlása alatt 1740-1848. *Budán*, 1860.

Hungary.—ANSTED, D. T. A Short Trip in H. . . . in . . . 1862.
Lond., 1863.
——— ARNOLD, J. A Középkori Szobrászat Magyarországon.
Pesten, 1863.
——— Merin's Journey to the Mines in H. CHURCHILL. Vol. IV.
——— Edmund and Edward, the Sonnes of King Edmund Ironside. Voyage into A., 1017. HAKLUYT. Vol. I.
——— Voyage of a certaine Englishman . . . into . . . H., 1243. HAKLUYT. Vol. I.
——— Browne, E. Description of . . . H., *etc.* HARRIS, J. Vol. II.
——— ——— Travels through H. into Thessaly, *etc.* HARRIS, J. Vol. II.
——— Dutens, J. V. Travels in Upper and Lower H. . . . in 1806. PELHAM. Vol. II.
——— Keysler, John George. Travels through . . . H. 1729. VOYAGES and TRAVELS. The World displayed. Vol. XIX.
———, **Lower.** BRIGHT, R. Travels . . . through L. H., *etc.*
Edinb., 1818.
HUNS.—SAINT-MARTIN, V. DE. Les H. Blancs, *etc.* *Par.,* 1849.
Hunter, River.—DANGAR, H. Index . . . to Map of the Conntry bordering upon the . . . H., *etc.* 1828.
Hu-pih.—RICHTHOFEN, BARON F. F. VON. Reports on the Provinces of . . . H., *etc.* *Shangh.,* 1870.
Huron.—CANADA, UPPER.—Remarks . . . containing a description of . . . H. . . . Territory. *Quebec,* 1861.
———, **Lake.**—HEAD, G. Forest Scenes . . . on the Borders of Lakes H. and Simcoe. 1829.
——— ——— LOGAN, SIR W. E. Plans of various Lakes and Rivers between Lake H. and the . . . Ottawa, *etc.* *Toronto,* 1857.
Hyapura, River.—See JAPURA.
Hyderabad.—BURGESS, J. Memorandum . . . with lists of the Rock-Excavations, Temples, &c. in . . . Haidarabad. *Bombay,* 1870.
Hydra.—CASTELLAN, A. L. Lettres sur la Morée . . . H., *etc.*
Par., 1808.
Hyères.—Fischer, C. A. Travels to H. . . . 1806. VOYAGES and TRAVELS. A Collection, *etc.* 1805. Vol. V.
Hyrcania.—REINAUD, M. Relations Politiques et Commerciales de l'Empire Romain avec . . . (l'Hyrcanie) pendant les cinq premiers siècles, *etc.* *Par.,* 1863.
——— Cartwright, J. The Preacher's Travels . . . through . . . H., *etc.* CHURCHILL. Vol. VII.
Hyurus, River.—See JAPURA.

I.

Icaria.—Zeno, N. and A. Voyage to the yles of . . . I . . . 1380. HAKLUYT. Vol. III.
Iceland.—GUDBRANDUS THORLACIUS, BISHOP OF HOLEN. Letter concerning the ancient state of Island, *etc.*

Q

Iceland.

Iceland.—ANDERSON, J. Nachrichten von Island, *etc.* *Hamb.*, 1746.
——— ——— Description . . . de l'Islande. *Par.*, 1764.
——— KERGUELEN TRÉMAREC, M. DE. Relation d'une Voyage . . . aux Côtes d'Islande, *etc.* *Par.*, 1771.
——— VON TROIL, U. Letters on I., *etc.* *Lond.*, 1783.
——— MACKENZIE, SIR G. S. Travels in I. during 1810. *Edin.*, 1811.
——— ——— Travels in I. during 1810. *Edin.*, 1812.
——— HOOKER, SIR W. J. Journal of a Tour in I. in 1809. 1813.
——— HENDERSON, E. Journal of a Residence in I. . . . 1814-15.
Edin., 1818.
——— PAULY, F. Topographie von Dänemark einschliesslich Islands, *etc.*
Altona, 1828.
——— BJÖRNER, GUNNLAUGI FILIUS. De mensura et delineatione Islandiæ Interioris, *etc.* *In Monast. Voleyensi*, 1834.
——— BARROW, J. Visit to I., *etc.* 1835.
——— MARSH, G. P. Compendious Grammar of the Old-Northern or Ice Language, *etc.* *Burlington, U. S.*, 1838.
——— GAIMARD, P. Voyage en Islande . . . pendant 1835 et 1836, *etc.*
Par., 1838-40.
——— DILLON, HON. A. A Winter in I., *etc.* 1840.
——— SCHLEISNER, P. A. Island undersögt fra et lægevidenskabeligt Synspunkt. *Copenh.*, 1849.
——— PFEIFFER, I. Journey to I., *etc.* 1852.
——— MILES, P. Nordurfari; or Rambles in I. 1854.
——— CHAMBERS, R. Tracings of I., *etc.* *Lond. Edin.*, 1856.
——— DUFFERIN, LORD. Letters . . . being an Account of . . . I., *etc.*
1857.
——— DAYMAN, J. Deep-Sea Soundings . . . between I. and Newfoundland, *etc.* 1858.
——— HOGG, J. On the History of I., *etc.* 1859.
——— STREVE, D. Beskrivelse over dans φ Islandia, *etc.* *Kjöb.*, 1859.
——— THOMSEN, G. The Northmen in I., *etc.* 1859.
——— FORBES, C. S. I.; its Volcanoes, *etc.* 1860.
——— IRMINGER, C. Strømninger og Iisdrift ved Island. *Kjøb.*, 1861.
——— , LINDSAY, W. L. The Flora of I. *Edin.*, 1861.
——— LOKOMAN, W. Suggestions for the Exploration of I. 1861.
——— WINKLER, G. G. Island, seine Bewohner, *etc.* *Braunsch.*, 1861.
——— MAS, M. BARLATIER DE. Instructions nautiques sur les Côtes d'Islande, *etc.* *Par.*, 1862.
——— SYMINGTON. A. J. Pen and Pencil Sketches of . . . I., *etc.*
1862.
——— BARING-GOULD, S. L, *etc.* 1863.
——— IRMINGER, C. Notice sur les Pèches . . . de l'Islande, *etc.*
Par., 1863.
——— THOYON, M. Renseignements sur quelques Mouillages de la Côte d'Islande, *etc.* *Par.*, 1865.

Iceland.—Paijkull, C. W. Bidrag till Kännedomen om Islands Bergabyggnad. *Stockh.*, 1867.
——— Shepherd, C. W. The N.-W. Peninsula of I.: being the Journal of a Tour, *etc.* *Lond.*, 1867.
——— Mohn, H. Institut Météorologique de Norvège. Température de la Mer entre l'Islande, l'Ecosse, *etc.* *Christ.*, 1870.
——— La Peyrère. Account of I., *etc.* Churchill. Vol. II.
——— Henderson, E. Voyage on Islands, 1814-15. Eyries. Vol. VII.
——— Hooker. Voyage en Islande, 1809. Eyries. Vol. VII.
——— Arthur, King. Voyage to Island . . . 517. Hakluyt. Vol. I.
——— A briefe commentarie of the true state of Island. Hakluyt. Vol. I.
——— Malgo, King. Voyage to Island . . . 580. Hakluyt. Vol. I.
——— Voyage . . . of . . . the ships *Sunshine* and *Northstarre* . . . to discover a passage betweene Groenland and Iseland, 1587. Hakluyt. Vol. III.
——— Zeno, N. and A. Voyage to . . . Island . . . 1380. Hakluyt. Vol. III.
——— A Voyage . . . containing an Account of . . . I., *etc.* Harris, J. Vol. II.
——— Discovery of I. by the Norwegians in the ninth century. Kerr. Vol. I.
——— Islands. Laharpe, J. Vol. XVI.
——— Von Troil's Letters on I. Pinkerton. Vol. I.
——— Blefkens, D. Voyages and History of Island . . . 1563. Purchas. Vol. III.
——— Iver Boty. Treatise of the Course from Island to Groneland, 1608. Purchas. Vol. III.
——— Jonas, A. Chrymogœa or History of I., 1609. Purchas. Vol. III.
——— Nicolo, M. M. and Zeni, A. Discoveries in I. . . . 1380. Purchas. Vol. III.
——— Zeno, N. and A. Dello scoprimento dell' Isola . . . Eslanda, *etc.* Ramusio. Vol. II.
——— Besondere Geschichte von Island. Voyages and Travels. Allgemeine Historie, *etc.* Vol. XIX.
——— Olafsen and Povelsen. Travels in I., 1800-01. Voyages and Travels. A Collection, *etc.* 1805. Vol. II.

Ida, Mount.—Tozer, H. F. Researches . . . Including Visits to Mounts I., *etc.* *Lond.*, 1869.
——— ——— Hunt, Dr. Journey . . . Ascent to the Summit of I. . . . 1799. Walpole, R. Memoirs, *etc.*

Idumæa.—*See* Edom.
Ieso.—*See* Jesso.
Iesd.—*See* Yezd.
Ile Maurice.—*See* Mauritius.
Iles Æoliennes.—*See* Lipari Islands.

Îles de la Mer des Indes — India.

Îles de la Mer des Indes.—*See* ARCHIPELAGO, INDIAN.
Îles de l'Ouest.—*See* HEBRIDES.
Îles Lucayes.—*See* BAHAMA ISLANDS.
Illinois.—BRADBURY, J. Travels in . . . I., *etc.* *Liver.,* 1817.
——— PECK, J. M. Guide for Emigrants to . . . I., *etc.* *Bost.,* 1836.
——— ——— Gazetteer of I., *etc.* *Phil.,* 1837.
——— GRAHAM, J. D. Report of the Harbours, &c. in . . . I., *etc.*
 Wash., 1857.
——— DANA, J. D. On . . . Fossil Insects from the Carboniferous Formation in I., *etc.* *New Hav.,* 1863-64.
Illyria.—TAFEL, T. L. F. De Via Militari Romanorum Egnatia, qua Illyricum Macedoniam et Thraciam jungebantur, *etc.* *Tubingæ,* 1842.
——— LEAR, E. Journal of a Landscape Painter in . . . I., *etc.* 1852.
Imerethi.—*See* IMERITIA.
Imeritia.—SPENCER, E. Travels . . . including a Tour through I., *etc.*
 1838.
Imiritia.—*See* IMERITIA.
In-Câlah.—*See* INSALAH.
India.—RITTER, C. Der Elephant Indiens, *etc.*
——— RITTER, C. Die Stupa's oder die Architektonischen Denkmale an der grossen Königstrasse zwischen Indien, Persien, *etc.* *Berlin.*
——— RITTER, C. Indische Feigenbaum, Asvattha, *etc.* *Berlin.*
——— TAVERNIER, J. B. Remarks and Observations in his Travels through the Indies, *etc.*
——— TRAMEZZINO, M. Diversi avisi particolari dall' India di Portogallo ricevuti, dall' anno 1551 fino al 1558, *etc.*
——— WYLD, J. Index to Map of I., *etc.*
——— MARTYR, P. De rebus Oceanicis . . . Item de rebus . . . Indicis . . . opuscula. *Coloniæ,* 1574.
——— MAFFEUS, J. P. Historiarum Indicarum libri XVI., *etc.*
 Florent., 1588.
——— IARRIC, P. DU. Thesaurus Rerum Indicarum, *etc.*
 Col. Agripp., 1615.
——— DAPPER. Asia . . . en een groot gedeelte van Indien, *etc.*
 Amst., 1672.
——— VALLE, P. DELLA. Viaggi . . . Parte terza L' I., *etc.*
 Venetia, 1681.
——— STRUYS, J. Les Voyages de, . . . aux Indes, *etc.* *Lyon,* 1682.
——— THEVENOT, M. DE. Troisième partie des Voyages de, contenant la relation de l'Indostan, *etc.* *Par.,* 1684.
——— ARRIAN. Expeditionis Alexandri, et historia Indica, *etc.*
 Lugd. Bat., 1704.
——— TELLEZ, B. Travels . . . Travels of P. Teixeira from I. to Italy, *etc.* 1710.
——— JESUITS, Travels of several . . . into . . . I., *etc.* 1714.

India.

India.—RENAUDOT, E. Ancient Accounts of I. and China . . . in the 9th century, etc. Lond., 1733.
— D'ANVILLE, J. B. BOURGUIGNON. Éclaircissemens géographiques sur la Carte de l'Inde. Par., 1753.
— LA-CROZE, V. Histoire du Christianisme des Indes. La Haye, 1757.
— FERISHTA, M. C. The History of Hindostan, etc. Lond., 1770.
— SCRAFTON, L. Reflections on the Government of Indostan, etc. Lond., 1770.
— IVES, E. Voyage . . . to I. in 1754, etc. 1773.
— OEXMELIN, A. O. Histoire des Aventuriers Flibustiers qui se sont signalés dans les Indes. Lyon, 1774.
— CORYAT, T. Crudities . . . Letters from I., etc. 1776.
— LETTRES édifiantes et curieuses, etc. Vol. 10-16, 25. Indes. Par., 1780-83.
— RAYNAL, G. T. Histoire . . . des Européens dans les deux Indes. Genève, 1781.
— RENNELL, J. Memoir of a Map of Hindoostan, etc. 1785.
— MARSDEN, W. On the Chronology of the Hindoos. 1790.
— MAURICE, T. The History of Hindostan, etc. 1790.
— RENNELL, J. Memoir of a Map of Hindoostan, etc. 1793.
— TAYLOR, J. Travels . . . to I., in 1789, etc. 1799.
— MAURICE, T. I. n Antiquities, etc. Lond., 1806-1800.
— JOHNSON, J. The Oriental Voyager . . . a Voyage to I., etc. Lond., 1807.
— CAMPBELL, D. Narrative . . . comprising the occurrences of Four Years in an Overland Journey to I. 1808.
— VALENTIA, VISCOUNT. Voyages and Travels to I. . . . 1802-6. 1811.
— HEYNE, B. Tracts . . . on I., etc. 1814.
— ELPHINSTONE, HON. M. Account of . . . Caubul, and its Dependencies in . . . I., etc. 1815.
— DUBOIS, J. A. Description of . . . the People of I., etc. 1817.
— HAMILTON, W. Geographical . . . description of Hindostan, etc. 1820.
— INDIA. Fifteen Years in I., etc. 1823.
— —— An Historical Sketch of the Princes of I., etc. Edin., Lond., 1823.
— PRINSEP, H. T. History of the Political and Military Transactions in I. . . . 1813-1823, etc. Lond., 1825.
— CATROU, F. History of the Mogul Dynasty in I. . . . 1399-1657, etc. Lond., 1826.
— MALCOLM, SIR J. Political History of I. from 1784 to 1823. 1826.
— ALEXANDER, SIR J. E. Travels from I. to England, etc. 1827.
— KEPPEL, HON. G. Personal Narrative of a Journey from I. to England . . . 1824. 1827.
— INDIA. Slavery in I. Abstracts of . . . Correspondence, etc. 1828.

India.

India.—HEBER, BISHOP. Narrative of a Journey through the Upper Provinces of I., etc. 1828.
—— INDIA AND CHINA, Papers relating to the Trade with, etc. 1829.
—— ELWOOD, MRS. COL. Journey Overland . . . to I. 1830.
—— PRINSEP, G. A. An Account of . . . Steam Navigation in British I. *Calc.*, 1830.
—— JOHNSTON, J. H. Précis of Reports . . . on the Navigation of the Rivers of I. by Steam-Vessels, etc. *Lond.*, 1831.
—— SKINNER, T. Excursions in I., etc. 1832.
—— STOCQUELER, J. H. Fifteen Months' Pilgrimage . . . in a Journey from I. to England, etc. 1832.
—— BERGHAUS, H. Asia . . . Memoir zur Erklärung . . . der reduzirten Karte von Hinterindien, etc. *Gotha*, 1832-35.
—— ARCHER, MAJOR. Tours in Upper I., etc. 1833.
—— ELLIOTT, R. Views in the East; comprising I., etc. 1833.
—— JACQUEMONT, V. Correspondance . . . pendant son Voyage dans l'Inde, etc. *Par.*, 1833.
—— NEUMANN, C. F. Pilgerfahrten Buddhistischer Priester von China nach Indien. *Leip.*, 1833.
—— BURNES, SIR A. Travels . . . from I. to Cabool, etc. 1834.
—— FORBES, J. Oriental Memoirs: a Narrative of Seventeen Years' Residence in I., etc. *Lond.*, 1834.
—— INDIA. Report . . . on Steam Navigation to I., etc. 1834.
—— JERVIS, T. B. Expediency of establishing the Meteorological and Monetary Systems throughout I., on a scientific . . . basis, etc. *Bomb.*, 1834.
—— PEMBERTON, R. B. Report on the E. n frontier of British I., etc. *Calc.*, 1835.
—— EICHHOFF, F. G. Parallèle des Langues de l'Europe et de l'Inde, etc. *Par.*, 1836.
—— HORSBURGH, J. I. Directory, etc. 1836.
—— WELLESLEY, MARQUIS. Despatches, Minutes, and Correspondence of, during his administration in I. 1836-7.
—— GRINDLAY, M. View of the present state of the question as to Steam-Communication with I., etc. 1837.
—— HARKNESS, H. Ancient and Modern Alphabets of the popular Hindu languages of the S. Peninsula of I. 1837.
—— ROBERTS, E. Scenes and Characteristics of Hindostan, etc. 1837.
—— THUGS. Illustrations of the history and practices of the Thugs . . . of I., etc. *Lond.*, 1837.
—— THUILLIER, H. L. General Report on the Topographical Surveys of I. . . . 1868-69. *Lond.*, 1837.
—— WELLINGTON, DUKE OF. Despatches, during his . . . Campaigns in I., etc. 1837-39.
—— GAMBA, V. da. Roteiro da viagem que em descobrimento da I. . . . fez Dom V. da G. em 1497. *Porto*, 1838.

India.—Lassen, C. Zur Geschichte der Griechischen und Indoskythischen Könige in ... Indien. *Bonn*, 1838.
—— Ritter, C. Stupa's (Topes) oder die Architectonischen Denkmale an der Indo-Baktrischen Königstrasse, etc. *Berl.*, 1838.
—— Wiss, H. Analysis of One Hundred Voyages to and from I., etc. 1838.
—— Royle, J. F. Essay on the productive resources of I. 1840.
—— Ternaux-Compans, H. De la Position des Anglais aux Indes, etc. *Par.*, 1840.
—— Thornton, E. Chapters of the Modern History of British I. 1840.
—— Mill, J. History of British I., etc. 1840-48.
—— India. Handbook for I., etc. 1841.
—— Moorcroft and Trebeck. Travels in the Himalayan Provinces of Hindustan, 1819 to 1825. 1841.
—— Parbury, G. Hand-Book for I. and Egypt, etc. *Lond.*, 1841.
—— Thornton, E. History of the British Empire in I. 1841-45.
—— Castro, J. de. Primeiro Roteiro da Costa da I. ... 1538-39. *Porto*, 1843.
—— Burnouf, E. M. Burnouf on the History of Buddhism in I. [A Review.] (1844.)
—— Fontanier, V. Voyage dans l'Inde, etc. *Par.*, 1844.
—— Galloway, J. A. Communication with I., etc. 1844.
—— Sleeman, Sir W. H. Rambles and Recollections of an Indian Official. 1844.
—— Warren, Comte E. de. L'Inde Anglaise en 1843, etc. [A Review.] *Par.*, 1844.
—— Reinaud, M. Relation des Voyages faits par les Arabes et les Persans dans l'Inde ... dans le IX° siècle. 1845.
—— Von Orlich, L. Travels in I., etc. 1845.
—— Santarem, Viscount de. Sur la véritable date des Instructions données à un des premiers Capitaines qui sont allés dans l'Inde, après Cabral. *Par.*, 1846.
—— Shahamet Ali. The Sikhs and Afghans in connection with I. and Persia, etc. 1847.
—— Hoffmeister, W. Travels in Ceylon and Continental I., etc. *Edin.*, 1848.
—— Hooker, J. D. Notes of a Tour in the Plains of I., etc. *Lond.*, 1848.
—— Bourne, J. I. River Navigation, etc. 1849.
—— Reinaud, M. Mémoire Géographique ... sur l'Inde antérieurement au milieu du XI°. siècle, etc. *Par.*, 1849.
—— Sykes, W. H. Discussion of Meteorological Observations taken in I. at various heights, etc. 1850.
—— Egypt. The Present Crisis in Egypt, in relation to our Overland Communication with I. 1851.
—— India. First Report ... on Steam Communications with I., etc. *Lond.*, 1851.

India.

India.—Soares, J. P. C. Bosquejo das Possessões Portuguezas no . . . I., etc.   *Lisboa,* 1851.
—— Soltykoff, Prince A. Voyages dans l'Inde, *etc.*   *Par.,* 1851.
—— Buist, G. Index to Books and Papers on . . . I.   *Bomb.,* 1852.
—— Falliatti, J. Zur Statistik des Flächenraums und der Volkszahl von Britisch-Indien.   *Tüb.,* 1852.
—— India. The Results of Missionary Labour in I.   *Lond.,* 1852.
—— Perry, Sir E. On the Geographical Distribution of the principal Languages of I., *etc.*   1853.
—— Capper, J. The three Presidencies of I., *etc.*   *Lond.,* 1853.
—— Corsetjee, M. A few passing Ideas for the benefit of I., *etc.*   *Bomb.,* 1853.
—— Dickinson, J. I.; its Government under a Bureaucracy.   1853.
—— Hiouen-Thsang. Histoire de . . . ses Voyages dans l'Inde, depuis l'an 629 jusqu'en 645, *etc.*   *Par.,* 1853.
—— India. Statistical Papers relating to I.   1853.
—— Power, W. T. Recollections . . . including Peregrinations in . . . I., *etc.*   *Lond.,* 1853.
—— Prinsep, H. T. The I. Question in 1853.   *Lond.,* 1853.
—— Schonberg, Baron E. von. Travels in I., *etc.*   1853.
—— Thompson, J. B. The Euphrates Valley Route to I.   1853.
—— India. Selections from the Records of the Government of I., *etc.*   *Calc.,* 1853, *etc.*
—— Grant, C. W. Indian Irrigation, *etc.*   1854.
—— Thornton, E. A Gazetteer of the Territories under the Government of the E. I. Company, and of the Native States . . . of I.   *Lond.,* 1854.
—— Allen, W. The Dead Sea, a new route for I.   1855.
—— Hooker, J. D., and Thomson, T. Introductory Essay to the Flora Indica, *etc.*   *Lond.,* 1855.
—— Knighton, W. Tropical Sketches; or Reminiscences of an I. n Journalist.   1855.
—— Perry, Sir E. A Bird's-Eye View of I., *etc.*   1855.
—— Taylor, H. Visit to I. . . . in 1853.   1855.
—— Andrew, W. P. The Scinde Railway and its relations to the routes to India.   1856.
—— Euphrates Valley Route to I., *etc.*   1856.
—— Speir, Mrs. Life in Ancient I.   1856.
—— Hommaire, J. Instructions Nautiques sur les Mers de l'Inde, *etc.*   *Par.,* 1856-60.
—— Andrew, W. P. Memoir on the Euphrates Valley Route to I., *etc.*   1857.
—— Balfour, E. Cyclopædia of I., *etc.*   *Madras,* 1857.
—— Clarke, H. Colonization . . . in our Indian Empire.   1857.
—— Elphinstone, Hon. M. History of I., *etc.*   1857.

India.—FALKLAND, VISCOUNTESS. Chow-Chow; being selections from a Journal kept in I., etc. 1857.
——— MACFARLANE, C. History of British I., etc. 1857.
——— MARTINEAU, H. British Rule in I., etc. 1857.
——— WEBER, A. Indische Skizzen, etc. Berl., 1857.
——— IRVING, B. A. The Commerce of I., etc. 1858.
——— JOCHMUS, A. Memorandum on I., etc. Lond., 1858.
——— LUDLOW, J. M. British I., its Races, etc. Camb., 1858.
——— MILLS, A. I. In 1858. etc. 1858.
——— MUNDY, G. C. Pen and pencil Sketches in I., etc. 1858.
——— SAINT-MARTIN, V. DE. Étude sur la Géographie Grecque et Latine de l'Inde, etc. Par., 1858.
——— ——— ——— Mémoire analytique sur la Carte . . . de l'Inde construite . . . pour les Voyages de Hionen-Thsang, 020-645. Par., 1858.
——— WINTER, C. T. Six Months in British Burmah; or, I. beyond the Ganges in 1857. [Lond.] 1858.
——— CORREA, G. Lendas da I., etc. Lisb., 1858-63.
——— CLARKE, H. On the Organization of the Army of I., etc. 1859.
——— REINAUD, M. Question Scientifique et personnelle, au sujet des dernières découvertes sur . . . l'Inde. Par., 1859.
——— INDIA. Memoirs of the Geological Survey of I.; under the direction of T. Oldham. Calcutta, 1859-64.
——— ATKINSON, T. W. Travels . . . on the confines of I., etc. 1860.
——— BADDELEY, P. F. H. Whirlwinds . . . of I., etc. 1860.
——— ORME, R. A. History of the Military Transactions of the British Nation in Indostan, from . . . MDCCXLV., etc. Madras, 1861.
——— WAUGH, SIR A. S. Report on the Survey of I. for the Three Years ending 1858-59. 1861.
——— SCHLAGINTWEIT, H., A., and R. DE. Results of a Scientific Mission to I. . . . between . . . 1854 and 1858, etc. Leipz. and Lond., 1861-63.
——— INDIA. Palæontologia Indica, etc. Calc., 1861-64.
——— BALFOUR, E. The Timber trees . . . of I., etc. Madras, 1862.
——— MARKHAM, C. R. Travels in . . . I., etc. Lond., 1862.
——— WATSON, J. F. Classified . . . Catalogue of the I. n Department in the International Exhibition, 1862. 1862.
——— REINAUD, M. Relations Politiques et Commerciales de l'Empire Romain avec . . . (l'Inde) pendant les cinq premiers siècles, etc. Par., 1863.
——— SCHLAGINTWEIT, E. Buddhism in Tibet. . . With an account of the Buddhist Systems . . . in I. Leipz., 1863.
——— WALKER, J. T. Report of the Operations of the Great Trigonometrical Survey of I., 1862-63. Dehra Doon, 1863.
——— HORSBURGH, J. Instructions Nautiques. Traversées d'Europe aux différentes parties de l'Inde, etc. Par., 1864.
——— INDIA. Early Travels in I., etc. Calc., 1864.

India.

India.—INDIA. Report of the Geological Survey of I., etc. *Calc.*, **1864.**
—— —— Report on the Survey of I., by Sir A. Scott Waugh. **1864.**
—— CAMERON, J. Our Tropical Possessions in Malayan I., etc.
Lond., **1865.**
—— INDIA GEOLOGICAL SURVEY. Annual Report . . . Twelfth year, 1865-67. *Calc.*, **1866-68.**
—— STREET'S I.n and Colonial Mercantile Directory for 1867-8.
Lond., **1867.**
—— DUNCAN, G. Geography of I., etc. *Madras*, **1868.**
—— FERGUSSON, J. Tree and Serpent Worship . . . in I., etc.
Lond., **1868.**
—— HUNTER, W. W. A Comparative Dictionary of the (Non-Aryan) languages of I. and High Asia, etc. *Lond.*, **1868.**
—— INDIA. Report of the Ethnological Committee on Papers laid before them, etc. *Nagpore*, **1868.**
—— WALKER, J. T. General Report on the Operations of the Great Trigonometrical Survey of I., during 1867-69. *Dehra Doon*, **1868-69.**
—— GONVILLE, CAPITAINE DE. Compagnó du Navire l'Espoir . . . 1503-1505. Relation . . . du voyage . . . ès nouvelles terres des Indes, etc. *Par.*, **1869.**
—— INDIA. Annals of I.n Administration in . . . 1867-68, etc.
Seramp., **1869.**
—— —— East I. Maps and Statistics, etc. **1869.**
—— —— East I. Progress and Condition, etc., 1867-68. **1869.**
—— —— The projected Sub-Marine Telegraph Cable to L . . . considered, etc. *Lond.*, **1869.**
—— TRENCH, F. The Russo-Indian Question historically . . . considered, etc. *Lond.*, **1869.**
—— WALKER, J. T. General Report on the Operations of the Great Trigonometrical Survey of I., during 1868-69. *Dehra Doon*, **1869.**
—— CATALOGUES. A Catalogue of Maps of the British Possessions in I., etc. *Lond.*, **1870.**
—— FAYRER, J. H.R.H. the Duke of Edinburgh in I. *Calc.*, **1870.**
—— TAYLOR, A. D. On the Harbours of I. *Liverpool*, **1870.**
—— Account of the Portuguese Transactions in I. from 1516-21, etc. ASTLEY. Vol. I.
—— V. de Gama's Voyage to I. . . . 1497. ASTLEY. Vol. I.
—— Voyage of P. A. Cabral in 1500 to I. ASTLEY. Vol. I.
—— Voyages of the Portuguese in I., from 1503-7, etc. ASTLEY. Vol. I.
—— Voyage of Soleymán Bashá, from Suez to I. . . . 1530. ASTLEY. Vol. I.
—— Corverte, It. True . . . Report of an Englishman . . . to which is prefixed an account of I. Proper. CHURCHILL. Vol. VIII.
—— A Fragment on the Indian Trade, written in 1791. DALRYMPLE, A. Tracts, from 1764 to 1808. Vol. II.
—— —— Hindoostan. EYRIÈS. Vol. XIII.

India. 235

India.—Voyages . . . aux sources des rivières de l'Hindoustan. Hardwicke, Webb, etc. EYRIES. Vol. XIV.

——— Mandevil, Sir J. Voyage . . . to I. . . . 1322-1355. HAKLUYT. Vol. II.

——— Odoricus, Frier B. Voyage to . . . I. . . . about 1325. HAKLUYT. Vol. II.

——— SIGHELMUS, Bishop of Sbirburne. Memorable Voyage . . . unto S. Thomas of I., 883. HAKLUYT. Vol. II.

——— Rundall, T. Narratives of Voyages . . . in search of a passage to Cathay and I., 1496 to 1631, etc. HAKLUYT Soc. PUB. Vol. V.

——— I. in the Fifteenth Century . . . a collection of Narratives . . . Edited . . . by R. H. Major, 1857. HAKLUYT Soc. PUB. Vol. XXII.

——— Varthema, L. di. Travels in . . . I. . . . 1503 to 1508 . . . Edited . . . by G. P. Badger. 1863. HAKLUYT Soc. PUB. Vol. XXXII.

——— An Account of the descriptions left us by the Ancients of the E. and N. parts of the Indies, etc. HARRIS, J. Vol. I.

——— An Account of the Religion, Government . . . and Manners of the Indians, etc. HARRIS, J. Vol. I.

——— An Account of the several passages to the Indies . . . that have been attempted . . . by the Ancients. HARRIS, J. Vol. I.

——— An Account of the Travels of two Mahommedans through I. . . . in the ninth Century, etc. HARRIS, J. Vol. I.

——— History of the Empire of the Great Mogul, etc. HARRIS, J. Vol. I.

——— The History of I. in the earliest Ages. HARRIS, J. Vol. I.

——— Mandelsloe, J. A. de. The remaining Voyages through the Indies, etc. HARRIS, J. Vol. I.

——— Remarks . . . made in his passage from . . . Persia through . . . the Indies, 1638. HARRIS, J. Vol. I.

——— Of the Indian Commerce under the Persian Empire. HARRIS J. Vol. I.

——— TAVERNIER, J. D. An Account of the different Routes to all the great Cities . . . in the Indies. HARRIS, J. Vol. I.

——— Sigbelm. Voyage to I., in the reign of Alfred. KERR. Vol. I.

——— Travels of Two Mahometans into I. . . . in the ninth century. KERR. Vol. I.

——— Castaneda, H. L. de. History of the discovery and conquest of I. by the Portuguese, 1497-1505. KERR. Vol. II.

——— Letters from Lisbon in the beginning of the sixteenth century, respecting their recent discovery of the Route by Sea to I., etc. KERR. Vol. II.

——— Account of . . . I. at the beginning of the Sixteenth Century, etc. KERR. Vol. VI.

——— Almeyda, F. de. Voyage from Lisbon to I., etc. KERR. Vol. VI.

——— Continuation of the Account of the Portuguese Transactions in I., from 1541 to 1617, etc. KERR. Vol. VI.

——— Course of the I.n Trade before the discovery of the Route by the Cape of Good Hope, etc. KERR. Vol. VI.

India.—Particular Relation of the Expedition of Solyman Pacha from Suez to I., *etc.* KERR. Vol. VI.

——— Account of an Expedition of the Portuguese from I. to Madagascar, 1613. KERR. Vol. VII.

——— Continuation of the Transactions of the Portuguese in I., from 1617-40. KERR. Vol. VII.

——— First Voyage of the English to I. in 1591, *etc.* KERR. Vol. VII.

——— Fitch, R. Journey to I. overland, 1583. KERR. Vol. VII.

——— Frederic, C. Voyages and Travels in I., *etc.* 1563-81. KERR. Vol. VII.

——— Varthema, L. Voyages and Travels in . . . I. . . . in 1503-8. KERR. Vol. VII.

——— Barret, W. Of the Monsoons . . . in I. KERR. Vol. VIII.

——— Hawkins, W. Narrative of . . . Residence in the Dominions of the Great Mogul, 1608. KERR. Vol. VIII.

——— Michelburne, Sir E. Voyage to I., 1604. KERR. Vol. VIII.

——— Coryat, T. Journey from Jerusalem to the Court of the Great Mogul, 1615, 16. KERR. Vol. IX.

——— Downton, Capt. N. Voyage to I. in 1614, *etc.* KERR. Vol. IX.

——— Peyton, W. Voyage to I., in 1615, *etc.* KERR. Vol. IX.

——— Roe, Sir T., Ambassador . . . to . . . Hindostan, Journal of. KERR. Vol. IX.

——— Terry, E. Voyage to India, 1616, with Observations respecting the Dominions of the Great Mogul, *etc.* KERR. Vol. IX.

——— Whittington, N. Travels . . . in the Mogul Country. KERR. Vol. IX.

——— Voyages des Anglais . . . dans les Indes, *etc.* LAHARPE, J. Vol. I.

——— Continent de l'Inde . . . Voyage de T. Rhoé dans l'Indostan. LAHARPE, J. Vol. IV.

——— Continent de l'Inde. Voyage de Tavernier dans l'Indostan. LAHARPE, J. Vol. V.

——— Partie Orientale des Indes. Arrakan, Pégu, *etc.* LAHARPE, J. Vol. V.

——— Histoire Naturelle des Indes. LAHARPE, J. Vol. VI.

——— Europe, Africa, I. 1859. LATHAM, R. G. Descriptive Ethnology. Vol. II.

——— Hodges, W. Travels in I. during 1780-83. PELHAM. Vol. I.

——— Jackson, J. Journey from I. towards England in 1797, *etc.* PELHAM. Vol. II.

——— Roe, Sir T., Embassador to the Great Mogul, Journal of. PINKERTON. Vol. VIII.

——— Coryat, T. Letter from Jerusalem to the Court of the Great Mogol, 1615-16, *etc.* PURCHAS. Vol. I.

——— Extracts of a Tractate, written by N. Withington, which was left in the Mogul's Countrey . . . his . . . Travels therein. PURCHAS. Vol. I.

——— Finch, W. Observations . . . in 1607 . . . Occurrents in I., *etc.* PURCHAS. Vol. I.

India. 237

India.—Hawkins, W. Relation of the occurrents which happened ... in the Countie of the Great Mogoll ... 1608-13, etc. PURCHAS. Vol. I.

—— Mildenhall, J. Travailes into the Indies ... 1599. PURCHAS. Vol. I.

—— Rue, Sir T. Observations collected ... in the Mogol's Court ... 1614-17. PURCHAS. Vol. I.

—— Sigholmus, Mandevile, Stevens, Fitch ... their I.n Voyages. PURCHAS. Vol. I.

—— Salbanke, J. Voyage through L ... 1609. PURCHAS. Vol. I.

—— Barthema or Vertoman, L. Travels into ... I., 1503. PURCHAS. Vol. II.

—— Benjamin, the Son of Jonas. Peregrination of ... and relations of ... I., etc. PURCHAS. Vol. II.

—— Castro, J. Voyage which the Portugals made from I. to Zocz, 1540-41. PURCHAS. Vol. II.

—— Frederike, C. Extracts of his eighteene yeeres I.n observations, 1563-81. PURCHAS. Vol. II.

—— Pimenta, N. Indian Observations ... 1597-99. PURCHAS. Vol. II.

—— Trigantius, N. Letter touching his Voyage to I. ... 1618. PURCHAS. Vol. II.

—— Nunez, A. A true Relation concerning ... the Fleet in I., from 1527 to 1536. PURCHAS. Vol. IV.

—— Barthema, L. Itinerario dell' Egitto ... I.. etc. RAMUSIO. Vol. I.

—— Empoli, G. da. Viaggio fatto nell' I., 1503. RAMUSIO. Vol. I.

—— Stefano, D. de San. Viaggio nalle Indie, 1499. RAMUSIO. Vol. I.

—— Nunez, A. Relatione ... delle Indie ... 1527-36. RAMUSIO. Vol. III.

—— Memoires de Thomas Rhoë Ambassadeur ... près du Mogol, etc. THEVENOT. Vol. I.

—— Voyage de Edoüard Terry aux Etats du Mogol, etc. THEVENOT. Vol. I.

—— Relation de la Cour du Mogol par le Captaine Haukins. THEVENOT. Vol. I.

—— Avis d'un des Facteurs de la Compagnie Hollandoise sur le commerce des Indes. THEVENOT. Vol. II.

—— Goez, B. Reisen in des Mogols Reiche nach China, 1602. VOYAGES and TRAVELS. Allgemeine Historie, etc. Vol. VII.

—— Pinto, F. M. Reisen nach Indien, etc. VOYAGES and TRAVELS. Allgemeine Historie, etc. Vol. X.

—— Beschreibung von Indostan. VOYAGES and TRAVELS. Allgemeine Historie, etc. Vol. XI.

—— Mandelslo, J. A. Reise nach Indostan, 1638-39. VOYAGES and TRAVELS. Allgemeine Historie, etc. Vol. XI.

—— Rhoe, T. Reise nach Indostan, 1615-17. VOYAGES and TRAVELS. Allgemeine Historie, etc. Vol. XI.

India — India, North-West.

India.—Tavernier, Helaen· . . . 1665-66 . . . nach Indostan, *etc.*
VOYAGES and TRAVELS. Allgemeine Historie, *etc.* Vol. XI.

——— Zustand der Franzosen in Indien bis 1755. VOYAGES and TRAVELS.
Allgemeine Historie, *etc.* Vol. XVIII.

——— I., an Account of a Voyage to . . . in H. M. S. *Caroline*, 1803-5.
etc. VOYAGES and TRAVELS. A Collection, *etc.* 1805. Vol. V.

——— Valentia, Viscount. Voyages and Travels to I. . . . 1802-6.
VOYAGES and TRAVELS. A Collection, *&c.* 1805. Vol. XI.

——— ——— Voyages and Travels to I. . . . 1802-0. VOYAGES and
TRAVELS. A Collection, *etc.* 1810. Vol. IV.

——— Fitzclarence, Lt.-Col. Journal of a Route across I. . . . 1817-18.
VOYAGES and TRAVELS, New. 1819. Vol. I.

——— Cramp, W. B. Narrative of a Voyage to I. . . . 1815-21. VOYAGES
and TRAVELS, New. 1819, *etc.* Vol. IX.

——— Jordan or Jourdain Catalani, F. Mirabilia descripta, sequitur de
. . . I., *etc.* VOYAGES and TRAVELS. Recueil, *etc.* Vol. IV.

——— The Voyage of Vasco de Gama to I. 1497. VOYAGES and TRAVELS.
The World displayed. Vol. VIII.

——— *See also* BRAHMINS.—DIU.—MAIRWARA.

———, **Central.**— MORRIS, J. H. Report on the Administration of the
Central Provinces . . . 1867-68. *Nagpore.*

——— ——— MALCOLM, SIR J. Memoir of C. I., *etc.* **1832.**

——— ——— CUNNINGHAM, A. The Bhilsa Topes; or, Buddhist Monuments of Central I., *etc.* *Lond. and Bomb.*, **1854.**

——— ——— INDIA. Tables of Heights in . . . Central I., *etc.*
Calc., **1863.**

——— ——— WALKER, J. T. Tables of Heights in · . . . C. I., *etc.*
Calc., **1863.**

——— ——— HISLOP, S. Papers relating to the Aboriginal Tribes of the
Central Provinces, *etc.* [*Nagpore*] **1866.**

——— ——— INDIA. Gazetteer of the Central Provinces.
Nagpore, **1867-68.**

——— ——— BURGESS, J. Memorandum . . . with lists of the Rock-
Excavations, Temples, &c., in the . . . Central Provinces, *etc.*
Bombay, **1870.**

——— ——— Blanford, W. T. On the Traps of . . . Central I. INDIA
GEOLOGICAL SURVEY. Memoirs, *etc.* Vol. VI.

———, **East.**—MARTIN, R. M. The History . . . of E.n I., *etc.*,
Lond., **1838.**

———, **North.**—FORSTER, G. Journey . . . through the N. part of I.,
etc. **1798.**

——— ——— CONOLLY, A. Journey to the N. of I., *etc.* **1838.**

———, **North-West.**—FORBES, F. Thesis on . . . Plague as observed
in the N.W. Provinces of I. *Edin.*, **1840.**

——— ——— THORNTON, E. Gazetteer of the Countries adjacent to I. on
the N.W., *etc.* **1844.**

India, North-West. RAIKES, C. Notes on the N.W. Provinces of I. *Lond.*, 1852.

—— —— INDIA. Selections from the Records of Government: N.W.n Provinces. *Agra*, 1855-64.

—— —— SAINT-MARTIN, V. DE. Étude sur la Géographie ... du Nord-Ouest de l'Inde, *etc.* *Par.*, 1860.

—— —— DAVIES, R. H. Report on ... the Countries on the N.W. Boundary of British I. *Lahore*, 1862.

—— —— WALKER, J. T. Tables of Heights in ... the ... N.W. Provinces, *etc.* *Calc.*, 1863.

—— —— COTTON, SIR S. Nine Years on the N.-W. Frontier of I., *etc.* *Lond.*, 1868.

——, **South.**—NEWBOLD, T. J. Mineral Resources of S.n I.

—— —— —— On some ancient Mounds of Scoriceus Ashes in S.n I.

—— —— TAYLOR, T. G. and CALDECOTT, J. Observations on the ... Terrestrial Magnetic Force in S.ern I. *Madras*, 1839.

—— —— MULLENS, J. Missions in S. I. visited and described. 1854.

—— —— CLEGHORN, H. The Forests and Gardens of S. I. 1861.

—— —— FOOTE, R. B. On the Distribution of Stone Implements in S. I. 1868.

—— —— Stoliczka, F. The Gastropods of the Cretaceous Rocks of S.n I. INDIA, GEOLOGICAL SURVEY. Palæontologia Indica, *etc.* Series III.

—— —— —— Additional Observations regarding the Cephalopodous Fauna of the S. I.n Cretaceous Deposits. INDIA, GEOLOGICAL SURVEY. Records, *etc.*, Vol. I.

—— —— —— General Results obtained from an examination of the Gastropodous Fauna of the S. I.n Cretaceous Deposits. INDIA, GEOLOGICAL SURVEY. Records, *etc.*, Vol. I.

——, **West.** JERVIS, T. B. Contributions to the Statistics of W.n I., in 1823-30. 1830.

—— —— TOD, LIEUT.-COL. J. Travels in W.n I., *etc.* *Lond.*, 1839.

—— —— BERNCASTLE, DR. A Voyage to China; including a Visit to ... the Cave Temples of W.n I., *etc.* *Lond.*, 1850.

—— —— MACKAY, A. Western I. Reports, *etc.* 1853.

—— —— INDIA. Geological Papers on W.n India ... edited by H. J. Carter. *Bomb.*, 1857.

—— —— INDIA. Atlas to Geological Papers on W.-n I., *etc.* *Bomb.*, 1857.

—— —— BLANFORD, W. T. On the Traps of W.n and Central I. INDIA, GEOLOGICAL SURVEY. Memoirs, *etc.* Vol. VI.

India America.—*See* AMERICA, SOUTH.
—— **Occidentalis.**—*See* WEST INDIES.
Indian Archipelago.—*See* ARCHIPELAGO, INDIAN.
—— **Islands.**—*See* ARCHIPELAGO, INDIAN.

Indian Ocean.—GENTIL, M. LE. Voyage dans les Mers de l'Inde . . . 1761 et . . . 1769. *Par.*, **1779-81.**
—— VINCENT, W. The Commerce and Navigation of the Ancients in the I. O. **1807.**
—— OWEN, W. F. W. Tables of Latitudes and Longitudes . . . of places in the . . . I. O., *etc.* *N. Y.*, **1827.**
—— MORRELL, B. Narrative of four Voyages to the . . . I. . . . O., *etc.* *N. Y.*, **1832.**
—— RENNELL, J. Investigation of the Currents . . . which prevail between the I. O. and the Atlantic, *etc.* **1832.**
—— PIDDINGTON, H. Ten Memoirs on the law of Storms as applying to the Tempests of the I. and Chinese Seas. *Calc.*, **1839-43.**
—— —— —— The Horn-Book of Storms for the I. and China Seas. *Calc.*, **1845.**
—— THOM, A. Inquiry into the Nature and Course of Storms in the I. O. South of the Equator, *etc.* **1845.**
—— KERHALLET, C. P. DE. Considérations générales sur l'Ocean Indien, *etc.* *Par.*, **1851.**
—— MELDRUM, C. A Meteorological Journal of the I. O. for March, 1853, *etc.* *Mauritius*, **1858.**
—— DENHAM, H. M. Hydrographic Notices . . . I. O., *etc.*
1858-59.
—— MELDRUM, C. On the Hurricane and Weather in the I. O., from the 6th to the 18th Feb., 1860. **1860.**
—— GRAS, M. A. LE. Phares des Mers des Indes . . . Corrigés 1862, 63. *Par.*, **1862, 63.**
Indiana.—BRADBURY, J. Travels in . . . I., *etc.* *Liver.*, **1817.**
—— PECK, J. M. Guide for Emigrants to . . . I., *etc.* *Bost.*, **1836.**
—— GRAHAM, J. D. Report of the Harbours, &c., in I., *etc.*
Wash., **1857.**
Indies.—*See* INDIA.
Indo-China.—*See* SIAM.
Indo-Pacific Islands.—*See* ARCHIPELAGO, INDIAN.
Indostan.—*See* INDIA.
Indus.—MACARTNEY, J. Memoir of a Map of the Countries W. of the I., *etc.* MS.
—— BURNES, SIR A. Travels . . . also a Voyage on the I., *etc.* **1834.**
—— BOILEAU, A. W. E. Tour through . . . Rajwara . . . and visit to the I., *etc.* *Calc.*, **1837.**
—— WOOD, J. Personal Narrative of a Journey to the Source of the . . . OXUS, by . . . the I., *etc.* **1841.**
—— ZIMMERMANN, C. Der Kriegs-Schauplatz in Inner-Asien, oder Bemerkungen zu der Uebersichtskarte von . . . dem Lande am untern I. *Berl.*, **1842.**
—— ANDREW, W. P. The I. and its provinces, *etc.* **1857.**
—— SCINDE RAILWAY. S. R.: the I. Steam Flotilla . . . Reports of the Directors . . . Sept. 1863. **1863.**

Indus — Ireland. 241

Indus.—ANDREW, W. P. On the Completion of the Railway System of the Valley of the I., etc. *Lond.*, 1869.
—— Nearchus. Voyage from the Mouth of the . . . I. up the Persian Gulph, etc. HARRIS, J. Vol. I.
—— Arrian's Voyage of Nearchus, from the I. to the Euphrates, etc. VINCENT, W. The Commerce, etc. Vol. I.
Ingur.—RADDE, G. Berichte, etc. (Jahrg. 1. Reisen . . . in . . . I.) *Tyflis*, 1866.
Inishcaltra.—See INNISCALTHRA.
Inniscalthra.—BRASH, R. R. Inishcaltra and its Remains. 1868.
Insalah.—MALTE-BRUN, V. A. Resumé historique et géographique de l'exploration de G. Rohlfs . . . à In-Çalah, etc. *Par.*, 1866.
Inseln des Grünen Vorgeburges.—See CAPE VERDE ISLANDS.
Ionian Islands.—HOLLAND, H. Travels in the I. I., etc. 1819.
—— NAPIER, C. J. The Colonies . . . the I. I. in particular. 1833.
—— GIFFARD, E. A Short Visit to the I. I., etc. *Lond.*, 1837.
—— MURRAY. Hand-Book for Travellers in the I. I., etc. *Lond.*, 1840.
—— DAVY, J. Notes . . . on the I. I., etc. 1842.
—— SPENCER, E. Travels in European Turkey . . . with a Visit to . . . the I. I., etc. 1851.
—— Müller, C. Journey through . . . the I. I., 1821. VOYAGES and TRAVELS, New. 1819, etc. Vol. VIII.
Iowa.—OWEN, D. D. Reports of a Geological Reconnoissance of the N.n part of I. *Wash.*, 1848.
—— OWEN, D. D. Report of a Geological Survey of . . . I., etc. *Phil.*, 1852.
—— HALL, J. and WHITNEY, J. D. Report on the Geological Survey of . . . I., etc. *Iowa*, 1858.
Irawadee, Irawadi.—See IRRAWADDY.
Ireland.—BETTS, J. Exercises on . . . I.
—— HALL, Mr. and Mrs. S. C. I.: its Scenery, etc. *Lond.*
—— IRELAND. Post-Chaise Companion . . . through I., etc. *Dublin.*
—— BARTON, R. Lectures . . . upon . . . Lough Neagh in I. *Dubl.*, 1751.
—— BEAUFORT, D. A. Memoir of a Map of I., etc. *Dubl.*, 1792.
—— DODD, J. S. Traveller's Directory through I. *Dubl.*, 1801.
—— FRASER, J. B. Gleanings in I., etc. *Lond.*, 1802.
—— IRELAND. Reports of the Commissioners appointed to enquire into the . . . Bogs in I., etc. 1810-14.
—— BICHENO, J. E. I. and its economy. 1830.
—— BARROW, J. Tour round I., etc. 1836.
—— HUDDART, J. Piloting Directory for . . . all the Coasts of I., etc. 1837.
—— JONNÈS, A. M. Statistique de . . . l'Irlande. *Par.*, 1837.
—— MUDGE, W. and FRAZER, G. A. Sailing Directions for the N.E., N., and N.W. Coasts of I. 1842.

R

Ireland.—IRELAND. A Plan for the Improvement of I., etc. 1844.
——— PARLIAMENTARY GAZETTEER of I., etc. *Dubl., Lond., Edinb.,* 1846.
——— PETTY, W. History of the Survey of Ireland, commonly called "the Down Survey," A. D. 1655-6, etc. *Dubl.,* 1851.
——— WORSAAE, J. J. A. Account of the Danes and Norwegians in . . . I. 1852.
——— CALVERT, J. Gold Rocks of . . . I., etc. 1853.
——— CAMERON, CAPT. Ordnance Survey: Abstract of principal Lines of Spirit-Levelling in I. 1855.
——— BURWOOD, J., and YULE, C. B. Tide-Tables for the . . . Irish Ports, etc. 1855-63.
——— JAMES, SIR H. Ordnance Survey. Meteorological Observations taken . . . 1829-52 . . . in I. *Dubl.,* 1856.
——— WELD, C. R. Vacations in I. 1857.
——— WILDE, W. R. Essay . . . Illustrative of the Ancient Animals of I. *Dubl.,* 1860.
——— BEAVEN, H. J. C. Six Weeks in I., etc. 1862.
——— Berius. Voyage into I., 684. HAKLUYT. Vol. I.
——— Hamilton's Letters on the N.n Coast of I. PINKERTON. Vol. III.
——— Young's Tour in I., an Abstract of. PINKERTON. Vol. III.
——— I., Journal of a Tour in, 1804, etc. VOYAGES and TRAVELS. A Collection, etc. 1803. Vol. III.
——— Carr, J. Stranger in I.; or a Tour . . . 1805. VOYAGES and TRAVELS. A Collection, etc. 1805. Vol. V.
——— **South Coast.**—PURDY, J., and FINDLAY, A. G. Sailing Directory for the . . . S.ern Coasts of I. 1849.
——— ——— WHITE, M., and PURDAY, J. Portulan . . . de la Côte Sud d'Irlande, etc. *Par.,* 1855.
Irish Channel.—English and I. Channels and Ports Tide-Tables, etc. 1835-53.
Irrawaddy.—YULE, H. Narrative . . . with . . . Notes on the Geological Features of the Banks of the River I., etc. *Calc.,* 1856.
Iscardo.—*See* ISKARDOH.
Iseland.—*See* ICELAND.
Iskanderoon.—*See* ISKANDERUN.
Iskanderun.—TAYLOR. J. Travels . . . to India, in 1789, by Scandaroon, etc. 1799.
Iskardoh.—VIGNE, G. T. Travels in . . . I., etc. 1842.
Island, Islandia. *See* ICELAND.
Ispahan.—BUCKINGHAM, J. S. Travels . . . including . . . Researches in I., etc. 1830.
——— Steel, R., and Crowther, J. Journey from Agimere to I., 1615-16. KERR. Vol. IX.
——— Hobbs, G. Travaile from Musco to Spahan, 1620. PURCHAS. Vol. I.

Ispahan.—Steel, R., and Crowther, J. Journal of a Journey from Ammere
... to Spahan ... 1615-16. Purchas. Vol. I.
—— Cartwright, J. Observations in his Voyage from Aleppo to Hispaan
... about 1603. Purchas. Vol. II.
Issini.—*See* Assinee.
Isthme Américain.—*See* Panama, Isthmus of.
Istria.—Vernon, F. Travels ... through I., *etc.* Ray, J.
—— Careri, L. F. Travels in I. ... 1702, *etc.* Voyages and Travels. A Collection, *etc.* 1805. Vol. I.
Italia.—*See* Italy.
Italy.—Sandys, G. A Relation of a Journey begun ... 1610. Containing a description of ... the remote parts of I., *etc.* 1615.
—— Italy. De Principibus Italiæ Commentarius, *etc.* *Lugd. Bat.*, 1631.
—— Tellez, B. Travels ... Travels of P. Teixeira from India to I., *etc.* 1710.
—— Addison, J. Remarks on several parts of Italy ... in 1701-1703. *Lond.*, 1726.
—— Pollnitz, C. L., Baron de. Memoirs ... in his ... Travels through ... I., *etc.* 1737.
—— Drummond, A. Travels through ... I., *etc.* 1754.
—— Nugent, Mr. The Grand Tour ... through ... I., *etc.* 1778.
—— Bernouilli, J. Nachrichten von Italien, *etc.* *Leipz.*, 1782.
—— Dupaty, Pres. Travels through I., *etc.* 1788.
—— Stolberg, Count F. L. zu. Reise in ... Italien, *etc.* *Königsb. u. Leip.*, 1794.
—— Chauchard, Capt. Geographical description of ... I., *etc.* *Lond.*, 1800.
—— Germany ... I. ... Geographical ... description of, *etc.* 1800.
—— Italy. Itinéraire d'Italie. *Flor.*, 1801.
—— Denina, C. Tableau ... de la Haute-Italie. *Par.*, 1805.
—— Dessiou, J. F. Le Petit Neptune Français ... To which is added, the Coast of I., *etc.* 1805.
—— Barbiellini, C. A. Nuova descrizione ... d'Italia, *etc.* *Mil.*, 1808.
—— MacGill, T. Travels in ... I., *etc.* 1808.
—— Stersberg, C. G. von. Reise durch Tyrol in die Oesterreichischen Provinzen Italiens. *Wien und Triest*, 1811.
—— Italy. Itinéraire d'Italie. *Mil.*, 1814.
—— Eustace, J. C. Classical Tour through I., 1802. 1815.
—— Baillie, M. First Impressions of ... I., *etc.* 1819.
—— Hoare, Sir R. C. Classical Tour in I., *etc.* 1819.
—— Cadell, W. A. Journey in ... I., *etc.* *Edin.*, 1820.
—— Galiffe, J. A. I. and its Inhabitants, *etc.* 1820.

Italy.

Italy.—HAAR, H. Nachweisungen für Reisende in Italien. *Leipz.*, 1821.
—— LAURENT, P. Classical Tour through ... I. in 1818-19. 1821.
—— ITALY. Itinerario Italiano. *Milan*, 1822.
—— ITALY. Itinéraire Classique d'Italia. *Par.*, 1823.
—— FORSYTH, J. Remarks on ... I. 1824.
—— BROCKEDON, W. Illustrations of the Passes ... by which I. communicates with France, etc. 1828.
—— CRAMER, J. A. Geographical ... description of Ancient I. *Oxford*, 1832.
—— STRAUSSEN, J. J. Reise durch Italien ... 1647-1673. *Gotha*, 1832.
—— RICHARD. Guide du Voyageur en I. *Par.*, 1833.
—— BECKFORD, W. I., etc. 1834.
—— SCHOUW, J. F. Tableau du Climat ... de l'Italie. *Copenh.*, 1839.
—— SERRISTORI, COUNT L. Statistica dell'Italia, etc. *Firenze*, 1839.
—— GRIBERG, COUNT J. Relazioni Commerciali del Egitto ... coi Porti dell' Italia, etc. *Firenze*, 1841.
—— EGYPT. Notes ... of a Visit to Egypt ... by way of I., etc. *Lond.*, 1844.
—— SCHOUW, J. F. De italienske Naaletraeers geographiske og historiske Forhold. *Copenh.*, 1844.
—— RANUZZI, A. Annuario Geografico Italiano. *Bologna*, 1844-45.
—— ALPS. Le Alpi che cingono l'Italia. *Torino*, 1845.
—— BALBI, A. Miscellanea Italiana, etc. *Mil.*, 1845.
—— BIANCONI, J. J. De Mari olim occupante planities et colles Italiæ, etc. *Bonon.*, 1846-52.
—— RÓNAY, J. Jellemisme, vagy az ... Olasz ... Nemzet ... Jellemzése, etc. *Györött*, 1847.
—— SCHOUW, J. F. Ege-og Birke-Familiens geographiske og historiske Forhold i Italien. *Copenh.*, 1847.
—— BALBI, A. Saggio ... delle strade ferrate ... Italiche. *Mil.*, 1848.
—— WHITESIDE, J. I. in the Nineteenth Century, etc. 1848.
—— LAMALLE, M. DUREAU DE. Climatologie comparée de l'Italie et de l'Andalousie, etc. *Par.*, 1849.
—— MAURY, L. F. A. Histoire ... des Forêts ... de l'Italie. *Par.*, 1850.
—— MURCHISON, SIR R. I. On the Earlier Volcanic Rocks of the Papal States, and the adjacent parts of I. 1850.
—— PEPE, LIEUT.-GEN. Scenes and Events in I., etc. 1850.
—— BELDAM, J. Recollections of Scenes ... in I., etc. 1851.
—— PFEIFFER, I. Visit to ... I., etc. 1853.
—— SPENCER, E. Tour of Inquiry through ... I., etc. 1853.
—— LAING, S. Notes ... on ... I., etc. 1854.
—— CHAMIER, CAPT. My Travels ... through ... I. 1855.

Italy.

Italy.—BROUGHTON, LORD. I.; Remarks made ... from 1816 to 1854. 1859.
—— NIGRI, C. La Grandezza Italiana. *Torino*, 1864.
—— GASTALDI, B. Lake Habitations and Pre-historic remains in N. n and Central I., *etc.* *Lond.*, 1865.
—— BROWN, S. On the Statistical Progress of ... I. *Lond.*, 1866.
—— ELLIS, R. An Enquiry into the Ancient Routes between I. and Gaul, *etc.* *Camb. and Lond.*, 1867.
—— FAIRMAN, E. ST. J. A Treatise on the Petroleum Zones of I. *Lond.*, 1868.
—— —— I Petrolii in Italia, *etc.* *Firenze*, 1869.
—— Skippon, Sir P. Journey through ... I., *etc.* CHURCHILL. Vol. VI.
—— France and I., a Tour in, made by an English Gentleman, 1675. CHURCHILL. Vol. VII.
—— Hawkwood, J. Travailes ... in diverse places of I. HAKLUYT. Vol. II.
—— Burnet, Bishop G. Travels through ... part of I. ... 1685-86. HARRIS, J. Vol. II.
—— Misson, M. Travels through a great part of I., *etc.* HARRIS, J. Vol. II.
—— Thevenot, J. Voyages ... from I. to Constantinople, 1655. HARRIS, J. Vol. II.
—— Stolberg, Count F. L. Travels through ... I., *etc.* PELHAM. Vol. II.
—— Spallanzani's Travels in I. PINKERTON. Vol. V.
—— Smith, Capt. J. Travels .. thorow ... Italie ... about 1596. PURCHAS. Vol. II.
—— Ray, J. Travels through ... I., *etc.* RAY, J. Collection, *etc.*
—— Küttner, C. G. Travels through ... part of I., 1798-99. VOYAGES and TRAVELS. A Collection, *etc.* 1805. Vol. I.
—— Kotzebue, A. v. Travels through I., 1804-5. VOYAGES and TRAVELS. A Collection, *etc.* 1805. Vol. IV.
—— Salvo, Marquis de. Travels from I. to England ... 1806. VOYAGES and TRAVELS. A Collection, *etc.* 1805. Vol. VI.
—— Semple, R. Observations on a Journey through Spain and I. ... 1805. VOYAGES and TRAVELS. A Collection, *etc.* 1805. Vol. VIII.
—— Paris, Travels from, through ... I., 1801-2, *etc.* VOYAGES and TRAVELS. A Collection, *etc.* 1805. Vol. IX.
—— Paris, Travels from, through ... I., 1801-2. VOYAGES and TRAVELS. A Collection, *etc.* 1810. Vol. II.
—— Semple, R. Journey through Spain and I. VOYAGES and TRAVELS. A Collection, *etc.* 1810. Vol. VI.
—— Chateauvieux, F. Lillin de. Travels in I. ... 1812-13. VOYAGES and TRAVELS. New. 1819. Vol. I.
—— Hoare, Sir R. C. Classical Tour through I. ... 1790. VOYAGES and TRAVELS, New. 1819. Vol. I.

Italy.—Rose, W. S. Letters from I. Voyages and Travels, New. 1819. Vol. I.

—— Castellan, A. L. Letters on I., 1820. Voyages and Travels, New. 1819. Vol. III.

—— Friedländer, H. Views in I. during a Journey in 1815-16. Voyages and Travels, New. 1819. Vol. V.

—— Montémont, A. Tour . . . in I., 1820. Voyages and Travels, New. 1810, etc. Vol. IX.

—— Misson, M. Travels through Germany and I. Voyages and Travels. The World displayed. Vol. XVIII, XIX.

—— Addison, Joseph. Travels through I. and Swisserland, 1699. Voyages and Travels. The World displayed. Vol. XIX.

——, **Central.** Murray. Hand-Book for Travellers in C. I., etc. *Lond.*, 1843.

—— —— —— Hand-Book for Travellers in N. I., etc. Pt. I., II. *Lond.*, 1842.

——, **North.** —— Hand-Book for Travellers in N. I., etc. *Lond.*, 1858.

——, **South.** —— Hand-Book for Travellers in S. I., etc. *Lond.*, 1853.

Itasca, Lake. Schoolcraft, H. R. Summary Narrative of an . . . Expedition to the . . . Mississippi . . . the discovery of its Origin in I. L., etc. *Phil.*, 1855.

Ithaca. Gell, Sir W. Geography . . . of I. 1807.

—— Goodisson, W. Historical . . . Essay upon . . . I., etc. 1822.

—— Bowen, G. F. I. in 1850. 1854.

Ivahy, River. Silva Coutinho, J. M. da. Annexo P. . . (Exploração do Rio I. [by A. A. de Padua Fleury].) [1885.]

Ivory Coast. Of the I. C. Astley. Vol. II.

Ivrea. Bertolotti, A. Passeggiate nel Canavese. *Lond.*, 1867-70.

Izalco. Palacio, D. G. de. Description of the Ancient Provinces of . . . I. . . . 1576. Squier. Collection. No. I.

J.

Jaboo.—Avezao, M. d'. Notice sur le Pays et le Peuple des Yébous, etc. *Par.*, 1845.

Jalofs.—Roger, Baron. Recherches philosophiques sur la langue Onolofe, etc. *Par.*, 1829.

—— Beschreibung von den Jalofern, etc. Voyages and Travels. Allgemeine Historie, etc. Vol. III.

Jamaica.—Sloane, H. Voyage to . . . J., etc. 1707.

—— Florida. Description of . . . the Course of the British Trading-Ships to and from . . . J., etc. 1739.

—— Edwards, B. Historical . . . Account of the Maroon Negroes in . . . J. in 1793-4, etc. 1801.

—— Latrobe, C. J. Report on Negro Education in J., etc. 1838.

Jamaica — Japan. 247

Jamaica.—Purdy, J., and Findlay, A. G. Sailing Directory for . . . J., etc. **1848.**
—— Bigelow, J. J. in 1850, etc. *N. Y.,* **1851.**
—— Martin, R. M. Report to the Shareholders of the Liguanea and General Mining Company of J., etc. **1851.**
—— Pim, B. The Negro and J. *Lond.,* **1866.**
—— Harvey, T. and Brewin, W. J. in 1866, etc. *Lond.,* **1867.**
—— Parker, W. Voyage to . . . J. . . . 1506-97. Hakluyt. Vol. IV.
—— Sherley, Sir A. Voyage to . . . J. . . . 1598. Hakluyt. Vol. IV.
—— Weltere Eroberungen der Castilianer in . . . J. . . . 1511. Voyages and Travels. Allgemeine Historie, etc. Vol. XIII.
—— Englândische Inseln. Reisen . . . in J., etc. Voyages and Travels. Allgemeine Historie, etc. Vol. XVII.

James of Compostella, Saint.—*See* Santiago de Compostella.

Jan Mayen.—Dufferin, Lord. Letters . . . being an Account of . . . J. M., etc. **1857.**
—— History of . . . Mayen Island . . . 1585-1746. Harris, J. Vol. II.
—— Îles de J. M. . . . Climat, minéraux, animaux. Laharpe, J. Vol. XVI.
—— Supplement. Description of . . . John M.'s Island, etc. 1711. Voyages. Account of several late, etc.
—— Beschreibung der Insel J. M. oder den Dreyeinigkeits-Insel. Voyages and Travels. Allgemeine Historie, etc. Vol. XIX.

Japan.—Japan. Nuovi Avvisi del Giapone, etc. *Venetia,* **1586.**
—— Guzman, P. L. Historia de las Missiones . . . de la Compañia de Jesus . . . en . . . la . . . Japon. *Alcalá,* **1601.**
—— Letters. Litterae Japonicae annorum M. DC. IX. et X., etc. *Antverp.,* **1615.**
—— Montanus, A. Gedenkwaerdige Gesantschappen der Oost-Indische Maetschappy in 't vereenigde Nederland aen . . . J., etc. *Amst.,* **1669.**
—— Montanus, A. Atlas Japannensis, etc. **1670.**
—— Moxon, J. A Brief Discourse of a Passage by the North Pole to J., etc. *Lond.,* **1697.**
—— Mandelslo, J. A. de. Voyage . . . Contenants une description . . . du Japon, etc. *Amst.,* **1727.**
—— Kaempfer, E. Histoire . . . du Japon, etc. *La Haye,* **1729.**
—— Thunberg, C. P. Reisen . . . vorzüglich in J. . . . 1770 bis 1779, etc. *Berl.,* **1792-94.**
—— —— Travels . . . in J., etc. **1796.**
—— —— Voyages au Japon . . . 1770-1778, etc. *Par.,* **1796.**
—— Golownin, Capt. Recollections of J., etc. **1819.**
—— Siebold, P. F. de. Nippon. Archiv zur Beschreibung von J., etc. *Leyden,* **1832.**
—— Straussen, J. J. Reise durch . . . J. . . . 1647-1673. *Gotha,* **1832.**

Japan.

Japan.—PARKER, P. Journal of an Expedition ... to J., *etc.* **1838.**

——— SIEBOLD, P. F. DE. Voyage au J. pendant 1823-30, *etc.*
Par., **1836-40.**

——— JAPAN. Manners and Customs of the J.ese in the Nineteenth Century. **1841.**

——— SIEBOLD, P. F. VON. Manners and Customs of the J.ese, in the Nineteenth Century, *etc.* *Lond.,* **1841.**

——— ALCOCK, R. Elements of Japanese Grammar, *etc.* *Shanghai,* **1851.**

——— MAC FARLANE, C. J., an Account, *etc.* **1852.**

——— SIEBOLD, P. F. VON. Nippon. Archiv zur Beschreibung von J., *etc.* *Leyden,* **1852.**

——— BUTTON, SIR T. Some particulars ... of a North-West Passage to ... J., 1612. **1853.**

——— TAYLOR, B. Visit to ... J. in 1853. **1855.**

——— HALLORAN, A. L. Wae Yang Jin. Eight Months' Journal kept ... during visits to ... J., *etc.* *Lond.,* **1856.**

——— PERRY, M. C. Narrative of the Expedition of an American Squadron to ... J., in 1852-54, *etc.* *Wash.,* **1856.**

——— SPALDING, J. W. J. ... an account of three Visits, *etc.* **1856.**

——— HABERSHAM, A. W. My last Cruise ... Visits to ... J., *etc.* *Phil.,* **1857.**

——— PALMER, A. H. Documents ... illustrating the origin of the Mission to J. ... May, 1851. *Wash.,* **1857.**

——— COEN, C. J. Reize van M. G. Vries in 1643 naar het Noorden en Oosten van J., *etc.* *Amst.,* **1858.**

——— CORNWALLIS, K. Two Journeys to J., 1856-7. **1859.**

——— GRAS, M. A. LE. Renseignements hydrographiques sur ... la Mer ... les Îles du Japon, *etc.* *Par.,* **1859.**

——— OLIPHANT, L. Narrative of the Earl of Elgin's Mission to ... J. in 1857-59. *Edin.,* **1859.**

——— OSBORN, S. Cruise in J. ese Waters. **1859.**

——— TRONSON, J. M. Narrative of a Voyage to J., *etc.* **1859.**

——— COLLINS, P. Mc D. A Voyage ... with ... incidental notices of ... J. *N. Y. and Lond.,* **1860.**

——— OSBORN, S. J.ese, with facsimiles of Illustrations by Artists of Yedo. **1861.**

——— PERREY, A. Documents sur les Tremblements de Terre et les phénomènes Volcaniques au Japon. *Lyon,* **1862.**

——— SAINSBURY, W. N. Calendar of State Papers ... J. ... 1513-1616, *etc.* *Lond.,* **1862.**

——— ALCOCK, SIR R. The Capital of the Tycoon, *etc.* *Lond.,* **1863.**

——— PEREIRA, F. A. M. Viagem ... á Capital do Japão, 1860. *Lisboa,* **1863.**

——— FRAISSINET, É. Le Japon, histoire et description, *etc.* *Par.,* **1864.**

——— HUMBERT, A. La Mer Intérieure du Japon. [*Geneva,* **1866.**]

Japan.—PUMPELLY, R. Notice of an Account of Geological Observations in ... J., etc. [1866.]
——— CHIJS, J. A. VAN DER. Nederlands Streven tot openstelling van J. voor den Wereldhandel, etc. *Amst.*, 1867.
——— SILVER, J. M. W. Sketches of J. ese manners and customs, etc. *Lond.*, 1867.
——— POMPE VAN MEERDERVOORT, J. L. C. Vijf Jaren in J., etc. *Leiden*, 1867, 68.
——— ALABASTER, C. and others. Reports of Journeys in ... J., etc. *Lond.*, 1869.
——— ARMINJON, V. F. Il Giappone ... nel 1866. *Genova*, 1869.
——— Adams, W. Voyage to J. etc. ASTLEY. Vol. I.
——— Cocks, R. Some particulars ... of J. from 1614-20. ASTLEY. Vol. I.
——— Saris, J. Voyage to ... J. in 1611. ASTLEY. Vol. I.
——— Curious Remarks on ... J., etc. CHURCHILL. Vol. I.
——— Voyage en Asie, Japon. EYRIÈS. Vol. XII.
——— Gualle, F. Voyage ... by the ... Isles of J. ... to Acapulco, 1582-84. HAKLUYT. Vol. III.
——— Rundall, T. Memorials of the Empire of J. in the XVI. and XVII. centuries, etc. 1850. HAKLUYT Soc. PUB. Vol. VIII.
——— Adams, W. Account of the adventures of, who resided ... in J., 1609-1631. HARRIS, J. Vol. I.
——— KÆO, D. An authentick ... description of J., etc. HARRIS, J. Vol. II.
——— Adams, W. Voyage to J. in 1598, etc. KERR. Vol. VIII.
——— Voyage of Capt. Saris to J., etc. KERR. Vol. VIII.
——— Peyton, W. Voyage ... in 1615 ... with the Ports ... between the Cape of Good Hope and J., 1616. KERR. Vol. IX.
——— Pring, Capt. Voyage ... to ... J. KERR. Vol. IX.
——— Japon. Voyage de Kæmpfer, etc. LAHARPE, J. Vol. VIII.
——— Caron's Account of J. PINKERTON. Vol. VII.
——— Kempfer's History of J. PINKERTON. Vol. VII.
——— J., Diary on the Coast of, 1673. PINKERTON. Vol. VII.
——— Adams, W. Voyage ... to J., 1598-1611. PURCHAS. Vol. I.
——— Cockes, R. Relation ... Whereunto are added divers Letters ... for the better knowledge of Japonian affaires. PURCHAS. Vol. I.
——— Brown, A. Extracts of a Journal ... sayling divers times ... to ... J., etc. 1617-22. PURCHAS. Vol. II.
——— Cocks, R. Letter concerning ... occurrents in J., 1622. PURCHAS. Vol. II.
——— Hatch, A. Letter touching J. ... 1623. PURCHAS. Vol. II.
——— Trigautius N. Letter touching ... the state of Christianitie in ... J., 1618. PURCHAS. Vol. II.
——— A general collection ... of the Jesuites entrance into J. and China ... 1542-90. PURCHAS. Vol. III.

Japan.—Ramusio. Informationi dell' Isola Giappan, *etc.* Ramusio. Vol. I.
— Autre avis sur le commerce du Japon. Thevenot. Vol. II.
— Relation du Japon.—Martyrs du Japon. Thevenot. Vol. II.
— Wood, J. Attempt to discover a N.-E. Passage to . . . J. 1711. Voyages. Account of several late, *etc.*
— Verhoeven, P. W. Reis . . . 1607-11 . . . nach J. Voyages and Travels. Allgemeine Historie, *etc.* Vol. VIII.
— Beschreibung der Japonischen Inseln. Voyages and Travels. Allgemeine Historie, *etc.* Vol. XI.
— Kampfern, F. Reise nach J. . . . 1690-91. Voyages and Travels. Allgemeine Historie, *etc.* Vol. XI.

Japan, Sea of. Montravel, M. L. de Tardy de. Instructions . . . sur la Mer du J., *etc.* *Par.*, 1857.
— —— Account of the grounds upon which a N.-E. passage into the Sea of J. has been sought for, *etc.* Harris, J. Vol. II.

Japfo.—*See* Japan.

Japura, River.—Silva Coutinho. J. M. de. Considerações geraes sobre os rios que descem da cordilheira dos Andes . . . cachoeiras do Purús e Hyuruá. 1863.
— —— Annexo P. Exploração do Rio Hyapura, *etc.* [1865.]
— —— Rocaud y Paz-Soldan, M. Nota . . . sobre la Exploracion del Rio Yavari, *etc.* [1867.]

Jask.—Swan, R. Journal of a Voyage to Surat and Jasques, 1660. Kerr. Vol. IX.
— Childe, A. Journal from England . . . to Jasques . . . 1616. Purchas. Vol. I.
— Swan, R. Extract of a Journal of a Voyage . . . to Jasques, *etc.* Purchas. Vol. I.

Jasques.—*See* Jask.

Java.—Thunberg, C. P. Travels . . . in J., *etc.* 1796.
— Raffles, Sir T. S. Substance of a Minute . . . on the . . . Internal Management . . . of J. 1814.
— Daendels, H. W. Brieven . . . bevattende eene beoordeeling van een Werkje . . . getiteld : J., *etc.* *Amst.*, 1816.
— Hogendorp, Count C. S. W. de. Coup-d'œil sur l'Île de J., *etc.* *Bruxelles*, 1830.
— Raffles, Sir T. S. History of J. 1830.
— Saxe-Weimar-Eisenach, Bernard, Duke de. Précis de la Campagne de J., en 1811. *La Haye*, 1834.
— Humboldt, W. von. Über die Kawi-Sprache auf der Insel J., *etc.* *Berl.*, 1836.
— Earl, G. W. The Eastern Seas . . . comprising a Tour of . . . J., *etc.* 1837.
— Moor, J. H. Notices of . . . J., *etc.* *Singapore*, 1837.
— Davidson, G. F. Trade and Travel . . . Recollections of . . . J., *etc.* *Lond.*, 1846.

JAVA.—SELBERG, E. Reis naar J., *etc.* *Amst.*, **1846.**
——— JUKES, J. B. Narrative of . . . an Excursion into the Interior of the E. part of J. **1847.**
——— STURLER, W. L. DE. Redevoering over de natuurlijke voordeelen van bodem en luchtstreek op J., *etc.* *Gron.*, **1847.**
——— VAN DE VELDE, C. W. M. Toelichtende Aanteekeningen behoorende bij de Kaart van . . . J. *Leiden*, **1847.**
——— JUNGHUHN, F. Rückreise von J. nach Europa . . . 1848, *etc.* *Leip.*, **1852.**
——— MELVILL OF CARNBEE, AND SMITS, H. D. A. Seaman's Guide rond J. to the . . . East, *etc.* **1853.**
——— WINTER, C. F. Het Boek Adji-Sâhâ, oude fabelachtige geschiedenis van J., *etc.* *Amst.*, **1857.**
——— MONEY, J. W. B. J.; or How to manage a Colony, *etc.* **1861.**
——— JUNGHUHN, Fr. Staat . . . aantoonende de vermeerdering der Kinaplanten op J. . . , Julij 1858 tot December 1862. **1863.**
——— D'ALMEIDA, W. B. Life in J., *etc.* *Lond.*, **1864.**
——— JAGOR, F. Singapore . . . J. Reiseskizzen. *Berl.*, **1866.**
——— JAVA. Zeilaanwijzingen van J. naar het Kanaal, *etc.* *Utrecht*, **1868-70.**
——— Scot, E. Account of J. . . . 1602-5. ASTLEY. Vol. I.
——— Voyage of Capt. D. Middleton to J. . . . in 1609. ASTLEY. Vol. I.
——— East Indies. Description of a Voyage . . . 1595-97: to which is added the Sea Journal of the Hollanders into J. CHURCHILL. Vol. VIII.
——— Sumatra, J., *etc.* EYRIES. Vol. XII.
——— The prosperous . . . Voyage to J. . . . performed by 8 ships of Amsterdam from Texell . . . 1598-99. HAKLUYT. Vol. V.
——— Scot, E. Account of J. . . . 1603-5. KERR. Vol. VIII.
——— Stavorinus. Account of J. . . . from the Voyages of. PINKERTON. Vol. XI.
——— Middleton, D. Voyage to J. and Banda, 1609. PURCHAS. Vol. I.
——— Scot, E. Discourse of J. . . . 1602-5. PURCHAS. Vol. I.
——— Zweyte Reise, des J. C. van Neck und W. van Warwick, nach . . . J., 1598-1600. VOYAGES and TRAVELS. Allgemeine Historie, *etc.* Vol. VIII.
——— Tavernier. Reisen . . . 1665-66 . . . nach J., *etc.* VOYAGES and TRAVELS. Allgemeine Historie, *etc.* Vol. XI.
——— Prior, J. Voyage to . . . J. . . . 1810-11. VOYAGES and TRAVELS, NEW. 1819. Vol. I.
——— *See also* BANTAM.—PASSOEROEAN.

Jaxartes.—*See* SIR-DARIA.
Jean Mayen.—*See* JAN MAYEN.
Jeddo.—FORTUNE, R. Yedo and Peking: a Narrative, *etc.* *Lond.*, **1863.**
——— Kämpfer, E. Reise nach . . . Jedo, 1690-91. VOYAGES and TRAVELS. Allgemeine Historie, *etc.* Vol. XI.

Jedo — Jerusalem.

Jedo.—*See* JEDDO.
Jedso.—*See* JESSO.
Jenné.—GALARSO, COUNT J. Viaggio del Signor . . . R. Caillié à . . . J., *etc.* 1830.
Jericho.—JERICHO. An Excursion from J. to the Ruins of . . . Gerasa and Amman, *etc.* 1852.
——— Biddulph, W. Travels of four Englishmen . . . into . . . J. . . . in 1600 and 1611. CHURCHILL. Vol. VII.
Jersey.—RICHARDS, J. The J. Island Pilot, *etc.* Lond., 1868.
——— ——— Routier de l'Ile J., *etc.* Par., 1866.
Jerusalem.—BARTLETT, W. H. Walks about . . . J.
——— BUZGO, G. B. DE. Viaggio . . . Con la descrittione di Gierusalem, *etc.* Milano, [1666.]
——— FALCONER, D. Journey from Joppa to J., in 1751. 1753.
——— SYRIA. Viaggio da Gerusalemme per le coste della Soria, *etc.* Livorno, 1787.
——— MAUNDRELL, H. Journey from Aleppo to J. . . . A.D. 1697, *etc.* 1810.
——— RICHARDSON, R. Travels . . . as far as . . . J., *etc.* Lond., 1822.
——— HENNIKER, SIR F. Notes during a Visit to . . . J. 1824.
——— SÆWULF. Relation des Voyages de, à J. . . . 1102-3. *Par.*, 1839.
——— BORRER, D. A Journey from Naples to J., *etc.* 1845.
——— ROBINSON, E. Topography of J., *etc.* N. Y., 1846.
——— FERGUSSON, J. Essay on the Ancient Topography of J. 1847.
——— WILLIAMS, G. Historical and descriptive Memoir on . . . J. 1849.
——— ——— The Holy City . . . Notices of J., *etc.* Lond., 1849.
——— BARTLETT, W. H. J. revisited. 1855.
——— THRUPP, J. F. Antient J. A new Investigation, *etc.* Camb., 1855.
——— DUPUIS, H. L. The Holy Places . . . Two Years' Residence in J., *etc.* 1856.
——— BARCLAY, J. T. City of the Great King; or, J., *etc.* Phil., 1857.
——— WEY, W. The Itineraries of W. Wey . . . to J., A.D. 1458 and A.D. 1462, *etc.* Lond., 1857.
——— TOBLER, T. Dritte Wanderung nach Palästina . . . und Nachlese in J. Gotha, 1859.
——— WHITTY, J. I. Proposed Water Supply . . . for J., *etc.* Lond., 1863.
——— JERUSALEM. J. Water Relief Society, *etc.* [Prospectus.] Lond., [1864.]
——— WHITTY, J. I. Water Supply of J., ancient and modern. Lond., 1864.
——— MORRISON, W. The Recovery of J. A Narrative, *etc.* Lond., 1871.

Jerusalem.

Jerusalem.—BIDDULPH, W. Travels of four Englishmen ... into ... J. ... in 1600 and 1611. CHURCHILL. Vol. VII.
—— Alderney, L. Voyage to ... J. ... 1581. HAKLUYT. Vol. II.
—— Alured, Bp. of Worcester. Voyage unto J., 1058. HAKLUYT. Vol. II.
—— Beauchamps, Voyage made by diverse of the ... family of ... to J., 1096. HAKLUYT. Vol. II.
—— Edgar. Voyage to J. ... 1102. HAKLUYT. Vol. II.
—— Gutuere, an English Lady, etc. Voyage toward J., 1097. HAKLUYT. Vol. II.
—— Helena, Empresse. Voyage to J., 337. HAKLUYT. Vol. II.
—— Ingulphus, Abbot of Croiland. Voyage unto J., 1064. HAKLUYT. Vol. II.
—— Lacy, J. Voyage to J., 1173. HAKLUYT. Vol. II.
—— Lok, J. Voyage to J., 1553. HAKLUYT. Vol. II.
—— Lord John of Holland, Earle of Huntington. Voyage to J. ... 1394. HAKLUYT. Vol. II.
—— Mandeville, W., Erle of Essex. Voyage to J., 1177. HAKLUYT. Vol. II.
—— Mowbrey, T. L., Duke of Norfolk. Voyage to J., 1399. HAKLUYT. Vol. II.
—— Petrus de Rupibus, Bp. of Winchester. Voyage to J., 1231. HAKLUYT. Vol. II.
—— Richard I. Famous Voyage ... for the recovering of J. ... 1190. HAKLUYT. Vol. II.
—— Swanus, one of the Sonnes of Earl Godwin. Voyage unto J., 1052. HAKLUYT. Vol. II.
—— William, Archb. of Tyre. Voyage to J. ... 1130. HAKLUYT. Vol. II.
—— Voyage of the Bp. of Winchester to J., 1417. HAKLUYT. Vol. II.
—— Bertrandon de la Brocquière. Voyage ... de J. en France par la Voie de Terra ... 1432-33. HAKLUYT. Vol. IV.
—— Maundrell, H. Journey from Aleppo to J., 1696. HARRIS, J. Vol. II.
—— Alured. Pilgrimage to J., 1058. KERR. Vol. I.
—— Ingulphus. Pilgrimage to J., 1064. KERR. Vol. I.
—— Leucander, A. Travels to J. in the eleventh century. KERR. Vol. I.
—— Swanus. Voyage to J., 1052. KERR. Vol. I.
—— Coryat, T. Journey from J. to the Court of the Great Mogul, 1615-16. KERR. Vol. IX.
—— Maundrell's Journey from Aleppo to J. PINKERTON. Vol. X.
—— Coryat, T. Letter from J. to the Court of the Great Mogul, 1615-16, etc. PURCHAS. Vol. I.
—— Biddulph, W. Part of a letter from J. PURCHAS. Vol. II.
—— Continuation of the J. Expedition ... gathered out of Matthew Paris ... 1118-1292. PURCHAS. Vol. II.

Jerusalem.—Coryates, T. Travels to . . . J., 1612-14. PURCHAS. Vol. II.
——— Folcherius Carnotensis. Acta of the Pilgrimes in their Expedition to J. . . . 1095-1124. PURCHAS. Vol. II.
——— The Historie of the first Expedition to J., by Godfrey of Bullen . . . 1095. PURCHAS. Vol. II.
——— Pilgrimage to J., written in very old English Rime. PURCHAS. Vol. II.
——— Timberley, H. Report of the Voyage from Cairo . . . to J., 1601. PURCHAS. Vol. II.
——— Relation des Voyages de Sæwulf, à J., . . . 1102-3, *etc.* VOYAGES and TRAVELS. Recueil, *etc.* Vol. IV.
——— Maundrell, Henry. Travels from Aleppo to J., 1606. VOYAGES and TRAVELS. The World displayed. Vol. XI.

Jesd.—*See* YEZD.

Jesso.—SIEBOLD, P. F. DE. Nippon. Archiv zur Beschreibung von Japan . . . Jezo, *etc.* *Leyden*, 1832.
——— ——— Nippon. Archiv zur Beschreibung von Japan . . . Jezo, *etc.* *Leyden*, 1852.
——— BICKMORE, A. S. The Ainos, or Hairy Men of Yesso, *etc.* *New Haven*, 1868.
——— History of . . . Yedzo, *etc.* 1585-1746. HARRIS, J. Vol. II.
——— Intelligence concerning . . . J., *etc.* KERR. Vol. IX.
——— Relation de la découverte de la terre de Iesso. THEVENOT. Vol. II.
——— Castell, P. Abhandlung über . . . Kamtschatka und J., *etc.* VOYAGES and TRAVELS. Allgemeine Historie, *etc.* Vol. XIX.

Jessulmere.—BOILEAU, A. W. E. Tour through . . . Jesulmer, *etc.* *Calc.*, 1837.

Jesulmer.—*See* JESSULMERE.

Jesus.—RAIMONDI, A. Analisis de las . . . Aguas Minerales de J., *etc.* *Arequipa*, 1864.

Jeypoor.—DASEVI, J. P. Report on . . . the J. Territory. *Mussorie*, 1863.

Jeypore.—*See* JEYPOOR.

Jeso.—*See* JESSO.

Jihoon.—*See* SIR-DARIA.

Joajacarta.—Schouten, G. Reisen nach . . . Mataram (J.) . . . 1658-65. VOYAGES and TRAVELS. Allgemeine Historie, *etc.* Vol. XII.

Jodhpoor.—*See* JOUDPORE.

Jœgersprlis.—VANDRING gjennem J.'s Have og Lund, *etc.* *Kjö.*, 1858.

Johanna.—Prior, J. Voyage . . . to . . . J. . . . 1813. VOYAGES and TRAVELS, New. 1819. Vol. II.

John Mayen's Island.—*See* JAN MAYEN.

Johor.—*See* JOHORE.

Johore.—Voyage to Pullicatt . . . Narrative of . . . Occurrences in . . . J., *etc.* KERR. Vol. VIII.

Johora.—Matelief, C. Reise . . . 1605-8 . . . Verrichtungen zu J., etc.
Voyages and Travels Allgemeine Historie, etc. Vol. VIII.
Joppa.—Falconer, D. Journey from J. to Jerusalem in 1751. **1753.**
―― Hardine. Voyage . . . which arrived at J., 1102. Hakluyt. Vol. II.
―― Voyage . . . of Englishmen, Danes, and Flemings, who arrived at J. . . . 1109. Hakluyt. Vol. II.
Jordan.—Seetzen, M. Brief Account of the Countries adjoining the J., etc. *Bath,* **1810.**
―― Buckingham, J. S. Travels . . . east of the . . . J. **1822.**
―― Ritter, C. Der J. und die Beschiffung des Todten Meeres. *Berl.,* **1850.**
―― Kennedy, J. The J. and the Dead Sea. **1851.**
―― Lynch, W. F. Official Report of the U. S. Expedition to explore the . . . J. *Balt., U. S.,* **1852.**
―― Graham, W. The J. and the Rhine, etc. **1854.**
―― Macgregor, J. The 'Rob Roy' on the J., etc. *Lond.,* **1869.**
Joudpore.—Boileau, A. W. E. Tour through . . . Jodhpoor, etc. *Calc.,* **1837.**
Juan de Ulloa, San.—*See* San Juan de Ulloa.
Juan Fernandez.—Sutcliffe, T. The Earthquake of J. F. . . . in the year 1835, etc. *Manchest,* **1839.**
Jucatan.—*See* Yucatan.
Judæa.—Bellonius, P. Plurimarum . . . rerum in . . . J. . . . conspectarum observationes, etc. *Antw.,* **1589.**
―― Harant, K. Gesta . . . do Země Judské, etc. *v. Praze,* **1854.**
―― Tobler, T. Dritte Wanderung nach Palästina . . . Fussreisen in Gebirge Judäas, etc. *Gotha,* **1859.**
―― Biddulph, W. Travels of four Englishmen . . . into . . . J. . . . in 1600 and 1611. Churchill. Vol. VII.
―― Mandevil, Sir J. Voyage from England to J. . . . from 1322 to 1855. Hakluyt. Vol. II.
Jujuy.—Moneta, P. Informe sobre la Practicabilidad do la Prolongacion del Ferrocarril Central Argentino desde Cordoba hasta J. *Buen. A.,* **1867.**
Julia, Island.—Pasvoer, C. Notes sur l'Île J., etc.
Jumna.—Fraser, J. B. Tour . . . to the sources of the J., etc. **1820.**
―― Skinner, T. Excursions . . . including a Walk . . . to the Sources of the J., etc. **1832.**
Jupiter Ammon, Oasis of.—Belzoni, G. Narrative of . . . a journey . . . to the Oasis of J. A. **1822.**
Jura.—Marcou, J. Lettres sur les Roches du J., etc. *Par.,* **1857.**
Justinopolis.—*See* Orfah.
Jutland.—Forchhammer, G. Notitser angaende den sandsynlige Forekomst af Juraformationen i det nordlige Jylland.

Jutland — Kalabar.

Jutland.—SCOTT, C. H. Danes and the Swedes ... with a Peep into J. 1856.
—— MARRYAT, H. Residence in J., etc. 1860.
——, **South.**—See SLESWICK.
Jylland.—See JUTLAND.
Jyntsea.—BERGHAUS, H. Asia ... Memoir zur Erklärung ... der reduzirten Karte von ... Djyntia, etc. *Gotha*, 1832-35.

K.

Kabah.—NORMAN, B. W. Rambles in Yucatan ... including a Visit to ... K., etc. *N. Y.*, 1843.
Kabinda.—See CABENDA.
Kabool.—VIGNE, G. T. Personal Narrative of a visit to ... K., etc.
—— ELPHINSTONE, HON. M. Account of ... Caubul, etc. 1815.
—— BURNES, SIR A. Travels ... from India to Cabool, etc. 1834.
—— LASSEN, C. Zur Geschichte der Griechischen und Indoskythischen Könige in ... K., etc. *Bonn*, 1838.
—— VIGNE, G. T. A personal Narrative of a Visit to ... K., etc. *Lond.*, 1840.
—— JERVIS, T. B. Review of a Narrative of the Campaign ... in ... K. in 1838-39. *Bomb.*, 1841.
—— MOORCROFT and TREBECK. Travels in ... K. ... 1819 to 1825. 1841.
—— WOOD, J. Personal Narrative of a Journey to the Source of the Oxus, by ... K., etc. 1841.
—— BURNES, SIR A. Cabool, etc. 1843.
—— BARR, W. Journal of a March ... to Cabul, etc. *Lond.*, 1844.
—— HÜGEL, BARON C. VON. Das Kabul-Becken, etc. *Wien*, 1850.
Kabylia.—HERBER. Dictionnaire Français-Berbère; dialects écrit ... par les Kabailes de la Division d'Alger. *Par.*, 1844.
—— DAUMAS, ET FABAR. La Grande Kabylie, etc. *Par.*, 1847.
—— AUCAPITAINE, BARON H. Les Kabyles, etc. *Par.*, 1864.
——, **Upper.** AUCAPITAINE, BARON H. Mollusques ... dans la Haute Kabylie. 1862.
Kachao.—See CACHAO.
Kachemire.—See CASHMERE.
Kaffa.—BEKE, C. T. Enquiry into M. A. d'Abbadie's Journey to K., etc. 1851.
Kaffir Land.—See CAFFRARIA.
Kahlen Mountains.—SCHMIDL, A. A. Der Mons Cetius des Ptolemäus. *Wien*, 1856.
Kajaaga, Kajaaja.—See GALAM.
Kakongo.—See CACONGO.
Kalabar.—See CALABAR.

Kalahari Desert.—BALDWIN, W. C.—African Hunting . . . including
. . . the K. D., *etc.* **1863.**

Kalaniddee.—MARSHALL, T. Statistical Reports on . . . K., *etc.*
Bomb., **1822.**

Kalat.—*See* KELAT.

Kamschatska.—*See* KAMTCHATKA.

Kamtchatka.—KRASHENINNIKOV, S. P. The History of K., *etc.*
Glocester, **1764.**

——. KRASCHENINNIKOW, S. Beschreibung des Landes K. *Lemgo,* **1766.**

—— STELLERS, G. W. Beschreibung von . . . K., *etc.* *Frankf.,* **1774.**

—— COCHRANE, J. D. Narrative of a pedestrian Journey . . . to . . .
K. **1824.**

—— DOBELL, P. Travels in K., *etc.* **1830.**

—— ERMAN, A. Ueber Ebbe und Fluth an den Ochosker und Kämtschatkischen Kusten des Grossen Oceans. **1845.**

—— HABERSHAM, A. W. My last Cruise . . . Visits to . . . K., *etc.*
Phil., **1857.**

—— KITTLITZ, F. H. v. Denkwürdigkeiten einer Reise . . . durch K.
Gotha, **1858.**

—— TRONSON. J. M. Narrative of a Voyage to . . . K., *etc.* **1859.**

—— COLLINS, P. McD. A Voyage . . . with . . . incidental notices
of . . . K., *etc.* *N. Y. and Lond.,* **1860.**

—— Account of . . . K. HARRIS, J. Vol. II.

—— Islands . . . K., climat, mineraux, animaux. LAHARPE, J. Vol. XVI.

—— K., Habitans, Découverte, *etc.* LAHARPE, J. Vol. XVII.

—— Lesseps, M. de. Travels in K., in 1787-88. PELHAM. Vol. II.

—— Castell, P. Abhandlung über . . . K. und Jesso, *etc.* VOYAGES
and TRAVELS. Allgemeine Historie, *etc.* Vol. XIX.

—— Cranz. Historie . . . von Grönland . . . K., *etc.* VOYAGES and
TRAVELS. Allgemeine Historie, *etc.* Vol. XIX.

—— Reisen . . . durch Nordosten nach K. zu gehen. VOYAGES and
TRAVELS. Allgemeine Historie, *etc.* Vol. XIX.

—— Reise nach K. durch Sibirien. VOYAGES and TRAVELS. Allgemeine
Historie, *etc.* Vol. XIX.

——, Sea of.—STÆHLIN, J. VON. An Account of the New Northern
Archipelago lately discovered . . . in the Seas of K. and Anadir, *etc.*
Lond., **1774.**

Kano.—Relation de Ghanal (K.), *etc.* VOYAGES and TRAVELS. Recueil, *etc.*
Vol. II.

Kansas.—FREMONT, J. C. Life . . . and Adventures in K., *etc.*
N. Y., **1856.**

—— ROBINSON, S. T. L. K.; its Interior . . . Life.
Bost. U. S., **1856.**

—— SHUMARD, B. F., and SWALLOW, G. C. Descriptions of New Fossils,
from . . . K. *St. Louis,* **1859.**

Kansas, River.—BECKWITH, E. G. Report of Exploration . . . from the Mouth of the K., *etc.* *Wash.*, 1854.
——— Pike. Voyage . . . anx sources . . . du K. . . . 1805-7. ETZEKA, Vol. IX.
Kansès, River.—*See* KANSAS.
Kanton.—*See* CANTON.
Kanuri.—*See* BORNU.
Karaboghas Bay.—ZIMMERMANN, C. Denkschrift über den untern Lauf des Oxus zum Karabugas Haff, *etc.* *Berl.*, 1845.
Karabugas-Haff.—*See* KARABOGHAS BAY.
Karakorum Mountains.—DIARY. The Diary of a Hunter from the Punjab to the K. M. *Lond. and Norw.*, 1863.
Karamania.—*See* CARAMANIA.
Karazm.—*See* KARISM.
Kardo.—*See* ISKARDOH.
Karena.—PAYRE, LIEUT.-COL. Report on . . . his Tour among the K. Mountain Tribes, *etc.* 1861.
Karism. Description of . . . Karazm, *etc.* ASTLEY. Vol. IV.
Karlsbad.—*See* CARLSBAD.
Karpathos.—*See* SCARPANTO.
Kars.—KMETY, G. Narrative of the defence of K., Sep. 29, 1855, *etc.* 1856.
——— MONTEITH, W. K. and Erzeroum, *etc.* 1856.
——— SANDWITH, H. Narrative of the Siege of K., *etc.* 1856.
Karst.—SCHMIDL, A. A. Guide du Voyageur dans . . . les Cavernes . . . du K. *Vienne*, 1854.
——— Wegweiser in die . . . Höhlen des Karstes. *Wien*, 1858.
Kasan. *See* KAZAN.
Kasbin.—*See* CASBIN.
Kaschmir.—*See* CASHMERE.
Kashgar.—DEROHAUS, H. Asia . . . Memoir zur Erklärung . . . der reduzirten Karte von . . . Katschhar, *etc.* *Gotha*, 1832-35.
——— VAIJENANOF, CAPTAIN. A Journey to K. in 1858, *etc.* [1868.]
——— HAYWARD, G. Statements of Routes between . . . K. . . . and British Territory. 1869.
——— Description of . . . K., *etc.* ASTLEY. Vol. IV.
——— Beschreibung der Kleinen Bukharey oder des Königreichs K. VOYAGES and TRAVELS. Allgemeine Historie, *etc.* Vol. VII.
Kashmir.—*See* CASHMERE.
Kasos.—DAPPER. Beschryving van . . . K., *etc.* 1688.
Kaspisches Meer.—*See* CASPIAN SEA.
Katay.—*See* CHINA.
Kathiawad.—*See* KATTYWAR.
Katmandu.—*See* KHATMANDOO.
Katschhar.—*See* KASHGAR.

Kattiawar.—See KATTYWAR.
Kattywar.—BUIST, G. Notes on a Journey through part of Kattiawar, etc.
1855.
—— BURGESS, J. Notes of a Visit to . . . places in Kathiawad, etc.
Bombay, 1869.
Kaukasien, Kaukasische Lander, Kaukasus. See CAUCASUS.
Kawau Island.—NEW ZEALAND GEOLOGICAL SURVEY. Abstract Report . . . Together with reports on . . . K. I., etc. *Well.*, 1869.
Kawhaw Island.—See KAWAU ISLAND.
Kaybar.—GOTTBERG, E. DE. Des Cataractes . . . de K. *Par.*, 1867.
Kayor, Lake.—DRUE, A. Attempt for a discovery of the Lake of K. in 1711, etc. ASTLEY. Vol. II.
—— Brüe, A. Versuch die See K. zu entdecken, 1714. VOYAGES and TRAVELS. Allgemeine Historie, etc. Vol. II.
Kasan.—KNORR, E. Meteorologische Beobachtungen aus . . . Kasan. 1835-36. *Kasan*, 1841.
Kazbek.—FRESHFIELD, D. W. Travels . . . including . . . Ascents of K., etc. *Lond.*, 1869.
Kazvin.—See CASBIN.
Keang-Chu.—Journey of J. de Fontaney . . . from Peking to Kyang Chew . . . in 1688. ASTLEY. Vol. III.
Ke-oho.—See CACHAO.
Kedah, Kedda.—See QUEDAH.
Kedje.—Ross, E. C. Report on a Visit to Kej, etc.
1865.
Kej.—See KEDJE.
Kelat.—MASSON, C. Narrative of . . . Journeys in . . . K., etc. 1844.
Kentucky.—BRADBURY, J. Travels in . . . K., etc. *Liver.*, 1817.
—— COLLINS, L. Historical sketches of K., etc. *Cincin.*, 1847.
—— OWEN, D. D. Second and third Reports of the Geological Survey in K., etc. *Frankfort, Ken.*, 1857.
—— Michaux, F. A. Travels . . . in . . . K. . . . 1802. VOYAGES and TRAVELS. A Collection, etc. 1805. Vol. I.
Kertch.—M'PHERSON, D. Antiquities of K., etc.
1857.
—— THOMPSON, B. and HOGG, J. Sketches of K., etc.
1857.
—— ABICH, H. Einleitende Grundzüge der Geologie der Halbinseln K., etc.
St. Pet., 1865.
—— —— Karten und Profile zur Geologie der Halbinseln K., etc.
Tiflis, 1866.
—— HELMERSEN, G. VON. Die . . . Naphthaquellen . . . bei K., etc.
1867.
Kertsch.—See KERTCH.
Kew.—HOOKER, SIR W. J. Report on . . . the Royal Gardens of K., from 1853 to 1859.
1859.

s 2

Kew.—SABINE, MAJOR-GEN. F. Results of the Magnetic Observations at the K. Observatory from 1857 . . . to 1862 inclusive.
Lond., **1863.**

Khanapoor.—MARSHALL, T. Statistical Reports on . . . K., etc.
Bomb., **1822.**

Khanbalek.—Travels of the Ambassadors . . . of Persia . . . to K. in Kathay, 1419. KEHR. Vol. I.

Kharacène.—See CHARACENE.

Khartoum.—See KHARTUM.

Khartum.—MELLY, G. Khartoum and the Blue and White Niles.
1851.

——— HAMILTON, J. Sinai . . . Wanderings . . . from Sawakin to Chartum. **1857.**

——— HEUGLIN, M. T. VON. Reise nach . . . Chartûm, etc.
Jena, **1869.**

Khatmandoo.—OLIPHANT, L. A Journey to Katmandu, etc.
Lond., **1852.**

Khio.—See SCIO.

Khiva.—MOURAVIEV, N. Voyage . . . à K., 1819-20, etc. *Par.,* **1823.**

——— GENS, GENERAL MAJOR. Nachrichten über Chiwa, etc.
St. Pet., **1839.**

——— HELMERSEN, G. VON. Nachrichten über Chiwa, etc.
St. Pet., **1839.**

——— VIGNE, G. T. A personal Narrative of a visit to Ghuzni . . . with notices of . . . K., etc. *Lond.,* **1840.**

——— ZIMMERMANN, C. Geographische Analyse eines Versuches zur Darstellung des Kriegstheaters Russlands gegen Chiwa. *Berl.,* **1840.**

——— ABBOTT, CAPT. J. Journey from Herant to K., etc. **1843.**

——— BASINER, T. F. J. Naturwissenschaftliche Reise . . . nach Chiwa.
St. Pet., **1848.**

——— LAMANSKY, E. Esquisse Géographique . . . et quelques traits des Mœurs des Habitants de . . . K., etc. *Par.,* **1858.**

——— VAMBÉRY, A. Travels . . . to K., etc. *Lond.,* **1864.**

——— Mouraviev, N. Voyage . . . à K. EYRIÈS. Vol. XIV.

Khokan.—GENS, GENERAL MAJOR. Nachrichten über . . . Chokand, etc. *St. Pet.,* **1839.**

——— HELMERSEN, G. VON. Nachrichten über . . . Chokand, etc.
St. Pet., **1839.**

——— LAMANSKY, E. Esquisse Géographique . . . et quelques traits des Mœurs des Habitants de . . . K. *Par.,* **1858.**

——— Nazarov, P. Voyage dans le K., 1813-14. EYRIÈS. Vol. XIV.

Khokhan.—See KHOKAN.

Kholmogory.—Burrough, S. Voyage from Colmogro to Russia to Wardhouse . . . 1557. HAKLUYT. Vol. I.

——— Southam, T. and Sparke, J. Voyage . . . from Colmogro to Novogrod . . . 1566. HAKLUYT. Vol. I.

Khondistan.—CAMPBELL, MAJOR-GENERAL J. A Personal Narrative of Thirteen Years' Service among the Wild Tribes of K., etc.
Lond., 1864.

Khorassan.—FRASER, J. B. Journey into Korassán in 1821-2, etc. 1825.

Khotan.—HAYWARD, G. Statements of Routes between ... K., and British Territory. 1869.

Khuzistan.—STOCQUELER, J. H. Fifteen Months' Pilgrimage through ... K., etc. 1832.

—— See also ARABISTAN.

Khyber Pass.—BARR, W. Journal ... including ... a Narrative of Operations in the K. P.: ... in 1839. Lond., 1844.

Kilkenny.—TIGHE, W. Statistical Observations relative to ... K., etc.
Dubl., 1802.

Killarney.—KILLARNEY, a Description of. 1776.

Kilwah.—See QUILOA.

Kimoll.—See ARGENTIERA.

King George's Islands.—Byron, Comm. Voyage ... to ... K. G. I., 1764-66, HAWKESWORTH, J. Vol. 1.

King George's Sound. EYRE, E. J. Journals of Expeditions ... Overland from Adelaide to K. G. S., etc. 1845.

Kingston.—CANADA. Estimates of the Expense of ... Water Communications ... from the Ottawa to K., etc. 1828.

King's Town.— DANGAR, H. Index ... with ... ground-plan ... ... of K. T., New South Wales. 1828.

Kirghis Steppes.—See STEPPES, KIRGHIZ.

Kirgisensteppe.—See STEPPES, KIRGHIZ.

Kirkby Thore.—SMYTH, ADMIRAL, W. H. On some Roman Vestigia recently found at K. T.; in Westmoreland. 1845.

Kistnah.—India. Reports of the ... effects of the Godavery and Krishna Annicuts, etc. Madras, 1858.

Kleczandw.—ZEUSCHNER, HERR. Ueber die neuentdeckte Silurformation von K., etc. 1869.

Klein Asie.—See ASIA MINOR.

Knaresborough.—HIRON. The Tourist's Companion; being a ... description ... of ... K., etc. Ripon, 1828.

Kokan.—See KHOKAN.

Kok-si-Kon.—RICHARDS, J. China. Harbours of K.-s.-K., etc. 1855.

Kolzum, Sea of.—See RED SEA.

Kongo.—See CONGO.

Konkun.—See CONCAN.

Koonawur.—GERARD, A. Account of K., etc. 1841.

Kooral.—SIEBOLD, P. F. VON. Nippon. Archiv zur Beschreibung von Japan ... K., etc. 1852.

Koordistan, Koordistaun.—See KURDISTAN.

Korasan.—See KHORASSAN.

Kordofan.—RÜPPEL, E. Reisen in ... K. etc. 1829.
Korea.—See COREA.
Korfu.—See CORFU.
Koristan.—See KUZISTAN.
Koromandel.—See COROMANDEL.
Korsetzko.—ZEUCHNER, HERR. Ueber das Vorkommen von Diceras arietina in K., etc. 1868.
Kostantínah.—See CONSTANTINE.
Koto.—See KOTOU.
Kotou.—The Kingdoms of Koto and Popo. ASTLEY. Vol. III.
Krafto.—See SAGHALIEN.
Krain.—See CARNIOLA.
Království České.—See BOHEMIA.
Krim Tartary.—See TARTARY, CRIMEAN.
Krishna.—See KISTNAH.
Krym.—See CRIMEA.
Kuddapah.—See CUDDAPAH.
Kulwah.—See QUILOA.
Kumaon.—INDIA. Official Reports on the Province of K., etc. *Agra*, 1851.
Kunduz.—MOORCROFT AND TREBECK. Travels in ... K. ... 1819 to 1825. 1841.
Kurdistan.—KINNEIR, J. M. Journey through ... K. in 1813-14, etc. 1818.

— KEPPEL, HON. G. Personal Narrative of a Journey from India ... by ... Curdistan, etc. 1827.
— FRASER, J. B. Travels in Koordistan, etc. *Lond.*, [1835 ?]
— RICH, C. J. Narrative of a Residence in K., etc. 1836.
— MIGNAN, R. Winter Journey ... into K. 1839.
— FOWLER, G. Three Years in Persia, with ... adventures in K. 1841.
— JONES, J. F. Narrative of a Journey through ... K., etc. *Bomb.*, 1849.
— LAYARD, A. H. Nineveh ... with ... a Visit to the Chaldean Christians of K., etc. 1849.
— BADGER, G. P. The Nestorians ... with ... a Mission to Coordistan, etc. 1852.
— LAYARD, A. H. Discoveries ... with Travels in ... K., etc. 1853.
— WAGNER, M. Travels in ... K., etc. 1856.
— MILLINGEN, F. Wild Life among the Koords. *Lond.*, 1870.
— Jackson, J. Journey ... in 1797, through Curdistan, etc. PELHAM. Vol. II.

Kurile Islands—KRASCHENINNIKOV, S. P. The History of ... the Kurilsky I., etc. *Glocester*, 1764.

Kurile Islands.—SIEBOLD, P. F. DE. Nippon. Archiv zur Beschreibung von Japan . . . den Südlichen Kurilen, *etc.* *Leyden*, 1832.

―――― Nippon. Archiv zur Beschreibung von Japan . . . den Südlichen Kurilen, *etc.* *Leyden*, 1852.

―――― DICKMORE, A. S. The Ainos, or Hairy Men of . . . the K. I. *New Haven*, 1868.

Kurilsky Islands.—*See* KURILE ISLANDS.

Kurland.—*See* CURLAND.

Kurnool.—King, W. On the Kuddapah and K. Formations. INDIA, GEOLOGICAL SURVEY. RECORDS, *etc.* Vol. II.

Kurrachee.—ANDREW, W. P. Port of K., *etc.* 1857.

―――― RAWLINSON, SIR H. C. Notes on the direct Overland Telegraph from Constantinople to K. 1861.

Kurrachi.—*See* KURRACHEE.

Kwo'ra, River.—*See* NIGER, RIVER.

Kyang Chew.—*See* KEANG-CHU.

L.

Laas.—SCHMIDL, A. A. Die Grotten und Höhlen von . . . L. *Wien*, 1854.

Labin.—Description of the Empire of Catay and Labin, *etc.* PURCHAS. Vol. III.

Labrador.—CARTWRIGHT, G. A Journal of Transactions and Events . . . on the Coast of L. *Newark*, 1792.

―――― CHAPPELL, LIEUT. Voyage of H. M. S. Rosamond to . . . the N. Coast of L. 1818.

―――― CRANTZ, D. History . . . of the Mission in L. 1820.

―――― HIND, H. Y. Explorations in the Interior of the L. Peninsula, *etc.* 1863.

―――― Terre de L. EYRIES. Vol. VIII.

Labuan.—FORBES, F. E. Five Years in China . . . with an account of the Occupation of . . . L., *etc.* 1848.

Laconia.—Sibthorpe, Dr. Journal relating to . . . L., *etc.* WALPOLE, R. Travels, *etc.*

Lac-Tchou.—IBBACHÈRE, M. DE LA. État actuel . . . des royaumes de . . . Lac-thu, *etc.* *Par.*, 1812.

Ladac, Ladak.—*See* LADAKH.

Ladakh.—MOORCROFT and TREBECK. Travels . . . in L. . . . 1819 to 1825. 1841.

―――― VIGNE, G. T. Travels in . . . L., *etc.* 1842.

―――― CUNNINGHAM, A. Ladák, Physical, Statistical, *etc.* 1854.

―――― MARKHAM, F. Shooting in . . . Ladac, *etc.* *Lond.*, 1854.

―――― TORRENS, H. D. Travels in L., *etc.* *Lond.*, 1862.

―――― LEITNER, G. W. Results of a Tour in . . . L., *etc.* *Lahore, Lond.*, [1868.]

Ladoga, Lake.—DÖLLEN, W. Resultate einer astronomisch-geodätischen Verbindung zwischen Pulkowa und den Ufern des Ladogasees. **1858.**

Ladrone Islands.—Beschreibung der Marianischen Inseln. VOYAGES and TRAVELS. Allgemeine Historie, *etc.* Vol. XI.

Lago Maggiore.—BERTOLOTTI, D. Viaggio ai . . . Laghi . . . M.
Como, **1825.**

La Guayra.—Techo, F. N. del. History of . . . Guaira, *etc.* CHURCHILL. Vol. IV.

La Hacha, Rio de.—*See* RIO DE LA HACHA.

Lahor.—*See* LAHORE.

Lahore.—BURNES, SIR A. Travels . . . also a . . . Voyage . . . from the sea to L., *etc.* **1834.**

——— BARR, W. Journal . . . including . . . a Visit to . . . L., *etc.*
Lond., **1844.**

——— PUNJAB. An Account of the formal commencement of the Punjab Railway at L., *etc.* **1859.**

——— B., M. V. From London to L. Lond., **1868.**

——— Travels of . . . B. Goës . . . from L. . . . to China in 1002. ASTLEY. Vol. IV.

——— Goës. Travels from L. to China. PINKERTON. Vol VII.

——— Finch, W. Observations . . . in 1607 . . . Description of . . . L., *etc.* PURCHAS. Vol. I.

——— Goes, B. Travels from L. to China . . . 1603. PURCHAS. Vol. III.

Lake of the Woods.—KEATING. W. H. Narrative of an expedition to the . . . L. of the W., *etc.* **1825.**

Lake Superior.—FOSTER, J. W., and WHITNEY, J. D. Report on the Geology . . . of . . . the L. S. Land District, *etc.* Pt. I., II.
Wash., **1850, 51.**

——— DAWSON, S. J. Report on . . . the Country between L. S. and the Red River Settlement, *etc.* Toronto, **1859.**

Lancashire.—CLARKE, J.—Survey of the Lakes of . . . L., *etc.* **1789.**

——— MURRAY, HON. MRS. S. Guide to . . . the Lakes of . . . L., *etc.*
1799.

——— HOUSMAN, J. Descriptive . . . Guide to . . . L., *etc.*
Carlisle, **1816.**

——— BLACK, J. Memoir on the Roman Garrison at Mancunium and its probable influence on . . . S. L. Edin., **1856.**

Lancaster Sound.—GOODSIR, R. A. Arctic Voyage to . . . L. S., *etc.*
1850.

Lankeran.—MORITZ, A. [The Thermal Springs of L.] *Russian*
[*Tiflis*] **1865.**

Lango.—FRANCESETTI, L. Lettres sur les Vallées de L. Turin, **1823.**

Laongo.—*See* LOANGO.

Laos.—BISSACHÈRE. M. DE LA. État actuel . . . des royaumes de . . . L., *etc.* Par., **1812.**

Laos.—Mouhot, H. Travels in . . . L., *etc.* Lond., 1864.
——— Kao, D. An authentick . . . description of . . . L., *etc.* Harris, J. Vol. II.
——— Beschreibung der Königreiche L. und Cambaja, 1691. Voyages and Travels. Allgemeine Historie, *etc.* Vol. XVIII.

Lapland.—Ihre, J. Lexicon Lapponicum, *etc.* Holmiæ, 1780.
——— Acerbi, J. Travels through . . . L. . . . to the North Cape, *etc.* 1802.
——— Svanberg, J. Exposition des Opérations faites en Lapponie, pour la détermination d'un Arc du Méridien, en 1801-3, *etc.* Stockh., 1805.
——— Linnæus, C. Lachesis Lapponica, or a Tour in L., *etc.* Lond., 1811.
——— Brooke, Sir A. de C., Bart. Winter in L., *etc.* 1827.
——— Everest, R. A Journey through . . . L., *etc.* Lond., 1829.
——— Rask, R. K. Ræsonneret Lappisk Sproglære, *etc.* Köbenh., 1832.
——— Baer, K. E. von. Expédition . . . en Lapponie.
St. Pet., 1837, 38.
——— Clarke, E. D. Travels in . . . L., *etc.* 1838.
——— Dillon, Hon. A. A Winter in . . . L. 1840.
——— Struve, W. Exposé historique des Travaux . . . 1851 . . . Suivi de deux Rapports de M. G. Lindhagen . . . sur les Opérations de Lapponie, 1851. St. Pet., 1852.
——— M'Douoall, G. F. Directions . . . including a description of . . . the Coast of . . . L, *etc.* 1858.
——— Taylor, B. Northern Travel . . . Pictures of . . . L., *etc.* 1858.
——— Reinere, M. Description hydrographique . . . de la . . . Côte de la Lapponie, *etc.* *Par.*, 1860-62.
——— A Voyage . . . containing an Account of the . . . Laplands, *etc.* Harris, J. Vol. II.
——— Leem's Account of Danish L. Pinkerton. Vol. I.
——— Reynard's Journey to L. Pinkerton. Vol. I.
——— Maupertius, H. von. Reise nach L., 1736-7. Voyages and Travels. Allgemeine Historie, *etc.* Vol. XVII.
——— Outhier, Abt. Reise nach L., 1837. Voyages and Travels. Allgemeine Historie, *etc.* Vol. XVII.
——— Regnard. Reise nach L., 1681. Voyages and Travels. Allgemeine Historie, *etc.* Vol. XVII.
——— Högström, P. Historische Beschreibung des Schwedischen Lapplandes. Voyages and Travels. Allgemeine Historie, *etc.* Vol. XIX.
——— See also Arsina.—Windso.

La Plata.—Lopez, J. J. Ueber die . . . Beziehungen Deutschlands mit den La- P. Staaten, *etc.* Berlin.
——— Azara, F. de. Apuntamientos para la historia natural . . . del . . . Rio de la P. Mad., 1802.

La Plata — La Plata, River.

La Plata.—Rio de la P. Noticias ... de las Provincias Unidas del Rio de La P., etc. **1826.**

—— Angelis, P. de. Coleccion de obras ... relativos á la historia ... del Rio de la P., etc. *Buen. A.,* **1836, 37.**

—— Parish, Sir W. Buenos Ayres and the Provinces of the Rio de La P., etc. **1839.**

—— Fitz-Roy, Rear-Adml. R. Sailing directions for ... La P., etc. **1848.**

—— Parish, Sir W. Buenos Ayres and the Provinces of the Rio de la P., etc. **1852.**

—— —— Buenos Aires y las Provincias del Rio de la P., etc. *Buen. A.,* **1853.**

—— Kerst, S. G. Die Plata-Staaten, etc. *Berl.,* **1854.**

—— Mansfield, C. B. Paraguay ... and the Plate, in 1852-53, etc. *Camb.,* **1856.**

—— Page, T. J. La P., the Argentine Confederation, etc. *N. Y.,* **1859.**

—— Wheelwright, W. Introductory Remarks on the Provinces of the L. P., etc. *Lond.,* **1861.**

—— Hinchliff, T. W. South American Sketches, or, a Visit to ... La P., etc. **1863.**

—— Neori, C. L'Emigrazione Italiana al Plata. **1863.**

—— Poucel, B. Mes Itinéraires dans les provinces du Rio de la P., 1854-1857, etc. *Par.,* **1864.**

—— Poucel, B. Les Otages de Durazno. Souvenirs de Rio de la P. ... 1845 à 1851. *Par.,* **1864.**

—— Sturz, J. J. Neue Beiträge über ... die L. P.-Länder. *Berlin,* **1865.**

—— La Plata. The River Plate ... as a Field for Emigration, etc. *Lond.* **[1866.]**

—— La Plata. No. 1 (1868). Correspondence respecting Hostilities in the River Plate, etc. *Lond.,* **1868.**

—— Latham, W. The States of the River Plate, etc. *Lond.,* **1868.**

—— Techo, F. N. del. History of ... Rio de la P., etc. Churchill. Vol. IV.

—— Dalrymple, A. Catalogue of Authors ... on Rio de la P., etc. Dalrymple, A. Collection of Nautical Memoirs, etc.

—— Küste der Statthalterschaft Rio de la P. bis nach Brasilien. Voyages and Travels. Allgemeine Historie, etc. Vol. XVI.

—— *See also* Argentine Confederation. Buenos Ayres.

——, **River.**—Azara, F. de. Voyages ... contenant la description ... de la Rivière de la P., etc. *Par.,* **1809.**

—— —— Du Périer, Lieut. Notes sur l'Atterrissage du Rio de la P., etc. *Par.,* **1842.**

—— —— Purvis, Commodore. Sobre las Avances del, en el Rio de la P. *Buen. A.,* **1843.**

—— —— Robertson, J. P. and W. P. Letters ... comprising Travels on the Banks of the ... Rio de la P. **1843.**

La Plata, River.—CHIRON DU BROSSAY. Instructions nautiques sur l'atterage et la navigation de la P.   *Par.,* 1845.
——— ——— HADFIELD, W. Brazil, the River Plate, *etc.*   1854.
——— ——— PAGE, T. J. Report of the Exploration and Survey of the ... L. P., *etc.*   *Wash.,* 1859.
——— ——— BONCABUT, A. Manuel de la Navigation dans le Rio de la P., *etc.*   *Par.,* 1857.
——— ——— SNOW, W. P. Two Years' Cruise ... in the River Plate.   1857.
——— ——— MOUCHEZ, E. Nouveau Manuel de la Navigation dans le Rio de la P., *etc.*   *Par.,* 1862.
——— ——— Drake, J. Voyage up the River Plate, 1582. HAKLUYT. Vol. IV.
——— ——— Voyage of two Englishmen to the River Plate, 1527. HAKLUYT. Vol. IV.
——— ——— Battell, A. Voyage to the River of Plate, *etc.* PURCHAS. Vol. II.
——— ——— Las Casas, B. de. Briefe Narration of ... the River la P., *etc.* PURCHAS. Vol. IV.
——— ——— Schmidel, H. Travels, from 1534-54. His Voyage up the River Plate, *etc.* PURCHAS. Vol. IV.
——— ——— Relation des Voyages du sieur Acarete sur la Rivière de la Platte, *etc.* THEVENOT. Vol. IV.
——— ——— Reisen auf dem Flusse de la P., *etc.* Cabot, 1526-27.— Mendoza, 1535-36.—Cabrera, 1538. VOYAGES and TRAVELS. Allgemeine Historie, *etc.* Vol. XVI.

Laponie.—*See* LAPLAND.
Lappland.—*See* LAPLAND.
Lappmark-Asele.—*See* ASELE-LAPPMARK.
Lapponie.—*See* LAPLAND.
Larissa.—BROWNE, E. Travels ... a Description ... of L., *etc.* HARRIS, J. Vol. II.
Laurium.—Walpole, R. and the Earl of Aberdeen. On the Mines of L. WALPOLE, R. Memoirs, *etc.*
Lausanne.—RAZOUMOWSKY, COUNT G. DE. Œuvres. Contenant, Voyage Minéralogique ... de Bruxelles à L., *etc.*   *Laus.,* 1784.
Lazistan.—SANDWITH, H. Narrative of ... Travels in ... L.   1856.
Lea.—THORNE, J. Rambles by Rivers; the ... L., *etc.*   1847.
Lebanon.—ALEPPO. Journey from Aleppo to Damascus ... with ... an account of Mount Libanus, *etc.*   1737.
——— LIGHT, H. Travels in ... Mount L. ... 1814. *Lond.,* 1818.
——— PALESTINE. Three Weeks in Palestine and L.   1836.
——— CHURCHILL, COL. Mount L., *etc.*   1853.
——— CHARMAUD, G. W. The Druses of the L., *etc.* *Lond.,* 1855.
——— PORTER, J. L. Five Years in Damascus ... with Travels ... in ... L., *etc.*   *Lond.,* 1855.

Lebanon.—Carnarvon, Earl of. Recollections of the Druses of the L., *etc.* **1860.**
—— Dandini, J. Voyage to Mount Libanus, *etc.* Churchill. Vol. VII.
—— Dandini's Voyage to Mount Libanus. Pinkerton. Vol. X.
Leeds.—Fenteman, T. Historical Guide to L., *etc.* *Leeds*, **1858.**
—— Wright, R. On the Early History of L., *etc.* *Leeds*, **1864.**
Leeward Islands.—Latrobe, C. J. Negro Education, Windward and L. I. **1838.**
—— Murchison, Sir R. I. On the . . . value of certain Phosphate Rocks of the Anguilla Isles in the L. I. **1859.**
Leghorn.—Grimbro, Count J. Relazioni Commerciali del Egitto . . . coi Porti dell'Italia, e . . . con quello di Livorno. *Firenze*, **1841.**
—— Cialdi, A. Risultati di Studj . . . sul Porto di Livorno.
Firenze, **1853.**
—— Davis, W. A True . . . description of . . . L, *etc.* Churchill. Vol. VII.
Le Maire, Straits of.—Frezier. Reise durch die Strasse des Le M., 1711-14. Voyages and Travels. Allgemeine Historie, *etc.* Vol. XII.
Lemnos.—Hunt, Dr. L. Walpole, R. Travels, *etc.*
Lena.—Reisen . . . durch die L. in das Eismeer . . . zu gehen. Voyages and Travels. Allgemeine Historie, *etc.* Vol. XIX.
Lenkeran.—*See* Lankeran.
Lequeos.—*See* Lieu-Kieu Islands.
Lero.—Sibthorp, Dr. Voyage . . . L., *etc.* Walpole, R. Travels, *etc.*
Letto.—*See* Lithuania.
Leucadia.—Goodisson, W. Historical . . . Essay upon . . . L., *etc.*
1822.
Levanna.—Gastaldi, R. Alcuni dati sulle Punte Alpini situate fra la L. ed il Rocciamelone. *Torino*, **1868.**
Levant.—Thevenot, M. de. Travels into the L., *etc.* **1687.**
—— Lucas, P. Voyage au L., *etc.* *La Haye*, **1709.**
—— Tournefort, M. Voyage into the L., *etc.* **1741.**
—— Shaw, T. Travels, or Observations relating to . . . the L. **1757.**
—— Lettres edifiantes et curieuses, *etc.* Vol. 1-5. L.
Par., **1780-83.**
—— Saint-Sauveur, A. Grasset. Voyage . . . dans les Isles et Possessions ci-devant Vénitiennes du L., *etc.* *Par.*, **1810.**
—— Galt, J. Letters from the L. **1813.**
—— Forbin, Count. Voyage dans le L. en 1817 et 1818. *Par.*, **1819.**
—— Turner, W. Journal of a Tour in the L. **1820.**
—— Grimbro, Count J. Observations authentiques sur la Peste du L., *etc.* *Florence*, **1841.**
—— Crowe, E. E. Greek and the Turk, or . . . Prospects in the L.
1853.

Levant.—ARNOLD, R. A. From the L., *etc.* *Lond.*, **1868.**
—— Blount, H. Voyage into the L. CHURCHILL. Vol. VII.
—— Blount's Voyage to the L. PINKERTON. Vol. X.
—— The Travels of Mr. John Thevenot, in the L. 1655. VOYAGES and TRAVELS. The World displayed. Vol. XI. XII.

Lewchew.—*See* LIEU-KIEU.

Liambey, River.—COOLEY, W. D. Dr. Livingstone's Reise vom Fluss L. nach Loanda ... beleuchtet. *Gotha*, **1855.**

Libanon, Libanus.—*See* LEBANON.

Liberia.—ASHMUN, J. The L. Farmer, *etc.* *Phil.*, **1835.**
—— GURLEY, R. R. Report ... in respect to L. *Wash.*, **1850.**
—— STOCKWELL, G. S. The Republic of L.; its Geography, *etc.*
N. Y., **1868.**

Libya.—FAIDHERBE, GENERAL. L. Voyage des cinq Nasamons d'Hérodote dans l'intérieur de la Libye. *Alger*, **1867.**
—— Jannequin, C. Abstract of a Voyage to L., *etc.* ASTLEY. Vol. II.
—— Of Ægypt ... L. ... and of their Religions. PURCHAS. Vol. V.
—— Jannequin, C. Auszug von einer Reisebeschreibung nach L., *etc.* 1637. VOYAGES and TRAVELS. Allgemeine Historie, *etc.* Vol. II.
—— Scholz, J. M. A. Travels in ... the L.n Desert ... 1821. VOYAGES and TRAVELS, New. 1819, *etc.* Vol. VIII.

Libyan Desert.—HOSKINS, G. A. Visit to the Great Oasis of the L. D., *etc.* **1837.**

Liefland.—*See* LIVONIA.

Liege.—VANDER MAELEN, P. Statistique ... de L., *etc.* *Brussels*, **1830.**
—— —— Dictionnaire Géographique de la Province de L., *etc.*
Brux., **1831.**
—— VAUX, H. DEL. Dictionnaire Géographique ... de la Province de L. *Liège*, **1835.**

Lieu-Kieu Islands.—HALL, B. Account of a Voyage ... to ... the Great Loo-Choo Island, *etc.* **1818.**
—— —— MACLEOD, J. Voyage of H.M.S. *Alceste* to ... the Island of Lewchew, *etc.* **1819.**
—— —— SIEBOLD, P. F. DE. Nippon. Archiv zur Beschreibung von Japan ... mit ... den Liukiu Inseln. *Leyden*, **1832.**
—— —— PARKER, P. Journal of an Expedition ... to Japan, with a visit to Loo-Choo. **1838.**
—— —— SIEBOLD, P. F. von. Nippon. Archiv zur Beschreibung von Japan ... den Linkiu-Inseln, *etc.* *Leyden*, **1852.**
—— —— SMITH, BP. G. Narrative of a Visit to Lewchew ... in 1850, *etc.* **1853.**
—— —— HALLORAN, A. L. Wae Yang Jin. Eight Months' Journal kept ... during visits to Loochoo, *etc.* *Lond.*, **1856.**
—— —— HABERSHAM, A. W. My last Cruise ... Visits to the ... Loo-Choo Islands, *etc.* *Phil.*, **1857.**

Lieu-Kieu Islands.—Gras, M. A. i.e. Renseignements hydrographiques sur les Iles . . . Lou-Tchou, *etc.* *Par.*, 1859.
— Iles Lieou-Kieou. Eyriès. Vol. XIII.
— Gualle, F. Voyage . . . by the Lequeos . . . to Acapulco, 1582-84. Hakluyt. Vol. III.

Liguria.—Laouze. Descrizione delle Riviere dello Stato Ligure.
Genova, 1780.

Lima.—Helms, A. Z. Travels from Buenos Ayres . . . to L. 1806.
— Smyth, W., and Lowe, F. Narrative of a Journey from L. to Para, *etc.* 1836.
— Scarlett, Hon. P. C. South America . . . comprising a Journey . . . to . . . L, *etc.* 1838.
— Smith, A. Peru as it is: a Residence in L., *etc.* 1839.
— Lima. A True . . . Relation of the . . . Earthquake . . . at L. . . . on the 28th October, 1746, *etc.* 1848.
— Rocafu y Paz-Soldan, M. Resumen de las Observaciones Meteorologicas hechas in L. . . . 1869 . . . Sobre la posicion geografica de L. *Lima*, 1870.
— Von unserer Reise nach L. Rückreise von L. nach Quito, *etc.* Voyages and Travels. Allgemeine Historie, *etc.* Vol. IX.
— Beschreibungen . . . von . . . L., *etc.* Voyages and Travels. Allgemeine Historie, *etc.* Vol. XV.
— Helms, A. Z. Travels from Buenos Ayres . . . to L., *etc.* Voyages and Travels. A Collection, *etc.* 1805. Vol. V.

Limbourg.—*See* Limburg.

Limburg.—Vander Maelen, P. Statistique . . . de L., *etc.*
Bruxels, 1830.
— — Dictionnaire Géographique du L. *Brux.*, 1835.

Lipari Islands.—Dolomieu, D. de. Voyage aux Iles de L., *etc.*
Par., 1783.
— — Hovels Reisen durch . . . die L. schen Inseln, *etc.*
Gotha, 1797.

Lipetsk.—*See* Lipetzk.

Lipetzk.—Struve, O. Détermination des Positions Géographiques de . . . L., *etc.* *St. Pet.*, 1843.

Lisbon.—Baillie, M. L. in 1821-23. 1825.
— Hadfield, W. Brazil . . . including notices of L., *etc.* 1854.
— Valdez, F. T. Da Oceania a Lisboa viagem. *Rio de Jan.*, 1866.
— Almeyda, F. de. Voyage from L. to India, *etc.* Kerr. Vol. VI.
— Navegação de Lisboa á Ilha de S. Thomé, *etc.* Portugal. Collecção de Noticias, *etc.* Vol. II.
— Alvares, P. Navigatione da L. in Calicut. Ramusio. Vol. I.
— Navigatione da L. all' Isola di San Thomé, *etc.* Ramusio. Vol. I.

Lisbona.—*See* Lisbon.

Lithuania.—Henry IV., King. Voyage into Prussia and Letto, 1390. Hakluyt. Vol. I.

Lithuania — London. 271

Lithuania.—Guagnino, A. Descrittione della Sarmatia Europea ... L., *etc.* Ramusio. Vol. II.
Liukiu Inseln.—*See* Lieu-Kieu Islands.
Liverpool.—Telford, T. Reports ... and Plans, for improving the Road from London to L. 1829.
——— Liverpool.—The Stranger in, *etc.* *Liverp.*, 1831.
——— Laird, W. Letters on the Export Coal Trade of L. *Liverp.*, 1850.
——— Burton, R. F. Wanderings ... from L. to Fernando Po. 1863.
——— Boult, J. Further Observations on the alleged Submarine Forests on the Shores of L. Bay, *etc.* *Liv.*, 1866.
——— ——— Speculations on the former Topography of L., *etc.* *Liv.*, 1866.
Livonia.—Ferber, J. J., and Fischer, J. B. Physische Erdbeschreibung von Kurland und Naturgeschichte von Liefland. *Riga*, 1784.
——— Straussen, J. J. Reise durch ... Liefland ... 1647-1673.
——— Struve, W. Resultate der in ... 1816 bis 1819 ausgeführten astronomisch-trigonometrischen Vermessung Livlands. *St. Pet.*, 1844.
——— Iljoerth, J. Description des Côtes. ... de la Livonie, *etc.* *Par.*, 1855.
——— Guagnino, A. Descrittione della Sarmatia Europen ... L., *etc.* Ramusio. Vol. II.
——— Salvo, Marquis de. Travels ... through ... L., 1806. Voyages and Travels. A Collection, *etc.* 1805. Vol. VI.
——— *See also* Narva.
Livorno.—*See* Leghorn.
Loanda.—Cooley, W. D. Dr. Livingstone's Reise vom Fluss Liambey nach L. ... beleuchtet. *Gotha*, 1855.
Loango.—A Description of ... Loango, *etc.* Astley. Vol. III.
——— Proyart's History of L., *etc.* Pinkerton. Vol. XVI.
——— Of the Province of Engoy and other Regions of L., *etc.* Purchas. Vol. II.
——— Eine Beschreibung der Königreiche L., *etc.* Voyages and Travels. Allgemeine Historie, *etc.* Vol. IV.
Lobeid.—Cuny, C. Journal de Voyage de Siout à El-Obéid 1857-58, *etc.* *Par.*, 1863.
Lochaber.—Darwin, C. Observations on the Parallel Roads of ... parts of L., *etc.* 1839.
Locris.—Gell, Sir W. Itinerary of Greece; containing ... Routes in L. ..., *etc.* 1819.
Lombardy.—Barrow, J. Tour in Austrian L., *etc.* 1841.
——— Ray, J. Travels through ... L., *etc.* Harris, J. Vol. II.
——— **and Venice.**—Lombardo Veneto. Elenco Alfabetico dei Comuni ... appartenenti al Regno Lombardo-Veneto. *Mil.*, 1819.
London.—Montémont, A. Londres, Voyage à cette Capitale, *etc.* *Paris*.
——— London Docks, Reasons in favour of the. 1797.

London — Loreto.

London.—Pennant, T. The Journey from Chester to L., etc.
Lond., **1811.**
—— Turnpike Roads. Reports of the Commissioners of the Metropolis Turnpike Roads N. of the Thames. **1827-28.**
—— Telford, T. Reports ... and Plans, for improving the Road from L. to Liverpool. **1829.**
—— Howard, L. The Climate of L., etc. *Lond.,* **1833.**
—— Booth, A. The Stranger's Intellectual Guide to L., etc. **1839.**
—— Bowerbank, J. S. A History of the Fossil Fruits & Seeds of the L. Clay. *Lond.,* **1840.**
—— Cunningham, P. Handbook for L., etc. **1849.**
—— New York. Plan for shortening the time of Passage between New York and L. *Portland, U. S.,* **1850.**
—— Rafn, C. C. Remarks on a Danish Runic Stone, from the eleventh century, found in ... L. *Copenh.,* **1854.**
—— Barlow, P. W. On some ... Features of the ... L. Basin, etc. **1855.**
—— Burn, J. H. Descriptive Catalogue of the L. ... Tokens, etc. **1855.**
—— London. Reports ... on the Metropolis Water Supply, etc. **1856.**
—— Mackrill, T. Water Supply of L., etc. *London,* **1866.**
—— B., M. V. From L. to Lahore. *Lond.,* **1868.**
—— Ravenstein, E. G. Reisehandbuch für L., etc. *Hildburgh.,* **1870.**
—— Harborne, W. Voyage overland from Constantinople to L., 1588. Hakluyt. Vol. II.
—— An Itinerary from L. to Constantinople ... 1794. Voyages and Travels. A Collection, etc. 1805. Vol. I.

Londonderry.—Sampson, G. V. Statistical Survey of the County of L., etc. *Dubl.,* **1802.**
—— Colby, Col. Ordnance Survey of the County of L. *Dubl.,* **1837.**
—— Portlock, J. E. Report on the Geology of ... L., etc. *Dubl.,* **1843.**

Long River.—La Hontan, Baron de. Reise auf dem langen Flusse, 1688. Voyages and Travels. Allgemeine Historic, etc. Vol. XVI.

Loo-Choo Islands.—*See* Lieu-Kieu Islands.

Lope Gonsalvo, Cape.—*See* Lopez, Cape.

Lopez, Cape.—Africa. Renseignements sur la partie de la Côte entre le Cape Négro et le Cap L. *Par.,* **1850.**
—— The Coast from Old Kalabar River to Cape Lope Gonsalvo. Astley. Vol. III.

Lord Howe Island.—Hill, E. S. L. H. I. Official Visit, etc.
Sydney, **1869.**

Lord's Island.—Pickering, J. Memoir on the language and inhabitants of L. I. *Camb., U. S.,* **1845.**

Loreto.—Raimondi, A.—Apuntes sobre la Provincia Litoral de L. (Peru.)
Lima, **1862.**

Lorraine.—Razoumowsky, Count G. de. Œuvres. Contenant, Voyage Minéralogique ... à ... L., *etc.* *Lausanne*, 1784.

Losaini.—*See* Osero.

Lota.—Barrio, P. del. Noticia sobre el Terreno Carbonifero de Coronel l L. *Santiago*, 1867.

Lough Neagh.—Barton, R. Lectures ... upon ... L. N., *etc.* *Dubl.*, 1751.

Louisburg.—Shirley, W. Letter ... with a Journal of the Siege of L., *etc.* 1746.

Louisiade Archipelago.—Macgillivray, J. Narrative ... including Discoveries ... in ... the L. A., *etc.* 1852.

Louisiana.—Laval, P. Voyage de la Louisiane, 1720, *etc.* *Par.*, 1728.

——— Louisiana, The present State of, *etc.* 1744.

——— Pike, Z. M. Exploratory Travels through ... the Interior of L., *etc.* 1811.

——— Bradbury, J. Travels in ... Upper L., *etc.* *Liver.*, 1817.

——— Dache, A. D. Additional Notes of ... Tidal Obervations ... at Cat Island, L. *New Hav.*, 1852.

——— Pike. Voyage dans l'ouest de la L. ... 1805-7. Eyries. Vol. IX.

——— Charlevoix, P. de. Reise nach L. ... 1721-22. Voyages and Travels. Allgemeine Historie, *etc.* Vol. XVI.

——— Perrin Du Lac. Travels through the Two L. a ... 1801-3. Voyages and Travels. A Collection, *etc.* 1805. Vol. VI.

See also Red River.

Lou-Tchou, Islands.—*See* Lieu-Kieu.

Low Archipelago.—Paschappe, M. and March M. de la. Observations ... faites en 1853, dans l'Archipel des Pomotous. *Par.*, 1857.

Low Countries.—*See* Netherlands.

Loyalty Islands.—Grimouilt, M. Renseignements Nautiques sur ... les Isles L. *Par.*, 1859.

——— Chambeyron et Banare, MM. Instructions Nautiques ... Suivies d'une Note sur les Iles L. par M. Jouan. *Par.*, 1869.

Lucayan Islands. *See* Bahama Islands.

Lucca.—Lucca, Guida ... per la Città di. *Lucca*, 1820.

Lucerne.—Businger. Itinéraire et description ... de L. *Lucerne*, 1815.

Lucknow.—Rees, L. E. R. Personal Narrative of the Siege of L., *etc.* 1858.

Luçones.—*See* Philippine Islands.

Ludlow.—Murchison, Sir R. I. Note on the relative position of the Strata, near L., containing the Ichthyolites described by Sir P. Egerton. 1857.

Lueg.—Schmidl, A. A. Die Grotten und Höhlen von ... L., *etc.* *Wien*, 1854.

Lugano, Lake of.—Bertolotti, D. Viaggio ai ... Laghi di ... L., *etc.* *Como*, 1825.

Luristan.—De Bode, Baron C. A. Travels in L., *etc.* 1845.

Lusitania.—*See* Portugal.

T

Luxemburg.—Razoumowsky, Count G. de. Œuvres. Contenant, Voyage Minéralogique . . . . de Bruxelles à . . . L., etc. *Lausanne*, 1784.
——— Van Kampen, N. G. Staat-en Aardrijkskundige beschrijving van het . . . Groot-Hertogdom L. *Haarlem*, 1827.
——— Vander Maelen, P. Statistique . . . de L., etc. *Brussels*, 1830.
——— Luxembourg Railway Company, Report, etc. 1846.
Lybia.—See Libya.
Lycia.—Fellows, Sir C. Account of discoveries in L. 1841.
——— Spratt, T. A. B. and Forbes, E. Travels in L., etc. 1847.
——— Fellows, Sir C. Travels and Researches . . . more particularly in . . . L. 1852.
——— See also Xanthus.
Lydia.—Rennell, J. Illustrations . . . of the . . . Retreat of the Ten Thousand . . . to . . . L. 1816.
Lynyan.—Blanford, W. T. On the neighbourhood of L., etc. in Sind. India Geological Survey. Memoirs. Vol. VI.
Lyons.—Fournier, C. I. N. Guide de l'Étranger à L. 1826.

M

Maas.—See Meuse.
Macao.—Andrade, J. I. Memoria . . . da entrada . . . dos Inglezes na cidade do M. *Lisb.*, 1835.
——— Gualle, F. Voyage from . . . Acapulco . . . to M. . . . 1582-84. Hakluyt. Vol. III.
——— Brown, A. Extracts of a Journal . . . sayling divers times . . . to . . . M., etc. 1617-32. Purchas. Vol. II.
Macassar.—Stavorinus, J. S. Voyage . . . à M. 1774-78. *Par.*, 1800.
——— Rhodes, A. Reise nach . . . M., etc. Voyages and Travels. Allgemeine Historie, etc. Vol. X.
——— See also Celebes.
Macau.—See Macao.
Macedonia.—Lucas, P. Voyage de, dans . . . la Macédoine, etc. *Par.*, 1712.
——— Holland, H. Travels in . . . M., etc. 1819.
——— Tafel, T. L. F. De Via Militari Romanorum Egnatia, qua Illyricum, M. et Thracia jungebantur, etc. *Tubingæ*, 1842.
——— Spencer, E. Travels . . . through . . . M., etc. 1851.
——— Belon, Mr. Remarks in . . . Creta . . . Journey . . . wherein the Gold and Silver Mines of M., etc. are described. Ray, J.
——— Pouqueville, F. C. H. L. Travels in . . . M. . . . 1805. Voyages and Travels, New. 1819. Vol. IV.
Madagascar.—Tellez, B. Travels . . . Voyage to M. . . . by F. Cauche. 1710.
——— Flacourt, E. de. Histoire de . . . M. *Par.*, 1758.
——— Rochon, Abbé. A Voyage to M., etc. *Lond.*, 1792.

Madagascar.—WINTERTON, EAST INDIAMAN. A Narrative of the Loss of the *Winterton* . . . on the coast of M. in 1792, etc. *Edin.*, 1820.
——— COPLAND, S. History of . . . M., etc. 1822.
——— DRURY, R. The pleasant . . . Adventures of R. D., during . . . Captivity on . . . M., etc. *Lond.*, 1826.
——— OWEN, W. F. W. Narrative of Voyage to explore the shores of . . . M., etc. 1833.
——— ELLIS, W. History of M. 1838.
——— MOORE, W. Log-Book of the . . . *Eliza Scott* . . . during her Voyage . . . to M., etc. 1838-39.
——— LAVERDANT, D. Colonisation de M. *Par.*, 1844.
——— JEHENNE, CAPIT. Sur Nossi-Be, Nossi-Mitsiou, Bavatoubé (Côte N. O. de M.). *Par.*, 1847.
——— FREEMAN, J. J. Tour in S. Africa, with notices of . . . M., etc. 1851.
——— ELLIS, W. Three Visits to M., etc. 1858.
——— ——— Three Visits to M., etc. *Lond.*, 1859.
——— LACAILLE, L. Connaissance de M. *Par.*, 1863.
——— MACLEOD, J. L. M. and its People. 1865.
——— OLIVER, S. P. M. and the Malagasy, etc. *Lond.*, [1865.]
——— ELLIS, W. M. revisited, etc. *Lond.*, 1867.
——— OLIVER, S. P. Les Hovas et autres tribus caractéristiques de M. *Guernesey*, 1869.
——— Boothby, R. A brief discovery . . . of M., etc. CHURCHILL. Vol. VIII.
——— Invorarity, D. Memoir of a Chart of the N.W. Coast of M., 1803, etc. DALRYMPLE, A. Collection of Nautical Memoirs, etc.
——— Account of an Expedition of the Portuguese from India to M., 1613. KERR. Vol. VII.
——— Rochon, Abbé. Voyage to M., etc. PELHAM. Vol. II.
——— Rochon's Voyage to M. PINKERTON. Vol. XVI.
——— Discorso d'un gran Capitano di Mare Francese . . . sopra . . . di San Lorenzo [M.], etc. RAMUSIO. Vol. III. Isola
——— Rennefort. Reise nach . . . M., 1665, 66. VOYAGES and TRAVELS. Allgemeine Historie, etc. Vol. VIII.
——— *See also* TAMATAVE.

Madeira.—SLOANE, H. Voyage to . . . M., etc. 1707.
——— BOWDITCH, T. E. Excursions in M., etc. 1825.
——— DRIVER, J. Letters from M., in 1834. 1838.
——— PURDY, J. Brasilian Navigator . . . with . . . Directions for . . . M., etc. 1844.
——— DIX, J. A. A Winter in M., etc. *N. Y.*, 1851.
——— HARCOURT, E. V. Sketch of M., etc. 1851.
——— WHITE, R. M., its Climate and Scenery, etc. *Lond. and Mad.*, 1851.

Madeira.—WILDE, W. R. Narrative of a Voyage to M., *etc.* *Dubl.*, 1852.

—— GRIFFIN, J. A plain ... system of ... Astronomy ... including a Journey from London to M., *etc.* 1854.

—— HADFIELD, W. Brazil ... including notices of ... M., *etc.* 1854.

—— TURNBULL, W. The Mariner's Daily Assistant ... with the Journal of a Voyage from London to M., *etc.* 1854.

—— KERHALLET, C. P. DE. Description Nautique de Madère, *etc.* *Par.*, 1858.

—— NORIE, J. W. A Complete Epitome of ... Navigation ... including a Journal of a Voyage from London to M., *etc.* *Lond.*, 1864.

—— OLIVEIRA, B. Letters upon ... the climate and general history of ... M. *Lond.*, 1864-5.

—— GRABHAM, M. C. The Climate and Resources of M., *etc.* *Lond.*, 1870.

—— Nichols, T. Description of ... M., *etc.* ASTLEY. Vol. I.

—— Voyage of Macham, the first discoverer of ... M., 1344. HAKLUYT. Vol. II.

—— Carteret, Capt. Voyage from Plymouth to M. ... 1766-69. HAWKESWORTH, J. Vol. I.

—— Discovery of M. KERR. Vol. II.

—— Nicola, T. Beschreibung der Canarischen Eylande und M. ... 1580. VOYAGES and TRAVELS. Allgemeine Historie, *etc.* Vol. II.

——, **River.**—SILVA COUTINHO, J. M. DE. Annexo P. ... Relatorio da Exploração do Rio M., *etc.* [1865.]

—— —— KELLER, J. and F. Relatorio da Exploração do Rio M., *etc.* *Rio de Jan.*, 1869.

—— —— —— Fonseca, J. G. da. Navegação feita da Cidade do Gram Pará, até á Bocca do Rio de M., 1749. PORTUGAL. Collecção de Noticias, *etc.* Vol. IV.

Madera.—*See* MADEIRA.

Madison.—MADISON, Charter of the City of. *Mad.*, 1856.

—— DRAPER, L. C. M. the Capital of Wisconsin, *etc.* *Mad.*, 1857.

Madras.—HAMILTON, F. Journey from M. through ... Mysore, *etc.* 1807.

—— HEBER, BISHOP. Narrative of a Journey ... to M., *etc.* 1829.

—— MADRAS, Meteorological Observations made at, *etc.* *Mad.*, 1841-54.

—— GOLDINGHAM, J. and TAYLOR, J. G. Meteorological Register kept ... at M. ... 1822-43. *Mad.*, 1844.

—— INDIA. Selections from the Records of the M. Government. *Mad.*, 1855, *etc.*

—— Prior, J. Voyage ... to M. ... 1810-11. VOYAGES and TRAVELS, New. 1819. Vol. I.

—— M., a Visit to ... 1811. VOYAGES and TRAVELS, New. 1819. Vol. V.

Madrid.—MADOZ, P. Dic. Geol. Estad. Hist. M., *etc.* *Madr.*, 1848-50.

Madrid,—MADRID. Anuario del Real Observatorio de M. . . . 1862.
Madr., 1861.

Madura.—SELBERG, E. Reis naar Java en bezoek op het Eiland Madura, etc. *Amst.*, 1846.

——— Beschreibung der Königreiche . . . M., *etc.* VOYAGES and TRAVELS. Allgemeine Historie, *etc.* Vol. XVIII.

——— *See also* CUMBOM VALLEY.

Madura.—*See* MADURA.
Mae-khan, River.—*See* MEKONG.
Maes.—*See* MEUSE.

Magalhaens, Straits of.—GAMBOA, P. S. DE. Viage al Estrecho de Magallanes en . . . 1579 y 1580. *Madr.*, 1768.

——— ——— MAGALHAENS. Relacion del último viage al Estrecho de Magallanes de la Fregata de S. M. Santa Maria de la Cabeza, *etc.*
Madr., 1788.

——— ——— MAGELLAN, Strait of. Viage. Relacion del último Viage al Estrecho de Magallanes . . . 1785 y 1786, *etc.* *Madrid*, 1788-93.

——— ——— MACDOUGALL, J. Narrative of a Voyage . . . through the Straits of M. . . . in 1826-27. 1833.

——— ——— Voyage of the *Delight* . . . to the Streights of Magellan, 1589. HAKLUYT. Vol. IV.

——— ——— Winter, J. Voyage into the South Sea by the Streight of Magellan, 1577. HAKLUYT. Vol. IV.

——— ——— Weert, S. de. Remarkable Voyage to . . . the Streights of Magellan, 1598-1600. HARRIS, J. Vol. I.

——— ——— Byron, Comm. Voyage . . . up the Streight of Magellan . . . 1764-66. HAWKESWORTH, J. Vol. I.

——— ——— Carteret, Capt. Voyage . . . through the Streight of Magellan . . . 1766-69. HAWKESWORTH, J. Vol. I.

——— ——— Weert, S. de. Voyage to the . . . Straits of Magellan, 1598. KERR. Vol. X.

——— ——— Adams, W. Voyage by the M. Streights to Japon, 1598-1611. PURCHAS. Vol. I.

——— ——— Ellis, J. A Briefe Note . . . in his Voyage through the Strait of M. . . . 1593. PURCHAS. Vol. IV.

——— ——— Le Maire, J. Reise eine neue Durchfahrt Sudwärts unter der Magellanischen Strasse zu entdecken, 1615-16. VOYAGES and TRAVELS. Allgemeine Historie, *etc.* Vol. XI.

——— ——— Frogers Reise . . . nach der Magellanischen Strasse, 1695-96. VOYAGES and TRAVELS. Allgemeine Historie, *etc.* Vol. XII.

——— ——— Wood, H. Reise durch die Magellanische Strasse. VOYAGES and TRAVELS. Allgemeine Historie, *etc.* Vol. XII.

——— ——— Quiroga, P. Reise nach der Küste des Magellanischen Landes, 1745-46. VOYAGES and TRAVELS. Allgemeine Historie, *etc.* Vol. XVI.

——— ——— Cordova, A. de. Voyage of Discovery to the S. of M., *etc.* VOYAGES and TRAVELS, New. 1819. Vol. II.

Magallanes, Strait of.—*See* MAGALHAENS.
Magellan, Strait of.—*See* MAGALHAENS.
Maggior Spagna.—*See* MEXICO.
Magindanao.—FORREST, T. Voyage to New Guinea . . . including an account of M., *etc.* 1780.
——— Sumatra, . . . Mindanao, *etc.* EYRIES. Vol. XII.
——— Carteret, Capt. Voyage . . . to . . . Mindanao . . . 1766-69. HAWKESWORTH, J. Vol. I.
Magna.—*See* MAINA.
Magnesia.—STRICKLAND, H. E. Ancient Colossal Statue near M. 1842.
Magyar Nemzet.—*See* HUNGARY.
Magyarország.—*See* HUNGARY.
Mahavillaganga.—BROOKE, R. Extracts from the Journal of an Excursion to explore the M. *Colombo*, 1833.
Mahratta Country.—BROUGHTON, T. D. Letters written in a M. Camp during . . . 1800, *etc.* *Lond.*, 1813.
——— MARSHALL, T. Statistical Reports on the . . . S.n M. C., *etc.* *Bomb.*, 1822.
——— BERNCASTLE, DR. A Voyage to China; including a Visit to the . . . M. C., *etc.* *Lond.*, 1850.
Mähren.—*See* MORAVIA.
Maiella.—*See* MAIELLO.
Maiello.—TENORE E GUSSONE. Viaggio . . . alla Maiella.
Mailapur.—*See* ST. THOME.
Main, River.—MEIDINGER, H. Statistische Uebersicht der Mainschifffahrt . . . im 1840, *etc.* *Frankf. a. M.*, 1841.
Maina.—Morritt, Mr. Account of a Journey through . . . M., in the Morea, 1795. WALPOLE, R. Memoirs, *etc.*
Maine.—JACKSON, C. T. On the Geology of the Public Lands . . . of . . . M., *etc.* *Bost.*, 1838.
——— AGASSIZ, L. Glacial Phenomena in M. *Bost.*, 1867.
Maire, Le, Straits of.—*See* LE MAIRE.
Mairwara.—DIXON, C. J. Sketch of M., *etc.* 1850.
Maisnr, Maisur.—*See* MYSORE.
Ma-kiang, River.—*See* MEKONG.
Malabar.—BALDAEUS, P. Naauwkeurige Beschryvinge van M., *etc.* *Amst.*, 1672.
——— HAMILTON, F. Journey . . . through . . M., *etc.* 1807.
——— MIGNAN, R. Notes . . . during a tour through a part of M., *etc.* *Bombay*, 1834.
——— Baldeus, P. A true . . . description of . . . M., *etc.* CHURCHILL. Vol. III.
——— Almeyda, F. de. Voyage . . . with an account of . . . M. KERR. Vol. VI.

Malabar — Maldive Islands. 279

Malabar.—Buchanan's Journey through . . . M. PINKERTON. Vol. VIII.
—— Dellon. Reise nach . . . der M. ischen Küste, 1670-72. VOYAGES and TRAVELS. Allgemeine Historie, *etc.* Vol. X.
—— Beschreibung der M. ischen Küste. VOYAGES and TRAVELS. Allgemeine Historie, *etc.* Vol. XII.
—— Schouten, G. Reisen nach . . . M. ischen Küste . . . 1658-65. VOYAGES and TRAVELS. Allgemeine Historie, *etc.* Vol. XII.
—— Zusatz zu der Beschreibung von M. VOYAGES and TRAVELS. Allgemeine Historie, *etc.* Vol. XVIII.
Malacca.—ANDERSON, J. Observations on . . . restoration of . . . M. to . . . Dutch, *etc.* *P. of W. I.*, **1824.**
—— CROOCKEWIT, J. H. Banka, M. . . . in 1849-50. *Te Sgrav.*, **1852.**
—— CAMERON, J. Our Tropical Possessions . . . being a descriptive Account of . . . M., *etc.* *Lond.*, **1865.**
—— JACOB, F. Singapore, M. . . . Reiseskizzen. *Berl.*, **1866.**
—— Lancaster, J. Memorable Voyage . . . as far as . . . M. . . . 1591. HAKLUYT. Vol. II.
—— Matelief, C. Reise . . . 1605-8. Seefahrt bis nach M., *etc.* VOYAGES and TRAVELS. Allgemeine Historie, *etc.* Vol. VIII.
—— Rhodes, A.. Reise nach . . . M., *etc.* VOYAGES and TRAVELS. Allgemeine Historie, *etc.* Vol. X.
—— **Straits of.**—NEWBOLD, T. J. Political and Statistical Account of the British Settlements in the Straits of M., *etc.* *Lond.*, **1839.**
—— —— BERNCASTLE, DR. A Voyage to China; including a Visit to . . . the S. of M., *etc.* *Lond.*, **1850.**
—— —— Weg, welchen Man nehmen muss, um durch die Strassen von M. . . . zu kommen. VOYAGES and TRAVELS. Allgemeine Historie, *etc.* Vol. XVIII.
Malaghetta Coast.—*See* GRAIN COAST.
Malakka.—*See* MALACCA.
Malay Archipelago.—*See* ARCHIPELAGO.
—— **Islands.**—Habersham, A. W. My last Cruise . . . Visits to the M. . . . I., *etc.* *Phil.*, **1857.**
—— **Peninsula.**—*See* MALAYA.
Malaya.—EARL, G. W. The Eastern Seas . . . comprising . . . visits to . . . the Malay Peninsula, *etc.* **1837.**
—— Moor, J. H. Notices of . . . M. P., *etc.* *Singapore*, **1837.** *See* also BANCA.—COLONG.—MALACCA.—QUEDAH.—PERAK.—SALANGOR.
Maldive Islands.—MOARSBY, R. Nautical Directions for the M. I., *etc.* **1840.**
—— Laval, F. Pirard de. Voyage to the East Indies . . . Shipwreck amongst the M., *etc.*, 1601-11. HARRIS, J. Vol. I.
—— Pyrard de Laval, F. Voyage to . . . the M. . . . 1601-11, *etc.* PURCHAS. Vol. II.

Maldive Islands — Manan.

Maldive Islands.—Pirard de Laval, Francis. A description of the Maldiva I., 1601. VOYAGES and TRAVELS. The World displayed. Vol. X.
Mallpur.—*See* ST. THOME.
Mallorca.—PAGENSTECHER, H. A. Die Insel M. Reiseskizze.
                                                                                        Leipz., 1867.
Malta.—BRYDONE, P. Voyage en Sicile et à Malthe, *etc.*   *Amst.*, 1776.
—— HOVELS Reisen durch . . . M., *etc.*   *Gotha*, 1797.
—— BOISGELIN, L. DE. Ancient and Modern M., *etc.*   *Lond.*, 1805.
—— BRYDONE, P. A Tour through Sicily and M., *etc.*   *Lond.*, 1806.
—— GAZE, A. Meletica Geographia, *etc.* *Gr.*   *Benetia*, 1807.
—— GIACINTO, P. C. Saggio di Agricoltura per le Isole di M. e Gozzo.
                                                                                   Messina, 1811.
—— FALCONER, W. Dissertation on St. Paul's Voyage . . . and Shipwreck on . . . Melite, *etc.*   *Oxf.*, 1817.
—— BADGER, G. P. Description of M., *etc.*   *Malta*, 1838.
—— MURRAY. Hand-Book for Travellers in . . . M.   *Lond*, 1840.
—— DAVY, J. Notes . . . on . . . M., *etc.*   1842.
—— SPRATT, T. A. B. Report of Deep Soundings between M. and the Archipelago, *etc.*   1857.
—— CLEGHORN, H. Notes on the Botany . . . of M., *etc.*
                                                                     Edin., 1870.
—— FALCONER, W. Dissertation on St. Paul's . . . Shipwreck on the Island Melite, *etc.*   *Lond.*, 1870.
—— Davis, W. A True . . . description of . . . M., *etc.* CHURCHILL. Vol. VII.
—— Day, J. Travels through . . . M., *etc.* HARRIS, J. Vol. II.
—— NICHOLAY, N. Description of . . . M., *etc.* PURCHAS. Vol. II.
—— Collins, F. Voyages to . . . M., *etc.* 1706-1801. VOYAGES and TRAVELS. A Collection, *etc.* 1805. Vol. X.
—— —— Voyages to . . . M., *etc.* 1796-1801. VOYAGES and TRAVELS. A Collection, *etc.* 1810. Vol. VI.
Malthe.—*See* MALTA.
Maluco Islands.—*See* MOLUCCA ISLANDS.
Man, Isle of.—MACCULLOCH, J. Description of . . . the I. of M., *etc.*
                                                                        Edin., 1819.
—— —— TEIGNMOUTH, LORD. Sketches of . . . the I. of M. 1836.
—— —— QUIGGIN. Guide through the I. of M.   *Douglas*, 1842.
—— —— CUMMING, J. G. I. of M. ; its history, *etc.*   1848.
—— —— Guide to the I. of M., *etc.*   1861.
—— —— Edwin, the Saxon King of Northumberland. Conquest of the Isles of Anglesey and M. HAKLUYT. Vol. I.
—— —— Robertson's Tour through the I. of M. PINKERTON. Vol. II.
Manan.—*See* MENAN.

Mánasarówar, Lake.—LLOYD, SIR W. Narrative . . . And Captain A. Gerard's account of an attempt to penetrate . . . to . . . Lake M., etc. *Lond.*, **1840.**

—— STRACHEY, H. Narrative of a Journey to the Lakes . . . Cho-Mapan, or M., etc. *Calc.*, **1848.**

Manche.—MONNIER, P. Mémoire sur les Courants de la M., etc. **1835-39.**

—— KELLER, F. A. E. Exposé du régime des Courants observés dans la M., etc. *Par.*, **1855.**

—— WITTE, M., and PURDAY, J. Portulan des Côtes de la M., etc. *Par.*, **1855.**

—— KING, J. W. Pilote de la M., etc. *Par.*, **1869.**

Manchester.—*See also* MANCUNIUM.

Manchooria, Manchuria.—*See* MANDCHOORIA.

Mancunium.—BLACK, J. Memoir on the Roman Garrison at M., etc. *Edinb.*, **1856.**

Mandchooria.—PALMER, A. H. Memoir . . . on the present state . . . of . . . M., etc. *Wash.*, **1848.**

—— COLLINS, P. McD. A Voyage . . . with . . . incidental notices of M., etc. *N. Y. and Lond.*, **1860.**

—— FLEMING, G. Travels on Horseback in Mantchu Tartary, etc. *Lond.*, **1863.**

—— WILLIAMSON, A. Journeys in . . . Manchuria, etc. *Lond.*, **1870.**

Mandchuria.—*See* MANDCHOORIA.

Mandinga.—*See* MANDINGO.

Mandingo.—MANDINGO. Vocabulary of the M. Language. *MS.* **1837.**

—— MACBRAIR, R. M. Grammar of the M. Language, etc.

—— Portuguese sent to . . . East Indies by Land, with . . . account of M., etc. ASTLEY. Vol. I.

—— Account of the M. s. ASTLEY. Vol. II.

Mangi.—Nicolo di Conti. Voyage to . . . M., etc. PURCHAS. Vol. III.

Mangischlak.—*See* MANGISHLAK.

—— HELMERSEN, G. VON. Geognostiche Bemerkungen über die Halbinsel Mangyschlak, etc. *St. Pet.*, **1848.**

Mangkassar.—*See* MACASSAR.

Mangyschlak.—*See* MANGISHLAK.

Manihi.—KULCZYCKI, A. Determination des Longitudes . . . Observations pour . . . M., etc. *Par.*, **1851.**

Manikesocke.—Of the Provinces of Bongo . . . M., etc. PURCHAS. Vol. II.

Manilla.—MAC MICKING, R. Recollections of M., etc. **1851.**

—— Gualle, F. Voyage from . . . Acapulco . . . to . . . M. 1582-84. HAKLUYT. Vol. III.

—— Drown, A. Extracts of a Journal . . . sayling divers times . . . to . . . M. s, etc. 1617-22. PURCHAS. Vol. II.

Manitch, River.—Helmersen, G. von. Geognostische Bemerkungen über die Steppengegend zwischen den Flüssen Samara . . . und M., *etc.*
St. Pet., **1846.**

Mankassar.—*See* Macassar.

Mantchu Tartary, Mantchuria.—*See* Manchooria.

Manytsch, River.—*See* Manitch.

Maoria.—Shortland, E. New Zealand Exhibition, 1865. A short Sketch of the M. Races. *Dunedin*, **1865.**

Mar Maggiore.—*See* Black Sea.

Mar Oceano.—*See* Pacific Ocean.

Maragnon, River.—*See* Amazon.

Maranham.—Lago, A. P. D. do. Survey of the Coast of . . . M., *etc.*
1821.

—— —— Estatistica historica-geografica da Provincia do M.
Lisboa, **1822.**

—— Memorias para a Historia da Capitania do M. . . . 1614. Portugal. Collecção de Noticias, *etc.* Vol. I.

Maranjon, Maranon.—*See* Amazon.

Marathon.—Squire, Col. The Plain of M., *etc.* Walpole, R. Memoirs, *etc.*

Marava.—Beschreibung der Königreiche . . . M., *etc.* Voyages and Travels. Allgemeine Historie, *etc.* Vol. XVIII.

Marawyny.—*See* Maroni.

Margarita.—Parker, W. Voyage to M. . . . 1596-97. Hakluyt. Vol. IV.

—— Shorley, Sir A. Voyage to . . . M. . . . 1500. Hakluyt. Vol. IV.

Maria Island.—Mortimer, G. Observations . . . during a Voyage to . . . M. I., *etc.*
Lond., **1791.**

Marianne Islands.—*See* Ladrone Islands.

Marienbad.—Grieben, T. Grieben's Reise-Bibliothek. No. 38 . . . M., *etc.*
Berl., **1861.**

Marienburg.—Rosenheyn, M. Die M., *etc.* *Leipz.*, **1858.**

Mariestadt.—*See* Skaraborg.

Marietta.—Sargent, W. Plan of an ancient Fortification at M., Ohio, *etc.*

Marignan.—*See* Marionana.

Marignana.—Beschreibung von . . . der Insel M., *etc.* Voyages and Travels. Allgemeine Historie, *etc.* Vol. XVI.

Marmora, Sea of.—Lechevalier, J. B. Voyage de la Propontide, *etc.*
Par., **1800.**

—— —— Purdy, J. New Sailing Directory for . . . the S. of M., *etc.*
1834.

—— —— Gras, M. A. Le. Sailing Directions for the . . . S. of M., *etc.*
1855.

Marmorice.—Hume, Dr. Extracts . . . and a description of the Bay of M., *etc.* Walpole, R. Travels, *etc.*

Marocco. —*See* MOROCCO.
Maroni.—Relation . . . and . . . Observations of the River of Marwin, *etc.* PURCHAS. Vol. IV.
Marony.—*See* MARONI.
Marowyne.—*See* MARONI.
Marquesas Islands.—VINCENDON-DUMOULIN, C. A. and DESGRAZ, C. Iles Marquises ou Nouka-Hiva. Histoire, géographie, *etc..*
Par., **1843.**

——— MELVILLE, H. Typee; a narrative of . . . Residence among the Natives . . . of the M. I., *etc.* **1847.**

——— GAUSSIN, P. L. J. B. Du Dialecte . . . des îles Marquises, *etc.*
Par., **1853.**

Marrawini.—*See* MARONI.
Marseilles.—CHARTON, M. Tableau . . . de M., *etc.* *Murs.*, **1829.**

——— ——— Tableau des Noms anciens et nouveaux . . . de M.
Mars., **1830.**

Martaban.—MENDEZ PINTO, F. Historia Oriental de las peregrinaciones de F. Mendez Pinto . . . en . . . Martauan, *etc.* *Madrid*, **1627.**

——— BAKER, T. T. The recent operations of the British Forces at . . . M.
Lond., **1862.**

Martauan.—*See* MARTABAN.
Martinique.—MONNIER, P. Description Nautique des Côtes de la M., *etc.*
Par., **1828.**

——— Reisen nach M. VOYAGES and TRAVELS. Allgemeine Historie, *etc.*
Vol. XVII.

Martyr Islands.—*See* FLORIDA KAYS.
Marwin.—*See* MARONI.
Maryland.—DUCATEL, J. T. Report on the New Map of M., 1834.
Annap., **1834.**

——— DUCATEL, J. T. and ALEXANDER, J. H. Reports . . . on the New Map of M., 1835-6. *Balt.*, **1836-37.**

——— ——— Annual Report of the Geologist of M., 1837 and 1838, *etc.*
Annap., **1837-8.**

——— - MARYLAND. Message . . . in relation to the Intersection of the Boundary Lines of M., *etc.* *Wash.*, **1850.**

——— KENNEDY, J. C. G. History and Statistics of . . . M., *etc.*
Wash., **1852.**

——— GRAHAM, J. D. Reports in relation to the . . . Boundary Lines of . . . M., *etc.* *Chicago*, **1862.**

Mas-Afuera.—CARTERET, Capt. Voyage . . . to M. . . . 1760-69.
HAWKESWORTH, J. Vol. I.

Masafuero.—*See* MAS-AFUERA.
Mas-a-Tierra.—*See* JUAN FERNANDEZ.
Maskat.—CARTER, H. J. Geological observations on the Igneous Rocks of M., *etc.* *Bombay*, **1851.**

Massachusetts.—HITCHCOCK, E. Report on the Geology . . . of M. *Amherst*, 1833.
——— ——— Report on a Re-examination of the . . . Geology of M. *Bost.*, 1838.
——— JACKSON, C. T. On the Geology of the Public Lands . . . of M., *etc.* *Bost.*, 1838.
——— MASSACHUSETTS. Reports of the Commissioners on the Zoological Survey of the State. *Bost.*, 1838.
——— MASSACHUSETTS. Report and Resolves in relation to the N. E.n Boundary. *Bost.*, 1838.
——— MASSACHUSETTS. Abstract of the . . . School Returns for 1838-9 and 1845-6. *Bost.*, 1839-46.
——— AUSTIN, J. Y. Annual Report of . . . M. *Wash.*, 1840.
——— MASSACHUSETTS. Abstract of the Returns of Inspectors and Keepers of Jails, *etc.* *Bost.*, 1840.
——— MASSACHUSETTS. Documents relating to the State Prison. *Bost.*, 1840.
——— PALFREY, J. G. Annual Reports of Births, Marriages, and Deaths in M., 1844-46. *Bost.*, 1845-6.
——— CHICKERING, J. Statistical View of the Population of M. from 1765 to 1840. *Bost.*, 1846.
——— MASSACHUSETTS. Abstract of the Census . . . 1855, *etc.* *Bost.*, 1857.
——— MASSACHUSETTS. Abstract of the Census, 1865, *etc.* *Bost.*, 1867.
——— MASSACHUSETTS. Returns of the Railroad Corporations in M., 1866, *etc.* *Bost.*, 1867.
——— GOULD, A. A. Report on the Invertebrata of M., *etc.* *Bost.*, 1870.

Massangana.—Description of the divers Nations . . . in Brasill . . . also . . . M., *etc.* PURCHAS. Vol. IV.

Masulipatam.—INDIA. Reports of the . . . effects of the Godavery and Krishna Annicuts, in . . . M., *etc.* *Madras*, 1858.
——— Voyage . . . to M. KERR. Vol. VIII.
——— Floris, P. W. Extracts of his Journal . . . 1610-15. Voyage to . . . M., *etc.* PURCHAS. Vol. I.
——— Report of W. Nicols, which travelled by land from Bramport to M. . . . 1612. PURCHAS. Vol. I.

Masulipatan.—*See* MASULIPATAM.

Mataram.—*See* JOCJACARTA.

Materan.—*See* JOCJACARTA.

Matto Grosso.—BOLIVIA. Notizen über den Minenbetrieb in . . . M. G., *etc.* *Berl.*, [1867.]

Maulevrier.—WALCKENAER, BARON C. A. and JOMARD. Rapport sur un Pied Romain trouvé dans la forêt de M., *etc.* *Par.*, 1839.

Mauritius.—MAURITIUS. A Voyage to . . . M., *etc.* *Lond.*, 1775.
——— GRANT, C. VISCOUNT DE VAUX. The History of M., *etc.* *Lond.*, 1801.

Mauritius.—FLINDERS, M. Voyage to Terra Australis . . . with an Account of the . . . M., etc. 1814.
——— MAURITIUS, Papers relating to the Colonial Trade of the. 1825.
——— ——— Papers . . . relative to the Slave Trade at the M. . . . 1811-25. 1826.
——— ——— A Return of the Dependencies of, etc. 1826.
——— BOUTON, L. Travaux de la Société d'Histoire Naturelle de l'Ile Maurice, etc. *Port Louis*, 1846.
——— PRIDHAM, C. England's Colonial Empire. Vol. I. The M., etc. 1846.
——— FREEMAN, J. J. Tour in S. Africa, with notices of . . . M., etc. 1851.
——— MAURITIUS, A Transport Voyage to the, etc. 1851.
——— MOUAT, F. J. Rough Notes of a trip to . . . the M., etc. *Cal.*, 1852.
——— BEATON, P. Creoles and Coolies; or Five Years in M. *Lond.*, 1859.
——— MAURITIUS, Report of . . . a Census of . . . April, 1861. *Maur.*, 1861.
——— WEST INDIES. Return showing the number of Immigrants and Liberated Africans admitted into . . . the M., 1847-60. 1861.
——— FLEMING, F. P. M. . . . being an account, etc. *Lond.*, 1862.
——— Guignes, M. de. Observations on . . . the Isle of France. PINKERTON. Vol. XI.
——— Beschreibung der Eylande Bourbon und Frankreich. VOYAGES and TRAVELS. Allgemeine Historie, etc. Vol. X.
——— St. Vincent, J. B. G. M. Bory de. Voyage to . . . [Isle of France] 1801-2, etc. VOYAGES and TRAVELS. A Collection, etc. 1805. Vol. II.
——— Price, J. Voyage . . . to the . . . Isles of . . . France, etc. 1810-11. VOYAGES and TRAVELS, New. 1819. Vol. I.
——— *See also* PORT LOUIS.

Mawooshen.—The King's Patent . . . for the plantation of New Scotland . . . with a description of M. . . . 1602-9. PURCHAS. Vol. IV.

Mayen Island.—*See* JAN MAYEN.

Mayomba.—Of the Provinces of Bongo, M., etc. PURCHAS. Vol. II.

Mayotta.—JEHENNE, CAPIT. Renseignements Nautiques . . . sur l'Ile M. *Par.*, 1843.

Maze.—*See* MEDSE.

Mecca.—GALLAND, M. Recueil des Rits et Cérémonies du Pélérinage de la Mecque, etc. *Amst.*, 1754.
——— BURTON, R. F. Personal Narrative of a Pilgrimage to . . . M. 1855.
——— MALTZAN, BARON H. DE. Pélerinage à la Macque, etc. [1860.]
——— AUCAPITAINE, BARON H. Étude sur la Caravane de la Mecque, etc. *Par.*, 1861.

Mecca.—Avril, A. d'. L'Arabie contemporaine, avec la description du pélérinage de la Mecque. *Par.*, 1868.
——— Journey from Grand Cairo to M. Ray, J.
——— Itinéraire de Constantinople à la Mecque, etc. Voyages and Travels. Recueil, etc. Vol. II.
——— Pitts, Joseph. Of the Religion of the Mahometans, with a description of M. . . . 1678. Voyages and Travels. The World displayed. Vol. XVII.

Meccah.—*See* Mecca.

Mechod.—*See* Meschrd.

Media.—Buckingham, J. S. Travels in . . . M., etc. 1830.
——— Straussen, J. J. Reise durch . . . Medien . . . 1047-1678. *Gotha*, 1832.
——— Cartwright, J. The Preacher's Travels . . . through . . . M., etc. Churchill. Vol. VII.
——— Chardin, Sir J. Travels . . . through . . . M. . . . 1672. Harris, J. Vol. II.
——— Borough, C. Reports of sixt voyage into . . . M. . . . 1579-81. Purchas. Vol. III.
——— Of the . . . Medes . . . and of their Religions. Purchas. Vol. V.

Medina.—Burton, R. F. Personal Narrative of a Pilgrimage to El-M., etc. 1855.
——— Pitts, Joseph. Of the Religion of the Mahometans, with a description of . . . M. 1678. Voyages and Travels. The World displayed. Vol. XVII.

Mediterranean Islands.—Alfred, the Great. A description . . . of the M. I., etc. 1855.
——— **Sea.**—Purdy, J. New Sailing Directory for the . . . W. ern Division of the M. S., etc.
——— Crescentio, B. Nautica Mediterranea. *Roma*, 1607.
——— Toriño de San Miguel, V. Derrotero de las Costas de España en el Mediterraneo, etc. *Madr.*, 1787.
——— Sandwich, John, Earl of. Voyage round the M. in 1738-39, etc. *Lond.*, 1799.
——— Dessiou, J. F. Le Petit Neptune Français . . . for . . . the . . . M., etc. 1805.
——— Lamalle, M. Dureau de. Géographie physique . . . de la Méditerranée, etc. *Par.*, 1807.
——— Gorgoglione, S. Portulano del Mare Mediterraneo. *Legh.*, 1813.
——— Richardson, R. Travels along the M. . . . 1816-17-18, etc. *Lond.*, 1822.
——— Purdy, J. New Sailing Directory for . . . the E. ern. . . . Division of the M. S., etc. 1834.
——— Temple, Sir G. T. Excursions in the M., etc. 1835.
——— Fairbairn, H. A Letter . . . on the . . . advantages of a Steam Passage to the East Indies, by the Gulf of Mexico . . . as compared with the proposed Route by the . . . M. S. 1837.

Mediterranean Sea.—Flotte d'Argençon, Comte M. de. Nouveau Portulan de la Méditerranée, etc. *Toulon*, 1830.
—— Wellsted, J. R. Travels . . . along the Shores of the . . . M., etc. 1840.
—— Mediterranean, The Shores and Islands of the, drawn from Nature by Sir G. Temple, etc. *Lond.*, 1843.
—— Vetch, J. Inquiry into the means of establishing a Ship Navigation between the M. and the Red Seas. 1843.
—— Smyth, Admiral W. H. The M., a Memoir, etc. 1844.
—— Purdy, J. Sailing Directions for . . . the M. S., etc. 1846.
—— Barth, H. Wanderungen durch die Küstenländer des Mittelmeeres, etc. *Berl.*, 1849.
—— Christmas, H. Shores and Islands of the M., etc. 1851.
—— Dabondeau, M. R. Tableau Général des Phares et Fanaux des Côtes de la Mediterranée, etc. *Par.*, 1852.
—— Wilde, W. R. Narrative of a Voyage . . . along the Shores of the M., etc. *Dubl.*, 1852.
—— Ainsworth, W. Report on . . . Telegraphic Communication between the M. S. and . . . Persian Gulf. 1856.
—— Mediterranean. The Lighthouses of the M. . . . Corrected to 1856. 1856.
—— Denham, H. M. Hydrographic Notices . . . M. S., etc. 1856-59.
—— Mediterranean. The Lights of the M. . . . Corrected to 1857, 58, 59. 1857-59.
—— Schaub, F. Magnetische Beobachtungen in Östlichen Theile des Mittelmeeres, ausgeführt in 1857. *Triest*, 1858.
—— Dunsterville, F. The Admiralty List of the Lights of the M. . . . Corrected to 1860, 61, 62. 1860-62.
—— Gras, M. A. le. Phares de la Mer Mediterranée . . . Corrigés 1862, 63. *Par.*, 1862-63.
—— Gras, A. Le. Considérations générales sur la Mer Mediterranée, etc. *Par.*, 1866.

Medway.—Purdy, J. and Findlay, A. G. New Piloting Directory for the . . . M., etc. 1846.
—— North Sea. Mer du Nord. IVe. Partie . . . La M., etc. *Par.*, 1864.
—— Foster, C. Le N. and Topley, W. On the Superficial Deposit of the Valley of the M., etc. 1865.

Meerut.—Delhi Railway. Opening of the M. and Umballa Section, etc. *Lond.*, 1869.

Méjico.—*See* Mexico.

Meklnes.—*See* Mequinez.

Mekong, River.—Thorel, C. Notes Médicales du Voyage d'Exploration du M., etc. *Par.*, 1870.

Mekran.—Ross, E. T. Notes on M. 1865.
—— Ross, E. C. Report on a . . . Route through M., etc. 1865.

Mekran.—Ross, E. C. Report on the Coast of M. from Cape Jusk to Gwadur. 1867.
Melbourne.—Smyth, R. B. Results of Meteorological Observations . . . M., etc. *Melb.*, 1855, 6.
——— Stoney, H. B. Victoria; with a description of . . . M., etc. 1856.
——— Abbott, F. Results . . . To which is added a Meteorological Summary for . . . M., etc. *Hob. Town*, 1866.
——— Crinole, T. pseud. Australian Sand-bar Harbours . . . with hints on the Sea Defences of M. *Melb.*, 1866.
——— Neumayer, G. Discussion of the Meteorological and Magnetical Observations made at . . . M. . . . 1858-63. *Mannheim*, 1867.
——— ——— On the Lunar Atmospheric Tide at M. 1867.
——— Nicholls, C. F. Probability of a Deep Lead of Gold round M. *Melb.*, 1869.
Meliapor.—*See* St. Thome.
Melite.—*See* Malta.
Melos.—*See* Milo.
Memel River.—*See* Niemen.
Memphis.—Drovetti, Chev. Lettre sur une nouvelle Mesure du Coudée trouvée à M. *Par.*, 1827.
Menam-Kong, River.—*See* Mekong.
Menan, Grand.—Shortland, P. F. Bay of Fundy Pilot . . . including the G. M. Island. 1857.
Mendana Islands.—*See* Marquesas Islands.
Mengrelia.—*See* Mingrelia.
Mentz.—Browne, E. Voyage . . . to Holland, with a Journey . . . through the Electorates of . . . M. . . . 1668. Harris, J. Vol. II.
Mequinez.—Comelin, F. P. de la Motte, and Bernard, J. Voyage to Barbary . . . M., etc. 1735.
——— Windus, J. A Journey to M. . . . in . . . 1721. *Lond.*, 1725.
——— Windhus's Journey to M. Pinkerton. Vol. XV.
——— Windus, Mr. A Journey to M. . . . 1720. Voyages and Travels. The World displayed. Vol. XVII.
Mer d'Allemagne.—*See* North Sea.
Mer de Baffin.—*See* Baffin's Bay.
Mer des Antilles.—*See* Caribbean Sea.
Mer du Sud.—*See* Pacific Ocean.
Mer Glaciale.—*See* Arctic Ocean.
Mer Polaire.—*See* Arctic Ocean.
Mer Vermeille.—*See* California, Gulf of.
Meroe.—Caillaud, F. Voyage à M., etc. *Par.*, 1826.
——— Hoskins, G. A. Travels in Ethiopia . . . illustrating . . . the ancient . . . M. 1835.
Merrimac, River.—Thoreau, H. D. A Week on the Concord and M. Rivers. *Bost. and Camb.*, 1849.

Mers du Nord.—See ARCTIC OCEAN.
Mers Polaires.—See ARCTIC OCEAN.
Mersey.—BOULT, J. Further Observations on the alleged Submarine Forests on the Shores of . . . the River M. *Liv.*, **1866**.
Meshed.—TRUILHIER, CAPIT. Mémoire descriptif de la Route de Téhran à Mechad, *etc.* *Par.*, **1841**.
——— SÉDILLOT, M. Notice sur une Carte Routière de M. à Bokhara, *etc.* *Par.*, **1852**.
Meschid.—See MESHED.
Mésène.—See MESSENIA.
Meshed.—See MESHED.
Mesopotamia.—DAPPER. Naukeurige Beschryving van . . . M., *etc.* *Amst.*, **1680**.
——— POCOCKE, R. Description of . . . M., *etc.* **1743-45**.
——— BUCKINGHAM, J. S. Travels in M., *etc.* **1827**.
——— FRASER, J. B. Travels in . . . M., *etc.* *Lond.* [**1835?**]
——— AINSWORTH, W. F. Travels . . . in . . . M., *etc.* **1842**.
——— FLETCHER, J. P. Notes . . . and Travels in M., *etc.* **1850**.
——— BADGER, G. P. The Nestorians . . . with . . . a Mission to M., *etc.* **1852**.
——— CLÉMENT, A. Souvenirs d'un Séjour en Mésopotamie. [**1866?**]
——— Biddulph, W. Travels of four Englishmen . . . into . . . M. . . . in 1600 and 1611. CHURCHILL. Vol. VII.
——— Cartwright, J. The Preacher's Travels . . . through . . . M., *etc.* CHURCHILL. Vol. VII.
——— Rauwolf, L. Journey into . . . M., *etc.* RAY, J.
Messenia.—HEINAUD, M. Mémoire sur le Commencement et la Fin du Royaume de la Mésène, *etc.* *Par.*, **1861**.
——— Sibthorp, Dr. Journal relating to . . . M., *etc.* WALPOLE, R. Travels, *etc.*
Mesurado, Cape.—Phillips, Capt. Journal of . . . Voyage . . . to Cape Mounserrados, *etc.* CHURCHILL. Vol. VI.
Meta, Mount.—TENORE E GUSSONI. Viaggio alla M., *etc.*
——— **River.**—MICHELENA Y ROJAS, F. Exploracion Oficial . . . del M., *etc.* *Bruselas*, **1867**.
Meta Incognita.—A generall . . . description of . . . M. I. HAKLUYT. Vol. III.
——— Voyage . . . for the finding of a N.W. Passage . . . to M. I., *etc.* HAKLUYT. Vol. III.
Meuse.—VAN RHIJN, A. Beschrijving van de Hydrograp. Kaart der Zeegaten van . . . de Maas. **1839**.
Mexican Sea.—See MEXICO, GULF OF.
Mexico.—MEXICO. Geographical Positions, *etc.* MS.
——— GOMARA, L. DE. Historia de M., *etc.* *Anvers*, **1554**.
——— GAGE, T. Nouvelle Relation des voyages dans la Nouvelle Espagne, *etc.* *Amst.*, **1695**.

U

Mexico.—GAGE, T. Survey of the Spanish West Indies . . . Also . . . Voyage . . . to . . . M., etc. 1702.

—— CHAPPE D'AUTEROCHE, J. Voyage . . . à travers le Mexique, etc. *Par.*, 1772.

—— AUTEROCHE, ABBÉ CHAPPE D'. A Voyage . . . with . . . description of the Author's Route through M., etc. *Lond.*, 1778.

—— CLAVIGERO, F. S. History of M., etc. 1787.

—— HUMBOLDT, A. VON. Essai politique sur . . . la Nouvelle Espagne. 1811.

—— PIKE, Z. M. Exploratory Travels through . . . the N.E.n Provinces of New Spain, in 1805-7. 1811.

—— BULLOCK, W. Six Months . . . in M., etc. 1825.

—— HALL, B. Extracts from a Journal written on the Coasts of . . . M. in 1820-22. *Edin.*, 1825.

—— SOLIS, A. DE. Historia de la Conquista de M., etc. *Par.*, 1827.

—— BEAUFOY, M. Mexican Illustrations, etc. 1828.

—— WARD, H. G. M. in 1827. 1828.

—— GRIBERG, COUNT J. Recueil de Voyages . . . and Historical Researches on the Conquest of . . . M. . . . in the thirteenth Century, by J. Ranking. 1829.

—— THOMPSON, G. A. Narrative of an Official Visit to Guatemala from M. 1829.

—— BURKART, J. Aufenthalt und Reisen in M., etc. *Stutt.*, 1836.

—— LATROBE, C. J. The Rambler in M., 1834. 1836.

—— NEBEL, C. Voyage . . . dans la partie la plus intéressante du Mexique. *Par.*, 1836.

—— AMERICA. Message from . . . President . . . concerning the Boundary between the U. S. and M. *Phil.*, 1837.

—— MEXICO. Diario del Gobierno de la República Mejicana. 1839-40.

—— FOOTE, H. S. Texas and the Texans . . . including a History of . . . Events in M., etc. *Phil.*, 1841.

—— FALCONER, T. Expedition to Santa Fé. An Account of its journey . . . through M., etc. *N. Orleans*, 1842.

—— BARCA, C. DE LA. Life in M., etc. 1843.

—— DIAZ DEL CASTILLO, C. B. The Memoirs of . . . containing the discovery . . . of M., etc. *Lond.*, 1844.

—— MAYER, B. M. as it was, and as it is. *N. Y.*, 1844.

—— PRESCOTT, W. H. History of the Conquest of M., etc. *Lond.*, 1844.

—— RUXTON, G. F. Adventures in M., etc. *Lond.*, 1847.

—— WISLIZENUS, A. Memoir of a Tour to Northern M., etc. *Wash.*, 1848.

—— LYON, G. F. Journal of a Residence . . . in . . . M. in 1826, etc. *Wash.*, 1849.

—— SMITH, M. L., and HARDCASTLE, E. L. F. Survey of the Valley of M. *Wash.*, 1849.

Mexico.

Mexico.—Mayer, B. M., *etc.*   *Hartf. U. S.*, 1852.
—— Robertson, W. P. Visit to M., *etc.*   1853.
—— Wilson, R. A. M. and its Religion, with Incidents of Travel, *etc.*
    Lond., N. Y., 1856.
—— Emory, W. H. Report on the United States and Mexican Boundary
Survey, *etc.*   *Wash.*, 1857.
—— Olmsted, F. L. Journey through . . . the Border Country of
. . . M.   1857.
—— Brasseur de Bourbourg, E. C. Histoire des Nations civilisées du
Mexique . . . durant les siècles antérieurs à C. Colomb, *etc.*
    Par., 1857-59.
—— Domenech, E. Missionary Adventures in . . . M., *etc.*   1858.
—— Tempsky, G. F. von Mitla. A Narrative of . . . a Journey in
M., *etc.*   1858.
—— Fröbel, J. Seven Years' Travel in . . . Northern M., *etc.* 1859.
—— Wilson, R. A. A New History of the Conquest of M., *etc.*
    Lond., 1859.
—— Hill, S. S. Travels in . . . M.   1860.
—— Tylor, E. B. Anahuc, or M. . . . Ancient and Modern. 1861.
—— Lempriere, C. Notes on M. in 1861 and 1862, *etc.*   *Lond.*, 1862.
—— Saussure, H. de. Coup-d'œil sur l'Hydrologie du Mexique, *etc.*
    Genève, 1862.
—— Valois, A. de. Mexique . . . Notes de Voyage.   *Par.* [1862.]
—— Virlet d'Aoust, M. Coup-d'œil générale sur la topographie . . .
du Mexique, *etc.*   *Par.* [1865.]
—— Bullock, W. H. Across M. in 1864-5.   *Lond. and Cam.*, 1866.
—— Mexico. The Republic of M. restored.   *Mexico*, 1867.
—— Bodenham, R. Voyage to . . . M., 1564. Hakluyt. Vol. III.
—— Chilton, J. Voyage to all the principall parts of Nueva Espanna,
etc. Hakluyt. Vol. III.
—— Hawkins, Sir J. Voyages to Nueva Espanna . . . 1562-68. Hakluyt. Vol. III.
—— Hawks, H. Voyage to Nueva Espanna . . . 1572. Hakluyt.
Vol. III.
—— Phillips, M. Voyage, 1568 . . . to M., *etc.* Hakluyt. Vol. III.
—— Tomson, R. Voyage into New Spains, 1555. Hakluyt. Vol. III.
—— Champlain, S. Narrative of a Voyage to . . . M. in 1599-1602
. . . Edited by N. Shaw. 1859. Hakluyt Soc. Pub. Vol. XXIII.
—— The conclusion of H. Cortes's Expedition . . . to the reduction of
. . . M., 1520-21. Harris, J. Vol. II.
—— Cortes, H. Expedition for the reduction of New Spain, 1518.
Harris, J. Vol. II.
—— Diaz del Castillo. History of the discovery . . . of M., *etc.* Kerr.
Vol. IV.
—— F. Cortez. Découverte du M. Laharpe, J. Vol. IX.

Mexico.—Mexique. Hernandez de Cordove. LAHARPE, J. Vol. IX.

—— Mexique. Prise de M. Nouvelle-Espagne, etc. LAHARPE, J. Vol. X.

—— Acosta, J. Mexican Antiquities, etc. PURCHAS. Vol. III.

—— —— Of the Ancient Superstitions of the Mexicans, etc. PURCHAS. Vol. III.

—— Cortes, H. Conquest of M. . . . 1518-30. PURCHAS. Vol. III.

—— Gomara, F. L. de. Relations of . . . Mexican Citie and Temple, etc. PURCHAS. Vol. III.

—— Historie of the Mexican Nation . . . 1324-1502. PURCHAS. Vol. III.

—— Divers Expeditions from M. . . . by divers Spaniards in a hundred yeeres space. PURCHAS. Vol. IV.

—— Gusman, N. di. Relation of New Spaine, 1530. PURCHAS. Vol. IV.

—— Of New France . . . New Spaine . . . and of their Religions. PURCHAS. Vol. V.

—— Alvarado, P. Lettera due a F. Cortese, del discoprimento nella Nuova Spagna. RAMUSIO. Vol. I.

—— Cortese, F. Relationi seconda, terza e quarta . . . della . . . Nuova Spagna, 1519-24. RAMUSIO. Vol. III.

—— D'un Gentil' huomo del F. Cortese, Relatione della gran Città del Temistitan Messico, e d'altre Cose della Nuova Spagna. RAMUSIO. Vol. III.

—— Godoi, D. Lettera a F. Cortese, del discoprimento nella Nuova Spagna. RAMUSIO. Vol. III.

—— Gusman, N. Relatione dell' imprese fatte in acquistare molte Provincie e Città nella Maggior Spagna, 1530. RAMUSIO. Vol. III.

—— Mendozza, A. Lettera del discoprimento della Terra Firma della Nuova Spagna . . . 1539. RAMUSIO. Vol. III.

—— Ixtlilxôchitl, F. d'Alva. Cruautés horribles des Conquérants du Mexique, Mémoire, 1519-24. TERNAUX-COMPANS. Voyages. Vol. VIII.

—— Recueil de Pièces relatives à la Conquête du Mexique, 1518-87. TERNAUX-COMPANS. Voyages. Vol. X.

—— Zurita, A de. Rapport sur les . . . Chefs de la Nouvelle-Espagne. TERNAUX-COMPANS. Voyages. Vol. XI.

—— Second Recueil de Pièces sur le Mexique, etc. TERNAUX-COMPANS. Voyages. Vol. XVI.

—— Histoire de l'Empire Mexicain representée par figures. THEVENOT. Vol. IV.

—— Relation du Mexique . . . par Thomas Gages. THEVENOT. Vol. IV.

—— Beschreibung von M., etc. VOYAGES and TRAVELS. Allgemeine Historie, etc. Vol. XIII.

—— Cortes, F. Reise, Entdeckung . . . des Reiches M., 1516-22. VOYAGES and TRAVELS. Allgemeine Historie, etc. Vol. XIII.

Mexico.—Grijalva, J. Reise und allererste Entdeckung Neuspaniens, 1517-18. VOYAGES and TRAVELS. Allgemeine Historie, etc. Vol. XIII.

—— Saavedra, A. Reise nach M., 1526. VOYAGES and TRAVELS. Allgemeine Historie, etc. Vol. XVIII.

—— The Conquest of M., by Hernando Cortes. 1518. VOYAGES and TRAVELS. The World displayed. Vol. IL

See also ACAPULCO.—GUATULCO.—TEHUANTEPEC.

——, **Gulf of.**—FAIRBAIRN, H. A Letter . . . on the . . . advantages of a Steam Passage to the East Indies, by the G. of M., etc. **1837.**

—— SMITH, J. W. Report to the Mexican Gulf Railway Company.
 Liverp., **1847.**

—— —— PURDY, J., and FINDLAY, A. G. Colombian Navigator. Vol. II. Sailing Directory for . . . the Mexican Sea, etc. **1848.**

—— —— ANDREWS, I. D. Report on . . . the G. of M., etc.
 Wash., **1853.**

—— —— VARNHAGEN, F. A. DE. Vespuce et son premier Voyage; on Notice d'une découverte . . . primitive du Golfe du Mexique en 1497 et 1498. *Par.*, **1858.**

—— —— SCHOTT, C. A. New Discussion on the distribution of the Magnetic Declination on the Coast of the G. of M.   *Wash.*, **1861.**

—— —— Gras, M. A. Le. Phares . . . du Golfe de Mexique. Corrigés 1862, 63.   *Par.*, **1862, 63.**

—— —— Manuel de la Navigation . . . dans le Golfe du M.
 1862-3.

—— —— Gras, A. Le. Phares . . . du Golfe du Mexique.
 Par., **1869.**

—— —— King, W. Voyage to the Bay of M., 1592. HAKLUYT. Vol. IV.

—— —— Michelson, W. and Mace, W. Voyage to the Bay of M., 1589. HAKLUYT. Vol. IV.

——, **New.** *See* NEW MEXICO.

Michigan.—PECK, J. M. Guide for Emigrants to . . . M., etc.
 Bost., **1836.**

—— BLOIS, J. T. Gazetteer of . . . M., etc.   *Detroit*, **1838.**

—— GRAHAM, J. D. Report of the Harbours, &c. in . . . M., etc.
 Wash., **1857.**

——, **Lake.**—GRAHAM, J. D. Report on the Harbours of Lake M.
 Wash., **1857.**

—— —— A Lunar Tidal Wave in Lake M. demonstrated.
 Phil., **1860.**

—— —— —— Report on the Improvement of the Harbours of Lakes M., etc.   *Wash.*, **1860.**

Middlesex.—MIDDLETON, J. View of the Agriculture of M., etc.
 Lond., **1807.**

Mikronesia.—KITTLITZ, F. H. v. Denkwürdigkeiten einer Reise . . . nach Mikronesien, etc.   *Gotha*, **1858.**

Milan — Mississippi, River.

Milan.—Sɛᴀᴛɪ, D. G. Piante delle Città, *etc.* di Milano.   *Mil.*, **1707.**
——— Rossi, L. Guida di Milano.   *Mil.*, **1818.**
——— ——— Guide des Étrangers à M., *etc.*   *Mil.*, **1819.**
——— Cᴀʀᴛᴀ, J. R. Description . . . de M.   *Mil.*, **1819.**
——— Mɪʟᴀɴ. Notizie statistiche della Provincia di M. . . . 1818.
    Milano, **1819.**
——— Zᴜᴄᴄᴏʟɪ, L. Descrizione di Milano.   *Mil.*, **1841.**
Milford Haven.—Pᴀɢᴇ, T. Report on the eligibility of M. H. for Ocean
    Steam Ships, *etc.*   **1859.**
Milo.—Lᴇʏᴄᴇsᴛᴇʀ, Lɪᴇᴜᴛ. Greek Inscriptions discovered in . . . Santorin
    and M.
Milyas.—Sᴘʀᴀᴛᴛ, T. A. B. and Foʀʙᴇs, E. Travels in . . . M., *etc.*
    1847.
Mina, Castle of.—*See* Sᴀɪɴᴛ Gᴇᴏʀɢᴇ ᴅᴇʟ Mɪɴᴀ.
Minch.—*See* Mɪɴsʜ.
Mindanao.—*See* Mᴀɢɪɴᴅᴀɴᴀᴏ.
Mindoro Sea.—Bʀɪᴅɢᴇs, Sɪʀ F. and Bᴀᴛᴇ, W. T. China Pilot . . .
    Observations on . . . the Sulu and M. Seas, *etc.*   **1859.**
Mingrelia.—Sᴘᴇɴᴄᴇʀ, E. Travels . . . including a Tour through . . .
    M., *etc.*   **1838.**
——— Mᴏɴᴛᴘéʀᴇᴜx, F. D. ᴅᴇ. Voyage . . . en Colchide, *etc.*
    Par., **1839.**
——— Rᴀᴅᴅᴇ, G. Berichte, *etc.* (Jahrg. I. Reisen im Mingrelischen
    Hochgebirge, *etc.*)   *Tiflis*, **1866.**
——— Chardin, Sir J. Travels . . . through . . . M. . . . 1672.
    Hᴀʀʀɪs, J. Vol. II.
——— De la Colchide ou Mengrelie. Tʜᴇᴠᴇɴᴏᴛ. Vol. I.
——— Chardin, Sir J. Travels through M. . . . into Persia. 1671.
    Voʏᴀɢᴇs and Tʀᴀᴠᴇʟs. The World displayed. Vol. XV., XVI.
Minnesota.—Pᴏᴘᴇ, J. Report of an Exploration of the Territory of M.
    Wash., **1850.**
——— Owᴇɴ, D. D. Report of a Geological Survey of . . . M., *etc.*
    Phil., **1852.**
——— Oʟɪᴘʜᴀɴᴛ, L. M. and the Far West.   **1855.**
Minorca.—Aʀᴍsᴛʀᴏɴɢ, J. History of . . . M.   **1752.**
Minsh, Little.—Oᴛᴛᴇʀ, H. C. Scotland, N.W. Coast. Little M. **1859.**
——— ——— Iɴsᴋɪᴘ, G. H. Instructions Nautiques sur . . . le Petit
    M., *etc.*   *Par.*, **1862.**
Mississippi, River.—Cʜᴀɪx, P. Le Bassin du M. au seizième siècle.
——— ——— Pɪᴋᴇ, Z. M. Exploratory Travels . . . from St. Louis, on
    the M., to the Source of that River, *etc.*   **1811.**
——— ——— Sᴄʜᴏᴏʟᴄʀᴀғᴛ, H. R. Travels in . . . the M. Valley, *etc.*
    N. Y., **1825.**
——— ——— Fʟɪɴᴛ, T. History and Geography of the M. Valley, *etc.*
    Cincin., **1832.**

Mississippi, River.—CUMMINGS, S. The Western Pilot, containing Charts of the . . . M., etc. *Cincin.*, 1840.
—— —— NICOLLET, J. N. Report intended to Illustrate a Map of the Hydrographical Basin of the Upper M. R. *Wash.*, 1843.
—— —— FALCONER, T. On the discovery of the M., etc. 1844.
—— —— MARR, R. A. Observations on the M. . . . at Memphis, etc. *Wash.*, 1853.
—— —— WHIPPLE, A. W. Report of Explorations for a Railway Route . . . from the M. . . . to the Pacific Ocean. *Wash.*, 1854.
—— —— SCHOOLCRAFT, H. R. Summary Narrative of an . . . Expedition to the Sources of the M. . . . in 1820, etc. *Phil.*, 1855.
—— —— AMERICA. Reports of . . . Surveys . . . for a Railroad from the M. to the Pacific, etc. *Wash.*, 1855-60.
—— —— MÜLLHAUSEN, B. Diary of a Journey from the M. to the . . . Pacific, etc. 1858.
—— —— HUMPHREYS, A. A. and ABBOT, H. L. Report upon . . . the M. River, etc. *Phil.*, 1861.
—— —— FOSTER, J. W. The M. Valley, etc. *Chicago, Lond*, 1869.
—— —— Pike. Voyage aux sources du M., 1805-6. EYRIÈS. Vol. IX.
—— —— Ashe, T. Travels . . . 1806, for . . . exploring the . . . M. VOYAGES and TRAVELS. A Collection, etc. 1805. Vol. X.

Missouri.—PECK, J. M. Guide for Emigrants to . . . M., etc. *Bost.*, 1836.
—— WETMORE, A. Gazetteer of the State of M., etc. *St. Louis*, 1837.
—— SHUMARD, B. F. and SWALLOW, G. C. Descriptions of New Fossils, from . . . M., etc. *St. Louis*, 1858.
—— SWALLOW, G. C. Geological Report of the Country along the . . . S.W. Branch of the Pacific Railroad, State of M., etc. *St Louis*, 1859.
—— SCHOOLCRAFT, H. R. Journal of a Tour into the Interior of M. . . . 1818-19. VOYAGES and TRAVELS, New. 1819. Vol. IV.
—— *See also* FORT LEAVENWORTH.
——, River.—LEWIS, and CLARKE, CAPTS. Travels to the Sources of the M. . . . in 1804-6. 1814.
—— —— —— Travels to the Source of the M. . . . in 1804-6. 1815.
—— —— FEATHERSTONHAUGH, G. W. Geological Report of . . . the elevated country between the M. and Red Rivers. *Wash.*, 1835.
—— —— UNION PACIFIC RAILROAD: the great National Highway between the M. R. and California, etc. *Chicago*, 1868.
—— —— HAYDEN, F. V. Geological Report of the Exploration of the . . . M., etc. *Wash.*, 1869.
—— —— Brackenbridge. Voyage au M., 1811. EYRIÈS. Vol. IX.
—— —— Lewis et Clarke. Voyage aux sources du M. . . . 1804-6. EYRIÈS. Vol. IX.
—— —— LEWIS and CLARK, CAPTS., and others. Travels . . . exploring the M. . . . 1805. VOYAGES and TRAVELS. A Collection, etc. 1805. Vol. VI.

Missouri, River.—Perrin Du Lac. Travels . . . among the Savage Nations of the M. . . . 1801-3. Voyages and Travels. A Collection, *etc.* 1805. Vol. VI.

Misti.—*See* Arequipa, Volcano of.

Mistir.—*See* Monastir.

Mitis.—Gould and Dowie. Instructions for making . . . M. . . . in the River St. Lawrence. 1832.

Mittelmeer.—*See* Mediterranean Sea.

Mocha.—M. Account of the King of M. and of his Country. Churchill. Vol. VI.

—— Sixth Voyage, in 1610 . . . Transactions at M., *etc.* Kerr. Vol. VIII.

—— Voyage of the *Ann-Royal* from Surat to M., 1618. Kerr. Vol. IX.

—— Heynes, E. Voyage from Surat to M. . . . 1618. Purchas. Vol. I.

—— Reise von Aden nach M., *etc.* Voyages and Travels. Allgemeine Historie, *etc.* Vol. XI.

Mocka.—*See* Mocha.

Moenemoezi.—Cooley, W. D. Inner Africa laid open . . . with the routes to . . . M., *etc.* 1852.

Moeris, Lake.—Belleforde, L. de. Mémoire sur le lac M. *Alex.*, 1843.

—— Borrer, D. A Journey . . . with . . . M. Linant de Bellefond's Mémoire sur le lac M. 1845.

Mogadore.—Morocco. Observations on . . . Morocco . . . 1830. Memorandum respecting . . . M., *etc. MS.*

—— Lemprière, W. Tour from Gibraltar to . . . M., *etc.* 1791.

—— Beaumier, A. Itinéraire de M. à Maroc, *etc.* *Par.*, 1868.

Mogan.—Jordan ou Jourdain Catalani, P. Mirabilia descripta, sequitur de . . . M., *etc.* Voyages and Travels. Recueil, *etc.* Vol. IV.

Mogodor.—*See* Mogadore.

Mogul Country.—*See* India.

Moha.—*See* Mocha.

Mokha.—*See* Mocha.

Moldavia.—Carra, M. Histoire de la Moldavie, *etc.* *Neuchatel*, 1781.

—— Thornton, T. The Present State of . . . M., *etc.* *Lond.*, 1807.

—— Hagemeister, J. de. Commerce of . . . M., *etc.* 1836.

—— Demidoff, A. de. Travels in . . . M. during 1837. 1837.

—— Elek, P. G. A'Moldvai Magyar Telepekrül. *Budán*, 1838.

—— Spencer, E. Travels . . . including a Tour through . . . M., *etc.* 1838.

—— Macarius, Travels of . . . Pt. I. . . . M., *etc.* 1849.

—— Leger, E. Trois Mois de séjour en Moldavie. *Par.*, 1861.

—— Austel, H. Voyage . . . through M. . . . 1556. Hakluyt. Vol. II.

Moldavia — Molucca Islands.   297

Moldavia.—Campenhausen, Baron. Travels through . . . M.
  1805. VOYAGES and TRAVELS. A Collection, etc. 1806. Vol. VIII.
Moldval.—See MOLDAVIA.
Mole, River.—THORNE, J. Rambles by Rivers; the . . . M., etc. **1847.**
Molucca Islands.—FORREST, T. Voyage to . . . the M., etc. **1780.**
——— KOLF, D. H. Reize door den . . . zuidelijken Molukschen Archipel,
  etc.   Amst., **1826.**
——— KOLF, D. H. Voyages through . . . the M. n Archipelago, etc.
    1840.
——— VAN DER HART, C. Reize . . . naar eenige der Molukache Eilanden,
  in 1850.   Te' Sgravenhage, **1853.**
——— Saris, J. Voyage to the . . . Molukkos . . . in 1611. ASTLEY.
  Vol. I.
——— Voyage of . . . D. Middleton to . . . the Molukkos in 1607.
  ASTLEY. Vol. I.
——— Camper, M. de N. du. Remarques sur les . . . Moluques, etc.
  1821-25. EYRIES. Vol. XII.
——— The prosperous . . . Voyage to Java . . . performed by 8 ships of
  Amsterdam . . . whereof 4 went forward . . . for the M., 1598-99.
  HAKLUYT. Vol. V.
——— Middleton, Sir H. Voyage to . . . the Maluco Islands . . . edited
  by B. Corney. 1855. HAKLUYT Soc. PUB. Vol. XIX.
——— Middleton, D. Voyage to . . . the M., 1607. KERR. Vol. VIII.
——— Second Voyage in 1604 . . . to . . . the M. KERR. Vol. VIII.
——— Expediciones al Maluco. Viage de Magallanes y de Elcano, años
  1518-21. NAVARETTE. Coleccion. Vol. IV.
——— Expediciones al M. Viages de Loaisa, y de Saavedra, años 1522-27.
  NAVARETTE. Coleccion. Vol. V.
——— Rebello, G. Informação das Cousas de Maluco. PORTUGAL. Col-
  lecção de Noticias, etc. Vol. VI.
——— Albuquerque's Exploits, and the first Knowledge of the M. PURCHAS.
  Vol. I.
——— Fitz-Herbert, H. Pithy description of the chiefe Ilands of . . .
  M. s., 1621. PURCHAS. Vol. I.
——— Middleton, Sir H. Voyage to the M. s. . . . 1620. PURCHAS.
  Vol. I.
——— Schot, A. Discourse of the present state of the M. s. PURCHAS.
  Vol. I.
——— Gaetan, J. Relatione del discoprimento dell'Isole Molucche . . .
  1542-43. RAMUSIO. Vol. I.
——— Ulloa, F. Navigatione per discoprire l' Isole delle Specierie . . .
  1532-39. RAMUSIO. Vol. III.
——— Beschreibung der Moluckischen Insel. VOYAGES and TRAVELS.
  Allgemeine Historie, etc. Vol. VIII.

Molucca Islands.—Zumts zur Beschreibung der Molunkischen Inseln. VOYAGES and TRAVELS. Allgemeine Historie, etc. Vol. XVIII.
Molukkos, Molukache Eilanden, Moluques.—See MOLUCCA ISLANDS.
Mombaca. See MOMBAS.
Mombas.—EMERY, LIEUT. J. B. Letters . . . on the Geography of M., etc. MS. 1833-34.
Mombasah, Mombassa.—See MOMBAS.
Monastir.—GUBERNATIS, E. DE. Lettere . . . sulle province di Susa e M., etc. *Firenze*, 1867.
Mongolia.—TIMKOWSKI, G. Travels of the Russian Mission through M. . . . 1820-21, etc. 1827.
——— ——— Voyage à Péking à travers la Mongolie, en 1820 et 1821, etc. *Par.*, 1827.
——— PRINSEP, H. T. Tibet, Tartary, and M., etc. *Lond.*, 1852.
——— ATKINSON, T. W. Oriental . . . Siberia . . . Adventures in . . . M., etc. 1858.
——— PUMPELLY, R. Notice of an Account of Geological Observations in . . . M. [1866.]
——— WILLIAMSON, A. Journeys in . . . E. n M., etc. *Lond.*, 1870.
——— Ysbrants Ides, E. Travels . . . through the Countries of the Mongul Tartars . . . 1692-95. HARRIS, J. Vol. II.
Monmouthshire.—HASSALL, C. General View of the Agriculture of . . . M., etc. *Lond.*, 1812.
——— WILLETT, M. History, Antiquities, and Scenery of M., etc. *Chepstow*, 1813.
——— MURCHISON, SIR R. I. The Silurian System, founded on Geological Researches in . . . M., etc. 1839.
Monomopata.—Account of . . . M., from De Faria y Sousa. ASTLEY. Vol. III.
——— A Description of the . . . Hottentots . . . of M. ASTLEY. Vol. III.
——— M. LAHARPE, J. Vol. III.
——— Beschreibung . . . worinnen eine Nachricht von . . . M. enthalten ist. VOYAGES and TRAVELS. Allgemeine Historie, etc. Vol. V.
Monongahela.—Ashe, T. Travels . . . 1806, for . . . exploring the . . . M., etc. VOYAGES and TRAVELS. A Collection, etc. 1806. Vol. X.
Mont Blanc.—PICTET J. P. Itinéraire des Vallées autour du M.-B. *Geneva*, 1818.
——— HOWARD, W. Narrative of a Journey to the summit of M. B., made in July, 1819. *Baltimore*, 1821.
——— FELLOWS, SIR C. Ascent of M. B. 1827.
——— SHERWILL, CAPT. M. Ascension . . . à la première Sommite de M. B. en 1825, etc. *Par.*, 1827.
——— AULDJO, J. Ascent . . . of M. B. 1828.

Mont Blanc.—AULDJO, J. Ascent . . . of M. B.   1830.
——— WILBRAHAM, E. B. Ascent of M. B. in 1830.   1832.
——— BARRY, M. Ascent of M. B., *etc.*   *Edin.*, 1836.
——— MANGET, J. L. Chamounix, le M. B., *etc.*   *Geneva*, 1843.
——— SENÉ, M. Le Relief du M.-B., *etc.*   *Genève*, 1844.
——— DELEBEAU, LE COMM. Notice sur les Altitudes du M.-B. et du Mont-
      Rose, *etc.*   *Versailles*, 1851.
——— SMITH, A. M. B., *etc.*   1860.
——— BARROW, J. Expeditions on . . . M. B., *etc.*   1864.
——— GLACIERS. Expeditions . . . including an ascent of M. B., *etc.*
                                                                 1864.
——— FAVRE, A. Recherches Géologiques dans les parties . . . voisines
      du M. B., *etc.*   *Par., Genève*, 1867.
——— Saussure's Attempts to reach the summit of M. B. PINKERTON.
      Vol. IV.
——— **Buét.** GLACIERS. Expeditions . . . including an ascent of . . .
      M. B., *etc.*   1864.
——— **Muét.** BARROW, J. Expeditions on . . . M. M.   1864.
——— **Perdu.** RAMOND, L. Voyages au M.-P., *etc.*   *Par.*, 1801.
——— Ramond's Journey to the summit of M. P. PINKERTON. Vol. IV.
——— **Rose.**—*See* MONTE ROSA.

Monte Pisano.—PUGAARD, C. Mémoire sur les calcaires plutonisés . . .
      du M. P.   *Par.*, 1860.
——— **Rosa.**—ULRICH, M. Die Seitenthäler des Wallis und der M.
                                                     Zürich, 1850.
——— DELCROS, LE COMM. Notice sur les Altitudes du Mont-Blanc et du
      Mont-Rose, *etc.*   *Versailles*, 1851.
——— SCHLAGINTWEIT, A. and H. Observations sur la Hauteur du Mont-
      Rose, *etc.*   *Turin*, 1853.
——— ——— Épreuves de Cartes Géographiques . . . du Mont-Rose, *etc.*
                                                     Leips., 1854.
——— HINCHLIFF, T. W. Summer Months among the Alps, with the
      Ascent of M. R.   1857.
——— BARROW, J. Expeditions on . . . M. R., *etc.*   1864.
——— GLACIERS. Expeditions . . . including an ascent of . . . M. R.,
      etc.   1864.
——— **Santo.**—*See* ATHOS, MOUNT.
——— **Video.**—DAVIE, J.C. Letters . . . describing . . . M. V., *etc.*
                                                                 1805.
——— VIDAL, E. E. Picturesque Illustrations of . . . M. V., *etc.* 1830.

Montecatini.—GRABERG, COUNT J. Cenni storici . . . . sulla . . . Cava
      di Caporciano, presso M., *etc.*   *Firenze*, 1847.
Montenegro.—WILKINSON, SIR J. G. Dalmatia and M., *etc.*   1848.
——— WINGFIELD, W. F. Tour in . . . M., *etc.*   1859.

Montenegro.—Strangford, Viscountess. The E.n Shores of the Adriatic . . . with a visit to M. *Lond.*, 1864.
———— Sommières, L. C. Vialla de. Travels in M. . . . 1806. Voyages and Travels, New. 1819. Vol. IV.
Monterey.—Blake, W. P. Notice of remarkable Strata . . . in . . . M., etc. *W'ash.*, 1855.
Montgomery.—Murchison, Sir R. I. The Silurian System, founded on Geological Researches in . . . M., etc. 1839.
Montpellier.—Fischer, C. A. Letters written during a Journey to M., 1804. Voyages and Travels. A Collection, etc. 1805. Vol. III.
Montreal.—Canada. Estimates of the Expense of . . . Water Communications . . . between M. and the Ottawa, etc. 1828.
———— Greig, W. Hochelaga depicts; or the history . . . of M., etc. *Mont.*, 1839.
Montserrat. — Engländische Inseln. Reisen . . . in . . . M., etc. Voyages and Travels. Allgemeine Historie, etc. Vol. XVII.
Mooab.—*See* Mouab.
Moon, Mountains of the.—Beke, C. C. Essay on the Sources of the Nile in the M. of the M. *Edin.*, 1848.
———————— Cooley, W. D. Claudius Ptolemy . . . and the authenticity of the M. of the M. *Lond.*, 1854.
———— ———— Beke, C. T. On the . . . "M. of the M.," etc. *Edin.*, 1861.
Moorzook.—*See* Mourzuk.
Moravia.—Schwoy, F. J.—Topographie vom Markgrafthum Mähren. *Wien*, 1793-4.
———— Spencer, E. Travels . . . including a Tour through . . . M., etc. 1836.
———— Kohl, J. G. Austria . . . M., etc. *Lond.*, 1844.
———— Browne, E. Voyage . . . to Holland, with a Journey . . . through M. . . . 1668. Harris, J. Vol. II.
———— De Bris, J. Appendix to Stolberg's Travels, extracted from a Journey in M. . . . in 1804. Pelham. Vol. II.
Morea.—Morea. Memorie istorico geografiche della M., etc. *Venezia*, 1687.
———— Dapper. Naukeurige Beschryving van M., etc. *Amst.*, 1688.
———— Castellan, A. L. Lettres sur la Morée, etc. *Par.*, 1808.
———— Gell, Sir W. Itinerary of the M., etc. 1817.
———— ———— Narrative of a Journey in the M. 1823.
———— Leake, W. M. Travels in the M. *Lond.*, 1830.
———— Giffard, E. A Short Visit to . . . the M. *Lond.*, 1837.
———— Leake, W. M. Peloponnesiaca, a supplement to Travels in the M. *Lond.*, 1846.
———— Schaub, C. Excursion en Morée, en 1840. *Genève*, 1859.
———— Pouqueville, F. C. H. L. Travels through the M. . . . 1798-1801. Voyages and Travels. A Collection, etc. 1805. Vol. III.

Morea — Morocco.

Morea.—Morritt, Mr. Account of a Journey through . . . Maina, in the M., 1795. Walpole, R. Memoirs, etc.
Morgenland.—See East.
Morgenländisches Meer.—See Red Sea.
Morlachia.—Dutens, J. V. Travels in . . . M., in 1806. Pelham. Vol. II.
Morocco.—Morocco. Observations on the W. n Coast of . . . M. . . . 1830, etc. MS.
——— Addison, L. West Barbary; or a short Narrative of the Revolutions of . . . M., etc.   Oxf., 1671.
——— Tellez, B. Travels of the Sieur Mouette in . . . M., etc.   1710.
——— Chenier, M. The present state of the Empire of M., etc.   Lond., 1788.
——— Lempriere, W. Tour from Gibraltar . . . to M.   1791.
——— Saugnier, M. Relations de plusieurs voyages . . . à Maroc, etc.   Par., 1792.
——— Damberger, C. F. Travels . . . from the Cape of Good Hope to M., etc.   1801.
——— Jackson, J. G. Account of . . . M., etc.   1809.
——— ——— An Account of . . . M., etc.   Lond., 1814.
——— Ali Bey. Travels in M., etc.   1816.
——— Beauclerk, G. A Journey to Marocco, in 1826.   Lond., 1828.
——— Caillié, R. Travels . . . across the Great Desert to M., etc.   1830.
——— Brooke, Sir A. de C., Bart. Sketches in . . . M.   1831.
——— Gräberg, Count J. Das Sultanat Mogh'rib-ul-Aksá, oder Kaiserreich Marokko, etc.   Stutt. u. Tub., 1833.
——— ——— Specchio . . . del' Impero di Marocco.   Genova, 1834.
——— ——— Prospetto del Commercio di Marocco.   Firenze, 1835.
——— Scott, Colonel. A Journal . . . of Travels in M., etc.   Lond., 1842.
——— Urquhart, D. The Pillars of Hercules; or, a narrative of travels in Spain and M., etc.   Lond., 1850.
——— Power, W. T. Recollections . . . including l'eregrinations in . . . M., etc.   Lond., 1853.
——— Durrieu, X. The present state of M., etc.   1854.
——— Snider-Pellegrini, A. Du Développement du Commerce de l'Algérie . . . précédé d'Observations sur . . . le Maroc.   Par., 1857.
——— Vincendon-Dumoulin, C. A., and Kerhallet, C. P. de. Description Nautique de la Côte N. du Maroc.   Par., 1857.
——— Murray, Mrs. E. Sixteen Years . . . in M., etc.   1859.
——— Richardson, J. Travels in M., etc.   1860.
——— Montefiore, Sir M. Narrative of a Mission to . . . M., 1863-64.   1864.

Morocco.—Oliveira, B. A Visit to the Spanish Camp in M., during the late War. *Lond.*, **1865.**
———— Rohlfs, G. Tagebuch seiner Reise durch M. nach Tuat 1864. *Gotha*, **1865.**
———— Beaumier, A. Itinéraire de Mogador à Maroc, *etc.* *Par.*, **1868.**
———— Lambert, P. Notice sur la Ville de Maroc. [*Par.* **1868.**]
———— Rohlfs, G. Reise durch Marokko, *etc.* *Bremen*, **1868.**
———— Hogan, E. Voyage ... to the Emperour of M., 1577. Hakluyt. Vol. II.
———— Roberts, H. Voyage and Ambassage to Mully Hamet, Emperor of M., 1585. Hakluyt. Vol. II.
———— Hogan, E. Account of the Embassy to M., 1577. Kerr. Vol. VII.
———— Roberts, H. Account of the Embassy ... to M., 1585. Kerr. Vol. VII.
———— Lemprière's Tour to M. Pinkerton. Vol. XV.
Morone.—Tenore e Gussoni. Viaggio ... al M., *etc.*
Morrone.—*See* Morone.
Moschovia, Moscovia.—*See* Russia.
Moscow.—Idem, E. Y. Three Years' Travels from M. ... to China, *etc.* *Lond.*, **1706.**
———— Macmichael, W. Journey from M. to Constantinople, *etc.* *Lond.*, **1819.**
———— Keppel, Hon. G. Personal Narrative of a Journey from India ... by ... M., *etc.* **1827.**
———— Straussen, J. J. Reise durch ... Moskau ... 1647-1673. *Gotha*, **1832.**
———— Schnitzler, J. H. M.: Tableau statistique, *etc.* *St. Pet.*, **1834.**
———— Abbott, Capt. J. Journey from Herant to ... M., *etc.* **1843.**
———— Struve, O. Détermination des Positions Géographiques de ... M., *etc.* *St. Pet.*, **1843.**
———— Hill, S. S. Travels ... to M. **1854.**
———— Horsey, Master J. Voyage over land from M. ... to England, 1584. Hakluyt. Vol. I.
———— Jenkinson, A. Voyage from ... M. ... to Boghar in Bactria, 1558. Hakluyt. Vol. I.
———— Hobbs, G. Travails from Musco to Spahan, 1820. Purchas. Vol. I.
———— Jenkinson, A. Voyage from ... M. ... to ... Boghar ... 1558. Purchas. Vol. III.
———— Reinbeck, G. Travels ... through M. ..., 1805. Voyages and Travels. A Collection, *etc.* 1805. Vol. VI.
———— Macmichel, W. Journey from M. to Constantinople, 1817-18. Voyages and Travels, New. 1819. Vol. I.
Moselle.—Quin, M. J. Steam Voyages on ... the M., *etc.* **1843.**
Mosqueto Kingdom, Mosquito Shore.—*See* Mosquito Territory.

Mosquito Territory.—Mosquito, Nicaragua and Costa-Rica. 1850.
—— Bard, S. A. Adventures on the M. Shore. 1857.
—— Mosquito Kingdom in America, a familiar description of the, etc. Churchill. Vol. VI.
Mostar.—Wilkinson, Sir J. G. Dalmatia and Montenegro, with a Journey to M., etc. 1848.
Motimbas.—Of the Provinces of Bongo ... M., etc. Purchas. Vol. II.
Mouab.—Reise von Aden ... nach M., etc. Voyages and Travels. Allgemeine Historie, etc. Vol. XI.
Moulmein.—McLeod, W. C. Copy of Papers relating to ..., Route ... from M. to ... China, etc. Lond., 1869.
Mounseradoe, Cape.—See Mesurado.
Mourzouk.—See Mourzuk.
—— Hornemann, F. Travels from Cairo to M. ... in 1797-8. 1802.
—— Richardson, J. Travels in the Great Desert ... including a description of ... M. 1848.
Mosambique.—Bowditch, T. E. Account of the Discoveries of the Portuguese in ... M., etc. 1824.
—— Macleod, J. L. Travels ... with a Narrative of a Residence in M. 1860.
—— Voyage dans ... l'Afrique. M. Thomas.-Salt. Evrika. Vol. XIV.
—— Prior, J. Voyage ... to M. ... 1813. Voyages and Travels, New. 1819. Vol. II.
—— **Channel.**—Barnard, Lieut. A Three Years' Cruise in the M. C., etc. Lond., 1848.
—— Nolloth, M. S. Notes during a Cruise in the M. Lond., 1857.
—— Hornby, A. F. R. de. Routier ... comprenant les îles du Canal de M., etc. Par., 1866.
Muab.—See Mouab.
Mukran.—See Mekran.
Museepoor.—Berghaus, H. Asia ... Memoir zur Erklärung ... der reduzirten Karte von ... Muniper, etc. Gotha, 1832-35.
Munich.—Lamont, J. Ueber das Magnetische Observatorium der Königl. Sternwarte hei M. Münch., 1841.
—— Kuhn, C. Ueber das Klima von München. Münch., 1854.
Muniper.—See Museepoor.
Murau. Germany. Anzeige, etc. Hohenmessungen in der Gegend von M. ... Von Dr. F. Rolle.
Muropue.—Cooley, W. D. Inner Africa laid open ... with the routes to the M., etc. 1852.
Murray River. Kinloch, A. The M. R., etc. Adel., 1853.
Murzuk. See Mourzuk.
Musa Wadi.—See Petra.
Musardu.—Anderson, B. Narrative of a Journey to M., etc. N. Y., 1870.

Muscat.—Shaik Mansur. History of Seyd Said, Sultan of M., etc.
Lond., 1819.
Musco.—See Moscow.
Muscovia, Muscovy.—See Russia.
Mushed.—See Meschkd.
Muttra.—Longbridge, J. A. The Hooghly and the M., etc. 1864.
Mysore.—Hobr, Mr. Select Views in M., etc. Lond., 1784.
—— Hamilton, F. Journey ... through M., etc. 1807.
—— Buchanan's Journey through M., etc. Pinkerton. Vol. VIII.
—— Beschreibung der Königreiche ... Maisur, etc. Voyages and Travels. Allgemeine Historie, etc. Vol. XVIII.

N.

Nacion Arjentina.—See Argentine Republic.
Naciones Bascas.—See Basque Provinces.
Nagpore.—Jenkins, R. Report on the Territories of the Rajah of N.
Calc., 1827.
—— Blanford, W. T. Notes on Route from Poona to Nagpur, etc. India, Geological Survey. Records, etc. Vol. I.
—— On ... Coal near Nagpur. India, Geological Survey. Records, etc. Vol. I.
Nagpur. See Nagpore.
Nakus.—Newbold, T. J. Visit from Wadi Tor to Gebel N., etc.
Namur.—Vander Maelen, P. Statistique ... de N. Brussels, 1830.
—— Dictionnaire Geographique de la Province de N.
Brux., 1832.
Nancy.—Lepage, H. La Ville de N. et ses environs, etc. Nancy, 1844.
Nanking.—Journey of J. de Fontancy ... from ... Kyang Chew ... to N. in 1688. Astley. Vol. III.
Naples.—Fergola, F. Relazione delle Operazioni geodetiche raccolte nelle Provincie Settentrionali del Regno di Napoli, etc.
—— Naples. Istorie della Chiesa Greca in Napoli esistente.
Nap., 1790.
—— Giustiniani, L. Dizionario geografico-ragionato ... di Napoli.
Nap., 1797-1816.
—— Alfano, G. M. Compendio ... di tutte le ... provincie che compongono il regno di Napoli. Nap., 1798.
—— Pulli, P. Trattato ... su la raccolta del Nuro di Napoli.
Nap., 1813-17.
—— Vasi, M. dl. Itinerario ... da Roma a Napoli, etc. Roma, 1816.
—— Stendhall, Count de. Rome, N. ... in 1817. 1818.
—— Del Re, G. Napoli. Calendario, 1819-24. 1819-24.
—— Craven, Hon. R. K. Tour through the S. Provinces of N. 1821.
—— Josio, A. de. Plan de la Ville de N. 1826.

Naples.—GALANTI, G. M. Napoli e Contorni, etc. *Nap.*, 1829.
—— D'AFFLITTO, D. L. Guida di Napoli. *Nap.*, 1834.
—— JORIO, A. DE. Napoli e Contorni. *Nap.*, 1835.
—— VISCONTI, F. Sistema Metrico della Città di Napoli. *Nap.*, 1838.
—— BORRER, D. A Journey from N. to Jerusalem, etc. 1845.
—— Davies, W. A True ... description of ... N., etc. CHURCHILL. Vol. VII.
—— RAY, J. Travels through the Kingdom of N., etc. HARRIS, J. Vol. II.
—— Semple, R. Observations on a Journey ... to N., 1805. VOYAGES and TRAVELS. A Collection, etc. 1805. Vol. VIII.
——, **Gulf of.**—NOBILE, A. Memoria sulle Maree del Golfo di Napoli. *Nap.*, 1841.
—— **and Sicily.**—SWINBURNE, H. Travels in the Two Sicilies, 1777-1780. *Lond.*, 1783-85.
—— —— SPALLANZANI, L. Travels in the Two Sicilies, etc. 1798.
—— —— VENEZIA, B. Dizionario Statistico ... delle due Sicilie. *Nap.*, 1818.
—— —— DEL RE, G. Descrizione ... del ... Regno delle due Sicilie. *Nap.*, 1830-36.
—— —— ANNALI CIVILI ... delle due Sicilie. 1833-1840. *Nap.*, 1833-46.
—— —— RIVERA, C. A. DE. Tavola di Riduzione dei Pesi e delle Misure delle due Sicilie in 1840. *Nap.*, 1841.
Napo.—OSCULATI, G. Esplorazione delle Regioni Equatoriali lungo il N., etc. *Milano*, 1860.
Narova.—HELMERSEN, G. VON. Die Geologische Beschaffenheit des untern N.thals, etc. 1860.
Narue.—See NARVA.
Narva.—BURROUGH, CAPT. W. Voyage ... to the Narue in Liefland, 1570. HAKLUYT. Vol. I.
Nassau.—CRAMER, L. W. Vollständige Beschreibung des Berg-Hütten und Hammerwesens in den ... N.-Usingischen Landen. *Frankf. a. M.*, 1805.
—— TWINING, T. Letters on the condition of the Working Classes of N. 1853.
Natal.—NATAL. Emigration to N. ... with full description, etc. *Lond.*
—— BANISTER, J. W. Memoir respecting British Interests ... at ... N., etc. 1836.
—— DELEGORGUE, A. Voyage ... notamment dans le territoire de N., etc. *Par.*, 1847.
—— FREEMAN, J. J. Tour in South Africa, with notices of N., etc. 1851.
—— HOLDEN, W. C. History of the Colony of N., etc. 1855.
—— MASON, G. H. Life with the Zulus of N. 1855.
—— SHOOTER, J. The Kafirs of N., etc. 1857.

Natal.—Irons, W. The Settlers' Guide to . . . N., etc. 1858.
—— Mann, R. J. The Colony of N. An Account, etc. 1859.
—— Vetch, J. Plans and Papers on the subject of a Harbour at Port N., S. Africa. 1859.
—— Baldwin, W. C. African Hunting from N. to the Zambesi, etc. 1863.
—— Robinson, J. N.; a practical Guide Book, etc. 1863.
—— Chapman, J. Travels . . . with Journeys . . . from N. to Walvisch Bay, etc. *Lond.,* 1868.
—— Natal Colony of N. [A Collection of letters.] *Lond.* [1869.]
—— —— N. Land & Colonization . . . Correspondence . . . hints, etc. *Lond.,* 1869.

Natchez.—Gräberg, Count J. Recueil de Voyages . . . and Historical Researches on the Conquest of . . . N. . . . in the thirteenth Century, by J. Ranking. 1829.

Natiscotec.—*See* Anticosti.

Natolia.—*See* Anatolia.

Nauheim.—Beneke, F. W. On the Warm Saline Springs of N., etc. *Lond. and Edin.,* [1860.]

Navarre.—De Rancy, M. Description . . . de la N. *Toulouse,* 1817.

Nebraska.—Owen, D. D. Report of a Geological Survey of . . . a portion of N. Territory, etc. *Phil.,* 1852.
—— Fremont, J. C. Life . . . and Adventures in . . . N., etc. *N. Y.,* 1856.
—— Warren, G. K. Letter to the Hon. G. W. Jones, relative to his explorations of N. Territory. *Wash.,* 1858.
—— Humphreys, A. A. Report . . . Exploration in N., etc. *Wash.,* 1859.

Neckar.—Meidinger, H. Statistische Uebersicht der N.-Schifffahrt und Flösserei. *Frankf. a. M.,* 1850.

Neelgherry Mountains.—*See* Neilgherry Hills.

Neenah, River.—Abert, Col. J. J. Reports . . . for the Improvement of the N., etc. *Wash.,* 1840.

Negro, Rio.—*See* Rio Negro.

Negroland.—*See* Caffraria.

Nehrwalla.—Tod, Lieut.-Col. J. Travels . . . with an account of the ancient city of N. *Lond.,* 1839.

Neilgherry Hills.—Harkness, H. A Description of a singular Aboriginal Race inhabiting the summit of the N. Hills, etc. *Lond.,* 1832.
—— Baikie, R. Observations on the N., etc. *Calc.,* 1834.
—— Jervis, T. Narrative . . . with . . . account of the N. Hills. *Lond.,* 1834.
—— Mignan, R. Notes . . . during a tour . . . among the Neilgherries, etc. *Bomb.,* 1834.

Neilgherry Hills.—KING, W. R. The Aboriginal Tribes of the Nilgiri H. *Lond.*, 1870.

See also DODABETTA.

Nelson.—HAAST, J. Report of a Topographical ... Exploration of the Western Districts of the N. Province, *etc.* *Nelson*, 1861.

—— HOCHSTETTER, F. VON. New Zealand ... with special reference to N. ... *etc.* *Stuttg.*, 1867.

Német Nemzet.—*See* GERMANY.

Nepal.—*See* NEPAUL.

Nepaul.—KIRKPATRICK, COLONEL. An Account of ... N. ... in ... 1793. 1811.

—— HAMILTON, F. Account of the Kingdom of N., *etc.* *Edin.*, 1819.

—— HOFFMEISTER, W. Travels in Ceylon .. Nepal, *etc. Edin.*, 1848.

—— HOOKER, J. D. On the Climate and Vegetation ... of E. N., *etc. Lond.*, 1849.

—— CAVENAGH, O. Rough Notes on ... N., *etc.* *Calc.*, 1851.

—— SMITH, T. Narrative of a Five Years' Residence at N., from 1841-45. 1852.

—— Népal Kirkpatrick. Hamilton. EYRIÈS. Vol. XIV.

—— *See also* KHATMANDOO.

Nerbudda.—FALCONER, H. Descriptive Catalogue of ... Fossil Remains ... from ... the N., *etc. Calc.*, 1859.

——, **Lower.**—BLANFORD, W. T. On Geology of the Taptee and L. N. Valleys. INDIA GEOLOGICAL SURVEY. Memoirs, *etc.* Vol. VI.

Netherlands.—GUICCIARDINI, L. Descrittione di tutti i Paesi Bassi, *etc. Anversa*, 1567.

—— GROTIUS, H. De Rebus Belgicis; or the Annals ... of the Low Countrey Warrs. 1665.

—— NUGENT, MR. The Grand Tour ... through the N., *etc.* 1778.

—— VOLKMANN, J. J. Neueste Reisen durch die Vereinigten Niederlande, *etc. Leipzig*, 1783.

—— CHAUCHARD, CAPT. Geographical ... description of, ... the N., *etc. Lond.*, 1800.

—— GERMANY ... the N. ... Geographical ... description of, *etc.* 1800.

—— WILSON, W. R. Travels in ... N., *etc.* *Lond.*, 1826.

—— GAUTIER, J. Le Voyageur dans le Royaume des Pays-Bas. *Brussels*, 1827.

—— VAN KAMPEN, N. G. Staat-en Aardrijkskundige beschrijving van het Koningrijk der Nederlanden, *etc. Haarlem*, 1827.

—— WELLINGTON, DUKE OF. Despatches, during his ... Campaigns in ... the Low Countries, *etc.* 1837-39.

—— BELGIUM. Belgian, N. ... Lighthouses, corrected to 1848 and 1851, *etc.* 1848-51.

—— Skippon, Sir P. Journey through part of the Low Countries, *etc.* CHURCHILL. Vol. VI.

Netherlands.—Burnet, Bishop G. Travels through . . . the Low Countries, 1685-86. HARRIS, J. Vol. II.

——— Misson, M. Travels through . . . the Spanish Low Countries . . . 1687-88. HARRIS, J. Vol. II.

——— Ray, J. Travels through the Low Countries . . . 1663. HARRIS, J. Vol. II.

——— Travels through the Low Countries, etc. RAY, J. Collection, etc.

——— Holcroft, T. Travels . . . through . . . the N., etc. VOYAGES and TRAVELS. A Collection, etc. 1805. Vol. II.

———, **Austrian.**—OUDIETTE, C. Dictionnaire géographique . . . des treize . . . Départemens qui composaient les Pays-Bas Autrichiens, etc. *Par.*, **1804-5.**

Neufchâtel.—NOEL, S. B. J. Premier Essai sur . . . N., etc. *Rouen*, **1795.**

Neuland.—See NEW ISLAND.

Neumarkt.—GERMANY Anzeige, etc. Hohenmessungen in der Gegend von . . . N. . . . Von Dr. F. Rolle.

Neuwied.—HIBBERT, S. History of the Extinct Volcanoes of the Basin of N., etc. *Edin.*, **1832.**

Neva.—CHAIX, P. Des Canaux qui unissent à la N. le Bassin du Volga. *Genève*, **1856.**

Nevada.—See also COMSTOCK LODE.

Nevis.—SLOANE, H. Voyage to . . . Nieves, etc. **1707.**

——— Engländische Inseln. Reisen . . . in . . . N., etc. VOYAGES and TRAVELS. Allgemeine Historie, etc. Vol. XVII.

New Andalusia.—Niederlassungen in Neuandalusien von dem Orinoko bis an Rio de la Hacha. VOYAGES and TRAVELS. Allgemeine Historie, etc. Vol. XVI.

New Britain.—CARTERET, Capt. Voyage . . . to . . . Nova Britannia . . . 1766-69. HAWKESWORTH, J. Vol. I.

New Brunswick.—BOUCHETTE, J. The British dominions in N. America . . . a . . . description of . . . N. B., etc. **1832.**

——— NEW BRUNSWICK, Practical Information to Emigrants . . . relative to. *Lond.*, **1832.**

——— ——— Report of the Directors of the N. B. and Nova Scotia Land Company. *Lond.*, **1832.**

——— KENDALL, E. N. Reports on . . . N. B., etc. **1835.**

——— WEDDERBURN, A. Statistical . . . Observations relative to the Province of N. B. *St. John*, **1835.**

——— YULE, P. Remarks on the disputed N.-W.n Boundary of N.B., etc. **1838.**

——— REDFIELD, W. C. Remarks relating to the Tornado which visited N.B., June 10, 1835. *N. Y.*, **1841.**

——— PERLEY, M. H. Hand-book of Information for Emigrants to N.B. *St. John's*, **1854.**

——— Gordon, Hon. A. Wilderness Journeys in N. B. GALTON, F. Vacation Tourists . . . in 1862-3.

New Caledonia.—MONTRAVEL, M. L. DE TARDY DE. Instructions sur la Nouvelle-Calédonie, etc. *Par.,* **1857.**

—— BOUZET, E. DU. Instructions . . . aux batiments venant en Nouvelle-Calédonie par le Cap de Bonne-Espérance. *Par.,* **1858.**

—— GRIMOULT, M. Renseignements Nautiques sur la Nouvelle Calédonie, etc. *Par.,* **1859.**

—— CHAMBEYRON EL BANARÉ, MM. Instructions Nautiques sur la Nouvelle-Calédonie, etc. *Par.,* **1869.**

—— MULOUCALL, G. F. Instructions nautiques pour la côte Sud-Est de la Nouvelle-Ecosse, etc. *Par.,* **1869.**

New Castile.—See CUZCO.

Newcastle, N. S. W.—NICOL, W. On Fossil Woods from N., etc. *Edin.,* **1833.**

New Continent.—See AMERICA.

New England.—See AMERICA.

Newe Worlde.—See WEST INDIES.

Newfoundland.—AUTEROCHE, ABBÉ CHAPPE D'. A Voyage . . . Also a Voyage to N. . . . by M. de Cassini. *Lond.,* **1778.**

—— CHAPPELL, LIEUT. Voyage of H.M.S. Rosamond to N., etc. **1818.**

—— BOUCHETTE, J. The British dominions in N. America . . . a . . . description of . . . N., etc. **1832.**

—— LAVAUD, C. Instructions pour naviguer sur la Côte Orientale de l'Ile de Terre-Neuve, etc. *Par.,* **1838.**

—— BONNYCASTLE, SIR R. H. N. in 1842, etc. **1842.**

—— JUKES, J. B. Excursions in and about N., etc. **1842.**

—— PURDY, J. and FINDLAY, A. G. British American Navigator. Sailing Directory for . . . N., etc. **1847.**

—— CORMACK, W. E. Narrative of a Journey across . . . N. *St. John's,* **1856.**

—— FIELD, C. W. Statement of . . . Advantages attendant upon making St. John's, N., a Port of Call, etc. **1856.**

—— BAYFIELD, ADMIRAL H. W. Maritime Positions . . . in N., etc. **1857.**

—— MAURY, M. F. Letter . . . on Nautical Directions for sailing from Valentia to N. *Wash.,* **1857.**

—— DAYMAN, J. Deep-Sea Soundings . . . between Iceland and N., etc. **1858.**

—— AVEZAC, M. D'. Les Navigations Terre-Neuviennes de J. & S. Cabot. Lettre, etc. *Par.,* **1869.**

—— BROWN, R. A History of the . . . Discovery . . . of . . . N. *Lond.,* **1869.**

—— CLOUÉ, G. C. Pilote de Terre-Neuve. *Par.,* **1869.**

—— GÉARE, A. Ebenezer . . . with considerations of the Trade of N. CHURCHILL. Vol. VIII.

—— A briefe Extract concerning the Discovery of N. HAKLUYT. Vol. III.

Newfoundland — New Granada.

Newfoundland.—Cartier, J. Voyages to N. . . . 1534, 40. HAKLUYT. Vol. III.

——— Gilbert, Sir H. Voyage to N., 1583. HAKLUYT. Vol. III.

——— Hore, M. Voyage to N. . . . in 1536. HAKLUYT. Vol. III.

——— Notes and observations . . . for some part of N., etc. HAKLUYT. Vol. III.

——— Sherley, Sir A. Voyage to . . . N., 1506. HAKLUYT. Vol. IV.

——— Cabot, S. Discovery of N., 1479. KERR. Vol. VI.

——— Cartier, J. Voyages . . . to N. . . . 1534-37. KERR. Vol. VI.

——— Thorne, R. Brief notice of the Discovery of N. KERR. Vol. VI.

——— Third Voyage toward Nova Zembla and . . . N. . . . 1608, etc. PURCHAS. Vol. III.

——— Whitbourne, R. Voyages to N. . . . 1611-18. PURCHAS. Vol. IV.

——— Newfoundland, The Patent for, and the Plantation there made . . . 1610, etc. PURCHAS. Vol. IV.

New France.—See CANADA.

New Galicia.—See NUEVA GALICIA.

New Granada.—ACOSTA, J. Compendio histórico del Descubrimiento . . . de la Nueva G., en el siglo décimo sexto. *Par.,* 1848.

——— JOMARD, E. F. Rapport sur la Carte de la Nouvelle-Grenade de M. le Col. Acosta. *Par.,* 1848.

——— CALDAS, F. J. DE. Semanario de la Nueva G., etc. *Par.,* 1849.

——— PANAMA. Contract between . . . N. G. and the Panama Railway Company. *N. Y.,* 1850.

——— CUERVO, A. B. Resúmen de la Geografía . . . de la Nueva G. *De Torres Amaya,* 1852.

——— MOLINA, F. Costa-Rica y Nueva G.; Exámen de la cuestion de Limites, etc. *Wash.,* 1852.

——— MOSQUERA, T. C. DE. Memoria sobre . . . la Nueva G. *N. Y.,* 1852.

——— NEW GRANADA and Costa Rica. The Boundary Question . . . examined, etc. *Lond.,* 1852.

——— MOLINA, F. Costa Rica and N. G.; an Inquiry into the question of Boundaries, etc. *Wash.,* 1853.

——— MOSQUERA, T. C. DE. Memoir of the . . . Geography of N. G., etc. *N. Y.,* 1853.

——— TRAUTWINE, J. C. Rough Notes of an Exploration for an Inter-Oceanic Canal Route . . . in N. G., etc. *Phil.,* 1854.

——— CULLEN, E. Republic of N. G., as a Field for Emigration. *Dubl.,* 1858.

——— NEW GRANADA. Jeografía . . . de la Nueva G. [By Colonel Codazzi.] [*Bogota,* 1858.]

——— NEW GRANADA. N. G. as a Field for Emigration. *Lond.,* 1859.

——— BOLLAERT, W. Antiquarian . . . Researches in N. G., etc. 1860.

New Granada — New Holland.

New Granada.—NEW GRANADA. Second edition. N. G. as a Field for Emigration. *Lond.*, 1860.
—— FOWLER, J. D. N. G.: its internal resources. *Lond.*, 1863.
—— Neues Königreich G. VOYAGES and TRAVELS. Allgemeine Historie, etc. Vol. XVI.
—— See also PANAMA, CITY OF.

New Guinea.—SONNERAT, M. Voyage à la Nouvelle Guinée, etc. *Par.*, 1776.
—— FORREST, T. Voyage to N. G., etc. 1780.
—— KOLF, D. H. Reize ... langs de ... Zuidwest Kust van Nieuw-G., in 1825-26. *Amst.*, 1828.
—— MODERA, J. Verhaal van eene Reize naar en langs de Zuid-West Kuist van Nieuw-G. in 1828. *Haarlem*, 1830.
—— KOLF, D. H. Voyages ... along the ... S.n Coast of N. G., in 1825-26, etc. 1840.
—— JUKES, J. D. Narrative of the Surveying Voyage of H.M.S. *Fly*, in ... N. G., etc. 1847.
—— MACGILLIVRAY, J. Narrative ... including Discoveries to ... N. G., etc. 1852.
—— LAUTS. Naam der Straat, tusschen Nieuw-Holland en Nieuw G. 1861.
—— MÜLLER, J. Die Humboldts-Bai und Cap Bonpland in Neu-G. ethnographisch und physikalisch untersucht, etc. *Berl.*, 1864.
—— FINSCH, O. Neu-G. und seine Bewohner. *Bremen*, 1865.
—— Dampier, W. Voyage to ... N. G. ... 1699-1701. HARRIS, J. Vol. I.
—— Eylande der Papue bey Neuguinea. VOYAGES and TRAVELS. Allgemeine Historie, etc. Vol. XVIII.
—— Geographische Beschreibung einer Küste von Neuguinea, 1705. VOYAGES and TRAVELS. Allgemeine Historie, etc. Vol. XVIII.
—— Keyts, J. Reise nach Neuguinea, 1678. VOYAGES and TRAVELS. Allgemeine Historie, etc. Vol. XVIII.
—— Vink. Reise nach Neuguinea, 1663. VOYAGES and TRAVELS. Allgemeine Historie, etc. Vol. XVIII.

New Hampshire.—HITCHCOCK, C. H. First Annual Report upon the Geology ... of N. H. *Manchester*, 1869.

New Holland.—EARL, G. W. Observations on the ... capabilities of the N. Coast of N. H., etc. 1836.
—— SOMMER, F. VON. Catalogus der Geologische Bestanddeelen van N. H. *Batavia*, 1849.
—— LAUTS. Naam der Straat, tusschen Nieuw-H. en Nieuw Guinea. 1861.
—— FOY, R. Renseignements Nautiques sur quelques Ports ... de la Nouvelle Hollande, etc. *Par.*, 1866.
—— Haas. Histoire de la découverte du détroit entre la Nouvelle Hollande et la Terre Van Dieman, 1705. EYRIES. Vol. IV.
—— Dampier, W. Voyage to N. H. ... 1699-1701. HARRIS, J. Vol. I.

New Holland—New South Wales.

New Holland.—Pelsart, F. Voyage and Shipwreck of, on the Coast of N. H. . . . 1629. Harris, J. Vol. I.
——— Dampier's Account of N. H. Pinkerton. Vol. XI.
New Island.—Reisen und Niederlassungen in der Insel Neuland. Voyages and Travels. Allgemeine Historie, etc. Vol. XVII.
New Jersey.—Rogers, H. D. Report on the Geological Survey of . . . N. J. *Phil.*, 1836.
——— ——— Geology of . . . N. J.; being a final Report. *Phil.*, 1840.
——— New Jersey. Annual Report of the State Geologist of N. J. for 1869. *Trenton*, 1870.
New Mexico.—Falconer, T. Notes of a Journey through . . . N. M. in . . . 1841 and 1842.
——— M'Call, G. A. Reports in Relation to N. M. *Wash.*, 1851.
——— Mayer, B. Mexico . . . Notices of N. M., etc. *Hartf. U. S.*, 1852.
——— Bartlett, J. R. Personal . . . explorations . . . in . . . N. M., etc. *N. Y.*, 1854.
——— Clever, C. P. N. M.: her Resources, etc. *Washington*, 1868.
——— Hayden, F. V. Preliminary Field Report of the U. S. Geological Survey of . . . N. M. *Wash.*, 1869.
——— Pike. Voyage dans l'ouest de la Louisiane . . . et . . . excursion au Nouveau Mexique, 1805-7. Eyriès. Vol. IX.
——— Espejo, A. de. Voyage from . . . Nueva Galicia, to N. M., 1582. Hakluyt. Vol. III.
——— Ruis, Frier A. Voyage to the 15 Provinces of N. M., 1581. Hakluyt. Vol. III.
——— Toletus, L. T. Letter . . . touching J. de Onate his discoveries in N. M. . . . 1605. Purchas. Vol. IV.
——— Voyages of Frier M. de Niça . . . into N. M. . . . 1539-90. Purchas. Vol. IV.
——— See also Bogota. Rocky Mountains. Santa Fé.
New Netherlands.—Netherlands, New. Remonstrance of N. N., and the Occurrences there, etc. *Alb.*, 1856.
New Plymouth.—Shurtleff, N. B. Records of the Colony of N. P. . . . 1633-94. *Bost., U. S.*, 1855-7.
New Russia.—Hagemeister, J. de. Commerce of N. R., etc. 1836.
New Scotland, N. Amer.—See Nova Scotia.
——— ———, S. Africa.—Pratt, J. J. Sheep and Stock Farming . . . with information relative to the Settlement of N. S. *Lond.*, [1867.]
New South Wales.—White, J. Journal of a Voyage to N. S. W. *Lond.*, 1790.
——— Collins, D. Account of . . . N. S. W., etc. 1798.
——— Wentworth, W. C. Statistical . . . description of . . . N. S. W., etc. 1819.

New South Wales — New World.

New South Wales.—OXLEY, J. Journals of two expeditions into the Interior of N. S. W., in 1817-18. 1820.

——— WALLIS, J. An historical account of ... N. S. W., etc. Lond., 1821.

——— FIELD, B. Geographical Memoirs on N. S. W., etc. 1825.

——— BANISTER, J. W. On Emigration to ... N. S. W., etc. 1831.

——— NEW SOUTH WALES. Copies of the Royal Instructions ... as to the ... disposing of Crown Lands. 1831.

——— DUARY, J. Authentic Information relative to N. S. W., etc. Lond., 1832.

——— NEW SOUTH WALES. Land Regulations, etc. 1832.

——— BENNETT, G. Wanderings in N. S. W., etc. 1834.

——— BRETON, LIEUT. Excursions in N. S. W., etc. 1834.

——— STURT, C. Two Expeditions ... with Observations on ... N. S. W. 1834.

——— LHOTSKY, J. A Journey ... with ... information respecting ... N. S. W. Syd., 1835.

——— LANG, J. D. Historical ... Account of N. S. W., etc. 1837.

——— MITCHELL, SIR T. L. Three Expeditions ... with descriptions of ... N. S. W. 1839.

——— WHEELER, D.—Extracts from the Letters and Journals of ... in ... N. S. W., etc. 1839.

——— NEW SOUTH WALES. Debate in the Legislative Council ... on the subject of Immigration to the Colony. Syd., 1840.

——— GIPPS, Sir G. Report of the progressive discovery ... of N. S. W., etc. 1841.

——— STRZELECKI, P. E. DE. Physical description of N. S. W., etc. 1845.

——— BRAIM, T. H. History of N. S. W., etc. 1846.

——— SIDNEY, S. The Three Colonies of Australia,—N. S. W., etc. 1853.

——— NEW SOUTH WALES and Victoria. Despatches ... relative to the discovery of Gold, etc. 1855.

——— HEYWOOD, B. A. A Vacation Tour ... through ... N. S. W., etc. 1863.

——— WILKINS, W. The Geography of N. S. W., etc. Sydney, 1863.

——— Colonie Anglaise de la Nouvelle Galles Méridionale depuis ... 1788 jusqu'en 1822. EYRIÈS. Vol. IV.

——— Tableau physique de la Nouvelle Galles du Sud, etc. EYRIÈS. Vol. V.

——— Cramp, W. B. Narrative ... and a description of N. S. W., 1815-21. VOYAGES and TRAVELS, New. 1819, etc. Vol. IX.

——— See also BLUE MOUNTAINS. KING'S TOWN. NEWCASTLE. PORT PHILIP. WINDSOR.

New Spain.—See MEXICO.

New World.—See AMERICA.

New York.

New York.—NEW YORK. Communication from the Governor relative to the Geological Survey of . . . N. Y., 1838. *N. Y.*, **1838.**

——— Communication from the Governor relative to the Geological Survey of the State, *etc.* **1839-40.**

——— BECK, L. C. and others. The N. Y. Geological . . . Reports for 1837. *Alb.*, **1840.**

——— PRESTON, T. R. Three Years' Residence in Canada . . . with Notes on a Winter Voyage to N. Y., *etc.* **1840.**

——— TANNER, H. S. The Traveller's Handbook for the State of N. Y., *etc.* *N. Y.*, **1844.**

——— BRODHEAD, J. R. Reports . . . relative to the Colonial History of N. Y. *N. Y.*, **1845.**

——— SCHOOLCRAFT, H. R. Notes on the Iroquois, or contributions to the . . . Ethnology of Western N. Y. *N. Y.*, **1846.**

——— O'CALLAGHAN, E. B. Documentary History of the State of N. Y., *etc.* *Alb. U. S.*, **1850.**

——— NEW YORK. Plan for shortening the time of Passage between N. Y. and London. *Portland U. S.*, **1850.**

——— SQUIER, E. G. Antiquities of the State of N. Y., *etc.* *Buffalo*, **1851.**

——— NEW YORK. Catalogue of the Cabinet of Natural History, *etc.* *Alb.*, **1853.**

——— ——— Annual Report of the State Engineer and Surveyor on the Railroad Statistics . . . 1853-55. *Alb.*, **1853-5.**

——— CAPRON, E. S. History of California . . . with a Journal of the voyage from N. Y., *etc.* *Bost.*, **1854.**

——— HOUGH, F. B. Results of . . . Meteorological Observations, made . . . in . . . N. Y., from 1826 to 1850. *Alb.*, **1855.**

——— NEW YORK. Annual Report of the Canal Commissioners, *etc.* *Alb.*, **1855.**

——— ——— Report of the State Engineer and Surveyor on the Canals . . . 1854. *Alb.*, **1855.**

——— ——— Annual Report of the Governors of the Alms House, for 1854-56. *N. Y.*, **1855-57.**

——— ——— Report of the Commissioners of Emigration . . . 1854 and 1856. *N. Y.*, **1855-57.**

——— BRODHEAD, J. R. Documents relative to the Colonial History of . . . N. Y., *etc.* *Alb.*, **1856-8.**

——— NEW YORK. First Annual Report on the Improvement of the Central Park, N. Y. *N. Y.*, **1857.**

——— ——— Report of the Railroad Commissioners . . . 1856. *Alb.*, **1857.**

——— ——— Report of the Regents of the University . . . 1857, 1860-61. *Alb.*, **1857-61.**

——— HALL, J. Contributions to the Palæontology of N. Y., *etc.* *N. Y.*, **1858.**

——— NEW YORK. Annual Report of the State Engineer and Surveyor on the Railroads, *etc.* *Alb.*, **1858.**

New York.—Dix, J. A. Address delivered before the N. Y. State Agricultural Society, etc. *Alb.*, **1859.**
——— New York. Report . . . on the condition of the State Cabinet of Natural History, etc. *Alb.*, **1860-61.**
——— Kohl, J. G. Travels . . . through . . . N. Y., etc. *Lond.*, **1861.**
——— New York. Report of the Trustees of the N. Y. State Library, 1862. *Alb.*, **1862.**
——— Wilson, H. Trow's N. Y. City Directory . . . May 1, 1868. *N. Y.*, **[1868.]**

New Zealand.—Best, A. D. Journal of an excursion into the Interior of the Northern Island of N. Z.
——— New Zealand, Some particulars concerning. *Lond.*
——— Collins, D. Account of . . . N. Z., etc. **1798.**
——— Nicholas, J. L. Narrative of a Voyage to N. Z. In 1814-15, etc. **1817.**
——— Busby, J. Authentic Information relative to . . . N. Z. *Lond.*, **1832.**
——— M'Donnell, T. Extracts from his MS. Journal, containing Observations on N. Z. *Lond.*, **1834.**
——— New Zealand, The British Colonization of, etc. **1837.**
——— Polack, J. S. N. Z., being a Narrative of Travels, etc. **1838.**
——— Moore, W. Log-Book of the . . . *Eliza Scott* . . . during her Voyage . . . to N. Z., etc. MS. **1838-9.**
——— Swainson, W. Observations on the Climate of N. Z., etc. *Lond.*, **1840.**
——— Dieffenbach, E. N. Z. and its Native Population. **1841.**
——— Drury, Capt. Revised Sailing Directions . . . for the N. part of . . . N. Z. *Auckl.*, **1841.**
——— Ritter, C. The Colonization of N. Z., etc. *Lond.*, **1842.**
——— Terry, C. N. Z.: its advantages, etc. **1842.**
——— Dieffenbach, E. Travels in N. Z., etc. **1843.**
——— Sutton, G. The Culture of the Grape-Vine and the Orange in . . . N. Z. **1843.**
——— Wakefield, E. J. Adventure in N. Z., from 1839 to 1844, etc. **1845.**
——— Wood, J. N. Z. and Its Claimants, etc. **1845.**
——— Fitz-Roy, Rear-Adml. R. Remarks on N. Z. **1846.**
——— New Zealand, On the British Colonization of, etc. *Lond.*, **1846.**
——— Power, W. T. Sketches in N. Z., etc. **1849.**
——— Africa. The Lights of . . . N. Z. Corrected to 1849, 51, 52, 56, 57, 58, 59. **1849-59.**
——— Australia. Report of . . . Proceedings . . . for . . . establishment of Steam Communication with . . . N. Z. **1850.**
——— Boyd, A. Steam to . . . N. Z. **1850.**

New Zealand.—INDIA. First Report . . . on Steam Communications with . . . N. Z. *Lond.*, 1851.

—— MELVILLE, H. The present state of Australia, including . . . N. Z., *etc.* 1851.

—— POWER, W. T. Recollections . . . including Peregrinations in . . . N. Z. *Lond.*, 1853.

—— TAYLOR, R. To Ika a Maui, or N. Z. and its inhabitants, *etc.* *Lond.*, 1855.

—— COOPER, J. R. N. Z. Settler's Guide, *etc.* 1857.

—— PUSELEY, D. The Rise and Progress of . . . N. Z., *etc.* 1858.

—— FENTON, F. D. Observations on the state of the Aboriginal Inhabitants of N. Z. *Auckl.*, 1859.

—— RICHARDS, G. H. and EVANS, J. F. N. Z. Pilot. 1859.

—— THOMSON, A. S. Story of N. Z., *etc.* 1859.

—— NEW ZEALAND, Statistics of, for 1853-62 . . . Including . . . a Census . . . taken Dec. 16, 1861. *Auckl.*, 1859-63.

—— DUNSTERVILLE, E. The Admiralty List of the Lights of . . . N. Z. Corrected to 1860, 61, 62. 1860-62.

—— NEW ZEALAND, Papers relating to the Recent Disturbances in, *etc.* 1861.

—— NEW ZEALAND. Census . . . Dec. 1861, *etc.* *Auckl.*, 1862.

—— YATES, J. On the excess of Water in the Region . . . about N. Z., *etc.* 1862.

—— GRAS, M. A. LE. Phares . . . de . . . Nouvelle Zélande. Corrigés 1862, 63. *Par.*, 1862, 63.

—— HEYWOOD, B. A. A Vacation Tour . . . through . . . N. Z., *etc.* 1863.

—— NEW ZEALAND GOVERNMENT, THE, and the Maori War of 1863-4, with especial reference to the confiscation of Native Lands, *etc.* 1864.

—— NOVARA, FRIGATE. Reise der Österreichischen Fregatte Novara um die Erde, *etc.* (Geologischer Theil. Bd. I. Geologie von Neu-Seeland . . . von Dr. F. von Hochstetter.) *Wien*, 1864.

—— WILSON, J. A. Remarks on Australian and N. Z. Climatology, *etc.* 1864.

—— BULLER, W. N. Z. Exhibition, 1865. Essay on the Ornithology of N. Z. *Dunedin*, 1865.

—— COLENSO, W. N. Z. Exhibition, 1865. Essay on the Botany of the N. Island of N. Z. *Dunedin*, 1865.

—— CRAWFORD, HON. J. C. N. Z. Exhibition, 1865. Essay on the Geology of the North Island of N. Z. *Dunedin*, 1865.

—— NEW ZEALAND GEOLOGICAL SURVEY. Geological Survey of N. Z. First general Report on the Coal Deposits of N. Z., *etc.* *Well.*, 1866.

—— HOCHSTETTER, F. VON. N. Z., its physical geography, *etc.* *Stutt.*, 1867.

—— HAYNES, S. L. A Ramble in the N. Z. Bush. *Lond.* [1868.]

—— HECTOR, J. Meteorological Report, 1868 . . . for N. Z., *etc.* *Well.*, 1869.

New Zealand — Nicaragua.   317

New Zealand.—NEW ZEALAND GEOLOGICAL SURVEY. Abstract Report on the Progress of the Geological Survey of N. Z. . . . 1864-9, etc. *Well.*, 1869.

—— Scheme of a Voyage to convey the Conveniences of Life to N. Z. 1771. DALRYMPLE, A. Tracts, from 1769 to 1793.

—— Nicholas, J. L. Voyage à la Nouvelle Zélande, 1814-15. EYRIES. Vol. V.

—— ——— Suite du Voyage à la Nouvelle Zélande. EYRIES, Vol. VI.

—— *See also* AUCKLAND. CANTERBURY. NELSON. OTAGO.

'Ngami, Lake.—ANDERSSON, C. J. A Journey to Lake 'N., *etc.* 1854.

—— ——— HOLDEN, W. C. History of . . . the Great Lake 'N., *etc.* 1855.

—— ——— ANDERSSON, C. J. Lake 'N., *etc.* 1856.

—— ——— BALDWIN, W. C. African Hunting. . . . including Lake N., *etc.* 1863.

—— ——— BAINES, T. Explorations . . . from Walvisch Bay to Lake N., *etc.* *Lond.*, 1864.

—— ——— CHAPMAN, J. Travels . . . with . . . visits to Lake N., *etc. Lond.*, 1868.

Niagara.—BARTRAM, J. Observations on . . . N. [By P. Kalm.] 1751.

—— DE VEAUX, S. The Traveller's Own Book to . . . N. Falls, *etc. Buff.*, 1841.

—— NIAGARA. Engineers' Opinion of the Marine Railway around the Falls of N. *N. Y.*, 1865.

Niandaha.—SCHIEBEN, C. Der N., *etc.*   *Riga*, 1856.

Nias.—MOOR, J. H. Notices of . . . N., *etc. Singapore*, 1837.

Nicaragua.—GAGE, T. Nouvelle Relation des Voyages dans la Nouvelle Espagne . . . et . . . retour par . . . N., *etc. Amst.*, 1695.

—— ——— Survey of the Spanish West Indies . . . describing N., *etc.* 1702.

—— M'QUEEN, J. A General Plan for a Mail Communication . . . to which are added Geographical Notices of . . . N., *etc. Lond.*, 1838.

—— LIOT, W. B. Panamá, N., *etc.* 1849.

—— BAILY, J. Central America . . . N., *etc.* 1850.

—— CHALONER and FLEMING. The Mahogany-Tree . . . with notices of the projected . . . communication of . . . N., *etc. Liverp.*, 1850.

—— MOLINA, F. Memoria sobre las Cuestiones de Limites . . . entre . . . Costa-Rica y . . . N. *Madr.*, 1850.

—— MOSQUITO, N. and Costa-Rica. 1850.

—— DARIEN. The N. and Darien Ship-Canal Routes. 1853.

—— SQUIER, E. G. Travels . . . particularly in N., *etc. N. Y.*, 1853.

—— CARSON, E. S. History of California . . . with a Journal of the voyage . . . viâ N., *etc. Bost.*, 1854.

—— SCHERZER, K. VON. Travels in . . . N., *etc.* 1857.

Nicaragua.—COLLINSON, J. Descriptive Account of Captain B. Pim's project for an International ... Railway across N., etc. *Lond.*, 1866.

—— BELLY, F. À travers l'Amérique Central. Le N , etc.
Par., 1867.

—— DOYLE, F. A Ride ... through N., etc. *Lond.*, 1868.

—— Oviedo y Valdés, G. F. Histoire du N. TERNAUX-COMPANS. Voyages. Vol. XIV.

——, Lake.—MERCER, A. Report on ... Inter-Oceanic connection ... by the way of Lake N., etc. *Wash.*, 1839.

Nicaria.—DAPPER. Beschryving van ... N., etc. 1688.

Nice.—SOLMS, M. DE N. *Florence*, 1854.

Nicobar Islands.—LEJOH, W. II. Reconnoitering Voyages ... including visits to the N. ... Islands, etc. *Lond.*, 1839.

—— —— Reconnoitering Voyages ... Including visits to N., etc.
1840.

—— NICOBAR ISLANDS, [Some odd pages relating to the.] 1858.

—— MAURER, F. Die Nikobaren, etc. *Berlin*, 1867.

Nicoala.—Dandini, J. Voyage to ... also a description of ... N., etc. CHURCHILL. Vol. VII.

Nicoya.—GAGE, T. Survey of the Spanish West Indies ... describing ... N., etc. 1702.

Niemen, River.—KOPPIN. Der Memelstrom in Hydrotechnischer Beziehung. *Berl.*, 1861.

Nieves.—*See* NEVIS.

Niger.—BARTH, H. Dr. B. Baikie's Thätigkeit am unteren N., etc.
Berlin.

—— GRABERG, Count J. Sulla scoperta dell' Imboccatura del N., etc.

—— HUTTON, W. Voyage to Africa ... with remarks on ... the N., etc. 1821.

—— LYON, G. F. Narrative ... with geographical Notices of ... the Course of the N. 1821.

—— M'QUEEN, J. Geographical ... View of ... Africa, containing a particular account ... of the ... N., etc. *Edin.*, 1821.

—— DONKIN, SIR R. Dissertation on the course ... of the N. 1829.

—— LANDER, R. and J. Journal of an Expedition to explore ... the N., etc. 1833.

—— LAIRD, M. and OLDFIELD, R. A. K. Narrative of an Expedition into the Interior of Africa, by the ... N., etc. 1837.

—— SCHÖN, J. F. and CROWTHER, C. Journals relating to the Expedition up the N. in 1841. 1842.

—— NIGER, Papers relative to the Expedition to the. 1843.

—— ALLEN, W. and THOMSON, T. R. H. Narrative of ... expedition to the ... N. in 1841. 1848.

—— BEKE, C. T. Observations sur la Communication supposée entre le N. et le Nil. 1850.

Niger — Nile.

Niger.—HUTCHINSON, T. J.   Narrative of the N. . . . . Exploration, *etc.*   1855.

—— BAIKIE, W. B.   Narrative of . . . Voyage up the . . . N., *etc.*   1856.

—— CROWTHER, S., and TAYLOR, J. C.   The Gospel on the Banks of the N.   Journals, *etc.*   1859.

—— BAIKIE, W. D.   Despatches . . . from . . . the N. Expedition, *etc.*   1862.

—— —— Reports on the Geographical Position of the Countries in the Neighbourhood of the N., *etc.*   [1862.]

—— CROWTHER, S., and TAYLOR, J. C.   No. 2.   Journals . . . of the Native Missionaries in the . . . N., 1862.   1863.

—— NIGER.   Journals and Notices of the Native Missionaries on the . . . N., 1862.   1863.

—— —— Copy of Correspondence on the subject of . . . establishing Steamers on the . . . N.   1864.

—— Janucquin, C.   Abstract of a Voyage to . . . Senega, on the . . . N.   ASTLEY.   Vol. II.

Nigritia — *See* SOUDAN.

Nijegorod. — *See* NIJNY NOVGOROD.

Nijny Novgorod. — KEPPEL, Hon. G.   Personal Narrative of a Journey from India . . . by . . . N. N., *etc.*   1827.

Nilbecken. — *See* NILE.

Nile. — BARTH, H.   Dr. D. Baikie's Thätigkeit am . . . Niger, mit besonderer Berücksichtigung der Flusschwellen . . . des Tsad-und Nillbeckens.   *Berlin.*

—— GILBERT, M. P.   Observations sur la Carte du Nil de M. Minni.   *Bruxelles.*

—— JOMARD, E. F.   Remarques au sujet de la Notice de M. Fresnel sur les Sources du Nil.   *Paris.*

—— VOSSIUS, I.   De Nilo et aliorum fluminum origine.   *Hagæ Com.*, 1666.

—— NILE, A short Relation of the River, *etc.*   1673.

—— LUCAS, P.   Voyage au Levant . . . Cours du Nil, *etc.*   *La Haye,* 1709.

—— LOBO, FATHER J.   Voyage to Abyssinia . . . a description of the N., *etc.*   *Lond.,* 1735.

—— MAXX, M. L'ABBÉ.   Mémoire . . . Dissertation sur les Sources du Nil . . . Par M. d'Anville.   1779.

—— BRUCE, J.   Travels into Abyssinia to discover the source of the N.   1790.

—— —— —— Travels to discover the source of the N., in 1768-1773.   *Edin.,* 1790.

—— NILE.   A short relation of the R. N.: of its Source and Current, *etc.*   *Lond.,* 1791.

—— RICHARDSON, R.   Travels . . . as far as the second Cataract of the N., *etc.*   *Lond.,* 1822.

Nile.—RENNELL, J. The Geographical System of Herodotus examined . . . with dissertations on . . . the Alluvions of the N., etc. 1830.

—— PROKESCH, A. VON. Land zwischen den Katarakten des Nil. 1831.

—— BERGHAUS, H. Asia . . . nebst Bemerkungen über . . . dem Nil-Lande. *Gotha,* 1832-35.

—— RITTER, C. Blick in das Nil Quelland. *Berlin,* 1844.

—— BEKE, C. T. Essay on the Sources of the N., etc. *Edin.,* 1848.

—— —— Mémoire justificatif en réhabilitation des Pères P. Paez et J. Lobo en ce qui concerne leurs visites à la Source de l'Abaï, etc. *Par.,* 1848.

—— PRISSE, E. Oriental Album . . . Life in the Valley of the N., etc. *Lond.,* 1848.

—— BEKE, C. T. On the Sources of the N., etc. 1849.

—— BARTLETT, W. H. The N. Boat, etc. 1850.

—— BEKE, C. T. Observations sur la Communication supposée entre le Niger et le Nil. 1850.

—— ABBADIE, A. D'. Observations relatives au cours du Nil, etc. *Par.,* 1851.

—— BEKE, C. T. Enquiry into M. A. d'Abbadie's Journey . . . to discover the source of the N. 1851.

—— —— A Summary of recent Nilotic discovery. 1851.

—— MELLY, G. Khartoum, and the Blue and White N.s. 1851.

—— CHUBI, J. H. Sea N., the Desert, etc. *Lond.,* 1853.

—— COOLEY, W. D. Claudius Ptolemy and the N., etc. *Lond.,* 1854.

—— THIBAUT, M. Journal de l'Expédition à la Recherche des Sources du Nil, 1839-40. *Par.,* 1856.

—— MALTE-BRUN, V. A. Sur l'Expédition aux Sources du Nil, etc. *Par.,* 1857.

—— SPRATT, T. A. B. Delta of the N. An Investigation, etc. *Lond.,* 1859.

—— —— An Investigation on the effect of the prevailing Wave Influence on the N.'s Deposits. *Lond.,* 1859.

—— BEKE, C. T. The Sources of the N., etc. 1860.

—— KRAPF, J. L. Travels . . . with an appendix respecting the Sources of the N., etc. 1860.

—— BEKE, C. T. On the Mountains forming the E. side of the Basin of the N., etc. *Edin.,* 1861.

—— —— Who discovered the Sources of the N.?, etc. 1863.

—— SPEKE, J. H. Journal of the discovery of the Source of the N. *Edin. and Lond.,* 1863.

—— BEKE, C. T. Lecture on the Sources of the N., etc. 1864.

—— BURTON, R. F., and MCQUEEN, J. The N. Basin, etc. 1864.

—— LOMBARDINI, E. Saggio Idrologico sul Nilo. *Milano,* 1864.

—— MCQUEEN, J. The N. Expeditions and Controversy, etc. 1864.

—— NARDI, F. Sulla Scoperta delle Origini del Nilo fatta da Speke e Grant, etc. *Roma,* 1864.

Nile.—Pastuey, H. Las über deu Oberlauf des Nil nach Ptolemæus.
Berl., 1864.

—— Speke, J. H. What led to the discovery of the Source of the N?
Edin., 1864.

—— Baker, Sir S. W. The Albert N'yanza, Great Basin of the N., *etc.*
Lond., 1866.

—— Kotschy, T. Der Nil, seine Quellen, *etc.* *Wien,* 1866.

—— Egli, J. J. Die Entdeckung der Nilquellen, *etc.* *Zürich,* 1867.

—— Findlay, A. G. Remarks on Dr. Livingstone's last journey, in relation to the probable ultimate Sources of the N. [*Lond.*] 1867.

—— Fraas, O. Aus dem Orient. Geologische Beobachtungen am Nil, etc. *Stuttgart,* 1867.

—— Gottberg, F. de. Des Cataractes du Nil, *etc.* *Par.,* 1867.

—— Schweinfurth, G. Pflanzen-geographische Skizze des gesammten Nil-Gebiets, *etc.* [*Gotha,* 1868.]

—— Macgregor, J. The "Rob Roy" on the ... N., *etc.*
Lond., 1869.

—— Fracastoro, H. Risposta sopra il detto crescimento del Nilo. Ramusio. Vol. I.

—— Ramusio. Discorso sopra il crescer del Fiume Nilo. Ramusio. Vol. I.

—— Relation du Père Jeronimo Lobo ... des sources du Nil, *etc.* Thevenot. Vol. IV.

—— Light, Capt. Journal of a Voyage up the N. ... 1814. Walpole, R. Memoirs, *etc.*

——, Upper.—Jomard, E. F. Notices sur la pente du Nil Supérieur, *etc.*
Paris.

—— —— Klöden, G. A. von. Das Stromsystem des Oberen Nil, *etc.*
Berl., 1856.

——, White.—Bimbachi, S. Premier Voyage à la Recherche des Sources du ... Nil-Blanc, *etc.* *Paris.*

—— —— Cailliaud, F. Voyage ... au Fleuve Blanc, *etc.*
Par., 1826.

—— —— Linant, M. Journal of a Navigation on the Bahr-el-Abiad, *etc.* 1826.

—— —— Arnaud, M. d'. Second Voyage à la Recherche des Sources du Bahr-el-Abiad, *etc.* *Par.,* [1842.]

—— —— Bimbachi, S. Voyage à la Recherche des Sources du ... Nil Blanc. *Par.,* 1842.

—— —— Jomard, E. F. Second Voyage à la Recherche des Sources du ... Nil Blanc, *etc.* *Par.,* 1842.

—— —— Arnaud, M. d'. Documents et Observations sur le cours du Bahr-el Abiad, *etc.* [1843.]

—— —— Ebn-Omar El-Tounsy, Chaykh Mohammed. Voyage au Darfour ... et préface ... sur la Région du Nil-Blanc supérieur.
Par., 1845
Y

Nile, White.—ABBADIE, A. D'. Note sur le Haut Fleuve Blanc.
  Par., **1849.**
—— —— WERNE, F. Expedition to discover the Sources of the W. N. in 1840-41, *etc.* **1849.**
—— —— BRUN-ROLLET, M. Le Nil Blanc, *etc.* *Par.*, **1855.**
—— —— BELTRAME, G. Di un Viaggio sul Fiume Bianco, *etc.*
  Verona, **1861.**
—— —— PENEY, A. Le Dr. A. Peney et ses dernières Explorations dans la Région du Haut Fleuve Blanc, *etc.* **1863.**
—— —— PONCET, J. Le Fleuve Blanc; notes géographiques, *etc.*
  Par., **1863.**
—— —— HEUGLIN, M. T. VON. Reise in das Gebiet des Weissen Nil, *etc.* *Leip. u. Heid.*, **1869.**
—— ——, **Upper.** JOMARD, E. F. Observations . . . sur le Nil-Blanc Supérieur. *Par.*, **1845.**
—— —— —— —— Rapport sur le Concours pour le Prix Annuel. Lettre sur le Haut Fleuve Blanc, *etc.* *Par.*, **1852.**
—— ——, PENEY, A. Les dernières Explorations dans la Région du Haut Fleuve Blanc, *etc.* *Par.*, **1863.**
Nile Basin.—*See* NILE.
Nilgiri Hills.—*See* NEILGHERRY HILLS.
Nimes.—MENARD, M. Histoire . . . de N., *etc.* *Nîmes*, **1838.**
Nineveh.—POTT, R. G. N.: a Review of its . . . history, *etc.*
—— BUCKINGHAM, J. S. Travels . . . with Researches on the Ruins of N., *etc.* **1827.**
—— RICH, C. J. Narrative of a Residence . . . on the Sites of Ancient N., *etc.* **1836.**
—— LAYARD, A. H. N. and its Remains, *etc.* **1849.**
—— FLETCHER, J. P. Notes from N., *etc.* **1850.**
—— FERGUSSON, J. The Palaces of N. . . . restored, *etc.* *Lond.*, **1851.**
—— VAUX, W. S. W. N. and Persepolis: an historical sketch, *etc.*
  1851.
—— WALPOLE, HON. F. The Ansayrii and the Assassins . . . including a Visit to N. **1851.**
—— WEISSENBORN, H. J. C. Ninive und sein Gebiet, *etc.* *Erfurt*, **1851.**
—— LAYARD, A. H. Discoveries in the Ruins of N., *etc.* **1853.**
Ning-Po.—Travels of five French Jesuits from N. to Pekíng in 1687. ASTLEY. Vol. III.
Ninive.—*See* NINEVEH.
Nishney Novogorod.—*See* NIJNY NOVGOROD.
Nismes.—*See* NIMES.
Nishnee Novgorod.—*See* NIJNY NOVGOROD.
Nob.—NEWBOLD, T. J. On the Site of . . . N., *etc.*
Nombre de Dios.—DAVIE, J. C. Letters . . . describing . . . N. de D., *etc.* **1805.**

Nombre de Dios.—DRAKE, SIR F. Voyages to N. de D. and Dariene, about 1572. HAKLUYT. Vol. IV.

Nora.—ERDMANN, A. Beskrifning öfver Dalkarlsbergs Jernmalmsfält utí N. Socken, etc. *Stockh.*, 1858.

Nordland, West.—See HERNOSAND.

Norfolk.—YOUNG, A.—General View of the Agriculture of the County of N. 1804.

—— WOODWARD, S. Descriptive Outline of the Roman Remains in N. 1831.

—— **Estuary.**—GORDON, L. D. B. Report on the Scheme proposed ... under the "N. E. Act," 1846. *Glasg.*, 1846.

—— ———— Report ... on the N. E. Scheme. *Lond.*, 1846.

—— **Island.** PHILLIP, A. Voyage to Botany Bay, with an account of ... N. I., etc. 1789.

—— MURRAY, T. B. Pitcairn ... To which is added a short Notice ... of N. I. 1860.

—— Brampton et Alt. Voyage de l'Ile N. à Batavia ... 1793. EYRIÈS. Vol. IV.

—— Philip, Governor. Voyage to Botany Bay, with an account of ... N. I., etc. PELHAM. Vol. I.

Norge.—See NORWAY.

Norioum.—MANNERT, K. Germania ... N. ... nach den Begriffen der Griechen und Römer, etc. *Leips.*, 1820.

Normandy.—ST. JOHN, J. A. Journal of a Residence in N. *Edin.*, 1831.

—— NORMANDY. Recherches sur l'Origine ... de quelques noms de lieu en Normandie. *Par.*, 1835.

—— KNIGHT, H. G. An Architectural Tour in N., etc. *Lond.*, 1841.

—— MUSGROVE, G. M. Ramble through N., etc. *Lond.*, 1855.

Norrland, West.—See HERNOSAND.

North. FORSTER, J. R. History of the Voyages and Discoveries made in the N., etc. 1786.

—— Neue Reisen der Engländer nach Norden, Barlow, 1719.—Scroggs, 1722.—Middleton, 1737.—Ellis, 1740. VOYAGES and TRAVELS. Allgemeine Historie, etc. Vol. XVII.

—— Reisen der Russen nach Norden, Beerings, 1725.—Spanberg, 1739.— Tchirikow, 1741. VOYAGES and TRAVELS. Allgemeine Historie, etc. Vol. XVII.

—— **Cape.**—GRÅBERG, COUNT J. Viaggio al Capo Nord 1799, del G. Acerbi.

—— ACERBI, J. Travels ... to the N. C., etc. 1802.

—— BROOKE, SIR A DE C., BART. Travels ... to the N. C. 1823.

North-East.—Reisen der Holländer nach Nordost, Parentz, 1594-95.— Heemskerke, 1596, 97. VOYAGES and TRAVELS. Allgemeine Historie, etc. Vol. XVII.

—— **Passage.**—Pontanus, J. J. Dissertation concerning the N.-E. P. PINKERTON. Vol. I.

—— Kotzebue, O. von. Voyage ... in search of a N.-E. P., 1815-18. VOYAGES and TRAVELS, New. 1819. Vol. VI.

Y 2

North Pole — North Sea.

North Pole.—Moxon, J. A Brief Discourse of a Passage by the N. P. to Japan, etc. *Lond.*, **1697.**

—— Phipps, C. J. A Voyage towards the N. P., etc. *Lond.*, **1774.**

—— Barrington, Hon. D. The possibility of approaching the N. P. asserted, etc. **1818.**

—— Parry, Sir W. E. Narrative of an attempt to reach the N. P. . . . in 1827. **1828.**

—— Ross, Sir J. C.—The Position of the N. Magnetic P. **1834.**

—— Beechey, F. W. Voyage . . . towards the N. P. . . . in . . . 1818, etc. **1843.**

—— Lambert, G. Projet de Voyage au Pole Nord. *Par.*, **1866.**

—— Martins, C. Sur la possibilité d'atteindre le Pole Nord. *Par.*, **1866.**

—— Lambert, G. La Question du Pole Nord, etc. *Par.*, **1867.**

—— Morsier, F. de. Expédition au Pole Nord. Esquisse des projets, etc. **[1867.]**

—— Petermann, A. Die deutsche Nordpol-Expedition, 1868. *Gotha*, **1868.**

—— Nicolaus de Linna. Voyage to all the Regions situate under the N. P., 1860. Hakluyt. Vol. I.

—— History of the Countries lying round the N. P., etc. 1585-1746. Harris, J. Vol. II.

—— Phipp's Journal of a Voyage to the N. P. Pinkerton. Vol. I.

—— Discoveries towards the N. P., 1607, etc. Purchas. Vol. III.

—— Freminville's Voyage towards the N. P., 1806. Voyages and Travels, New. 1810. Vol. II.

—— **Sea.** Kerguelen Trémarec, M. de. Relation d'une Voyage dans la Mer du Nord, etc. *Par.*, **1771.**

—— Braumüller, J. G. Der wichtigste Kanal in Europa, durch eine Vereinigung des Schwarzen Meeres mit der Ost-und Nord-See, etc. *Berl.*, **1815.**

—— North Sea, Directions for the, etc. **1832.**

—— Monnier, P. Mémoire sur les Courants de la . . . Mer d'Allemagne, etc. **1835-39.**

—— Beechey, F. W. Report on . . . Tidal Streams of the . . . N. S. **1851.**

—— Keller, F. A. E. Exposé du régime des Courants observés . . . dans . . . la Mer d'Allemagne, etc. *Par.*, **1855.**

—— North Sea Pilot, etc. **1857-1863.**

—— North Sea. Mer du Nord. Traduction du Pilote, etc. *Par.*, **1859-60.**

—— Gras, M. A. le. Phares de la Mer du Nord . . . Corrigés 1859, 61, 62, 64. *Par.*, **1859-64.**

—— Dunsterville, E. The Admiralty List of Lights in the N. S. Corrected to 1861 and 1862. **1861-2.**

—— Murray, J. On the N. S., etc. **1862.**

North Sea — North West Passage.

North Sea.—NORIE, J. W. Guide du Marin . . . sur les côtes est de la Mer du Nord, etc.   *Par.*, 1863.

——— NORTH SEA. Mer du Nord, IV⁰ Partie . . . Les Côtes, etc.   *Par.*, 1864.

——— GRAS, A. LE. Phares de la Mer du Nord, etc.   *Par.*, 1869.

North-West Passage.—JAMES, T. The dangerous Voyage of, in his intended discovery of a N. W. P., etc.   1740.

——— SMITH, F. An Account of a Voyage for the discovery of a N.-W. P. . . . in 1746 and 1747, etc.   1748.

——— HEARNE, S. A Journey . . . for the discovery of . . . a N.-W. P., etc. 1769-72.   1795.

——— BARRINGTON, HON. D. The possibility of . . . a N.-W. P. etc.   1818.

——— ROSS, CAPT. SIR J. Voyage . . . for . . . inquiring into the probability of a N.-W. P.   1819.

——— PARRY, SIR W. E. Journal of a Voyage for the discovery of a N.-W. P. . . . in 1819-20, etc.   1821.

——— ——— Journal of a second Voyage for the discovery of a N.-W. P. . . . in 1821-23, etc.   1824.

——— ——— Journal of a third Voyage for the discovery of a N.-W. P. . . . 1824-25, etc.   1826.

——— BRAITHWAITE, S. Supplement to Sir J. Ross's second Voyage in search of a N.-W. P.   1835.

——— HUISH, R. The last Voyage of Capt. Sir J. Ross . . . for the discovery of the N.-W. P., etc.   1835.

——— ROSS, CAPT. SIR J. Narrative of a second Voyage in search of a N.-W. P., etc.   1835.

——— M'CLURE, R. LE M. Discovery of the N.-W. P. . . . 1850-54, etc.   1856.

——— OSBORN, S. Discovery of the N.-W. P. by H. M. S. *Investigator*, etc.   1856.

——— ARMSTRONG, A. Personal narrative of the discovery of the N.-W. P., etc.   1857.

——— BROWN, J. The N.-W. P., etc.   1858.

——— ——— A Sequel to the N.-W. P.   1860.

——— MILTON, VISCOUNT, and CHEADLE, W. B. The N.-W. P. by Land, etc.   *Lond.*, [1865].

——— James, Capt T. Strange . . . Voyage in his intended discovery of the N.-W. P. . . . in 1631-32, etc.   CHURCHILL. Vol. II.

——— Gatonbe, J. Voyage into the N.-W. P.   CHURCHILL. Vol. VI.

——— Cabot, S. Voyage . . . for the discovery of a N.-W. P. . . . 1497. HAKLUYT. Vol. III.

——— Davis, J. Voyages for the discovery of a N. W. P., 1585-6. HAKLUYT. Vol. III.

——— Gilbert, Sir H. Discourse to prove a passage by the N. W. to Cataya, etc. HAKLUYT. Vol. III.

North-West Passage.—Rundall T. Narratives of Voyages towards the N.W., in search of a Passage . . . 1496 to 1631, etc.. 1849. HAKLUYT Soc. Pub. Vol. V.

——— JAMES, Capt. T. Voyage for the discovery of a passage into the South Seas, by the N.-W. . . . 1631-33. HARRIS, J. Vol. II..

——— Philosophical motives for seeking a passage into the South Seas, by the N. W. . . . with the History of the Attempts . . . for . . . 130 years. HARRIS, J. Vol. II.

——— Frobisher's Three Voyages for the discovery of the N.-W. P., in 1576-78, etc. PINKERTON. Vol. XII.

——— Abstract of . . . Journall for the Discoverie of the N.-W. P., 1610. PURCHAS. Vol. III.

——— Baffin, W. A briefe . . . relation of . . . the fift Voyage, for the discovery of a passage In the N.-W., 1616. PURCHAS. Vol. III.

——— True Relation of . . . the fourth Voyage for . . . the N.-W. P., 1615. PURCHAS. Vol. III.

——— Cabot, Sir S., and others. Voyages to the N.-W., 1497-1583. PURCHAS. Vol. III.

——— Knight, J. Voyage for the discovery of the N.-W. P., 1606. PURCHAS. Vol. III.

——— Second Voyage for finding a passage . . . by the N.-W., written by H. Hudson, 1608. PURCHAS. Vol. III.

——— Weymouth, G. Voyage . . . for the discovery of the N.-W. P. . . . 1602. PURCHAS. Vol. III.

——— Neue Reisen gegen Nordwest; Weimouth, 1602.—Hudson, 1607-10.—Dutton, 1612.— Baffin, 1616.— Fox, 1631.—James, 1631, etc. VOYAGES and TRAVELS. Allgemeine Historie, Vol XVII.

——— Reisen der Dänen und Spanier zur Entdeckung einer Fahrt durch Norden; Munk, 1619.—D'Aguilar, 1602.—De Fonte, 1640. VOYAGES and TRAVELS. Allgemeine Historie, etc. Vol. XVII.

——— Reisen gegen Nordwest, etc. Cabot, 1497.—Frobisher, 1579.—Davis, 1585-87. VOYAGES and TRAVELS. Allgemeine Historie, etc. Vol. XVII.

——— The Voyage of Captain Thomas James for the discovery of a N.-W. P. . . . 1631.—Ellis, Henry. Voyage for the discovery of a N.-W. P. . . . 1740. VOYAGES and TRAVELS. The World displayed. Vol. X.

Northern Dwina.—See DWINA.

Northern Ocean.—See ARCTIC OCEAN.

Norvegia.—See NORWAY.

Norway.—VERA, G. DI. Tre Navigationi fatte dagli Olandesi e Zelandesi, . . . nella Norvegia, etc. *Venet.*, **1599.**

——— PONTOPPIDAN, Br. E. Natural History of N., etc. **1755.**

——— MUMSEN, J. Reise nach Norwegen im 1788. *Hamb.*, **1789.**

——— BROOKE, SIR A. DE C., Bart. Travels through . . . N., etc. **1823.**

——— FORSELL, C. Sverige och Norwege eller Skandinavien. *Stock.*, **1826.**

——— WILSON, W. R. Travels in N., etc. *Lond.*, **1826.**

Norway.—EVEREST, R. A Journey through N., etc. *Lond.*, 1829.
—— ELLIOTT, C. B. Letters from . . . N., etc. 1832.
—— BARROW, J. Excursions in . . . N., etc. 1834.
—— FAYE, A. Udtog af Norges Riges Historie. *Christ.*, 1834.
—— PRICE, E. N. Views . . . and Journal. 1834.
—— INGLIS, H. D. A Personal Narrative of a Journey through N., etc. *Lond.*, 1835.
—— CLARKE, E. D. Travels in . . . N., etc. 1836.
—— BREMNER, R. Excursions in . . . N., etc. 1840.
—— MILFORD, J. N., and her Laplanders, in 1841, etc. *Lond.*, 1842.
—— NORWAY. Statistiske Tabeller vedkommende Underviisningsvæsenets Tilstand i Norge . . . 1840. *Christ.*, 1843.
—— TOETHE, M. B. Norges Statistik. *Christ.*, 1848.
—— ROAB, W. A. Yacht Voyage to N., etc. 1849.
—— ROQUETTE, M. DE LA. Norvège. Extrait, etc. *Par.*, 1849.
—— MUNCH, P. A. Symbolæ ad Historiam Antiquiorem rerum Norvegicarum. *Christ.*, 1850.
—— LAING, S. Journal of a Residence in N. during 1834-36. 1851.
—— PFEIFFER, J. Journey to Iceland, and Travels in . . . N., etc. 1852.
—— FORBES, J. D. N. and its Glaciers, etc. *Edin.*, 1853.
—— NORWAY. Beretning om Kongeriget Norges økonomiske Tilstand. *Christ.*, 1853-58.
—— FORESTER, T. Rambles in N., etc. 1855.
—— BUNBURY, S. A. A Summer in . . . N., etc. 1856.
—— METCALFE, F. Oxonian in N. 1856.
—— NORWAY. Statistiske Tabeller for Kongeriget N., etc. *Christ.*, 1856-58.
—— BRACE, C. L. The Norse-Folk; a visit to . . . N., etc. 1857.
—— HÖRBYE, J. C. Observations sur les Phénomènes d'Erosion en Norvège. *Christ.*, 1857.
—— NORWAY and SWEDEN, A Long Vacation Ramble in, by X. and Y. *Camb.*, 1857.
—— SCHÜBELER, F. C. Ueber die geographische Verbreitung der Obstbäume . . . in Norwegen. *Hamb.*, 1857.
—— HELMERSEN, G. VON. Geologische Bemerkungen auf einer Reise in . . . N. *St. Pet.*, 1858.
—— METCALFE, F. Oxonian in Thelemarken, or Notes of Travel in S.W.n N. 1858.
—— MURCHISON, SIR R. I. The Silurian Rocks and Fossils of N., etc. 1858.
—— TAYLOR, B. Northern Travel . . . Pictures of . . . N. 1858.
—— SARS, M. and KJERULF, T. Jagttagelser over den postpliocene eller Glaciale Formation i en del af det sydlige Norge. *Christ.*, 1860.

Norway — Norway, Coast of.

Norway.—Vibe, A. Höidemaalinger i Norge fra Aar 1774 til 1860.
Christ., 1860.
— Statistical Tables. S. T. Part VII. ... N., etc. 1861.
— Schübeler, F. C. Synopsis of the Vegetable Products of N., etc.
Christ., 1862.
— Holmboe, C. A. Norske Vægtlodder fra Fjortende Aarhundrede.
Christ., 1863.
— Sars, G. O. Norges Ferskvandskrebsdyr, etc. Christ., 1865.
— Kjerulf, T. The Terraces of N., etc. Lond., 1870.
— Mohn, H. Institut Météorologique de Norvège. Température de la Mer entre l'Islande ... et la Norvège. Christ., 1870.
— Malgo, King. Voyage to ... N., 680. Hakluyt. Vol. I.
— Other. Voyage to the N. parts beyond N., about 890. Hakluyt. Vol. I.
— A Voyage ... containing an Account of ... N., etc. Harris, J. Vol. II.
— Quirini, P. Voyage ... into N., 1431. Kerr. Vol. I.
— Nowel, T. Travels in ... N. ... in 1801. Pelham. Vol. II.
— Cox's Travels in N. Pinkerton. Vol. VI.
— Ancient Commerce betwixt England and N., etc. Purchas. Vol. III.
— Quirino, P. Shipwrecke of, on the Coast of N., 1431. Purchas. Vol. III.
— Veer, G. de. Voyages of W. Barents ... behind N. ... 1594-96. Purchas. Vol. III.
— Navigationi fatte da gli Olandesi ... nella Nornegia ... 1594-97. Ramusio. Vol. III.
— Schouten, G. Reisen nach ... Norwegen, 1658-65. Voyages and Travels. Allgemeine Historie, etc. Vol. XII.
— Hallberg, Baron Von. Sentimental Sketches, written during a Journey through ... N., about 1820. Voyages and Travels, New. 1819. Vol. V.
— Pontoppidan, E. The Natural History of N. Voyages and Travels. The World displayed. Vol. XX.
— **Coast of.**—Kerguelen Trémarec, M. de. Relation d'une Voyage ... aux Côtes ... de Norwège, etc. Par., 1771.
— Norway. Beskrivelse tel Kaartet over den Norske Kyst,
Christ., 1858-59.
— Belouim. Belgian ... and Norwegian Lighthouses, corrected to 1843, 51, 54, 57-59. 1843-59.
— Norway Pilot. Part 1. From the Naze to the Kattegat, etc. 1854.
— Long, Baron de. Pilote Norvégien, etc. Par., 1858.
— M'Dougall, G. F. Directions ... including a description of ... the Coast of N., etc. 1858.
— Dunsterville, F. The Admiralty List of the ... Norwegian Lights. Corrected to 1860. 1860.

Norway, Coast of.—Nobis, J. W. Guide du Marin ... sur les Côtes ouest de Norwège, etc. *Par.*, 1863.
——— Throton, M. Renseignements sur quelques Mouillages de la Côte ... de Norvège. *Par.*, 1865.
——— Norwegian Pilot. Den Norske Lods, etc. *Krist.*, 1867-68.

Norwège.—See Norway.
Norwood.—Weatherhead, G. H. An Account of the Beulah Saline Spa at N., etc. 1832.
Nossi-Be.—Jehenne, Capit. Sur N.-B., etc. *Par.*, 1847.
Nossi-Mitaiou.—Jehenne, Capit. Sur ... N.-M., etc. *Par.*, 1847.
Nouka-Hivn, Islands.—See Marquesas Islands.
Nouveau Continent, Nouveau Monde.—See America.
Nouvelle-Ecosse.—See Nova Scotia.
Nouvelle-France—See Canada.
——— **Galles Meridionale.**—See New South Wales.
Nova Britannia.—See New Britain.
——— **Francia.**—See Canada.
——— **Scotia.**—Nova Scotia. Copies of Communications ... on the subject of the Shubenacadie in N. S. 1830.
——— Banister, J. W. On Emigration to ... N. S., etc. 1831.
——— Bouchette, J. The British dominions in N. America ... a ... description of ... N. S., etc. 1832.
——— New Brunswick. Report of the Directors of the New Brunswick and N. S. Land Company. *Lond.*, 1832.
——— Lyell, Sir C. Travels ... with Geological Observations on ... N. S. 1845.
——— Purdy, J. and Findlay, A. G. British American Navigator. Sailing Directory for ... N. S., etc. 1847.
——— Poole, H. On the Meteorology of the Albion Mines, N. S. 1854.
——— Bayfield, Admiral H. W. N. S. Pilot ... including Halifax Harbour. 1856.
——— Maritime Positions ... on the S. Coast of N. S., etc. 1857.
——— ——— N. S. Pilot ... including Sable Island. 1860.
——— Gras, M. A. le. Routier ... de la Nouvelle-Ecosse. *Par.*, 1861.
——— Outram, J. A Hand Book of Information for Emigrants to N. S. *Halifax*, 1864.
——— Heatherington, A. A Practical Guide for ... the Gold Fields of N. S. *Montreal*, 1868.
——— Brown, R. A History of the ... Discovery ... of ... N.S., etc. *Lond.*, 1869.
——— Heatherington, A. 1860-1869. The Gold Yield of N. S. *Lond.*, 1870.

Nova Scotia.—The King's Patent . . . for the plantation of N. S. . . . 1602-9. PURCHAS. Vol. IV.

—— **Semlia.**—*See* NOVA ZEMBLA.

—— **Zembla.**—VERA, G. DE. Tre Navigationi fatte dagli Olandesi . . . dove scopersero . . . la Nuova Z., *etc.* *Venet.*, 1599.

—— BAER, K. E. VON. Expédition à Novaïa Zemlia, *etc.*
St. Pet., 1837, 38.

—— —— Ueber das Klima von Nowaja-Semlja, *etc.*
St. Pet., 1857.

—— Veer, G. de. True Description of three Voyages . . . by the Dutch in 1594-96; with their . . . residence of ten months in Nouaya Zemlya. . . . Edited by C. T. Beke. 1853. HAKLUYT Soc. Pub. Vol. XIII.

—— History of . . . N. Z. 1585-1746. HARRIS, J. Vol. II.

—— A Voyage . . . containing an Account of . . . Z., *etc.* HARRIS, J. Vol. II.

—— Islands . . . Nouvelle-Zemble . . . Climat, minéraux, animaux. LAHARPE, J. Vol. XVI.

—— Third Voyage toward N. Z. . . . 1609, *etc.* PURCHAS. Vol. III.

—— Navigationi fatti da gli Olandesi . . . dove scopersero . . . la N. Z. . . . 1594-97. RAMUSIO. Vol. III.

—— Flawes, W. Journal of a Voyage from N. Z. to England. VOYAGES. Account of several late, *etc.*

—— Von dem Russischen Neulande oder Nova Semlia. VOYAGES and TRAVELS. Allgemeine Historie, *etc.* Vol. XIX.

Novaia Zemlia.—Novaya Zemlya.—*See* NOVA ZEMBLA.

Novogorod.—STRUVE, O. Détermination des Positions Géographiques de N., *etc.* *St. Pet.*, 1843.

—— Southam, T. and Sparke, J. Voyage . . . from Colmogro to N. . . . 1566. HAKLUYT. Vol. I.

Novogrod.—*See* NOVOGOROD.

Nowaja-Semlja.—*See* NOVA ZEMBLA.

Nubia.—NORDEN, F. L. Travels in Egypt and N., *etc.* 1757.

—— LIGHT, H. Travels in . . . N. . . . 1814. *Lond.*, 1818.

—— BURCKHARDT, J. L. Travels in N. 1819.

—— BELZONI, G. Narrative of . . . Operations . . . in . . . N., *etc.* 1822.

—— IRBY, HON. C. L. and MANGLES, J. Travels in . . . N. . . . 1817 and 1818. 1823.

—— HENNIKER, SIR F. Notes during a Visit to . . . N., *etc.* 1824.

—— MADDEN, R. R. Travels in . . . N., *etc.* 1829.

—— RÜPPEL, E. Reisen in Nubien, *etc.* 1829.

—— GAISSAS, COUNT J. Tableau . . . de la Nubie, *etc.*
Gennaio, 1830.

—— ROSSELL, BP. M. N. and Abyssinia, *etc.* *Edin.*, 1832.

Nubia — Ob, River. 331

Nubia.—BOURCHIER, W. Narrative of ... Journeys across the N.n Desert, etc. 1834.
—— MADOX, J. Excursions in ... N., etc. 1834.
—— ROMER, Mrs. Pilgrimage to ... N., etc. 1846.
—— PEEL, W. A Ride through the N.n Desert. 1852.
—— Egypte. Nubia. Etaits. Vol. XIV.
—— Burckhardt, M. Some Account of the Travels of, in ... N., etc. VOYAGES and TRAVELS, New. 1819. Vol. II.

Nueva Espanna.—*See* MEXICO.

Nueva Galicia.—Forcjo, A. DE. Voyage from the Valley of S. Bartholomew, in N. G., to New Mexico, 1582. HAKLUYT. Vol. III.
—— Ulloa, F. de. Voyage by the Coasts of New G. ... into the Gulfe of California ... 1539. HAKLUYT. Vol. III.
—— Vasquez de Coronado, F. Voyage from N. G. to Cibola ... 1540. HAKLUYT. Vol. III.
—— Nunez, A. Relatione ... della N. G., 1527-36. RAMUSIO. Vol. III.

Numidia.—DAVIS, N. Ruined Cities within N.n ... Territories. Lond., 1862.
—— Of Ægypt ... N. ... and of their Religions. PURCHAS. Vol. V.

Nuneham.—OXFORD UNIVERSITY and City Guide: to which is added a description of ... N., etc. Oxf., 1831.

Nuova Spagna.—*See* MEXICO.

Nuremberg.—MAINBEROER, C. Une Semaine à N., etc. *Nur.*, 1836.
—— MAYER, F. Nürnberg im neunzehnten Jahrhundert, etc. *Nurnb.*, 1843.

Nyassa, Lake.—COOLEY, W. D. Inner Africa laid open ... with the routes to ... Lake N., etc. 1852.
—— —— LIVINGSTONE, D. and C. Narrative ... of the discovery of the Lakes Shirwa and N., etc. Lond., 1865.

O.

Oasis.—HORNEMANN, F. Voyage ... augmenté ... d'un Mémoire sur les O. ... par L. Langlès. *Par.*, 1803.
—— HENNIKER, SIR F. Notes during a Visit to ... the O., etc. 1824.
—— RENNELL, J. The Geographical System of Herodotus examined ... with dissertations on ... the O., etc. 1830.
—— RICHARDSON, J. Travels in the Great Desert ... including a description of the O., etc. 1848.
——, **Western.**—*See* DAKHEL.

Ootakamund.—MIGNAN, R. Notes ... including an account of the topography of O., etc. *Bombay*, 1834.

Oaxaca.—GAGE, T. Survey of the Spanish West Indies ... Also ... Journey through Guaxaca, etc. 1702.

Ob, River.—Burrough, S. Voyage towards the River of O. ... 1556. HAKLUYT. Vol. I.

Ob, River.—Voyage to Sibier and the River O. . . . in a letter written to Gerardus Mercator. HAKLUYT. Vol. I.

—— —— Cherry, F., and Lyndes, T. Report, touching a warme Sea to the S.-E. of the River O. PURCHAS. Vol. III.

—— —— Description of . . . Catay . . . and of the great river O. PURCHAS. Vol. III.

—— —— Marsh, A. Notes concerning the discovery of the River of O., 1584, etc. PURCHAS. Vol. III.

—— —— Pursglove, W. Travell from Pechora . . . to the River O., etc. PURCHAS. Vol. III.

Obéid, EL—See LODEID.
Oberkrain.—See CARNIOLA, UPPER.
Oberwölz.—GERMANY. Anzeige, etc.—Hohenmessungen in der Gegend von . . . O. . . . Von Dr. F. Rolle.
Obi.—LOGAN, J. R. The Rocks of Pulo Ubin, etc. *Singapore*, 1846.
Oceania.—RIENZI, G. L. D. DE. Océanie . . . Revue géographique, etc.
Par., 1836.

—— EICHTHAL, G. D'. Mémoire sur l'histoire primitive des Races Océaniennes, etc. *Par.*, 1843.

—— LOPES DE LIMA, J. J. Ensaios sobre a Statistica das Possessões Portuguezas . . . na O., etc. *Lisboa*, 1844-62.

—— EICHTHAL, G. D'. Études sur l'histoire primitive des Races Océaniennes, etc. *Par.*, 1845.

—— FOY, R. Renseignements Nautiques sur quelques Ports de l'Océanie, etc. *Par.*, 1866.

—— VALDEZ, F. T. Da O. a Lisboa viagem. *Rio de Jan.*, 1866.

—— JOHNSTON, A. K. Atlas of the British Empire in . . . O. . . . with . . . letterpress. *Edin. and Lond.*, [1870].

Ocha, Mount.—Hawkins, Mr. An Account of the discovery of a very antient Temple on Mount O., etc. WALPOLE, R. Travels, etc.

Oche, Mount.—See OCHA.
Ochosk.—See OKHOTSK.
Ochus.—See TEDZEN.
Odense.—SIMONSEN, VEDEL. Bidrag til O. Byes Aeldre Historie.
Odense, 1842.

Odessa.—KOCH, C. Crimea and O., etc. 1855.
Oesterreichische Monarchie.—See AUSTRIA.
Oetscher.—SCHMIDL, A. A. Die Höhlen des Ö. *Wien*, 1857.
Oetzthal.—GERMANY. Anzeige, etc.—Das O.er Eisgebiet. Von K. Sonklar.

—— SONKLAR, C. A. VON. Die O.er Gebirgsgruppe, etc. *Gotha*, 1860.

—— SONKLAR, K. VON. Die O.er Gebirgsgruppe, etc. *Gotha*, 1861.

Ogdensburgh.—PETERS, C. H. F. Report on the Longitude and Latitude of O. 1865.

Oggersheim.—Speyer. Bericht und Vollständiges Messungs- Protocoll, sammt allen Berechnungen über die im Jahre 1819 zwischen Speyer und O. gemessene Grund-Linie. *MS.* 1819.
Ohio.—Bradbury, J. Travels in . . . O., *etc.* *Liver.,* 1817.
—— Peck, J. M. Guide for Emigrants to . . . O., *etc.* *Bost.,* 1836.
—— Mather, W. Second Annual Report on the Geological Survey of . . . O. *Columbus,* 1838.
—— Michaux, F. A. Travels . . . in . . . O. . . . 1802. Voyages and Travels. A Collection, *etc.* 1805. Vol. I.
—— River.—Cummings, S. The Western Pilot, containing Charts of the O., *etc.* *Cincin.,* 1840.
—— —— Perrin Du Lac. Travels . . . along the O. . . . 1801-3. Voyages and Travels. A Collection, *etc.* 1805. Vol. VI.
—— —— Ashe, T. Travels . . . 1806, for . . . exploring the . . . O., *etc.* Voyages and Travels. A Collection, *etc.* 1805. Vol. X.
Ohosaka.—*See* Osacca.
Okavango, River.—Anderson, C. J. The O. River, *etc.* 1861.
Okhotsk.—Erman, A. Ueber Ebbe und Fluth an den Ochozker und Kämtschatkischen Küsten des Grossen Oceans. 1845.
——, Sea of.—Montravel, M. L. de Tardy de. Instructions . . . sur la Mer . . . d'O. *Par.,* 1857.
—— —— Geas, M. A. le. Renseignements hydrographiques sur . . . la Mer d'O. *Par.,* 1859.
Okotsk, Sea of. *See* Okhotsk.
Olancho.—Wells. W. V. Explorations and Adventures in . . . the Gold Regions of O., *etc.* *N. Y.,* 1857.
Olasz Nemzet.—*See* Italy.
Olinchy.—Macaulay, H. Directions for entering the Harbour of O., *etc.* Dalrymple, A. Collection of Nautical Memoirs, *etc.*
Olympus, Mount.—Tozer, H. F. Researches . . . including Visits to Mounts . . . O., *etc.* *Lond.,* 1869.
Oman, Gulf of.—Constable, G. C., and Stiffe, A. W. La Pilote du Golfe Persique, comprenant le Golfe d'Omman, *etc.* *Par.,* 1866.
Omderman.—Marno, E. Von Dabbeh nach O., *etc.* *Wien,* [1870.]
Omman.—*See* Oman.
Onega.—M'Dougall, G. F. Directions for . . . the White Sea, including . . . O., *etc.* 1858.
Onondaga.—Bartram, J. Observations on . . . O., *etc.* 1751.
—— Geddes, G. Report on . . . O., *etc.* *Albany,* 1860.
Ontario, Lake.—Bartram, J. Observations on . . . Lake O., *etc.* 1751.
—— —— Long, J. Voyages and Travels . . . with an account of the Posts situated on . . . Lake O., *etc.* *Lond.,* 1791.
—— —— Canada. Estimates of the Expense of . . . Water Communications . . . from Lake Erie to Lake O. 1828.

334 Ontario, Lake — Oregon.

Ontario, Lake.—Graham, J. D. Report on the Improvement of the Harbours of Lakes . . . O., *etc.* *Wash.*, 1860.

——, **Province of.**—Carling, J. Dominion of Canada. Emigration to the Province of O. *Toronto*, 1869.

Oormiah.—*See* Urumiyah.

Ooroomeyah.—*See* Urumiyah.

Ooscoroa.—*See* Ouroubi.

Ophir.—Joctans posteritie seated in the E. parts of Asia, amongst them O. . . . where . . . now is . . . Pegu, *etc.* Purchas. Vol. I.

—— Of the Gold, Silver, Gemmes . . . which Salomon's Fleet brought from O. Purchas. Vol. I.

—— Of O., divers opinions weighed and censured, *etc.* Purchas. Vol. I.

—— Probable conjectures of the Course taken in the Ophirian Voyage, *etc.* Purchas. Vol. I.

—— Salomons, King. Navis sent from Ezlongeber to O., *etc.* Purchas. Vol. I.

Ophrynium.—Calvert, F. Contributions to . . . Ancient Geography . . . Investigations relative to . . . O., *etc.* 1861.

Oran.—Comelin, F. P. de la Motte, and Bernard, J. Voyage to Barbary . . . with . . . exact draughts of . . . O., *etc.*

—— Bugraud, M. Mémoire sur notre Établissement dans la Province d'O., *etc.* *Par.*, 1838.

—— Morichrau et Bedeau. Projets de Colonisation pour les Provinces d'O. et de Constantine. *Par.*, 1847.

Orange River.—Holden, W. C. History of . . . the O.-R. Sovereignty, *etc.* 1855.

Orcades.—*See* Orkney Islands.

Oreb.—*See* Horeb.

Örebro.—Topografiska och Statistiska Uppgifter om Ö Län. *Stockh.*, 1844.

—— Erdmann, A. Beskrifning öfver Dalkarlsbergs Jernmalmsfält uti . . . Ö Län. *Stockh.*, 1858.

Oregon.—Cushing, Mr. Territory of O. Report, *etc.* *Wash.*, 1839.

—— Greenhow, R. The History of O, *etc.* *Bost.*, *U. S.*, 1844.

—— Mofras, Duflot de. Exploration du Territoire de l'O., *etc.* *Par.*, 1844.

—— Falconer, D. The O. Question, *etc.* 1845.

—— Fremont, J. C. Report of the Exploring Expedition to . . . O. . . . in 1843-4. *Wash.*, 1845.

—— Sturgis, W. The O. Question. *Bost.*, 1845.

—— Oregon Question. The O. Question, *etc.* *Lond.*, 1845-46.

—— Nicolay, C. G. The O. Territory, *etc.* *Lond.*, 1846.

—— Wallace, F. J. The O. Question determined, *etc.* 1846.

—— Coxe, Hon. H. J. A Ride . . . to O., *etc.* 1852.

—— Fremont, J. C. Life . . . and Adventures in . . . O., *etc.* *N. Y.*, 1856.

Orenberg.—MEYENDORFF, BARON G. DE. Voyage d' O. à Boukara . . . 1820, etc. *Par.*, 1826.
—— JOUKOVSKY, J. Review of remarkable events in the Province of O. *Russ.* *St. Pet.*, 1832.
—— MEYENDORFF, BARON G. DE. Journey of the Russian Mission from O. to Bokhara, etc. *Madras*, 1840.
—— BRADMORE, S. Report on the Inam Estate, situate in the Government of O., etc. *Lond.*, 1865.
Orenbourg, Orenburg.—See ORENBERG.
Orénoque.—See ORINOCO.
Orfah.—Notice sur la Carte générale des Paschaliks de . . . Orza, etc. VOYAGES and TRAVELS. Recueil, etc. Vol. II.
Organ Mountains.—HINCHLIFF, T. W. South American Sketches, or a Visit to . . . the O. M., etc. 1863.
Orient.—See EAST.
Orinoco, River.—HIPPISLEY, G. Narrative of the Expedition to the O., etc. 1819.
—— —— ROBINSON, J. H. Journal of an Expedition 1400 miles up the O., etc. 1822.
—— —— HUMBOLDT, A. VON. Tableaux de la Nature . . . les Cataractes de l'Orénoque, etc. *Par.*, 1828.
—— —— MICHELENA Y ROJAS, F. Exploracion Oficial . . . del O., etc. *Bruselas*, 1867.
—— —— APPUN, C. F. Unter den Tropen. Wanderungen . . . am O., etc. *Jena*, 1871.
—— —— BARROT, J. Description of the . . . Oronoque, etc. CHURCHILL. Vol. V.
—— —— Robinson, J. H. Voyage à l'Orénoque, 1818-19. EYRIÈS. Vol. IX.
—— —— SPARREY, F. Description of . . . the . . . O., 1602. PURCHAS. Vol. IV.
—— —— Reisen auf dem O., etc. VOYAGES and TRAVELS. Allgemeine Historie, etc. Vol. XVI.
Orissa.—STERLING, A. An Account . . . of O. Proper, or Cuttack, etc.
—— See also KHONDISTAN.
Orkney Islands.—KERGUELEN TRÉMAREC, M. DE. Relation d'une Voyage . . . aux Côtes . . . des Orcades, etc. *Par.*, 1771.
—— GORRIE, D. Summers and Winters in the O.s. *Lond.*, 1868.
—— ORKNEY ISLANDS. Handbook to the O. I. *Kirkwall* [1868].
—— Malgo, King. Voyage to . . . O. . . . 517. HAKLUYT. Vol I.
—— Brand's Description of the O., etc. PINKERTON. Vol. III.
Ormus.—See ORMUZ.
Ormuz.—Fitch, R. The long . . . voyage of . . . to O., etc. 1583-1591. HAKLUYT. Vol. II.
—— Relation of the War of O. . . . 1622. KERR. Vol. IX.
—— Fitch, R. Voyage to O. . . . 1583-91. PURCHAS. Vol. II.

Ormus.—Monoxe, E. Journal of the late O. business. Purchas. Vol. II.

——— Newbery, J. Letters relating to his . . . last Voyage into . . . O., 1583. Purchas. Vol. II.

——— Newberie, J. Two Voyages. One . . . to . . . O. . . . 1580-82 Purchas. Vol. II.

——— Finder, W. Relation of O. business, 1620-21. Purchas. Vol. II.

——— Relation of the Kings of O., etc. Purchas. Vol. II.

——— Relation of O., and of the late taking thereof, etc. Purchas. Vol. II.

——— Wilson, T. Letter . . . containing many particulars of the O. Warre, etc. Purchas. Vol. II.

Oronoque, River.—See Orinoco.

Oropia.—Finlay, G. Remarks on the Topography of O. and Diaeria.
Athens, 1838.

Orosz Nemzet.—See Russia.

Orpha.—See Orfah.

Orrhai.—See Orfah.

Oran.—See Orfah.

Orua, Oruba.—See Aruba.

Osacca.—Kaempfern, E. Reise nach . . . O., etc. 1690-91. Voyages and Travels. Allgemeine Historie, etc. Vol. XI.

———, **Gulf of.**—Coara. Description Hydrographique . . . du Golfe d'O., etc.
Par., 1861.

Osacka, Osaka.—See Osacca.

Osero.—Fortis, A. Travels . . . to which are added . . . Observations on . . . O., etc.
Lond., 1778.

Osmanen-Reich.—See Turkey.

Ost-See.—See Baltic Sea.

Ostiaks.—Besondere Nachricht von den Ostiaken. Voyages and Travels. Allgemeine Historie, etc. Vol. XIX.

Oswego.—Bartram, J. Observations on . . . O., etc. 1751.

Otagiti.—See Tahiti.

Otago.—Thomson, J. T. Sketch of the Province of O.
Dunedin, N. Z., 1858.

——— Lindsay, W. L. On the Geology of the Gold-Fields of O., etc.
1862.

Otaheite.—See Tahiti.

Otranto.—Canotti, F. Della ricchezza pubblica o privata della Terra d'O., etc.
Nap., 1861.

Ottawa.—Canada. Estimates of the Expense of . . . Water Communications . . . between Montreal and the O., etc.
1828.

——— Ottawa, the future Capital of Canada, etc.
Lond., 1858.

——— Canada, Upper. Remarks . . . containing a description of O. Territory.
Quebec, 1861.

Ottawa, River.—LOGAN, Sir W. E. Plans of various Lakes and Rivers between Lake Huron and the . . . O., etc.   *Toronto*, 1857.

Ottoman Empire.—See TURKEY.

Otuquis.—BACH, M. Descripcion . . . de O., etc.   *Buen. Aires*, 1843.

——— KERST, S. G. Die Plata-Staaten und die Wichtigkeit der Provinz O., etc.   *Berl.*, 1854.

Ouachita.—See WASHITA.

Ouaday.—See WADAY.

Oude.—SLEEMAN, Sir W. H. Journey through . . . O. in 1849-50, etc.   1858.

——— REES, L. E. R. O., its Past and its Future.   1859.

Ougoria.—Purglove, W. Travell from Pechora to . . . O., etc, PURCHAS. Vol. III.

Onolofa.—See JALOFA.

Ousouri.—MAACK, R. Journey along the Valley of the Usuri. *Russ. St. Pet.*, 1861.

Ouse, River.—RENNIE, Sir J. River O. Outfall Improvement,   *Lond.* [1839.]

Overijssel.—See OVERYSSEL.

Overyssel.—LAET, J. DE. Belgii Confœderati Respublica: seu . . . Transisal. . . . descriptio.   *Lugd. Bat.*, 1630.

Owhyhee.—See HAWAII.

Oxford.—OXFORD UNIVERSITY and City Guide, etc.   *Oxf.*, 1831.

Oxus.—WOOD, J. Personal Narrative of a Journey to the Source of the River O., etc.   1841.

——— ZIMMERMANN, C. Denkschrift über den untern Lauf des O., zum Karabugas Haff, etc.   *Berl.*, 1845.

P.

Pacific Ocean.—NAVARRETE, M. F. DE. Examination . . . and Notices of the principal Expeditions . . . in search . . . of a communication between the Atlantic Ocean and the South Sea. *MS. Port.*

——— HAWKINS, Sir R. The Observations of, in his Voyage to the South Sea, 1593.   1622.

——— SHARP, Capt. B. and others. Voyages and Adventures in the South Sea, etc.   1684.

——— SOUTH SEAS. A View of the Coasts, Countries, and Islands within the limits of the South-Sea Company, etc.   171L

——— FREZIER, M. Relation du Voyage de la Mer du Sud aux Côtes de Chili . . . 1712-14.   *Amst.*, 1717.

——— HERRERA, A. DE. Historia general de los hechos de los Castellanos en las Islas y Tierra Firme del Mar Océano.   *Madr.*, 1730.

——— FREZIER, M. Relation du Voyage de la Mer du Sud aux Côtes du Chily . . . 1712-14, etc.   *Par.*, 1732.

z

Pacific Ocean.—JAMES, T. The dangerous Voyage of, in his intended Discovery of a N.-W. Passage into the South Sea, etc. **1740.**

—— DOBBS, A. Remarks upon Capt. Middleton's . . . Voyage for discovering a passage from Hudson's Bay to the South Seas, etc. **1744.**

—— FORSTER, J. R. and G. Characteres Generum Plantarum, quas in itinere ad insulas Maris Australis collegerunt, etc. **1776.**

—— CROZET, M. Journaux de Nouveau Voyage à la Mer du Sud, etc. *Par.*, **1783.**

—— COOK, CAPT. J. and KING, J. Voyage to the P. O. . . . 1776-80. **1784.**

—— COLNETT, J. Voyage . . . into the P. O., etc. **1798.**

—— MACKENZIE, A. Voyages . . . to the Frozen and P. Oceans, in 1789 and 1793, etc. **1801.**

—— SARTCHEF, CAPT. Voyages along the . . . Arctic and P. O. . . . 1785 to 1793. *Russ.* *St. Pet.*, **1802.**

—— BURNEY, J. Chronological History of the Discoveries in the South Sea or P. O. **1803-17.**

—— HUMBOLDT, A VON. and BONPLAND, A. Recueil d'Observations de Zoologie . . . faites . . . dans la Mer du Sud, en 1799-1803. **1811.**

—— LEWIS, and CLARKE, CAPTS. Travels . . . to the P. O. in 1804-6. **1814.**

—— Travels . . . to the P. O., in 1804-6. **1815.**

—— KOTZEBUE, O. VON. A Voyage of Discovery into the South Sea . . . 1815-1818, etc. *Lond.*, **1821.**

—— KRUSENSTERN, A. J. DE. Recueil de Mémoires . . . pour servir d'explication à l'Atlas de l'Océan Pacifique. *St. Pet.*, **1824-27.**

—— PITMAN, R. B. On the Practicability of joining the Atlantic and P. Oceans by a Ship Canal, etc. **1825.**

—— DILLON, P. Narrative . . . of a Voyage to the South Seas, etc. **1829.**

—— MAW, H. L. Journal of a Passage from the P. to the Atlantic, etc. **1829.**

—— BEECHEY, F. W. Narrative of a Voyage to the P., etc. **1831.**

—— DRAKE, SIR F. Lives and Voyages of Drake . . . and Dampier; including . . . earlier Discoveries in the South Sea, etc. *Edin.*, **1831.**

—— MORRELL, B. Narrative of Four Voyages to the . . . P. O., etc. *N. Y.*, **1832.**

—— PACIFIC OCEAN. Three Years in the P., etc. **1835.**

—— CIRCUMNAVIGATION of the Globe . . . and progress of Discovery in the P. O., etc. *Edin.*, **1836.**

—— PACIFIC Steam Navigation Company, Plan of the intended operations of the. *Glasg.*, **1836.**

—— —— Steam Navigation, Documents relating to. *Lima*, **1836.**

—— REYNOLDS, J. N. Address on the subject of a Surveying . . . Expedition to the P. O., etc. *N. Y.*, **1836.**

—— FAIRBAIRN, H. A Letter . . . on the . . . advantages of a Steam Passage to the East Indies, by . . . the P. O., etc. **1837.**

Pacific Ocean.—SCARLETT, HON. P. C. South America and the P., *etc.* 1838.

——— WHEELWRIGHT, W. Statements and Documents relative to the Establishment of Steam Navigation in the P., *etc.* 1838.

——— MENCER, HON. C. F. Report on the ... connection of the Atlantic and P. Oceans by ... Lake Nicaragua, *etc.* *Wash.*, 1839.

——— WHEELER, D. Extracts from the Letters and Journals of ... in ... some of the Islands of the P. O., *etc.* 1839.

——— ANGELIS, P. DE. Historical sketch of Pepys' Island in the S. P. O. *Buen. Aires*, 1842.

——— PENDLETON, N. G. On Military Posts from Council Bluffs to the P. O. *Wash.*, 1842.

——— BEECHEY, F. W. Voyage ... towards the North Pole ... 1818; with a summary of ... early attempts to reach the P., *etc.* 1843.

——— WHEELWRIGHT, W. Report on Steam Navigation in the P., *etc.* 1843.

——— MEINICKE, C. E. Die Südseevölker und das Christenthum, *etc.* *Prenzlau*, 1844.

——— ERMAN, A. Ueber Ebbe und Fluth an den Ochozker und Kämtschatkischen Küsten des Grossen Oceans. 1845.

——— MOBO, G. Report of the Communication between the Atlantic and P. Oceans through the Isthmus of Tehuantepec. 1845.

——— MORO, G. Communication between the Atlantic and P. Oceans through ... Tehuantepec. Additional Observations, *etc.* 1845.

——— GARAY, J. DE. An Account of ... Tehuantepec ... with proposals for ... a communication between the Atlantic and P., *etc.* 1846.

——— HALE, H. Migrations in the P. O., *etc.* 1846.

——— COULTER, J. Adventures in the P., *etc.* *Dubl.*, 1847.

——— MELVILLE, H. Omoo: a narrative of adventures in the S. Seas. 1847.

——— CARMICHAEL-SMYTH, R. On ... the construction of a ... Railway between the Atlantic and the P., *etc.* 1849.

——— LIOT, W. B. Panamá ... Considerations upon the ... Communication between the Atlantic and P. Oceans. 1849.

——— ROCKWELL, J. A. Report on Canal and Railway Routes between the Atlantic and P., *etc.* *Wash.*, 1849.

——— WALPOLE, HON. F. Four Years in the P. ... 1844-48. 1849.

——— ATLANTIC AND PACIFIC OCEANS. Official Report ... on the communications between the Atlantic and P., *etc.* *Wash.*, 1850.

——— CHEEVER, H. T. Life in the Sandwich Islands; or the Heart of the P., *etc.* 1851.

——— DOULL, A. Employment ... for the Million, based upon ... Railway Communication from the Atlantic to the P., *etc.* *Lond.*, 1851.

——— FINDLAY, A. G. Directory for the Navigation of the P. O., *etc.* *Lond.*, 1851.

Pacific Ocean.—KERHALLET, C. P. DE. Considérations générales sur l'Océan Pacifique, *etc.* *Par.*, 1851.

—— AMERICA, CENTRAL. Description of . . . a Road . . . from . . . the Atlantic to . . . the P., *etc.* *Phil.*, 1852.

—— DOULL, A. Project for . . . a . . . passage between the Atlantic and P. O. by means of a Railway, *etc.* 1852.

—— ERMAN, A. Ortbestimmungen bei einer Fahrt durch den Grossen . . . Ocean, *etc.* 1852.

—— ERSKINE, J. E. Journal of a Cruise among the Islands of the Western P., *etc.* 1853.

—— BECKWITH, E. G. Report of Exploration . . . for the P. Railroad, *etc.* *Wash.*, 1854.

—— JOHNSON, E. F. Railroad to the P., *etc.* *N. Y.*, 1854.

—— REDFIELD, W. C. Cape Verde . . . Hurricane . . . 1853, with . . . notices of various Storms in the P., *etc.* *New Haven, U. S.*, 1854.

—— STEVENS, J. J. Report of Exploration of a Route for the P. Railroad, *etc.* *Wash.*, 1854.

—— WHIPPLE, A. W. Report of Explorations for a Railway Route . . . from the Mississippi River to the P. *Wash.*, 1854.

—— ATLANTIC AND PACIFIC OCEANS. The Practicability . . . of a . . . canal to connect the Atlantic and P., *etc.* *N. Y.*, 1855.

—— DENHAM, H. M. Report on some Islands and Reefs in the South-Western P. O. 1855.

—— TOTTEN, G. M. Communication . . . containing . . . Observations upon the Levels of the Atlantic and P. O. *N. Y.*, 1855.

—— AMERICA. Reports of . . . Surveys . . . for a Railroad from the Mississippi to the P., *etc.* *Wash.*, 1855-60.

—— KELLEY, F. M. On the Junction of the Atlantic and P. Oceans, *etc.* 1856.

—— KERHALLET, C. P. DE. Considérations générales sur l'Océan Pacifique, *etc.* *Wash.*, 1856.

—— KELLEY, F. M. Projet d'un Canal Maritime . . . entre l'Océan Atlantique et l'Océan Pacifique, *etc.* *Par.*, 1857.

—— REDFIELD, W. C. Observations in relation to the Cyclones of the Western P. *Wash.*, 1857.

—— BROWN, SIR R. European and Asiatic Intercourse . . . by . . . Railway from the Atlantic to the P., *etc.* 1858.

—— EUROPEAN and Asiatic Intercourse . . . by means of a . . . Railway from the Atlantic to the P. 1858.

—— MÖLLHAUSEN, B. Diary of a Journey from the Mississippi to the P., *etc.* 1858.

—— SWALLOW, G. C. Geological Report . . . with Memoir of the P. Railroad. *St. Louis*, 1859.

—— HÜGEL, BARON C. VON. Der Stille Ocean, *etc.* *Wien*, 1860.

—— HECTOR, J. On the Geology of the Country between Lake Superior and the P. O., *etc.* 1861.

Pacific Ocean.—Hood, T. H. Notes of a Cruise ... in the W. P. in 1862. *Edinb.*, 1863.
— Pim, B. The Gate of the P. 1863.
— Davis, Rear-Admiral C. H. Report on Interoceanic Canals and Railroads between the Atlantic and P., *etc.* *Wash.*, 1867.
— Rouhaud, M. Les Régions Nouvelles. Histoire du Commerce et de la Civilisation au Nord de l'Océan Pacifique. *Par.*, 1868.
— Verney, Sir H. A Route from the Atlantic to the P. through British Territory. *Lond.*, 1869.
— Collinson, J. and Bell, W. A. The Denver P. Railway, *etc.* *Lond.*, 1870.
— D'Entrecasteaux, Voyage de ... dans le Grand Océan, 1791-93. Everts. Vol. I.
— Découvertes ... dans le Grand Océan, par plusieurs navigateurs Anglais, 1768. Everts. Vol. III.
— Wilson, Capt. J. Voyage dans le Grand Océan, 1706-8. Everts. Vol. III.
— Mackenzie. Voyage ... du Fort Chipiouyan aux côtes du Grand Océan, 1789-93. Everts. Vol. VII.
— Candish, T. Voyages into the South Sea ... 1586-91. Hakluyt. Vol. IV.
— Drake, Sir F. Voyage into the South Sea ... 1577. Hakluyt. Vol. IV.
— Oxnam, J. Voyage ... into the South Sea, 1575. Hakluyt. Vol. IV.
— Winter, J. Voyage into the South Sea ... 1577. Hakluyt. Vol. IV.
— Hawkins, Sir R. Observations in his Voyage into the South Sea, 1593 ... edited by C. R. Drinkwater Bethune. 1847. Hakluyt Soc. Pub. Vol. I.
— Magllanes, or Magellan, F. Voyage from the South Seas to the East Indies, 1519-22. Harris, J. Vol. I.
— Weert, S. de. Remarkable Voyage to the South Seas ... 1598-1600. Harris, J. Vol. I.
— James, Capt. T. Voyage for the discovery of a passage into the South Seas, by the N. W. ... 1631-33. Harris, J. Vol. II.
— Middleton, C. Attempts ... for ... a passage to the South Seas from Hudson's Bay ... 1725-42. Harris, J. Vol. II.
— Philosophical motives for seeking a passage into the South Seas, by the N. W. ... together with the History of the Attempts ... for ... 130 years. Harris, J. Vol. II.
— Candish, Sir T. Second Voyage, intended for the South Sea, 1591. Kerr. Vol. X.
— Weert, S. de. Voyage to the South Sea ... 1598. Kerr. Vol. X.
— Bulkeley, J. and Cummins, J. Voyage to the South Seas in 1740-41, *etc.* Kerr. Vol. XVII.
— Byron, Hon. J. Narrative of the Shipwreck of the *Wager* in the South Seas, *etc.* Kerr. Vol. XVII.

Pacific Ocean—Pacific Ocean, South.

Pacific Ocean.—Nouveaux Voyages dans la Mer du Sud. Byron, Carteret, Wallis, Bougainville, Cook. LAHARPE, J. Vol. XVII.-XXIV.

—— Cook, Clerke, and Gore, Captains. Voyage to the P. O. ... in 1776-80. PELHAM. Vol. I.

—— S. de Wert. Voyage to the South Sea ... 1598-99. PURCHAS. Vol. I.

—— Briggs, Master. Discourse of the probability of a passage to the ... South Sea. PURCHAS. Vol. III.

—— Candish, T. Discourse of his fatall ... Voyage towards the South Sea ... 1591-93. PURCHAS. Vol. IV.

—— Dormer, T. Letter ... touching his Voyage for the South Sea, 1620. PURCHAS. Vol. IV.

—— Giros, or De Quir, P. F. Relation of the New Discoverie in the South Sea, 1609. PURCHAS. Vol. IV.

—— Hawkins, Sir R. Observations in his Voyage into the South Sea, 1593. PURCHAS. Vol. IV.

—— Knivet, A. Admirable Adventures ... of, which went with T. Candish to the South Sea, 1591-1601. PURCHAS. Vol. IV.

—— Narbrough, Sir J. Voyage to the South Sea, etc. 1711. VOYAGES. Account of several late, etc.

—— Nugnez de Balboa. Folge der Indianischen Begebenheiten und Entdeckung des Süd-Meeres, 1512-13. VOYAGES and TRAVELS. Allgemeine Historie, etc. Vol. XIII.

—— Anson. Zusatz zu der Reise ins Stille Meer, 1741-45. VOYAGES and TRAVELS. Allgemeine Historie, etc. Vol. XVIII.

—— Mindana, A. von. Andere Reise nach die Sudsee, 1595-96. VOYAGES and TRAVELS. Allgemeine Historie, etc. Vol. XVIII.

—— Kotzebue, O. von. Voyage of Discovery in the South Sea ... 1815-18. VOYAGES and TRAVELS, New. 1819. Vol. VI.

——, Islands of the.—See POLYNESIA.

——, North.—VANCOUVER, G. Voyage of Discovery to the N. P. O., etc. 1798.

——, —— PALMER, A. H. Memoir ... on the ... Asiatic Islands of the N. P. O. *Wash.*, 1848.

——, —— BROWN, R. On the ... Coal-Fields of the N. P. Coast. *Edin.*, 1869.

——, —— NORTH PACIFIC PILOT. Pts. I., II. *Lond.*, 1870.

——, —— Broughton. Voyage dans la partie septentrionale du Grand Océan, 1795-98. EYRIES. Vol. II.

——, —— Vancouver. Voyage ... dans le Grand Océan septentrional, 1791-5. EYRIES. Vol. II.

——, —— Billings et Saritcher. Voyage dans le Grand Océan boréal, 1785-94. EYRIES. Vol. VI.

——, —— Vancouver, G. Voyage of discovery of the N. P. O. ... in 1790-95. PELHAM. Vol. I.

——, South.—PACIFIC OCEAN, SOUTH. An Account of the Discoveries made in the S. P. O., previous to 1764. *Lond.*, 1767.

Pacific Ocean, South.—DALRYMPLE, A. Historical Collection of . . . Voyages and Discoveries in the S. P. O. 1770-71.
——, ——. FINDLAY, A. G. Directory for the Navigation of the S. P. O., etc. *Lond.*, 1863.
——, ——. An Account of . . . Discoveries . . . in the S. P. O. previous to 1764. DALRYMPLE, A. Tracts, from 1764 to 1808. Vol. I.
——, ——. Wilson, W. Missionary Voyage to the S. P. O., in 1796-98, etc. PELHAM. Vol. I.
Padshahpoor.—MARSHALL, T. Statistical Reports on . . . P., etc. *Bombay*, 1822.
Padshapoor.—*See* PADSHAHPOOR.
Padua.—MOSCHINI, G. Guida per la Città di Padova, etc. *Ven.*, 1817.
Paechoi Mountains.— RUSSIA. Der Nördliche Ural und das Küstengebirge Pai-Choi, untersucht . . . 1847-50, etc. *St. Pet.*, 1853-56.
Pai-Choi, Mountains.—*See* PAECHOI.
Palaestina, Palästina.—*See* PALESTINE.
Palaos.—*See* PELEW ISLAND.
Palatinate.—Browne, E. Voyage . . . to Holland, with a Journey . . . through . . . the Lower and Upper P. . . . 1668. HARRIS, J. Vol. II.
Palawan.—BATE, W. J. China Pilot . . . Sailing directions for P. Island and Passage, etc. 1855.
—— BELCHER, SIR E. and BATE, W. T. China Pilot . . . with Sailing Directions for P. Passage and Island. 1859.
Paleacatta.—*See* PULICAT.
Palembang.—PALEMBANG. De Heldhaftige Bevreding van P., etc. *Rotter.*, 1822.
—— STUBLER, W. L. DE. Proeve eener Beschrijving van het Gebied van P., etc. *Gron.*, 1843.
Palenque,—*See* SAN DOMINGO DE PALENQUE.
Palermo.—VALGUARNERA, M. Origine ed Antichità di P. *Pal.*, 1614.
Palestine.—SANDYS, G. A Relation of a Journey begun . . . 1610. Containing a description of . . . the Holy Land, etc. 1615.
—— RELANDUS, H. H. Relandi Palaestina ex monumentis veteribus illustrata. *Traj. Batav.*, 1714.
—— LA ROQUE, M. DE. Voyage dans la P., etc. *Amst.*, 1718.
—— LUCAS, P. Voyage fait en 1714 dans la . . . P., etc. *Amst.*, 1720.
—— HASIUS, J. M. Regni Davidici et Salomonaei descriptio, etc. *Nurimb.*, 1739.
—— POCOCKE, R. Description of . . . P., etc. 1743-45.
—— LIGHT, H. Travels in . . . Holy Land . . . 1814. *Lond.*, 1818.
—— BUCKINGHAM, J. S. Travels in P., etc. 1822.
—— BURCKHARDT, J. L. Travels in . . . the Holy Land. 1822.
—— LANDSEER, J. Sabaean Researches . . . Essays . . . on the engraved Hieroglyphics of . . . Canaan, etc. 1823.
—— BUCKINGHAM, J. S. Travels among the Arab Tribes . . . east of Syria and P., etc. 1825.

Palestine.

Palestine.—MADDEN, R. R. Travels in ... P., etc. 1829.
—— PROKESCH, A. VON. Reise ins Heilige Land, in 1829. *Wien,* 1831.
—— RUSSELL, M. P., or the Holy Land; from the earliest period, *etc.*
Edin., 1832.
—— FITZMAURICE, HON. W. E. Cruise to ... P., *etc.* 1834.
—— MADOX, J. Excursions in the Holy Land, *etc.* 1834.
—— LAMARTINE, A. DE. A Pilgrimage to the Holy Land in 1832-33.
1835.
—— PALESTINE. Three Weeks in P. and Lebanon. 1836.
—— BARTLETT, W. H. Syria, the Holy Land, *etc.* 1836-38.
—— NIEBUHR, C. Reisebeschreibung ... durch Palästina, *etc.*
Hamb., 1837.
—— ROBINSON, G. Travels in P., *etc.* 1837.
—— STEPHENS, G. Incidents of Travel in ... the Holy Land. 1838.
—— PAXTON, J. D. Letters from P. ... 1836-8. 1839.
—— SÆWULF, Relation des Voyages de ... en Terre Sainte, 1102-8.
Par., 1839.
—— DAMER, HON. MRS. G. L. D. Diary of a Tour in ... the Holy
Land. *Lond.,* 1841.
—— EGERTON, LADY F. Journal of a Tour in the Holy Land, *etc.*
Lond., 1841.
—— ROBINSON, E. Biblical Researches in P., *etc.* 1841.
—— EGYPT. Notes from a private Journal of a Visit to ... P., *etc.*
Lond., 1844.
—— KELLY, W. K. Syria and the Holy Land, *etc.* 1844.
—— KITTO, J. Pictorial History of P., *etc.* 1844.
—— HAHN-HAHN, COUNTESS I. Travels in ... the Holy Land, *etc.*
1845.
—— ROMER, MRS. Pilgrimage to ... P., *etc.* 1846.
—— LINDSAY, LORD. Letters on ... the Holy Land. 1847.
—— PALESTINE, Early Travels in, comprising the narratives of Arculf,
Willibald, Bernard ... Edited ... by T. Wright. 1848.
—— WOODCOCK, W. J. Scripture Lands; being a Visit to the Scenes of
the Bible, *etc.* 1849.
—— RAUMER, K. VON. Palästina. *Leip.,* 1850.
—— SPENCER, J. A. The East. Sketches of Travels in ... the Holy
Land. 1850.
—— FREEMAN, J. J. Tour in S. Africa, with notices of ... P. 1851.
—— NEALE, F. A. Eight Years in ... P., *etc.* 1852.
—— WILDE, W. R. Narrative of ... a Visit to ... P., *etc.* *Dubl.,* 1852.
—— PFEIFFER, I. Visit to the Holy Land, *etc.* 1853.
—— HABANT, K. Gesta ... do Zemé Svaté, *etc.* *v. Praze,* 1854.
—— SAULCY, F. DE. Narrative of a Journey ... in the Bible Lands,
1850-51, *etc.* 1854.

Palestine.

Palestine.—SEETZEN, U. J.   Reisen durch ... Palästina, *etc.*
Berl., **1854.**

——   VAN DE VELDE, C. W. M.   Narrative of a Journey through ...
P., *etc.*   **1854.**

——   DUPUIS, H. L.   The Holy Places ... Two Years' Residence in
... P., *etc.*   **1856.**

——   PETACHIA, RABBI.   Travels of; who, in the ... Twelfth Century,
visited ... the Holy Land, *etc.*   **1856.**

——   ROBINSON, E.   Biblical Researches in P., *etc.*   **1856.**

——   STANLEY, A. P.   Sinai and P. in connection with their history.
Lond., **1857.**

——   MURRAY.   Hand-Book for Travellers in Syria and P., *etc.*
Lond., **1858.**

——   VAN DE VELDE, C. W. M.   Memoir to accompany the Map of the
Holy Land constructed by C. W. M. van de V.   *Gotha,* **1858.**

——   THOMSON, W. M.   The Land and the Book ... Scenes and
Scenery of the Holy Land.   **1859.**

——   TOBLER, T.   Dritte Wanderung nach Palästina in 1857, *etc.*
Gotha, **1859.**

——   VAN DE VELDE, C. W. M.   Discours sur la P., *etc.*   *Genève,* **1864.**

——   BEKE, E.   Jacob's Flight; or a Pilgrimage ... Into the Promised
Land.   *Lond.,* **1865.**

——   DERENBOURG, J.   Essai sur l'histoire et la géographie de la P., *etc.*
Par., **1867.**

——   TOBLER, T.   Bibliographia geographica Palæstinæ, *etc.*
Leipz., **1867.**

——   MACGREGOR, J.   The "Rob Roy" ... A Canoe Cruise in P., *etc.*
Lond., **1869.**

——   Baumgarten, M.   Travels through ... P., *etc.*   CHURCHILL, Vol. I. ...

——   Biddulph, W.   Travels of four Englishmen ... into ... P. ...
in 1600 and 1611.   CHURCHILL.   Vol. VII.

——   Syrie et P.   EVARIA.   Vol. XIV.

——   Tristram, H. B.   Winter Ride in P.   GALTON, F.   Vacation Tourists
... in 1862-3.

——   Baldwine, Abp. of Canterbury.   Voyage unto ... Palæstina, 1190.
HAKLUYT.   Vol. II.

——   Gedericus.   Voyage ... unto the Holy Land, 1102.   HAKLUYT.
Vol. II.

——   Gulielmus Peregrinus.   Voyage to Palæstina, 1190.   HAKLUYT.
Vol. II.

——   Rainulph Glanville, Earle of Chester.   Voyage to the Holy Land
... 1218.   HAKLUYT.   Vol. II.

——   Richard surnamed Canonicus.   Voyage into ... Palæstina, 1190.
HAKLUYT.   Vol. II.

——   Voyage intended by Henry IV. to the Holy Land, 1413.   HAKLUYT.
Vol. II.

Palestine — Pampas.

Palestine.—Voyage of H. Rohun and Sacr Quincy to the Holy Land, 1222. HAKLUYT. Vol. II.

——— Voyage of certaine Englishmen . . . unto the Holy Land, 1147. HAKLUYT. Vol. II.

——— Voyage of Hainulph, Earle of Chester . . . to the Holy Land, 1218. HAKLUYT. Vol. II.

——— Whiteman, A., *alias* Leucander. Voyage to Palæstina, 1020. HAKLUYT. Vol. II.

——— Benjamin, the Son of Jonas. Peregrination of . . . and relations of . . . P., *etc.* PURCHAS. Vol. II.

——— The Churches Peregrination by the Holy Land Way, *etc.* PURCHAS. Vol. II.

——— Newberie, J. Two Voyages. One into the Holy Land, 1578-9, *etc.* PURCHAS. Vol. II.

——— Sanderson, J. Pilgrimage from Constantinople to the Holy Land . . . 1601. PURCHAS. Vol. II.

——— Scot, W. L. Travels in . . . the Holy Land . . . 1612. PURCHAS. Vol. II.

——— Supplement of the Holy Land Storie . . . out of . . . William, Archbishop of Tyrus, 1126-78. PURCHAS. Vol. II.

——— Of the . . . Regions and Religions of . . . P. PURCHAS. Vol. V.

——— Rauwolf, L. Journey into . . . P., *etc.* RAY, J.

——— Relation des Voyages de Sæwulf . . . en Terre Sainte . . . 1102-3, *etc.* VOYAGES and TRAVELS. Recueil, *etc.* Vol. IV.

——— Voyage de Bernard et de ses compagnons . . . en Terre-Sainte, *etc.* VOYAGES and TRAVELS. Recueil, *etc.* Vol. IV.

——— Forbin, Count de. Travels In . . . the Holy Land, 1817-18. VOYAGES and TRAVELS, New. 1819. Vol. I.

——— Scholz, J. M. A. Travels in . . . P. . . . 1821. VOYAGES and TRAVELS, New. 1819, *etc.* Vol. VIII.

——— Shaw, Thomas. Travels into Syria and the Holy Land. VOYAGES and TRAVELS. The World displayed. Vol. XI.

Palimbothra.—See PATNA.

Palitana.—BURGESS, J. Notes of a Visit to Satrunjaya Hill, near P., *etc.*
Bombay, 1869.

Palmas, Cape.—ADAMS, CAPT. J. Remarks on the Country . . . from Cape P. to the River Congo, *etc.* 1823.

——— SCHOENLEIN, P. Botanischer Nachlass auf Cape P. von Klotzsch. *Berl,* 1857.

Palmyra.—ADDISON, C. G. Damascus and P., *etc.* 1838.

——— PORTER, J. L. Five Years in Damascus . . . with Travels . . . in P., *etc.* *Lond.,* 1855.

——— A Journey to P.; or Tedmor in the Desart. VOYAGES and TRAVELS. The World displayed. Vol. XIII.

Pampas.—HEAD, F. B. Rough Notes . . . across the P., *etc.* 1826.

Pampas — Panama, Isthmus, of. 347

Pampas.—SCARLETT, Hon. P. C. South America . . . comprising a journey across the P., etc. 1838.

—— PARISH, Sir W. Buenos Ayres . . . and a description of the Geology . . . of the P. 1852.

—— BONELLI, L. H. DE Travels . . . across the P., etc. 1854.

Panama.—GAGE, T. Survey of the Spanish West Indies . . . describing . . . P., etc. 1702.

—— SCARLETT, Hon. P. C. South America . . . comprising a Journey . . . to . . . P., etc. 1838.

—— WHEELWRIGHT, W. Report . . . with an Account of the Coal Mines of . . . P. 1843.

—— LIOT, W. B. P., Nicaragua, etc. 1849.

—— CHALONER and FLEMING. The Mahogany Tree . . . with notices of the projected . . . communication of P., etc. *Liverp.*, 1850.

—— PANAMA. Contract between . . . New Granada and the P. Railway Company. *N. Y.*, 1850.

—— Von der Reise von Portobello nach P., etc. VOYAGES and TRAVELS. Allgemeine Historie, etc. Vol. IX.

—— **City of.**—EMORY, W. H. Observations . . . made . . . at . . . P., New Granada. *Camb., U. S.*, 1850.

—— **Isthmus of.**—WAFER, L. New Voyage and description of the Isthmus of America, etc. 1704.

—— —— M'QUEEN, J. A General Plan for a Mail Communication . . . to which are added Geographical Notices of the Isthmus of P., etc. *Lond.*, 1838.

—— —— KING, Hon. T. B. Railroad across the I. of P. *Wash.*, 1849.

—— —— EMORY, W. H. Observations . . . made at . . . I. of Darien, etc. *Camb., U. S.*, 1850.

—— —— CULLEN, E. I. of Darien Ship-Canal. 1852.

—— —— DUNLOP, A. Notes on the Isthmus of P., etc. *Lond.*, 1852.

—— —— GISBORNE, L. Darien Ship-Navigation, etc. 1852.

—— —— CULLEN, E. I. of Darien Ship Canal, etc. 1853.

—— —— DARIEN. The Isthmus of Darien in 1852. 1853.

—— —— —— The Nicaragua and Darien Ship-Canal Routes. 1853.

—— —— GISBORNE, L. The Isthmus of Darien in 1852, etc. 1853.

—— —— CAPRON, E. S. History of California . . . with a Journal of the Voyage . . . viâ P. *Bost.*, 1854.

—— —— TOTTEN, G. M. Communication of the Board of Directors of the P. Railroad Company to the Stockholders, etc. *N. Y.*, 1855.

—— —— CULLEN, E. Over Darien by a Ship Canal, etc. 1856.

—— —— M'DERMOT, W. The Darien Canal, etc. 1857.

—— —— MICHLER, N. Report of his Survey of an Interoceanic Ship Canal near the Isthmus of Darien. *Wash.*, 1861.

348   Panama, Isthmus of — Paraguay.

Panama, Isthmus of.—OTIS, F. N.   Illustrated History of the P. Railroad.   *N. Y.*, 1862.

——— ——— SAMPER, J. M.   Note sur les Sociétés . . . pour la Colonisation . . . de l'Isthme du Darien.   *Par.*, 1862.

——— ——— ROGER, P.   Percement de l'Isthme Américain par un Canal, etc.   *Par.*, 1864.

——— ——— MALTE-BRUN, V. A.   Canal Interocéanique du Darien Américque, etc.   *Par.* [1865.]

——— ——— COLOMBIAN CANAL.   International Company . . . for . . . cutting a Ship Canal across the Columbian Isthmus, etc.   *Par.*, 1867.

——— ——— CULLEN, E.   The Darien Indians and the Ship Canal.   [1867.]

Panjab.—*See* PUNJAB.

Pannonia.—MANNERT, K.   Germania . . . P., nach den Begriffen der Griechen und Römer, etc.   *Leipz.*, 1820.

Panuco.—HORTOP, J.   Travels to the North of P., 1580.   HAKLUYT.   Vol. III.

——— Philips, M.   Voyage, 1568, a little to the north of P., etc.   HAKLUYT.   Vol. III.

Papal States.—*See* STATES OF THE CHURCH.

Papua, Papua.—*See* NEW GUINEA.

Paquin.—*See* PEKING.

Para.—SMYTH, W. and LOWE, F.   Narrative of a Journey from Lima to P., etc.   1836.

——— Fonseca, J. G. da.   Navegação feita da Cidade do Gram Pará, até á Bocca do Rio da Madeira, 1749.   PORTUGAL.   Collecção de Noticias, etc.   Vol. IV.

——— Roteiro da Viagem da . . . P. até a's ultimas Colonias dos Dominios Portuguezes em os Rios Amazonas e Negro.   PORTUGAL.   Collecção de Noticias, etc.   Vol. VI.

Pará, River.—LANE, J. C.   Report of the Surveys of the . . . P., etc.   *N. Y.*, 1856.

Paraba, River.—Schmidel, H.   Travels, from 1534-54 . . . Expedition up the . . . P., etc.   PURCHAS.   Vol. IV.

Parabol, River.—*See* PARABA.

Paraetonium.—Scholz, J. M. A.   Travels in the Countries between Alexandria and P., etc.   VOYAGES and TRAVELS, New, 1819, etc. Vol. VIII.

Paraguay.—PARAGUAY.   Descripcion de la Provincia del P.-Conquista. *MS.*

——— CHARLEVOIX, FATHER.   The History of P., etc.   *Dublin*, 1769.

——— AZARA, F. DE.   Apuntamientos para la historia natural . . . del P., etc.   *Mad.*, 1802.

——— DAVIE, J. C.   Letters from P., etc.   1805.

——— AZARA, F. DE.   Voyages . . . contenant la description . . . du P., etc.   *Par.*, 1809.

——— DOBRIZHOFFER, M.   Account of the Abipones, an Equestrian People of P., etc.   1822.

Paraguay.—Rengger and Longchamps. The Reign of Dr. J. G. R. de Francia in P., etc. 1827.
——— Robertson, J. P. and W. P. Letters on P., etc. 1838.
——— Mansfield, C. B. P. ... in 1852-53, etc. Camb., 1856.
——— Page, T. J. La Plata ... and P., etc. N. Y., 1859.
——— Demersay, L. A. Histoire physique ... du P., etc. Par., 1860.
——— Graty, A. M. du. La République du P. Brux., 1862.
——— Quentin, C. An Account of P., etc. Lond., 1865.
——— Paraguay. La Guerra del P. Buen. A., 1867.
——— Hutchinson, T. J. The Paraná; with incidents of the P.n War, etc. Lond., 1868.
——— Thompson, G. The War in P., etc. Lond., 1869.
——— Sepp, F. F. A. and Behme, A. Account of a voyage from Spain to Paraquaria. Churchill. Vol. IV.
——— Techo, F. N. del. History of ... P., etc. Churchill. Vol. IV.
——— Dalrymple, A. Catalogue of Authors ... on ... P., etc. Dalrymple, A. Collection of Nautical Memoirs, etc.
——— Powell, D. The Republic of P. Galton, F. Vacation Tourists ... in 1862-3.

Parahiba.—Silva Coutinho, J. M. de. Annexo P. ... (Relatorio sobre a exploração das valles do P. e Pomba ... pelos engenheiros J. e F. Keller, 1864.) [1865.]

Paramaribo.—Suriman. Dagverhaal van eene Reis naar P., etc. Amst., 1842.
——— Waller, J. A. Voyage in the West Indies ... with some notices ... relative to ... P. ... 1807. Voyages and Travels, New. 1819. Vol. III.

Parana.—Wheelwright, W. Introductory Remarks ... P. and Conlova Railway, Report, etc. 1861.
——— Techo, F. N. del. History of ... P., etc. Churchill. Vol. IV.
———, River.—Robertson, J. P. and W. P. Letters ... comprising Travels on the Banks of the P., etc. 1843.
———, ——— Hinchliff, T. W. South American Sketches, or a Visit to ... the P. 1863.
———, ——— Hutchinson, T. J. The P., etc. Lond., 1868.
———, ——— Schmidel, H. Travels, from 1534-54 ... Expedition up the River of P., etc. Purchas. Vol. IV.

Paraquaria.—See Paraguay.

Paria.—Dudleley, Sir R. Voyage to ... the Coast of P. ... 1594, 5. Hakluyt. Vol. IV.

Paris.—Itinéraire des bateaux à vapeur de P. au Havre, etc. Par.
——— Paris. View of P. and Places adjoining. 1701.
——— Chappe d'Auteroche, J. Journey into Siberia ... and Level of ... roads from P. to Tobolsky. 1770.
——— Picquet, C. Table alphabétique ... des Rues ... de P., etc. Par., 1805.

Paris.—Cuvier, Baron G. and Brongniart, A.   Essai sur la Géographie minéralogique des environs de P.   *Par.*, 1811.
——— Frank, G.   Viaggio a Parigi, *etc.*   *Milano*, 1813.
——— Paris.   Recherches Statistiques sur la Ville de P., *etc.*
Par., 1823-29.
——— Gardner, A. K.   P. Illustrated.   1847.
——— Paris.   Reports on the P. Universal Exhibition.   *Lond.*, 1856.
——— Lister's Journey to P., 1698.   Pinkerton.   Vol. IV.
——— Kotzebue, A. von. Journey . . . through Switzerland to P., 1804. Voyages and Travels.   A Collection, *etc.*   1805.   Vol. I.
——— Holcroft, T. Travels . . . to P.   Voyages and Travels.   A Collection, *etc.*   1805.   Vol. II.
Parium.—Hunt, Dr.   Journey from P. to the Troad . . . 1799. Walpole, R. Memoirs, *etc.*
Parnassus.—Sibthorp, Dr.   P. and the Neighbouring District, 1794. Walpole, R.   Memoirs, *etc.*
Paro, River.—*See* Ucayala.
Parry Islands.—Markham, C. R.   Franklin's Footsteps ; a Sketch . . . of the P. Isles, *etc.*   *Lond.*, 1853.
Parthenon.—Wilkins, Mr.   On the Sculptures of the P.   Walpole, R. Travels, *etc.*
Parthia.—Cartwright, J.   The Preacher's Travels . . . through . . . P., *etc.*   Churchill.   Vol. VII.
——— Of the . . . Parthians . . . and of their Religions. Purchas. Vol. V.
Passaroean, Passaroewang, Passaruang.—*See* Passoeroean.
——— Domis, H. I.   De Residentie P. op het Eiland Java.   *s' Grav.*, 1836.
Pastoserak.—Gourdon, W.   Later Observations, in his wintering at Pustozera, 1614-15, *etc.*   Purchas.   Vol. III.
Patagonia.—Falkner, T.   Description of P., *etc.*   *Hereford*, 1774.
——— Byron, J.   Narrative of . . . Distresses suffered . . . on the Coast of P., 1740-46.   *Lond.*, 1832.
——— Douville, J. B.   Trente Mois de ma Vie . . . suivie . . . d'une description de . . . P.   *Par.*, 1833.
——— Macdouall, J.   Narrative of a Voyage to P. . . . in 1826-27.
1833.
——— FitzRoy, Rear-Adml. R.   Sailing Directions for . . . P., *etc.*
1848.
——— Bourne, B. F.   The Captive in P., *etc.*   *Bost.*, 1853.
——— Snow, W. P.   Two Years' Cruise off . . . P., *etc.*   1857.
——— St. André, M. D. de.   Renseignements Nautiques sur les Côtes de Patagonie.   *Par.*, 1862.
——— Cox, G. E.   Viaje en las Rejiones Septentrionales de la P., 1862, 63.
Sant. de Chile, 1863.
——— Byron, Comm.   Voyage . . . to . . . P. . . . 1764-66. Hawkesworth, J.   Vol. I.

Patagonia.—Wallis, Capt. Voyage to the Coast of P. ... 1766-68. HAWKESWORTH, J. Vol. I.
Patane.—*See* PATANI.
Patani.—Voyage to ... P., *etc.* KERR. Vol. VIII.
———— Pring, Capt. Voyage ... to P. and Japan. KERR. Vol. IX.
———— Floris, P. W. Extracts of his Journal ... 1610-15. Voyage to ... P., *etc.* PURCHAS. Vol. I.
———— Brown, A. Extracts of a Journal ... sayling divers times ... to .... P. ... 1617-22. PURCHAS. Vol. II.
Patania, Patany.—*See* PATANI.
Patapilly.—*See* POLLYPATTI.
Patmos.—Sibthorp, Dr. Voyage ... P., *etc.* WALPOLE, R. Travels, *etc.*
———— Whittington, Mr. Discovery of the Remains of the Acropolis of P. WALPOLE, R. Travels, *etc.*
Patna.—Iambulus, his Navigation to ... Palimbothra, *etc.* PURCHAS. Vol. I.
Pe-che-li, Gulf of. DENHAM, H. M. Hydrographic Notices ... Directions for the ... Gulf of Pe-Chile, *etc.* 1856-59.
Pe-Chile, Gulf of.—*See* PE-CHE-LI.
Pechora.—*See* PETCHORA.
Pedir.—BENNETT, G. Wanderings in ... P. Coast, *etc.* 1834.
Peermede.—MARKHAM, C. R. Chinchona Cultivation ... Expedition ... from P. to the Cumbum Valley, *etc.* 1865.
Pegu.—MENDEZ PINTO, F. Historia Oriental de las peregrinaciones de F. Mendez Pinto ... en ... Pegou, *etc.* *Madrid,* 1627.
———— SPRYE, R. H. F. and C. H. F. The British and China Railway ... through P., *etc.* 1858.
———— SPRYE, R. Commerce with Western and Interior China ... across British P., *etc.* 1860.
———— SPRYE, R. and R. H. F. Aërial Telegraph to Hong-Kong ... and a new commerce ... across E.n-P., *etc.* *Lond.,* 1862.
———— ———— The Western-Inland-Provinces of China Proper ... considered in connection with British-Eastern-P., *etc.* 1862.
———— Fitch, R. The long ... voyage of .... to ... P., *etc.* 1583-1591. HAKLUYT. Vol. II.
———— Voyage to Pullicatt ... Narrative of ... Occurrences in P., *etc.* KERR. Vol. VIII.
———— Balbi's Voyage to P. PINKERTON. Vol. IX.
———— Fitch's Voyage to P., *etc.* PINKERTON. Vol. IX.
———— Balbi, G. Voyage to P. ... 1579-83. PURCHAS. Vol. II.
———— Pimenta, N. Indian Observations ... principally relating to ... P. 1597-99. PURCHAS. Vol. II.
———— Beschreibung der Königreiche Golkonda und P. VOYAGES and TRAVELS. Allgemeine Historie, *etc.* Vol. X.
———— *See also* OPHIR.

Pegue.—See PEGU.
Pei Ho.—DENHAM, H. M. Hydrographic Notices ... Directions for the P. H., *etc.* **1856-59.**
Peiraeus.—RAFN, C. C. Inscription Runique du Pirée, interprétée. *Copenh.*, **1856.**
Pekin. See PEKING.
Peking. BARROW, SIR J. Travels ... from P. to Canton. **1804.**
——— TIMKOWSKI, G. Travels of the Russian Mission to .. and Residence in P. in 1820-21, *etc.* **1827.**
——— TIMKOVSKI, G. Voyage à P. à travers la Mongolie, in 1820 et 1821, *etc.* *Par.*, **1827.**
——— RIPA, FATHER. Memoirs of, during Thirteen Years' Residence at ... P., *etc.* **1844.**
——— FORTUNE, R. Yedo and P.: a Narrative, *etc.* *Lond.*, **1863.**
——— PEKING. Descriptive Notes on P., *etc.* *Shangh.*, **1866.**
——— LAMPREY, J. Notes of a Journey in the N.-W. Neighbourhood of Pekin. *Lond.*, **[1867.]**
——— Journey of A. Gaubil ... from Kanton to P. in 1722. ASTLEY. Vol. III.
——— Travels of five French Jesuits from Ning po fū to Peking in 1687. ASTLEY. Vol. III.
——— Journey of J. Douvet ... from P. to Kanton ... in 1693. ASTLEY. Vol. III.
——— Journey of J. de Fontancy ... from P. to Kyang Chew, *etc.* ASTLEY. Vol. III.
——— Ysbrants Ides, E. Travels ... to ... P. ... 1692-95. HARRIS, J. Vol. II.
——— Nicolo di Conti. Voyage to ... Cambalu (P), *etc.* PURCHAS. Vol. III.
——— Pontoia, Father D. Letter written in P. ... 1602, *etc.* PURCHAS. Vol. III.
——— Report of a Mahometan Merchant which had been in Cambalu (P.) 1500. PURCHAS. Vol. III.
———, **Gulf of.** STAUNTON, SIR G. Authentic Account of an Embassy to China ... with a relation of a Voyage to the ... G. of P. **1797.**
Pelew Island.—Neue Erläuterungen über die Insel Palaos, 1721-32. VOYAGES and TRAVELS. Allgemeine Historie, *etc.* Vol. XVIII.
——— Zusatz zu der Entdeckung der Palaos ... 1710. VOYAGES and TRAVELS. Allgemeine Historie, *etc.* Vol. XVIII.
——— **Islands.**—KEATE, G. Account of the P. I., *etc.* **1803.**
——— Mac Cluer. Voyage aux Iles Pelcou, 1796-93. EYRIES. Vol. II.
——— Wilson, Capt. Naufrage de l'Antilope, sur les Iles Pelcou, 1783. EYRIES. Vol. II.
Pelion, Mount.—TOZER, H. F. Researches ... including Visits to Mounts Ida ... and P., *etc.* *Lond.*, **1869.**

Peloponnesus—*See* MOREA.

Peluse, Bay of.—PHILIBERT, CAPIT. Canal Maritime de Suez. Observations hydrographiques dans la Baie de P. *Par.*, **1857.**

Pelusium.—SPRATT, T. A. B. A Dissertation on the true position of P., etc. *Lond.*, **1859.**

Pemba.—*See* BAMBA.

Pembroke.—MURCHISON, SIR R. I. The Silurian System, founded on Geological Researches in ... P., etc. **1839.**

Penang.—*See* PRINCE OF WALES ISLAND.

Peninsula Española.—*See* SPAIN.

Peninsule Hispanique.—*See* SPAIN.

Penjab.—*See* PUNJAB.

Pennine Alps.—*See* ALPS.

Pennsylvania.—BARTRAM, J. Observations on ... P., etc. **1751.**

—— ROGERS, A. D. Geology of P. First to Sixth Annual Reports. *Harrisb.*, **1836-42.**

—— INGERSOLL, J. R. Address at the Annual Meeting of the P. Colonization Society, etc. *Phil.*, **1838.**

—— PENNSYLVANIA. Report of the Board of Canal Commissioners. *Harrisb.*, **1838.**

—— TAYLOR, R. C. Two Reports on ... the Dauphin and Susquehanna Coal Company, and ... the Stony Creek Coal Estate, P., etc. *Phil.*, **1840.**

—— MARYLAND. Message ... in relation to the Intersection of the Boundary Lines of ... P., etc. *Wash.*, **1850.**

—— KOHL, J. G. Travels ... through ... P., etc. *Lond.*, **1861.**

—— GRAHAM, J. D. Reports in relation to the ... Boundary Lines of ... P., etc. *Chicago*, **1862.**

—— BACHE, A. D. Records of a Magnetic survey of P., etc. *Wash.*, **1863.**

Pentapole Libyque.—*See* PENTAPOLIS.

Pentapolis.—BEECHEY, F. W., and H. W. Proceedings ... comprehending an account ... of the Ancient Cities composing the P. **1828.**

—— Monte Cassiano, le R. P. Pacifique de. Relation succincte de la Pentapole Libyque, etc. VOYAGES and TRAVELS. Recueil, etc. Vol. II.

Pepper Coast.—*See* GRAIN COAST.

Pepys' Island.—ANOELIS, P. DE. Historical Sketch of P. I., etc. *Buen. Aires*, **1842.**

Pera.—Freizer. Reisen an den Küsten von P., 1713. VOYAGES and TRAVELS. Allgemeine Historie, etc. Vol. XV.

Perak.—ANDERSON, J. Observations ... the result of a ... Mission to ... P., etc. *P. of W. I.*, **1824.**

Perico.—Reise aus dem Hafen P. nach Guayaquil, etc. VOYAGES and TRAVELS. Allgemeine Historie, etc. Vol. IX.

2 A

Perigord.—LARTET, R., and CHRISTY, H. Reliquiæ Aquitanicæ; being Contributions to the Archæology and Palæontology of P., *etc.*
Lond., [1865].

Perim Island.—FALCONER, H. Descriptive Catalogue of ... Fossil Remains ... from ... P. I., *etc.* *Calc.*, **1859.**

Permia.—IDES, E. Y. Three Years' Travels ... Thro' ... P., *etc.*
Lond., **1706.**

——— Ysbrants Ides, E. Travels ... through ... P. .... 1692-95. HARRIS, J. Vol. II.

——— Purtglove, W. Travell from Prehora to P., *etc.* PURCHAS Vol. III.

Pernambuco.—PENISTON, W. M. Public Works in P., *etc.* **1863.**

——— Lancaster, J. Voyage to ... Fernambuck in Brasil, 1594. HAKLUYT. Vol. IV.

——— Prior, J. Voyage ... to ... P. ... 1813. VOYAGES and TRAVELS, New. 1810. Vol. II.

Perouse Islands.—PERROT. A. M. Rapport sur le Plan des Îles Wanikoro, ou de La P., gravé par M. Caplin. *Paris.*

Persepolis.—FRANCKLIN, W. Observations ... Together with a short Account of ... P., *etc.* *Lond.*, **1790.**

——— BUCKINGHAM, J. S. Travels ... including ... Researches in ... the Ruins of P. **1830.**

——— PRICE, W. Journal ... Also a Dissertation upon the Antiquities of P. **1833.**

——— RICH, C. J. Narrative of ... a Visit to ... P. **1836.**

——— LÖWENSTERN, I. Remarques sur la deuxième Écriture Cunéiforme de P. *Par.*, **1850.**

——— FERGUSSON, J. The Palaces of ... P. restored, *etc.* *Lond.*, **1851.**

——— VAUX, W. S. W. Nineveh and P.; an historical Sketch, *etc.*
1851.

——— Franklin, W. Observations on ... the Remains of the Palace of P. PELHAM. Vol. II.

——— Relation des Antiquitez de P., traduite d'Herbert. THEVENOT. Vol. I.

Persia.—MONTEITH, W. Notes on Georgia ... also a description of the Frontier of ... P., *etc.*

——— RITTER, C. Die Stupa's oder die Architektonischen Denkmale an der grossen Königstrasse zwischen Indien, Persien, *etc.* *Berlin.*

——— VALLE, P. DELLA. Viaggi ... Parte prima (seconda) In P., *etc.*
Venetia, **1661.**

——— STRUYS, J. Les Voyages de, en ... Perse, *etc.* *Lyon*, **1682.**

——— CHARDIN, SIR J. Travels into P., *etc.* **1686.**

——— THEVENOT, M. DE. Travels into ... P., *etc.* **1687.**

——— KAEMPFER, E. Amœnitatum exoticarum ... fasciculi V. quibus continentur variæ relationes ... rerum Persicarum, *etc.*
Lemgoviæ, **1712.**

——— MANDELSLO, J. A. DE. Voyage ... de Perse aux Indes Orientales, *etc.* *Amst.*, **1727.**

Persia.

Persia.—OLEARIUS, A. Voyages très-curieux ... faits en ... Perse, etc. *Amst.*, 1727.
——— RUSSIA. A Journey through Russia into P., by two English Gentlemen, 1739, etc. 1742.
——— HANWAY, J. Historical Account ... with ... Travels into P., etc. 1753.
——— PERSIA. An Historical Account of the present Troubles of, etc. 1756.
——— ZEND-AVESTA, ouvrage de Zoroastre, contenant ... plusieurs traits importans relatifs à l'ancienne Histoire des Perses, etc. *Par.*, 1771.
——— IVES, E. Voyage ... from P. to England, etc. 1773.
——— HISTOIRE des Découvertes ... dans plusieurs contrées ... de la Perse. *Lausanne*, 1784.
——— FRANCKLIN, W. Observations made on a Tour from Bengal to P. ... 1786-7, etc. *Lond.*, 1790.
——— FORSTER, G. Journey ... through ... P., etc. 1798.
——— OUSELEY, W. Epitome of the Ancient History of P., etc. 1799.
——— CHARDIN, SIR J. Voyages en Perse, etc. *Par.*, 1811.
——— MORIER, J. Journey through P. ... 1808-9. 1812.
——— KINNEIR, J. M. A Geographical Memoir of the P.n Empire. *Lond.*, 1813.
——— ELPHINSTONE, HON. M. Account of ... Caubul, and its Dependencies in P., etc. 1815.
——— MORIER, J. A Second Journey through P., etc. *Lond.*, 1818.
——— KOTZEBUE, M. VON. Narrative of a Journey into P. ... in 1817, etc. 1819.
——— OUSELEY, SIR W. Travels in ... P. in 1810-12. 1819.
——— JAUBERT, P. A. Voyage ... en Perse ... 1805 et 1806, etc. *Par.*, 1821.
——— PORTER, SIR R. K. Travels in ... P., etc. *Lond.*, 1821, 22.
——— FREYGAN, M., and MME. Letters from the Caucasus ... with ... a Journey into P. in 1812, etc. 1823.
——— FRASER, J. B. Travels ... with notices on the Geology and Commerce of P. 1826.
——— ALEXANDER, SIR J. E. Travels ... through P., etc. 1827.
——— PERSIA, Sketches of, etc. 1827.
——— MALCOLM, SIR J. History of P., etc. 1829.
——— BUCKINGHAM, J. S. Travels in ... P., etc. 1830.
——— ALCOCK, T. Travels in ... P., etc. 1831.
——— STOCQUELER, J. H. Fifteen Months' Pilgrimage through ... P., etc. 1832.
——— STRAUWEN, J. J. Reise durch ... Persien ... 1647-1673. *Gotha*, 1832.
——— GORDON, P. Fragment of the Journal of a Tour through P. in 1820. 1833.

Persia.—Price, W. Journal of Travels of the British Embassy to P., etc. 1833.

——— Brydges, Sir H. J. Account of ... Mission to ... P. in 1807-11, etc. 1834.

——— Burnes, Sir A. Travels ... from India to ... P., etc. 1834.

——— Fraser, J. B. Historical ... Account of P., etc. Edin., 1834.

——— Smith, E., and Dwight, H. G. O. Missionary Researches ... Including a Journey ... Into ... P., etc. 1834.

——— Conolly, A. Journey ... through ... P., etc. 1838.

——— Fraser, J. B. Winter Journey ... to Tehran, with Travels through ... P. 1838.

——— Persia. Correspondence relating to P. ... 1834-39. 1839.

——— Fowler, G. Three Years in P., etc. 1841.

——— Osculati, G. Note d'un Viaggio nella P. ... 1841-42. Monza, 1844.

——— Shahamet Ali. The Sikhs and Afghans, in connection with India and P., etc. 1847.

——— Jones, J. F. Narrative of a Journey through ... P., etc. Bomb., 1849.

——— Struve, O. Résultats Géographiques du Voyage en Perse en 1838-39. St. Pet., 1851.

——— Curzon, Hon. R. Armenia ... the Frontiers of ... P. 1854.

——— Stuart, Lieut.-Col. Journal of a Residence in Northern P., etc. 1854.

——— Ferrier, J. P. Caravan Journeys ... in P., etc. 1856.

——— Sheil, Lady. Glimpses of Life and Manners in P. 1856.

——— Wagner, M. Travels in P., etc. 1856.

——— Binning, R. B. M. Journal of two years' Travel in P., etc. 1857.

——— Hell, X. II. de. Extrait du Voyage ... en Perse ... 1846-8, etc. Par., 1859.

——— Barbier de Meynard, C. Dictionnaire géographique ... de la Perse, etc. Par., 1861.

——— Berchet, G. La Repubblica di Venezia e la P. Torino, 1865.

——— Filippi, F. de. Note di un Viaggio in P. nel 1862. Milano, 1865.

——— Khanikoff, N. de. Mémoire sur l'Ethnographie de la Perse. Par., 1866.

——— Pollington, Viscount. Half round the Old World ... a Tour in ... P., etc. Lond., 1867.

——— Persia. Banking in P. Lond., 1868.

——— Cartwright, J. The Preacher's Travels ... through ... P., etc. Churchill. Vol. VII.

——— Perse. Olivier. Malcolm. Morier, etc. Evaria. Vol. XIV.

——— Alcock, T., and others. Voyage into P., 1563. Hakluyt. Vol. I.

——— Banister, T., and Ducket, G. Voyage into P., 1568. Hakluyt. Vol. I.

Persia. 357

Persia.—Burrough, C. Sixth Voyage into P., 1597. HAKLUYT. Vol. I.
— Edwards, A., and others. Voyage into P., 1568. HAKLUYT. Vol. I.
— Jenkinson, A. Voyage ... into P. ... 1561. HAKLUYT. Vol. I.
— Johnson, R., and others. Voyage into P., 1565. HAKLUYT. Vol. I.
— Constantine, the Great. Voyage to ... P. ... 330. HAKLUYT. Vol. II.
— Odoricus, Frier B. Voyage to ... P. ... about 1325. HAKLUYT. Vol. II.
— Vertomannus, L. Navigation and Voyages to ... P. ... 1503. HAKLUYT. Vol. IV.
— Varthema, L. di. Travels in ... P. ... 1503 to 1508. ... Edited ... by G. P. Badger. HAKLUYT Soc. Pub. Vol. XXXII.
— Mandelsloe, J. A. de. Remarks ... made in his passage from ... P. through ... the Indies, 1638. HARRIS, J. Vol. I.
— Chardin, Sir J. Travels ... into P. Proper, 1672. HARRIS, J. Vol. II.
— Description of ... P., etc. HARRIS, J. Vol. II.
— View of the P.n History, etc. HARRIS, J. Vol. II.
— Contarini, A. Journey from ... Venice to ... P., 1473-6. KERR. Vol. II.
— Varthema, L. Voyages and Travels in ... P. ... in 1503-8. KERR. Vol. VII.
— Franklin, W. Observations made on a Tour from Bengal to P., in 1786-7, etc. PELHAM. Vol. II.
— Chardin's Travels in P., Extracts from. PINKERTON. Vol. IX.
— Forster's Travels, Extracts from, concerning the N.n parts of P. PINKERTON. Vol. IX.
— Francklin's Tour in the S. of P. PINKERTON. Vol. IX.
— Persia. Description, from Harris's Collection. PINKERTON. Vol. IX.
— Valle, P. della. Travels in P., Extracts from. PINKERTON. Vol. IX.
— Mildenhall, J. Travailes ... in ... P. ... 1599. PURCHAS. Vol. I.
— Salbanke, J. Voyage through ... P. ... 1609. PURCHAS. Vol. I.
— Barthema or Vertoman, L. Travels into ... P. ... 1503. PURCHAS. Vol. II.
— Newberie, J. Two Voyages. One ... to ... P. ... 1580-82. PURCHAS. Vol. II.
— Sherley, Sir R. A briefe memorial of the Travels of, in P. PURCHAS. Vol. II.
— Sherlie, Sir A. Travels into P. ... 1599. PURCHAS. Vol. II.
— Silva Figueroa, Don G. Letter ... touching matters of P., 1610. PURCHAS. Vol. II.

Persia — Persian Gulf.

Persia.—Borough, C. Reports of his voyage into ... P. ... 1579-81. PURCHAS. Vol. III.

——— Of the ... Persians ... and of their Religions. PURCHAS. Vol. V.

——— Barthema, L. Itinerario dell' Egitto ... P., etc. RAMUSIO. Vol. I.

——— Barbaro, J. Viaggio ... nella P., 1436-87. RAMUSIO. Vol. II.
——— Contarino, A. Viaggio nella P., 1473-77. RAMUSIO. Vol. II.
——— Viaggio d'un Mercante che fu nella P., 1507-20. RAMUSIO. Vol. II.
——— Zeno, C. Viaggio in P. ... 1450. RAMUSIO. Vol. II.

——— Extrait ... d'un Mémoire de M. de Hammer sur la Perse, etc. VOYAGES and TRAVELS. Recueil, etc. Vol. II.

——— Jordan on Jourdain Catalani, P. Mirabilia descripta, soquitur de ... Regno Persidis, etc. VOYAGES and TRAVELS. Recueil, etc. Vol. IV.

——— The Travels of the Ambassadors from ... Holstein into ... P. 1635. VOYAGES and TRAVELS. The World displayed. Vol. XIII., XIV.

——— The Travels of Mr. Jonas Hanway ... into P. ... 1743. VOYAGES and TRAVELS. The World displayed. Vol. XIV., XV.

——— Chardin, Sir J. Travels ... into P. 1671. VOYAGES and TRAVELS. The World displayed. Vol. XV., XVI.

——— See also CASBIN. SHIRAZ.

Persian Gulf.—MORIER, J. A Second Journey ... with a Journal of the voyage ... to the P. G., etc. Lond., 1818.

——— SHAIK MANSUR. History of Seyd Said ... together with an account of the Countries and People on the Shores of the P. G., etc. Lond., 1819.

——— BERGHAUS, H. Asia ... Memoir zur Erklärung ... der reduzirten Karte von ... Persischer Golf, etc. Gotha, 1832-35.

——— BEKE, C. T. On the ... advance of the Land at the head of the P. G. 1835.

——— ——— On the former extent of the P. G., etc. 1836.

——— WELLSTED, J. R. Travels ... along the Shores of the P. G., etc. 1840.

——— FONTANIER, V. Voyage dans ... le Golfe Persique, etc. Par., 1844.

——— AINSWORTH, W. Report on ... Telegraphic Communication between the Mediterranean Sea and ... P. G. 1856.

——— CONSTABLE, C. G., and STIFFE, A. W. Memorandum on the recent Surveying Operations in the P. G., etc. 1862.

——— PELLY, L. Remarks concerning the Pearl Oyster-beds [of the P. G.] 1865.

——— CONSTABLE, G. C., and STIFFE, A. W. Le Pilote du Golfe Persique, etc. Par., 1866.

——— Nearchus. Voyage ... up the P. G., etc. HARRIS, J. Vol. I.

Persian Gulf.—Salbanke, J. Voyage through . . . the P. G. . . . 1609. PURCHAS. Vol. I.
—— Coronli, A. Lettera . . . della Navigatione del . . . Sino Persico . . . 1517. RAMUSIO. Vol. I.

Peru.—VEGA, G. DE LA. Comentarios Reales, que tratan . . . de los Yncas . . . del P., etc.   *Lisb. y Cordova*, **1609-17.**
—— SKINNER, J. The Present State of P., etc.   **1805.**
—— MATHISON, G. F. Narrative of a Visit to . . . P., etc.   **1825.**
—— ORLARZO, COUNT J. Recueil de Voyages . . . and Historical Researches on the Conquest of P. . . . in the thirteenth century, by J. Ranking.   **1829.**
—— TEMPLE, E. Travels in . . . P., etc.   **1830.**
—— POEPPIG, E. Reise in . . . P., etc.   *Leipz.*, **1835.**
—— PACIFIC OCEAN. Three Years in the Pacific; containing Notices of . . . P., etc.   **1835.**
—— PERU. Pacto y Ley Fundamental de la Confederacion P.-Boliviana.   **1837.**
—— SMITH, A. P. as it is, etc.   **1839.**
—— SUTCLIFFE, T. Sixteen Years in Chile and P. from 1822 to 1839, etc.   *Lond.* **[1841.]**
—— TSCHUDI, J. J. VON. Travels in P. during 1838-42, etc.   **1847.**
—— FITZROY, REAR-ADML. R. Sailing Directions for . . . P., etc.   **1848.**
—— LIMA, A True . . . Relation of the . . . Earthquake . . . at Lima . . . 1746. With a description of . . P. in general, etc.   **1848.**
—— PERU. Arancel de la Republica del P., etc.   *Lima*, **1852.**
—— WEDDELL, H. A. Aperçu d'un Voyage dans . . la Bolivie, et . . . les parties voisines du Pérou.   *Paris*, **1852.**
—— —— Voyage dans . . . la Bolivie, et . . . les parties voisines du Pérou, etc.   *Par.*, **1853.**
—— MARKHAM, C. R. Cuzco . . . a Visit to . . . P.   *Lond.*, **1856.**
—— BOLLAERT, W. Antiquarian . . . Researches in . . . P., etc.   **1860.**
—— HILL, S. S. Travels in P., etc.   **1860.**
—— PERU. Documentos . . . que acreditan la posesion del P. sobre los Territorios de Quijos y Canelos, etc.   *Lima*, **1860.**
—— MARKHAM, C. R. Travels in P., etc.   *Lond.*, **1862.**
—— PAZ SOLDAN, M. Geografia del P., etc.   *Par.*, **1862.**
—— —— Géographie du Pérou, etc.   *Par.*, **1863.**
—— MARKHAM, C. R. Contributions towards a Grammar . . . of Quichua, the language of the Yncas of P.   *Lond.*, **1864.**
—— SPRUCE, R. Notes on the Valleys of Piura and Chira in Northern P., etc.   *Lond.*, **1864.**
—— PAZ SOLDAN, M. F. Historia del P. Independente . . . 1819-1822.   *Lima*, **1868.**
—— SQUIER, E. G. The Primeval Monuments of P. compared with those in other parts of the World.   **1870.**

Peru.

Peru.—Chilton, J. Voyage . . . to divers places in P., 1568. HAKLUYT. Vol. III.

——— Betagh, Capt. Observations on . . . P. . . . 1720. HARRIS, J. Vol. I.

——— Pizarro, F. The History of the discovery . . . of P., 1524, etc. HARRIS, J. Vol. II.

——— Zarate, A. Early History of P., etc. KERR. Vol. IV.

——— ——— History of the discovery . . . of P., etc. KERR. Vol. IV.

——— Vega, G. de la. Early History of P., from . . . 1549, etc. KERR. Vol. V.

——— Zarate, A. Early History of P. continued. Kerr. Vol. V.

——— Betagh, Capt. Observations on . . . P. KERR. Vol. X.

——— Découverte et Conquête du P. par F. Pizarro, etc. LAHARPE, J. Vol. X.

——— Pérou. Origine des Incas, etc. LAHARPE, J. Vol. XI.

——— Betagh's Account of P. PINKERTON. Vol. XIV.

——— Bouguer's Voyage to P. PINKERTON. Vol. XIV.

——— A Briefe Relation of an Englishman which had been 13 yeares Captive . . . in P. 1603. PURCHAS. Vol. IV.

——— Ellis, J. A Briefe Note . . . concerning . . . P., 1593. PURCHAS. Vol. IV.

——— Las Casas, B. de. Briefe Narration of . . . P., etc. PURCHAS. Vol. IV.

——— Pizarro, F. Brief Notes of his Conquest of P., 1531-34. PURCHAS. Vol. IV.

——— Sancho, P. Relations of Occurrents in the Conquest of P. after . . . 1534. PURCHAS. Vol. IV.

——— Urnino, A. Relation concerning . . . the secrets of P. . . . 1581. PURCHAS. Vol. IV.

——— Vega, J. G. de la. Observations of . . . the Incas, or Ancient Kings of P.—Suppliment, etc. PURCHAS. Vol. IV.

——— Xeres, F. de. Conquest of P. and Cusco . . . 1524-33. PURCHAS. Vol. IV.

——— Of Cumana . . . P. . . . and of their Religions. PURCHAS. Vol. V.

——— Relatione d'un Capitano Spagnuolo del discoprimento e conquista del P. . . . 1531. RAMUSIO. Vol. III.

——— Relatione d'un Secretario di F. Pizarro, della conquista . . . del P. . . . 1534. RAMUSIO. Vol. III.

——— Xerez, F. Relatione della Conquista . . . del P. . . . 1532-3. RAMUSIO. Vol. III.

——— Xérès, F. Relation véridique de la Conquête du Pérou . . . 1524-33. TERNAUX-COMPANS. Voyages. Vol. IV.

——— Balboa, M. C. Histoire du P. TERNAUX-COMPANS. Voyages. Vol. XV.

——— Montesinos, L. F. Mémoires historiques sur l'ancien P. TERNAUX-COMPANS. Voyages. Vol. XVII.

Peru.—Relation des Voyages du sieur Acarete . . . Jusqu'au Pérou, etc. THEVENOT. Vol. IV.
—— Reise nach . . . P. VOYAGES and TRAVELS. Allgemeine Historie, etc. Vol. IX.
—— Nugnez Balboa. Entdeckungen, welche den Weg nach P. bahneten. 1510. VOYAGES and TRAVELS. Allgemeine Historie, etc. Vol. XIII.
—— Beschreibungen . . . von . . . P., etc. VOYAGES and TRAVELS. Allgemeine Historie, etc. Vol. XV.
—— Correal, F. Reisen nach P., 1692-95. VOYAGES and TRAVELS. Allgemeine Historie, etc. Vol. XV.
—— Pizarro, F. Reise und Entdeckung von P. . . . 1524–41. VOYAGES and TRAVELS. Allgemeine Historie, etc. Vol. XV.
—— Ursprung, Regierung . . . u. d. gl. des alten Reiches P. VOYAGES and TRAVELS. Allgemeine Historie, etc. Vol. XV.
—— Naturgeschichte . . . von P. VOYAGES and TRAVELS. Allgemeine Historie, etc. Vol. XVI.
—— Quiros, F. Reise nach P. 1606. VOYAGES and TRAVELS. Allgemeine Historie, etc. Vol. XVIII.
—— The Conquest of P., by F. Pizarro. 1524. VOYAGES and TRAVELS. The World displayed. Vol. III.
——, **Coast of.**—FREZIER, M. Relation du Voyage de la Mer du Sud aux Côtes . . . du Pérou . . . 1712-14. *Amst.*, **1717.**
—— —— —— Relation du Voyage de la Mer du Sud aux Côtes . . . du Pérou, 1712-14, etc. *Par.*, **1732.**
—— —— HALL, B. Extracts from a Journal written on the Coasts of . . . P. . . . in 1820-22. *Edin.*, **1825.**
—— —— GARCIA Y GARCIA, A. Derrotero de la Costa del P. *Lima*, **1863.**
—— —— —— P.n Coast Pilot. *N. Y.*, **1866.**
Pesaro.—CIALDI, A. Sul Porto-Canale di P. *Pesa*, **1857.**
Peshawar.—*See* PESHAWUR.
Peshawur.—BAYLEY, E. C. On . . . Sculptures found in . . . P. *Calc.*
—— MOORCROFT and TREBECK. Travels in . . . P. . . . 1819 to 1825. **1841.**
—— BARR, W. Journal of a March from Delhi to P., etc. *Lond.*, **1844.**
Pesth.—PATON, A. A. The Goth and the Hun: or . . . P. . . . in 1850. **1851.**
Petapoli.—FLORIS, P. W. Extracts of his Journal . . . 1610-15. Voyage to . . . P., etc. PURCHAS. Vol. I.
Petchora.—GOURDON, W. Voyage made to P., 1611. PURCHAS. Vol. III.
—— Logan, J. Voyage to P. . . . 1611. PURCHAS. Vol. III.
—— Pursglove, W. Travell from P. to Permia, etc. PURCHAS. Vol. III.
—— —— Voyage to P. . . . 1611. PURCHAS. Vol. III.
Petra.—BARTLETT, W. H. Forty days in the Desert . . . a Journey . . . to P.
—— LABORDE, N. L. DE. Journey . . . to . . . the excavated City of P., etc. **1836.**

Petra.—KINNEAR, J. Cairo, P. . . . In 1839, etc. Lond., 1841.
Pfeffers.—ZIEGLER, J. M. Die Mineralquelle Pfäfers. Wintert. 1861.
Phanagoria.—See TAMAN.
Philadelphia.—SEWARD, W. Journal of a voyage from Savannah to P., etc. Lond., 1740.
Phillippeville.—MALTE-BRUN, V. A. Itinéraire . . . de P. à Constantine. Par., 1856.
Philippine Islands.—Zuñiga, M. de. Historical View of the P. I., etc. 1814.

—— BERGHAUS, H. Asia . . . Memoir zur Erklärung . . . der reinzirten Karte von . . Philippinen, etc. Gotha, 1832-35.
—— Moor, J. H. Notices of the . . . P. I., etc. Singapore, 1837.
—— PHILIPPINE ISLANDS. Informe sobre el estado de las Islas Filippinas en 1842, etc. Madr., 1843.
—— BOWRING, SIR J. A Visit to the P. I. 1850.
—— MAC MICKING, R. Recollections of . . . the P., etc. 1851.
—— GIRONIÈRE, P. DE LA. Twenty Years in the P., etc. 1853.
—— LECLERC, C. Bibliotheca Americana. Catalogue . . . d'une . . . Collection de Livres . . . sur . . . les Philippines. Par., 1867.
—— SEMPER, C. Die Philippinen und ihre Bewohner, etc. Würzburg, 1869.
—— Camper, M. de N. du. Remarques sur les P., etc. 1821-25. ETHIKA. Vol. XII.
—— Gualle, F. Voyage from . . . Acapulco to . . . the Philippines . . . 1582-84. HAKLUYT. Vol. III.
—— Dampier's Account of the P. PINKERTON. Vol. XI.
—— Guignes, M. de. Observations on the P. I., etc. PINKERTON. Vol. XI.
—— Gonzales de Mendoza, J. First discoverie of the Philippinas. PURCHAS. Vol. III.
—— Hermals, Friar M. de, and other Spaniards . . . returne to the Philippinas, about 1580. PURCHAS. Vol. III.
—— Lopez de Legaspi, M. First Plantation of the Philippinas. PURCHAS. Vol. III.
—— Spanish Plantation of the Philippinas, etc. PURCHAS. Vol. III.
—— Trois Relations des Isles P. THEVENOT. Vol. II.
—— Rholen, A. Reise nach . . . den Philippinen, etc. VOYAGES and TRAVELS. Allgemeine Historie, etc. Vol. X.
—— Beschreibung der Philippinischen Inseln. VOYAGES and TRAVELS. Allgemeine Historie, etc. Vol. XI.

Philistäa.—See PHILISTIA.
Philistia.—TOBLER, T. Dritte Wanderung nach Palästina . . . Ritt durch P., etc. Gotha, 1859.
Phocis.—GELL, SIR W. Itinerary of Greece; containing . . . Routes in . . . P., etc. 1819.
—— Raikes, Mr. Journal through parts of . . . P., etc. WALPOLE, H. Memoirs, etc.

Phœnicia.—Sertzen, U. J. Reisen durch . . . Phönicien, etc.
Berl., **1854.**

——— William, Archb. of Tyre. Voyage to . . . Tyro in P., 1130. Hakluyt. Vol. II.

——— Of Tharsis . . . Of the P.n Antiquities. Purchas. Vol. I.

——— Of the . . . Regions and Religions of . . . P., etc. Purchas. Vol. V.

Phuxnan.—*See* Huc.

Pianosa.—Zuccagni-Orlandini, A. Die toscanische Insel P. und deren Colonisirung, etc. *Leipz.*, **1836.**

Picardy.—Costello, L. S. A Pilgrimage . . . from P. to Le Velay. **1842.**

Piedmont.—Michelotti, G. T. Saggio Idrografico del Piemonte. *Rome*, **1803.**

——— Gilly, W. S. Excursion to the Mountains of P. in 1823, etc. **1826.**

——— Baines, E. Visits to the Vaudois of P. **1855.**

——— St. John, B. Subalpine Kingdom; or, Experiences . . . in . . . P., etc. **1856.**

——— Gallenga, A. Country Life in P. **1858.**

——— Favre, A. Recherches Géologiques dans les parties du . . . Piémont . . . voisines du Mont Blanc, etc. *Par., Genève*, **1867.**

Pietermaritzburg.—Mann, R. J. Meteorological Observations made at P. during . . . 1865. **[1866.]**

Pimas.—Parke, J. G. Report of Explorations for . . . a Railway . . . between Dona Ana . . . and P. Villages, etc. *Wash.*, **1854.**

Pinang.—*See* Prince of Wales Island.

Pines, Isle of.—Lanier, A. H. Geografia de la Isla de Pinos, etc. *Habana*, **1836.**

Pirée.—*See* Peiraeus.

Pisa.—Morrona, A. da. P. antica e moderna. *Pisa*, **1821.**

Pisidia.—Arundell, F. V. J. A visit to . . . P., etc. **1828.**

——— Tchihatcheff, P. de. Dépôts Tertiaires . . . d'une partie septentrionale de la Pisidie, etc. *Par.*, **1854.**

——— Biddulph, W. Travels of four Englishmen . . . into . . . P. . . . in 1600 and 1611. Churchill. Vol. VII.

Pitcairn Island.—Shillibeer, J. Narrative of the *Briton's* Voyage to P. I., etc. **1818.**

——— Brodie, W. P. I. . . . in 1850, etc. **1851.**

——— Meinicke, C. E. Die Insel P. *Prenzlau*, **1858.**

——— Murray, T. B. P. : the Island, etc. **1860.**

——— Shillibeer, J. Voyage à l'Ile P., 1813-15. Eyriès. Vol. VI.

Pithiusian Islands.—St. Sauveur, A. G. de. Travels through the . . . P. I., 1801-6. Voyages and Travels. A Collection, etc. 1805. Vol. VIII.

Pithiusian Islands.—St. Sauveur, A. G. de. Travels through the . . . P. I., 1801-6. VOYAGES and TRAVELS. A Collection, *etc.* 1810. Vol. III.

Pittsburg.—JAMES, E. Account of an Expedition from P. to the Rocky Mountains, in 1819-20, *etc.* 1823.

——— Long, E. H. Voyage de P. aux Monts Rocailleux. EYRIÈS. Vol. IX.

Piura.—SPRUCE, R. Notes on the Valleys of P. and Chira, *etc.*
Lond., 1864.

Planina.—SCHMIDL, A. A. Die Grotten und Höhlen von . . . P., *etc.*
Wien, 1854.

Plata, Rio de la.—*See* LA PLATA.

Plate, River.—*See* LA PLATA.

Platte, La.—*See* LA PLATA.

Platte, River, U. S.—Pike. Voyage . . . aux sources . . . de la P. . . . 1805-7. EYRIÈS. Vol. IX.

Plimoth.—*See* PLYMOUTH.

Plymouth.—RENNIE, SIR J. An Historical . . . Account of the Breakwater in P. Sound.
Lond., 1848.

——— N. E.—Journall of a Plantation settled at P. . . . 1622. PURCHAS. Vol. IV.

Po.—MARTINS, C. and GASTALDI, B. Essai sur les Terrains Superficiels de la Vallée du P., *etc.*
Versailles.

Poitiers.—CHERUE, CH. DE. Le Guide du Voyageur à P., *etc.* Poit., 1851.

Poland.—CAROSI, J. P. VON. Reisen durch verschiedene Polnische Provinzen.
Leip., 1781.

——— COXE, W. Travels into P., *etc.* 1784.

——— MALTE-BRUN, V. A. Tableau de la Pologne ancienne et moderne, *etc.*
Par., Brux., 1830.

——— SCHNITZLER, J. H. Russie, la Pologne . . . Tableau statistique, *etc.*
Par., 1835.

——— PETACHIA, RABBI, Travels of; who in the . . . Twelfth Century visited P., *etc.*
1856.

——— PARAVEY, CHEV. DE. De l'origine Orientale des Polonais, *etc.*
Par., 1861.

——— Clark, W. G. Poland. GALTON, F. Vacation Tourists . . . in 1862-3.

——— Voyage of a certaine Englishman . . . into P. . . . 1243. HAKLUYT. Vol. I.

——— Austel. H. Voyage . . . through . . . Polonia . . . 1580. HAKLUYT. Vol. II.

——— Conner, D. A comprehensive account of . . . P., *etc.* HARRIS, J. Vol. II.

——— Coxe, W. Travels in P. PELHAM. Vol. II.

——— Guagnino, A. Descrittione della Sarmatia Europea . . . Polonia, *etc.* RAMUSIO. Vol. II.

——— Valesio, H. Compendio delle Chroniche di Polonia. RAMUSIO. Vol. II.

Poland.—Salvo, Marquis de. Travels ... through ... P. ... 1806.
VOYAGES and TRAVELS. A Collection, *etc.* 1806. Vol. VI.
—— Semple, J. G. Tour through ... P. ... 1805. VOYAGES and
TRAVELS. A Collection, *etc.* 1805. Vol. VII.
—— —— Tour through ... P. ... 1805. VOYAGES and TRAVELS. A Collection, *etc.* 1810. Vol. VI.
Polar Circle.—*See* ARCTIC REGIONS.
—— **Regions.**—*See* ARCTIC REGIONS.
—— **Sea.**—*See* ARCTIC OCEAN.
Pole Antarctique.—*See* SOUTH POLE.
Polonia.—*See* POLAND.
Polynesia.—WALCKENAER, C. A. Le Monde Maritime, ou Tableau ...
de la Polynésie, *etc.* *Par.*, 1819.
—— LANG, J. D. View of the Origin ... of the P.n Nation, *etc.*
1834.
—— SOUTH SEA ISLANDS, Review of various works on the. *Phil.*, 1836.
—— WILLIAMS, J. Narrative of Missionary Enterprises in the South
Sea Islands, *etc.* 1837.
—— BENNETT, F. D. Narrative ... comprising Sketches of P., *etc.*
1840.
—— ELLIS, W. Polynesian Researches, *etc.* 1853.
—— GAUSSIN, P. L. J. B. Du Dialecte de Tahiti ... et ... de la
Langue Polynésienne. *Par.*, 1853.
—— GREY, SIR G. P.n Mythology, *etc.* *Lond.*, 1855.
—— ST. JULIAN, C. Official Report of Central P.; with a Gazetteer, *etc.*
Sydney, 1857.
—— QUATREFAGES, A. DE. Les Polynésiens et leurs migrations.
Par., [1865 ?]
—— ANGAS, G. F. P.; a popular Description, *etc.* *Lond.*, [1866.]
—— On the P.n, or East-Insular Languages. 1834. MARSDEN, W.
Miscellaneous Works.
Pomba.—SILVA COUTINHO, J. M. DE. Annexo P. ... (Relatorio sobre a
exploração dos valles do Parahyba e P. ... polos engenheiros J. u
F. Keller, 1864.) [1866.]
Pomerania.—IJSBERTH, J. Description des Côtes ... de la Poméranie,
etc. *Par.*, 1855.
Pomotou Archipelago.—*See* LOW ARCHIPELAGO.
Pondicherry.—Niederlassung der Franzosen zu P. VOYAGES and TRAVELS. Allgemeine Historie, *etc.* Vol. X.
—— Zusatz zu der Französischen Niederlassung in P. seit 1741-55.
VOYAGES and TRAVELS. Allgemeine Historie, *etc.* Vol. XVIII.
Pont-Euxin.—*See* BLACK SEA.
Pontine Marshes.—POSZI, G. Storia naturale dell' Agro Pontino.
Roma, 1865.
Pontus.—HAMILTON, W. J. Researches in ... P., *etc.* 1842.

Poona.—Blanford, W. T. Notes on Route from P. to Nagpur, *etc.* INDIA, GEOLOGICAL SURVEY. Records, *etc.* Vol. I.

Poorna River.—Wynne, A. B. The Valley of the P., *etc.* INDIA, GEOLOGICAL SURVEY. Records, *etc.* Vol. II.

Poo-teon Chan.—*See* PUTO.

Pootoo.—*See* PUTO.

Popayan, River.—*See* JAPURA.

Popo.—The Kingdoms of Koto and P. ASTLEY. Vol. III.

Popocatepetl.—POPOCATEPETL. Ascensione al Volcano P.
Torino, 1856.

Port Denison.—MACDONALD, J. G. Journal . . . on an Expedition from Port D. to the Gulf of Carpentaria, *etc.* *Brisbane*, 1865.

—— **Desire.**—Byron, Comm. Voyage . . . to . . . P. D. . . . 1764-66. HAWKESWORTH, J. Vol. I.

—— **Famine.**—Byron, Comm. Voyage . . . to . . . P. F. . . . 1764-66. HAWKESWORTH, J. Vol. I.

—— **Jackson.**—PHILLIP, A. Voyage to Botany Bay, with an account of . . . P. J., *etc.* 1789.

—— WAGHORN, T. Two Letters on the extension of Steam Navigation from Singapore to Port J., *etc.* 1846, 47.

—— Philip, Governor. Voyage to Botany Bay, with an account of P. J., *etc.* PELHAM. Vol. I.

—— **Louis.**—St. Vincent, J. B. M. Bory de. Voyage . . . with a Narrative of the Passage of Capt. Baudin to P. L., *etc.* VOYAGES and TRAVELS. A Collection, *etc.* 1805. Vol. II.

—— **Phillip.**—HOVELL, W. H. and HUME, H. Journey of Discovery to P. P. . . . in 1824-5. *Sydney*, 1837.

—— JAMES, T. H. Six Months in S. Australia; with some account of P. P., *etc.* 1838.

—— HOVELL, W. H. Reply to "A brief statement of facts, in connection with an Overland Expedition from Lake George to P. P., in 1824," *etc.* *Sydney*, 1855.

—— HUME, H. A brief statement of Facts in connection with an Overland Expedition from Lake George to P. P. in 1824, *etc.* *Sydney*, 1855.

—— TUCKEY, J. H. Voyage pour établir une colonie au P. P. . . . 1803-4. EYRIÈS. Vol. IV.

—— —— Account of a Voyage to establish a Colony at P. P. . . . 1802-4. VOYAGES and TRAVELS. A Collection, *etc.* 1805. Vol. I.

Port Royal.—HILL, R. A Week at P.-R. *Montego B.*, 1855.

—— **Said.**—CIALDI, A. P.-S. A M. F. de Lesseps, *etc.* *Rome*, 1868.

—— SPRATT, T. A. B. On the Evidences of the rapid Silting in progress at P. S., *etc.* *Lond.*, 1870.

—— **Stephens, N. S. W.**—KING, P. P. Abstract from a Meteorological Journal kept at P. S. . . . 1843-47. *Launceston*.

Portingale.—*See* PORTUGAL.

Portland Bay.—JAMES, T. II. Six Months in S. Australia; with some account of ... P. B., etc. 1836.
Porto Bello.—GAGE, T. Survey of the Spanish West Indies ... describing ... P., etc. 1702.
――― Parker, W. The Taking of P. B. ... 1601. PURCHAS. Vol. IV.
――― Von der Reise von P. nach Panama, etc. VOYAGES and TRAVELS. Allgemeine Historie, etc. Vol. VIII.
Portogallo.—See PORTUGAL.
Porto Rico.—See PUERTO RICO.
――― **Santo.**—DOWDITCH, T. E. Excursions in ... P. S., etc. 1825.
Portugal.—MARTYR, P. De rebus Oceanicis ... Item de rebus ... Lusitanicis ... opuscula. *Colonia*, 1574.
――― PORTUGAL. Portugallia, sive de Regis Portugalliæ regnis et opibus Commentarius. *Lugd. Bat.*, 1641.
――― LAHONTAN, BARON. New Voyages ... an Account of ... P., etc. 1703-35.
――― CASTRO, J. B. Mappa de P. *Lisb.*, 1745-58.
――― CARDOSO, L. Diccionario geografico ... de P., etc. *Lisb.*, 1747-51.
――― MENEZES, L. DE. Historia de P. Restaurada. *Lisb.*, 1751.
――― OSORIO, J. History of the Portuguese, during the Reign of Emmanuel, etc. 1752.
――― PORTUGAL. Collecção de Noticias para a historia e geografia das Nações Ultramarinas, que vivem nos Dominios Portuguezes, etc. *Lisb.*, 1812-41.
――― Tofiño de San Miguel, V. España Maritima ... with the Coast of P., etc. 1814.
――― PORTUGAL. Mappa Chronologico do Reino de P., etc. *Lisb.*, 1815.
――― COUTINHO, J. DA C. DE AZEVEDO. Ensaio ... sobre o commercio de P. *Lisb.*, 1816.
――― BALBI, A. Essai ... sur le P., etc. *Par.*, 1822.
――― ASTILLON, I. Géographie ... du P. *Par.*, 1823.
――― MIÑAÑO, S. DE. Diccionario ... de España y P. *Madr.*, 1826-28.
――― PORTUGAL. The True Interests of the European Powers ... in reference to the existing affairs of P., etc. 1829.
――― WALTON. W. Letter relating to the Affairs of P. 1829.
――― BECKFORD, W. Italy; with sketches of ... P., etc. 1834.
――― WELLINGTON, DUKE OF. Despatches, during his Campaigns in ... P., etc. 1837-39.
――― DENMAN, HON. Practical Remarks on the Slave-Trade, and on the existing Treaties with P. 1839.
――― GAMA, A. DE S. DA. Memoria sobre as Colonias de P. ... na Costa Occidental d'Africa em 1814, etc. *Par.*, 1839.
――― PEREIRA, F. F. Taboa geografico-estatistica Lusitana, etc. *Porto*, 1839.

Portugal.

Portugal. —Costa, C. A. da. Revisão do Recenseamento des População de P. em 1838. *Lisb.*, **1840.**

—— Forrester, J. J. Correspondence with ... P., on ... his Map of the Douro Wine Districts. *Op.*, **1844.**

—— Kingston, W. H. G. Lusitanian Sketches of the Pen and Pencil. **1845.**

—— Balbi, A. Della popolazione del Portogallo, *etc.* *Mil.*, **1846.**

—— Santarem, Visconde de. Rapport sur l'ouvrage de M. Lopez ... "Essais statistiques sur les possessions Portugaises en Outre Mer." *Par.*, **1846.**

—— France. The Lighthouses on the N. and W. Coasts of ... P. Corrected to 1848, 52, 53, 54, 56, 57. **1846-57.**

—— Soares, J. P. C. Bosquejo das Possessões Portuguezas do Oriente, *etc.* *Lisb.*, **1851.**

—— Forrester, J. J. The Oliveira Prize-Essay on P., *etc.* **1853.**

—— Soares, J. P. C. Documentos Comprovativos do Bosquejo das Possessões Portuguezas no Oriente. *Lisbon*, **1853.**

—— Portugal. Portugaliæ Monumenta historica, *etc.* *Olisipone*, **1856-63.**

—— Santarem, Visconde de. Quadro elementar das Relações Politicas ... de P. com as diversas Potencias do Mundo desde o principio do xvi. seculo, *etc.* *Lisboa*, **1858-60.**

—— France. The Admiralty List of the Lights of the N. and W. Coasts of ... P. Corrected to 1859. **1859.**

—— Forrester, J. J. Companion to "P. and Its Capabilities," *etc.* *Op.*, **1860.**

—— Dunsterville, E. The Admiralty List of the Lights on the N. and W. Coasts of ... P. Corrected to 1860, 61, 62. **1860-62.**

—— Gras, M. A. le. Phares des Côtes ... Ouest. ... de P. Corrigés 1862-64. *Par.*, **1862-64.**

—— Portugal. Commissão geologica de P. Estudios geologicos, *etc.* *Lisbon*, **1867.**

—— Gras, A. Le. Description des Côtes ... de P. *Par.*, **1869.**

—— —— Phares ... des Côtes Ouest ... de P., *etc. Par.*, **1869.**

—— Drake, Sir F. Voyage to Cadiz ... and ... other places upon the Coast of Spaine and P. ... 1587. Hakluyt. Vol. II.

—— Voyage to Spaine and P., written (as it is thought) by Colonel A. Wingfield, 1589. Hakluyt. Vol. II.

—— True Coppie of a Discourse written by a Gentleman, employed in the late Voyage of Spanie and Portingale, 1589. Hakluyt. Vol. V.

—— Travels through P. ... by an English Gentleman, 1603. Harris, J. Vol. II.

—— Dillon, J. T. Travels through Spain, with notes ... from a Tour through ... P. in 1603, by C. A. Fischer. Pelham. Vol. II.

—— Link, H. F. Travels in P. Pelham. Vol. II.

Portugal.—Folque, F. Reflexões acerca . . . dos Dominios de P. o Hespanha na America Meridional. PORTUGAL. Collecção de Noticias, etc. Vol. VII.
—— The P.s discontent and compromise with the Spaniard, etc. PURCHAS. Vol. I.
—— Brief relation of the Embassage . . . from . . . Ethiopia to . . . P., etc. PURCHAS. Vol. II.
—— Wingfield, Col. A. Discourse of the P. Voyage, 1589, under Sir J. Norris, etc. PURCHAS. Vol. IV.
—— Oceum Chamnam. Reise nach Siam und P., 1684-86. VOYAGES and TRAVELS. Allgemeine Historie, etc. Vol. X.
—— Spain and P., a Tour through . . . 1803, etc. VOYAGES and TRAVELS. A Collection, etc. 1805. Vol. III.
—— Collins, F. Voyages to P., etc. 1796-1801. VOYAGES and TRAVELS. A Collection, etc. 1805. Vol. X.
—— —— Voyages to P., etc. 1796-1801. VOYAGES and TRAVELS. A Collection, etc. 1810. Vol. VI.
—— Spain and P., a Tour through . . . 1803. VOYAGES and TRAVELS. A Collection, etc. 1810. Vol. VI.
—— Graham, W. Travels through P. and Spain . . . 1812-14. VOYAGES and TRAVELS, New. 1819. Vol. III.
—— A Description of Spain and P. VOYAGES and TRAVELS. The World displayed. Vol. XX.
—— See also ALGARVE.

Portugall Indies.—See GOA.

Posen.—POSEN. A Narrative of Recent Occurrences in. 1848.
—— GERLACHLAEGER, E. P. Kurz gefasste Geschichte und Beschreibung der Stadt, etc. *Posen*, 1866.

Potosi.—HELMS, A. Z. Travels . . . by P. to Lima. 1806.
—— ANDREWS, CAPT. Journey from Buenos Ayres . . . to P., etc. 1827.
—— Relation des Voyages du sieur Acarete . . . au P. THEVENOT. Vol. IV.
—— Helms, A. Z. Travels . . . by P. to Lima, etc. VOYAGES and TRAVELS. A Collection, etc. 1805. Vol. V.

Potsdam.—BERLIN. Guide de . . . P., etc. *Berl.*, 1793.

Pozzuoli.—FALCONER, W. Dissertation on St. Paul's Voyage from Cæsarea to Puteoli, etc. *Oxf.*, 1817.
—— —— Dissertation on St. Paul's Voyage from Cæsarea to Puteoli, etc. *Lond.*, 1870.

Prague.—KOHL, J. G. Austria . . . P., etc. *Lond.*, 1844.
—— FARRSCH, K. Kalender der Flora des Horizontes von Prag, etc. 1852.
—— PODIEBRAD, D. J. Alterthümer der Prager Josefstadt, Israelitischer Friedhof, etc. *Prag*, 1855.

Prairie du Chien.—Brunson, A. P. du C., etc. *Milwauk.*, 1857.

2 B

Predazzo.—RICHTHOFEN, F. F. VON. Geognostische Beschreibung der Umgegend von P., etc. *Gotha*, 1860.

Prester John, Empire of.—*See* ABYSSINIA.

Priaman.—TATTON, J. Voyage of Capt. S. Castleton to P. in 1612. ASTLEY. Vol. I.

—— Voyage of Capt. R. Rowles to P., etc. ASTLEY. Vol. I.

—— Voyage of Capt. R. Rowles to . . . P. KERR. Vol. VIII.

—— The unhappie Voyage of the *Union*, till she arrived at P., 1609, etc. PURCHAS. Vol. I.

Prince Albert Land.—HALL, J. Proposed Settlement of P. A. L. *Melb. and Syd.*, 1862.

Prince Edward's Island.—BOUCHETTE, J. The British dominions in N. America . . . a . . . description of . . . P. E., etc. 1832.

Prince of Wales Island.—ANDERSON, J. Observations on . . . Pinang, etc. *P. of W. I.*, 1824.

—— Prince of Wales Island, Exposition of the political and commercial relations of the Government of, with the . . . E. Coast of Sumatra, etc. *P. of W. I.*, 1824.

—— CAMERON, J. Our Tropical Possessions . . . being a descriptive Account of . . . P., etc. *Lond.*, 1865.

Princes' Islands.—Sibthorp, Dr. Voyage . . . P. I., etc. WALPOLE, R. Travels, etc.

Prome.—FRASER, A. Note . . . on a proposal . . . to promote the construction of a Railway from Rangoon to P. *Rangoon*, 1867.

Promised Land.—*See* PALESTINE.

Propontis, Propontide.—*See* MARMORA, SEA OF.

Providence, U.S.—REDFIELD, W. C. Replies to Dr. Hare's Objections . . . with some evidence of the Whirling Action of the P. Tornado of Aug. 1838. *N. Y.*, 1842.

Pruang.—STRACHEY, H. Narrative of a Journey to . . . the Valley of P., in Tibet, etc. *Calc.*, 1848.

Prusa.—*See* BRUSSA.

Prussia.—CHAUCHARD, CAPT. Geographical . . . description of . . . P., etc. *Lond.*, 1800.

—— FÖRSTER, F. Statistisch- Topographisch- Historische Uebersicht des Preussischen Staats. *Berl., u. Leip.*

—— EBERHARD, L. D. Wegweiser durch die Preussischen Staaten. *Berl.*, 1831.

—— ELLIOTT, C. B. Letters from . . . P., etc. 1832.

—— MURRAY. Hand-Book for Travellers . . . through . . . P., etc. *Lond.*, 1836.

—— BELGIUM. Belgian . . . Prussian . . . Lighthouses, corrected to 1843, 51, 54, 57-59. 1843-59.

—— LAING, S. Notes . . . on . . . P., etc. 1854.

—— UNDINE. Our Cruise in the *Undine* . . . through . . . P., etc. *Lond.*, 1854.

Prussia.—Hjorth, J. Description des Côtes . . . de la P., etc.
Par., 1855.
—— Prussia. Tabellen und amtliche Nachrichten über den Preussischen Staat, etc. Berl., 1858.
—— Dunsterville, E. The Admiralty List of the . . . Prussian . . . Lights. Corrected to 1860. 1860.
—— Statistical Tables. S. T. Part VII. . . . P., etc. 1861.
—— Prussia. Erläuterungen zu der Karte über die Production . . . der mineralischen Brennstoffe in Preussen, in 1862. Berl., 1863.
—— Prussia. The History of P. . . . to the Occupation of Hanover, 1867, etc. Lond., 1869.
—— Henry IV., King. Voyage into P. and Letto, 1390. Hakluyt. Vol. I.
—— Thomas . . . Duke of Gloucester. Voyage into P., 1391. Hakluyt. Vol. I.
—— Benjamin, the Son of Jonas. Peregrination of . . . and relations of . . . P., etc. Purchas. Vol. II.
—— Guagnino, A. Descrittione della Sarmatia Europea . . . P., etc. Ramusio. Vol. II.
—— Carr, J. A Northern Summer; or, Travels . . . through . . . P. . . . 1804. Voyages and Travels. A Collection, etc. 1805. Vol. III.

Puebla de los Angelos. Gage, T. Survey of the Spanish West Indies . . . Also . . . Voyage . . . to . . . Ciudad de los A., etc. 1702.

Puerto Cabello.—Parker, W. Voyage to . . . P. de Cavallos . . . 1596-97. Hakluyt. Vol. IV.
—— **de Cavallos.**—See Puerto Cabello.
—— **Escoces.**—Parsons, J. West India Directory, Sailing directions from P. E. to Samardi, etc. 1854.
—— **Rico.**—Turnbull, D. Travels in the West . . . with Notices of P. R., etc. 1840.
—— Pert, Sir T., and Cabot S. Voyage to . . . San Juan de P. R., 1516. Hakluyt. Vol. III.
—— Newport, C. Voyage to . . . S. Juan de P. R. . . . 1591. Hakluyt. Vol. IV.
—— Drake, Sir F. His Voyage, 1595 . . . with the Spanish account of D.'s Attack on P. R.; edited . . . by W. D. Cooley. 1849. Hakluyt Soc. Pub. Vol. IV.
—— Pert, Sir T., and Cabot, S. Voyage to . . . P. R., about 1516. Kerr. Vol. VI.
—— Cumberland, Earl of. Voyage to S. John de P. R. Purchas. Vol. IV.
—— Layfield, E. Large Relation of the P. R. Voyage, etc. Purchas. Vol. IV.
—— Pongo, J. Reise nach Borriquen oder P. R. . . . 1508-9. Voyages and Travels. Allgemeine Historie, etc. Vol. XIII.

Puget's Sound.—Montgomerie, J. E., and Horsey, A. F. B. do. A few words collected from . . . the Indians in the neighbourhood of . . . P. S. 1848.

372 Puglia — Punjab.

Puglia.—*See* APULIA.
Pulicat.—Voyage to Pulicatt, *etc.* KERR. Vol. VIII.
—— Floris, P. W. Extracts of his Journal . . . 1610-15. Voyage to Palecatto, *etc.* PURCHAS. Vol. 1.
Pulkowa.—*See* BULKA.
Pullicatt.—*See* PULICAT.
Pullypattl.—Voyage to . . . Patapilly, *etc.* KERR. Vol. VIII.
Pulney Hills.—MARKHAM, C. R. Chinchona Cultivation . . . on the P. H., *etc.* 1865.
Pulo Ubin.—*See* OBI.
Punjab.—MACARTNEY, J. Memoir of a Map of the P., *etc.* MS.
—— WYLD, J. Notes on Map of . . . P., *etc.*
—— MALCOLM, LIEUT.-COL. Sketch of the Sikhs . . . who inhabit the Provinces of the Penjab, *etc.* *Lond.*, 1812.
—— HÜGEL, BARON C. VON. Kaschmir und das Reich der Siek. *Stutt.*, 1840-41.
—— MOORCROFT and TREBECK. Travels in the Himalayan Provinces of . . . the P. . . . 1819 to 1825. 1841.
—— ZIMMERMANN, C. Der Kriegs-Schauplatz in Inner-Asien, oder Bemerkungen zu der Uebersichts-Karte von . . . dem Penjab, *etc.* *Berl.*, 1842.
—— BARR, W. Journal . . . including Travels in the P., *etc.* *Lond.*, 1844.
—— MASSON, C. Narrative of Journeys in . . . the P., *etc.* 1844.
—— THORNTON, E. Gazetteer of the . . . P., *etc.* 1844.
—— HÜGEL, Baron C. VON. Travels into Kashmir and the P., *etc.* 1845.
—— VON ORLICH, L. Travels in India, including . . . the P., *etc.* 1845.
—— LAL, MOHAN. Travels in the P., *etc.* 1846.
—— EDWARDES, H. B. A Year on the P. Frontier, *etc.* 1851.
—— HONIGBERGER, J. M. Thirty-five Years in the East. Adventures . . . relating to the P., *etc.* 1852.
—— PUNJAUB. General Report upon the Administration of the Punjaub Proper, for 1849-51, *etc.* *Lond.*, 1854.
—— ANDREW, W. P. The Punjaub Railway, *etc.* 1857.
—— PUNJAUB. An Account of the formal commencement of the Punjaub Railway at Lahore, *etc.* 1859.
—— DIARY. The Diary of a Hunter from the P. to the Karakorum Mountains. *Lond. and Norw.*, 1863.
—— INDIA. Tables of Heights in . . . the P., *etc.* *Calc.*, 1863.
—— SCINDE RAILWAY. Scinde Railway . . . the P. Railway . . . Reports of the Directors . . . Sept., 1863. 1863.
—— WALKER, J. T. Tables of Heights in . . . the P., *etc.* *Calc.*, 1863.

Punjab.—INDIA. Selections from the Records of the Government of the P. etc. **1868,** etc.
—— NEIL, A. Annual Report on Meteorological Observations, registered in the P. 1868. *Lodiana,* **1869.**
—— PUNJAB. Report on the Sanitary Administration of the Panjab, 1869. *Lahore,* **1870.**
Punjaub.—*See* PUNJAB.
Purus, River.—SILVA COUTINHO, J. M. DE. Relatorio da exploração do Rio P. **1862.**
—— —— Considerações geraes sobre os rios que descem da cordilheira dos Andes . . . cachoeiras do P., etc. **1863.**
Pustosera.—*See* PASTOSSERA.
Puteoli.—*See* POZZUOLI.
Pu Teon Shan.—*See* PUTO.
Puto.—HALLORAN, A. L. Wae Yang Jin. Eight Months' Journal, kept . . . during visits to . . . Pootoo. *Lond.,* **1856.**
Puy, Le.—DOUE, J. M. B. DE. De la Fréquence comparée des Vents supérieurs et inférieurs sous le climat du P. en Velay, etc.
Versailles, [**1851.**]
Puy en Velay.—*See* PUY, LE.
Puzzuoli.—*See* POZZUOLI
Pyrenees.—PYRENEES. Essai sur la Minéralogie des Monts-P.
Par., **1784.**
—— RAMOND, L. Observations faites dans les P., etc. *Par.,* **1789.**
—— PASUMOT, F. Voyages Physiques dans les P. en 1788 et 1789, etc.
Par., **1797.**
—— RAMOND, L. Voyages au Mont-Perdu, et dans la partie adjacente des Hautes-Pyrénées. *Par.,* **1801.**
—— DRALET, M. Description des P., etc. *Par.,* **1813.**
—— RAMOND, L. Travels in the P., etc. **1813.**
—— PALASSOU, M. Histoire Naturelle des P., etc. *Pau,* **1815-19.**
—— CORABOEUF, M. Les Opérations Géodésiques des P. *Par.,* **1831.**
—— CHAUSENQUE, M. Les P., etc. *Par.,* **1834.**
—— PARIS, T. C. Letters from the P., etc. *Lond.,* **1843.**
—— TAINE, H. Voyage aux P., etc. *Par.,* **1860.**
—— VIGNOLES, C. International Exhibition of 1862 . . . Model of the Passage of the Tudela and Bilboa Railway across the Chain of the Cantabrian P., etc. *Lond.,* **1862.**
See also MONT PERDU.

Q.

Quebec.—SILLIMAN, B. Tour to Q., 1819. VOYAGES and TRAVELS, New. 1819. Vol. VII.
Queda.—*See* QUEDAH.

Quedah.—OSBORN, S. Q., or Stray Leaves from a Journal in Malayan Waters. 1857.

Queen Charlotte Islands.—INSKIP, G. H. Q. C. I. . . . Sailing Directions, *etc.* 1856.

—— Carteret, Capt. Voyage . . . to . . . Q. C. I. . . . 1766–69. HAWKESWORTH, J. Vol. I.

Queensland.—PUGH, T. P. Brief Outline of the . . . Colony of Q. *Brisbane,* 1861.

—— HEYWOOD, B. A. A Vacation Tour . . . through . . . Q., *etc.* 1863.

—— ALLEN, C. H. A Visit to Q., *etc.* *Lond.,* 1870.

Quelpaert.—Hamel, H. Reisen einiger Holländer nach Korea, nebst . . . ihrem Schiffbruche an . . . Q., 1658–68. VOYAGES and TRAVELS. Allgemeine Historie, *etc.* Vol. VI.

Quijos. PERU. Documentos . . . que acreditan la possesión del Perú sobre los Territorios de Q., *etc.* *Lima,* 1860.

Quiloa.—Prior, J. Voyage . . . to . . . Q. . . . 1813. VOYAGES and TRAVELS, New. 1819. Vol. II.

Quinsai.—*See* QUINSAY.

Quinsay.—Monfart. Continuation of the Jesuites Acts . . . in C. . . . Of Hancou or Q. . . . 1618. PURCHAS. Vol. III.

—— Nicolo di Conti. Voyage to . . . Q., *etc.* PURCHAS. Vol. III.

Quisai.—*See* QUINSAY.

Quito.—QUITO. Memoria sobre las oscilaciones de la Brujula en Q., *etc.* *Quito,* 1868.

—— Velasco, J. de. Histoire du Royaume de Q. TERNAUX-COMPANS. Voyages. Vol. XVIII., XIX.

—— Beschreibung der Provinz Q., *etc.* VOYAGES and TRAVELS. Allgemeine Historie, *etc.* Vol. IX.

—— Dieses begreift die Reise von Guayaquil nach . . . Q., *etc.* VOYAGES and TRAVELS. Allgemeine Historie, *etc.* Vol. IX.

—— Beschreibungen . . . von . . . Q., *etc.* VOYAGES and TRAVELS. Allgemeine Historie, *etc.* Vol. XV.

Quivira.—Vasquez de Coronado, F. Voyage . . . to . . . Q. . . . 1540. HAKLUYT. Vol. III.

R.

Radnor.—MURCHISON, Sir R. I. The Silurian System, founded on Geological Researches in . . . R., *etc.* 1839.

Raffles' Bay.—EARL, G. W. Observations on . . . the establishment of a Settlement in the vicinity of R. B. 1836.

Ragusa.—WILKINSON, Sir J. G. Dalmatia and Montenegro . . . History of . . . R., *etc.* 1848.

—— WINGFIELD, W. F. Tour in Dalmatia . . . with . . . Sketch . . . of R. 1859.

—— Austel, H. Voyage . . . to R. . . . 1586. HAKLUYT. Vol. II.

Rairoa.—KULCZYCKI, A. Determination des Longitudes . . . Observations pour . . . R., etc. *Par.*, 1851.

Rajahmundry.—INDIA. Reports of the . . . effects of the Godavery and Krishna Ancients, in R., etc. *Madras*, 1858.

Rájast'hán.—*See* RAJPOOTANA.

Rajpoot States.—*See* RAJPOOTANA.

Rajpootana.—TOD, J. Annals and Antiquities of Rájast'hán, etc. 1829.

—— BOILEAU, A. W. E. Tour through the W. States of Rajwara in 1835, etc. *Calc.*, 1837.

—— MEDLICOTT, H. B. The Boundary of the Vindhyan Series in R. INDIA, GEOLOGICAL SURVEY. Records, etc. Vol. I.

Rajwara.—*See* RAJPOOTANA.

Rakaia, River.—HAAST, J. Report on the Headwaters of the . . . R. *Christch.*, 1866.

Rákas Tal.—*See* CHO-LAGAN.

Ramea.—DRAKE, G. Voyage to the Isle of R., 1593. HAKLUYT. Vol. III.

—— The first discovery of the Isle of R. . . . 1591. HAKLUYT. Vol. III.

—— LEIGH, C. Voyage to . . . the Isle of R., 1597. HAKLUYT. Vol. III.

Ramgurh.—BALL, V. On the R. Coal Field. INDIA GEOLOGICAL SURVEY, Memoirs. Vol. VI.

Ramisseram.—CORDINER, J. Description of Ceylon . . . and a Journey to R. in 1804. 1807.

Rangoon.—BAKER, T. T. The recent operations of the British Forces at R., etc. *Lond.*, 1852.

—— FAYRER, J. Abstract of the Meteorological Register kept at R. from May, 1852, to April, 1853. *Rangoon*, 1853.

—— SPRYE, R. H. F. and C. H. F. The British and China Railway; from . . . R., etc. 1858.

—— SPRYE, R. and R. H. F. The Western-Inland Provinces of China Proper . . . considered in connection with . . . R. 1858.

—— SPRYE, R. and R. H. F. The Western-Inland-Provinces of China Proper . . . considered in connection with . . . R. *Lond.*, 1862.

—— CHINA. Memorial . . . on . . . Commerce with the West of China from . . . R. 1864.

—— WILLIAMS, J. M. Memorandum on Railway Communication with Wn. China . . . from . . . R., etc. *Lond.*, 1865.

—— FRASER, A. Note . . . on a proposal . . . to promote the construction of a Railway from R. to Prome. *Rangoon*, 1867.

—— WILLIAMS, J. J., and LUARD, C. H. Copies of . . . Survey Report . . . respecting R., etc. *Lond.*, 1867.

Rascien.—*See* RASHAN.

Rashan.—THOEMMEL, G. Geschichtliche . . . Beschreibung . . . der Rascien. *Wien*, 1867.

Rätien.—*See* RHÆTIA.

Ravenna.—GINANNI, F. Istoria . . . delle Pinette Ravennati, etc. *Roma*, 1774.

R'Dâmes.—See GHADAMES.

Recca.—SCHMIDL, A. A. Ueber den unterirdischen Lauf der R. 1851.

Red River.—FEATHERSTONHAUGH, G. W. Geological Report of . . . the elevated country between the Missouri and R. Rivers. *Wash.*, 1835.

—— MARCY, R. B., and M'CLELLAN, G. B. Exploration of the R. R. of Louisiana, in 1852, etc. *Wash.*, 1854.

—— POPE, J. Report of Exploration . . . from the R. R. to the Rio Grande. *Wash.*, 1854.

—— HIND, H. Y. Narrative of the Canadian R. R. Exploring Expedition of 1857, etc. 1858.

—— DAWSON, S. J. Report on . . . the Country between Lake Superior and the R. R. Settlement, etc. *Toronto*, 1859.

—— HEAD, SIR E. Papers relative to the Exploration . . . between Lake Superior and the R. R. Settlement. 1859.

—— Lewis and Clark, Capts., and others. Travels . . . exploring the . . . R. R. . . . 1805. VOYAGES and TRAVELS. A Collection, etc. 1805. Vol. VI.

——, **Sea.**—LOBO, FATHER J. Voyage to Abyssinia . . . with a description of the Coasts of the R. S., etc. 1735.

—— IRWIN, E. A Series of Adventures in . . . the R. S., etc. *Lond*, 1780.

—— VALENTIA, VISCOUNT. Voyages and Travels to . . . the R. S. . . . 1802-6. 1811.

—— BELZONI, G. Narrative of . . . a journey to the Coast of the R. S., etc. 1822.

—— ELWOOD, MRS. COL. Journey Overland . . . by . . . the R. S. to India. 1830.

—— ELLIOTT, R. Views in the East; comprising . . . the Shores of the R. S., etc. 1833.

—— BOURCHIER, W. Narrative of . . . Shipwreck . . . in the R. S., etc. 1834.

—— EHRENBERG, C. G. Natur und Bildung der . . . Corallenbänke in Rothen Meer. *Berl.*, 1834.

—— FAIRBAIRN, H. A Letter . . . on the . . . advantages of a Steam Passage to the East Indies, by the Gulf of Mexico . . . as compared with the proposed Route by the R. . . . S. 1837.

—— BEKE, C. T. On the Passage of the R. S. by the Israelites, etc. 1838.

—— HURICOURT, C. R. DE. Considérations . . . sur le Golfe Arabique, etc. *Par.*, 1841.

—— MORESBY, R., and ELWON, T. Sailing Directions for the R. S. 1841.

—— ROBINSON, F. Refutation of Lieut. Wellsted's Attack upon Lord Valentia's Work upon the R. S., etc. 1842.

—— VETCH, J. Inquiry into the means of establishing a Ship Navigation between the Mediterranean and the R. Seas. 1843.

—— FONTANIER, V. Voyage dans l'Inde . . . par . . . la Mer Rouge. *Par.*, 1844.

Red Sea.—HERICOURT, C. R. D'. Second Voyage sur les deux rives de la Mer Rouge, etc. *Par.*, 1846.

—— LACTURE, COUNT D'ESCAYRAC DE. De l'influence que le Canal des deux Mers exercera sur le Commerce . . . de la Mer Rouge, etc. *Par.*, 1855.

—— BEKE, C. T. The French and English in the R. S. 1862.

—— FOY, R. Renseignements Nautiques sur quelques Ports . . . de la Mer Rouge. *Par.*, 1866.

—— SCHWEINFURTH, G. Pflanzen-geographische Skizze . . . der Uferländer des Rothen Meeres. [*Gotha*, 1868.]

—— MACGREGOR, J. The "Rob Roy" on the . . . R. S., etc. *Lond.*, 1869.

—— Description of the . . . R. S., etc. ASTLEY. Vol. I.

—— Dounton, Lieut.-Gen. N. Journal of . . . Voyage to the R. S. . . . in 1610. ASTLEY. Vol. I.

—— Middleton, Sir H. Voyage to the R. S. . . . in 1610. ASTLEY. Vol. I.

—— Saris, J. Voyage to the R. S. in 1611. ASTLEY. Vol. I.

—— Biddulph, W. Travels of four Englishmen . . . into . . . the R. S., in 1600 and 1611. CHURCHILL. Vol. VII.

—— Bissell, A. Voyage . . . to the R. S. . . . 1798-99. DALRYMPLE, A. Collection of Nautical Memoirs, etc.

—— Eighth Voyage, in 1611 . . . Occurrences . . . in the R. S., etc. KERR. Vol. VIII.

—— —— Middleton, Sir H. Journey to Zenan . . . Voyage from the R. S. to Surat, etc. KERR. Vol. VIII.

—— Voyages des Anglais . . . dans la Mer Rouge, etc. LAHARPE, J. Vol. I.

—— A briefe narration of the . . . Discoverie of the R. S. PURCHAS. Vol. I.

—— Of Ezion Geber . . . and the R. S., etc. PURCHAS. Vol. I.

—— Arriano. Navigatione del Mar Rosso, fino all' Indie Orientali, etc. RAMUSIO. Vol. I.

—— Corsali, A. Lettera . . . della Navigatione del Mar Rosso . . . 1517. RAMUSIO. Vol. I.

—— Ramusio. Discorso sopra la Navigatione dal Mar Rosso, fino all' Indie Orientali: scritta per Arriano. RAMUSIO. Vol. I.

—— Viaggio scritto per un Comito Venetiano, dal Mar Rosso fino al Diu . . . 1537-8. RAMUSIO. Vol. I.

—— Valentia, Viscount. Voyages and Travels to . . . the R. S. . . . 1802-6. VOYAGES and TRAVELS. A Collection, etc. 1805. Vol. XI.

—— —— Voyages and Travels to . . . the R. S. . . . 1802-6. VOYAGES and TRAVELS. A Collection, etc. 1810. Vol. IV.

—— Erste Reisen der Franzosen nach dem glücklichen Arabien durch das Morgenländische Meer, 1708. VOYAGES and TRAVELS. Allgemeine Historie, etc. Vol. XI.

Ree, Lough.—WOLFE, J. Sailing Directions, etc., with some Hydrographic Notices of L. R., etc. 1850.

Reggio, in Lombardy.—Affarosi, D. C. Notizie istoriche della Città di R., etc. *Padova*, 1755.

Regnum Davidicum.—See PALESTINE.

Reich der Siek.—See PUNJAB.

Reichenau.—JULIUS, W. A. Semmering und R. Führer, etc. *Wien*, 1858.

República Mejicana.—See MEXICO.

République Française.—See FRANCE.

Repulse Bay.—LYON, G. F. A brief Narrative of an unsuccessful attempt to reach R. B., etc. *Lond.*, 1825.

Respublica Batavica.—See HOLLAND.

Reunion.—See BOURBON, ISLAND of.

Rey, River.—PERKINS, G. Relacion de la Expedicion á el R. en el Chaco. *Rosario*, 1867.

Rhadames.—See GHADAMIS.

Rhætia.—MANNERT, K. Germania, R. ... nach den Begriffen der Griechen und Römer, etc. *Leipz.*, 1820.

——— STEUB, L. Ueber die Urbewohner Rätiens, etc. *München*, 1843.

Rhamnus.—STUART, J. and REVETT, N. The Antiquities of Athens ... R., etc. 1825-33.

——— Halkes, Mr. Journal through parts of ... R., etc. WALPOLE, R. Memoirs, etc.

Rhat.—See GUAT.

Rheinbayern.—See BAVARIA, RHENISH.

Rhenish Bavaria.—See BAVARIA, RHENISH.

Rhine.—ENGELMANN, J. B. Résumé de l'histoire ... des Villes principales du Rhin. *Heidelb.*

——— LIBEUR, L'ABBÉ. Voyage pittoresque sur le Rhin, etc. *Francf. s. l. M.*, 1807.

——— RHINE. An Autumn near the R., etc. *Lond.*, 1821.

——— TOMBLESON, W. Tombleson's Views of the R., etc. *Lond.*, 1832.

——— MURRAY. Hand-Book for Travellers ... along the R., etc. *Lond.*, 1836.

——— QUIN, M. J. Steam Voyages on ... the R., etc. 1843.

——— GRAHAM, W. The Jordan and the R., etc. 1854.

——— NOBILING. Nachrichten über den Zustand des Rheinstroms innerhalb des Preussischen Gebietes, etc. *Berl.*, 1856.

———, Upper.—TOMBLESON, W. Tombleson's U. R. *Lond.*, [1840 ?]

Rhodes.—DAPPER. Beschryving van ... Rhodes, etc. 1688.

——— WILDE, W. R. Narrative of ... a Visit to ... R., etc., *Dubl.* 1852.

——— Greaves, J. Account of the Latitude of ... R. RAY, J.

Rhodos.—See RHODES.

Rhone.—HANNIBAL. Dissertation sur le passage du R. et des Alpes par Annibal, etc. *Par.*, 1821.
——— PARDOE, Miss. The River and the Desert; or, Recollections of the R., etc. *Lond.*, 1838.
——— DESJARDINS, E. R. et Danube, etc. *Par.*, 1870.

Riazan.—STRUVE, O. Détermination des Positions Géographiques do . . . R., etc. *St. Pet.*, 1843.

Richborough.—BATTELY, J. Opera posthuma. Antiquitates Rutupinæ, etc. *Oxon.*, 1745.

Righi.—BUSINGER. Itinéraire du Mont-R., etc. *Lucerne*, 1815.

Rimouski.—GOULD and DOWIE. Instructions for making . . . R. in the River St. Lawrence. 1832.

Rio Bravo del Norte.—EMORY, W. H. Notes of a Military Reconnoissance . . . including parts of the D. N., etc. *N. Y.*, 1848.
——— WEBSTER, J. D. Report of a Survey of the Gulf Coast at the Mouth of the Rio Grande. *Wash.*, 1850.
——— PARKE, J. G. Report of Explorations for . . . a Railway . . . between Dona Ana on the Rio Grande, and Pimas Villages on the Gila. *Wash.*, 1854.
——— POPE, J. Report of Exploration . . . from the Red River to the Rio Grande. *Wash.*, 1854.
——— UHDE, A. Die Länder am untern R. B. del N. *Heidelb.*, 1861.

Rio das Velhas.—*See* VELHAS.

Rio de Janeiro.—NAVARRO E CAMPOS, Sr. Itinerary of a Journey . . . in 1808, from Bahia to R. de J. *MS. Portug.*
——— HINCHCLIFF, T. W. South American Sketches, or a Visit to R. J., etc. 1863.
——— MICHELENA Y ROJAS, F. Exploracion Oficial . . . Viaje a R. de J., etc. *Bruselas*, 1867.
——— Byron, Comm. Voyage . . . to R. de J. . . . 1764-66. HAWKESWORTH, J. Vol. I.
——— Nodal, G. de. Reise nach R. J., etc. 1618. VOYAGES and TRAVELS. Allgemeine Historie, etc. Vol. XVIII.
——— Prior, J. Voyage . . . to . . . R. de J. . . . 1813. VOYAGES and TRAVELS, New. 1819. Vol. II.

Rio de la Hacha.—Statthalterschaften R. de la H. und St. Martha. VOYAGES and TRAVELS. Allgemeine Historie, etc. Vol. XVI.

Rio de la Plata.—*See* LA PLATA.

Rio Dulce.—Sherley, Sir A. Voyage . . . 30 leagues up R. D. . . . 1596. HAKLUYT. Vol. IV.

Rio Grande del Norte.—*See* RIO BRAVO DEL NORTE.

Rio Grande do Sul.—*See* SAN PEDRO DO RIO GRANDE.

Rio Janeiro.—*See* RIO DE JANEIRO.

Rio Negro.—WALLACE, A. R. Narrative of Travels on the . . . Rio N., etc. 1853.
——— MICHELENA Y ROJAS, F. Exploracion Oficial . . . del . . . R.-N., etc. *Bruselas*, 1867.

Rio Negro.—Roteiro da Viagem de . . . Pará até a's ultimas Colonias dos Dominios Portuguezes em os Rios . . . N. PORTUGAL. Collecção de Noticias, *etc.* Vol. VI.

Rio Seatro.—Account of the Inland Countries between Sierra Leone and R. S. ASTLEY. Vol. II.

Rioja Minor.—DAVIE, J. C. Letters . . . describing . . . R. M., *etc.*
1805.

Rion.—RADDE, G. Berichte, *etc.* (Jahrg. I. Reisen. . . . in . . . R., *etc.*)
Tiflis, 1866.

Ripon.—HIPON. The Tourist's Companion; being a . . . description . . . of R., *etc.*
Rip., 1828.

Ritzebüttel.—ABENDROTH, SENATOR. R., *etc.*
Hamb., 1818.

River of Canada.—*See* SAINT LAWRENCE.

Rocciamelone.—CASTALDI, B. Alcuni dati sulle Punte Alpini situate fra la Levanna ed il R.
Torino, 1868.

Roche-Mélon.—*See* ROCCIAMELONE.

Rock, River.—ABERT, Col. J. J. Reports . . . for the Improvement of the . . . R., *etc.*
Wash., 1840.

Rocky Mountains.—JAMES, E. Account of an Expedition . . . to the R. M., in 1819, '20, *etc.*
1823.

—— Cox, R. Adventures . . . including . . . a residence of Six Years on the W. side of the R. M., *etc.*
1831.

—— FREMONT, J. C. Report of the Exploring Expedition to the R. M. in 1842, *etc.*
Wash., 1845.

—— RUXTON, G. F. Adventures in Mexico and the R. M.
Lond., 1847.

—— COKE, HON. H. J. A Ride over the R. M., *etc.*
1852.

—— STANSBURY, H. Exploration . . . including a Reconnoissance of a New Route through the R. M.
Phil., 1852.

—— MARCOU, J. Geology of N. America; with Reports on . . . the R. M., *etc.*
Zurich, 1858.

—— ———— Notes pour servir à une description géologique des Montagnes Rocheuses.
Genève, 1858.

—— BLAKISTON, T. W. Report of . . . Exploration of . . . the R. M. in 1858.
Woolwich, 1859.

—— BURTON, R. F. City of the Saints, and across the R. M. to California.
1861.

—— MILTON, VISCOUNT, and CHEADLE, W. B. The North-West Passage by Land. Being . . . a Route . . . to British Columbia . . . by one of the Northern Passes in the R. M.
Lond., [1865.]

—— Long, E. H. Voyage de Pittsbourg aux Monts Rocailleux. EYRIES. Vol. IX.

Roknia.—FAIDHERBE, GENERAL L. Recherches anthropologiques sur les Tombeaux Mégalithiques de R.
Bone, 1868.

Romania.—*See* ROUMANIA.

Rome.—MARLIANUS, B. Urbis Romae Topographia, *etc.*
Basileae, 1550.

—— ADAM, A. Roman Antiquities.
Edinb., 1797.

Rome.—Uggeri, A. A. Journée pittoresque des Édifices de R. Ancienne.
Roma, 1800.
——— ——— Édifices de R. Antique, *etc.* *Roma*, 1816.
——— Vasi, M. de. Itinerario ... da Roma a Napoli, *etc.* *Roma*, 1816.
——— Stendhall, Count de. R. ... in 1817. 1818.
——— Nibby, A. Viaggio Antiquario no' contorni di R. *Roma*, 1819.
——— Vasi, M. de. Itinerario di Roma antica e moderna. 1819-20.
——— Kelsall, C. Classical Excursion from R. to Arpino.
Geneva, 1820.
——— Fea, C. Descripțion de R. *Rome*, 1821.
——— Venuti. Descrizione topografica delle Antichità di Roma.
Roma, 1824.
——— Rome in the Nineteenth Century. *Edin.*, 1826.
——— Gell, Sir W. Topography of R., *etc.* 1834.
——— Gibbon, E. History of the Decline and Fall of the Roman Empire,
etc. 1836.
——— Yates, J. On the Limes Rhaeticus and Limes Transrhenanus of
the Roman Empire. 1852.
——— Smith, W. Dictionary of Greek and Roman Geography. *etc.*
1856.
——— Burgess, R. On the Egyptian Obelisks in R, *etc.* 1858.
——— Scarfellini, C. Sulli Terremoti avvenuti in Roma ... 1858 e
1859, *etc.* *Roma*, 1860.
——— Reinaud, M. Relations Politiques et Commerciales de l'Empire
Romain avec l'Asie Orientale ... pendant les cinq premiers siècles,
etc. *Par.*, 1863.
——— Forchhammer, P. W. Die Gründung Roms. *Kiel*, 1868.
——— Misson, M. Arrival at R., to his departure out of Italy. Harris, J.
Vol. II.
——— Kelsall, C. Classical Excursion from R. to Arpino, 1820. Voyages and Travels, New. 1819. Vol. IV.
Romelia.—*See* Roumania.
Rona.—Mackenzie, Sir G. Account of Hirta and R. Pinkerton. Vol. III.
Rosario.—Rosario. Breve Noticia y documentos relativos a la Colonia
Agricola del R. Oriental, *etc.* *Montevideo*, [1859.]
——— Argentine Railway. Central Argentine Railway from R. to Cordova, *etc.* 1863.
Ross.—Murchison, Sir R. L. Supplementary Remarks on the Strata of the
Ooliric Series . . . in ... R., *etc.* 1827.
Rouen.—Licquet, T. R. Précis de son Histoire, *etc.* *Rouen*, 1831.
Roumania.—Macarius, Travels of ... Pt. 1 ... Romelia, *etc.*
1849.
——— Moltke, Baron von. The Russians in ... Rumelia in 1828-29.
1854.
——— Jackson, J. Journey ... in 1797, through ... Romelia, *etc.*
Pelham. Vol. II.

Rugen.—Rugen, A Tour through . . . 1805, etc. Voyages and Travels. A Collection, etc. 1805. Vol. V.

——— Rugen, A Tour through . . . 1805. Voyages and Travels. A Collection, etc. 1810. Vol. VI.

Rumburg.—Dresden und die umliegende Gegend bis . . . II., etc. *Dresd.,* **1804.**

Rumelia.—*See* Roumania.

Russia.—Erman, A. Beiträge zur Klimatologie des Russischen Reiches.

——— Mayerberg, Baron A. de. Iter in Moschoviam . . . anno M.DC.LXI., etc.

——— Monteith, W. Notes on Georgia . . . also a description of the Frontier of R., etc.

——— Wesselowsky, C. Tabellen über mittlere Temperaturen im Russischen Reiche.

——— Wyld, J. Notes on the Distribution of Gold throughout . . . R.

——— Vera, G. di. Tre Navigationi fatto dagli Olandesi . . . nella . . . Moscovia, etc. *Venet.,* **1599.**

——— Struys, J. Les Voyages de, en Moscovie, etc. *Lyon,* **1682.**

——— Olearius, A. Voyages très-curieux . . . faits en Moscovie, etc. *Amst.,* **1727.**

——— Straulenberg, P. J. von. Das Nord-und Ostliche Theil von Europa und Asia, in so weit solches das gantze Russische Reich . . . begreiffet . . . vorgestellet, etc. *Storkh.,* **1730.**

——— Russia. A Journey through R. into Persia, by two English Gentlemen, 1739, etc. **1742.**

——— Hanway, J. Historical Account . . . with . . . Travels . . . through R., etc. **1753.**

——— Russia. Authentic Narrative of the R.n Expedition against the Turks by Sea and Land. **1772.**

——— Lepechin, I. Tagebuch der Reise durch verschiedene Provinzen des Russischen Reiches in 1768-9, etc. *Altenburg,* **1774.**

——— Coxe, W. Travels into . . . R., etc. **1784.**

——— Gmelin, S. G. Reise durch Russland, etc. *St. Pet.,* **1784.**

——— Histoire des Découvertes . . . dans plusieurs contrées de la R., etc. *Lausanne,* **1784.**

——— Pallas, P. S. Voyages en différentes Provinces de l'Empire de Russie, etc. *Par.,* **1788-93.**

——— Pleschejeff S. Survey of the R.n Empire, etc. *Lond.,* **1792.**

——— Chantreau. Voyage . . . en Russie . . . 1788 et 89. *Hamb.,* **1794.**

——— Georgi, J. G. Geographisch-physikalische . . . Beschreibung des Russischen Reichs. *Königsb.,* **1797.**

——— Forster, G. Journey . . . into R., by the Caspian Sea. **1798.**

——— Ozorof, J. G. [A Russian Translation of G.'s 'Russland,' etc.] [*St. Pet.*] **1799.**

——— Levesque, P. C. Histoire de Russie, etc. *Hamb. et Brunsw.,* **1800.**

Russia. 383

Russia.—Coxe, W. Account of the ... Commerce between R. and China. 1804.
——— MacGill, T. Travels in ... R., etc. 1808.
——— Porter, R. K. Travelling Sketches in R., etc. 1809.
——— Cochrane, J. D. Narrative of a pedestrian Journey through R., etc. 1824.
——— Griberg, Count J. L'Empire Russe comparé aux principaux états du Monde, par Balbi, etc. 1829.
——— Schnitzler, J. H. Statistique et Itinéraire de la Russie. *Par.*, 1829.
——— Alcock, T. Travels in R., etc. 1831.
——— Elliott, C. B. Letters from ... R., etc. 1832.
——— Stocqueler, J. H. Fifteen Months' Pilgrimage through ... R., etc. 1832.
——— Russia. Hydrographie de l'Empire de Russie. *St. Pet.*, 1833.
——— Vsevolojsky, N. S. Dictionnaire Géographique-Historique de ... R., etc. *St. Pet.*, 1833.
——— Barrow, J. Excursions in ... R., etc. 1834.
——— Schnitzler, J. H. Russie ... Tableau statistique, etc. *Par.*, 1835.
——— Kreeft, C. First R.n Railroad, etc. 1837.
——— Krusenstern, A. J. de. L'Instruction publique en Russie. *Warsaw*, 1837.
——— Kupffer, A. T. Observations Météorologiques et Magnétiques faites dans l'Empire de Russie, 1835, 36. *St. Pet.*, 1837.
——— Conolly, A. Journey ... through R., etc. 1838.
——— Elliott, C. B. Travels in ... R., etc. 1838.
——— Daemner, R. Excursions in the Interior of R. 1839.
——— Bulgarin, T. Russlands-Geschichte. *Riga*, 1839.
——— ——— Russlands-Statistik. *Riga*, 1839.
——— Mignan, R. Winter Journey through R., etc. 1839.
——— Kupffer, A. T. Annuaire Magnétique et Météorologique du Corps des Ingénieurs des Mines de Russie. *St. Pet.*, 1839-48.
——— Baer, K. E. von, and Helmersen, Count von. Beiträge zur Kenntniss des Russischen Reiches, etc. *St. Pet.*, 1839-58.
——— Adelung, F. Ueber die älteren ausländischen Karten von Russland. *St. Pet.*, 1840.
——— Karpinski, Capt. On the Gold-Washings in R. *St. Pet.*, 1840.
——— Neumann, C. F. Russland und die Tscherkessen. *Stutt. und Tüb.*, 1840.
——— Zimmermann, C. Geographische Analyse eines Versuches zur Darstellung des Kriegstheaters Russlands gegen Chiwa. *Berl.*, 1840.
——— Erman, A. Archiv für wissenschaftliche Kunde von Russland. *Berl.*, 1841-52.

Russia.—MULLER, G. F. and PALLAS, P. S. Conquest of Siberia, and the History of the Transactions . . . between R. and China from the earliest period. **1842.**
—— KOHL, J. G. R., *etc.* **1843.**
—— STRUVE, W. Table des Positions Géographiques principales de Russie. *St. Pet.*, **1843.**
—— ADELUNG, F. VON. Kritisch-literärische Übersicht der Reisenden in Russland bis 1700, *etc.* *St. Pet., Leipz.*, **1846.**
—— KUPFFER, A. T. Resumé des Observations Météorologiques faites en Russie. *St. Pet.*, **1846.**
—— STRUVE, F. G. W. and O. W. Expédition Chronométrique . . . pour la détermination de la Longitude Géographique de l'Observatoire Central de Russie. *St. Pet.*, **1846.**
—— HAMEL, J. Tradescant der Aeltere 1618 in Russland. **1847.**
—— HÓNAY, J. Jellemismse, vagy az . . . Orosz . . . Nemzet . . . Jellemzése, *etc.* *Györött*, **1847.**
—— KUPFFER, A. T. Annales de l'Observatoire Physique Central de Russie, *etc.* *St. Pet.*, **1850-64.**
—— BODE, A. Notizen gesammelt auf einer Forstreise durch einen Theil des Europäischen Russlands. *St. Pet.*, **1854.**
—— CHESNEY, F. R. Russo-Turkish Campaigns of 1828 and 1829.
1854.
—— COLE, J. W. R. and the Russians, *etc.* **1854.**
—— CURZON, HON. R. Armenia . . . the Frontiers of R., *etc.* **1854.**
—— CUSTINE, M. DE. R., *etc.* **1854.**
—— GOLOVIN, I. The Nations of R. and Turkey, *etc.* **1854.**
—— HAMEL, J. England and R., *etc.* **1854.**
—— LATHAM, R. G. The Native Races of the R.n Empire.
Lond., **1854.**
—— M'CULLOCH, J. R. R. and Turkey, *etc.* **1854.**
—— RUSSIA. Observations on the Climate of R. *Russ. St. Pet.*, **1854.**
—— SPENCER, E. Turkey, R., *etc.* **1854.**
—— BELGIUM. The Belgian . . . Russian . . . Lights. Corrected to 1854, 57-59. **1854-59.**
—— HARRISON, R. Nine Years' Residence in R., from 1844 to 1853.
1855.
—— SEYMOUR, H. D. R. on the Black Sea and Sea of Azof, *etc.* **1855.**
—— TEGOBORSKI, M. L. DE. Commentaries on the Productive Forces of R. **1855.**
—— VESELOWSKY, C. Du Climat de la Russie. *St. Pet.*, **1855.**
—— HAXTHAUSEN, BARON VON. The R.n Empire, *etc.* **1856.**
—— MILNES, T. R.; its Rise and Progress, *etc.* **1856.**
—— PETACHIA, RABBI. Travels of; who, in the . . . Twelfth Century visited . . . R., *etc.* **1856.**
—— MURCHISON, SIR R. I. The Silurian Rocks and Fossils . . . of the Baltic Provinces of R., *etc.* **1858.**

Russia. 385

Russia.—Russia. By a recent Traveller. 1859.
—— —— Six Years' Travel in R., by an English Lady. 1859.
—— Sala, G. A. Journey due North, being Notes of a Residence in R. in 1850. 1858.
—— Dunsterville, E. The Admiralty List of the ... Russian ... Lights. Corrected to 1860. 1860.
—— Reinkee, M. Description hydrographique des Côtes Septentrionales de la Russie, etc. *Par.*, 1860-62.
—— Struve, O. Ueber einen vom General Schubert an die Akademie gerichteten Antrag, betreffend die Russisch-Scandinavische Meridian-Gradmessung. 1861.
—— Statistical Tables. Part VII. R., etc. 1861.
—— Gerstfeldt, Herr. Der Verkehr Russlands mit Westasien. [1862.]
—— Blaramberg, Lieut. Gen. Catalogue of Trigonometrical and Astronomical Positions determined in the R. Empire ... up to 1860. *Russ. St. Pet.*, 1863.
—— Russia. Catalogue of Trigonometrical and Astronomical Positions determined in the R.n Empire ... to 1860, etc. *St. Pet.*, 1863.
—— —— Geographical Dictionary of the R.n Empire, etc. *Russ. St. Pet.*, 1863.
—— Helmersen, G. von. [Explanatory Notes on the Geological Map of R.] *Russ.* [*St. Pet.*] 1865.
—— Lumley, J. S. Report on the Tea Trade of R., etc. *Lond.*, 1867.
—— Pollington, Viscount. Half round the Old World ... a Tour in R., etc. *Lond.*, 1867.
—— Helmersen, G. von. Studien über die Wanderblöcke und die Diluvialgebilde Russlands. *St. Pet.*, 1869.
—— Taesch, F. The Russo-Indian Question historically ... considered, etc. *Lond.*, 1869.
—— —— Voyage and Travels of A Jenkinson from R. to Boghar ... in 1557. Astley. Vol. IV.
—— —— Muscovy, a description of, etc. Churchill. Vol. VII.
—— —— Jenkinson, A. Voyage into R. .... 1557. Hakluyt. Vol. I.
—— —— —— Voyage through R. ... 1561. Hakluyt. Vol. I.
—— —— —— Third Voyage into R., 1566. Hakluyt. Vol. I.
—— —— —— Fourth Voyage into R., 1571. Hakluyt. Vol. I.
—— —— Herberstein, Baron S. von. Notes upon R. .... Translated and edited ... by R. H. Major. 1851-52. Hakluyt Soc. Pub. Vol. X. XI.
—— —— Russia at the Close of the Sixteenth Century. Edited by E. A. Bond. 1856. Hakluyt Soc. Pub. Vol. XX.
—— —— Ysbrants Ides, E. Travels from Muscovy ... to ... China ... 1692-95. Harris, J. Vol. II.
—— —— Finland and R. 1849. Murray. Hand-Book for Northern Europe. Pt. II.

2 o

Russia.

Russia.—Tooke, W. View of the R. n Empire. PELHAM. Vol. II.
—— Willoughby, Sir H. and others. Voyages to the N. n parts of R., etc. PINKERTON. Vol. I.
—— Coxe's Travels in R. PINKERTON. Vol. VI.
—— Benjamin, the Son of Jonas. Peregrination of ... and relations of ... R. PURCHAS. Vol. II.
—— Sherley, Sir A. Voyage ... thorow R. ... 1601. PURCHAS. Vol. II.
—— The beginning of the English Discoveries towards the North ... also Voyages by R., etc. PURCHAS. Vol. III.
—— The first voyage ... in which ... Muscovia was discovered ... 1553. PURCHAS. Vol. III.
—— Fletcher, G. Treatise of R. ... 1588. PURCHAS. Vol. III.
—— Jenkinson, A. First Voyage ... toward ... R. 1557. PURCHAS. Vol. III.
—— Russia, The late changes and manifold alterations in ... 1570-1615. PURCHAS. Vol. III.
—— Veer, G. de. Voyages of W. Barents ... behind ... Muscovia ... 1594-96. PURCHAS. Vol. III.
—— Campense, A. Lettera intorno le Cose di Moscovia. RAMUSIO. Vol. II.
—— Guagnino, A. Descrittione della Sarmatia Europea ... Moscovia, etc. RAMUSIO. Vol. II.
—— Jovio, P. Historico delle Cose della Moscovia. RAMUSIO. Vol. II.
—— Sigismondo Libero Barone in Habenstan. Commentari della Muscovia et della R., 1559. RAMUSIO. Vol. II.
—— Navigationi fatte da gli Olandesi ... nella ... Moscovia ... 1594-97. RAMUSIO. Vol. III.
—— Jenkinson, A. Reise aus Russland nach ... Bokhara, 1557. VOYAGES and TRAVELS. Allgemeine Historie, etc. Vol. VII.
—— Carr, J. A Northern Summer; or, Travels ... through ... R. ... 1804. VOYAGES and TRAVELS. A Collection, etc. 1805. Vol. III.
—— Senme, J. G. Tour through ... R. ... 1805. VOYAGES and TRAVELS. A Collection, etc. 1805. Vol. VII.
—— Campenhausen, Baron. Travels through several Provinces of the R. n Empire ... 1805. VOYAGES and TRAVELS. A Collection, etc. 1805. Vol. VIII.
—— —— Travels through several Provinces of the R. n Empire. VOYAGES and TRAVELS. A Collection, etc. 1810. Vol. III.
—— Senme, J. G. Tour through ... R. ... 1805. VOYAGES and TRAVELS. A Collection, etc. 1810. Vol. VI.
—— The Travels of the Ambassadors from ... Holstein into Moscovy ... 1635. VOYAGES and TRAVELS. The World displayed. Vol. XIII. XIV.
—— The Travels of Mr. Jonas Hanway ... through R. ... 1743. VOYAGES and TRAVELS. The World displayed. Vol. XIV., XV.

Russia, Central—HELMERSEN, G. VON. Die Steinkohlen des mittleren Russlands, etc. *St. Pet.*, 1867.

———, **East.**—SPOTTISWOODE, W. A Tarantasse Journey through E. n R. in 1856. 1857.

———, **European.**—MURCHISON, SIR R. I., AND OTHERS. On the Geological Structure of the Central and Southern Regions of R. in Europe, *etc.* 1842.

——— ——— ——— The Geology of R. in Europe, *etc.* *Lond. and Par.*, 1845.

——— ——— STRUVE, F. G. W. Ueber den Flächeninhalt der 37 Westlichen Gouvernements und Provinzen des Europäischen Russlands. *St. Pet.*, 1848.

——— ——— RUSSIA. Explanation of the Agricultural and Statistical Atlas of E. R. *Russ.* *St. Pet.*, 1851.

———, **North.**—SAUER, M. Account of a geographical . . . Expedition to the N. n parts of R., *etc.* 1802.

———, **South.**—CASPIAN SEA. Description . . . d'un Voyage fait 1784 dans la partie méridionale de la Russie. *Par.*, 1793.

——— ——— GOEBEL, AND OTHERS. Reise in die Steppen des Südlichen Russlands. *Dorpat*, 1838.

——— ——— BROOKS, S. Russians of the South. 1854.

——— ——— DEMIDOFF, A. DE. Travels in S. R. . . . during 1837. 1855.

Rutupia.—See RICHBOROUGH.

S.

Sabine, River.—GRAHAM, J. D. Observations . . . of the Magnetic Declination at two positions on the River S., *etc.* *Phil.*, 1846.

Sable Island.—BAYFIELD, ADMIRAL H. W. Nova Scotia Pilot . . . including S. I. 1860.

Saffi.—BEAUMIER, A. Itinéraire de . . . Maroc à Saffy, *etc.* *Par.*, 1868.

Saffy.—*See* SAFFI.

Saghalien.—SIEBOLD, P. F. VON. Nippon. Archiv zur Beschreibung von Japan . . . Krafto, *etc.* *Leyden*, 1852.

——— DICKMORE, A. S. The Ainos, or Hairy Men of . . . S., *etc.* *New Haven*, 1868.

Saghalin.—*See* SAGHALIEN.

Saguenay.—Cartier, J. Voyages to . . . S., 1534, 40. HAKLUYT. Vol. III.

——— La Roche, J. F. de. Voyage . . . to . . . S., 1542. HAKLUYT. Vol. III.

——— Cartier, J. Voyages . . . to . . . S. . . . 1534-37. KERR. Vol. VI.

———, **River.** SAGUENAY. Hints for entering the River S., *etc.* 1840.

Sahara.—*See* DESERT, GREAT.

Saint Augustine — Saint Helena.

Saint Augustine.—Finch, W. Observations ... touching ... S. A., etc. Purchas. Vol. I.

—— **Bernard, Mount.**—Mabget, J. L. Chamounix ... et les deux St. B.s. *Geneva*, 1843.

—— **Cassian.**—Richthofen, F. F. von. Geognostische Beschreibung der Umgegend von ... Sanct C., etc. *Gotha*, 1860.

—— **Catherine, Mount.**—Harant, K. Gesta ... do ... Sv. Kateriny, etc. *v. Praze*, 1854.

————— Lord John of Holland, Earle of Huntington. Voyage to ... S. Katherine Mount, 1394. Hakluyt. Vol. II.

—— **Christopher.** Sloane, H. Voyage to ... S. C.s, etc. 1707.

————— Reisen und Niederlassungen in der Insel St. C., 1027. Voyages and Travels. Allgemeine Historie, etc. Vol. XVII.

—— **Clair, Lake.**—Graham, J. D. Report on the Improvement of the Harbours of Lakes ... St. C., etc. *Wash.*, 1860.

—— **Croix.**—Patten, R. Report on the Locating Survey of the S. C. and Lake Superior Railroad. *Madison*, 1856.

—— **Domingo.**—*See* Hayti.

Sainte Alousie.—*See* Santa Lucia.

Saint Elias, Mount.—*See* Ocha.

—— **Eustatius.**—*See* Eustatius.

—— **Geneviève.**—Vincent, M. C. Report on the St. G. Glass-Sand Property, etc. *Lond.*, 1869.

—— **George Del Mina.**—Towrson, W. Three Voyages to ... Castle D. M., in 1555-57. Antley. Vol. I.

————— Three Voyages to ... the Castle of M. ... 1555-57. Hakluyt. Vol. II.

—— **George's Channel.**—Monnier, P. Mémoire sur les Courants de ... Canal de St. G., etc. 1835-39.

————— Huddart, J. Piloting Directory for ... S. G. C., etc. 1837.

————— Pass.—Logan, P. Journal of a Journey from Brisbane Town to St. G. P., etc. *Syd.*, 1826-30.

—— **Germain.**—Paris. Itinéraire ... de Paris au Havre ... précédé d'une Notice historique sur le chemin de fer de Paris à S.-G. *Par.*

—— **Gothard.**—Lardy, C. Essai sur la Constitution Geognostique du St. G. *Lausanne*, 1832.

—— — **Helen.**—M'Cord, J. S. Meteorological Observations made on the Island of St. H. in the River St. Laurence, etc. *Montreal*, 1842.

—— **Helena.**—Beatson, Major-Gen. A. Tracts relative to ... St. H. 1816.

————— Brooke, T. H. History of the Island of S. H., etc. *Lond.*, 1824.

————— Leith, W. H. Reconnoitering Voyages ... including visits to ... St. H., etc. *Lond.*, 1839.

————— Reconnoitering Voyages ... including visits to ... St. H., etc. 1840.

Saint Helena.—MAURITIUS. A Transport Voyage to the Mauritius ... touching at ... St. H. 1851.
——— ——— Prior, J. Voyage ... to ... St. H. ... 1813. VOYAGES and TRAVELS, New. 1819. Vol. II.
——— James of Compostella.—*See* SANTIAGO DE COMPOSTELLA.
——— John.—DAVIE, J. C. Letters from Paraguay, describing ... St. J., etc. 1805.
——— ——— de Ulhua.—*See* SAN JUAN DE ULLOA.
——— Kilda.—Mackenzie, Sir G. Account of Hirta and Rona. PINKERTON, Vol. III.
——— ——— Martin's Voyage to St. K. PINKERTON. Vol. III.
——— Kitt's.—*See* SAINT CHRISTOPHER.
——— Laurence, Island of.—*See* MADAGASCAR.
——— Lawrence, County.—HOUGH, F. B. History of St. L. and Franklin Counties, *etc.* *Albany*, 1853.
——— ——— Gulf of.—WELLESLEY, Hon. W. Private Letter Book of H.M.S. *Sapphire* during her Voyage ... to ... G. of St. L., *etc.* 1830-33.
——— ——— ——— BAYFIELD, ADMIRAL H. W. Sailing Directions for the G. ... of St. L. 1837.
——— ——— ——— PURDY, J., and FINDLAY, A. G. British American Navigator. Sailing Directory for ... the Gulf and River of St. L. *etc.* 1847.
——— ——— ——— BAYFIELD, ADMIRAL H. W. Maritime Positions in the Gulf ... St. L., *etc.* 1857.
——— ——— ——— ——— St. L. Pilot, *etc.* 1860.
——— ——— ——— ——— Pilote du Golfe ... St. Laurent, *etc.* *Par.*, 1863.
——— ——— ——— Cartier, J. Voyages to ... the Gulfe of S. L. ... 1534, 40. HAKLUYT. Vol. III.
——— ——— ——— Voyage of the *Grace* ... up the Gulfe of S. L. ... 1594. HAKLUYT. Vol. III.
——— ———, River. LONG, J. Voyages and Travels ... with an account of the Posts situated on the River S. L., *etc.* *Lond.*, 1791.
——— ——— ——— MACKENZIE, A. Voyages ... on the River St. L. ... in 1789 and 1793, *etc.* 1801.
——— ——— ——— GOULD AND DOWIE. Instructions for making Gangs ... in the River St. L. 1832.
——— ——— ——— BAYFIELD, ADMIRAL H. W. Sailing Directions for the ... River of St. L. 1837.
——— ——— ——— ——— Maritime Positions in the ... River St. L., *etc.* 1857.
——— ——— ——— ——— St. L. Pilot, *etc.* 1860.
——— ——— ——— ——— Pilote ... du fleuve Saint-Laurent, *etc.* *Par.*, 1863.
——— ——— ——— Cartier, J. Voyages ... up the River of Canada ... 1534, 40. HAKLUYT. Vol. III.

Saint Lawrence, River.—Notes and Observations . . . for . . . the River Canada. HAKLUYT. Vol. III.

———— **Louis.**—TARVER, M. St. L., its Early History. *St. Louis*, 1849.

————, **Island.**—Sénégambie, Îles St. L. et Gorée. EYRIÈS. Vol. X.

————, ———— Durand, J. P. L. Voyage . . . from . . . St. L. to Galam, 1785-80. VOYAGES and TRAVELS. A Collection, *etc*. 1805. Vol. IV.

———— **Mary.**—DAVIE, J. C. Letters from Paraguay, describing . . . St. M., *etc.* 1805.

———— **Paul, Island.**—Prior, J. Voyage . . . to . . . St. P. . . . 1810-11. VOYAGES and TRAVELS, New. 1819. Vol. I.

———— **Peter, River.**—KEATING, W. H. Narrative of an Expedition to the Source of St. P.s River, *etc.* 1825.

———— **Petersburg.**—WRAXALL, N. A Tour through . . . St. P. 1776.

———— ———— KEPPEL, HON. G. Personal Narrative of a Journey from India . . . by . . . St. P., *etc.* 1827.

———— ———— GRANVILLE, A. B. St. Pet., *etc.* 1828.

———— ———— ABBOTT, CAPT. J. Journey from Herant to . . . St. P., *etc.* 1843.

———— ———— GALITZIN, PRINCE E. La Finlande; Notes . . . pendant une excursion de St. P. à Tornea. *Par.*, 1852.

———— ———— JERMANN, E. Pictures from St. P., *etc.* 1852.

———— ———— HELMERSEN, G. VON. Die Alexandersäule zu St. P.' *St. Pet.*, 1868.

———— ———— St. Petersburg, Voyage to, in 1814, *etc.* VOYAGES and TRAVELS, New. 1819. Vol. II.

———— **Thomá.**—*See* ST. THOME, MADRAS.

Saint Thomas, Island of.—Phillips, T. Abstract of a Voyage . . . to . . . the Island of St. T. . . . in 1693. ASTLEY. Vol. II.

———— ———— Phillips, Capt. Journal of . . . Voyage . . . to . . . the Island of S. T., *etc.* CHURCHILL. Vol. VI.

———— ———— Navegação de Lisboa á Ilha de S. Thomé, *etc.* PORTUGAL. Collecção de Noticias. *etc.* Vol. II.

———— ———— Navigatione da Lisbona all' Isola di San Thomé, *etc.* RAMUSIO. Vol. I.

———— ———— Phillips, T. Beschreibung einer Reise . . . nach . . . St. T. . . . 1693. VOYAGES and TRAVELS. Allgemeine Historie, *etc.* Vol. III.

Saint Thome, Madras.—MENDEZ PINTO, F. Historia Oriental de las peregrinaciones de F. Mendez Pinto . . . en . . . Calamiñam, *etc.* *Madrid*, 1627.

———— ———— Haiens de la Reise . . . 1670-72 . . . Verrichtungen zu St. Thomá. VOYAGES and TRAVELS. Allgemeine Historie, *etc.* Vol. VIII.

Saint Vincent.—EDWARDS, B. Historical Survey of . . . Saint Domingo . . . Also a Tour through . . . St. V., *etc.* 1801.

———— Parker, W. The Taking of St. V. . . . 1601. PURCHAS. Vol. IV.

Saint Vincent, Province.—*See* SAÕ PAULO.
Sakae, Sakair.—*See* OSACCA.
Sakhalian.—*See* SAGHALIEN.
Salado, River.—HUTCHINSON, T. J. Buenos Ayres ... with extracts from a diary of S. Exploration, *etc.* *Lond.,* **1865.**
Salamas.—SMITH, E., and DWIGHT, H. G. O. Missionary Researches ... including ... a Visit to the Nestorian ... Christians of ... Salmas, *etc.* **1834.**
Salamias.—*See* SALAMAS.
Salamina.—*See* ST. THOME.
Salangor.—ANDERSON, J. Observations ... the result of a ... Mission to ... Salengore, *etc.* *P. of. W. I.,* **1824.**
Saldanha.—Downton, N. Journal ... 1611-12. Their coming to S., *etc.* PURCHAS. Vol. I.
Saldanha Bay.—RAYMOND, W. S. B. Harbour, its special capabilities for Colonization. *Lond.,* **1867.**
——— Downton, Capt. N. Journal ... between S. B. and Socotora, *etc.* KERR. Vol. VIII.
Saldania.—*See* SALDANHA.
Salé, Salee.—*See* SALLEE.
Salem.—DYKES, J. W. B. S., an Indian Collectorate. *Lond.,* **1853.**
Salengore.—*See* SALANGOR.
Sallee.—AUTEROCHE, ABBE CHAPPE D'. A Voyage ... Also a Voyage to ... S. By M. de Cassini. *Lond.,* **1778.**
——— LEMPRIERE, W. Tour from Gibraltar to ... S., *etc.* **1791.**
Salmas.—*See* SALAMAS.
Salomon Islands.—A Fragment concerning the discovery of the Islands of S. CHURCHILL. Vol. IV.
Salop.—*See* SHROPSHIRE.
Salt Lake.—*See* GREAT SALT LAKE.
Salta.—ANDREWS, CAPT. Journey ... through ... S., *etc.* **1827.**
Salvador.—BAILY, J. Central America ... S., *etc.* **1850.**
——— SQUIER, E. G. Notes on ... San S., *etc.* *N. Y.,* **1855.**
——— BRASSEUR DE BOURBOURG, E. C. Aperçus d'un Voyage dans ... San S., *etc.* *Par.,* **1857.**
——— SCHERZER, K. VON. Travels in ... San S. **1857.**
——— TEMPSKY, G. F. VON MITLA. A Narrative of ... a Journey in ... S., *etc.* **1858.**
Salzburg.—SCHMIDL, A. A. Das Kaiserthum Oesterreich. Das Erzherzogthum Oesterreich mit S., *etc.* *Stuttg.,* **1836, 39.**
Samana.—DOMINICAN REPUBLIC, the ... and a Glance at ... S., *etc.* *Phil.,* **1852.**
Samara.—HELMERSEN, G. VON. Die Bohrversuche zur Entdeckung von Steinkohlen auf der S. halbinsel, *etc.* **1867.**

Samara, River.—HELMERSEN, G. VON. Geognostische Bemerkungen über die Steppengegend zwischen den Flüssen S., Wolga, etc.
St. Pet., **1846.**

Samarang.—STAVORINUS, J. S. Voyage . . . à S. . . . 1774-78.
Pur., **1800.**

Samarcand.—VÁMBÉRY, A. Travels . . . to . . . S., etc.
Lond., **1864.**

——— Clavijo, R. G. de. Narrative of the Embassy of, to . . . S., 1403-6. Translated, with notes . . . by C. R. Markham. 1859. HAKLUYT Soc. Pub. Vol. XXVI.

Samaria.—Biddulph, W. Travels of four Englishmen . . . into . . S. in 1600 and 1611. CHURCHILL. Vol. VII.

Samen.—FERRET, A., and Galinier. Voyage . . . dans les provinces . . . du S., etc. *Par.*, **1847.**

Samoeds.—*See* SAMOIEDIA.

Samoiedia.—Johnson, R. Landing among the Samoeds, 1556. HAKLUYT. Vol. I.

——— A Voyage . . . containing an Account of . . . S., etc.. HARRIS, J. Vol. II.

——— Samoièdes et Ostiaks, par un Anonyme. LAHARPE, J. Vol. VIII.

——— Samoiedia, a new account of, etc. PINKERTON. Vol. I.

——— Description of . . . S. . . . 1612. PURCHAS. Vol. III.

——— Neue Nachricht von Samyedien, etc. VOYAGES and TRAVELS. Allgemeine Historie, etc. Vol. XIX.

Samoyedes.—*See* SAMOIEDIA.

San Antonio, Cape.—Hawkins, Sir J. Voyages to . . . the Cape of S. Anton . . . 1562-68. HAKLUYT. Vol. III.

San Diego.—EMORY, W. H. Notes of a Military Reconnoissance from Fort Leavenworth . . . to S. D. *N. Y.*, **1848.**

——— COOKE, P. ST. G. Official Journal of a March . . . to S. D. in Upper California. *Wash.*, **1849.**

——— WHIPPLE, A. W. Report of an Expedition from S.-D. to the Colorado, etc. *Wash.*, **1851.**

——— BLAKE, W. P. Observations on . . . the Coast of California, from Bodega Bay to S. D. *Wash.*, **1855.**

San Domingo de Palenque.—DEL RIO, A. Description of the Ruins of an Ancient City discovered near P., etc. **1822.**

——— Warden, M. Description des Ruines découvertes près de P., etc. VOYAGES and TRAVELS. Recueil, etc. Vol. II.

San Francisco.—BENJAMIN, J. B. Reise in . . . S. F. *Hannov.*, **1862.**

San Juan, River.—MERCER, Hon. C. F. Report on . . . Inter-Oceanic connection . . . by the way of . . . the River St. J. *Wash.*, **1839.**

——— TRAUTWINE, J. C. Rough Notes of an Exploration . . . of the . . . S. J., etc. *Phil.*, **1854.**

San Juan de Puerto Rico.—*See* PORTO RICO.

San Juan de Ulloa.—GAGE, T. Survey of the Spanish West Indies . . . Also . . . Voyage . . . to S. John de Ulhua, etc. **1702.**

San Juan de Ulloa.—Polenham, R. Voyage to S. J. de Ulloa . . . 1564. HAKLUYT. Vol. III.
San Lorenzo, Island.—*See* MADAGASCAR.
San Marino.—BRIZI ARETINO, O. Quadro . . . della . . . Republica di S. M. *Firenze*, 1842.
——— BALBI, A. S. M. 1846.
San Remo.—DAUBENY, H. The Climate of S. R., *etc.* *Lond.*, 1865.
San Salvador, State of.—*See* SALVADOR.
San Thomé.—*See* SAINT THOMAS, ISLAND OF.
San Vicente.—*See* SAÕ PAULO.
Sanaga.—*See* SENEGAL.
Sanohi.—FERGUSSON, J. Tree and Serpent Worship . . . From the sculptures of the Buddhist Topes at S., *etc.* *Lond.*, 1868.
Sancta-Cruz.—*See* BRASIL.
Sancti Edmundi Burgus.—*See* BURY SAINT EDMUND'S.
Sancto Domingo del Darien.—*See* DARIEN, PROVINCE OF.
Sandwich Islands.—MORTIMER, G. Observations . . . during a Voyage to . . . S. I., *etc.* *Lond.*, 1791.
——— MATHISON, G. F. Narrative of a Visit to . . . the S. I., *etc.* 1825.
——— ELLIS, W. Narrative . . . with Remarks on . . . the S. I. 1826.
——— SANDWICH ISLANDS. Voyage of H.M.S. *Blonde* to the S. I. . . . 1824-25. *Lond.*, 1826.
——— JARVES, J. J. History of the S. I., *etc.* *Bost. U. S.*, 1843.
——— SIMPSON, A. The S. I. Progress of Events, *etc.* 1843.
——— CHEEVER, H. T. Life in the S. I., *etc.* 1851.
——— COKE, HON. H. J. A Ride . . . with a glance at . . . the S. I., *etc.* 1852.
——— ELLIS, W. Polynesian Researches, during a residence of nearly eight years in the . . . S. I. 1853.
——— HILL, S. S. Travels in the S. . . . I. 1856.
Santa Catharina.—BRITO, P. J. M. DE. Memoria . . . sobre . . . S. C., *etc.* *Lisb.*, 1829.
Santa Cruz.—MOROCCO. Observations on . . . Morocco . . . 1830 . . . Description of S. C., *etc. MS.*
——— LEMPRIERE, W. Tour from Gibraltar to . . . S. C., *etc.* 1791.
Santa Fé.—FALCONER, T. Expedition to S. F. An Account, *etc.* *N. Orleans*, 1842.
——— KENDALL, G. W. Narrative of an Expedition . . . from Texas to S. F., *etc.* *Lond.*, 1845.
——— COOKE, P. ST. G. Official Journal of a March from S. F. . . . to San Diego, *etc.* *Wash.*, 1849.
——— SIMPSON, J. H. Report of the Route from Fort Smith . . . to S. F., *etc.* *Wash.*, 1850.

Santa Fè.—Perkins, G. Las Colonias de S. F., etc.
Rosario de S. F., 1864.

—— Santa Fè. Registro oficial de la Provincia de S. F., etc.
S. F., 1864.

—— Burmeister, J. de. Memoria sobre . . . los Terrenos cedidos a la empresa del Ferro-Carril Central Argentino en . . . S. F.
Rosario, 1866.

Santa Fè de Bogota.—*See* Bogotá.

Santa Lucia.—Breen, H. H. St. L., etc. 1844.

—— Nicol, J. True Relation of the . . . Massacre of . . . 67 men in S. L. . . . 1605. Purchas. Vol. IV.

—— Reisen nach . . . Insel St. L., etc. Voyages and Travels. Allgemeine Historie, etc. Vol. XVII.

Santa Maria.—Julian, A. La Perla de la America, Provincia de S. M., reconocida, etc. *Madr.*, 1787.

Santa Martha.—Pizarro, F. Reisen . . . an der Kuste von St. M. . . . 1534-41. Voyages and Travels. Allgemeine Historie, etc. Vol. XV.

—— Statthalterschaften Rio de la Hacha und St. M. Voyages and Travels. Allgemeine Historie, etc. Vol. XVI.

Santa Maura.—Dapper. Naukeurige Beschryving van . . . S. M., etc.
Amst., 1688.

Santiago.—Andrews, Capt. Journey . . . to S. de Chili, etc.
1827.

—— Sherley, Sir A. Voyage to . . . S. J. . . . 1596. Hakluyt. Vol. IV.

—— Beschreibungen . . . von . . . Sant Jago. Voyages and Travels. Allgemeine Historie, etc. Vol. XV.

Santiago de Compostella.—Wey, W. The Itineraries of W. Wey . . . to Saint James of Compostella, A.D. 1456, etc. *Lond.*, 1857.

Santo Stefano.—Dapper. Beschryving van . . . S. S., etc. 1688.

Santorin.—Leycester, Lieut. Greek Inscriptions discovered in . . . S. and Milo.

Saõ Francisco, River.—Liais, E. Exploração dos Rios S. F. e Das Valhas. [*Rio de Jan.*, 1863.]

—— Burton, R. F. Explorations . . . Also, Canoeing down 1500 miles of the . . . S. F., etc. *Lond.*, 1869.

Saõ Paulo.—Gaspar, F. Memorias para a historia da Capitania de S. Vicente, hoje chamada de S. P., etc. *Lisb.*, 1797.

—— Aubertin, J. J. Eleven Days' Journey in . . . S. P., etc.
Lond., 1866.

—— Joseph de Anchieta. Epistola quamplurimarum Rerum Naturalium, quæ S. Vincentii (nunc S. Pauli) Provinciam Incolunt, sistens descriptionem. Portugal. Colleçção de Noticias. Vol. I.

Saõ Pedro do Rio Grande.—Vereker, Hon. H. P. British Shipmaster's Hand-Book to Rio Grande do Sul. 1860.

Sapienza.—Lease, W. M. On the claim to the Islands of Carvi and S.
Lond., 1850.

Saratoga Springs.—MEADE, W. An ... Inquiry into the chemical properties, &c., of the Mineral Waters of ... S., etc. *Phil.*, 1817.
—— DE VEAUX, S. The Traveller's Own Book to S. S., etc. *Buff.*, 1841.

Sarawak.—BRERETON, C. D. An Address, with a proposal for ... a Church ... at S., etc. 1846.
—— Low, H. S., its Inhabitants, etc. 1848.

Sardinia.—CHAUCHARD, CAPT. Geographical ... description of ... S., etc. *Lond.*, 1800.
—— SMYTH, ADMIRAL W. H. Sketch of the present state of ... S. 1828.
—— CASALIS, G. Diccionario geografico ... degli Stati di ... Sardegna. *Turino*, 1840-46.
—— BIONDELLI, B. Sullo stato attuale della Sardegna. *Mil.*, 1841.
—— TYNDALE, J. W. The Island of S., etc. *Lond.*, 1849.
—— HOGG, J. On the Sicilian and Sardinian languages. 1856.
—— FORESTER, T. Rambles in ... S., etc. 1858.
—— MARMORA, COUNT A. DE LA. Itinéraire de ... Sardaigne, etc. *Turin*, 1860.

Sardis.—RENNELL, J. Illustratrons ... of the ... Expedition of Cyrus from S. to Babylonia, etc. 1816.

Sark.—See SERK.

Sarmatia.—Guagnino, A. Descrittione della S. Europæa, etc. RAMUSIO. Vol. I.
—— M. di Micheovo. Descrittione delle due Sarmatie. RAMUSIO. Vol. II.

Sasardi.—PARSONS, J. West India Directory. Sailing directions from Puerto Escocés to S., etc. 1854.

Saskatchewan.—HIND, H. Y. Narrative of the ... S. Exploring Expedition of 1858. 1859.
—— DAWSON, S. J. Report on ... the Country between ... the Red River Settlement ... and S. *Toronto*, 1859.

Saugor Island.—PRINSEP, G. A. Sketch of the ... S. I. Society and its Lessees. *Calc.*, 1831.

Saugur Island.—See SAUGOR ISLAND.

Saumur.—DODIN, J. F. Recherches historiques sur ... S. *Saum.*, 1812.

Savannah.—SEWARD, W. Journal of a voyage from S. to Philadelphia, etc. *Lond.*, 1740.

Save.—SEEN, DIE, der Vorzeit in Oberkrain und die Felsenschliffe der Save, von F. B. M. *Laibach*, 1863.

Savoy.—BOURRIT, M. Journey to the Glaciers in ... S., etc. *Norwich*, 1776.
—— —— Description des ... Glaciers de Savoye. *Genève*, 1785.
—— BEAUMONT, J. F. A. Description ... de la Savoie. *Par.*, 1802-6.

Savoy.—Forbes, J. D. Travels through the Alps of S., *etc.* *Edin.*, 1843.
—— —— Norway ... with Excursions in the High Alps of ... S. *Edin.*, 1853.
—— St. John, D. Subalpine Kingdom ; or, Experiences ... In S., *etc.* 1856.
—— Favre, A. Mémoire sur les terrains liasique et keupérien de la S. *Genève*, 1859.
—— —— Recherches Géologiques dans les parties de la Savoie ... voisines du Mont Blanc, *etc.* *Par., Genève*, 1867.
Savoye.—*See* Savoy.
Sawakin.—Hamilton, J. Sinai ... Wanderings ... from S. to Chartum. 1857.
Saxon Switzerland.—*See* Saxony.
Saxony.—Saxony. Nachtrag zu dem Verzeichnisse der im Königreichs Sachsen ... abzuhaltenden Messen ... 1836-40, *etc.*
—— Charpentier, J. F. W. Mineralogische Geographie der Chur-sächsischen Lande. *Leip.*, 1778.
—— Lindau, W. A. Vergissmeinnicht. Ein Taschenbuch für den Besuch der sächsischen Schweiz, *etc.* *Dresd.*, 1823.
—— Elliott, C. B. Letters from ... S. 1832.
—— Saxony. Uebersicht der im Königreiche Sachsen bestehenden öffentlichen Gelehrtenschulen, *etc.* *Dresd.*, 1835.
—— —— Mittheilungen des Statistischen Vereins für ... Sachsen. 1834-48, *etc.* *Dresd.*, 1835-49.
—— Alphabetisches Orts-Verzeichniss des Königreichs Sachsen. *Dresd.*, 1837.
—— Saxony. Uebersicht der im Jahre 1836 in ... Sachsen ... statt-gefundenem Getreide-und Victualienpreise, *etc.* *Dresd.*, 1837.
—— Saxony. Allgemeine Uebersicht des Königreichs Sachsen in Statistischer Beziehung. *Leipz.*, 1839.
—— Schiffner, A. Beschreibung von Sachsen, *etc.* *Stuttg.*, 1840.
—— Murchison, Sir R. I. On the development of the Permian System in S., *etc.* 1842.
—— Saxony. Statistische Mittheilungen aus ... Sachsen, *etc.* *Dresd.*, 1851.
—— Browne, E. Voyage ... to Holland, with a Journey ... through ... S. ... 1668. Harris, J. Vol. II.
Saypan.—Byron, Comm. Voyage ... to ... S. ... 1764-66. Hawkesworth, J. Vol. I.
Scandaroon, Scanderun.—*See* Iskanderun.
Scandinavia.—Grænero, Count J. Scandinavia vengée de l'accusation d'avoir produit les peuples barbares qui détruisirent l'Empire de Rome. *Lyons*, 1822.
—— Forsell, C. Sverige och Norwege aller Skandinavien. *Stockh.*, 1826.
—— Clarke, E. D. Travels in ... S., *etc.* 1838.

Scandinavia — Scotland.

Scandinavia.—NILSSON, S. Report on the primitive Inhabitants of S., etc. *Lond.*, 1848.
—— LLOYD, D. S.n Adventures, etc. 1854.
—— STRUVE, O. Ueber einen vom General Schubert an die Akademie gerichteten Antrag, betreffend die Russisch-Scandinavische Meridlain-Gradmessung. 1861.
Scarborough.—AINSWORTH, W. The S. Guide. *York*, 1811.
Scarpanto.—DAPPER. Beschryving van ... Karpathos, etc. 1688.
Schaffhausen.—GEMÄLDE DER SCHWEIZ ... S., etc. *Bern*, 1834-38.
Schantaren.—*See* SHANTAR ISLANDS.
Schettland.—*See* SHETLAND ISLANDS.
Schiringsheal.—BELL, W. Ein Versuch den Ort S. ... enthaltend, etc. 1847.
—— Forster, J. R. Remarks on the situation of S., etc. KERR. Vol. I.
Schleswig-Holstein.—*See* SLESWICK and HOLSTEIN.
Schneeberg.—EMDHL, J. X. Schilderung der Gebirgs-Gegenden um den S. in Oesterreich. *Wien*, 1803.
—— SCHMIDL, A. A. Der S. in unter Oesterreich. *Wien*, 1831.
Schönbrunn.—SCHÖNBRUNN'S Pflanzengarten und Menagerie. *Wien*, 1856.
Schwalbach.—GENTH, A. The Iron Waters of S., etc. *Wiesb.*, 1855.
Schwetzingen.—SCHWETZINGEN, Description du Jardin de.
Schwyz.—GEMÄLDE DER SCHWEIZ ... S., etc. *Bern*, 1834-38.
Sciacca.—*See* XACCA.
Scilly Islands.—THOUTBECK, J. Survey and present state of the S. Islands. *Sherborne*,
—— HEATH, R. Natural ... Account of the Islands of S. 1750.
—— Heath's Account of ... S. PINKERTON. Vol. II.
Scinde.—*See* SINDE.
Scio.—BODENHAM, R. Voyage to ... Chio, 1550.
—— Voyage ... to ... Chio, about 1534. HAKLUYT. Vol. II.
—— Another Voyage unto ... Chio. 1535. HAKLUYT. Vol. II.
—— Jordan ou Jourdain Catelani, P. Mirabilia descripta, sequitur de ... Insula Chio, etc. VOYAGES and TRAVELS. Recueil, etc. Vol. IV.
Soloto.—VOLNEY, C. F. Tableau ... des Etats-Unis ... suivi d'eclaircissements ... sur la Colonie Française au S., etc. *Par.*, 1803.
Sciringes-heal.—*See* SCHIRINGSHEAL.
Sclavonia.—*See* SLAVONIA.
Scotland.—BETTS, J. Exercises on ... S., etc.
—— GLAISHER, J. On the Meteorology of S., etc.
—— SINCLAIR, SIR J. The Statistical Account of S., etc. *Edin.*, 1791.
—— FAUJAS SAINT-FOND, B. Voyage ... en Écosse, etc. *Par.*, 1797.
—— ———— Travels in ... S., etc. 1799.
—— MURRAY, HON. Mrs. S. Guide to the Beauties of S., etc. 1799.

Scotland.—Mawe, J. Mineralogy ... with a description of ... Mines in ... S., etc. **1802.**

——— Scotland, Highlands of. The Traveller's Guide through S., etc. *Edin.*, **1811.**

——— Cary, J. Itinerary of the Great Roads throughout ... S. **1812.**

——— Frank, G. Viaggio ... per una gran parte ... della Scozia, etc. *Milano*, **1813.**

——— Webster, D. Topographical Dictionary of S. *Edin.*, **1817.**

——— Sinclair, Sir J. Analysis of the Statistical Account of S., etc. *Lond.*, **1826.**

——— Scotland. Fourteenth Report ... relative to ... Roads and Bridges in S., etc. **1828.**

——— Sedgwick, A. and Murchison, Sir R. I. On the Structure ... of the Deposits ... between the Primary Rocks and the Oolitic Series in the N. of S. **1828.**

——— Scotland, Highlands of, Journal of a Tour through the ... 1829. *Norton Hall*, **1830.**

——— Scottish Tourist and Itinerary, etc. *Edin.*, **1834.**

——— Teignmouth, Lord. Sketches of the Coasts and Islands of S., etc. **1836.**

——— Scotland, Highlands of. Topographical ... Gazetteer of S. *Glasg.*, **1842.**

——— Scotland. Report ... on the Harbours of S. **1848.**

——— Johnson, A. K. Historical Notice of the progress of the Ordnance Survey in S. *Edin.*, **1851.**

——— Murchison, Sir R. I. Memoirs on the Geology of S., etc. S., etc. **1851-62.**

——— Worsaae, J. J. A. Account of the Danes and Norwegians in ... **1852.**

——— Scotland, Highlands of. Letters on the Ordnance Survey of S., etc. **1853.**

——— Black's Picturesque Tourist of S. *Edinb.*, **1859.**

——— Otter, H. C. Scotland N. W. Coast, etc. **1859.**

——— Murchison, Sir R. I. Supplemental Observations on the Order of the Ancient Stratified Rocks of the N. of S. **1860.**

——— James, Sir H. Ordnance Survey. Abstracts of the principal Lines of Spirit Levelling in S. **1861.**

——— Frickmann, M. Instructions pour la navigation de la Côte Ouest d'Écosse. *Par.*, **1869.**

——— Mohn, H. Institut Météorologique de Norvège. Température de la Mer entre l'Islande, l'Écosse, etc. *Christ.*, **1870.**

——— Ravenstein, E. G. Reisehandbuch für ... Schottland. *Hildburgh.*, **1870.**

——— Gonzales. Voyage to England and S. Pinkerton. Vol. II.

——— Pennant, T. Two Tours in S. Pinkerton. Vol. III.

Scotland.—Gleanings of a Wanderer, in . . . S. . . . 1804. Voyages and Travels. A Collection, etc. 1805. Vol. II.

——— Saussure, L. A. Necker de. Travels in S., etc. Voyages and Travels, New. 1819. Vol. VI.

———, **Western Islands of.**—*See* Hebrides.

Scosia.—*See* Scotland.

Scythia.—Rennell, J. The Geographical System of Herodotus examined . . . with dissertations on . . . the Expedition of Darius Hystaspes to S., etc. **1830.**

——— Of the . . . Scythians . . . and of their Religions. Purchas. Vol. V.

Sebastopol.—Porter, Major W. Life in the Trenches before S. **1856.**

Segestan, Seglstan.—*See* Seistan.

Seine, Department of the.—Paris. Recherches Statistiques sur . . . le Département de la S. *Par.*, **1823-29.**

——— **Inférieure.**—Noel, S. B. J. Premier Essai sur le département de la S. I., etc. *Rouen*, **1795.**

———, **River.**—Quin, M. J. Steam Voyages on the S., etc. **1843.**

Sels Alp.—Richthofen, F. F. von. Geognostische Beschreibung der Umgegend von . . . der Seissor Alpe, etc. *Gotha*, **1860.**

Seistan.—Sroistan, ovvero il Corso del Fiume Hindmend secondo Abu Ishak-el-Farssi-el-Istachri, etc. *Milano*, **1842.**

Sejistan.—*See* Seistan.

Selborne.—White, G. Natural History of S. **1813.**

Seleucia.—Mignan, R. Travels . . . with Observations on the Sites of . . . S., etc. **1829.**

Semmering.—Julius, W. A. S. und Reichenau. Führer, etc. *Wien*, **1858.**

Senega.—*See* Senegal.

Senegal.—Saugnier, M. Relations de plusieurs voyages . . . au S., etc. *Par.*, **1792.**

——— Thévenot, J. P. F. Traité des Maladies des Européens . . . au S., etc. *Par.*, **1840.**

——— Panet, M. Instructions . . . pour le Voyage de M. Panet du S. en Algérie. *Par.*, **1849.**

——— Snider-Pellegrini, A. Du Développement du Commerce de l'Algérie . . . et d'une Route . . . au S. par Tombouctou, etc. *Par.*, **1857.**

——— Faidherbe, L. Notice sur la Colonie du S., etc. *Par.*, **1859.**

——— Hutchinson, T. J. Ten Years' Wanderings . . . from S. to Gaboon. **1861.**

——— Jannequin, C. Abstract of a Voyage . . . to the Kingdom of S., etc. Astley. Vol. II.

——— Le Maire, Sieur, Voyages of, to . . . S., etc. Churchill. Vol. VIII.

——— Voyages au S. . . . Cadamosto, A. Brue. Laharpe, J. Vol. I.

Senegal—Senegambia.

Senegal.—Voyages au S. jusqu'à Sierra Leone. LAHARPE, J. Vol. II.
—— —— Adamson's Voyage to S., etc. PINKERTON. Vol. XVI.
—— —— Brüe, A. · Dritte Reise nach Sanaga, 1715. VOYAGES and TRAVELS. Allgemeine Historie, etc. Vol. II.
—— —— Eine Nachricht von dem Lande gegen Norden von Sanaga, etc. VOYAGES and TRAVELS. Allgemeine Historie, etc. Vol. II.
—— —— Jannequin, C. Auszug von einer Reisebeschreibung . . . nach . . . Sanaga . . . 1637. VOYAGES and TRAVELS. Allgemeine Historie, etc. Vol. II.
—— —— Durand, J. P. L. Voyage to S., etc. VOYAGES and TRAVELS. A Collection, etc. 1805. Vol. IV.
—— —— Durand, J. P. L. Voyage to S., 1785–86. VOYAGES and TRAVELS. A Collection, etc. 1810. Vol. I.
——, **River.**—MOLLIEN, G. Travels . . . to the Sources of the S. and Gambia, etc. 1820.
—— —— BOUET-VILLAUMEZ, COUST E. Description Nautique des Côtes . . . comprises entre le S. et l'Equateur. *Par.*, 1849.
—— —— Voyages of R. Rainolds and T. Dassel to the . . . S. . . . 1591. ASTLEY. Vol. I.
—— —— Account of the Country to the N. of the Sanaga, etc. ASTLEY. Vol. II.
—— —— —— Brue, A. Description of the . . . Sanaga, etc. ASTLEY. Vol. II.
—— —— —— First Voyage up the Sanaga in 1627. ASTLEY. Vol. II.
—— —— —— Second Voyage up the Sanaga . . . in 1698. ASTLEY. Vol. II.
—— —— —— Third Voyage up the Sanaga in 1715, etc. ASTLEY. Vol. II.
—— —— Voyages . . . containing . . . an account of the . . . Sanaga, etc. ASTLEY. Vol. II.
—— —— Mollien, M. Voyage aux sources du S. . . . 1818. EYRIÈS. Vol. XI.
—— —— Rainolds, R. and Dassel, T. Voyage to the . . . Senega . . . 1591. HAKLUYT. Vol. III.
—— —— —— Voyage to the S. . . . 1591. Kerr. Vol. VII.
—— —— Brüe, A. Beschreibung des Flusses Sanaga, etc. VOYAGES and TRAVELS. Allgemeine Historie, etc. Vol. II.
—— —— Reise auf der Sanaga, 1697. VOYAGES and TRAVELS. Allgemeine Historie, etc. Vol. II.
—— —— Le Maire. Reise nach . . . der Sanaga . . . 1682. VOYAGES and TRAVELS. Allgemeine Historie, etc. Vol. III.
—— —— A Description of the Country up the S. VOYAGES and TRAVELS. The World displayed. Vol. XVII.

Senegambia.—BRUNNER, S. Reise nach Senegambien, etc. *Bern*, 1840.
—— —— Sénégambie, Îles Saint Louis et Gorée. EYRIÈS. Vol. X.
—— —— See also GALAM.—TIMBO.

Sennaar.—Poncet, Monsieur. A Voyage to Ethiopia ... Describing ... likewise ... S., etc. *Lond.*, 1709.
―――― Dongola. Narrative of the Expedition to ... S., etc. 1822.
―――― Cailliaud, F. Voyage ... de S. à Syouah, etc. *Par.*, 1826.
―――― Werne, F. African Wanderings; or an Expedition from S. to Taka, etc. 1852.

Sennâr.—*See* Sennaar.

Serbal, Mount.—Hogg, J. Remarks on Mount S., etc. 1849.

Sercq.—*See* Serk.

Seringapatam.—Beatson, Major-Gen. A. View of the ... siege of S. 1800.

Serio.—Ponte, G. M. da. Osservazioni sul Dipartimento del S. *Bergamo*, 1803.

Serk.—Guernsey. The Guernsey Island Pilot ... S., etc. *Lond.*, 1863.

Servia.—Boué, A. Les Serbes et les Croates.
―――― Paton, A. A S., the youngest Member of the European Family, etc. *Lond.*, 1845.
―――― Ranke, L. History of S., etc. 1847.
―――― Spencer, E. Travels ... through ... S., etc. 1851.
―――― Kiss, K. Hunyadi Janos Utolsó Hadjárata Bolgár és Szerhorszá;ghan 1454-ben, etc. *Pest*, 1856.
―――― Érdy, J. A Bozma és Szerb Régi Érmek. *Pest*, 1857.
―――― Abbutenot, G. Herzegovina ... with a brief account of S., etc. 1862.
―――― Greive, W. T. The Church and People of S. Galton, F. Vacation Tourists ... in 1862-3.

Se-Shan.—Knight, S. The Coals from S.-S., etc. *Shanghai*, 1867.

Sestos, River.—*See* Sestro.

Sestro, River.—Towrson, W. Three Voyages to ... the River Sestos, 1555-57. Hakluyt. Vol. II.

Sevier, River.—Beckwith, E. G. Report of Exploration ... from the Mouth of the Kansas to S. River, etc. *Wash.*, 1854.

Seville.—Cerquero, J. S. Memoria sobre la posicion geografica de Sevilla. *S. Fernando*, 1832.

Sewalik Mountains.—Falconer, H. Descriptive Catalogue of ... Fossil Remains ... from the S. Hills, etc. *Calc.*, 1859.

Seychelles.—Mauritius. Papers ... relative to the Slave Trade at ... the S. ... 1811-25. 1826.
―――― Prior, J. Voyage ... to ... S. ... 1810-11. Voyages and Travels, New. 1819. Vol. I.

Shan States.—Williams, J. M. Memorandum on Railway Communication with ... the ... S. S. from ... Rangoon, etc. *Lond.*, 1865.
―――― Wakefield Chamber of Commerce. Direct Commerce with the S. S. ... Memorial, etc. *Lond.*, 1869.

Shannon.—Wolfe, J. Sailing Directions for the Lower S., etc. 1843.

2 D

Shanse.—RICHTHOFEN, BARON F. F. VON. Reports on the Provinces of
 . . . S. *Shangh.*, **1870.**
Shantar Islands.—MIDDENDORFF, A. T. VON. Bericht uber die Beendigung der Expedition . . . auf die Schantaren, *etc.* *St. Pet.*, **1845.**
Sheeraz.—*See* SHIRAZ.
Shetland Islands.—SINCLAIR, C. S. and the Shetlanders. *London.*
—— KERGUELEN-TRÉMAREC, M. DE. Relation d'une Voyage . . . aux Côtes . . . de Schetiland, *etc.* *Par.*, **1771.**
—— HIBBERT, S. Description of the S. I., *etc.* *Edin.*, **1822.**
—— Brand's Description of . . . S. PINKERTON. Vol. III.
Shillong.—Medlicott, H. B. Geological Sketch of the S. Plateau. INDIA, GEOLOGICAL SURVEY. Records, *etc.* Vol. II.
Shiras, Shirau, Shirauz.—*See* SHIRAZ.
Shiraz.—WARING, E. S. A Tour to S., *etc.* **1807.**
—— RICH, C. J. Narrative of . . . a Visit to S., *etc.* **1836.**
—— PELLY, L. Remarks on a recent Journey to S., *etc.* *Bomb.*, **1863.**
—— Waring, E. S. Tour to S. . . . 1802, *etc.* VOYAGES and TRAVELS. A Collection, *etc.* 1805. Vol. VI.
Shirwa, Lake.—LIVINGSTONE, D. and C. Narrative of . . . the discovery of the Lakes S. and Nyassa, *etc.* *Lond.*, **1865.**
Shoa.—HERICOURT, C. R. D'. Considérations . . . sur . . . le Royaume de Choa. *Par.*, **1841.**
—— ISENBERG, C. W. and KRAPF, J. L. Journals of . . . in S., *etc.* **1843.**
—— JOHNSTON, C. Travels . . . through . . . Adal to . . . S. **1844.**
—— HERICOURT, C. R. D'. Second Voyage . . . dans . . . le Royaume de Choa. *Par.*, **1846.**
Shropshire.—PLYMLEY, J. General View of the Agriculture of S., *etc.*
—— MURCHISON, SIR R. I. The Silurian System, founded on Geological Researches in . . . Salop, *etc.* **1839.**
—— BOTFIELD, B. S., its History, *etc.* **1860.**
Siam.—MENDEZ PINTO, F. Historia Oriental de las peregrinaciones de F. Mendez Pinto . . . en . . . Sornao, que vulgarmente se llama S., *etc.* *Madrid,* **1627.**
—— CHAUMONT, MONS. DE. Relation de l'ambassade de, à la Cour . . . de S. *Par.*, **1687.**
—— MANDELSLO, J. A. DE. Voyage . . . Contenants une description . . . de S., *etc.* *Amst.*, **1727.**
—— FINLAYSON, G. The Mission to S. . . . in 1821-2, *etc.* *Lond.*, **1826.**
—— CRAWFURD, J. Journal of an Embassy to . . . S., *etc.* **1830.**
—— EARL, G. W. The Eastern Seas . . . comprising . . . visits to . . . S. *etc.* **1837.**
—— MOOR, J. H. Notices of . . . S., *etc.* *Singapore,* **1837.**

Siam. 403

Siam.—Pallegoix, Mgr. Description du Royaume Thai ou S., etc.
Lugny, 1854.

—— Bowring, Sir J. The Kingdom ... of S., etc. 1857.

—— Spyre, R. H. F. and C. H. F. The British and China Railway; from ... Rangoon ... to S., etc. 1859.

—— Mouhot, H. Travels in the central parts of Indo-China (S.), etc.
Lond., 1864.

—— Bastian, A. Die Voelker des Oestlichen Asien, etc. (Vol. 3. Reisen in S. ... 1863.) *Leipz.,* 1866, 67.

—— Gréhan, A. Le Royaume de S. *Par.,* 1868.

—— Marten, N. Voyage of Capt. A. Hippon to ... S. in 1611. Astley. Vol. I.

—— A full ... relation of the ... Revolution in ... S., etc. Churchill. Vol. VIII.

—— Sa, P. de. Description of S. Churchill. Vol. VIII.

—— Fitch, R. The long ... voyage of ... to ... S., etc. 1583-1591. Hakluyt. Vol. II.

—— Voyage to ... S., etc. Kerr. Vol. VIII.

—— Observations sur le Royaume de S., tirées des Mémoires de Forbin. Laharpe, J. Vol. V.

—— Voyage du Père Tachard à S. Laharpe, J. Vol. V.

—— Partie Orientale des Indes. S. Laharpe, J. Vol. VI.

—— Turpin's History of S. Pinkerton. Vol. IX.

—— Floris, P. W. Extracts of his Journal ... 1610-15. Voyage to ... S., etc. Purchas. Vol. I.

—— Relation du Royaume de S. par Schouten, etc. Thevenot. Vol. I.

—— Comte et Fontaney. Reise von S. nach Ning po fu, etc. Voyages and Travels. Allgemeine Historie, etc. Vol. V.

—— Beschreibung des Königreichs S. Voyages and Travels. Allgemeine Historie, etc. Vol. X.

—— Chaumont, Ritter von. Reise nach S., 1685. Voyages and Travels. Allgemeine Historie, etc. Vol. X.

—— Fontenay, P. von. Reise von S. nach China, 1686. Voyages and Travels. Allgemeine Historie, etc. Vol. X.

—— Occum Chamnam. Reise nach S. und Portugall, 1684-86. Voyages and Travels. Allgemeine Historie, etc. Vol. X.

—— Tachard, G. Reise nach S., 1685. Voyages and Travels. Allgemeine Historie, etc. Vol. X.

—— De Challes. Letzte Nachricht von dem Schicksale der Franzosen zu S., 1690-91. Voyages and Travels. Allgemeine Historie, etc. Vol. XVIII.

—— Des Farges. Bericht von denen 1688 in S. vorgefallenen Reichsveränderungen. Voyages and Travels. Allgemeine Historie, etc. Vol. XVIII.

—— Forbin, G. von. Auszug aus der Reisebeschreibung in S., 1685-88. Voyages and Travels. Allgemeine Historie, etc. Vol. XVIII.

2 D 2

Siam.—*See also* BANGKOK.

—— , **Gulf of.**—RICHARDS, J. China Pilot. Appendix, No. I. Gulf of S., *etc.* **1858.**

Siberia.—IDES, E. Y. Three Years' Travels ... Thro' ... S., *etc.* *Lond.*, **1706.**

—— STRAHLENBERG, P. J. VON. Das Nord-und Ostliche Theil von Europa und Asia, in so weit solches ... Siberien ... begreiftet ... vorgestellet, *etc.* *Stockh.*, **1730.**

—— CHAPPE D'AUTEROCHE, J. Journey into S., *etc.* **1770.**

—— ANTIDOTE. The Antidote; or an enquiry into ... "A Journey into S., made in MDCCLXI., *etc.*" *Lond.*, **1772.**

—— SARYCHEF, CAPT. Voyages along the N.E. Coast of S. ... 1785 to 1793. *Russ.* *St. Pet.*, **1802.**

—— COXE, W. Account of ... the Conquest of S., *etc.* **1804.**

—— DOBELL, P. Travels in ... S. *etc.* **1830.**

—— LEDYARD, J. Travels ... in S., *etc.* **1834.**

—— WRANGELL, F. VON. Reise längs der Nordküste von S. ... 1820-24, *etc.* *Berlin*, **1839.**

—— MIDDENDORFF, A. T. VON. Geognostische Beobachtungen auf seiner Reise durch Sibirien, *etc.* **1840.**

—— COTTRELL, C. H. Recollections of S., *etc.* **1842.**

—— MULLER, G. F. and PALLAS, P. S. Conquest of S., *etc.* **1842.**

—— ERMAN, A. Travels in S., *etc.* **1848.**

—— PALMER, A. H. Memoir ... on the present state ... of S., *etc.* *Wash.*, **1848.**

—— HILL, S. S. Travels in S. **1854.**

—— HABERSHAM, A. W. My last Cruise ... Visits to ... S., *etc.* *Phil.*, **1857.**

—— ATKINSON, T, W. Oriental and Western S., *etc.* **1858.**

—— THOMSON, J. M. Narrative of a Voyage to ... S., *etc.* **1859.**

—— COLLINS, P. MoD. A Voyage ... with a Land Journey through S., *etc.*, *N. Y. and Lond.*, **1860.**

—— MIDDENDORFF, A. T. VON. Sibirische Reise, *etc.* *St. Pet.*, **1860.**

—— —— Über die Nothwendigkeit von Vorbereitungen für den Empfang vorweltlicher Siberischer Riesenthiere. **1860.**

—— SCHMIDT, F. B. [Historical summary of the physico-geographical investigations of the Chief of the Physical Division of the S.n Expedition, *etc.*] *Russ.* *St. Pet.*, **1866.**

—— Voyage to Sibier ... in a Letter written to Gerardus Mercator. HAKLUYT. Vol. I.

—— A Voyage ... containing an Account of ... S., *etc.* HARRIS, J. Vol. II.

—— Ysbrants Ides, E. Description of S. HARRIS, J. Vol. II.

—— —— Travels ... through ... S. ... 1692-95. HARRIS, J. Vol. II.

—— Sibérie. Voyage de Gmelin. LAHARPE, J. Vol. VIII.

Siberia — Sicily.   405

Siberia.—Willoughby, Sir H. and others. Voyages to . . . S. Pinkerton. Vol. I.
— Description of . . . S. . . . 1612. Purchas. Vol. III.
— Relation of two Russe Cossacks Travailes out of S. to Catay . . . 1610. Purchas. Vol. III.
— Chappe d'Auteroche, Abt. Auszug aus Reise nach Sibirien, 1760-61. Voyages and Travels. Allgemeine Historie, etc. Vol. XIX.
— Gmelin. Auszug aus dem Tagebuche . . . in Sibirien. 1733-43. Voyages and Travels. Allgemeine Historie, etc., Vol. XIX.
— Reise nach Kamtschatka durch Sibirien. Voyages and Travels. Allgemeine Historie, etc. Vol. XIX.
— Sarytschew, G. Account of a Voyage . . . to the N.-E. of S. . . . 1785. Voyages and Travels. A Collection, etc. 1805. Vol. V.
— — Voyage . . . to the N.E. of S. Vol. II. Voyages and Travels. A Collection, etc. 1805. Vol. VI.
— — Voyage of discovery to the N.E. of S., 1785. Voyages and Travels. A Collection, etc. 1810. Vol. VI.
— See also Berezow.
— —, **East.**—Hoffman, E. Reise nach dem Goldwäschen Ost-Sibiriens.
St. Pet., 1847.
— — Dultchef, I. Travels in E. S. Russ. St. Pet., 1856.
— — Hansteen, C., and Due, Lieut. Resultate magnetischer . . . Beobachtungen auf einer Reise nach dem östlichen Sibirien . . 1828-30. Christ., 1863.
— — Radde, G. Reisen im Süden von Ost-Sibirien . . . 1855-1859, etc. St. Pet., 1863.
— —, **West.**—Fedrow, W. Vorläufige Berichte ueber die von Ihm . . . in West-Sibirien ausgeführten astronomisch-geographischen Arbeiten, etc. St. Pet., 1838.
— — Middendorff, A. T. von. Voyage Scientifique dans la Sibérie Occidentale. 1844.
Sibler.— See Siberia.
Sichen.—Murchison, Sir R. I. On the Slaty Rocks of the S., etc. 1851.
Sicily.—Fazello, T. Historia di Sicilia, etc. Palermo, 1628.
— Callejo y Angulo, P. del. Description . . . de Sicile, etc.
Amst., 1734.
— Byng, Admiral Sir G. An Account of the Expedition of the British Fleet to S. . . . 1718-20, etc. Lond., 1739.
— Amico e Statella, V. M. Lexicon topographicum Siculum, etc.
Pan. et Catan., 1757-60.
— Brydone, P. Voyage en Sicile et à Malthe, etc. Amst., 1776.
— Bernouilli, J. Nachrichten von Italien . . . Sicilien, etc.
Leipz., 1782.
— Stolberg, Count F. L. zu. Reise in . . . Sicilien.
Königsb. u. Leip., 1794.
— Hovel's Reisen durch Sizilien, etc. Gotha, 1797.

Sicily.—Chaucharo, Capt. Geographical . . . description of . . . S., etc.
Lond., 1800.
—— Dessiou, J. F. Le Petit Neptune Français . . . with the N. Coast of S., etc. 1805.
—— Drydone, P. A Tour through S. and Malta, etc. *Lond.*, 1806.
—— Hoare, Sir R. C. Classical Tour in . . . S. 1819.
—— Ortolani, G. E. Nuovo Dizionario . . . della Sicilia, etc.
Palermo, 1819.
—— Hughes, T. S. Travels in S., etc. 1820.
—— Welz, G. de. Saggio su i mezzi da moltiplicare prontamente le ricchezze della Sicilia. *Parigi*, 1822.
—— Smyth, Admiral W. H. Memoir descriptive of . . . S., etc.
1824.
—— Knight, H. G. The Normans in S., etc. *Lond.*, 1838.
—— Ebn Khaldoun. Histoire . . . de la Sicile, sons la domination Musulmane, etc. *Par.*, 1841.
—— Hogg, J. Catalogue of Sicilian Plants; with some Remarks on . . . S. *Lond.*, 1842.
—— —— On some Grecian Antiquities observed in S. 1847.
—— —— On the Sicilian and Sardinian languages. 1856.
—— Amari, M. Bibliotheca Arabo-Sicula, etc. *Lips.*, 1857.
—— Cleghorn, H. Notes on the Botany . . . of . . . S.
Edin., 1870.
—— Hay, J. Travels through . . . S., etc. Harris, J. Vol. II.
—— Stolberg, Count F. L. Travels through . . . S. Pelham. Vol. II.
—— Benjamin, the Son of Jonas. Peregrination of . . . and relations of . . . S., etc. Purchas. Vol. II.
—— Collins, F. Voyages to . . . S., etc., 1796-1801. Voyages and Travels. A Collection, etc. 1805. Vol. X.
—— —— Voyages to . . . S., etc. 1796-1801. Voyages and Travels. A Collection, etc. 1810. Vol. VI.
—— Hoare, Sir R. C. Classical Tour through . . . S., 1790. Voyages and Travels, New. 1819. Vol. I.
—— Russell, G. Tour through S., 1815. Voyages and Travels, New. 1819. Vol. I.
—— Gourbillon, M. Travels in S. . . . 1819. Voyages and Travels, New. 1819. Vol. IV.
—— Frobin, Count de. Recollections of S., 1820. Voyages and Travels. New. 1819, etc. Vol. IX.
See also Acræ.

Siden.—Bonar, H. The Land of Promise . . . a journey from Beersheba to S. 1858.

Siebenbürgen.—*See* Transylvania.

Sierra Leone.—Falconbridge, A. M. Two Voyages to S. L., etc.
Lond., 1794.

Sierra Leone — Silesia. 407

Sierra Leone.—Sierra Leone. Accounts relating to ... the Colony of S. L. 1825.
—— Sierra Leone. Report of the Commissioners of Inquiry into the State of the Colony of S. L. 1827.
—— Sierra Leone. Papers relating to the Colony of S. L. 1830.
—— Sierra Leone. Report from the Select Committee on ... S. L., *etc.* 1830.
—— Shreeve, W. W. S. L.; the principal British Colony on the W. Coast of Africa. 1847.
—— Poole, T. E. Life in S. L., *etc.* 1850.
—— Cada Mosto, A. da. Voyage of ... P. de Cintra to S. L. Astley. Vol. I.
—— Account of the Inland Countries between S. L. and Rio ... Sestro. Astley. Vol. II.
—— The Customs ... common to the Inhabitants of Bûlmberro or S. L. Astley. Vol. II.
—— Voyages ... sur les Côtes d'Afrique jusqu'à S. L. Cadamasto, A. Brue. Labarre, J. Vol. I.
—— Voyages au Sénégal jusqu'à S. L. Labarre, J. Vol. II.
—— Finch, W. Observations ... touching S. L., in 1607, *etc.* Purchas. Vol. I.
—— Cintra, P. de. Reise ... nach S. L., 1462. Voyages and Travels. Allgemeine Historie, *etc.* Vol. II.
—— Atkins, H. Beschreibung von S. L., 1721. Voyages and Travels. Allgemeine Historie, *etc.* Vol. III.
—— Barbot, J. Beschreibung von S. L., 1678. Voyages and Travels. Allgemeine Historie, *etc.* Vol. III.
—— Finch, W. Beobachtungen über S. L., 1607. Voyages and Travels. Allgemeine Historie, *etc.* Vol. III.
—— Labat. Beschreibung von S. L. 1729. Voyages and Travels. Allgemeine Historie, *etc.* Vol. III.
—— Villault de Bellefond. Beschreibung von S. L., 1668. Voyages and Travels. Allgemeine Historie, *etc.* Vol. III.
—— **Nevada.**—Marcou, J. Geology of N. America; with Reports on ... the S. N., *etc.* *Zurich*, 1856.
—— Whitney, J. D. The Yosemite Guide-Book ... and the adjacent Region of the S. N., *etc.* *Camb.*, 1869.
Sihun.—*See* Sir-Daria.
Si Kiang.—Denham, H. M. Hydrographic Notices ... Directions for the S. K., *etc.* 1856-59.
Silesia.—Martiny, F. W. Handbuch für Reisende nach dem Schlesischen Riesengebirge, *etc.* *Breslau*, 1812.
—— Spencer, E. Travels ... including a Tour through ... S., *etc.* 1838.
—— Austel, H. Voyage ... through ... S. ... 1586. Hakluyt. Vol. II.

Silesia, Upper.—HAMMARDS. Reise durch Oberschlesien . . . nach der Ukraine. *Gotha*, 1787.

—— MAUVE, C. Erläuterungen zu der Flötzkarte des Oberschlesischen Steinkohlengebirges zwischen Bouthen, Gleiwitz, *etc.* *Bresl.*, 1860.

Silhet.—Duvaucel, A. Voyage dans le S. EYRIES. Vol. XIV.

Simcoe, Lake.—HEAD, G. Forest Scenes . . . on the Borders of Lakes Huron and S. 1829.

Simplon, Department of the.—SCHINER, M. Description du Département du S., *etc.* *Sion*, 1812.

Sina.—*See* CHINA.

Sinai.—ROBBER, D. A Journey from Naples to Jerusalem, by way of . . . the Peninsula of S., *etc.* 1845.

—— LEPSIUS, R. A Tour from Thebes to the Peninsula of S., 1845. 1846.

—— HOGG, J. Remarks on . . . the Sinaic Inscriptions. 1849.

—— FORSTER, C. The One Primeval Language traced . . . from the Rocks of S., *etc.* 1851.

—— LEFEVRE, R. Discoveries in . . . the Peninsula of S., in 1842-45, *etc.* 1852.

—— HOGG, J. Further Notice respecting the Sinaic Inscriptions. 1854.

—— LOTTIN DE LAVAL, M. Voyage dans la Péninsule Arabique du S., *etc.* *Par.*, 1855-59.

—— FORSTER, C. The Israelitish authorship of the Sinaitic Inscriptions vindicated, *etc.* 1856.

—— HAMILTON, J. S., the Hedjaz, and Soudan, *etc.* 1857.

—— STANLEY, A. P. S. and Palestine in connection with their history. *Lond.*, 1857.

—— FRAAS, O. Aus dem Orient. Geologische Beobachtungen . . . auf der S.-Halbinsel, *etc.* *Stuttgart*, 1867.

—— Tyrwhitt, R. St. J. Sinai. GALTON, F. Vacation Tourists . . . in 1862-3.

——, **Mount.**—BARTLETT, W. H. Forty days in the Desert . . . a Journey . . . to Mount S., *etc.*

—— —— CLOONER, ROBERT, BISHOP OF. A Journal from Grand Cairo to Mount S., *etc.* *Lond.*, 1753.

—— —— MACNDBELL, H. Journey . . . from Grand Cairo to Mount S., *etc.* 1810.

—— —— HENNIKER, SIR F. Notes during a Visit to . . . M. S., *etc.* 1824.

—— —— LABORDE, N. L. DE. Journey . . . to Mount S., *etc.* 1836.

—— —— BEKE, C. T. On . . . the situation of Mount S. 1838.

—— —— ROBINSON, E. Biblical Researches in . . . Mount S., *etc.* 1841.

Sinai, Mount.—HOGG, J. On the Geography . . . of the Peninsula of Mount S., etc. *Edinb.*, 1850.
—— —— CLAYTON, Dr. R. Journal from Grand Cairo to M. S., etc. *Lond.*, 1853.
—— —— HARANT, K. Gesta . . . do . . . S., etc. *v. Praze*, 1854.
—— —— BEKE, C. T. A few words . . . on . . . the position of Mount S. 1862.
—— —— Cairo, Journey from, to Mount S. PINKERTON. Vol. X.
—— —— Mount Sinai . . . described out of . . . Breidenbach, etc. PURCHAS. Vol. II.
—— —— Fazakerley, J. N. Journey from Suez to Mount S. WALPOLE, R. Travels, etc.

Sinde.—POTTINGER, H. Travels in . . . S., etc. 1816.
—— BURNES, J. A Narrative of a Visit to the Court of S., etc. *Edin. and Lond.*, 1831.
—— BRUNTON, J. Description of the . . . S. Railway, etc. 1839.
—— BURNES, SIR A. Leech, Lord, and Woods; Reports . . . on Scinde, etc. *Calc.*, 1839.
—— OUTRAM, J. Rough Notes of the Campaign in S. . . . in 1838-9. 1840.
—— JERVIS, T. B. Review of a Narrative of the Campaign . . . in S. . . . 1838-39. *Bomb.*, 1841.
—— POSTANS, T. Personal Observations on S., etc. 1843.
—— THORNTON, E. Gazetteer of . . . S., etc. 1844.
—— VON ORLICH, L. Travels in India, including S., etc. 1845.
—— BURTON, R. F. Scinde; or the Unhappy Valley. 1851.
—— NAPIER, SIR W. History of General Sir C. Napier's administration of Sind, etc. *Lond.*, 1851.
—— ELLIOTT, SIR H. Appendix to the 'Arabs in S.,' etc. *Cape Town*, 1853.
—— ANDREW, W. P. The Scinde Railway, etc. 1856.
—— INDIA. Geological Papers on W.n India, including . . . S., etc. *Bomb.*, 1857.
—— INDIA. Tables of Heights in S., etc. *Calcutta*, 1863.
—— SCINDE RAILWAY . . . Reports of the Directors . . . Sept. 1863. 1863.
—— WALKER, J. T. Tables of Heights in S., etc. *Calc.*, 1863.
—— BURGESS, J. Memorandum . . . with lists of the Rock-Excavations, Temples, &c. in Sindh, etc. *Bombay*, 1870.
—— Sindhy. EYRIKA. Vol. XIV.

Sindh, Sindhy.—*See* SINDE.

Singapore.—BENNETT, G. Wanderings in . . . S., etc. 1834.
—— EARL, G. W. The Eastern Seas . . . also an Account of . . . S., etc. 1837.

Singapore.—Parker, P. Journal of an Expedition from S. to Japan, etc.
1838.
—— Davidson, G. F. Trade and Travel . . . Recollections of . . . S., etc.
Lond., 1846.
—— Waghorn, T. Two Letters on the extension of Steam Navigation from S. to Port Jackson, etc.
1846, 47.
—— Berncastle, Dr. A Voyage to China; including a Visit to . . . S., etc.
Lond., 1850.
—— Elliott, C. M. Meteorological Observations made . . . at S., 1841-45.
Madras, 1850.
—— Cameron, J. Our Tropical Possessions . . . being a descriptive Account of S., etc.
Lond., 1865.
—— Jagor, F. S. . . . Reiseskizzen.
Berl., 1866.

Singbhum.—See Singhbhoom.

Singhbhoom.—Ball, V. On the Occurrence of Gold in the District of S., etc. India, Geological Survey. Records, etc. Vol. II.

Sino Persico.—See Persian Gulf.

Sloot.—See Siut.

Siouah.—See Siwah.

Siout.—See Siut.

Sir.—See Sir-Daria.

Sir-Daria.—Lobysevitsch, T. La Ligne Militaire du Syr-D.
St. Pet., 1865.

Sirhind.—Lloyd, Sir W. Narrative of a Journey . . . viâ . . . S., etc.
Lond., 1840.

Siria.—See Syria.

Siriana.—Ides, E. Y. Three Years' Travels . . . Thro' . . . S., etc.
Lond., 1706.
—— Ysbrants Ides, E. Travels . . . through . . . S. . . . 1692-95.
Harris, J. Vol. II.

Siut.—Cuny, C. Journal de Voyage de S. à El-Obéid 1857, 58, etc.
Par., 1863.
—— Drovetti. Itinerary . . . from S. to Dongolah, etc. Voyages and Travels, New. 1819. Vol. VII.

Siwah.—Siouah, Fezzan, et Intérieur de l'Afrique. Eyriès. Vol. XIV.
—— Schulz, J. M. A. Travels in . . . S. . . . 182L Voyages and Travels, New. 1819, etc. Vol. VIII.

Skaraborg.—Topografiska och Statistiska Uppgifter om S.s Län.
Stockh., 1845.

Skardo.—See Iskardoh.

Sla.—See Sallee.

Slavonia.—Safarík, P. J. Slowansky Národopis.
Praze, 1849.
—— Dolena, J. V. Travels in . . . S. . . . in 1806. Pelham. Vol. II.

Sleswick.—Sleswick. On Nationality and Language in . . . S. or South Jutland.
Copenh., 1848.

Sleswick.—Hafn, C. C. Inscriptions Runiques du Sleswick Méridional interprétées, etc. *Copenh.*, 1861.
—— **and Holstein.**—Scott, C. H. Danes and the Swedes . . . Including Schleswig-H., etc. 1856.
—— —— Paton, J. On the Sea Dykes of Schleswig and H., etc.
Land. On reclaiming Land, etc.
Smyrna.—Price, W. Journal of Travels of the British Embassy to . . . S., etc. 1833.
—— Vernon, F. Travels . . . to S. Ray, J.
—— Browne, W. G. Price of Commodities at S., in 1780, 1790, 1800, and 1812. Walpole, R. Travels, etc.
Snake Island.—*See* Anguilla.
Soane Valley.—Hooker, J. D. Observations made . . . in the S. V., etc. *Calc.*, 1848.
Söborg.—Frederick VII., King of Denmark. Vestiges d'Asserbo et de S., découverts par . . . Frédéric VII., etc. *Copenh.*, 1855.
Socatora.—*See* Socotra.
Society Islands.—Ellis, W. Polynesian Researches, during a residence of nearly eight years in the S. . . . I., etc. 1853.
—— Hill, S. S. Travels in the . . . S. I. 1856.
Socotora.—*See* Socotra.
Socotra.—Wellsted, J. R. Travels . . . including . . . a Tour on the Island of S. 1840.
—— —— Ward, C. Y. Pilote du Golfe d'Aden, Sokotra, etc. *Par.*, 1866.
—— Downton, N. Journal . . . between Saldanha Bay and S., etc. Kerr. Vol. VIII.
—— Eighth Voyage, in 1611. . . . Occurrences at S., etc. Kerr. Vol. VIII.
—— Downton. N. Journal . . . 1611-12. Their coming . . . to S., etc. Purchas. Vol. I.
—— Finch, W. Observations . . . touching . . . S., etc. Purchas. Vol. I.
Sodom.—Saulcy, F. de. Narrative . . . including an account of the discovery of the Sites of S. and Gomorrah, etc. 1854.
Sokotra.—*See* Socotra.
Solor.—Benachbarte Eylande um Timor und S. Voyages and Travels. Allgemeine Historie, etc. Vol. XVIII.
Solothurn.—Gemälde der Schweiz . . . S., etc. *Bern*, 1834-38.
Somali.—Waan, C. Y. Pilote du Golfe d'Aden . . . Côtes de S., etc. *Par.*, 1866.
Somers' Islands.—*See* Bermuda Islands.
Somma, Mount.—Scacchi, A. Sopra le specie di Silicati del Monte di S., etc. *Nap.*, 1852.
Somme, Department of the.—Somme, Department of the. Notions générales sur la Géologie . . . de la S. *Abbeville* [1857.]
Somnath.—Burgess, J. Notes of a Visit to S., etc. *Bombay*, 1869.

Sonde.—*See* SONDA.

Söndmör.—STRÖM, H. Physisk ... Beskrivelse over Fogderiet S., *etc.*
Sorōe, 1762.

Sonora.—BARTLETT, J. R. Personal ... explorations ... in ... S., *etc.*
N. Y., 1854.

—— MOWRY, S. The Geography and Resources of ... S., *etc.*
San F. and N. Y., 1863.

—— MALTE-BRUN, V. A. La S. et ses Mines, *etc.* *Par.*, 1864.

Sooloo.—*See* SULU ISLANDS.

Soongaria.—LEDEBOUR, C. F. VON. Reise durch ... die Soongarische Kirghisen-Steppe.
Berl., 1829.

Soria.—*See* SYRIA.

Sornao.—*See* SIAM.

Sorrento.—PUGAARD, C. Description géologique de la Péninsule de S., *etc.*
Copenh. et Leip., 1856.

—— Notice sur les calcaires plutonisés de la Péninsule de S.
Par., 1859.

Soudan.—HODGSON, W. B. Remarks on the recent Travels of Dr. Barth in ... S.

—— LYON, G. F. Narrative ... with geographical Notices of S., *etc.*
1821.

—— HODGSON, W. B. Notes on ... the S., *etc.* *N. Y.*, 1844.

—— CHURI, J. H. Sea Nile ... and Nigritia, *etc.* *Lond.*, 1853.

—— LAUTURE, COUNT D'ESCAYRAC DE. Le Désert et le S. Études, *etc.*
Par., 1853.

—— TRÉMEAUX, M. Voyage au S. Oriental ... 1847-48. *Par.*, 1853.

—— ST. JOHN, B. Travels of an Arab Merchant in S., *etc.*
Lond., 1854.

—— BRUN-ROLLET, M. Le Nil Blanc et le S., *etc.* *Par.*, 1855.

—— LAUTURE, COUNT D'ESCAYRAC DE. Mémoire sur le S., *etc.*
Par., 1855-56.

—— HAMILTON, J. Sinai, the Hedjaz and S., *etc.* 1857.

—— CUNY, C. Observations générales sur le Mémoire sur le S. de M. le Comte d'Escayrac de Lauture.
Par., 1858.

—— PETHERICK, J. Egypt, the S., *etc.* *Edin. and Lond.*, 1861.

—— STUCKLÉ, H. Le Commerce de la France avec le S. *Par.*, 1864.

—— HEUGLIN, M. T. VON. Reise nach ... Ost-Sudán, *etc.*
Jena, 1868.

—— *See also* HORNIA.

Sound.—LÖVENORN, CHEV. DE. New Sailing Directory for the ... S., *etc.*
1844.

—— Sound. Letters on the S.-Dues Question, *etc.* *N. Y.*, 1855.

—— Oether. Second Voyage into the S., *etc.* HAKLUYT. Vol. I.

—— Wolstana. Navigation into the East Sea, or the S., *etc.* HAKLUYT. Vol. I.

Soungaria.—*See* SOONGARIA.
South.—Reisen nach den Sudländern, Pelfart, 1629.—Tasmann, 1642-3.—Dampier, 1699-1700. Reise zweyer Französischen Schiffe nach den S. VOYAGES and TRAVELS. Allgemeine Historie, *etc*. Vol. XII.

—— Solis, J. Diaz de. Letzte Reise und Entdeckungen nach Süden, 1516. VOYAGES and TRAVELS. Allgemeine Historie, *etc*. Vol. XIII.

—— Gonneville, B. P. Erste Entdeckung der Südlichen Welt, 1504. VOYAGES and TRAVELS. Allgemeine Historie, *etc*. Vol. XVIII.

—— Vesputius, A. Erste Entdeckung der Südlichen Welt, 1502. VOYAGES and TRAVELS. Allgemeine Historie, *etc*. Vol. XVIII.

—— Vlaming, W. Reise nach den Südländern, 1696. VOYAGES and TRAVELS. Allgemeine Historie, *etc*. Vol. XVIII.

South African Republic.—*See* TRANSVAAL REPUBLIC.
South Pole.—BISCOE, J. Journal of a Voyage towards the S. P. . . . 1830-32. *MN*.

—— COOK, CAPT. J. Voyage towards the S. P., *etc*. 1777.

—— —— Voyages dans l'Hemisphère Austral, *etc*. *Par*., 1778.

—— WEDDELL, J. Voyage towards the S. P., 1822-24, *etc*. 1827.

—— D'URVILLE, ADMIRAL J. D. Expédition au Pole Antarctique, *etc*. *Par*., 1840.

—— —— Voyage au Pole Sud . . . pendant 1837-40, *etc*. *Par*., 1843.

South Sea.—*See* PACIFIC OCEAN.
South Sea Islands.—*See* POLYNESIA.
Southampton.—BULLAR, J. Hints to assist . . . Visitors . . . in S., *etc*. *South*., 1846.

Spa.—SPA. Le Guide des Curieux qui visitent les Eaux de S. *Verviers*, 1814.

—— BILDERBECK, L. VON. Wegweiser für . . . Anchen . . . nebst einem Ausflug nach S. *Aachen*, 1825.

—— SPA. Guide aux Eaux et aux Jeux de S. *Spa*, 1885.

Spahan.—*See* ISPAHAN.
Spain.—MARTYR, P. De rebus Oceanicis . . . Item de rebus . . . Hispanicis opuscula. *Colonia*, 1574.

—— LAET, J. DE. Hispania, *etc*. *Lugd. Bat*., 1629.

—— GAGE, T. Survey of the Spanish West Indies . . . Also . . . Voyage from S. to S. John de Ulhua, *etc*. 1702.

—— VAYRAC, ABBÉ DE. État présent de l'Espagne. *Amst*., 1719.

—— BOWLES, W. Introduccion á la Historia Natural y á la Geografía . . . de España. *Madr*., 1775.

—— DILLON, J. T. Travels through S., *etc*. *Lond*., 1782.

—— TOFIÑO DE SAN MIGUEL, V. Derrotero de las Costas de España en el Mediterraneo, *etc*. *Madr*., 1787.

—— TOWNSEND, J. A Journey through S. in 1786-87, *etc*. *Lond*., 1792.

Spain.

Spain.—SPAIN. Ordenanza General de Correos, Postas, Caminos, etc.
Madrid, 1794.

—— BOURGOING, J. F. Tableau de l'Espagne moderne. *Par.*, 1797.

—— FISCHER, F. A. Travels in S. in 1797 and 1798. 1802.

—— SPAIN. Diccionario Geográfico Histórico de España.
Madrid, 1802.

—— LABORDE, COUNT A. DE. View of S., etc. 1809.

—— JACOB, W. Travels in the South of ... S. 1811.

—— TOFIÑO DE SAN MIGUEL, V. España Maritima, or Spanish Coasting Pilot, etc. 1814.

—— MURPHY, J. C. History of the Mahometan Empire in S., etc.
1816.

—— AMERICA, SPANISH. Outline of ... War ... between S. and Spanish American, etc. 1817.

—— ANTILLON, I. Géographie ... de l'Espagne, etc. *Par.*, 1823.

—— SPAIN. Atlas del Itinerario Descriptivo de España, etc.
Valencia, 1826.

—— MIÑAÑO, S. DE. Diccionario ... de España y Portugal.
Madr., 1826-28.

—— LABORDE, COUNT A. DE. Itinéraire descriptif de l'Espagne, etc.
Par., 1827-30.

—— SUCHET, LE MARÉCHAL. Mémoires sur ses campagnes en Espagne 1808-14. *Par.*, 1828.

—— CABANES, F. X. DE. Guia general ... de España. *Mad.*, 1830.

—— BROOKE, SIR A. DE C., BART. Sketches in S., etc. 1831.

—— BECKFORD, W. Italy; with Sketches of S., etc. 1834.

—— COOK, S. E. Sketches in S. in 1829-32. 1834.

—— WELLINGTON, DUKE OF. Despatches, during his ... Campaigns in ... S., etc. 1837-39.

—— SANTAREM, VISCOUNT DE. L'Introduction des procédés relatifs à la Fabrication des Etoffes de Soie dans la Péninsule Hispanique, sous la domination des Arabes. *Par.*, 1838.

—— BORROW, G. Zincali, or an account of the Gypsies of S. 1843.

—— MADOZ, P. Diccionario ... de España, etc. *Mad.*, 1846.

—— RÓNAY, J. Jellemisme, vagy az ... Spanyol Nemzet ... Jellemzése, etc. *Györött*, 1847.

—— FRANCE. The Lighthouses on the N. and W. Coasts of ... S. ... Corrected to 1848, 52, 53, 54, 56, 57. 1848-57.

—— URQUHART, D. The Pillars of Hercules; or, a narrative of travels in S., etc. *Lond.*, 1850.

—— DIX, J. A. A Winter in Madeira and a Summer in S., etc.
N. Y., 1851.

—— HOSKINS, G. A. S. as it is. 1851.

—— TORRE, J. M. DE LA. Nuevo Compendio de Geografía ... de la Monarquía Española. *Habana*, 1852.

Spain.—Powrs, W. T. Recollections . . . including Peregrinations in S., etc. Lond., 1853.
―― Hammer-Purgstall, Baron. Über die Arabische Geographie von Spanien. Wien, 1854.
―― Coello, F. Projecto de las lineas generales de Navegacion y de Ferro-Carriles en la Peninsula Española. Madr., 1855.
―― Murray. Hand-Book for Travellers in S., etc. Lond., 1855.
―― Verneuil, M. de. Notes pour accompagner le Tableau Orographique d'une partie de l'Espagne. Par., 1855.
―― ―― and others. Note sur les progrès de la Géologie en Espagne pendant 1854. Caen, 1855.
―― Spain. Border Lands of S. and France, etc. 1856.
―― Adolphus, J. L. Letters from S., etc. 1858.
―― Avezac, d'. Les Voyages de A. Vespuce au compte de l'Espagne, etc. 1858.
―― Spain. Censo de la Poblacion de España 1857, etc. Madrid, 1858.
―― ―― Nomenclátor de los Pueblos de España, etc. Madrid, 1858.
―― Coello, F. and others. Reseñas geográfica, geologica, y agrícola de España. Madr., 1859.
―― France. The Admiralty List of the Lights of the N. and W. Coasts of . . . S. . . . Corrected to 1859. 1859.
―― Murray, Mrs. E. Sixteen Years . . . in . . . S., etc. 1859.
―― Andros, A. C. Pen and Pencil Sketches of a Holiday Scamper in S. Lond., 1860.
―― Dunsterville, F. The Admiralty List of the Lights on the N. and W. Coasts of . . . S. . . . Corrected to 1860, 61, 62. 1860-62.
―― Spain. Anuario Estadistico de España, 1859-61, etc. Madrid, 1860-63.
―― Vignoles, C. International Exhibition of 1862 . . . Model of the Passage of the Tudela and Bilbao Railway . . . through the Basque Provinces in the N. of S. Lond., 1862.
―― Gras, M. A. le. Phares des Côtes . . . Ouest d'Espagne . . . Corrigés 1862-64. Par., 1862-64.
―― Markham, C. R. Report on the Irrigation of E. n S. Lond. [1867.]
―― Edwards, M. B. Through S. to the Sahara. Lond., 1868.
―― Spain. Censo de la Ganaderia de España . . . 1865, etc. Madrid, 1868.
―― ―― A Winter Tour in S., etc. Lond., 1868.
―― Delamarre, C. La Situation économique de l'Espagne, etc. Par., 1869.
―― Gras, A. le. Phares . . . des Côtes Ouest d'Espagne, etc. Par., 1869.
―― ―― Routier des Côtes N. O., Ouest et Sud d'Espagne. Par., 1869.

Spain.

Spain.—MURRAY's HANDBOOKS. A Handbook for Travellers in S., etc.
Lond., 1869.

—— Sepp, F. F. A. and Behme, A. Account of a voyage from S. to Paraquaria. CHURCHILL. Vol. IV.

—— Drake, Sir F. Voyage to Cadiz ... and ... other places upon the Coast of S. and Portugale ... 1587. HAKLUYT. Vol. II.

—— Gurney, M. Voyage against the Moores of Algir to ... S. HAKLUYT. Vol. II.

—— Voyage ... to the Coast of S. ... 1591. Reported by R. Flick. HAKLUYT. Vol. II.

—— Voyage to S. and Portugale, written (as it is thought) by Colonel A. Wingfield, 1589. HAKLUYT. Vol. II.

—— True Coppie of a Discourse written by a Gentleman, employed in the late Voyage of Spanie and Portingale, 1589. HAKLUYT. Vol. V.

—— Benjamin, Rabbi. Travels ... from S. to China, 1160-1173. HARRIS, J. Vol. I.

—— Travels through ... S. ... by an English Gentleman, 1693. HARRIS, J. Vol. II.

—— Willoughby, F. Travels through S., 1664. HARRIS, J. Vol. II.

—— Benjamin, Rabbi. Travels from S. to China in the twelfth century. KERR. Vol. I.

—— Dillon, J. T. Travels through S., etc. PELHAM. Vol. II.

—— Bourgoanne's Travels in S. PINKERTON. Vol. V.

—— Folque, F. Reflexões acerca ... dos Dominios de ... Hespanha na America Meridional. PORTUGAL. Colecção de Noticias, etc. Vol. VII.

—— Willughby, F. Travels through great part of S. RAY, J.

—— Spain and Portugal, a Tour through ... 1803, etc. VOYAGES and TRAVELS. A Collection, etc. 1805. Vol. III.

—— Semple, R. Observations on a Journey through S. ... 1805. VOYAGES and TRAVELS. A Collection, etc. 1805. Vol. VIII.

—— Beargoing, J. F. Travels in S. ... down to 1806. VOYAGES and TRAVELS. A Collection, etc. 1805. Vol. IX.

—— Collins, F. Voyages to ... S., etc. 1796-1801. VOYAGES and TRAVELS. A Collection, etc. 1805. Vol. X.

—— Bourgoing, J. F. Travels in S., 1806. VOYAGES and TRAVELS. A Collection, etc. 1810. Vol. II.

—— Collins, F. Voyages to ... S., etc. 1796-1801. VOYAGES and TRAVELS. A Collection, etc. 1810. Vol. VI.

—— Semple, R. Journey through S. and Italy. VOYAGES and TRAVELS. A Collection, etc. 1810. Vol. VI.

—— Spain and Portugal, a Tour through ... 1803. VOYAGES and TRAVELS. A Collection, etc. 1810. Vol. VI.

—— Bowring, J. Observations on ... S., made ... in 1819. VOYAGES and TRAVELS, New. 1819. Vol. III.

—— Graham, W. Travels through ... S. ... 1812-14. VOYAGES and TRAVELS, New. 1819. Vol. III.

Spain.—A description of S. and Portugal. VOYAGES and TRAVELS. The World displayed. Vol. XX.

Spanie.—*See* SPAIN.

Spanyol Nemzet.—*See* SPAIN.

Spartel, Cape.—AFRICA. New Sailing Directions . . . from Cape S. . . . to the Cape of Good Hope, *etc.* **1799.**

——— ——— ——— African Pilot . . . from Cape S. to the River Cameroons. **1856.**

——— ——— Report of the casting away of the Ship *Tobie*, neere Cape Espartel . . . 1593. HAKLUYT. Vol. III.

Spartivento, Cape.—DESSIOU, J. F. Le Petit Neptune Français . . . the Coast of Italy, from the River Var to Cape S., *etc.* **1805.**

Spencer's Gulf.—SHÜRMANN, C. W. Vocabulary of the Parnkalla Language, spoken by the Natives inhabiting the Western Shores of S. G., *etc.* *Adel.,* **1844.**

Spetsbergen.—*See* SPITZBERGEN.

Speyer.—SPEYER UND OGGERSHEIM. Bericht und Vollständiges Messungs-Protocoll, sammt allen Berechnungen über die im Jahre 1819 zwischen S. und Oggersheim gemessene Grund-Linie. *MS.* **1819.**

Spice Islands.—*See* MOLUCCA ISLANDS.

Spitzbergen.—FABVRE, CAPIT. Retour en France de . . . *la Recherche*; Rapport sur la seconde campagne . . . au Spitzberg. *Par.,* **1839.**

——— DUFFERIN, LORD. Letters . . . being an Account of . . . S., *etc.* **1857.**

——— LANDTAGEN, D. G. Geografiska Ortsbestämningar på Spetsbergen af Prof. A. E. Nordenskiöld, *etc.* *Stockh.,* **1863.**

——— NORDENSKIÖLD, A. E. Geografisk och grognostisk Beskrifning öfver Nordöstra Delarne af Spetsbergen, *etc.* *Stockh.,* **1863.**

——— Two Journals . . . The second, kept . . . in 1633-4 . . . at S. CHURCHILL. Vol. II.

——— Veer, G. de. True Description of three Voyages . . . by the Dutch in 1594-96; with their discovery of S. . . . Edited by C. T. Beke. 1853. HAKLUYT Soc. PUB. Vol. XIII.

——— Collection of Documents on S. and Greenland. Edited . . . by A. White. 1855. HAKLUYT Soc. PUB. Vol. XVIII.

——— History of . . . S. . . . 1596-1746. HARRIS, J. Vol. II.

——— Backstrom's Voyage to S. PINKERTON. Vol. I.

——— Spitzbergen, Journal of seven Seamen left at. PINKERTON. Vol. I.

——— Marten, F. Observations made in S., *etc.* 1711. VOYAGES. Account of several late, *etc.*

——— Beschreibung . . . von S. VOYAGES and TRAVELS. Allgemeine Historie, *etc.* Vol. XVII.

———, **East.**—STÆHLIN, J. VON. An Account, *etc.* (Adventures of Four Russian Sailors . . . on the desert Island of East-S. By P. L. Le Roy, *etc.*) *Lond.,* **1774.**

Spitzbergen, East.—Le Roy's Narrative of Four Russian Sailors cast upon the Island of E. S. PINKERTON. Vol. I.

——— **Sea.**—See ARCTIC OCEAN.

Spoleto.—SPOLETO. [Istoria]. Orazione Academica. *Spol.*, 1838.

Stafford.—MURCHISON, SIR R. I. The Silurian System, founded on Geological Researches in . . . S., *etc.* 1839.

Staten Island.—FITZROY, REAR-ADML. R. Sailing Directions for . . . S. I., *etc.* 1848.

States of the Church.—CALINDRI, G. Saggio statistico-storico del Stato Pontificio. *Perugia*, 1829.

——— MURCHISON, SIR R. I. On the Earlier Volcanic Rocks of the Papal States, *etc.* 1850.

——— Ray, J. Travels through . . . the Ecclesiastical State, *etc.* HARRIS, J. Vol II.

Stato Pontificio.—See STATES OF THE CHURCH.

Stenosa.—Sibthorp, Dr. Voyage . . . S., *etc.* WALPOLE, R. Travels, *etc.*

Steppes.—POTOCKI, COUNT J. Voyage dans les Steps d'Astrakhan et du Caucase, *etc.* *Par.*, 1829.

——— GOEBEL and others. Reise in die Steppen des Südlichen Russlands. *Dorpat*, 1838.

——— HELMERSEN, G. VON. Geognostische Bemerkungen über die Steppengegend zwischen den Flüssen Samara, Wolga, *etc.* *St. Pet.*, 1846.

——— HELL, X. H. DE. Travels in the S. of the Caspian Sea, *etc.* 1847.

——— NÖSCHEL, A. Bemerkungen über die Naturhistorischen . . . Verhältnisse der Steppe zwischen den Flüssen Or und Turgai, *etc.* *St. Pet.*, 1856.

——— MARNI, N. BARBOT DE. Beschreibung der Astrachankischen oder Kalmücken-Steppe. *St. Pet.*, 1863.

———, **Kirghis.**—LEDEBOUR, C. F. VON. Reise durch . . . die Soongarische Kirgisen-Steppe. *Berl.*, 1829.

——— ——— BAER, K. E. VON. Klima der Kirgisen-Steppe. 1840.

——— ——— LEVCHINE, A. DE. Description des Hordes et des Steppes des Kirghiz-Kazaks, *etc.* *Par.*, 1840.

——— ——— HELMERSEN, G. VON. Reise nach . . . der Kirgisensteppe . . . 1835. 1841.

——— ——— LEVCHINE, A. DE. Descrizione delle Orde e delle Steppe dei Kirghizi-Kazaki, *etc.* *Mil.*, 1840.

——— ——— BASINER, T. F. J. Naturwissenschaftliche Reise durch die Kirgisensteppe nach Chiwa. *St. Pet.*, 1848.

——— ——— ATKINSON, T. W. Oriental . . . Siberia . . . Adventures in . . . the K. S., *etc.* 1858.

———, **Tartar.**—ATKINSON, Mrs. Recollections of T. S., *etc.* 1862.

Steyermark.—See STYRIA.

Stockholm.—WRAXALL, N. A Tour through . . . S., *etc.* 1776.

Stone.—SMYTH, ADMIRAL W. H. Letter on a "Double Faced" Brass in S. Church, *etc.* 1860.

Stone.—SMYTH, ADMIRAL W. H. A Word more on the "Double-Faced" Brass in S. Church, *etc.* 1861.

Styria.—KLETLE, F. F. Rückerinnerungen an eine Reise in ... Steyermark ... 1810. *Wien,* 1814.

—— SEDGWICK, A., and MURCHISON, SIR R. I. A Sketch ... with Sections ... through the Tertiary Deposits of S., *etc.* 1831.

—— WEIDMANN, F. C. Darstellungen aus dem Steyermärkischen Oberlande. *Vienna,* 1834.

—— SCHMIDL, A. A. Das Kaiserthum Oesterreich ... Das Erzherzogthum Stelermark. *Stuttg.,* 1836, 39.

—— KOHL, J. G. Austria ... S., *etc.* *Lond.,* 1844.

—— BROWNE, E. Journey ... through S., *etc.* HARRIS, J. Vol. II.

—— Salvo, Marquis de. Travels ... through ... S. ... 1806. VOYAGES and TRAVELS. A Collection, *etc.* 1805. Vol. VI.

——, **Lower.**—HALL, D. Schloss Hainfeld; or a Winter in L. S. 1836.

Sudetes.—ASSMANN, C. G. De Itinere per Montes Sudetos, *etc.* *Viteb.,* 1789.

Suez.—DARBY, G. F. Notes on S., *etc.* *Constant.,* 1859.

—— Voyage of Don S. de Gama, from Goa to S. in 1540, *etc.* ASTLEY. Vol. I.

—— Voyage of Soleyman Basha, from S. to India ... 1539. ASTLEY. Vol. I.

—— Castro, J. de. Voyage of Don S. de Gama from Goa to S., in 1540, *etc.* KERR. Vol. VI.

—— Particular Relation of the Expedition of Solyman Pacha from S. to India, *etc.* KERR. Vol. VI.

—— Castro, J. Voyage which the Portugals made from India to Zoez, 1540-41. PURCHAS. Vol. II.

—— Fazakerley, J. N. Journey from S. to Mount Sinai. WALPOLE, R. Travels, *etc.*

——, **Isthmus of.**—MEREWETHER, W. L. [Report on places lately visited, between Aden and S.]

—— RENNELL, J. The Geographical System of Herodotus examined ... with dissertations on the ... Canal of S., *etc.* 1830.

—— LATRONNE. L'Isthme de S. Le Canal ... sous les Grecs, les Romains et les Arabes. *Par.,* 1841.

—— GALLOWAY, J. A. Communication with India ... with remarks on ... the S. Railroad. 1844.

—— SUEZ. Société d'Études de l'Isthme de S. ... Travaux ... Rapport, *etc.* *Par.,* 1847.

—— LESSEPS, F. DE. The I. of S. Question. 1855.

—— —— New Facts and Figures relative to the I. of S. Canal, *etc.* 1856.

—— —— Percement de l'Isthme de S. Rapport, *etc.* *Par.,* 1856.

Suez, Isthmus of — Sulu Islands.

Suez, Isthmus of.—Suez. Compagnie Universelle du Canal Maritime de S. Firman de Concession, etc. *Par.,* 1856.

——— ——— Griffith, C. D. Speech on the . . . S. Canal, etc. 1857.

——— ——— Lesseps, F. de. Inquiry into the opinions of the Commercial Classes of Great Britain on the S. . . . Canal. 1857.

——— ——— Paleocapa, P. Observations sur le discours prononcé par M. Stephenson, de l'Isthme de S. *Par.,* 1857.

——— ——— Philibert, Capit. Canal Maritime de S. Observations hydrographiques, etc. *Par.,* 1857.

——— ——— Saint-Hilaire, J. B. Egypt and the Great S. Canal, etc. 1857.

——— ——— Dupin, Baron C. Canal Maritime de S. Deux Rapports, etc. *Par.,* 1857-58.

——— ——— Conrad, F. W. Canal de S.; état de la question. *La Haye,* 1858.

——— ——— Kotschy, T. Die Vegetation und der Canal . . . von S. *Wien,* 1858.

——— ——— Scarpellini, E. Memorandum di la Scienzia—l'Istmo di S., etc. *Roma,* 1858.

——— ——— Spratt, T. A. B. An Inquiry into . . . the Practicability of the S. Canal. *Lond.,* 1858.

——— ——— Coninck, F. de. Du Percement de l'Isthme de S., etc. *Havre,* 1859.

——— ——— Lange, D. A. The I. of S. Canal question, etc. 1859.

——— ——— Badger, G. P. Visit to the I. of S., etc. 1862.

——— ——— Hawkshaw, J. Report . . . on the S. Canal, etc. *Westminster,* 1863.

——— ——— Oliveira, B. A Few Observations upon the Works of the I. of S. Canal . . . 1863. 1863.

——— ——— Lavallet, A. Extrait . . . Communication . . . sur les Travaux . . . de l'Isthme de S. *Par.,* 1866.

——— ——— Suez, Compagnie Universelle, etc. Assemblée générale des Actionnaires . . . Rapport de M. F. de Lesseps, etc. *Par.,* 1866.

——— ——— Richards, G. H., and Clarke, A. Report on the Maritime Canal, connecting the Mediterranean . . . with the Red Sea, etc. 1870.

Suira.—*See* Mogadore.

Sulden.—Sonklar, C. A. von. Der neuerliche Ausbruch des Suldnergletschers in Tirol. *Wien,* 1857.

Sulou.—*See* Sulu Islands.

Sulu Islands.—Forrest, T. Voyage to New Guinea . . . including an account of . . . Sooloo, etc. 1780.

——— Berghaus, H. Asia . . . Memoir zur Erklärung . . . der reducirten Karte von . . . S. Ins., etc. *Gotha,* 1832-35.

——— Moor, J. H. Notices of the . . . Sulus, etc. *Singapore,* 1837.

——— Sumatra . . . Sulou. Everka. Vol. XII.

Sulu Sea.—BELCHER, SIR E., and BATE, W. T. China Pilot . . . Observations on . . . the S. and Mindoro Seas, *etc.* 1858.
Sumatra.—MARSDEN, W. Remarks on the Su. Languages. 1780.
——— History of S., *etc.* 1811.
——— HEYNE, B. Tracts . . . on India . . . also an Account of S. 1814.
——— PRINCE OF WALES ISLAND, Exposition of the political and commercial Relations of the Government of, with . . . the E. Coast of S., *etc.* *Prince of W. I.*, 1824.
——— ANDERSON, J. Mission to the E. Coast of S., in 1823, *etc.* *Edin., Lond.*, 1826.
——— MOOR, J. H. Notices of . . . S., *etc.* *Singapore*, 1837.
——— MULLER, S. Berigten over S., *etc.* *Amst.*, 1837.
——— BOELHOUWER, J. C. Herinneringen van mijn verblijf op S.'s Westkust gedurende . . . 1831-34. *s'Grav.*, 1841.
——— MICHIELS, A. V. Nederlands Souvereiniteit over de schoonsten en rijkste gewesten van S. *Amst.*, 1848.
——— KORTHALS, P. W. Topographische Schets van een Gedeelte van N. *Leyden*, 1847.
——— Sumatra. Java, *etc.* EYRIES. Vol. XII.
——— Peyton, W. Voyage . . . in 1615. Occurrences . . . at S., *etc.* KERR. Vol. IX.
——— Discorso d'un gran Capitano di Mare Francese . . . sopra . . . S. RAMUSIO. Vol. III.
——— Beaulieu, A. Reise . . . 1610-21 . . . Beschreibung der Insel S. VOYAGES and TRAVELS. Allgemeine Historie, *etc.* Vol. X.
——— See also PRIAMAN.
Summatra.—See SUMATRA.
Summer Islands.—See BERMUDA ISLANDS.
Sunda Islands.—THUNBERG, C. P. Voyages au Japon, par . . . les Îles de la Sonde . . . 1770-1778, *etc.* *Par.*, 1796.
———, **Straits of.**—BERNCASTLE, DR. A Voyage to China; including a Visit to . . . the Straits of . . . S., *etc.* *Lond.*, 1850.
——— ——— HONG-KONG. Directions for . . . Passage to Hong-Kong, through S. S., *etc.* 1857.
Sunderland.—JOHNSON, E. J. Sailing Directions from S. Point to Berwick, *etc.* 1836.
Sunium.—STUART, J. and REVETT, N. The Antiquities of Athens . . . S., *etc.* 1825-33.
Superior, Lake.—SCHOOLCRAFT, H. R. Summary Narrative . . . Report of the Copper Mines of Lake S., *etc.* *Phil.*, 1855.
——— ——— PATTEN, R. Report on the Locating Survey of the St. Croix and L. S. Railroad. *Madison*, 1856.
——— ——— HEAD, SIR E. Papers relative to the Exploration . . . between L. S. and the Red River Settlement. 1859.
——— ——— KOHL, J. G. Kitchi-Gami. Wanderings round Lake S. 1860.

Superior, Lake.—HECTOR, J. On the Geology of the Country between L. S. and the Pacific Ocean, etc. 1861.

Surat.—OMBECK, P. A Voyage . . . Together with a Voyage to Suratte, by O. Toreen, etc. *Lond.*, 1771.

—— STAVORINUS, J. S. Voyage . . . à Suratz, en 1774-78. *Par.*, 1800.

—— Downton, Lieut.-Gen. N. Journal of . . . Voyage to . . . S. in 1610. ASTLEY. Vol. I.

—— Middleton, Sir H. Voyage to . . . S. in 1610. ASTLEY. Vol. I.

—— Bernier, F. Voyage to S., etc. CHURCHILL. Vol. VIII.

—— Wynne, A. B. Geological Notes on the S. Collectorate. INDIA, GEOLOGICAL SURVEY. Records, etc. Vol. I.

—— Finch, W. Observations of, who accompanied Capt. Hawkins to S., etc. KERR. Vol. VIII.

—— Middleton, Sir H. Journey to Zenan . . . Voyage from the Red Sea to S., etc. KERR. Vol. VIII.

—— Elkington, T. Voyage to S., etc. KERR. Vol. IX.

—— Swan, R. Journal of a Voyage to S. and Jasques, 1860. KERR. Vol. IX.

—— Tenth Voyage, in 1612 . . . to S., etc. KERR. Vol. IX.

—— Voyage of the Ann-Royal from S. to Mokha, 1618. KERR. Vol. IX.

—— Childe, A. Journal from England to S. . . . 1616. PURCHAS. Vol. I.

—— Downton, N. Journal . . . 1611-12. Their coming to Saklania . . . and after that to S. PURCHAS. Vol. I.

—— Heynes, E. Voyage from S. to Moha . . . 1618. PURCHAS. Vol. I.

—— Hores, W. Discourse of his Voyage from S. to Achen . . . 1618-19. PURCHAS. Vol. I.

—— Swan, R. Extract of a Journal of a Voyage to S., etc. PURCHAS. Vol. I.

—— Ovington, J. Reise nach S. . . . 1690-93. VOYAGES and TRAVELS. Allgemeine Historie, etc. Vol. X.

—— Rhoden, A. Reise nach . . . S., etc. VOYAGES and TRAVELS. Allgemeine Historie, etc. Vol. X.

—— Tavernier. Reisen . . . 1665-66 . . . von Surata nach Goa, etc. VOYAGES and TRAVELS. Allgemeine Historie, etc. Vol. XI.

Surata, Surate, Suratte.—*See* SURAT.

Surinam.—STEDMAN, J. G. Narrative of . . . Expedition against the revolted Negroes of S. . . . 1722-27, etc. 1796.

—— SURINAM. Aanteckeningen, betrekkelyk de Kolonie S. *Arnhem*, 1826.

—— LANS, W. H. Bijdrage tot de Kennis der Kolonie S. *s'Grav.*, 1842.

—— SURINAM. Dagverhaal van eene Reis naar Paramaribo en verdere omstreken in . . . S. *Amst.*, 1842.

—— SURINAM. Verzameling van Stukken aangaande de Surinaamsche Aangelegenheden, etc. *s'Gravenh.*, 1845.

Surinam.—Radems, Baron R. F. van. De Vestiging van Nederlanders te Suriname aanbevolen. *s'Grav.*, **1854.**

——— Warren, G. Description of S., upon the Continent of Guiana, etc. Churchill. Vol. VIII.

——— *See also* Paramaribo.

Surrey.—Stevenson, W. General View of the Agriculture of . . . S. **1809.**

Susa.—Jackson, J. G. An Account of . . . S., *etc.* *Lond.*, **1814.**

——— Gubernatis, E. de. Lettere . . . sulle province di S., *etc.* *Firenze*, **1867.**

——— Notice of some remarkable Monuments of Antiquity discovered on the Site of the Ancient S., *etc.* Walpole, R. Travels, *etc.*

Susiana.—Loftus, W. K. Travels . . . in . . . S., *etc.* **1857.**

——— Cartwright, J. The Preacher's Travels . . . through . . . . S., *etc.* Churchill. Vol. VII.

Susoo.—*See* Susu.

Susu.—Susoo Language, A Grammar and Vocabulary of the . . . the Names of some of the S. Towns, *etc.* *Edin.*, **1802.**

Sutherland.—Murchison, Sir R. I. Supplementary Remarks on the Strata of the Oolitic Series . . . in . . . S., *etc.* **1827.**

Sutlej.—*See* Sutluj.

Sutluj.—Hugel, Baron C. von. Das Kabul-Becken und die Gebirge zwischen dem Hindu Kusch und dem Sutlej. *Wien*, **1850.**

Svecia.—*See* Sweden.

Sv. Katerina.—*See* Saint Catherine, Mount.

Swall.—Francisco, D. Examination of, taken in Swally Rode . . . aboord the *Gift*, Feb. 20, 1614. Purchas. Vol. I.

Swally.—*See* Swall.

Swan River.—Cowen, J. R. Hints on Emigration to . . . the S. and Canning Rivers, *etc.* **1829.**

——— Swan River Settlement. Copies of the Correspondence of the Colonial Department, *etc.* **1829.**

——— Banister, J. W. On Emigration to . . . the S. R. **1831.**

——— Swan River Settlement, Returns relative to the, *etc.* **1831.**

——— Irwin, F. C. State and position of . . . S. R. Settlement. **1835.**

——— Moore, Hon. G. F. Evidences of an Inland Sea, collected from the Natives of the S. W. Settlement. *Dubl.*, **1837.**

Sweden.—Murchison, Sir R. I. On the Superficial Detritus of S., *etc.*

——— Sweden. Svecia, sive de Suecorum. Regis Dominiis et opibus Commentarius Politicus. *Lugd. Bat.*, **1631.**

——— Denmark. An Account of . . . S.: as it was in . . . 1688, *etc.* *Lond.*, **1738.**

——— Whitelocke, Sir B. A Journal of the Swedish Ambassy in 1653 and 1654, from . . . England, *etc.* *Lond.*, **1772.**

——— Coxe, W. Travels into . . . S., *etc.* **1784.**

Sweden.

Sweden.—Acerbi, J. Travels through S. . . . to the North Cape, *etc.* 1802.
—— Porter, R. K. Travelling Sketches in . . . S., *etc.* 1809.
—— Thomson, T. Travels in S. in 1812. 1813.
—— Brooke, Sir A. de C., Bart. Travels through S., *etc.* 1823.
—— Sweden, Guide through. *Gothenburg*, 1824.
—— Forsell, C. Sverige och Norwege eller Skandinavien.
Stock., 1826.
—— Wilson, W. R. Travels in . . . S., *etc.* *Lond.*, 1826.
—— Brooke, Sir A. de C., Bart. Winter in . . . S. · 1827.
—— Nilsson, S. Petrifacta Suecana . . . descripta, *etc.*
Lond., Goth., 1827.
—— Everest, R. A Journey through . . . part of S., *etc.*
Lond., 1829.
—— Elliott, C. B. Letters from . . . S., *etc.* 1832.
—— Forsell, C. Statistik öfver Sverige. *Stock.*, 1833.
—— Barrow, J. Excursions in . . . S., *etc.* 1834.
—— Inglis, H. D. A Personal Narrative of a Journey through . . . part of S., *etc.* *Lond.*, 1835.
—— Clarke, E. D. Travels in . . . S., *etc.* 1838.
—— Laing, S. Tour in S. in 1838, *etc.* 1839.
—— Bremner, R. Excursions in . . . S. 1840.
—— Forsart, P. A. F. K. Handbuch für Reisende in S.
Pforzheim, 1841.
—— Belgium. Belgian . . . Swedish . . . Lighthouses, corrected to 1843, 51, 54, 57-59. 1843-59.
—— Murchison, Sir R. I. On the Silurian Rocks . . . in . . . S., *etc.* 1847.
—— Sweden. Rambles in S. . . . by Sylvanus. 1847.
—— Ross, W. A. Yacht Voyage to . . . S. 1849.
—— Pfeiffer, I. Journey to Iceland, and Travels in S., *etc.* 1852.
—— Bunbury, S. A. A Summer in . . . S, *etc.* 1856.
—— Scott, C. H. Danes and the Swedes . . . a Visit, *etc.* 1856.
—— Brskow, B. v. Om förflutna tiders Svenska Ordboks-företag.
Stock., 1857.
—— Brace, C. L. The Norse-Folk; a visit to . . . S. 1857.
—— Norway and S., A Long Vacation Ramble in, by X. and Y.
Camb., 1857.
—— Helmersen, G. von. Geologische Bemerkungen auf einer Reise in S., *etc.* *St. Pet.*, 1858.
—— Taylor, B. Northern Travel . . . Pictures of S., *etc.* 1858.
—— Dunsterville, E. The Admiralty List of the . . . Swedish . . . Lights. Corrected to 1860. 1860.
—— Ziegler, J. M. Notiz über Ausbeutung einer Waldung in Schweden.
Wintert., 1860.

Sweden — Switzerland.   425

Sweden.—Edlund, E. Meteorologiska Jakttagelser i Sverige . . . 1859-61.
                  Stock., **1860-63.**
—— Statistical Tables. . . . Part VII. . . . 8., *etc.*   **1861.**
—— Erdmann, A. Sveriges Geologiska Undersökning, *etc.*
                   Stockh., **1862.**
—— Marryat, H. One Year in S., *etc.*   *Lond.*, **1862.**
—— Sweden. Sveriges Geologiska Undersökning, *etc.*
                   Stockh., **1862-64.**
—— Erdmann, A. Exposé des Formations Quaternaires de la Suède.
                   Stockh., **1868.**
—— Story, J. Travels through S., *etc.* Churchill. Vol. VII.
—— An Impartial Account of . . . S., *etc.* Harris, J. Vol. II.
—— Nowel, T. Travels in . . . S., in 1801. Pelham. Vol. II.
—— Fortia's Travels in S. Pinkerton. Vol. VI.
—— Küttner, C. G. Travels through . . . S. . . . 1798-99. Voyages and Travels. A Collection, *etc.* 1805. Vol. I.
—— Carr, J. A Northern Summer; or, Travels . . . through . . . S. . . .1804. Voyages and Travels. A Collection, *etc.* 1805. Vol. III.
—— Seume J. G. Tour through . . . S. . . . 1805. Voyages and Travels. A Collection, *etc.* 1805. Vol. V.
—— Macdonald, J. Travels through . . . part of S., 1800. Voyages and Travels. A Collection, *etc.* 1805. Vol. XI.
—— Travels through . . . part of S., 1609. Voyages and Travels. A Collection, *etc.* 1810. Vol. VI.
—— Seume, J. G. Tour through . . . S. . . . 1805. Voyages and Travels. A Collection, *etc.* 1810. Vol. VI.
—— Hallberg, Baron Von. Sentimental Sketches, written during a Journey through . . . S. . . . 1820. Voyages and Travels, New. 1819. Vol. V.
—— A description of S. Voyages and Travels. The World displayed. Vol. XX.

Switzerland.—Hyer, O. Recherches sur le Climat . . . du Pays Tertiaire, *etc.*   *Winterthur.*
—— Switzerland. [An Article from an Encyclopædia.]
—— Ebel, J. G. Anleitung auf die nützlichste und genussvollste Art in der Schweitz zu reisen.   *Zurich*, **1793.**
—— Coxe, W. Travels in S., *etc.*   **1794.**
—— Stolberg, Count F. L. zu. Reise in . . . der Schweiz, *etc.*
                Königsb. u. Leip., **1794.**
—— Muller, J. Histoire des Suisses, *etc.*   *Laus., Par.*, **1795-97.**
—— Laharpe, F. C. La Neutralité des Gouvernans de la Suisse, 1797.
                  Par., **1797.**
—— Ebel, J. G. Schilderung der Gebirgsvölker der Schweiz.
                 Leipz., **1798-1802.**
—— Chauchard, Capt. Geographical . . . description of . . . S.,
 etc.   *Lond.*, **1800.**

Switzerland.—GERMANY . . . S. . . . Geographical . . . description of, etc. 1800.

—— WAHLENBERG, G. De Vegetatione et Climate in Helvetia Septentrionali, etc. *Turici Helvet.*, 1813.

—— BAILLIE, M. First Impressions of . . . S., etc. 1819.

—— LUTZ, M. Geographisch Statistisches Handlexikon der Schweiz, etc. *Aarau,* 1822.

—— SIMOND, L. S. in 1817-19, etc. 1823.

—— BROCKEDON, W. Illustrations of the Passes . . . by which Italy communicates with . . . S., etc. 1828.

—— GEMÄLDE DER SCHWEIZ, etc. *Bern,* 1834-38.

—— MURRAY. Hand-Book for Travellers . . . through . . . S. *Lond.,* 1836.

—— MEYER VON KNONAU. Erdkunde der Schweizerischen Eidgenossenschaft. *Zürich,* 1838-39.

—— BEATTIE, W. S., etc. 1839.

—— ESCHMANN, J. Ergebnisse der Trigonometrischen Vermessungen in der Schweiz. *Zürich,* 1840.

—— BACH, J. F. Introduction à la connaissance . . . de la Suisse, etc. *Par.,* 1842.

—— MURCHISON, SIR R. I. Additional Remarks on the deposit of Æningen in S. 1846.

—— FERGUSON, R. Swiss Men and Swiss Mountains. 1853.

—— ZIEGLER, J. M. Hypsométrie de la Suisse, etc. *Zürich,* 1853.

—— KELLER, F. Die Keltischen Pfahlbauten in den Schweizerseen. *Zürich,* 1854.

—— LAING, S. Notes . . . on . . . S., etc. 1854.

—— CHAMIER, CAPT. My Travels . . . through . . . S., etc. 1855.

—— HEER, O. Flora Tertiaria Helvetiæ, etc. *Winter.,* 1855-59.

—— GISTEL, J. Die Sudwestbayerische Schweiz, etc. *Straubing,* 1857.

—— ZIEGLER, J. M. Die Gewerbthätigkeit und die Eisenbahnen der Schweiz aus dem vaterländischen Standpunkte. *Winter.,* 1858.

—— —— Geographische Karte der Schweizerischen Gewerbthätigkeit. *Wintert.,* 1858.

—— SWITZERLAND. Practical Swiss Guide, etc. 1859.

—— DENZLER, H. H. Die Meereshöhe des Chasseral, als Grundlage der Schweizerischen Höhenmetzen. 1864.

—— FAVRE, A. Recherches Géologiques dans les parties . . . de la Suisse voisines du Mont Blanc, etc. *Par., Genève,* 1867.

—— ZIEGLER, J. M. Notice sur l'Hypsométrie de la Suisse, etc. *Genève,* 1867.

—— HIRSCH, A. and PLANTAMOUR, E. Nivellement de précision de la Suisse, etc. *Genève et Bale,* 1867, 68, 70.

—— SWITZERLAND. Procès-verbal de la septième Séance de la Commission Geodésique Suisse, etc. 1868.

Switzerland — Syria.

Switzerland.—FINLAY, G. Παρατηρήσεις επι της εν Ελβετια ... προιστορικης αρχαιολογιας. Εν Αθηναις, 1869.
—— Burnet, Bishop G. Travels through S. ... 1685-86. HARRIS, J. Vol. II.
—— Ray, J. Travels through ... S., etc. HARRIS, J. Vol. II.
—— Stolberg, Count L. Travels through ... S., etc. PELHAM. Vol. II.
—— Coxe's Travels in S. PINKERTON. Vol. V.
—— Kotzebue, A. von. Journey ... through S. to Paris, 1804. VOYAGES and TRAVELS. A Collection, etc. 1805. Vol. I.
—— Paris, Travels from, through S. and Italy, 1801-2, etc. VOYAGES and TRAVELS. A Collection, etc. 1805. Vol. IX.
—— Paris, Travels from, through S. and Italy, 1801-2. VOYAGES and TRAVELS. A Collection, etc. 1810. Vol. II.
—— and France, Letters from, etc. VOYAGES and TRAVELS, New. 1819. Vol. VI.
—— Simond, L. Travels in S., 1817-19. VOYAGES and TRAVELS, New. 1810. Vol. VII.
—— Addison, Joseph. Travels through ... S. 1699. Keysler, John George. Travels through S., etc. 1729. VOYAGES and TRAVELS. The World displayed. Vol XIX.
—— *See also* ALPS.
——, **Saxon.** *See* SAXONY.
Sydney.—BLACKWOOD, F. P. Sailing Directions ... from S. to Torres Strait. 1847.
—— KING, P. P. Sailing Directions ... from S. to Torres Strait. 1847.
—— CHIMMO, W. Voyage ... from S. to the Gulf of Carpentaria, etc. 1857.
—— ABBOTT, F. Results ... To which is added a Meteorological Summary for ... S., etc. *Hob. Town*, 1866.
Syouah.—CAILLIAUD, F. Voyage ... de Fâzogl ... à S., etc. *Par.*, 1826.
Syout. *See* SIUT.
Syr-Daria.—*See* SIR-DARIA.
Syria.—ALEPPO. Journey from Aleppo to Damascus; with a description of ... parts of S., etc. 1737.
—— HASIUS, J. M. Regni Davidici ... descriptio ... una cum delineatione Syriæ, etc. *Nurimb.*, 1739.
—— POCOCKE, R. Description of ... S., etc. 1743-45.
—— SYRIA. Viaggio da Gerusalemme per le coste della Soria. *Livorno*, 1787.
—— VOLNEY, C. F. Voyage en Syrie, etc. *Par.*, 1787.
—— NOTES GÉOGRAPHIQUES pour servir d'Index à la Carte de Syrie relative à l'histoire de l'Expédition du Bonaparte en Orient. *Par.*, 1803.
—— BROWNE. W. G. Travels in ... S., etc. 1806.

Syria.

Syria.—ALI BEY. Travels in ... S., *etc.* 1816.
—— BURCKHARDT, J. L. Travels in S., *etc.* 1822.
—— IRBY, HON. C. L. and MANGLES, J. Travels in ... S. ... 1817 and 1818. 1823.
—— BUCKINGHAM, J. S. Travels among the Arab tribes ... east of S. and Palestine, *etc.* 1825.
—— BERGHAUS, H. Asia ... nebst Bemerkungen über ... Syrien, *etc.* Gotha, 1832-35.
—— MADOX, J. Excursions in ... S., *etc.* 1834.
—— BARTLETT, W. H. S., *etc.* 1836-38.
—— NIEBUHR, C. Reisebeschreibung ... durch Syrien, *etc.* Hamb., 1837.
—— ROBINSON, G. Travels in Palestine and S. 1837.
—— ADDISON, C. G. Damascus ... with a sketch of ... S., *etc.* 1838.
—— MACBRAIR, R. M. Sketches of a Missionary's Travels in ... S., *etc.* 1839.
—— GRÄBERG, Conut J. Relazioni Commerciali ... della Siria, coi Porti dell' Italia, *etc.* Firenze, 1841.
—— KINNEAR, J. Cairo ... with Remarks on ... S. Lond., 1841.
—— KELLY, W. K. S. and the Holy Land, *etc.* 1844.
—— WILSON, T. Nozráni in Egypt and S. 1846.
—— FLETCHER, J. P. Notes ... and Travels in ... S. 1850.
—— NEALE, F. A. Eight Years in S., *etc.* 1852.
—— GRAHAM, W. The Jordan and the Rhine ... Five Years in S., *etc.* 1854.
—— SEETZEN, U. J. Reisen durch Syrien, *etc.* Berl., 1854.
—— VAN DE VELDE, C. W. M. Narrative of a Journey through S., *etc.* 1854.
—— PORTER, J. L. Greek Inscriptions from S., *etc.* Lond., 1855.
—— JOCHMUS, A. Der Syrische Krieg, *etc.* Frankf. a. M., 1856.
—— PETACUIA, RABBI. Travels of; who, in the ... Twelfth Century visited ... S., *etc.* 1856.
—— WORTABET, O. M. S. and the Syrians, *etc.* 1856.
—— FALKLAND, VISCOUNTESS. Chow-Chow; being Selections from a Journal kept in ... S. 1857.
—— MURRAY. Hand-Book for Travellers in S. and Palestine, *etc.* Lond., 1858.
—— GRAHAM, C. C. Additional Inscriptions from the ... E. Desert of S., *etc.* 1859.
—— HOGG, J. On ... the E. Desert of S., *etc.* Edin., 1860.
—— PHILLIPS, J. S. Interpretations ... the Re-settlement of the Seed of Abraham in S., *etc.* 1860.
—— DESMOULINS, M. Renseignements Hydrographiques ... sur la Côte de S. Par., 1862.
—— SYRIA. Rambles in the Deserts of S., *etc.* Lond., 1864.

Syria. 429

Syria.—BERCHET, G. Relazione dei Consoli Veneti nella Siria. *Torino,* 1866.

——— FRAAS, O. Aus dem Orient. Geologische Beobachtungen ... in Syrien. *Stuttgart,* 1867.

——— Baumgarten, M. Travels through ... S., etc. CHURCHILL. Vol. I.

——— Biddulph, W. Travels of four Englishmen ... into ... S. ... in 1600 and 1611. CHURCHILL. Vol. VII.

——— CARTWRIGHT, J. The Preacher's Travels ... through ... S., etc. CHURCHILL. Vol. VII.

——— Syrie et Palestine. FRARIA. Vol. XIV.

——— Baldwine, Abp. of Canterbury. Voyage unto S. 1190. HAKLUYT. Vol. II.

——— Edward, Prince. Voyage into S., 1270. HAKLUYT. Vol. II.

——— Fitch, R. The long ... voyage of ... by way of Tripolis in S., to Ormuz, etc. 1583-1591. HAKLUYT. Vol. II.

——— The honourable Voyage of Richard, Earle of Cornwall ... into S., 1240. HAKLUYT. Vol. II.

——— Hubert, Walter, Bp. of Salisbury. Voyage unto S., 1190. HAKLUYT. Vol. II.

——— Pelagius Cambrensis. Voyage into ... S., 390. HAKLUYT. Vol. II.

——— Richard surnamed Canonicus. Voyage into S. ... 1190. HAKLUYT. Vol. II.

——— Turneham, R. Voyage into S., 1270. HAKLUYT. Vol. II.

——— Wrag, R. Description of a Voyage to ... S., 1593-95, etc. HAKLUYT. Vol. II.

——— Vertomannus, L. Navigation and Voyages to ... S. ... 1503. HAKLUYT. Vol. IV.

——— Varthema, L. di. Travels in ... S. ... 1503 to 1508 ... Edited ... by G. P. Badger. 1863. HAKLUYT Soc. Pub. Vol. XXXII.

——— Voyages and Travels in ... S. ... in 1503-8. KERR. Vol. VII.

——— Volney, C. F. Travels through S. ... in 1783-85. PELHAM. Vol. II.

——— Barthema or Vertoman, L. Travels into ... S. ... 1503. PURCHAS. Vol. II.

——— Benjamin, the Son of Jonas. Peregrination of ... and relations of ... S., etc. PURCHAS. Vol. II.

——— Of the ... Regions and Religions of ... S., etc. PURCHAS. Vol. V.

——— Barthema, L. Itinerario dell' Egitto, Soria, etc. RAMUSIO. Vol. I.

——— Federici, C. de'. Viaggio nell' India Orientale, ed oltra ... per via di Soria, 1563-69. RAMUSIO. Vol. III.

——— Rauwolf, L. Journey into ... S., etc. RAY, J.

——— Schols, J. M. A. Travels in ... S., 1821. VOYAGES and TRAVELS, New. 1819, etc. Vol. VIII.

Syria.—SHAW, T. Travels into S., *etc.* VOYAGES and TRAVELS. The World displayed. Vol. XI.

——— Squire, Col. Travels through part of . . . S. Salutaris. WALPOLE, R. Travels, *etc.*

——— *See also* BAALBEC. TRIPOLI.

Syria, Greater.—CELLA, P. DELLA. Narrative . . . with instructions for navigating the (I. S. 1822.

——— ——— BEECHEY, F. W. and H. W. Proceedings . . . comprehending an account of the G. S., *etc.* 1828.

Sserb.—*See* SERVIA.

Sserborsság. *See* SERVIA.

Saillitze.—SCHMIDL, A. A. Die Baradla-Höhle . . . und die Lednica-Eishöhle bei S., *etc.* *Wien*, 1857.

T.

Tabreea.—*See* TABRIZ.

Tabriz.—FRESHFIELD, D. W. Travels . . . including Visits to . . . Tabreez, *etc.* *Lond.*, 1869.

Tadmor.—*See* PALMYRA.

Taff Vale.—MEREWETHER, MR. SERJEANT. Speech . . . on the T. V. Railway Bill 1840.

Tafilelt.—JACKSON, J. G. An Account of . . . T., *etc.* *Lond.*, 1814.

——— ROHLFS, G. Reise . . . Exploration der Oasen von T., *etc.* *Bremen*, 1868.

Tagus, River.—BIDDLECOMBE, G. Directions for entering the . . . T. 1848, 1854.

Tahiti.—GARNIER, J. Excursion autour de l'Ile de T.

——— RODRIGUEZ, M. Relacion diaria, Viage de la Isla de Amat, alias Otagiti, 1774. *MS.*

——— MORTIMER, G. Observations . . . during a Voyage to . . . Otaheite, *etc.* *Lond.*, 1791.

——— KULCZYCKI, A. Determination des Longitudes . . . Observations pour . . . Taiti, *etc.* *Par.*, 1851.

——— GAUSSIN, P. L. J. B. Du Dialecte de T., *etc.* *Par.*, 1853.

———Bligh, G. Voyage à Taïti . . . 1787-89. (Second Voyage. 1792-3.) EYRIÈS. Vol. III.

——— Edwards, Capt. Voyage . . . à Taïti pour saisir les révoltés du *Bounty* . . . 1790-92. EYRIÈS. Vol. III.

——— Wallis, Capt. Voyage to . . . Otaheite . . . 1766-68. HAWKESWORTH, J. Vol. I.

——— Relation d'un Voyage à l'Ile d'Amat ou Taiti, *etc.* VOYAGES and TRAVELS. Recueil, *etc.* Vol. IV.

Taiti.—*See* TAHITI.

Tai-Wan.—*See* FORMOSA.

Takau-Kon.—RICHARDS, J. China. Harbours of . . . T.-K., *etc.* 1855.

Talca — Tartary.

Talca.—Domeyko, D. I.   Viaje á las Cordilleras de T., etc.   1849.
Talcmeco.—Graberg, Count J.   Recueil de Voyages . . . and Historical Researches on the Conquest of . . . T., in the thirteenth Century, by J. Ranking.   1828.
Taman.—Abich, H.   Einleitende Grundzüge der Geologie der Halbinseln Kertsch und T.   *St. Pet.*, 1865.
—— ——   Karten und Profile zur Geologie der Halbinseln Kertsch und T., etc.   *Tiflis*, 1866.
—— Helmersen, G. von.   Die . . . Naphthaquellen . . . bei . . . T.   1867.
Tamatave.   Oliver, S. P.   Madagascar . . . With Sketches in the Provinces of T., etc.   *Lond.* [1865.]
—— Wilkinson, T.   The Trip from T. to the Capital.   [1867.]
Tamise.—See Thames.
Tampico.—Fisher, G.   Memorials of, relating to the Expedition of General Mexia against T. in 1835, etc.   *Houston, Tex.*, 1840.
Tana.—See Azov.
Tangier.—Lempriere, W.   Tour from Gibraltar to T., etc.   1791.
Tanjore.—India.   Reports of the . . . effects of the . . . Coleroon Annicuts, in T., etc.   *Madras*, 1858.
—— Beschreibung der Königreiche Tanjur, etc.   Voyages and Travels. Allgemeine Historie, etc. Vol. XVIII.
Tanjur.—See Tanjore.
Tanna.—See Azov.
Tannasseri.—See Tenasserim.
Täplies.—Dresden und die umliegende Gegend bis . . . T., etc.   *Dresd.*, 1804.
Taptee.—Blanford, W. T.   On Geology of the T. and Lower Nerbudda Valleys.   India, Geological Survey.   Memoirs, etc.   Vol. VI.
Taraki.—See Saghalien.
Taranaki.—Hector, J.   Report on the Petroleum found at T.   1866.
Tarasp.—Killias, F.   The Mineral Waters and Baths of T., etc.   *Coire*, 1866.
Tarca.—Kulczycki, A.   Determination des Longitudes . . . Observations pour . . . T., etc.   *Par.*, 1851.
Tarrakai.—See Saghalien.
Tarshish.—Of Tharsis . . . whether it be the same with Ophir, etc.   Purchas. Vol. I.
Tartar Steppes.—See Steppes, Tartar.
Tartaria.—See Tartary.
Tartary.—Vera, G. di.   Tre Navigationi fatte dagli Olandesi . . . nella . . . Tartaria, etc.   *Venet.*, 1599.
—— Mendez Pinto, F.   Historia Oriental de las peregrinaciones de F. Mendez Pinto . . . en . . . Tartaria, etc.   *Madrid*, 1627.
—— Struys, J.   Les Voyages de, en . . . T., etc.   *Lyon*, 1682.

Tartary.

Tartary.—Ides, E. Y. Three Years' Travels ... Thro' ... Gnat T., *etc.*
Lond., 1706.

—— Olearius, A. Voyages très-curieux ... faits en ... Tartarie, *etc.*
Amst., 1727.

—— Strahlenberg, P. J. von. Das Nord-und Ostliche Theil von Europa und Asia, in so weit solches das gantze Russische Reich mit ... der grossen Tatarey ... begreiffet ... vorgestellet, *etc.*
Stockh., 1730.

—— Radcliffe, W. The Natural History of East T., *etc.* Lond., 1789.

—— Elphinstone, Hon. M. Account of ... Caubul and its Dependencies in ... T., *etc.* 1815.

—— Rémusat, A. Recherches sur les langues Tartares, *etc.*
Par., 1820.

—— Straussen, J. J. Reise durch ... die Tatarei ... 1047-1673.
Gotha, 1832.

—— Burnes, Sir A. Travels ... from India to ... T., *etc.* 1834.

—— Schott, W. Versuch über die Tatarischen Sprachen. Berl., 1836.

—— Carpin, J. du Plan de. Relation des Mongols ou Tartares, *etc.*
Par., 1838.

—— Huc, M. Recollections of a Journey through T. ... 1844-46, *etc.*
1852.

—— Prinsep, H. T. Tibet, T. and Mongolia, *etc.* Lond., 1852.

—— Huc, M. Souvenirs d'un Voyage dans la Tartarie ... 1844-40.
Par., 1853.

—— —— Christianity in ... T., *etc.* 1857-8.

—— Collinson, Admiral. The Coasts of China and T., *etc.* 1858.

—— Tronson, J. M. Narrative of a Voyage to ... T., *etc.* 1859.

—— Spyre, R. Commerce with ... T., *etc.* 1860.

—— Torrens, H. D. Travels in ... T., *etc.* Lond., 1862.

—— Travels of J. de Plano Carpini ... into T. in 1246. Astley.
Vol. IV.

—— Travels of Marco Polo into T, in 1272. Astley. Vol. IV.

—— Travels through T. ... to ... China. Astley. Vol. IV.

—— Voyage of a certaine Englishman into Tartarie ... 1243. Hakluyt.
Vol. I.

—— Mandevil, Sir J. Voyage ... to ... T. ... 1322-1355.
Hakluyt. Vol. II.

—— D'Orléans, Père P. J. History of the ... two journeys into T. of ... F. Verbiest ... edited by the Earl of Ellesmere, *etc.* 1854.
Hakluyt Soc. Pub. Vol. XVII.

—— Rubruquis, W. de. The remarkable Travels of ... into T. and China, 1253. Harris, J. Vol. I.

—— Haitho, Prince of Armenia. Travels in T., 1254. Kerr. Vol. I.

—— Plano Carpini, J. de. Travels in T., 1246. Kerr. Vol. I.

—— Rubruquis, W. de. Travels in T., about 1253. Kerr. Vol. I.

Tartary. 433

Tartary.—Schildtberger, J. Travels into T., 1394. KERR. Vol. I.
——— Sketch of the Revolutions in T. KERR. Vol. I.
——— Travels of an Englishman in T., 1242. KERR. Vol. I.
——— Bacon, R. Tartarian . . . Relations, *etc.* PURCHAS. Vol. III.
——— The beginning of the English Discoveries towards the North . . . also Voyages . . . thorow divers Regions of Tartaria. PURCHAS. Vol. III.
——— Bronionius de Biezerfedea, M. Description of Tartaria, *etc.* PURCHAS. Vol. III.
——— Chaggi Memet. Travels and observations in the Country of the Great Can. PURCHAS. Vol. III.
——— Goes, B. Travels . . . thorow the Tartar's Countrie, 1603. PURCHAS. Vol. III.
——— Historie of Ayton . . . especially touching the Tartars. PURCHAS. Vol. III.
——— Mendez Pinto, F. Observations of . . . T. . . . 1521-45. PURCHAS. Vol. III.
——— Relations touching the Tartars, taken out of . . . Roger Wendover and Matthew Paris. PURCHAS. Vol. III.
——— Veer, G. de. Voyages of W. Barents . . . behind . . . Tartaria . . . 1594-96. PURCHAS. Vol. III.
——— Of the . . . Tartarians . . . and of their Religions. PURCHAS. Vol. V.
——— Alcmini. Due Viaggi in Tartaria, 1247. RAMUSIO. Vol. II.
——— Guagnino, A. Descrittione della Sarmatia Europea . . . de tutti Tartari campestri. RAMUSIO. Vol. II.
——— Hayton Armeno. Dell' origine e successione de' Gran Cani Imperadori Tartari, 1253-1303. RAMUSIO. Vol. II.
——— Marco Polo. Viaggi delle cose de Tartari . . . 1250, *etc.* RAMUSIO. Vol. II.
——— Navigationi fatte da gli Olandesi . . . nella . . . Tartaria . . . 1594-97. RAMUSIO. Vol. III.
——— Ascelin, Mönch. Reisen des, und seiner Gefährten, zu den Tartarn, 1247. VOYAGES and TRAVELS. Allgemeine Historie, *etc.* Vol. VII.
——— Carpini, J. de Plano. Reisen nach der T., 1246. VOYAGES and TRAVELS. Allgemeine Historie, *etc.* Vol. VII.
——— Marco Polo. Reisen in die T., 1272. VOYAGES and TRAVELS. Allgemeine Historie, *etc.* Vol. VII.
——— Pinto, F. M. Reise nach . . . T., *etc.* VOYAGES and TRAVELS. Allgemeine Historie, *etc.* Vol. X.
——— Carpin, J. du Plan de. Relation des Mongols ou Tartares, pendant 1245-47, *etc.* VOYAGES and TRAVELS. Recueil, *etc.* Vol. IV.
——— Jordan, ou Jourdain Catalani, P. Mirabilia descripta, sequitur de . . . Magno Tartaro, *etc.* VOYAGES and TRAVELS. Recueil, *etc.* Vol. IV.

2 F

Tartary — Tasmania.

Tartary.—The Travels of the Ambassadors from . . . Holstein into . . . T. . . . 1635. VOYAGES and TRAVELS. The World displayed. Vol. XIII., XIV.

——, **Asiatic.**—WAGNER, J. C. Das mächtige Kayser-Reich Sina, und die Asiatische Tartarey vor Augen gestellet, etc. Jugsb., 1688.

——, **Chinese.**—DU HALDE, J. B. Description . . . de la Tartarie Chinoise, etc. La Haye, 1736.

—— —— —— A Description of . . . C. T., etc. Lond., 1738.

—— —— STAUNTON, SIR G. Authentic Account of an Embassy to China . . . including . . . part of C. T., etc. 1797.

—— —— MARKHAM, F. Shooting in . . . C. T., etc. Lond., 1854.

—— —— ATKINSON, T. W. Oriental . . . Siberia . . . Adventures in . . . C. T., etc. 1858.

—— —— Description of T. subject to China, etc. ASTLEY. Vol. IV.

—— —— Tartarie Chinoise, etc. LAHARPE, J. Vol. VIII.

—— —— Beschreibung von der Tartarey, die unter China gehöret. VOYAGES and TRAVELS. Allgemeine Historie, etc. Vol. VII.

——, **Crimean.**—SPENCER, E. Travels in . . . Krim T., etc. 1837.

——, **East.**—Description of . . . E. T., etc. ASTLEY. Vol. IV.

—— —— Verbiest, F. Reise in die ostliche Tartarey, 1682. VOYAGES and TRAVELS. Allgemeine Historie, etc. Vol. VII.

——, **Independent.**—Tartarie Indépendante, etc. LAHARPE, J. Vol. VIII.

—— —— T., accounts of I. PINKERTON. Vol. IX.

——, **Little.**—PETACHIA, RABBI. Travels of ; who, in the . . . Twelfth Century, visited . . . L. T., etc. 1856.

—— —— Whittington, Mr. Account of a Journey through part of Little T., etc. WALPOLE, R. Travels, etc.

——, **Mantchu.**—See MANDCHOORIA.

——, **Mongol.**—See MONGOLIA.

——, **Siberian.**—COCHRANE, J. D. Narrative of a pedestrian Journey through . . . S. T., etc. 1824.

——, **West.**—Gerbillon, J. F. Travels into W. T. . . . between 1688 and 1698. ASTLEY. Vol. IV.

—— —— Beschreibung . . . der westlichen Tartarey, etc. VOYAGES and TRAVELS. Allgemeine Historie, etc. Vol. VI.

—— —— Gerbillon, J. F. Reisen in die westliche T. . . . 1688-98. VOYAGES and TRAVELS. Allgemeine Historie, etc. Vol. VII.

Tarudant.—See TEBODANT.

Tasmania.—MILLIGAN, J. Vocabulary of Dialects of Aboriginal Tribes of T. Tasmania.

—— WENTWORTH, W. C. Statistical . . . description of . . . Van Diemen's Land. 1819.

—— FIELD, B. Geographical Memoirs . . . and . . . Meteorology of . . . Van Diemen's Land. 1825.

Tasmania.—Bannister, J. W. On Emigration to . . . Van Diemen's Land, etc. **1831.**

——— New South Wales. Copies of the Royal Instructions to the Governors of . . . Van Diemen's Land . . . as to the . . . disposing of Crown Lands. **1831.**

——— Van Diemen's Land, Copies of all Correspondence . . . on . . . the Military Operations lately carried on against the Aboriginal Inhabitants of Van Diemen's Land. **1831.**

——— Bischoff, J. Sketch of the History of Van Diemen's Land, etc. **1832.**

——— Breton, Lieut. Excursions in . . . Van Diemen's Land, etc. **1834.**

——— Montagu, J. Statistical Returns of Van Diemen's Land, from 1824-35, etc. *Hobart T.*, **1836.**

——— Frankland, G. Report on the Transactions of the Survey Department of Van Diemen's Land, etc. *Hob.*, **1837.**

——— Tasman, A. J. Sketches of Tasman's Peninsula, etc. *V. D.s L.*, **1837.**

——— Montagu, J. Statistical Returns of Van Diemen's Land, from 1824 to 1830, etc. *Hobart T.*, **1839.**

——— Wheeler, D. Extracts from the Letters and Journals of . . . in . . . Van Diemen's Land, etc. **1839.**

——— Strzelecki, P. E. de. Physical description of . . . Van Diemen's Land. **1845.**

——— Africa. The Lights of . . . T. . . . Corrected to 1849, 51, 52, 56, 57, 58, 59. **1849-59.**

——— Meredith, Mrs. C. My home in T., during . . . Nine Years. **1852.**

——— Tasmania. T.n Contributions to the Universal Exhibition of Industry at Paris, 1855. *Tasman.*, **1855.**

——— Stoney, H. B. Residence in T., etc. **1856.**

——— Pugsley, D. The Rise and Progress of . . . T., etc. **1858.**

——— Hull, H. M. The Experience of Forty Years in T., etc. *Lond.*, **1859.**

——— Dunsterville, E. The Admiralty List of the Lights of . . . T. . . . Corrected to 1860, 61, 62. **1860-62.**

——— Whiting, G. The Products and Resources of T., etc. *Hobart Town*, **1862.**

——— Gras, M. A. le. Phares . . . de . . . Terre de Van Diemen . . . Corrigés 1862, 63. *Par.*, **1862, 63.**

——— Heywood, B. A. A Vacation Tour . . . through . . . T., etc. **1863.**

——— Gould, C. Report upon . . . Gold in . . . Van-Diemen's Land, etc. **1864.**

——— Bonwick, J. The last of the T.ns, etc. *Lond.*, **1870.**

——— Hull, H. M. T. in 1870, etc. *Hob. T.*, **1870.**

Tasman's Peninsula.—*See* Tasmania.

Tatarei.—See TARTARY.

Taunus.—RHINE, An Autumn near the . . . with a Tour in the T. Mountains in 1820, etc. *Lond., 1821.*

Taurida.—PALLAS, P. S. Tableau physique et topographique de la Tauride, etc. *St. Pet., 1795.*
—— See also CRIMEA.

Tauris.—See TABRIZ.

Tawa.—Blanford, W. T. On the Coal Seams of the T. Valley, etc. INDIA, GEOLOGICAL SURVEY. Records, etc. Vol. I.

Tawat.—See TUAT.

Tay.—SORBY, H. C. On the Terraces in the Valley of the T., etc. *Edin., 1856.*

Taywan.—See FORMOSA.

Tchadda, River.—See CHADDA.

Tcherkessia.—See CIRCASSIA.

Tchoka.—See SAGHALIEN.

Tebris.—See TABRIZ.

Teco.—See TICNO.

Teouanapa.—See TEHUANTEPEC.

Tedjen.—See TEDZEN.

Tedmor.—See PALMYRA.

Tedshen.—See TEDZEN.

Tedzen.—ZIMMERMANN, C. Denkschrift über . . . die Strombahn Ochus oder T. der Neueren, zur Balkan-Bay. *Berl., 1845.*

Teheran.—FRASER, J. B. Winter Journey from Constantinople to T., etc. 1838.
—— TRUILHIER, CAPIT. Mémoire descriptif de la Route de Téhran à Meched, etc. *Par., 1841.*
—— VAMBERY, A. Travels . . . from T., etc. *Lond., 1864.*

Tehuantepec.—ORBEGOZO, J. DE. Reconocimiento del Istmo de T. en 1825. *Jalapa, 1831.*
—— GARAY, J. DE. Reconocimiento . . . de T., etc. 1844.
—— —— Survey of . . . T., etc. 1844.
—— Moro. G. Communication between the . . . Oceans through . . . T. Additional Observations, etc. 1845.
—— —— Report of the Communication between the . . . Oceans through . . . T. 1845.
—— GARAY, J. DE. An Account of . . . T., etc. 1846.
—— LIOT, W. B. Panamá . . . T., etc. 1849.
—— CHALONER and FLEMING. The Mahogany-Tree . . . with notices of the projected . . . communication of . . . T. *Liverp., 1850.*
—— DALE, R. Notes of an Excursion to the Isthmus of T., etc. 1851.
—— WILLIAMS, J. J. Report . . . upon the location of the T. Railway and Carriage Road across the Isthmus, etc. [*N. Y.*] 1870.
—— Relation of the Haven of Tecuanapa, etc. HAKLUYT. Vol. III.

Tellus.—See WORLD.

Telmessus.—WILDE, W. R. Narrative of . . . a Visit to . . . T., etc.
Dubl., 1852.

Tempe.—Hawkins, Mr. On . . . the Vale of T., etc. WALPOLE, R. Memoirs, etc.

Tenasserim.—Relation des Royaumes de . . . Tannasari . . . par wilhem Meibold, etc. THEVENOT. Vol. I.

Teneriffe.—MORTIMER, G. Observations . . . during a Voyage to . . . T., etc.
Lond., 1791.

——— WILDE, W. R. Narrative of a Voyage to . . . T., etc.
Dubl., 1852.

——— SMYTH, C. P. Report on the T. Astronomical Experiment of 1856.
Lond. and Edin., 1858.

——— ——— T., an Astronomer's Experiment, etc. Lond., 1858.

——— OLIVEIRA, D. Letters upon the capabilities of . . . T. as a Winter Residence, etc.
Lond., 1864-5.

——— FRITSCH, K. VON, and OTHERS. Teneriffe geologisch topographisch dargestellt, etc.
Winterthur, 1867.

——— FRITSCH, K. VON, and REISS, W. Geologische Beschreibung der Insel Teneriffe, etc.
Winterthur, 1868.

——— St. Vincent, J. B. G. M. Bory de. Voyage to . . . [T.] 1801-2, etc. VOYAGES and TRAVELS. A Collection, etc. 1805. Vol. II.

Tennessee.—BRADBURY, J. Travels in . . . T., etc. Liver., 1817.

——— SAFFORD, J. M. Geological Reconnoissance of the State of T.
Nashville, 1856.

——— Michaux, F. A. Travels . . . in . . . T., 1802. VOYAGES and TRAVELS. A Collection, etc. 1805. Vol. I.

——— Cornelius E. Tour in . . . T., etc. 1818. VOYAGES and TRAVELS, New. 1819. Vol. III.

Teplitz.—HOFER, C. E. Beschreibung . . . (von T.), etc. Prag, 1798.

——— GRIEBEN, T. Grieben's Reise-Bibliothek. No. 38 . . . T., etc.
Berl., 1861.

Terceira.—De Chaste's Voyage to T. PINKERTON. Vol. I.

——— Of certaine notable . . . accidents that happened in T. . . . 1589-92. PURCHAS. Vol. IV.

Tercera.—See TERCEIRA.

Terodant.—LEMPRIERE, W. Tour from Gibraltar to . . . Tarudant, etc.
1791.

Terra Australia.—See AUSTRALIA.

Terra del Fuego.—WEDDELL, J. Voyage . . . to T. del F., etc. 1827.

——— MACDOUALL, J. Narrative of a Voyage to . . . T. del F. . . . . in 1826-27. 1833.

——— SNOW, W. P. Two Years' Cruise of T. d. F., etc. 1857.

Terra Firma.—Hawkins, Sir J. Voyages to the Coast of T. F. . . . 1562-68. HAKLUYT. Vol. III.

Terra Firma.—Barker, A.   Voyage to the Coast of T. F. . . . 1576.
    HAKLUYT. Vol. IV.
——   Sherley, Sir A. Voyage . . . along the Coast of T. F. . . . 1596.
    HAKLUYT. Vol. IV.
——   Ursino, A. Relation concerning the Coast of T. F. . . . 1581.
    PURCHAS. Vol. IV.
——   Von der Reise von Cartagena nach T. F., etc. VOYAGES and
    TRAVELS. Allgemeine Historie, etc. Vol. IX.
——   Beschreibungen . . . von . . . T. F., etc. VOYAGES and
    TRAVELS. Allgemeine Historie, etc. Vol. XV.
Terra Incognita.—TASMAN, J. Discoveries on the Coast of the S. T. I.
    VOYAGES. Account of several late, etc.   1711.
Terra Nova.—*See* NEWFOUNDLAND.
Terre Australe.—*See* AUSTRALIA.
Terre du Prêtre Jean.—*See* ABYSSINIA.
Terre-Neuve.—*See* NEWFOUNDLAND.
Terres Australes.—*See* AUSTRALIA.
Territoire Chinois.—*See* CHINA.
Tessin.—GEMÄLDE DER SCHWEIZ . . . T., etc.   *Bern*, 1834-38.
Tetuan.—MOROCCO. Observations on . . . Morocco . . . 1830 . . .
    Description of . . . T., etc. MS.
Tevere.—*See* TIBER.
Texas.—FALCONER, T. Notes of a Journey through T. . . . in . . .
    1841 and 1842.
——   EDWARDS, C. T. and Coahuila, etc.   *N. Y.*, 1834.
——   EDWARD, D. B. The History of T., etc.   *Cincin.*, 1836.
——   HOLLEY, MRS. M. A. T.   *Lexington*, 1836.
——   TEXAS. A Visit to T., etc.   *N. Y.*, 1836.
——   —— The War in T., etc.   *Phil.*, 1836.
——   ELLIS, S. The Emigrant's Guide to T., etc.   *New Orl.*, 1839.
——   HUNT, R. S. and RANDEL, J. F. Guide to . . . T. *N. Y.*, 1839.
——   BONNELL, G. W. Topographical description of T., etc.
                                                  Austin, Tex., 1840.
——   LECLERC, F. Le T. et sa Révolution.   *Par.*, 1840.
——   MOORE, F. Description of T., etc.   *Phil.*, 1840.
——   FOOTE, H. S. T. and the Texans, etc.   *Phil.*, 1841.
——   IKIN, A. T.; its History, etc.   1841.
——   KENNEDY, W. T., etc.   1841.
——   AMERICA. Message of . . . President . . . in relation to . . .
    Boundary between the U. S. and . . . T.   *Wash.*, 1842.
——   FALCONER, T. Expedition to Santa Fé. An account of its journey
    from T., etc.   *N. Orleans*, 1842.
——   MAILLARD, N. D. History of . . . T., etc.   1842.

Texas — Thessalonica. 439

Texas.—KENDALL, G. W. Narrative of an Expedition ... from T. to
Santa Fé, etc. *Lond.*, **1845.**

—— PURDY, J. and FINDLAY, A. G. Colombian Navigator. Vol. I.
Sailing Directory for ... T., etc. **1847.**

—— SMITH, E. Account of a Journey through N.-E.n. T., etc. **1849.**

—— BARTLETT, J. R. Personal ... explorations ... in T., etc.
N. Y., **1854.**

—— OLMSTED, F. L. Journey through T., etc. **1857.**

—— CORDOVA, J. DE. T., her capabilities and resources, etc.
Manchester, **1858.**

—— DOMENECH, E. Missionary Adventures in T., etc. **1858.**

—— MARCOU, J. Geology of N. America; with Reports on the Prairies
of ... T., etc. *Zurich*, **1858.**

Texel.—The prosperous ... Voyage to Java ... performed by 8 ships
of Amsterdam from T. ... 1598-99. HAKLUYT. Vol. V.

Texell.—*See* TEXEL.

Texcuco.—Ixtlilxochitl, F. d'Alva. Histoire des Chichimèques, ou des
anciens Rois de T., etc. TERNAUX-COMPANS. Voyages. Vol. XII.
XIII.

Thai.—*See* SIAM.

Thames.—LAURIE, R. H. and WHITTLE, J. New Piloting Directory for
the ... T., etc. *Lond.*, **1816.**

—— PURDY, J. and FINDLAY, A. G. New Piloting Directory for the
... T., etc. **1846.**

—— THORNE, J. Rambles by Rivers; the T., etc. **1847.**

—— NORTH SEA. Mer du Nord. IV* Partie. La Tamise, etc.
Par., **1864.**

—— N. Z.—NEW ZEALAND GEOLOGICAL SURVEY. Abstract Report ...
Together with Reports on ... T. Gold Fields, etc. *Well.*, **1869.**

—— —— NEW ZEALAND GEOLOGICAL SURVEY. Second Report on
the T. Gold Fields, etc. *Well.*, **1869.**

Tharsis.—*See* TARSHISH.

Thebais.—IRWIN, E. A Series of Adventures in the course of a ...
Route through the Deserts of T., etc. *Lond.*, **1780.**

—— Relation du Voyage ... de la Thebaïde fait en 1668 par les
Capucins Missionaires en Egypte. THEVENOT. Vol. IV.

Thebes.—LEPSIUS, R. A Tour from T. to the Peninsula of Sinai, 1845.
1846.

—— FORCHHAMMER, P. W. Topographia Thebarum Heptapylarum.
Kilice, **1854.**

—— —— Cailliaud, F. Travels in the Oasis of T. ... 1815-19.
VOYAGES and TRAVELS, New. 1810. Vol. VII.

Therouanne.—ELLIS, SIR H. Representation of the Siege of Therouenne,
in France, A.D. 1553.

Thessalonica.—TAFEL, T. L. F. De T. ... dissertatio geographica.
Berlin, **1839.**

Thessaly.—GELL, SIR W. Itinerary of Greece; containing ... Routes in ... T. 1819.
—— HOLLAND, H. Travels in ... T., *etc.* 1819.
—— BROWNE, E. Travels through Hungary into T., *etc.* HARRIS, J. Vol. II.
—— POUQUEVILLE, F. C. H. L. Travels in ... T., 1805. VOYAGES and TRAVELS, New. 1819. Vol. IV.
Thibet.—*See* TIBET.
Thoricus.—STUART, T. and REVETT, N. The Antiquities of Athens ... T., *etc.* 1825-33.
Thrace.—POCOCKE, R. Description of ... T., *etc.* 1743-45.
—— TAFEL, T. L. F. De Via Militari Romanorum Egnatia, qua Illyricum, Macedonia et Thracia jungebantur, *etc.* *Tubingœ*, 1842.
—— SPENCER, E. Travels ... through ... T., *etc.* 1851.
—— Biddulph, W. Travels of four Englishmen ... into ... T. ... In 1600 and 1611. CHURCHILL. Vol. VII.
Thua Thien.—*See* HUÉ.
Thurgau.—GEMÄLDE DER SCHWEIZ ... T., *etc.* *Bern*, 1834-38.
Thüringerwald.—MURCHISON, SIR R. I. and MORRIS, J. On the Palæozoic ... Rocks of the T., *etc.* 1855.
Thuringia.—RICHTER, R. Das Thüringische Schiefergebirge. 1869.
Tian-schan.—*See* TIEN-SHAN.
Tibbet.—*See* TIBET.
Tiber.—CIALDI, A. Navigazione del Tevere, *etc.* *Roma*, 1845.
—— Sul Tevere, *etc.* *Roma*, 1847.
Tiberias, Lake of.—SEETZEN, M. Brief Account of the Countries adjoining the L. of T., *etc.* *Bath*, 1810.
Tibet.—DU HALDE, J. R. A Description of ... T., *etc.* *Lond.*, 1738.
—— TURNER, S. Account of an Embassy to ... T., *etc.* 1806.
—— HOFFMEISTER, W. Travels in Ceylon ... and ... to the borders of Thibet, *etc.* *Edin.*, 1848.
—— HOOKER, J. D. Elevation of the Great Table Land of T. 1849.
—— HUC, M. Recollections of a Journey through ... T. ... 1844-46, *etc.* 1852.
—— PRINSEP, H. T. T., Tartary and Mongolia, *etc.* *Lond.*, 1852.
—— THOMSON, A. S. Western Himalaya and T., a ... Journey, *etc.* 1852.
—— HUC, M. Souvenirs d'un Voyage dans ... le T. ... 1844-46. *Par.*, 1853.
—— MARKHAM, F. Shooting in ... T., *etc.* *Lond.*, 1854.
—— STRACEY, H. Physical Geography of Western T. 1854.
—— HUC, M. Christianity in ... T. 1857-8.
—— SPRYE, R. Commerce with ... T., *etc.* 1860.
—— KNIGHT, CAPTAIN. Diary of a Pedestrian in Cashmere and Thibet. *Lond.*, 1863.

Tibet.—Schlagintweit, E. Buddhism in T., *etc.*   *Leipz.,* **1863.**
——— Description of Korea . . . and T. Astley. Vol. IV.
——— Description of Tartary . . . T., *etc.* Astley. Vol. IV.
——— Travels through Tartary, T., and Bukhâria to . . . China. Astley. Vol. IV.
——— Travels through T., to and from China, by several Missioners. Astley. Vol. IV.
——— T. et Boutan. Bogle. Turner. Etmits. Vol. XIV.
——— Thibet. Laharpe, J. Vol. VIII.
——— T., a description of. Pinkerton. Vol. VII.
——— T., Travels through, by several Missionaries. Pinkerton. Vol. VII.
——— Beschreibung von . . . T. Voyages and Travels. Allgemeine Historie, *etc.* Vol. VI.
——— Beschreibung von T., *etc.* Voyages and Travels. Allgemeine Historie, *etc.* Vol. VII.
——— Desiderius, H. Reisen nach T., 1714. Voyages and Travels. Allgemeine Historie, *etc.* Vol. VII.
——— Horaz della Penna, Bruder. Nachricht vom Anfange . . . der Capucinermission in T., 1741. Voyages and Travels. Allgemeine Historie, *etc.* Vol. VII.
——— *See also* Cho-Lagan. Mánasarówar.-Pruano.
———, **Little.**—Leitner, G. W. Results of a Tour in . . . L. Thibet, *etc.*   *Lahore, Lond.* [**1868.**]

Ticco.—Hores, W. Discourse of his Voyage from Surat to . . . Tecco . . . 1618-19. Purchas. Vol. I.

Tidikelt.—Rohlfs, G. Reise . . . Exploration der Oasen von . . . T., *etc.*   *Bremen,* **1868.**

Tien-Shan.—Osten-Sacken, Baron F. R. v. D., and Ruprecht, F. J. Sertum Tianschanicum. Botanische Ergebnisse einer Reise, *etc.*   *St. Pét.,* **1869.**

Tien-Tain Ho.—*See* Pei Ho.

Tigré, Abyssinia.—Ferret, A., and Galinier. Voyage . . . dans les provinces du T., *etc.*   *Par.,* **1847.**

Tigre, River.—*See* Tigris.

Tigris.—D'Anville, J. B. L'Euphrate et le Tigre.   *Par.,* **1779.**
——— Rich, C. J. Narrative of . . . a Voyage down the T., *etc.*   **1836.**
——— Chesney, F. R. Expeditions for the Survey of the . . . T., in 1835-37, *etc.*   **1850.**
——— Weissenborn, H. J. C. Ninive . . . mit Rücksicht auf die neuesten Ausgrabungen im T.thale.   *Erfurt,* **1851.**

Tiguex.—Vasquez de Coronado, F. Voyage . . . to . . . T. . . . 1540. Hakluyt. Vol. III.

Timbo.—Watt et Winterbottom. Voyage à Timbuu, 1794. Evants. Vol. X.

Timbou.—See TIMBO.
Timbuctoo.—JACKSON, J. G. Account of . . . T., etc. 1809.
——— ——— An . . . interesting account of T., etc. *Lond.*, 1814.
——— ADAMS, R. The Narrative of; who . . . resided several months in the City of T., etc. 1816.
——— RILEY, J. Loss of the American brig *Commerce* . . . with an account of T., etc. 1817.
——— SHABEENY, EL HAGE ABD SALAM. Account of T., etc. 1820.
——— CAILLIÉ, R. Travels through Central Africa to T., etc. 1830.
——— GRÄBERG, COUNT J. Viaggio del Signor . . . R. Caillié à Tombuctù, etc. 1830.
——— SNIDER-PELLEGRINI, A. Du Développement du Commerce de l'Algérie . . . et d'une Route . . . au Sénégal par Tumbuctun, etc. *Par.*, 1857.
——— Jobson, R. Voyage for . . . the Golden trade of Tombuto in 1620-21. ASTLEY. Vol. II.
——— Two briefe Relations concerning . . . Tombuto and Gago . . . written in 1594. HAKLUYT. Vol. III.
——— Jobson, R. Reise zur Entdeckung . . . des Goldhandels in Tombuto, 1620-21. VOYAGES and TRAVELS. Allgemeine Historie, etc. Vol. III.

Timoan.—Byron, Comm. Voyage . . . to . . . T. . . . 1764-66. HAWKESWORTH, J. Vol. I.

Timor.—BLIGH, W. Narrative of . . . Voyage . . . from Tofoa . . . to T., etc. 1790.
——— Beschreibung des Eylandes T. VOYAGES and TRAVELS. Allgemeine Historie, etc. Vol. XII.
——— Benachbarte Eylande um T. und Solor. VOYAGES and TRAVELS. Allgemeine Historie, etc. Vol. XVIII.

Tingoeala.—Description of . . . T. . . . 1612. PURCHAS. Vol. III.

Tinian.—MORTIMER, G. Observations . . . during a Voyage to . . . T., etc. *Lond.*, 1791.
——— Byron, Comm. Voyage . . . to . . . T. . . . 1764-66. HAWKESWORTH, J. Vol. I.
——— Wallis, Capt. Voyage to . . . T. . . . 1766-68. HAWKESWORTH, J. Vol. I.

Tiperah.—See TIPPERAH.

Tipperah.—Tavernier. Reisen nach . . . Tipra . . . 1652. VOYAGES and TRAVELS. Allgemeine Historie, etc. Vol. X.
———, **Independent.**—LANE, C. Extracts from a Report by, on a portion of I. T., etc. *Dehra Doon*, 1883.

Tipra.—See TIPPERAH.

Tipuani.—WEDDELL, H. A. Voyage . . . ou Visite au District aurifère de T. *Par.*, 1853.

Tivoli.—CABRAL, G. E RE, F. DEL. Monumenti antichi . . . di T. *Roma*, 1779.

Tlaxcalla.—GAGE, T. Survey of the Spanish West Indies ... Also ... Voyage ... to ... T., etc. 1702.
Tobago.—EDWARDS, B. Historical Survey of ... Saint Domingo ... Also a Tour through ... T., etc. 1801.
Tobolsk.—CHAPPE D'AUTEROCHE, J. Journey into Siberia ... and Level of ... roads from Paris to T. 1770.
Tobolsky.—See TOBOLSK.
Todos los Santos, Bay.—See BAHIA DE TODOS OS SANTOS.
Tofoa.—BLIGH, W. Narrative of ... Voyage ... from T. ... to Timor, etc. 1790.
Tombouctou, Tombuctu, Tombûto.—See TIMBUCTOO.
Tonchino.—See TONQUIN.
Tonga Islands.—See FRIENDLY ISLANDS.
Tonglo.—HOOKER, J. D. Notes ... during an excursion from Darjiling to T., etc. *Calc.*, 1849.
Tonqueen.—See TONQUIN.
Tonquin.—RHODES, A. DE. Relazione de' felici successi della Santa Fede predicata ... nel Regno di Tunchino. *Milano*, 1651.
——— PALLU, F. Breve, e compendiosa Relatione de' Viaggi di tre Vescovi Francesi ... a i Regni della Cina ... e Tonchino, etc. *Roma*, 1669.
——— BISSACHÈRE, M. DE LA. État actuel du Tunkin, etc. *Par.*, 1812.
——— SPRYE, R. H. F. and C. H. F. The British and China Railway; from ... Rangoon ... to ... T., etc. 1858.
——— Baron, S. Description of ... Tonqueen. CHURCHILL. Vol. VI.
——— KAO, D. An authentick ... description of ... Tunkin, etc. HARRIS, J. Vol. II.
——— Baron's Description of T. PINKERTON. Vol. IX.
——— Richards's History of T. PINKERTON. Vol. IX.
——— Baron, Beschreibung von Tunkin, 1685. VOYAGES and TRAVELS. Allgemeine Historie, etc. Vol. X.
——— Rhodes, A. Reise nach ... Tunkin, etc. VOYAGES and TRAVELS. Allgemeine Historie, etc. Vol. X.
Tools.—See TULA.
Too Mapham, Lake.—See MANASAROWAR.
Toorkisthan.—See TURKESTAN.
Tor.—NEWBOLD, T. J. Visit from Wadi T. to Gebel Nakus, etc.
Tornea.—GALITZIN, PRINCE E. La Finlande; Notes ... pendant une excursion de St. Pétersb. urg à T. *Par.*, 1852.
Toronto.—SABINE, MAJOR-GEN. E. Observations made at the ... Observatory at T. ... 1840-48, etc. 1845-57.
——— MAGNETICAL OBSERVATIONS ... made at ... T., etc. *Tor.*, 1863.
——— TORONTO. Abstracts of Magnetical Observations made at ... T. ... 1856 to 1862, etc. *Tor.*, 1863.

Toronto.—TORONTO. Abstracts of Meteorological Observations made at
. . . T. . . . 1854 to 1859. *Tor.*, **1864.**
—— —— Results of Meteorological Observations made at . . . T.,
1860-62. *Tor.*, **1864.**
Torres Strait.—BLACKWOOD, F. P. Sailing Directions . . . from Sydney
to T. S. **1847.**
—— JUKES, J. D. Narrative of the Surveying Voyage of H.M.S. *Fly*, in
T. S., *etc.* **1847.**
—— KING, P. P. Sailing Directions . . . from Sydney to T. S. **1847.**
—— ROGUE, A. Steam to Australia . . . the expediency of . . . a
settlement at Cape York in T. S., pointed out, *etc.* *Sydney*, **1848.**
—— Brampton et Alt. Voyage de l'Ile Norfolk à Batavia, par le détroit
de T., 1793. EYRIÈS. Vol. IV.
Tortugas.—*See* FLORIDA KAYS.
Toscana.—*See* TUSCANY.
Touariks.—RICHARDSON, J. T. Alphabet . . . Vocabularies, *etc.*
Lond., **1847.**
Touat.—*See* TUAT.
Toula.—*See* TULA.
Toulouse.—TOULOUSE. L'Indicateur Toulousain, *etc.* *Toul.*, **1822.**
—— DREMOND, A. Le Guide Toulousain. *Toul.*, **1868.**
Tours.—CHERSÉ, CH. DE. Le Guide du Voyageur à Poitiers . . . suivi
de l'Itinéraire de T. à Poitiers, *etc.* *Poitiers*, **1851.**
Touzla.—*See* TOUZLA.
Touzla.—Hunt, Dr. Journey . . . the Salt Springs of T., *etc.* 1799.
WALPOLE, R. Memoirs, *etc.*
Trajectum.—*See* UTRECHT.
Transcaucasia.—ABICH, H. Meteorologische Beobachtungen in Trans-
caucasien. *Berlin.*
—— WILBRAHAM, R. Travels in the T. n Provinces, *etc.* **1839.**
—— HAXTHAUSEN, BARON VON. T. Sketches of the Nations, *etc.* **1854.**
—— OLIPHANT, L. The T.-C. n Campaign of the Turkish Army under
Omer Pasha. **1856.**
—— ABICH, H. Aperçu de mes Voyages en Transcaucasie en 1864.
Moscow, **1865.**
Transisalana.—*See* OVERYSSEL.
Transsilvania.—*See* TRANSYLVANIA.
Transvaal Republic.—PRATT, J. J. Sheep and Stock Farming . . .
Remarks on the S. African or T. R., *etc.* *Lond.* [**1867.**]
Transylvania.—WINDISCH, K. G. v. Geographie des Königreichs Ungarn
und Siebenbürgen. *Presburg*, 1780-90.
—— BECKER, W. G. E. Journal einer . . . Reise durch . . . Sieben-
bürgen. *Freyb.*, **1815.**
—— GERANDO, A. DE. La T., *etc.* *Par.*, **1845.**
—— PATON, A. A. The Goth and the Hun; or T. . . . in 1850.
1851.

Transylvania.—Paget, J.   Hungary and T., *etc.* 1855.
——— Ébny, J.   De Tabulis Ceratis in Transsilvania repertis, *etc.*
　　　　　　　　　　　　　　　　　　　　　　　　　　　Pest., 1856.
——— Mikó Imbe, Count.   Erdély Különválása Magyarországtól.
　　　　　　　　　　　　　　　　　　　　　　　　　　　Budan, 1860.
——— Anstrd, D. T.   A Short Trip in . . . T. in . . . 1862.
　　　　　　　　　　　　　　　　　　　　　　　　　　Lond., 1862.
——— Ébny, J.   Numi Transilvaniæ, *etc.*　　　　　　*Pesten*, 1862.
——— Boner, C.   T.; Its Products, *etc.*　　　　　　　*Lond.*, 1865.
——— Dutens, J. V.   Travels in . . . T. . . . in 1806.   Pelham.
　　Vol. II.
——— Jackson, J., Journey . . . in 1797, through . . . T., *etc.*   Pelham.
　　Vol. II.
——— Smith, Capt. J.   Travels . . . with his T.n Acts . . . about 1596.
　　Purchas.   Vol. II.
Trasimeno, Lago.—Gambini, R.   Dissertazioni intorno la storia e la fisica
　　del Lago T.　　　　　　　　　　　　　　　　　　　*Perugia*, 1826.
Travancora.—Markham, C. R.   Chinchona Cultivation in T., *etc.* 1865.
Trebisonde.—*See* Trebizond.
Trebizond.—Rennell, J.   Illustrations . . . of the . . . Retreat of the
　　Ten Thousand . . . to T., *etc.*　　　　　　　　　　　1816.
Tremiti, Islands of.   Gasparrini, G.   Descrizione delle Isole di T., *etc.*
　　　　　　　　　　　　　　　　　　　　　　　　　　　Nap., 1838.
Trent.—Misson, M.   Travels through . . . the Bishoprick of T. . . .
　　1687-88.   Harris, J.   Vol. II.
——— Ray, J.   Travels through . . . the Bishoprick of T., *etc.*   Harris,
　　J.   Vol. II.
Treves.—Browne, E.   Voyage . . . to Holland, with a Journey . . .
　　through the Electorates of . . . T. . . . 1668.   Harris, J.   Vol. II.
Trieste.—Agapito, Count G.   Descrizione di T.　　*Vienna*, 1830.
Trinidad.—Latrobe, C. J.   Negro Education, British Guiana and T.
　　　　　　　　　　　　　　　　　　　　　　　　　　　1838.
——— Verteuil, L. A. A. de   T.: its Geography, *etc.*　　1858.
——— Wall, G. P. and Sawkins, J. G.   Report on the Geology of T., *etc.*,
　　　　　　　　　　　　　　　　　　　　　　　　　　Lond., 1860.
——— Duddeley, Sir R.   Voyage to the Isle of T. . . . 1594-5.
　　Hakluyt.   Vol. IV.
——— Sparrey, F.   Description of . . . T. . . . 1602.   Purchas.
　　Vol. IV.
Trinity Island.—*See* Jan Mayen.
Tripoli.—Ali Bey.   Travels in . . . T., *etc.*　　　　　　1816.
——— Celia, P. della.   Narrative of an expedition from T. . . . to
　　. . . Egypt, *etc.*　　　　　　　　　　　　　　　　　　1822.
——— Beechey, F. W. and H. W.   Proceedings of . . . Expedition to
　　explore the N. Coast of Africa, from T. eastward, *etc.*   1828.
——— Grimshow, R.   History . . . of T., *etc.*   *Richmond*, U. S., 1835.

Tripoli.—Saint-Martin, V. de. Sur les Anciens Sites de la Tripolitaine.
Par., 1861.
—— Hoilfs, G. Reise . . . nach T. *Bremen*, 1868.
—— Dandini, J. Voyage to . . . also a description of . . . T., *etc.* Churchill. Vol. VII.
—— Aldersey, L. Voyage to . . . T., 1581. Hakluyt. Vol. II.
—— Eldred, J. Voyage to T. in Syria . . . 1583. Hakluyt. Vol. II.
—— Fitch, R. The long . . . voyage of, by way of T. in Syria, to Ormuz, *etc.* 1583-1591. Hakluyt. Vol. II.
—— Voyage . . . to T. in Barbary, 1583. Hakluyt. Vol. II.
—— Eldred, J. Voyage by Sea to T. in Syria, *etc.* 1583. Kerr. Vol. VIII.
—— Nicholay, N. Description of . . . T. Purchas. Vol. II.
—— Sanderson, J. Pilgrimage from Constantinople . . . to T. in Syria, 1601. Purchas. Vol. II.
—— —— Voyages to . . . T. 1584-1602. Purchas. Vol. II.
—— Cervelli, A. Relations inédites . . . Extrait du Journal d'une Expédition faite en 1811-12, de T. à Derne, *etc.* Voyages and Travels. Recueil, *etc.* Vol II.

Tripolis, Tripolitaine.—*See* Tripoli.

Troad.—Webb, P. B. Osservazioni intorno allo stato antico e presente dell' Agro Trojano. *Mil.*, 1821.
—— Hunt, Dr. Journey from Parium to the T. . . . 1799. Walpole, R. Memoirs, *etc.*
—— Morritt, Mr. Remarks on the T., *etc.* Walpole, R. Memoirs, *etc.*

Tronhiem, Tronyem.—*See* Drontheim.

Trossachs.—Garnet's Account of the Drosachs. Pinkerton. Vol. III.

Troy.—Napier, E. Remarks on Ancient T. and the Modern Troad.
London.
—— Chevalier, M. Description of the Plain of T., *etc.* *Edin.*, 1791.
—— Acland, H. W. The Plains of T. *Oxf.*, 1839.
—— Biddulph, W. Travels of four Englishmen . . . into . . . T. . . . in 1600 and 1611. Churchill. Vol. VII.
—— Fabulous Antiquities of the peregrinations . . . of . . . the Grecian Navie to T., *etc.* Purchas. Vol. I.

Truxillo.—Parker W. Voyage to . . . T. . . . 1596-97. Hakluyt. Vol. IV.

Tsad, Tsada, River.—*See* Chadda.
Tsadbecken.—*See* Chadda, River.
Tschad, Lake—*See* Chad.
Tschadda, River.—*See* Chadda.
Tscherkessen.—*See* Circassia.
Tshadda, River.—*See* Chadda.
Tsien-Tang, River.—*See* Tsien-Tang-Kiang.

Tsien-Tang-Kiang, River.—Macgowan, D. J. The Kagro of the T.-T. River. 1853.
Tekenis-Tsquali.—See Tekhenis-Tsthali.
Tekhenis-Tsthali.—Radde, G. Berichte, etc. (Jahrg. I. Reisen ... in ... Tekenis-Tsquali, etc.) *Tiflis*, 1866.
Tuat.—Rohlfs, G. Tagebuch seiner Reise durch Marokko nach T., 1864. *Gotha*, 1865.
———— Malte-Brun, V. A. Resumé historique et geographique de l'exploration de G. Rohlfs au Touat, etc. *Par.*, 1866.
———— Rohlfs, G. Reise ... Exploration der Oasen von ... T., etc. *Bremen*, 1868.
Tucuman.—Andrews, Capt. Journey ... through ... T., etc. 1827.
———— Techo, F. N. del. History of ... T., etc. Churchill. Vol. IV.
Tula.—Struve, O. Détermination des Positions Géographiques de ... Toula. *St. Pet.*, 1843.
Tulare Lakes.—Blake, W. P. On the Rate of Evaporation on the T. L. of California. *Wash.*, 1858.
Tunbridge Wells.—Britton, J. Descriptive Sketches of T. W., etc. 1832.
Tunis.—Temple, Sir G. T. Excursions in ... T. 1835.
———— Peyssonnel et Desfontaines. Voyages dans les Régences de T., etc. *Par.*, 1838.
———— Dunant, J. H. Notice sur la Régence de T. *Genève*, 1858.
———— Gubernatis, E. de. Lettere sulla Tunisia, etc. *Firenze*, 1867.
———— Davis, W. A True ... description of ... T., etc. Churchill. Vol. VII.
———— Henry IV. Voyage with an Armie ... to T. In Barbary. Hakluyt. Vol. II.
Tunisia.—See Tunis.
Tunkin.—See Tonquin.
Tur.—See Tor.
Turchia.—See Turkey.
Turcomanie, Turcomie.—See Turkestan.
Turin.—Paroletti, M. T. et ses Curiosités, etc. *Turin*, 1819.
———— ———— T., à la portée de l'Étranger, etc. *Turin*, 1838.
Turkestan.—Mouraviev, N. Voyage en Turcomanie ... 1819-20, etc. *Par.*, 1823.
———— Burslem, R. Peep into Toorkisthan. 1846.
———— Lal, Mohan. Travels in ... T., etc. 1846.
———— Ferrier, J. P. Caravan Journeys ... in ... T., etc. 1856.
———— Pashino, P. I. [T. in 1866.] *Russian*. [*St. Pet.*] 1868.
———— Description of ... T. Astley. Vol. IV.
———— Mouraviev, N. Voyage en Turcomie, etc. Eyriès. Vol. XIV.
———— T. Laharpe, J. Vol. VIII.

Turkestan — Turkey.

Turkestan.—Beschreibung des Landes T. Voyages and Travels. Allgemeine Historie, etc. Vol. VII.

Turkestan, Eastern.—Hayward, G. W. I. Vocabularies . . . IV. Re-calculated Elevations of Towns . . . in E.n T. *Lahore*, 1870.

Turkey.—Hogg, J. Further Account of . . . Antiquities in T., etc.

——— ——— On some ancient Assyrian and Egyptian Sculptures . . . in T.

——— Knolles, R. The Generall Historie of the Turkes, etc. *Lond.*, 1603.

——— Sandys, G. A Relation of a Journey begun . . . 1610. Containing a description of the Turkish Empire, etc. 1615.

——— Thevenot, M. de. Travels into . . . T., etc. 1687.

——— Lucas, P. Voyage fait en 1714 dans la Turquie, etc. *Amst.*, 1720.

——— Galland, M. Recueil des Rits et Cérémonies . . . auquel on a joint divers écrits relatifs . . . aux . . . Turcs. *Amst.*, 1764.

——— Eton, W. Survey of the Turkish Empire, etc. *Lond.*, 1799.

——— Bonnini, C. T. Travels in . . . T. 1801.

——— Thornton, T. The Present State of T., etc. *Lond.*, 1807.

——— Macgill, T. Travels in T., etc. 1808.

——— Hamilton, W. Remarks on several parts of T., etc. 1809.

——— Hobhouse, J. C. Journey through . . . T. in Europe and Asia, etc. 1813.

——— Ali Bey. Travels in . . . T., etc. 1816.

——— Walpole, R. Memoirs relating to European and Asiatic T., etc. *Lond.*, 1817.

——— Laurent, P. Classical Tour through . . . T. . . . in 1818-19. 1821.

——— Gaiberg, Count J. L'Empire Russe comparé aux principaux états du Monde . . . Quadro . . . della . . . Turchia . . . nel 1829. 1829.

——— Madden, R. R. Travels in T., etc. 1829.

——— Alcock, T. Travels in . . . T., etc. 1831.

——— Strauseen, J. J. Reise durch die Türkei . . . 1647-1673. *Gotha*, 1832.

——— Temple, Sir G. T. Travels in . . . T., etc. 1836.

——— Niebuhr, C. Reisebeschreibung . . . durch . . . T., etc. *Hamb.*, 1837.

——— Elliott, C. B. Travels in . . . T. 1838.

——— Spencer, E. Travels . . . Including a Tour through . . . T., etc. 1838.

——— Murray. Hand-Book for Travellers in . . . T., etc. *Lond.*, 1840.

——— Damer, Hon. Mrs. G. L. D. Diary of a Tour in . . . T., etc. *Lond.*, 1841.

——— Davy, J. Notes . . . on . . . T. 1842.

——— Hahn-Hahn, Countess I. Travels in T., etc. 1845.

Turkey. 449

Turkey.—Tchihatcheff, P. de. L'Asie Mineure et l'Empire Ottoman, état actuel, etc. *Par.*, 1850.

—— Turkey. Frontier Lands of the Christian and the Turk, etc. 1853.

—— Barker, W. B. Practical Grammar of the Turkish language, etc. 1854.

—— Carlisle, Earl of. Diary in Turkish . . . Waters. 1854.

—— Chesney, F. R. Russo-Turkish Campaigns of 1828 and 1829. 1854.

—— Curzon, Hon. R. Armenia . . . the Frontiers of T., etc. 1854.

—— Golovin, I. The Nations of Russia and T., etc. 1854.

—— M'Culloch, J. R. Russia and T., etc. 1854.

—— Porter, Sir J. T., its History, etc. 1854.

—— Smyth, Admiral W. H. Year with the Turks, etc. 1854.

—— Spencer, E. T., etc. 1854.

—— Stuart, Lieut.-Col. Journal of a Residence in . . . T. 1854.

—— Wyld, J. Geographical . . . Notes to accompany . . . Maps of the Ottoman Empire, etc. 1854.

—— Jochmus, A. Der Syrische Krieg und der Verfall des Osmanen-Reiches seit 1840. *Frankf. a. M.*, 1858.

—— Wortabet, G. M. Syria . . . or T. in the Dependencies. 1856.

—— Lauture, Count d'Escayrac de. La Turquie, etc. *Par.*, 1858.

—— Hell, X. H. de. Extrait du Voyage en Turquie . . . 1846-8, etc. *Par.*, 1859.

—— Pollington, Viscount. Half round the Old World . . . a Tour in . . . T., etc. *Lond.*, 1867.

—— Millingen, F. La Turquie sous le règne d'Abdul-Aziz, etc. *Par.*, 1868.

—— Tozer, H. F. Researches in the Highlands of T., etc. *Lond.*, 1869.

—— Millingen, F. Slavery in T. The Sultan's Harem. *Lond.*, 1870.

—— Daulphinois, N. N. Navigations . . . made into T. Churchill. Vol. VII.

—— Turkish Empire, a General Account of. Churchill. Vol. VII.

—— Voyage of five merchant Ships of London into T. . . . 1586. Hakluyt. Vol. II.

—— Thevenot, J. Account of the Customs . . . of the Turks, etc. Harris, J. Vol. II.

—— Salbanke, J. Voyage through . . . part of T. . . . 1609. Purchas. Vol. I.

—— Newberie, J. Two Voyages. One . . thorow T., 1580-82. Purchas. Vol. II.

—— Of the . . . Turkes . . . and of their Religions. Purchas. Vol. V.

—— Forbin, Count de. Travels in . . . T. . . . 1817, 18. Voyages and Travels, New. 1819. Vol. I.

2 G

Turkey.—Jordan on Jourdain Catalani, P. Mirabilia descripta, sequitur de ... Turquia. VOYAGES and TRAVELS. Recueil, *etc.* Vol. IV.

―――― Carlyle, J. D. Letters during his Residence in T. WALPOLE. Memoirs, *etc.*

――――, **Asiatic.**—Asie Turque. ETATS. Vol. XIV.

――――, **European.**—BURRO, G. B. DE. Viaggio di cinque anni in ... Europa del Turco, *etc.* *Milano,* [1688.]

―――― ―――― ALEXANDER, SIR J. E. Travels : ... through ... E. T., *etc.* **1827.**

―――― ―――― BOUÉ, A. Turquie d'Europe, *etc.* *Par.,* **1840.**

―――― ―――― STRUVE, F. G. W. Astronomische Ortsbestimmungen in der Europäischen Türkei, *etc.* *St. Pet.,* **1845.**

―――― ―――― SPENCER, E. Travels in E. T., *etc.* **1851.**

―――― ―――― BOUÉ, A. Itinéraire dans la Turquie d'Europe. *Vienne,* **1854.**

―――― ―――― MACINTOSH, A. F. Military Tour in E. T., *etc.* **1854.**

―――― ―――― VALENTINI, BARON DE. Description of the Seat of War in E. T., *etc.* **1854.**

―――― ―――― COSTAMBERT, E. Rapport sur ... la Turquie d'Europe, *etc.* *Par.,* **1857.**

―――― ―――― Sibthorp, Dr. Remarks relating to the Natural History of parts of E. T. WALPOLE, R. Travels, *etc.*

Turkie.—*See* TURKEY.

Turkistan.—*See* TURKESTAN.

Tuscany.—GRÅBERG, COUNT J. Atlante geografico-fisico ... del Granducato di Toscana, del A. Z. Orlandini.

―――― TOZETTI, J. T. Voyage Minéralogique ... en Toscane. *Par.,* **1792.**

―――― MARENIGH, J. Guide de Florence et d'autres villes ... de Toscane. *Flor.,* **1822.**

―――― REPETTI, E. Dizionario geografico ... della Toscana, *etc.* *Firenze,* **1833-45.**

―――― GRÅBERG, COUNT J. Dizionario Geografico ... della Toscana, di Repetti. **1836.**

―――― ―――― Memorie sul bonificamento della Maremme Toscane, del F. Tartini. *Firenze,* **1839.**

―――― MURCHISON, SIR R. I. On the Vents of Hot Vapour in T., *etc.* **1850.**

―――― SIMONIN, L. La Toscane et la Mer Tyrrhenienne. Études, *etc.* *Par.,* **1868.**

―――― Ray, J. Travels through ... T., *etc.* HARRIS. J. Vol. II.

Tuzla.—*See* TOUZLA.

Twat.—*See* TOAT.

Two Sicilies.—*See* NAPLES AND SICILY.

Tyre.—WILDE, W. R. Narrative of ... a Visit to ... T., *etc.* *Dubl.,* **1852.**

Tyre — Umballa. 451

Tyre.—William, Archb. of Tyre. Voyage to . . . T. . . . 1130. HAK-
LUYT. Vol. II.
Tyrol.—TAYLOR, J. Travels . . . to India, in 1789, by . . . the T., *etc.*
1799.
——— WOLF, P. P. Geschichte, Statistik und Topographie von T.
München, 1800.
——— STERNBERG, C. G. VON. Reise durch T., *etc.*
Wien und Triest, 1811.
——— SCHMIDL, A. A. Das Kaiserthum Oesterreich. Die gefürstete Grafschaft T. mit Vorarlberg. *Stuttg.*, 1837.
——— BARROW, J. Tour . . . through . . . T., *etc.* 1853.
——— WHITE, W. On Foot through the T. in 1855. 1856.
——— SONKLAR, K. VON. Der neuerliche Ausbruch des Suldnergletschers in T. *Wien*, 1857.
——— Misson, M. Travels through . . . T. . . . 1687-88. HARRIS, J. Vol. II.
——— Salvo, Marquis de. Travels . . . through the T. . . . 1806. VOYAGES and TRAVELS. A Collection, *etc.* 1805. Vol. VI.
———, **North.**—BARROW, J. Tour in . . . N. T., *etc.* 1841.
Tyrone.—POSTLOCK, J. E. Report on the Geology of . . . parts of T., *etc.*
Dubl., 1843.
Tyrrhenian Sea.—THIÉBAUT DE BERNEAUD, A. A Voyage to . . . Elba; with notices of the other Islands in the T. S., *etc.* *Lond.*, 1814.
——— SIMONIN, L. La Toscane et la Mer Tyrrhenienne. Études, *etc.*
Par., 1868.

U.

Ubin.—*See* OBI.
Ucayala, River.—MICHELENA Y RÓJAS, F. Exploracion Oficial . . . Arriba de las bocas del Ucayali, *etc.* *Bruselas*, 1867.
Ucayle, River.—*See* UCAYALA.
Udine.—VENERIO, G. Osservazioni Meteorologiche fatte in U. . . . 1803-42. *Udine*, 1851.
Udskoi.—MIDDENDORFF, A. T. VON. Bericht über die Reendigung der Expedition nach U. Ostrog, *etc.* *St. Pet.*, 1845.
Udskoy.—*See* UDSKOI.
Ukraine.—HAMMARDT. Reise durch Oberschlesien . . . nach der U.
Gotha, 1787.
——— Beauplan, Sieur de. Description of U., *etc.* CHURCHILL. Vol. I.
——— Mr. A short account of the U., *etc.* HARRIS, J. Vol. II.
Ulloa, San Juan de.—*See* SAN JUAN DE ULLOA.
Umarawutty.—FERGUSON, J. Tree and Serpent Worship . . . From the sculptures of the Buddhist Topes at . . . Amravati, *etc.*
Lond., 1868.
Umballa.—DELHI RAILWAY. Opening of the Meerut and U. Section, *etc.*
Lond., 1869.

2 G 2

452 Ummerapoora — United States of America.

Ummerapoora.—Cox, H. Journal of a Residence . . . at Amarapurah. 1821.
—— Yule, H. Narrative . . . with . . . Notes on the Geological Features of . . . the Country N. of . . . Amarapoora, by T. Oldham. *Calc.*, 1858.

Ungern.—*See* Hungary.

United Kingdom.—*See* Great Britain.

United States of America.—America. Inquiries respecting the . . . Indian Tribes of the U. S.
—— Fitch, A. The most pernicious species of U. S. Insects, *etc.*
—— Hall, J. Maps and Plates of the Geological Sections of the U. S. of A. *N. Y.*
—— Hassler, F. R. Report on the Survey of the Coast of the U. S. . . . 1837-39. *Washington.*
—— Redfield, W. C. Observations on the Hurricanes . . . of the . . . Coast of the U. S.
—— Winterbotham, W. Historical . . . View of the . . . U.S., *etc.* 1795.
—— Volney, C. F. Tableau du Climat et du Sol des États-Unis d'Amerique, *etc.* *Par.*, 1803.
—— Morse, J. Report of the Secretary of War of the U. S., on Indian Affairs, comprising a Tour in 1820, *etc.* *New-Haven*, 1822.
—— America. Excursion through the U. S., *etc.* 1824.
—— America. General outline of the U. S., *etc.* *Phil.*, 1824.
—— De Roos, Hon. F. F. Personal Narrative of Travels in the U. S., *etc.* 1827.
—— Darby, W. View of the U. S., *etc.* *Phil.*, 1828.
—— Waterton, C. Wanderings in . . . the N.-W. of the U. S., *etc.* 1828.
—— America. A connected view of the . . . Internal Navigation of the U. S., *etc.* *Phil.*, 1830.
—— Flint, T. History and Geography of the . . . U. S., *etc.* *Cincin.*, 1832.
—— Darby, W. and Dwight, T. A New Gazetteer of the U. S., *etc.* *Hartf.*, 1833.
—— Finch, J. Travels in the U. S., *etc.* 1833.
—— Poussin, G. T. Travaux d'Améliorations Intérieures. États-Unis . . . 1824-31. *Par.*, 1834.
—— Abdy, E. S. Journal of a Residence and Tour in the U. S., *etc.* *Lond.*, 1835.
—— Hassler, F. R. Second and third volumes of . . . documents relating to the Survey of the U. S. . . . 1834-1836. *N. Y.*, 1835.
—— Tyson, J. R. Discourse on the Surviving Remnant of the Indian Race in the U. S. *Phil.*, 1836.
—— America. Message from . . . President . . . concerning the Boundary between the U. S. and . . . Mexico. *Phil.*, 1837.

United States of America. 453

United States of America.—MITCHELL. Travellers' Guide through the U. S. *Phil.*, 1837.

—— ROCHELLE, M. ROUX DE. États-Unis d'Amérique; Histoire et Description, etc. *Par.*, 1837.

—— MITCHELL. Accompaniment to Reference and Distance Map of the U. S., etc. *Phil.*, 1839.

—— AMERICA. Commerce and Navigation. *Wash.*, 1840.

—— GALLATIN, A. The Right of the U. S. of A. to the N. E. Boundary, etc. *N. Y.*, 1840.

—— TANNER, H. S. American Traveller, or Guide through the U. S. *Phil.*, 1840.

—— —— Description of the Canals and Railroads of the U. S., etc. *N. Y.*, 1840.

—— AMERICA. Message of . . . President . . . in relation to . . . Boundary between the U. S. and . . . Texas. *Wash.*, 1842.

—— HINTON, J. H. The History and Topography of the U. S., etc. 1842.

—— LÖWENSTERN, I. Les États-Unis et la Havane, etc. *Par.*, 1842.

—— GALLATIN, A. Memoir on the N. E. Boundary [claimed by the U. S.], etc. *N. Y.*, 1843.

—— HASKEL, D. and SMITH, J. C. A complete . . . Gazetteer of the U. S., etc. *N. Y.*, 1843.

—— FALCONER, T. On . . . the S.-W., Oregon, and N.-W. Boundary of the U. S., etc. 1844.

—— MURRAY, H. The U. S. of A., their History, etc. *Edin.*, 1844.

—— BACHE, A. D. Reports of . . . Superintendent of . . . Coast Survey, etc. *Wash.*, 1844-62.

—— LYELL, SIR C. Travels . . . with Geological Observations on the U. S., etc. 1845.

—— WILKES, C. Narrative of the U. S. Exploring Expedition, 1838-42. *Phil.*, 1845.

—— GRAHAM, J. D. Observations of the Magnetic Dip, at several positions . . . of the U. S., etc. *Phil.*, 1846.

—— PURDY, J., and FINDLAY, A. G. Colombian Navigator. Vol. I. Sailing Directory for . . . the E. and S. Coasts of the U. S., etc. 1847.

—— LYELL, SIR C. Second Visit to the U. S., *etc.* 1849.

—— PEARCE, J. A. Speech on the Coast Survey of the U. S. *Wash.*, 1849.

—— M'ARTHUR, W. P. and BARTLETT, W. A. U. S. Coast Survey. Sailing Directions for the W.n Coast, etc. *Wash.*, 1850.

—— AMERICA. Lighthouses, Beacons, and Floating Lights of the U. S., corrected to 1850. *Phil.*, 1851.

—— AMERICA. Table of Post Offices in the U. S., etc. *Phil.*, 1851.

—— BACHE, A. D. Notices of the W. Coast of the U. S., *etc.* *Wash.*, 1851.

United States of America.

United States of America.—WILLIAMS, W. Traveller's ... Guide through the U. S., etc. *Phil.*, 1851.
—— SCHOOLCRAFT, H. R. Historical ... Information respecting the ... Indian Tribes of the U. S., etc. *Phil.*, 1851-53.
—— AMERICA. Report of ... Superintendent of ... Coast Survey, etc. *Wash.*, 1852-61.
—— AMERICA. The Seventh Census, etc. *Wash.*, 1853.
—— AMERICA, UNITED STATES. The Seventh Census of the U. S., etc. *Wash.*, 1853.
—— ANDREWS, I. D. Report on the ... Cotton crop of the U. S. *Wash.*, 1853.
—— DE BOW, J. D. Seventh Census of the U. S., 1850, etc. *Wash.*, 1853.
—— MELSHEIMER, F. E. Catalogue of the described Coleoptera of the U. S., etc. *Wash.*, 1853.
—— ROBERTSON, W. P. Visit to Mexico, by the ... U. S., etc. 1853.
—— DE BOW, J. D. Statistical View of the U. S., etc. *Wash.*, 1854.
—— BACHE, A. D. Tide Tables for the principal seaports of the U. S. *N. Y.*, 1855.
—— COOLIDGE, R. H. Army Meteorological Register, from 1843, etc. *Wash.*, 1855.
—— POEY, A. Sur les Tempêtes Électriques ... aux Étais-Unis, etc. *Versailles*, 1855.
—— WELD, C. R. Vacation Tour in the U. S., etc. 1855.
—— BACHE, A. D. The Tides of the Atlantic and Pacific Coasts of the U. S., etc. *New Hav.*, 1856.
—— DUNSTERVILLE, E. The Lighthouses ... and Floating Lights of the U. S. Corrected to 1856. 1856.
—— FLAGG, E. Report of the Commercial Relations of the U. S. *Wash.*, 1856.
—— HAVEN, S. F. Archæology of the U. S., etc. *Wash.*, 1856.
—— MURRAY, HON. A. M. Letters from the U. S., etc. 1856.
—— SHAW, J. Ramble through the U. S., etc. 1856.
—— EMORY, W. H. Report on the U. S. and Mexican Boundary Survey, etc. *Wash.*, 1857.
—— MURRAY, HON. H. A. Lands of the Slave and the Free; or ... the U. S., etc. 1857.
—— OLMSTED, F. L. Journey through ... the Border Country of the U. S. and Mexico. 1857.
—— PHILIPPS, J. M. The U. S. and Cuba. 1857.
—— BACHE, A. D. On the heights of the Tides of the U. S., etc. 1858.
—— DAVIDSON, G. Directory for the Pacific Coast of the U. S. *Wash.*, 1858.
—— VARNHAGEN, F. A. DE. Vespuce et son premier Voyage; ou Notice d'une découverte ... primitive ... des Côtes des Etats-Unis en 1497 et 1498. *Par.*, 1858.

United States of America.—AMERICA. Admiralty List of ... Lights of the U. S. Corrected to 1858, 59, 61. **1858-61.**
—— FRÖBEL, J. Seven Years' Travel in ... the Far West of the U. S. **1859.**
—— WARREN, G. K. Memoir to accompany the Map of the Territory of the U. S., etc. *Wash.*, **1859.**
—— DUNSTERVILLE, E. The Admiralty List of the Lighthouses ... and Floating Lights of the U. S. Corrected to 1860. **1860.**
—— JEWETT, C. C. Notices of Public Libraries in the U. S. of A., etc. *Wash.*, **1861.**
—— OLMSTED, F. L. Journeys and Explorations in the Cotton Kingdom, etc. *Lond.*, **1861.**
—— BENJAMIN, J. B. Reise in den östlichen Staaten der Union, etc. *Hannov.*, **1862.**
—— GILLISS, J. M. Astronomical and Meteorological Observations made at the U. S. Naval Observatory, during 1861. *Wash.*, **1862.**
—— MUNSON, E. Letter ... on Slavery in the S. ern States, etc. **1862.**
—— GRAS, M. A. LE. Phares ... des États Unis, 1862, 64. *Par.*, **1862-64.**
—— AMERICA, UNITED STATES. Report of the Superintendent of the Coast Survey ... 1861-64, 1866. *Wash.*, **1862-69.**
—— —— List of Distances, etc. *Wash.*, **1868.**
—— États-Unis. (Suite.) EYRIÈS. Vol. VIII. IX.
—— Perrin Du Lac. Travels ... in the U. S. ... 1801-3. VOYAGES and TRAVELS. A Collection, etc. 1805. Vol. VI.
—— Warden, M. Recherches sur les Antiquités des États-Unis, etc. VOYAGES and TRAVELS. Recueil, etc. Vol. II.

Unterwalden.—GEMÄLDE DER SCHWEIZ ... U., etc. *Bern*, **1834-38.**
Upsala.—TOPOGRAFISKA OCH STATISTISKA Uppgifter om U. LÄn. *Stock.*, **1850.**

Ural Mountains.—MURCHISON, SIR R. I., AND OTHERS. U. M.
—— —— On the Geological Structure ... of the U. M. **1842.**
—— —— The Geology of ... the U. M. *Lond. and Par.*, **1845.**
—— HUMBOLDT, A. VON. Travels ... including his Journey to the U. M., etc. **1853.**
—— RUSSIA. Der Nördliche U. ... untersucht ... 1847-50, etc. *St. Pet.*, **1853-56.**
—— HELMERSEN, G. VON. Die Steinkohlenformation des Urals, etc. **1866.**

Ural, River.—HELMERSEN, G. VON. Reise nach dem U. ... In ... 1833, etc. **1841.**
—— —— Geognostische Bemerkungen über die Steppengegend zwischen den Flüssen Samara ... U., etc. *St. Pet.*, **1846.**
—— —— Nachrichten über die ... Expedition zur Erforschung des Nördlichen U. *St. Pet.*, **1847.**

Urfah.—*See* ORFAH.
Uri.—GEMÄLDE DER SCHWEIZ . . . U., *etc.*   *Bern*, 1834-38.
Uruguay.—HOERNES, G. R. B. Medical Topography of . . . U., *etc.*
    Phil., 1845.
———— CONRING, VON. Noch einmal die Auswanderung nach U.
    Berl., 1864.
———— GRIESEN, A. H. U.; ist dieses Land für Wollproduction . . . zu empfehlen.   *Berl.*, 1864.
———— ———— U.; Viehzucht und Ackerbau, *etc.*   *Berl.*, 1864.
———— STCBE, J. J. Schafzucht und Wollproduction für deutsche Rechnung in U., *etc.*   *Berl.*, 1864.
Urumiah.—*See* URUMIYAH.
Urumiyah.—SMITH, F. AND DWIGHT, H. G. O. Missionary Researches . . . including . . . a Visit to the Nestorian . . . Christians of Oormiah, *etc.*   1834.
———— WILBRAHAM, R. Travels . . . along the S. n Shore of the Lakes of Van and U., *etc.*   1839.
Urvalca.—Techo, F. N del. History of . . . U., *etc.* CHURCHILL. Vol. IV.
Ustiga, Great.—IDES, E. Y. Three Years' Travels . . Thro' Great U., *etc.*   *Lond.*, 1706.
———— ———— Yabrants Ides, E. Travels . . . through Great U., *etc.* 1692-95. HARRIS, J. Vol. II.
Usuri.—*See* OUSOURI.
Utah.—STANSBURY, H. Exploration . . . of the Valley of the Great Salt Lake of U., *etc.*   *Phil.*, 1852.
———— CHANDLESS, W. Visit to . . . U.   1857.
———— SIMPSON, J. H. Report of Wagon Road Routes in U. Territory.
    Wash., 1859.
———— BURTON, R. F. City of the Saints, *etc.*   1861.
———— REMY, J. AND BRENCHLEY, J. Journey to Great-Salt-Lake City, *etc.*
    1861.
Utrecht.—LAET, J. DE. Belgii Confoederati Respublica; seu . . . Traject. . . . descriptio.   *Lugd. Bat.*, 1630.
Uveygatz.—*See* VAIGATS.
Uxmal.—NORMAN, B. W. Rambles in Yucatan . . . including a Visit to . . . U., *etc.*   *N. Y.*, 1843.

V.

Vaccas, Capo.—Nunez, A. Relatione dello Capo di V. . . . 1527-36. RAMUSIO. Vol. III.
Vaigats, Island.—Pet, A., and Jackman, E. Voyage . . . beyond the Iland of V., 1580. HAKLUYT. Vol. I.
———— **Strait.**—VERA, G. DL Tre Navigationi fatte dagli Olandesi . . . dove scopersero il Mare di Veygatz, *etc.*   *Venet.*, 1599.

Vaigats, Strait.—Navigationi fatte da gli Olandesi . . . dove scopersero il Mare di Uveygatz, etc. Ramusio. Vol. III.

Val Demone.—Calabria. Istoria . . . del Tremoto avvenuto . . . nel V. . . . 1783, etc. *Napoli*, 1784.

Val-Ferret.—Desor, E. Nouvelles Excursions . . . Accompagnées d'une Notice sur les glaciers . . . du V.-F., etc. *Neuch., Par.*, 1845.

Valachia.—*See* Wallachia.

Valais.—Simler, J. J. Simleri Vallesiæ . . . descriptio. *Lugd. Bat.*, 1633.

——— Razoumowsky, Count G. de. Voyages Minéralogiques dans . . . une partie du V. *Lausanne*, 1784.

——— Schiner, M. Description . . . de la ci-devant Republique du V. *Sion*, 1812.

Valdivia, River.—Vidal Gormaz, F. Continuacion de los trabajos de esploracion del Rio V., etc. *Sant. de Chile*, 1889.

Valentia, Ireland.—Airy, G. B. Determination of the longitude of V. etc.

——— ——— Maury, M. F. Letter . . . on Nautical Directions for sailing from V. to Newfoundland. *Wash.*, 1857.

Vallais.—*See* Valais.

Vallesia.—*See* Valais.

Valparaiso.—Scarlett, Hon. P. C. South America . . . comprising a Journey . . . to V., etc. 1838.

Van, Lake.—Wildraham, R. Travels . . . along the S.n Shore of the Lakes of V., etc. 1839.

Van Diemen's Land.—*See* Tasmania.

Vancouver Island.—Fitzgerald, J. E. An Examination of the . . . Proceedings of the Hudson's Bay Company, with reference to the Grant of V. I. 1847.

——— Martin, R. M. The Hudson's Bay Territories and V.'s Island, etc. *Lond.*, 1849.

——— Richards, G. H. V. I. Pilot, etc. 1861.

——— Barrett-Lennard, C. E. Travels . . . with . . . a . . . Voyage round V. I. 1862.

——— Forbes, C. Prize Essay. V. I., etc. *Victoria, V. I.*, 1862.

——— Macdonald, D. G. F. British Columbia and V. I., etc. 1862.

——— Mayne, R. C. Four Years in British Columbia and V. I., etc. *Lond.*, 1862.

——— Rattray, A. V. I. and British Columbia, etc. 1862.

——— Vancouver Island. V. I. Exploration. 1864. *Victoria*, 1864.

——— Macfie, M. V. I. and British Columbia, etc. *Lond.*, 1865.

——— Brown, R. Synopsis of the Birds of V. I. 1868.

Var, River.—Dessiou, J. F. Le Petit Neptune Français . . . the Coast of I. from the River V., etc. 1805.

Varallo.—Dupré Delorme, E. F. M. Voyage . . . (Guida al Sacro Monte di V., etc.). *Valence*, 1830.

Velay.—Costello, L. S. A Pilgrimage . . . from Picardy to Le V.
        1842.

Velhas, Rio das.—Liais, E. Exploração dos Rios S. Francisco e Das Valhas.
        [*Rio de Jan.*, 1863.]

Venezuela.—*See* Venezuela.

Venezuela.—Hawkshaw, J. Reminiscences of . . . Residence in V.
        Lond., 1838.

—— Baralt, R. M. Resúmen de la historia de V. . . . hasta 1797, etc.
        Par., 1841.

—— Baralt, R. M., and R. Diaz. Resúmen de la historia de V. desde 1797 hasta 1837.
        Par., 1841.

—— Codazzi, Le Col. Rapport sur les Travaux Géographiques . . . dans la V.
        1841.

—— Wappäus, J. E. Die Republiken von Südamerika . . . Part I. V.
        Göttingen, 1843.

—— Eastwick, E. B. V.; or Sketches of life, etc.
        Lond., 1868.

—— Paez, R. Travels and Adventures . . . First series: Life in the Llanos of V.
        Lond., 1868.

—— Appun, C. F. Unter den Tropen. Wanderungen durch V., etc.
        Jena, 1871.

—— Las Casas, B. de. Briefe Narration . . . of V., etc. Purchas, Vol. IV.

—— Pizarro, F. Reisen . . . an der Küste von . . . V. . . . 1524-41. Voyages and Travels. Allgemeine Historie, etc. Vol. XV.

Venice.—Sansovino, F. Venetia . . . descritta, etc.
        Ven., 1663.

—— Coronelli, J. Isolario dell' Atlante Veneto.
        Ven., 1696.

—— Formaleoni, V. Saggio sulla Nautica antica de' Veneziani, etc.
        Ven., 1783.

—— Taylor, J. Travels . . . to India, in 1789, by . . . V., etc.
        1799.

—— Zabla, P. Sulle antiche Mappe Idro-Geografiche lavorate in V., etc.
        Ven., 1818.

—— Quadri, A. Huit Jours à Venise.
        Ven., 1825.

—— Otto Giorni a Venezia, etc.
        Ven., 1826.

—— Venice. Guida per l'Arsenale di Venezia.
        Ven., 1829.

—— Quadri, A. Otto Giorni a Venezia.
        Ven., 1830.

—— Pepe, Lieut.-Gen. Scenes and Events in Italy . . . including the Siege of V.
        1850.

—— Berchet, G. La Repubblica di Venezia e la Persia.
        Torino, 1865.

—— Vacani, Baron C. Della Laguna di Venezia, etc.
        Firenze, 1867.

—— Austel, П. Voyage by V. to Ragusa . . . 1586. Hakluyt. Vol. II.

—— Browne, E. Journey from Vienna to V., etc. Harris, J. Vol. II.

—— Ray, J. Travels through . . . the State of V., etc. Harris, J. Vol. II.

Venice.—Barbaro, J.   Travels from V. to Tanna . . . 1436.   Kerr.
Vol. I.
———   Contarini, A.   Journey from . . . V. to . . .   Persia, 1473-6.
Kerr.   Vol. II.
———   Vernon, F.   Travels from V. through Istria.   Ray, J.
———, Gulf of.—*See* Adriatic Sea.
Venise.   *See* Venice.
Vera Cruz.—Iserri, J. I.   Prospectus of a Navigable Canal between V. C. and Alvarado.   *N. Y.*, **1827.**
Vera Paz.—Gage, T.   Survey of the Spanish West Indies . . . Also . . . Journey through . . . V. P., *etc.*   **1702.**
Veragua.—Rosencoat, M. de.   Reconnaissance hydrographique des Côtes Occidentales du Centre Amérique, Province de V., *etc.*   *Par.*, **1857.**
Veraguas.—*See* Veragua.
Vermejo, River.—Soria, P.   Informe del Comisionado de la Sociedad del Rio Bermejo, á los Senores Accionistas.   *Buen. A.*, **1831.**
———   ———   Arenales, J.   Noticias . . . sobre el . . . Rio Bermejo, *etc.*   *Buen. A.*, **1833.**
———   ———   Kerst, S. G.   Die Plata-Staaten und die Wichtigkeit . . . des Rio Bermejo, *etc.*   *Berl.*, **1854.**
Vermillion Sea.—*See* California, Gulf of.
Verona.—Verona, Guida e Compendio Storico della Città di, *etc.*   *Verona*, **1825.**
Vesteras.—*See* Westeras.
Vesuvius.—Auldjo, J.   Sketches of V., *etc.*   **1833.**
———   Scacchi, A.   Della humite e del Peridoto del Vesuvio Memoria.   *Nap.*, **1852.**
———   ———   Sopra le specie di Silicate . . . del Vesuvio, *etc.*   *Nap.*, **1852.**
———   Lobley, J. L.   Mount V., *etc.*   *Lond.*, **1868.**
Veygats.—*See* Vaigatu.
Vichy.—Murchison, Sir R. I.   On the . . . Origin of the Mineral Springs of V.   **1851.**
———   Vichy.   V., its Mineral Waters, *etc.*   *Par.*, [**1870.**]
Victoria.—Hopkins, E.   On . . . the Gold Fields of V.   *Melb.*, **1853.**
———   Sidney, S.   The Three Colonies of Australia . . . V., *etc.*   **1853.**
———   Archer, W. H.   Statistical Register of V., *etc.*   *Melb.*, **1854.**
———   New South Wales and V.   Despatches relative to the Discovery of Gold, *etc.*   **1855.**
———   Wathen, G. H.   The Golden Colony; or V. in 1854, *etc.*   **1855.**
———   Campbell, W.   Observations on the discovery of Gold in V., *etc.*   *Edin.*, **1856.**
———   Stoney, H. B.   V.: with . . . its principal Cities, *etc.*   **1856.**
———   Smyth, R. B.   V. Meteorological Reports, *etc.*   *Melb.*, **1856-58.**

Victoria.—VICTORIA. Meteorological Reports, etc. 1856-58.
Melb., **1856-59**.
—— MUELLER, F. The Plants indigenous to . . . V. *Melb.*, **1860-62**.
—— ARCHER, W. H. Statistical Notes on . . . V., etc. *Melb.*, **1861**.
—— VICTORIA. Catalogue of the V.n Exhibition, 1861, etc.
Melb., **1861**.
—— VICTORIA. Report of the Government Botanist and Director of the Botanic and Zoological Garden. *Melb.*, **1861**.
—— VICTORIA. The Victorian Government Prize Essays. 1860.
Melb., **1861**.
—— SELWYN, A. R. C. V. Geological Survey. Reports, etc.
Melb., **1862**.
—— HEYWOOD, B. A. A Vacation Tour . . . through V., etc. **1863**.
—— SELWYN, A. R. C., and ULRICH, G. H. F. Intercolonial Exhibition Essays, 1866. Notes on the Physical Geography . . . and Mineralogy of V. *Melb.*, **1866**.
—— VICTORIA. Mineral Statistics of V. for . . . 1867. *Melb.*, **1868**.
—— ALOAR, F. A Hand-book to the Colony of V. *Lond.*, **1869**.
—— BOOTH, E. C. Homes away from Home, and the Men who make them in V. *Lond.*, **1869**.
—— NEUMAYER, G. Results of the Magnetic Survey of . . . V. . . . 1858-64. *Mannheim*, **1869**.
—— Falls.—BAINES, T. Explorations . . . from Walvisch Bay to . . . the V. F. *Lond.*, **1864**.
—— CHAPMAN, J. Travels . . . with . . . visits to . . . the V. F.
Lond., **1868**.
——, Lake.—SWAYNE, G. C. Lake V.: a Narrative of Explorations, etc.
Edin. and Lond., **1868**.

Vienna.—TOWNSON, R. Travels . . . with a short account of V. in 1793,
1797.
—— BRIGHT, R. Travels from V. through Lower Hungary, etc.
Edinb., **1818**.
—— PEZZL, J. Beschrelbung von Wien, etc. *Wien*, **1826**.
—— BALBI, A. Essai . . . sur les Bibliothèques de Vienna.
Vienna, **1835**.
—— SCHMIDL, A. A. Wien's Umgebungen auf zwanzig Stunden in Umkreise, etc. *Wien*, **1836**.
—— KOHL, J. G. Austria. V., etc. *Lond.*, **1844**.
—— SCHMIDL, A. A. Wien und seine nachsten Umgebungen in malerischen Original-Ansichten, etc. *Wien*, **1847**.
—— PATON, A. A. The Goth and the Hun: or . . . V. in 1850.
1851.
—— SCHMIDL, A. A. Wien und seine nächsten Umgebungen, etc.
Wien, **1858**.
—— HÖRNES, M. Die Fossilen Mollusken des Tertiær-Beckens von Wien.
Wien, **1859-62**.

Vienna.—VIENNA. Bericht über die Erhebungen der Wasser-Versorgungs-Commission des Gemeinderathes der Stadt Wien. *Wien*, 1864.

—— Browne, E. Journey from V. to Venice, *etc.* HARRIS, J. Vol. II.

Vindhya Hills.—HOOKER, J. D. Observations made . . . on the Kymaon Branch of the V. H. *Calc.*, 1848.

—— Medlicott, H. B. The Boundary of the V.n Series in Rajpootana. INDIA, GEOLOGICAL SURVEY. Records, *etc.* Vol. I.

Vindya Hills.—*See* VINDHYA HILLS.

Virgin Islands.—Layfield, E. Large Relation . . . with a description of . . . the Virgines . . . 1596-98. PURCHAS. Vol. IV.

Virginia.—JEFFERSON, T. Notes on the State of V. *Lond.*, 1787.

—— SMITH, CAPT. J. The True Travels . . . of Capt. J. Smith . . . The Generall Historie of V., *etc.* *Richm.*, *U. S.*, 1819.

—— BLENDELL, B. The Contributions of J. L. Peyton to the History of V. . . . reviewed. *Lond.*, 1868.

—— MAURY, M. F. Physical survey of V., *etc.* *Richmond*, 1868.

—— Norwood, Col. Voyage to V. CHURCHILL. Vol. VI.

—— Voyages and Navigations of the English to V., *etc.* (First-fifth Voyage, 1584-90.) HAKLUYT. Vol. III.

—— V. richly valued. HAKLUYT. Vol. V.

—— Strachey, W. The Historie of Travaille into V. Britannia . . . Edited . . . by R. H. Major. 1849. HAKLUYT Soc. PUB. Vol. VI.

—— V., Discovery of, and Voyages to. PINKERTON. Vol. XII.

—— Smith's History of V., *etc.* PINKERTON. Vol. XIII.

—— Archer, G. Letter touching the . . . Fleet . . . which arrived at V. . . . 1609. PURCHAS. Vol. IV.

—— Argal, Capt. S. Voyage from James Towne in V. to seek the Ile of Bermuda . . . 1610. PURCHAS. Vol. IV.

—— Argal, Sir S. Briefe intelligence from V. . . . about 1624. PURCHAS. Vol. IV.

—— Argoll, Sir S. Letter touching his Voyage to V. . . . 1613. PURCHAS. Vol. IV.

—— Canner, T. Relation of the Voyage made to V., by Capt. B. Gilbert, 1603. PURCHAS. Vol. IV.

—— The First Plantation of English Colonies in V. . . . 1514-90. PURCHAS. Vol. IV.

—— Gosnol, Capt. Voyage to the N. part of V., 1602. PURCHAS. Vol. IV.

—— Hamor, R. Notes of V.n Affaires . . . 1614. PURCHAS. Vol. IV.

—— Letters of Sir T. Dale and A. Whitaker, from James Towne in V., 1614, *etc.* PURCHAS. Vol. IV.

—— Part of the first Patent granted by His Majestie for the plantation of V., April, 1606. PURCHAS. Vol. IV.

—— Percy, G. Observations gathered out of a Discourse of the Plantation of the Southerne Colonie in V. by the English, 1606. PURCHAS. Vol. IV.

Virginia.—Pringe, M. Voyage for the discovery of the N. part of V., 1603. PURCHAS. Vol. IV.
—— Proceedings of the English Colonie in V. . . . 1606-10. PURCHAS. Vol. IV.
—— Rosier, J. Extracts of a V.n Voyage made by Capt. G. Weymonth, 1604. PURCHAS. Vol. IV.
—— Notes of . . . Mace's Voyage to V., 1602. PURCHAS. Vol. IV.
—— Smith, Capt. J. Description of V., about 1600. PURCHAS. Vol. IV.
—— Stoneman, J. Voyage of H. Challons, intended for the N. Plantation of V., 1606, etc. PURCHAS. Vol. IV.
—— Strachy, W. True reportorie of . . . Sir T. Gates . . . his coming to V., 1610. PURCHAS. Vol. IV.
—— V.n affaires since 1620-24. PURCHAS. Vol. IV.
—— V.'s Verger: or a discourse showing the benefits . . . from American-English Plantations, etc. PURCHAS. Vol. IV.
—— Of New France, V. . . . . and of their Religions. PURCHAS. Vol. V.
—— Cornelius, E. Tour in V. . . . 1818. VOYAGES and TRAVELS, New. 1819. Vol. III.
—— **Britannia.**—See VIRGINIA.
—— **Water.**—WINDSOR. The Royal Windsor Guide, with a brief account of . . . V. W., etc. *Windsor.*

Visapour, Visapur.—See BEEJAPOOR.

Vistula.—BRAUNILLER, J. G. Der wichtigste Kanal in Europa . . . vermittelst der Weichsel, etc. *Berl.*, **1815.**
—— SCHMID, VON. Hydrotechnische Beschreibung des Weichselstroms, etc. *Berl.*, **1858.**
—— SPITTEL. Der Weichselstrom von Montauerspitze bis zur Mündung. *Berlin*, **1862.**

Vitl.—See FIJI.

Vitipour.—See BEEJAPOOR.

Volga.—MÜLLER, F. H. Historisch-geographische Darstellung des Stromsystems der Wolga. *Berl.*, **1839.**
—— HELMERSEN, G. VON. Geognostische Bemerkungen über die Steppengegend zwischen den Flüssen Samara, Wolga, etc. *St. Pet.*, **1846.**
—— OLIPHANT, L. The Russian Shores of the Black Sea . . . with a Voyage down the V., etc. **1854.**
—— CHAIX, P. Des Canaux qui unissent à la Néva le Bassin du V. *Genève*, **1856.**

Volta, River.—GONSALVO, L. Beschreibung der Küsten von Rio da V. bis an das Vorgebirge. VOYAGES and TRAVELS. Allgemeine Historie, etc. Vol. IV.

Voltore, Mount.—PALMIERI, L. and A. Scacchi, della regione vulcanica del Monte V. *Nap.*, **1852.**

Vorarlberg.—SCHMIDL, A. A. Das Kaiserthum Oesterreich. Die gefürstete Grafschaft Tirol mit V. *Stuttg.*, **1837.**

Vorarlberg — Wales. 463

Vorarlberg.—BERGMANN, J. Untersuchungen über die freien Walliser ... in ... V. *Wien*, 1844.
——— LINTH, A. E. v. D. Geologische Bemerkungen über das Nördliche V., etc. *Zurich*, 1853.
Voronez.—STRUVE, O. Détermination des Positions Géographiques de ... Vorontje, etc. *St. Pet.*, 1843.
  Var: Voronej — Vorontje. — Voronesh — Voroniej.
Vosges.—JOANNE, A. Collection des Guides-Joanne ... V., etc. *Par.*, 1868.

W.

Waday.—EBN-OMAR EL-TOUNSY, CHEYKH MOHAMMED. Voyage au Ouaday, etc. *Par.*, 1851.
Wadi Tor.—*See* TOR.
Wady Feiran.—*See* FEIRAN, WADI.
Waigatz.—*See* VAIGATZ.
Wai-ho, River.—*See* THAMES, N. Z.
Wales.—BETTS, J. Exercises on ... England and W., etc.
——— OGILBY, J. Britannia; or ... W. ... surveyed, etc. 1698.
——— OWEN, J. Britannia Depicta ... an actual Survey of ... W., etc. 1764.
——— MUDGE, W. AND DALBY, J. Trigonometrical Survey of ... W. ... 1784 to 1799. 1799-1801.
——— MAWE, J. Mineralogy ... with a description of ... Mines in ... W., etc. 1802.
——— BALDWIN, ARCHBISHOP. Itinerary through W., A. D. 1588, etc. 1806.
——— NICHOLSON, G. Cambrian Traveller's Guide. *Stourport*, 1808.
——— CARY, J. Itinerary of the Great Roads throughout ... W., etc. 1812.
——— CONYBEARE, W. D. AND PHILLIPS, W. Outlines of the Geology of England and W., etc. *Lond.*, 1822.
——— CARLISLE, N. Historical Account of ... Charities in ... W., etc. 1828.
——— PATERSON's Roads in England and W. ... Improved by E. Mogg. 1830.
——— BELL, J. New ... Gazetteer of ... W., etc. *Glasg.* 1837-38.
——— MURCHISON, SIR R. I. Map of the Silurian Region and adjacent Counties of ... W., etc. 1839.
——— PARLIAMENTARY GAZETTEER of England and W., etc. *Lond., Edin., Glasg.*, 1843.
——— ORWHYN. Guide to N. and S. W., etc. 1853.
——— BLACK's Picturesque Tourist of England and W. *Edin.*, 1854.
——— JAMES, SIR H. Ordnance Survey. Abstracts of the principal Lines of Spirit Levelling in England and W. 1861.

Wales.—RAVENSTEIN, E. G. Denominational Statistics of England and W.
　　　　　　　　　　　　　　　　　　　　　　　Lond., 1870.
――― Malkin's Tour through W. PINKERTON. Vol. II.
――― Skrine's Tour through W. PINKERTON. Vol. II.
――― W., a Tour in . . . 1805. VOYAGES and TRAVELS. A Collection, *etc.* 1805. Vol. IV.
――― W., a Tour in . . . 1805. VOYAGES and TRAVELS. A Collection *etc.* 1810. Vol. I.
―――, **North.**—ROSCOE, T. Wanderings and Excursions in N. W.
　　　　　　　　　　　　　　　　　　　　　　　Lond., 1853.
――― ――― Gleanings of a Wanderer in . . . N. W. . . . 1804. VOYAGES and TRAVELS. A Collection, *etc.* 1805. Vol. II.
―――, **South.** YOUNG, A. Six Weeks' Tour through the S. n Counties of . . . W. 　　　　　　　　　　　　　　　1768.
――― ――― DAVIES, W. General View of . . . S. W., *etc.*
　　　　　　　　　　　　　　　　　　　　　　　Lond., 1815.
――― ――― ROSCOE, T. Wanderings and Excursions in S. W., *etc.*
　　　　　　　　　　　　　　　　　　　　　　　Lond., 1854.
Wallachia.—CARRA, M. Histoire de la . . . Valachie, *etc.*
　　　　　　　　　　　　　　　　　　　　　　　Neuchatel, 1781.
――― THORNTON, T. The Present State of . . . W. *Lond.*, 1807.
――― HAGEMEISTER, J. DE. Commerce of . . . W., *etc.* 　1836.
――― DEMIDOFF, A. DE. Travels in . . . W. . . . during 1837, *etc.*
　　　　　　　　　　　　　　　　　　　　　　　　　　　1855.
――― Jackson, J. Journey . . . in 1797, through . . . W., *etc.* PELHAM. Vol. II.
――― Campenhausen, Baron. Travels through . . . W. . . . 1805. VOYAGES and TRAVELS. A Collection, *etc.* 1805. Vol. VIII.
Wallis.—*See* VALAIS.
Walvisch Bay.—BAINES, T. Explorations . . . from W. B. to Lake Ngami, *etc.* 　　　　　　　　　　　　　*Lond.*, 1864.
――― CHAPMAN, J. Travels . . . with Journeys . . . to W. B., *etc.*
　　　　　　　　　　　　　　　　　　　　　　　Lond., 1868.
Wanikoro, Islands.—*See* PEROUSE ISLANDS.
Wardhouse.—*See* WARDHUYS.
Wardhuys. Burrough, S. Voyage from Colmogro . . . to Wardhouse . . . 1557. HAKLUYT. Vol. I.
Warsaw.—Heinbeck, G. Travels . . . through . . . W. . . . 1805. VOYAGES and TRAVELS. A Collection, *etc.* 1805. Vol. VI.
Warwickshire.—MURCHISON, SIR R. I. and STRICKLAND, H. E. On the Upper Formations of the New Red Sandstone System in . . . W.
　　　　　　　　　　　　　　　　　　　　　　　　　　　1837.
Washita.—Lewis and Clark, Capts. and others. Travels . . . exploring the . . . W. . . . 1805. VOYAGES and TRAVELS. A Collection, *etc.* 1805. Vol. VI.
Wassanah.—RILEY, J. Loss of the American brig *Commerce* . . . With an account of . . . W. 　　　　　　　　　　　　1817.

Watertown.—WATERTOWN, Wisconsin, City of: its . . . Statistics.
Wat., 1856.

Watling Street.—MACLAUCHLAN, R. Memoir written during a Survey of the W. S., *etc.* 1852.

Weichsel, River.—*See* VISTULA.

Wellesley, Province.—CAMERON, J. Our Tropical Possessions . . . being a descriptive Account of . . . Province W., *etc. Lond.*, 1865.

Wellington.—WOOD, J. Twelve Months in W., Port Nicholson, *etc.*
1843.

—— **Channel.**—MASOLES, J. Illustrated Geography and Hydrography. W. C. Section. 1851.

—— M'CORMICK, R. Narrative of a Boat Expedition up the W. C. In 1852, *etc.* 1854.

Weltevreden.—GIBSON, W. M. The Prison of W., *etc.* *N. Y.*, 1856.

Wereld.—*See* WORLD.

West.—JULIEN, S. Mémoires sur les contrées Occidentales, traduits . . . en Chinois, en l'an 648, *etc.* *Par.*, 1857.

—— HALL, E. H. The Great W., *etc.* *Lond.*, 1867.

Westeraas.—*See* WESTERAS.

Westeras.—TOPOGRAFISKA och Statistiska Uppgifter om . . . W. Län.
Stockh., 1842.

West Indies.—REDFIELD, W. C. Observations on the Hurricanes . . . of the W. I., *etc.*

—— MARTYR, P. De rebus Oceanicis et Novo Orbe, decades tres, *etc.*
Colonia, 1574.

—— The Decades of the Newe Worlde, or W. India, *etc.* 1585.

—— LINSCROTEN, J. H. VAN. Discourse of Voyages into the E. and W. I. *Lond.*, 1598.

—— BENZONI, H. Novæ Novi Orbis Historiæ, *etc.* *Genevæ*, 1600.

—— CASE, B. DALLE. Istoria . . . della destruttione dell' India Occidentali. *Ven.*, 1626.

—— Conquista dell' Indie Occidentali. *Ven.*, 1645.

—— SHARP, CAPT. R. AND OTHERS. Voyages and Adventures in the South Sea . . . Sir H. Morgan, his expedition against the Spaniards in the W. I., *etc.* 1684.

—— GAGE, T. Survey of the Spanish W. I., *etc.* 1702.

—— RAYNAL, G. T. A Philosophical . . . History of the . . . Europeans in the E. and W. I., *etc.* *Lond.*, 1788.

—— WINTERBOTHAM, W. Historical . . . View of the . . . W. I.
1795.

—— SPENCE, W. The Radical Cause of the distresses of the W. India Planters pointed out, *etc.* 1807.

—— ALCEDO, A. DE. Geographical . . . dictionary of . . . the W. I., *etc.* 1812.

—— M'QUEEN, J. W. India Colonies vindicated, *etc.* *Lond.*, 1824.

2 H

West Indies.—COLERIDGE, S. T. Six Months in the W. I., *etc.* **1825.**

—— EAST AND WEST INDIA TRADE. Five Accounts of the ... Value of Exports ... to the British W. I., *etc.* **1827.**

—— WEST INDIES, An Account of the Extent and Situation of the Crown Lands in the, *etc.* **1828.**

—— —— Statements ... relating to the Commercial ... and Political State of the British W. I. Colonies, since May 18, 1830. **1831.**

—— —— Report from Select Committee on the Commercial State of the, *etc.* **1832.**

—— ALEXANDER, SIR J. E. Transatlantic Sketches, comprising ... scenes in ... the W. I. **1833.**

—— WEST INDIES. Observations relative to the Establishment of the W. I. Agricultural Company. **1836.**

—— MARTIN, R. M. Statistics of the Colonies ... in the W. I., *etc.* *Lond.*, **1839.**

—— CAPADOSE, LIEUT.-COL. Sixteen Years in the W. I. *Lond.*, **1845.**

—— LEWIS, M. G. Journal of a Residence among the Negroes in the W. I. **1845.**

—— LONG, PROF., and others. America and the W. I. geographically described. **1845.**

—— TEENSTRA, M. D. Beknopte Beschrijving van de Nederlandsche Overzeesche Bezittingen ... in Oost-en West-Indien, *etc.* *Gron.*, **1848.**

—— SIEBOLD, P. F. DE, and CARNBEE, P. MELVILL DE. Le Moniteur des Indes ... Occidentales, recueil de Mémoires, *etc.* *La Haye et Bat.*, **1847-49.**

—— PURDY, J. and FINDLAY, A. G. Colombian Navigator. Vol. II. Sailing Directory for the N. part of the W. I., *etc.* **1848.**

—— WEST INDIES, The Lighthouses of the ... Corrected to 1848, 53, 58, 59. **1848-59.**

—— CHALONER and FLEMING. The Mahogany-Tree ... in the W. I., *etc.* *Liverp.*, **1850.**

—— COKE, HON. H. J. A Ride ... with a glance at ... the W. I., *etc.* **1852.**

—— ROBERTSON, W. P. Visit to Mexico, by the West India Islands, *etc.* **1853.**

—— PARSONS, J. W. India Directory. Sailing directions, *etc.* **1854.**

—— DUNSTERVILLE, E. The Lights of the West India Islands ... Corrected to 1856. **1856.**

—— SHAW, J. Ramble through ... the W. I. **1856.**

—— POEY, A. Catalogue Chronologique des Tremblements de Terre ressentis dans les Indes-Occidentales de 1530 à 1858, *etc.* *Versailles*, **1858.**

—— WEST INDIES. The W. I. Labour Question, *etc.* **1858.**

West Indies.   467

West Indies.—Trollope, A. The W. I. and the Spanish Main. 1859.
——— Barnett, F. W. I. Pilot, *etc.*   1859-61.
——— Dunsterville, F. The Admiralty List of the Lights of the West India Islands . . . Corrected to 1860, 61, 62. 1860-62.
——— Underhill, E. B. and Brown, J. T. Two Addresses on Emancipation in the W. I.   1861.
——— West Indies. Return showing the number of Immigrants and Liberated Africans admitted into each of the British W. I. Colonies . . . 1847-60.   1861.
——— Poey, A. Table chronologique de quatre cent Cyclones qui ont sévi dans les Indes Occidentales, *etc.*   1862.
——— Underhill, E. B. The W. I., their . . . condition.   1862.
——— Atkins, J. Voyage to . . . the W. I. in 1721. Astley. Vol. II.
——— Description of the W. I. in general, *etc.* Hakluyt. Vol. III.
——— Hawkins, Sir J. Voyages to the W. I. . . . 1562-68. Hakluyt. Vol. III.
——— The most ancient Voyage and Discovery of the W. I. . . . by Madoc . . . 1170. Hakluyt. Vol. III.
——— Tison, T. Voyage to the W. I. before 1526. Hakluyt. Vol. III.
——— Drake, Sir F. Expedition to the W. I. . . . 1585-86. Hakluyt. Vol. IV.
——— Drake, Sir F. and Hawkins, Sir J. Last Voyage to the . . . W. I., 1595, *etc.* Hakluyt. Vol. IV.
——— Oxnam, J. Voyage to the W. I., 1575. Hakluyt. Vol. IV.
——— Preston, Sir A. Voyage to the W. I., 1595. Hakluyt. Vol. IV.
——— Hakluyt, R. Historie of the W. I., *etc.* Hakluyt. Vol. V.
——— Champlain, S. Narrative of a Voyage to the W. I. . . . in 1599-1602. . . . Edited by N. Shaw. 1859. Hakluyt Soc. Pub. Vol. XXIII.
——— ——— Second Voyage, to the W. I. . . . 1493-96. Harris, J. Vol. II.
——— Columbus, C. Third Voyage to the W. I. . . . 1498-1500. Harris, J. Vol. II.
——— Cortes, H. The History of the . . . discoveries . . . made by the Spaniards in the W. I., *etc.* Harris, J. Vol. II.
——— Summary of the Discoveries . . . of the Spaniards in the W. I., *etc.* Kerr. Vol. III.
——— Tison, S. Brief note of a Voyage to the W. I. before 1526. Kerr. Vol. VI.
——— Drake, Sir F. Voyage to the W. I., 1585. Kerr. Vol. VII.
——— Possessions in the W. I. Marshall, R. M. History of the British Colonies. Vol. II.
——— Colon, C. Relaciones . . . concernientes a los cuatro Viages para el descubrimiento de las Indias Occidentales. Navarette. Coleccion. Vol. I.
——— Colon's Discovery of the W. I. Pinkerton. Vol. XII.

2 H 2

West Indies.—Acosta, J. Observations gathered out of the four books of, touching . . . the W. I. PURCHAS. Vol. III.

—— Herrera, A. de. Description of the W. I., 1601. PURCHAS. Vol. III.

—— Oviedo, G. F. de. Extracts of his Summarie and the general Historie of the Indies. PURCHAS. Vol. III.

—— Las Casas, B. de. Briefe Narration of the destruction of the I. by the Spaniards, 1542. PURCHAS. Vol. IV.

—— Middleton, D. Notes of Voyage into the W. I. . . . 1601. PURCHAS. Vol. IV.

—— Martire, P. Sommario cavato della sua Historia del Nuovo Mondo . . . poi detto Indie Occidentali, 1492-1515. RAMUSIO. Vol. III.

—— Oviedo, G. F. Historia . . . dell' Indie Occidentali. RAMUSIO. Vol. III.

—— —— Relatione della . . . Terra Firma dell' Indie Occidentali, 1543. RAMUSIO. Vol. III.

—— —— Sommario . . . della sua Historia . . . dell' Indie Occidentali, etc. RAMUSIO. Vol. III.

—— Ramusio. Discorso sopra la Terra Firma dell' Indie Occidentali, etc. RAMUSIO. Vol. III.

—— Federmann, N. Narration du premier Voyage aux Indes de la Mer Océane, 1529-32. TERNAUX-COMPANS. Voyages. Vol. I.

—— Atkins, J. Reise nach . . . West-indien, 1721. VOYAGES and TRAVELS. Allgemeine Historie, etc. Vol. II.

—— Fernere Folge der Westindischen Entdeckungen . . . 1514-16. VOYAGES and TRAVELS. Allgemeine Historie, etc. Vol. XIII.

—— Waller, J. A. Voyage in the W. I. . . . 1807. VOYAGES and TRAVELS, New. 1819. Vol. III.

—— Montule, E. Voyage to . . . the W. I., 1817. VOYAGES and TRAVELS, New. 1819, etc. Vol. IX.

West River. *See* SI KIANG.

Western Islands.—*See* AZORES.—HEBRIDES.

—— **Lake.**—MIR LANG-TSZE. See Huo kea hwa koo kin wei tsih. [Guide to the Antiquities of the W. L., near Hangchow.] *Chinese.*
1780.

—— **Nordland.**—*See* HERNOSAND.

Westmoreland.—ROBINSON, T. Natural History of W., etc. 1709.

—— HUTCHINSON, W. Excursion to the Lakes in W., etc. 1776.

—— CLARKE, J. Survey of the Lakes of . . . W., etc. 1789.

—— MURRAY, HON. Mrs. S. Guide to . . . the Lakes of W., etc.
1799.

—— HOUSMAN, J. Descriptive . . . Guide to . . . W., etc.
Carlisle, 1816.

Westphalia.—LOTTNER, F. H. Geognostische Skizze des Westfälischen Steinkohlen-Gebirges. *Iserlohn,* 1863.

Westphalia.—Holcroft, T. Travels ... through W., etc. Voyages and Travels. A Collection, etc. 1805. Vol. II.
Wey.—Thorne, J. Rambles by Rivers; the ... W., etc. 1847.
Wheedah, Whidah, Whidaw.—See Whydah.
White Sea.—Mann, l'Abbé. Mémoire dans lequel on examine l'opinion ... que les Mers Noire ... & Blanche, ont anciennement communiqué ensemble, etc. 1779.
——— Hamel, J. England and Russia; comprising the voyages of J. Tradescant ... and others, to the W. S., etc. 1854.
——— Ommanney, E. Hydrographical Remarks on the W. S., in the Summer of 1854. *Lond.*, 1855.
——— M'Dougall, G. F. Directions for making the Passage from the Downs to the W. S., etc. 1858.
——— Gran, M. A. Le. Phares de ... la Mer Blanche. Corrigés 1859, 61, 62, 64. *Par.*, 1859-64.
——— Reineke, M. Description hydrographique ... de la ... Mer Blanche, etc. *Par.*, 1860-62.
——— Dunsterville, E. The Admiralty List of Lights in the ... W. S. Corrected to 1861 and 1862. 1861-2.
——— Norie, J. W. Guide du Marin sur les Côtes ... de la Mer Blanche, etc. *Par.*, 1863.
——— Gran, A. Le. Phares de ... la Mer Blanche, etc. *Par.*, 1869.
——— Ohthere, Voyages of, to the W. S. ... in the ninth century. Kerr. Vol I.
Whydah. Duncan, J. Travels ... from W. ... to Adofoodiah, etc. 1847.
——— Wildman, L. Remarks on the Produce of W., etc. 1862.
——— Phillips, T. Abstract of a Voyage to ... W. ... in 1693. Astley. Vol. II.
——— The Kingdom of W., etc. Astley. Vol. III.
——— Phillips, Capt. Journal of ... Voyage ... to Whidaw, etc. Churchill. Vol. VI.
——— Phillips, T. Beschreibung einer Reise ... nach W. ... 1693. Voyages and Travels. Allgemeine Historie, etc. Vol. III.
Wicklow.—Fraser, R. General View of ... W., etc. *Dubl.*, 1801.
Wiesbaden.—Verdan, D. Guide historique et descriptif de Wiesbade, etc. *Wiesb.* [1860.]
Wight, Isle of.—Clarke, J. The Delineator; or a ... description of the I. of W. *Newport*, 1812.
——— ——— Bullar, J. Hints ... on Objects worthy of attention in ... the I. of W., by J. Drew. *South.*, 1846.
——— ——— Sorby, H. C. On the Physical Geography of the Tertiary Estuary of the I. of W. *Edin.*, 1857.
——— ——— Hassell's Tour to the I. of W. Pinkerton. Vol. II.
Windso.—Manpertuis. Reise nach dem Denkmaale zu W., in dem nordlichen Lapplande. Voyages and Travels. Allgemeine Historie, etc. Vol. XVII.

Windsor.—Windsor. The Royal W. Guide, etc. *Windsor.*
—— **N. S. W.**—Tebbutt, J. Meteorological Observations made at ... W. ... 1863-66. *Sydney,* **1868.**
Windward Islands.—Latrobe, C. J. Negro Education, W. and Leeward Islands. **1838.**
Windward Passage.—Florida. Description of the W. P., etc. **1739.**
—— —— Purdy, J., and Findlay, A. G. Sailing Directory for the W. and Gulf Passages, etc. **1848.**
Winland.—*See* America.
Winnebago, Lake.—Abert, Col. J. J. Reports ... for ... a Pier at the N. extremity of W. Lake. *Wash.,* **1840.**
Winnepeek, Lake.—*See* Winnipeg.
Winnipeg, Lake.—Keating, W. H. Narrative of an Expedition to ... Lake Winnepeek, etc. **1825.**
Winterthur.—Biedermann, W. G. A. Chéloniens Tertiains des environs de W., etc. *Wint.*
—— —— Petrefacten aus der Umgegend von W., etc. *Wint.,* **1863.**
Wirtemberg.—Michaelis, E. H. Barometrische Höhenbestimmungen in ... Würtemburg. *Berlin.*
—— Memminger, J. D. G. Kleine Beschreibung von Würtemberg. *Stutt. u. Tüb.,* **1828.**
—— Schwabe, F. Reine natürliche Geographie von Würtemberg. *Stutt.,* **1832.**
—— Gistel, J. Das Heilbad zum Heiligen Kreuz- Brunner bei W. *Straubing,* **1856.**
Wisconsin.—Featherstonhaugh, G. W. Report of a Geological Reconnaissance ... by ... Green Bay and the W. Territory to the Coteau de Prairie. *Wash.,* **1836.**
—— Peck, J. M. Guide for Emigrants to ... W., etc. *Bost.,* **1836.**
—— Cram, T. J. Reports of the Topographical Bureau in relation to ... W. *Wash.,* **1840.**
—— Owen, D. D. Report of a Geological Survey of W., etc. *Phil.,* **1852.**
—— Smith, W. R. History of W., etc. *Madison,* **1854.**
—— Percival, J. G. Annual Report of the Geological Survey of ... W. *Madison,* **1856.**
—— Graham, J. D. Report of the Harbours, &c. in W., etc. *Wash.,* **1857.**
—— *See also* Chippewa.—Madison.—Prairie du Chien.
—— **River.**—Abert, Col. J. J. Reports ... for the improvement of the ... W., etc. *Wash.,* **1840.**
Wiskonsin.—*See* Wisconsin.
Wolf Rock.—Douglass, J. N. The W. R. Lighthouse, etc. *Lond.,* **1870.**
Wolga.—*See* Volga.
Wolofs.—*See* Jalofs.

Worcester, U. S.—LINCOLN, W. History of W., Massachusetts, etc. *Worc.*, **1837.**

Worcestershire.—MURCHISON, SIR R. I., and STRICKLAND, H. E. On the Upper Formations of the New Red Sandstone System in . . . W., etc. **1837.**

——— MURCHISON, SIR R. I. The Silurian System, founded on Geological Researches in . . . W., etc. **1839.**

World.—VANCOUVER, G. Voyage . . . round the W., in 1790-95.

——— DAMPIER, W. A New Voyage round the W., etc. **1697.**
——— FUNNELL, W. Voyage round the W., etc. **1707.**
——— SHELVOCKE, G. A Voyage round the W. . . . 1719-22, etc. *Lond.*, **1726.**
——— BETAGH, W. Voyage round the W. . . . begun 1719, etc. **1728.**
——— DAMPIER, W. A New Voyage round the W., etc. **1729.**
——— ANSON, LORD G. Voyage round the W., 1740-44, etc. **1748.**
——— SHELVOCKE, G. A Voyage round the W. . . . in . . . 1718, etc. *Lond.*, **1757.**
——— BYRON, COMM. Voyage round the W., etc. **1767.**
——— ——— A Voyage round the W., etc. *Lond.*, **1768.**
——— BOUGAINVILLE, BARON DE. Voyage autour du Monde . . . 1766-69. *Par.*, **1771.**
——— COOK, CAPT. J. Voyage . . . round the W., etc. **1777.**
——— FORSTER, G. Voyage round the W. . . . 1772-5. **1777.**
——— COOK, CAPT. J. Voyages . . . autour du Monde, etc. *Par.*, **1778.**
——— FORSTER, J. R. Observations made during a Voyage round the W., etc. **1778.**
——— WALES, W. Remarks on Mr. Forster's Account of Captain Cook's last Voyage round the W. in . . . 1772-1775. *Lond.*, **1778.**
——— SPARRMAN, A. Voyage . . . round the W. . . . 1772-76, etc. **1785.**
——— DIXON, G. Voyage round the W., etc. **1789.**
——— PORTLOCK, N. Voyage round the W. . . . 1785-88. **1789.**
——— VANCOUVER, G. Voyage . . . round the W. . . . 1790-95. **1798.**
——— MARCHAND, E. Voyage autour du Monde, 1790-92, etc. *Par.*, **1798-1800.**
——— LA PÉROUSE, J. F. G. DE. Voyage de, autour du Monde, 1780-88, etc. *Lond.*, **1799.**
——— PIGAFETTA, A. Primo Viaggio Intorno al Globo Terraqueo, etc. *Milano*, **1800.**
——— CLARET FLEURIEU, C. P. A Voyage round the W. . . . 1790-92, by E. Marchand, etc. *Lond.*, **1801.**
——— PIGAFETTA, A. Premier Voyage autour du Monde . . . 1519-22, etc. *Par. An. IX.* [**1801.**]
——— TURNBULL, J. Voyage round the W. in 1800-1804, etc. **1805.**

World.—KRUSENSTERN, A. J. DE. Voyage round the W., 1803-6, etc.
                     1813.

—— CAMPBELL, A. Voyage round the W., etc.   *Edin.*, **1816.**

—— ARAGO, J. Promenade autour du Monde . . . 1817-20, etc.
                   Par., **1822.**

—— FREYCINET, L. DE. Voyage autour du Monde . . . 1817-20.
                   Par., **1826.**

—— BELLINGSHAUSEN, CAPT. Voyage round the W. . . . 1819-21.
Russ.   *St. Pet.*, **1831.**

—— LAPLACE, CAPT. Voyage autour du Monde . . . 1830-32.
                 Par., **1833-35.**

— — — HOLMAN, J. A Voyage round the W. . . . 1827 to 1832.
                    1834-5.

—— MEYEN, F. J. F. Reise um die Erde . . . 1830-32.
                 Berl., **1834-35.**

—— REYNOLDS, J. N. Voyage of the . . . *Potomac* . . . during the Circumnavigation of the Globe, 1831-34, etc. *N. Y.*, **1835.**

—— WILSON, T. B. Narrative of a Voyage round the W., etc. **1835.**

—— LUTKE, F. Voyage autour du Monde . . . 1826-29, etc.
                 Par., **1835-36.**

—— ERMAN, A. Reise um die Erde . . . in 1828-30. **1835-48.**

—— CIRCUMNAVIGATION of the Globe, an historical account of the, etc.
                 Edin., **1836.**

—— LUTKE, F. Observationum Barometricarum . . . sub itinere circa Tellurem collectarum, computum instituit G. G. Haellstroem.
                 Petropoli, **1836.**

—— LUTKE, F. Voyage autour du Monde . . . 1826-29, etc.
                 St. Pet., **1836.**

—— WILLINCK, T. P. M. Reize om de Wereld . . . 1823-24, etc.
                 Breda, **1836.**

—— BOUGAINVILLE, BARON DE. Journal de . . . Navigation autour du Globe . . . 1824-26.   *Par.*, **1837.**

—— KUSCHENBROGER, W. S. W. Narrative of a Voyage round the W., during 1835-37, etc.   **1838.**

—— KING, P. P. and FITZ-ROY, R. Narrative . . . describing . . . the *Beagle's* Circumnavigation of the Globe. **1839.**

—— LAFOND, G. Quinze Ans de Voyages autour du Monde.
                 Par., **1840.**

—— TESSAN, C. DE. Voyage autour du Monde, etc. *Par.*, **1842-4.**

—— BELCHER, SIR E. Narrative of a Voyage round the W., etc. **1843.**

—— LAFOND, G. Voyages autour du Monde, etc. *Par.*, **1844.**

—— CHAMISSO, A. VON. Reise um die Welt . . . in 1815-18, etc.
                 Leip., **1846.**

—— SIMPSON, SIR G. Narrative of a Journey round the W. during 1841-42.   **1847.**

— — — BILLE, S. Beretning om . . . Reise omkring Jorden, 1845-47.
                Copen., **1849-51.**

World. 473

World.—PFEIFFER, I. Lady's Voyage round the W., etc. 1851.
—— —— A Woman's Journey round the W., etc. 1852.
—— GERSTAECKER, F. Narrative of a Journey round the W., etc. 1853.
—— SEEMANN, B. Narrative of the Voyage of H.M.S. *Herald*, 1845-51 ... being a Circumnavigation, etc. 1853.
—— ELWES, R. Sketcher's Tour round the W. 1854.
—— MOUCHEZ, E. Observations Chronométriques faites pendant la Campagne de Circumnavigation de ... *La Capricieuse.* *Par.*, 1855.
—— WILKES, C. Theory of the Winds: to which is added Sailing Directions for a Voyage round the W. *Phil.*, 1856.
—— VIRGIN, C. A. Kongliga Svenska Fregatten Eugenies, Resa omkring Jorden ... 1851-53, etc. *Stockh.*, 1857-61.
—— —— Voyage autour du Monde sur ... l'*Eugène* ... 1851-53, etc. *Stockh.*, 1858-61.
—— NOVARA, FRIGATE. Reise der Oesterreichischen Fregatte *Novara* um die Erde ... 1857-59, etc. *Wien*, 1860-61.
—— SCHERZER, K. VON. Narrative of the Circumnavigation of the Globe by the ... *Novara* in 1857-59. *Lond.*, 1861.
—— —— Reise der Oesterreichischen Fregatte *Novara* um die Erde, in 1857-59, etc. *Wien*, 1861, 62.
—— Careri, J. F. G. Voyage round the W., etc. CHURCHILL. Vol. IV.
—— Drake, Sir F. The W. encompassed, etc. CHURCHILL. Vol. VIII.
—— Portlock et Dixon. Voyage autour du Monde ... 1785-88. EYRIÈS. Vol. I.
—— Voyage de La Pérouse autour du Monde, 1785-86. EYRIÈS. Vol. I.
—— Marchand, E. Voyage autour du Monde ... 1790-2. EYRIÈS. Vol. II.
—— Vancouver. Voyage autour du Monde ... 1791-5. EYRIÈS. Vol. II.
—— Turnbull, J. Voyage autour du Monde, 1800-4. EYRIÈS. Vol. III.
—— Kotzebue. Voyage autour du Monde, 1815-18. EYRIÈS. Vol. VI.
—— Krusenstern. Voyage autour du Monde, 1803-6. EYRIÈS. Vol. VI.
—— Lisiansky. Voyage autour du Monde, 1803-6. EYRIÈS. Vol. VI.
—— Candish, T. Voyages ... round ... the whole earth, 1586-91. HAKLUYT. Vol. IV.
—— Drake, Sir F. Voyage ... about the Globe of the whole earth, 1577. HAKLUYT. Vol. IV.
—— Voyages ... the whole Globe being circompassed. HAKLUYT. Vol. IV.
—— Drake, Sir F. The W. encompassed ... Collated ... by W. S. Vaux. 1854. HAKLUYT Soc. Pub. Vol. XVI.
—— Anson, Comm. Account of the Expedition of, round the W., 1740-44. HARRIS, J. Vol. I.
—— Candish, or Cavendish, Sir T. Voyage round the W., 1586-88. HARRIS, J. Vol. I.

World.—Clipperton, J. Voyage round the W., 1719-22. Harris, J. Vol. I.
—— Cowley, Capt. Voyage round the W., 1683-86. Harris, J. Vol. I.
—— Dampier, W. First Voyage round the W. ... 1683-91. Harris, J. Vol. I.
—— Drake, Sir F. Voyage round the Globe, 1577-80. Harris, J. Vol. I.
—— Funnell, W. Voyage round the W., 1703-6. Harris, J. Vol. I.
—— Hermite, J. le. Voyage of the Nassau Fleet round the Globe, 1623-26. Harris, J. Vol. I.
—— Rogers, W. and Courtney, S. Voyage round the W., 1708-11. Harris, J. Vol. I.
—— Schouten, W. C. and Le Maire, J. Remarkable Voyage round the W. ... 1615-17. Harris, J. Vol. I.
—— Shelvocke, G. Voyage round the W., 1719-22. Harris, J. Vol. I.
—— Spilbergen, G. Voyage round the W., 1614-17. Harris, J. Vol. I.
—— Van Noort, O. Voyage round the W., 1598-1601. Harris, J. Vol. I.
—— Cook, Capt. Voyage round the W., 1768-71. Hawkesworth, J. Vol. II., III.
—— Candish, Sir T. Voyage round the W., 1586-88. Kerr. Vol. X.
—— Clipperton, J. Voyage round the W. ... 1719-22. Kerr. Vol. X.
—— Cooke, J. and others. Voyage round the W., 1683-91. Kerr. Vol. X.
—— Drake, Sir F. Voyage round the W., 1577-80. Kerr. Vol. X.
—— Funnell, Voyage round the W., 1703-6. Kerr. Vol. X.
—— Magellan, F. Voyage round the W., 1519-22. Kerr. Vol. X.
—— Rogers, W. and Courteny, S. Voyage round the W. ... 1708-11. Kerr. Vol. X.
—— Schouten, W. C. and Le Maire, J. Voyage round the W. ... 1615-17. Kerr. Vol. X.
—— Shelvocke, G. Voyage round the W., 1719-22. Kerr. Vol. X.
—— Spilbergen, G. Voyage round the W., 1614-17. Kerr. Vol. X.
—— Van Noort, O. Voyage round the W. ... 1598-1601. Kerr. Vol. X.
—— Voyage of the Nassau Fleet round the W., in 1523-6, etc. Kerr. Vol. X.
—— Anson, G. Voyage round the W., 1740-44. Kerr. Vol. XI.
—— Roggewein, Commodore. Voyage round the W., 1721-23. Kerr. Vol. XI.
—— Byron, Commodore. Voyage round the W. ... 1764-6. Kerr. Vol. XII.
—— Carteret, P. Voyage round the W. ... 1766-9, etc. Kerr. Vol. XII.
—— Wallis, S. Voyage round the W. ... 1766-8, etc. Kerr. Vol. XII.

World. 475

World.—Cook, J. First Voyage ... round the W., 1768-70. KERR. Vol. XII., XIII.

—— Bougainville, L. de. Abstract of a Voyage round the W., 1766-9. KERR. Vol. XIII.

—— Cook, J. Second Voyage ... round the W. 1772-5. KERR. Vol. XIV.

—— —— Third Voyage round the W., 1776-80. KERR. Vol. XV. XVI. XVII.

—— Voyages autour du Monde et aux Poles. LAHARPE, J. Vol. XV.

—— La Pérouse. Voyage round the W., during 1785-88. PELHAM. Vol. II.

—— Portlock, N. Voyage round the W. ... , in 1780-88, etc. PELHAM. Vol. II.

—— Pigafetta's Voyage round the W. PINKERTON. Vol. XI.

—— Candish, T. Letter ... touching ... his Voyage about the W., 1588. PURCHAS. Vol. I.

—— Drake, Sir F. Circumnavigation of the Earth, 1577-80. PURCHAS. Vol. I.

—— Magalianes, F. The occasion of his Voyage, and the particulars of ... the compassing of the W. ... 1519-22. PURCHAS. Vol. I.

—— Noort, O. Voyage round about the Globe, 1598-1601. PURCHAS. Vol. I.

—— Pretty, F. Voyage of T. Candish ... round about the Circumference of the whole Earth, 1586-88. PURCHAS. Vol. I.

—— Schouten, C. Circumnavigation ... 1615-17. PURCHAS. Vol. I.

—— Spilbergen, G. Voyage ... having encompassed the whole circumference of the Earth ...1614-17. PURCHAS. Vol. I.

—— Carder, P. Relation of a Voyage about the W. ... 1577-86. PURCHAS. Vol. IV.

—— Barlosa, O. Navigatione d'un Portoghese ... sopra la nave Vittoria, attorno il Mondo, 1519. RAMUSIO. Vol. I.

—— M. Transilvano. Epistola della ... Navigatione fatta per li Spagnuoli lo 1519-22, attorno il Mondo. RAMUSIO. Vol I.

—— Pigafetta, A. Viaggio atorno il Mondo, 1519-22. RAMUSIO. Vol. I.

—— Ramusio. Discorso sopra la Navigatione fatta da gli Spagnuoli attorno il Mundo, 1522-27. RAMUSIO. Vol. L

—— Anson, Lord. Reise um die Welt durch Südwest, 1740-44. VOYAGES and TRAVELS. Allgemeine Historie, etc. Vol. XII.

—— Dampier. Reise um die Welt, 1683-89. Careri, 1695-97. Gentil, Barbinais le, 1714-17. VOYAGES and TRAVELS. Allgemeine Historie, etc. Vol. XII.

—— Cowley. Reise um die Welt, 1684. VOYAGES and TRAVELS. Allgemeine Historie, etc. Vol. XVIII.

—— Turnbull, J. Voyage round the W., 1800-4. VOYAGES and TRAVELS. A Collection, etc. 1805. Vol. III.

—— Roquefeuil, C. de. Voyage round the W., 1816-19. VOYAGES and TRAVELS, New. 1819, etc. Vol. IX.

World.—The Voyage of Sir Francis Drake round the W.—The Voyage of Schouten and Le Maire round the W. VOYAGES and TRAVELS. The World displayed. Vol. V.

——— The Voyage of Capt. William Dampier round the W., 1685. The Voyage of Captain Woodes Rogers round the W. 1708. VOYAGES and TRAVELS. The World displayed. Vol. VI.

——— Commodore Anson's Voyage round the World. 1740. VOYAGES and TRAVELS. The World displayed. Vol. VII.

Woronesk, Woronetz.—See VORONEZ.
Würtemberg.—See WIRTEMBERG.
Wye.—Onwhyn. Guide to ... the W. 1853.

——— Roscoe, T. Wanderings ... in S. Wales, with the Scenery of the ... W. *Lond.*, 1854.

X.

Xacca.—BELLITTI, D. A. S. Delle Stufe e de' Bagni di Sciacca. *Palermo,* 1783.

Xalapa.—GAGE, T. Survey of the Spanish West Indies ... Also ... Voyage ... to X., etc. 1702.

Xanthus.—FELLOWS, SIR C. The Inscribed Monument at X., recopied in 1842. 1842.

——— ——— The Xanthian Marbles: their acquisition, etc. 1843.

——— ——— Account of the Ionic Trophy Monument excavated at X. 1848.

Xingú, River.—ADALBERT, PRINCE. Travels ... with a voyage up the ... X., etc. 1849.

Y.

Yang-tse-Kiang.—DENHAM, H. M. Hydrographic Notices ... Directions for the ... Y.-T.-K., etc. 1856-59.

——— BLAKISTON, T. W. Five Months on the Yang-Tszs, etc. 1862.

——— YANGTSZE, UPPER. Report ... on the Trade of the Upper Yang-tszo, etc. *Shanghai,* 1869.

Yang-Tsze.—See YANG-TSE-KIANG.
Yapura, River.—See JAPURA.
Yarkand.—HAYWARD, G. Statements of Routes between Y. ... and British Territory. 1869.

Yarmouth.—LAURIE, R. H., and WHITTLE, J. New Piloting Directory for the ... Thames; with the Navigation thence to Y., etc. *Lond.*, 1816.

Yavari, River.—See JAPURA.
Yébous, Yebu.—See JABOO.
Yeddo, Yedo.—See JEDDO.
Yedzo.—See JESSO.

Yellow River.—Biot, F. Mémoire sur les changemens du cours Inférieur du Fleuve Jaune. *Par.*, 1843.

Yellow Sea.—Staunton, Sir G. Authentic Account of an Embassy to ... China ... with a relation of a Voyage to the Y. S., *etc.* 1797.

Yellowstone River.—Hayden, F. V. Geological Report of the Exploration of the Y., *etc.* *Wash.*, 1869.

—— Pike. Voyage ... aux sources ... de la Pierre Jaune ... 1805-7. Eyriès. Vol. IX.

Yemen.—Middleton, Sir H. Journey to Zenan, in the Interior of Y., *etc.* Kerr. Vol. VIII.

Yesso.—*See* Jesso.

Yezd.—Truilhier, Capit. Mémoire descriptif de la Route ... de Meched à Iezd, *etc.* *Par.*, 1841.

York, Cape.—Queensland. Extracts from the Correspondence respecting the proposed Station near C. Y., *etc.* *Brisbane*, 1863.

Yorkshire.—Housman, J. Descriptive .. Guide to ... the West Riding of Y. *Carlisle*, 1816.

—— Topley, W. Notes on the Physical Geography of E. Y. *Hertford*, 1866.

Yosemite Valley.—Whitney, J. D. The Y. Guide-Book, *etc.* *Camb.*, 1869.

Yucatan.—Stephens, J. L. Incidents of Travel in ... Y. 1842.

—— Norman, B. W. Rambles in Y., *etc.* *N. Y.*, 1843.

—— Robertson, W. P. Visit to Mexico, by ... Y., *etc.* 1853.

—— Bollaert, W. Maya Hieroglyphic Alphabet of Y. [1865.]

—— Malte-Brun, V. A. Un Coup-d'œil sur le Y., *etc.* *Par.*, [1865.]

—— Hernandez de Cordove. Découverte de Y. Laharpe, J. Vol. IX.

—— Cordua, H. von. Reise und Entdeckung des Landes Y., 1517. Voyages and Travels. Allgemeine Historie, *etc.* Vol. XIII.

—— *See also* Campeachy.

Yugyakarta.—*See* Jocjacarta.

Yun-nan.—Speye, R. H. F. and C. H. F. The British and China Railway; from ... Rangoon ... to the Y. Province, *etc.* 1858.

Yura.—Raimondi, A. Analisis de las Aguas Termales de Y., *etc.*, *Arequipa*, 1864.

Z.

Zagros, Mount.—Mignan, R. Winter Journey ... across Mount Z., *etc.* 1839.

Zaire, River.—*See* Congo, River.

Zambesi.—Baldwin, W. C. African Hunting from Natal to the Z., *etc.* 1863.

—— Livingstone, D. and C. Narrative of an Expedition to the Z., *etc.* *Lond.*, 1865.

Zanskar.—Leitner, G. W. Results of a Tour in . . . Z., etc.
Par. [1865.]
Zante.—Dapper. Naukeurige Beschryving van . . . Zanten, etc.
Amst., 1688.
—— Castellan, A. L. Lettres sur la Morée . . . et Z. *Par.*, 1808.
—— Goodisson, W. Historical Essay upon . . . Z., etc. 1822.
—— Hawkins, Mr. On the Tar Springs of Z. Walpole, R. Travels, etc.
Zayl.—Norman, B. W. Rambles in Yucatan . . . including a Visit to . . . Z., etc. *N. Y.*, 1843.
Zealand.—Laet, J. de. Belgii Confœderati Respublica: seu . . . Zeland. . . . descriptio. *Lugd. Bat.*, 1630.
Zembla.—*See* Nova Zembla.
Zemé Judska.—*See* Judea.
—— **Svatá.**—*See* Palestine.
Zendero.—*See* Ginairo.
Zoes.—*Sy* Suez.
Zugspitz.—Schlagintweit, A. and H. Épreuves de Cartes Géographiques . . . de la Z. *Leips*, 1854.
Zulu Country.—Schreuder, H. P. S. Grammatik for Z.-Sproget, etc.
Christ., 1850.
—— Snooter, J. The Kafirs of Natal and the Z. C. 1857.
Zuni.—Marco de Niça, Friar. Voyage from . . . Culiacan, to . . . Cevola, or Cibola (Z.), etc. 1539. Hakluyt. Vol. III.
—— Vasquez de Coronado, F. Voyage from Nueva Galicia to Cibola (Z.) . . . 1540. Hakluyt. Vol. III.
—— Nizza, M. da. Relatione del Viaggio fatto per Terra à Cevola . . . . . . 1539. Ramusio. Vol. III.
—— Vasquez di Coronado, F. Sommario di due sue lettere, del Viaggio fatto da Fra Marco da Nizza alle sette Città di Cevola, 1539. Ramusio. Vol. III.
—— Castañeda de Nagera, P. de. Relation du Voyage de Cibola, en 1540. Ternaux-Compans. Voyages. Vol. IX.
——, **River.**—Sitgreaves, L. Report of an Expedition down the Z., etc.
Wash., 1854.
Zurich.—Gemälde der Schweiz. Z., etc. *Bern*, 1834-38.
—— Zurich, Meteorologische Beobachtungen . . . In, 1837-46-48.
Zür., 1846-48.

THE END.

www.ingramcontent.com/pod-product-compliance
Lightning Source LLC
Chambersburg PA
CBHW051239300426
44114CB00011B/809